ORIGINAL MEANINGS

POLITICS AND IDEAS IN THE MAKING OF THE CONSTITUTION

JACK N. RAKOVE

Alfred A. Knopf   New York 1996

THIS IS A BORZOI BOOK
PUBLISHED BY ALFRED A. KNOPF, INC.

Library of Congress Cataloging-in-Publication Data
Rakove, Jack N.
Original meanings: politics and ideas in the making of the Constitution/
Jack N. Rakove.—1st ed.
p.   cm.
Includes bibliographical references and index.
ISBN 0-394-57858-9
1. United States—Constitutional history.
2. United States—Constitutional law—Interpretation and construction.
I. Title.
KF4541.R35   1996
342.73´029—dc20
[347.30229]   95-44550
CIP

Manufactured in the United States of America
First Edition

ORIGINAL MEANINGS

For Helen

CONTENTS

ACKNOWLEDGMENTS

The second great pleasure in completing a book is to acknowledge all those who helped make it possible.

I have benefited, first, from the support of Project '87; the National Endowment for the Humanities, which awarded me both a Constitutional Fellowship for a full year of research and two opportunities to teach this subject to seminars of college teachers and law professors; and the Stanford Humanities Center. Numerous bicentennial conferences, seminars, and lectures along the way helped me to refine my ideas. I owe special thanks to Bernard Bailyn for encouraging me to develop the original version of my argument in *Perspectives in American History*; to Jack Beatty for allowing me to reach a serious popular audience in *The Atlantic*; to Michael Lacey of the Woodrow Wilson Center, who offered me a valuable opportunity to work out my ideas on the complicated question of rights; and to Jane N. Garrett, my editor, for taking the long view.

Professor Bailyn did not intend to start me on this subject a quarter century ago, when he suggested that I write a seminar paper on the early uses of *The Federalist*. For me his work has always illustrated what another scholar (writing of Sir Lewis Namier) called "the tremendous seriousness of the historian's quest." More recently, his analysis of the debates of 1787–88 provided much of the framework within which I have tried to make sense of the division between Federalists and Anti-Federalists.

I owe similar intellectual debts to a select group of scholars whose writings have served as a foundation for my own. The first task I undertook in that seminar paper of 1969 was to read Gordon Wood's dissertation; today I still return to the book it became to marvel at the sophistication of its arguments. My intellectual debt to Gordon is evident in nearly every chapter. In a field as massively researched as this one, it is impossible to cite all the scholars who have created the intellectual context within which my ideas have taken shape. But I wish to thank several colleagues whose writings have helped me most: John Phillip Reid, for providing a base point for my thinking on rights; Peter S. Onuf, whose work on federalism raises a host of theoretical and historical questions of the first magnitude; and Leonard Levy and Charles A. Lofgren, for their pioneering works in originalism. At a late date, an exchange of manuscripts and messages with Bruce Ackerman encouraged me to rethink the issues of legality and legitimacy surrounding ratification.

When I first took up this subject, my bemused colleagues Paul Brest and Thomas Grey of the Stanford Law School helped me to fathom the ongoing legal arguments over originalism. So did Robert Post of Boalt Hall, an old friend lost and found again across the Bay. A sometime lawyer, Elizabeth Kopelman, contributed much-needed research to some tangled questions of law and history.

Two other teams of lawyers contributed to this book. I acquired hands-on experience in a special form of originalism when I was retained by the law firm of Goodwin, Procter, & Hoar to work on *Oneida Indian Nation* v. *New York*, a case concerned with the original meaning of the Articles of Confederation. It is a distinct pleasure to acknowledge how much I learned about "law office history" from my association with Allan van Gestel, Jeffrey Bates, and Laura Carroll. Throughout the time I worked on this book, conferences and gigs of one kind or another took me to Washington, where I regularly enjoyed the hospitality of the prominent legal family of Jeffrey, the Honorable Ellen, Nikki, and Justin Huvelle.

Teaching in the country's most amiable history department has been another source of support. But my most valued colleagues at Stanford have been the undergraduates who took my seminar on the making of the Constitution. Their ideas helped me time and again to think through the problems discussed in this book, and they also tolerated (admittedly under duress) my numerous digressions and feeble attempts at humor. I thank them all, but especially: Diane Abt, Daniel Aladjem, John Bezmalinovic, Carleen Chou, C. R. Douglas, Noah Fogelson, Greg Gottesman, Allison Hartwell (Eid), Charles Hokanson, Carla Holmes, David Johanson, Russell Korobkin, Jason Moore, Beth Morgan, Rob Price (who knows the original meaning of Weltanschauung), Donna Regensburg, Fred Schnabel, Mark Toft, Wendie Schneider, Kim Walsh, and, above all,

Ourania Markou (Elbridge Gerry's biggest fan and my favorite source of baklava).

Two good friends read the completed manuscript and tried valiantly to curb my worst excesses. My collaboration with Ralph Lerner has now passed a decade, but in a sense it runs back to my boyhood and even my birthplace at the University of Chicago. As Ralph knows, there is more of Morgenthau than Strauss in my way of thinking, but in the ongoing debate between the *latke* and the *hamantasch*, I try to appreciate the virtues of both. James C. Turner is the one historian whose judgment I trust most, which is why I am doubly grateful that he was willing to read this work so closely despite a quarter century's knowledge of my penchant for malapropisms of all flavors. Now I know what Professor Bailyn meant when he was heard to remark (after Jim's orals) that "here is a historian who can be held accountable for a great many errors." If his scholarly interests were closer to my own, I would have expected Jim to catch all the errors that doubtless remain.

Were it not for the constant demands of my family, who made me high priest of their own cult of domesticity, I might have finished this book years ago. My sons, Rob and Dan, have been a great delight every day of their lives. My wife, Helen, has tolerated this project with mild bemusement, but her nightly accounts of the foibles of practicing law inspire me to awake each morning thankful that I was created a historian. She has waited too many years to have a book dedicated to her, but it's a debt of love long overdue.

Publication of this book will be a great relief to my mother, Shirley, and sister, Roberta, as well as to Michael and Max Plumpton. They know best how much it is a tribute to my father, Milton, and his memory. Everything I really know about politics, I learned from him.

PREFACE

This book has two ambitions. First, it is part of a broader effort to explore how Americans created a national polity during the Revolutionary era. Picking up where an earlier work* left off, it examines the politics of constitution-making and the major problems of constitutional theory and institutional design that Americans had to consider when they replaced the Articles of Confederation with a true national government. Second, in telling this story, I also address a question that recurs in legal and political controversies over the Constitution: What authority should its "original meaning" (or "original intention" or "understanding") enjoy in its ongoing interpretation? In its simplest form, the debate over this question can be reduced to two positions. The advocates of *originalism* argue that the meaning of the Constitution (or of its individual clauses) was fixed at the moment of its adoption, and that the task of interpretation is accord ingly to ascertain that meaning and apply it to the issue at hand. The critics of originalism hold that it is no easy task to discover the original meaning of a clause, and that even if it were, a rigid adherence to the ideas of the framers and ratifiers would convert the Constitution into a brittle shell incapable of adaptation to all the changes that distinguish the present from the past.

My interest in this second issue arose well before the call for a return to a "jurisprudence of original intention" sparked political controversy in the mid-1980s. It originated instead in my curiosity about the role that

---

The Beginnings of National Politics: An Interpretive History of the Continental Congress (New York, 1979).

appeals to historical evidence played in certain controversies of the previous decade—not so much those having to do with questions of rights and the meaning of the Fourteenth Amendment, as those concerned with issues of foreign relations, war powers, impeachment, and even the obscure question of whether members of Congress who hold commissions in the military reserves violate the prohibition found in Article I, Section 6. Because originalism depends on our knowledge of the past, it raises further questions beyond the normative problem of deciding whether or not it provides a sound theory of constitutional interpretation. How *do* we know what the Constitution originally meant? Do we simply read pertinent snatches of debate from the Federal Convention and salient passages of *The Federalist*, or must we undertake a more complicated inquiry?

The latter alternative obviously lies closer to my thinking. Chapter i explains why this enterprise is indeed a complicated one; the rest of the book offers a general model of how originalist inquiries might be conducted, with due respect for canons of historical research and explanation. That model in turn involves considering two general problems. First, to what extent did the structure of debate and decision-making in 1787–88 enable a coherent set of intentions and understandings to form around the text of the Constitution? This is the question pursued in Chapters II–IV, which carry the political story of constitutional reform through the adjournment of the Convention, and then in Chapters V and VI, which consider what it meant to ratify a constitution, and the general character of the public debate on which ratification depended. Second, when we do ask what the framers and ratifiers thought about particular subjects, how do we reconstruct their ideas and concerns? This is the question pursued in Chapters VII–X, which examine the development of American ideas on the issues that loomed largest in this debate: federalism, representation, the separation of powers, and rights.

Answering these questions has given this book a somewhat complicated architecture, and readers are warned that I have found a measure of repetition unavoidable. Chapter III, for example, is devoted to reconstructing James Madison's constitutional thinking in 1787–88, but I develop and elaborate these themes in every chapter that follows. Chapter IV is similarly concerned with analyzing the politics of the Federal Convention, but succeeding chapters return to Philadelphia in 1787 to explore how the framers approached particular issues.

These questions (and others) can be pursued at many levels of generality and with widely varying results. This is an enormous field and a subject of continuing inquiry, and I make no pretense of resolving its major theoretical problems, much less all the issues that American law and politics repeatedly generate. This book is *an* interpretation of the origins of the Constitution; it is selective in the topics it pursues and in the approach it takes; it attempts to identify the great sources of contention, but it does not address many of the lesser (and some major) questions that were also in dispute. I have tried to give the Anti-Federalists their due by allowing their most trenchant objections to the Constitution to lay a foundation for the response they elicited from their Federalist opponents. In sketching that response, I have been surprised to discover how much emphasis I have given to *The Federalist*. The reason for this is the obvious one: Nothing equals it in analytical breadth and conceptual power. Yet *how* one thinks about its eighty-five essays, in relation both to the private concerns of the two principal authors and to other Federalist writings of 1787–88, remains a critical problem to which later chapters repeatedly return.

Early in this project I considered examining some of the constitutional issues that have been agitated in recent years, but which the framers and ratifiers either ignored or considered only fleetingly or obviously could not foresee. Many of these issues can still be analyzed from an originalist perspective, and more or less plausible inferences can be drawn from the evidence of the 1780s. But the longer I pursued this project, the less enticing such questions became. It is hard enough for a working historian to keep up with all the constitutional questions that American law and politics repeatedly (and often surprisingly) bring before us. Shaping this narrative to take account of such questions would give this book a presentist skewing that would detract from its purpose of explaining how a national polity was in fact created. Equally important, because I firmly believe that the framers and many of the ratifiers were themselves decidedly empirical in their approach to politics, it seems rather beside the point to ask how they would act today. Whatever else we might say about their intentions and understandings, this at least seems clear: They would not have denied themselves the benefit of testing their original ideas and hopes against the intervening experience that we have accrued since 1789.*

Rather than attempt to resolve pressing problems of current controversy, therefore, I have sought to present a contextually grounded account

---

*I am often asked whether I think originalism offers a viable or valid theory of constitutional interpretation. My preferred answer is, I hope, suitably ambivalent. In the abstract, I think that originalism is vulnerable to two powerful criticisms. First, it is always in some fundamental sense anti-democratic, in that it seeks to subordinate the judgment of present generations to the wisdom of their distant (political) ancestors. Second, the real problems of reconstructing coherent intentions and understandings from the evidence of history raise serious questions about the capacity of originalist forays to yield the definitive conclusions that the advocates of this theory claim to find. On the other hand, I happen to like originalist arguments when the weight of the evidence seems to support the constitutional outcomes I favor—and that may be as good a clue to the appeal of originalism as any other.

of how the Constitution was drafted and ratified that will give those seeking to ascertain original meanings a more informed basis for considering what the entire process of its adoption entailed. That in part explains why I pay particular attention to James Madison. This emphasis may seem arbitrary—a "privileging" of one viewpoint among many—but it is well warranted for two reasons. First, Madison was the crucial actor in every phase of the reform movement that led to the adoption of the Constitution, from the agenda and strategy he set for the Federal Convention to his efforts to force a reluctant Congress to accept a bill of rights in 1789. We simply cannot understand how or why the Constitution took the form it did unless we make sense of Madison. He also became, for somewhat ironic reasons, the leading author of the theory of originalism itself (as Chapter XI explains). Second, modern understandings of the original meaning of the Constitution depend to a remarkable extent on his writings and speeches—but often as absorbed in the small if potent doses of his celebrated essays in *The Federalist*. By treating his concerns more broadly, I hope to restore a due measure of historical contingency to their origins and implications.

Beyond carrying forward the story of the creation of a national polity, this book also pursues my deeper agenda as a historian. For it is also concerned with the interplay between politics and political thought—between what Hannah Arendt called "the speech-making and decision-taking, the oratory and the business, the thinking and the persuading, and the actual doing" which Revolution required, and the conceptual creativity that enabled the revolutionaries to think their way through fundamental problems of government. Perhaps "it was not political theory in the grand manner," as Gordon Wood has concluded, "but it was political theory worthy of a high place in the history of Western thought"—and understanding what made it possible remains, in my view, a fascinating question.* Explaining how this great burst of intellectual creativity gave rise to the equally creative political innovations of the 1790s would require a further volume.

---

*Hannah Arendt, *On Revolution* (New York, 1963), 26; Gordon S. Wood, *The Creation of the American Republic, 1776–1787* (Chapel Hill, 1969), 615.

ORIGINAL MEANINGS

CHAPTER I

THE PERILS OF
ORIGINALISM

"THE INFANT PERIODS of most nations are buried in silence, or veiled in fable," James Madison observed in July 1819; "and perhaps the world may have lost but little which it need regret." This was no casual observation. Years earlier, Madison had mounted a serious historical project of his own, studying the "History of the most distinguished Confederacies, particularly those of antiquity," as part of his preparations for the great Federal Convention of 1787. It was "the curiosity I had felt during my researches," he recalled near the close of his life, "and the deficiency I found in the means of satisfying it more especially in what related to the process, the principles—the reasons, & the anticipations which prevailed in the formation" of these confederations, that convinced Madison to "preserve as far as I could an exact account of what might pass in the Convention" at Philadelphia. If the Convention fulfilled "its trust," his notes would enable future generations to recover "the objects, the opinions & the reasonings" from which the "new System of Govt." had taken its form. "Nor was I unaware of the value of such a contribution to the fund of materials for the History of a Constitution on which would be staked the happiness of a young people great even in its infancy, and possibly the cause of Liberty through[ou]t the world."[1]

Madison recorded these thoughts in the preface he wrote to accompany the posthumous publication of his notes of debates at Philadelphia. "A sketch never finished or applied," he called it—and in truth, this preface offered only a brief overview of the events leading to the calling of the Federal Convention. But its rough quality did not trouble Madison. For sound history, he believed, could never be written by the participants in great events, however momentous their deeds or intimate their knowledge. "It has been the misfortune of history," he wrote in 1823,

> that a personal knowledge and an impartial judgment of things rarely meet in the historian. The best history of our Country, therefore, must be the fruit of contributions bequeathed by contemporary actors and witnesses to successors who will make an unbiassed use of them. And if the abundance and authenticity of the materials which still exist in the private as well as public repositories among us should descend to hands capable of doing justice to them, the American History may be expected to contain more truth, and lessons certainly not less valuable, than those of any Country or age.[2]

So Madison urged friends and correspondents to preserve their vital papers, and he took great care to gather and safeguard his own: letters, memoranda, and, most prized of all, the notes of debates which he regarded as his great testamentary legacy to the American republic. Yet during the half century between the adoption of the Constitution and his death in 1836, Madison never thought to draft the first-person account of that momentous event that historians—with all their mistrust of memoirs—would dearly love to have.

Even so, a historian reading Madison's "Sketch" and his carefully preserved papers immediately recognizes a kindred spirit at work—so much so, in fact, that Madison may well be regarded as a patron saint of American history. Without his notes of debates, it would be nearly impossible to frame more than a bare-bones account of how the Constitution took shape. They alone make it possible to follow the *flow* of debate within the Convention, to detect the imprint of individual personalities and rhetorical styles, and, most important, to identify the shifting concerns that prevailed at different points during the deliberations.

Like so many of his colleagues and "cotemporaries," Madison was acutely and rightly aware that posterity would find his generation's experiments in self-government intensely interesting. In exchange for his own sensitivity to their needs, Madison asked only that those who later used his records should seek to write the "unbiassed" history the subject deserved. In one sense, his request sets an admirable standard to which all historians should naturally aspire: What self-respecting scholar sets out to write an avowedly "biased" history? Yet objectivity is, of course, an elusive ideal, and Madison's hopes express a faith in the possibilities of obtaining objective knowledge of the past that many modern scholars would find touchingly naïve. For two sets of reasons—one tied to the character of the Constitution itself, the other involving more general issues of historical knowledge—the task of "doing justice" to "The Founding" of the American republic is more demanding than Madison ever suspected.

Precisely because the Constitution has always played a central role in American politics, law, and political culture, as both a continuing source of dispute and a legitimating symbol of national values, the interpretation of its historical origins and meaning has rarely if ever been divorced from an awareness of contemporary ramifications. When the early-twentieth-century Progressive historians portrayed the framers as a propertied elite intent on preserving the powers of their own class, they were mindful of the uses of public power in an industrializing America.[3] Or again, the emphasis that political scientists such as James MacGregor Burns and Robert Dahl place on the anti-democratic tendencies of the Constitution is derived from a frustration with the seeming inability of the political system to fashion effective governing coalitions.[4] No less political is the celebratory attitude toward the higher wisdom of the founders that marks the work of recent conservative political theorists who prefer the framers' ideas of natural rights and federalism to the result-oriented reasoning of contemporary legal theory and its accompanying willingness to expand the authority of federal courts at the expense of the democratic autonomy of communities and states.[5] Because any portrait of the Founding and the Founders—whether cynical or heroic—affects how we imagine these great symbols of American political life, even the most objective scholar may find it difficult to avoid an appearance of bias, however slight or inadvertent.

Madison himself was not immune to this danger. In his own way, he sought to enhance the heroic aura that already surrounded the Convention. For if the origins of the Constitution would never be lost in the dim reaches of legend and fable, opportunity still remained to portray its adoption and its framers in mythic terms. While recognizing that the "character" of the Constitution "must be tested by the experience of the future," Madison used the final paragraph of his "Sketch" to

> express my profound and solemn conviction, derived from my intimate opportunity of observing and appreciating the views of the Convention, collectively and individually, that there never was an assembly of men, charged with a great and arduous trust, who were more pure in their motives, or more exclusively or anxiously devoted to the object committed to them, than were the members of the Federal Convention of 1787. . . .[6]

An "unbiassed" view of the framers, in other words, was one that would discover their political integrity and benevolence—and one that would provide an exemplary lesson in the possibilities of republican politics to a generation that the aging statesman of the 1830s feared was learning to prefer confrontation to accommodation.

A history written in that way would necessarily tell the story of the framing of the Constitution not only from the vantage point of the framers but even, perhaps, as they would most have wanted it to be told. Understanding events as participants themselves did has always been one of the great goals and challenges of historical writing. Yet in recent years historians have become ever more insistent on the limitations of any form of storytelling—that is, of the narrative conventions traditionally used in reconstructing the epochal events of the past. Historians may think they are writing objective accounts of definable phenomena. But in practice (it is argued) there can be no single story of any event—least of all, so complex an event as the adoption of the Constitution. Moreover, the composition of any narrative history requires decisions as to perspective and dramatic structure that differ little from the imaginative contrivances of the novelist.

Even if a historian confident in his empiricism can dismiss such radical doubts as the mischievous intrusion of overly refined literary theories, the problem of perspective remains crucial for another reason. Both the framing of the Constitution in 1787 and its ratification by the states involved processes of collective decision-making whose outcomes necessarily reflected a bewildering array of intentions and expectations, hopes and fears, genuine compromises and agreements to disagree. The discussions of both stages of this process consisted largely of highly problematic predictions of the consequences of particular decisions. In this context, it is not immediately apparent how the historian goes about divining the true intentions or understandings of the roughly two thousand actors who served in the various conventions that framed and ratified the Constitution, much less the larger electorate that they claimed to represent. Economists and political scientists have developed highly sophisticated models to analyze collective voting on complex issues, but the evidence on which historians of eighteenth-century America rely cannot readily be compared with the databases of contemporary social science.

For all these reasons, then, the ideal of "unbiassed" history remains an elusive goal, while the notion that the Constitution had some fixed and well-known meaning at the moment of its adoption dissolves into a mirage. Yet in the end, what is most remarkable about our knowledge of the adoption of the Constitution is not how little we understand but how much. Historians familiar with the extant records may well feel that Associate Justice Robert Jackson rather overstated the point when he complained that the ideas of the framers had to be "divined from materials almost as enigmatic as the dreams Joseph was called upon to interpret for Pharaoh."[7] However indeterminate some of our findings may be, however much more evidence we could always use, the origins of the Constitution are not "buried in silence or veiled in fable." Not only do Madison's notes and other sources allow us to track the daily progress of the deliberations at Philadelphia, but the records of the ensuing ratification debates reveal the range of meanings that the American political nation first attached to the proposed Constitution. Nor are the relevant sources confined to what was said and written during the intense debates of the late 1780s. The larger intellectual world within which the Constitution is often located—the Enlightened world of Locke and Montesquieu, Hume and Blackstone, plain whigs and real whigs, common lawyers and Continental jurists—has been the subject of extensive analysis. Nor is the prior political history of the Revolution a neglected episode in the study of the American past.

Questions of bias, perspective, and the intelligibility of collective action will remain vexatious, of course. But so they do in almost any kind of historical writing. Rather than fret about these problems in the abstract or bemoan the limits of the evidence, it makes more sense to ask how well particular types of sources can be brought to bear on the range of questions that arise when we ask what the Constitution originally meant, or what its framers originally intended, or what its ratifiers (and the electorate beyond them) originally understood they were being asked to endorse or reject.

MEANING, INTENTION, UNDERSTANDING—these are the three terms that the historians, political theorists, and legal scholars who engage in originalist analyses of the Constitution commonly use to title their research. The terms are often used loosely and synonymously, at some cost to the clarity that this interpretive method ostensibly seeks. But they are not fully interchangeable—or at least they need not be—and distinguishing them more carefully exposes some of the conceptual traps that ensnare the unwary.

The Constitution is the text whose meaning interpretation seeks to recover, and the term "original meaning" can accordingly be applied to the literal wording—the language—of its many provisions. For example, what does Article I mean when it talks of "commerce" (a word famously glossed in the most controversial twentieth-century exegesis of the Constitution, a cometary work which once blazed across the academic sky and has long since vanished beneath its horizon)?[8] What does Article II mean when it vests something called "the executive power" in the president (the question that underlay the most important disputes of the 1790s)? Or again, what is the "establishment of religion" that the First Amendment prohibits Congress from making any laws respecting?

Meaning must be derived from usage, however, and it is at this point that the alternative formulations of original intention and understanding become pertinent. *Intention* connotes purpose and forethought, and it is accordingly best applied to those actors whose decisions produced the constitutional language whose meaning is at issue: the framers at the Federal Convention or the members of the First Federal Congress (or subsequent congresses) who drafted later amendments. Theirs were the choices of wording that produced the literal text, adding the phrase "This Constitution" at the beginning of the supremacy clause, for example, or substituting "declare" for "make" in the war-power clause. Knowing why they preferred one term to another is surely relevant to recovering the original meaning of the Constitution. Original intention is thus best applied to the purposes and decisions of its authors, the framers.

Understanding, by contrast, may be used more broadly to cover the impressions and interpretations of the Constitution formed by its original readers—the citizens, polemicists, and convention delegates who participated in one way or another in ratification. Unlike the framers, they had no authorial control over the content of the Constitution, and the only intentions they were ultimately allowed to exercise were to confirm or reject it in its entirety, sometimes hoping, but not assuredly knowing, that subsequent amendments might allay their worst fears. But this public debate was nevertheless very much concerned with how the manifold provisions of the Constitution were commonly or popularly understood—though here, of course, the range of understandings that emerged often produced rather less than a consensus.

Perhaps these distinctions seem labored or overly precise. But the value of thinking rigorously about the separate elements of originalism is compounded by the different purposes that this theory may serve. If its purpose is merely to gain a general sense of what a term meant, or why a given provision was adopted, *without treating its original meaning as dispositive*, then it is permissible to slide promiscuously among these sources and even to regard early interpretations adopted after the Constitution took effect as reasonably authoritative because of their propinquity to the deliberations of 1787–88. The greater the remove in time from the moment of founding, the greater the inclination to collapse the distinct phases of framing, ratifying, and implementing the Constitution into one composite process of original interpretation.

But this latitudinarian attitude becomes less defensible if originalism seeks to provide something more than an informed point of departure for a contemporary decision. For the argument that the original meaning, once recovered, should be binding presents not only a strategy of interpretation but a rule of law. It insists that original meaning should prevail—regardless of intervening revisions, deviations, and the judicial doctrine of *stare decisis*—because the authority of the Constitution as supreme law rests on its ratification by the special, popularly elected conventions of 1787–88. The Constitution derives its supremacy, in other words, from a direct expression of popular sovereignty, superior in authority to all subsequent legal acts resting only on the weaker foundations of representation. If this becomes the premise of interpretation, it follows that the understanding of the ratifiers is the preeminent and arguably sole source for reconstructing original meaning. The prior editorial decisions and revisions of the Convention recede to the status of mere proposals, while actions taken by any branch of government *after* the Constitution took effect themselves become mere interpretations. Both may still offer corroboratory evidence of how the Constitution was understood, for its framers and early implementers shared a common political vocabulary with its ratifiers. But that elision should not erase the real distinction and premise upon which a strong theory of originalism logically depends.

Whether one pursues the loose or strict versions of this method of interpretation, it would be evident that all appeals to the original meaning, intention, and understanding of the Constitution are inherently historical in nature. This does not mean, however, that these are the kinds of questions historians would ordinarily ask. A historical account of a particular clause would certainly want to address why it became part of the Constitution and how its later interpretation evolved in response to events and the concerns of political leaders, jurists, particular interests, or the public at large. It would also have room to reflect on the ironic twists and turns that have often carried interpretation away from the apparent intentions and understandings of 1787–88. But historians have little stake in ascertaining the original meaning of a clause for its own sake, or in attempting to freeze or distill its true, unadulterated meaning at some pristine moment of constitutional understanding. They can rest content with—even revel in—the ambiguities of the evidentiary record, recognizing that behind the textual brevity of any clause there once lay a spectrum of complex views and different shadings of opinion. "It may be a necessary fiction for lawyers and jurists to believe in a 'correct' or 'true' interpretation of the Constitution, in order to carry on their business," Gordon Wood has observed, "but we historians have different obligations and aims." The foremost of these tasks is to explain why "contrasting meanings" were attached to the Constitution from its inception.⁹ And, if anything, this is a task that recent controversies over the feasibility of a "jurisprudence of original intention" have inspired historians to pursue with relish.¹⁰

To borrow a dictum from John Marshall, the great chief justice (and constitutional ratifier), historians can never forget that it is a debate they are interpreting. They have a further obligation not easily reconciled with the strong form of originalism. With its pressing ambition to find determinate meanings at a fixed moment, the strict theory of originalism cannot capture everything that was dynamic and creative, and thus uncertain and problematic, in the constitutional experiments of the Revolutionary era—which is why, after all, the debates of this era were so lively and remain so engaging. Where we look for precise answers, the framers and ratifiers were still struggling with complex and novel questions whose perplexities did not disappear in 1788.

Yet historians have other duties that complicate their relation to the recurring question of the role that originalism can play in constitutional controversy and adjudication. As critics, consultants, or citizens, they are called upon (or volunteer) to assess the historical claims that judges make while resolving a judicial case in controversy or which partisan advocates express while contesting political issues with constitutional implications. Like other experts, historians guard their professional terrain jealously, and they may rise in righteous anger when opinions they believe to be dubious and false are advanced with dogmatic certitude. But also like other experts, they possess valuable information which they can be enticed to yield up, and which may well suggest that one account of the original meaning of the Constitution appears more persuasive or better founded than another. It is one thing to say that few interpretations of the more ambiguous and disputable clauses of the Constitution can be established conclusively, another to treat all interpretations as equally plausible or representative of the prevailing ideas of the time. Historians who pursue or merely observe the ongoing quest for the Holy Grail of original meaning thus occupy an awkward position vis-à-vis other knights-errant. Their research can lay an evidentiary basis for originalist interpretation, but it can also undermine critical assumptions on which invocations of original meaning depend, and expose the flawed conclusions they reach. And as Leonard Levy, the dean of American constitutional historians, has argued, the Supreme Court's use of originalist evidence is best described as a mix of "law office history" and justificatory rhetoric which offers little reason to think that this method of interpretation can provide the faithful and accurate application of the original constitutional understandings its advocates promise. William E. Nelson reaches a similar conclusion in his study of the adoption and early interpretation of the Fourteenth Amendment.[11]

It is not the province of the historian to decide questions of law. But by thinking about the original meanings, intentions, and understandings of 1787–91 as a problem of historical knowledge, it may be possible to give this recurring motif of constitutional interpretation a rigor it often lacks.

FROM THE MOMENT OF ITS PUBLICATION in a special issue of the *Pennsylvania Packet* on September 19, 1787, Americans have endowed the Constitution with two complementary sets of meanings. Taken as a whole—which is how the ratifiers had to take it—the Constitution symbolizes the "more perfect union" its framers proposed to put in place of the "imbecile" Articles of Confederation. In practice, the sole choice the Federal Convention and its Federalist supporters succeeded in forcing upon the nation at large was binary: The Constitution could be either accepted or rejected, but it could be altered only after it had been ratified. Thus ratification ultimately depended on the gross comparison of the Confederation and the Constitution. Structuring the decision in this way gave the Federalists the crucial political advantage of being able to equate support for the Constitution with support for the Union. There was nothing ambiguous about the nature of this choice at the time it was made, but it certainly became so later, as southern states'-rights theorists argued that the states that had been the parties to the original compact retained a sovereign right to reverse their decision.[12]

The Constitution has thus always represented something more than the sum of its parts. But since 1789, most disputes about its meaning have necessarily centered on its individual clauses. No single clause or provision can be interpreted without considering its relation to the document as a whole. Yet in practice, the enterprise of interpretation often requires an intense analysis of key words and brief phrases that the Constitution itself does not define. No explanatory footnotes or midrashic columns encumber the text, defining what such key terms as "necessary and proper" or "the executive power" or an "establishment of religion" were meant or understood to signify.

These two conceptions of the meaning of the Constitution are complementary, not contradictory. But they do lead historians to ask different kinds of questions about its adoption. The task of explaining *why* the Constitution was adopted does not involve paying close attention to its actual drafting or the origin and evolution of particular clauses. The central issue instead is to identify the political and social alignments that favored or opposed the creation of a stronger national government. Thus long after Charles Beard offered his *Economic Interpretation of the Constitution* in 1913, many historians still view the adoption of the Constitution largely in the context of a political struggle between identifiable constituencies and interests. Though the terms used to describe these different coalitions have changed over time, the thrust of inquiry has shifted less than one might suppose. Even in Gordon Wood's monumental study, *The Creation of the American Republic*, the substance of the Constitution matters less than the way in which the struggle over its ratification catalyzed a larger gulf between democratic and aristocratic elements in American society.[13] Within this context, it is enough to identify the most conspicuous differences between the Articles of Confederation and the Constitution; the basic story will not be altered if many of the particularities of the Constitution are ignored. Indeed, some of the concerns that most troubled the framers at Philadelphia—such as the extended impasse between small and large states—may prove only marginally relevant.

By contrast, the task of recovering the original meaning of the Constitution in all its detail raises a series of complex questions. Where do we turn when the meaning of the text—or more accurately, the meaning of a particular passage embedded in a larger text—is open to dispute?

An avowedly historical approach to the problem of original meaning involves something more than aggregating all relevant references to a particular provision of the Constitution or an aspect of constitutional thinking. It requires us to assess the probative value of any piece of evidence as well as to think systematically about the different types of evidence with which we work. In practice, there are four sets of sources that can be brought to bear to solve problems or puzzles about the original meaning of the Constitution. Two of these sets of sources can be described as *textual* in the sense that they consist of the explicit discussion of the Constitution found in the records of debates of the federal and state conventions of 1787 and 1788, as well as the commentaries published during the campaign over its ratification. The other two sets of sources can be characterized as *contextual* in that they may enable us—when explicit commentary on particular points seems inadequate—to reconstruct a body of tacit assumptions and concerns that informed the way in which framers and ratifiers thought about the questions they were resolving. On the one hand, there were those broad notions of government that Americans had acquired through their absorption in the political theory of the Enlightenment. But the way in which the political actors of the 1780s thought about the Constitution also reflected their perceptions of what might be called the public-policy issues of their day. Lessons derived from recent experience were arguably as likely to influence their thinking as the maxims and axioms they found in Locke or Montesquieu or Blackstone.

Each of these sources has its virtues and its potential defects. A historical approach to the problem of original meaning has to ask what each contributes to the overall inquiry.

The obvious point of departure must be the records of the Federal Convention itself: the inadequate journal kept by its secretary, William Jackson; Madison's daily notes of debates; and the other notes, memoranda, and speeches preserved by other delegates at Philadelphia. Given the circumstances under which the delegates deliberated, theirs were the only intentions that in any literal sense affected the composition and substance of the Constitution. This was not only because the Convention met in secret but, equally important, because its results ran far beyond what even the most astute observers anticipated or even imagined it would propose. The absence of any accepted agenda prior to the opening of debate in late May 1787 and the fact that the delegates came to Philadelphia essentially uninstructed by their legislative constituents make the internal deliberations of the Convention the first and most salient set of sources for the original meaning of the Constitution.

Tried techniques of historical narration should, in theory, be easy to apply to the task of writing the interior "story" of the Convention. What kind of event could be more susceptible to standard narrative treatment than one involving a limited number of actors (including certifiable "great men") meeting for a brief period and making critical decisions that define the dramatic structure of the entire story? Yet in practice the numerous narrative histories of the Convention have added little of interpretive value to our understanding of the framing of the Constitution. Certain stock themes are so essential to all accounts of the Convention as to defy authors to show a spark of originality. No author can stray far from a heavy reliance on Madison's notes of debates. The central actors must also be cast true to character: Madison, bookish yet politically astute; George Washington, reserved yet charismatic; James Wilson, brilliant but arrogant; Benjamin Franklin, witty and wise; Luther Martin, inebriated and stultifying yet good for comic relief; Roger Sherman, a crabbed speaker but a dogged parliamentarian; Alexander Hamilton, the candid icono-clast; and Gouverneur Morris, rashly (if apocryphally) draping his arm around Washington's shoulder. And the dramatic structure of the story turns out to be misshapen, since the climactic "great compromise" of July 16 occurred a full two months before Franklin could finally conclude that it was a rising and not a setting sun he had long pondered on the back of Washington's chair.[14]

Even when the literary problems inherent in retelling a familiar, highly stylized story are put aside, the most that any merely narrative ap-proach to the Convention can offer is a dramatic backdrop to the more important analytical questions we want to ask about the making of the Constitution. The dramatic structure of the Convention thus matters far less than the intellectual and political structure of the issues the delegates sought to resolve. For the completed Constitution was not the sum of a series of decisions taken on discrete issues. It is better imagined (to pursue the mathematical metaphor) as the solution to a complex equation with a large number of dependent variables: change the value of one, and the values shift throughout. The central problem thus involves tracing the re-lation between (or among) individual decisions that often seem to con-cern discrete issues but were in fact closely connected. Breathless accounts of the changing moods of the delegates or evocations of the heat and hu-midity of a Philadelphia summer that was, in any case, reasonably mild[15] will not explain why the decision to allow the state legislatures to elect the Senate undermined Madison's proposal to give Congress an absolute veto over all state laws; or how the final tinkering over the mechanics of pres-idential election was designed to enlarge executive authority in foreign affairs.

The construction of the matrix of these decisions is complicated by the fact that the Convention addressed two distinct types of issues. At the most abstract level, the debates were indeed concerned with such funda-mental questions as the nature of representation and executive power, fed-eralism, the separation of powers, and the protection of individual and minority rights. It is evident, too, that the delegates believed that what they did would have lasting implications not only for their constituents but for a larger world. No one dissented when Madison and Hamilton both observed that the decisions of the Convention were destined to "de-cide for ever the fate of Republican Government."[16]

Yet the debates at Philadelphia also had an intensely pragmatic cast. Much of the Convention was spent on issues that the delegates approached as spokesmen for the particular interests of their constituents. Here their real challenge did not involve solving theoretical dilemmas posed by Hobbes or Locke or Montesquieu; it instead required efforts to accommodate the conflicting interests of different states and regions on such matters as the apportionment of representation and taxes, the regulation of commerce, and the extension of the slave trade. Rather than view the Convention as an advanced seminar in constitutional theory, historians and many political scientists have preferred to describe it as a cumulative process of bargaining and compromise in which a rigid adherence to principle yielded to the pragmatic tests of reaching agreement and building coalitions.[17] From this perspective, the politics of the Convention resemble that of any legislative body, and its votes become grist for the fine-milling techniques of roll-call analysis that are commonly used to explain decision-making in Congress, state legislatures, or, for that matter, any city council outside Cook County, Illinois. The key to understanding the "great compromise" may thus be found, one political scientist has suggested, through two- or five-factor solutions with the varimax rotation (ortho).[18]

Ideas or *interests*—these are the classic if hackneyed antinomies upon which much of the debate over the political and intellectual history of the entire Revolutionary era has long been conducted. It is not difficult to see how both affected the deliberations at Philadelphia in 1787. What is elusive is the interplay between them. Some of the arguments the framers advanced were doubtless designed to legitimate positions rooted in calculations of state or regional or class interest. Others carried deeper conviction on their merits, as attempts to resolve issues that were avowedly related to problems of constitutional theory, broadly considered. The true task is thus to find "the middle ground"—a Madisonian metaphor—between the clouded heights of principle and the familiar terrain of specific interests.

Yet precisely because these higher principles often prove difficult to distill from the political maneuvers or elliptical discussions of the Convention, many students of the original meaning of the Constitution prefer to give equal or even greater weight to the commentaries and debates of the ratification campaign. Foremost among these sources are the essays of *The Federalist*, whose sway over modern scholarship begs explanation in its own right. But for all its virtues, *The Federalist* presents only one facet of the wide-ranging debate that erupted with the publication of the Constitution. Nothing like the extraordinary mobilization of public interest the Constitution evoked had been seen since the crisis of independence a full decade earlier. Ratification, it might be argued, created more than a new framework of national governance. It also demonstrated the possibility of national politics, anticipating the equally noteworthy innovations that enabled Americans, against their expectations, to create effective political parties within a few years.

The records of the ratification campaign are more diverse than those of the Federal Convention. They consist of pamphlets and newspaper essays written to influence public opinion; private letters assessing both the Constitution and the changing state of politics; and the records of debates in the state conventions, whose assent alone gave the Constitution its ultimate legal force. This corpus of material can be put to two general uses.

First, the ratification records occasionally provide useful evidence bearing on the prior deliberations at Philadelphia. Individual framers were often asked to explain why the Convention had acted in one way or declined to act in another; sometimes their responses add significantly to our knowledge of the original debates at Philadelphia. Moreover, the arguments that these framers advanced in support of the Constitution might reflect reliable impressions or summaries of the considerations they felt had prevailed at Philadelphia—and thus attest to the original intentions underlying the text. Certainly some of the respect *The Federalist* commands is due not only to its lucid, comprehensive treatment of the Constitution but also to the privileged position its two principal authors, Madison and Hamilton, held as leading framers.

Far more important, however, is the second use to which the ratification records can be put. Taken as a whole, they provide our best evidence of how the Constitution and its provisions were understood at the moment of adoption. Again, this understanding (or these understandings) cannot be equated with the authorial intentions that gave the Constitution its actual content. It is entirely possible—even probable, indeed almost certain—that the intentions of the framers and the understandings of the ratifiers and their electors diverged in numerous ways, on points both major and minor. Given the highly charged and intensely political character of the ratification campaign, no other outcome was possible. True, the Federalist supporters of the Constitution had a natural incentive to rally around the most effective explanations for particular clauses, and thus to foster a measure of consensus as to their meaning. But their Anti-Federalist opponents could freely credit any objection their imaginations could conjure, no matter how wild. Some of their predictions echoed the hyperbole of eighteenth-century political rhetoric, and Federalists cited this extravagance and the inconsistencies in the Anti-Federalist brief against the Constitution to prove that their opponents were unreasoning and overwrought. Many historians have shared that view.[19] Yet whether extravagant or plausible, Anti-Federalist fears were part of the original understanding of the Constitution, not only in their own right but also because they influenced the arguments that were made in its support.

Our reconstruction of the original understanding(s) of the Constitution, then, cannot be divorced from the political context of the ratification struggle. This does not mean that we should dismiss all statements on either side of the question as so much propaganda, but it does require an evaluation of the expedient needs that particular arguments were made to serve. For both parties, the overriding imperative was to determine whether the Constitution would be adopted, not to formulate definitive interpretations of its individual clauses. Thus while arguments about particular provisions mattered a great deal, in the end, the sole decision the ratifiers took was that of approving the Constitution as proposed or rejecting it. The only understanding we can be entirely confident the majority of ratifiers shared was that they were indeed deciding whether the Constitution would "form a more perfect union" than the Articles of Confederation (even if it no longer claimed, as had the Articles, that this union would be "perpetual").[20]

Our knowledge of what the ratifiers understood they were adopting is further limited by the spotty character of the reporting of the debates at the state conventions and the obscurity of their members. Though a few speeches were reported in more detail than Madison provided in his corresponding efforts at Philadelphia, none of the records of the state conventions, with the possible exception of Virginia, match his notes in quality and breadth.[21] Yet notwithstanding their deficiencies, these records deserve careful scrutiny for one crucial reason that is, however, related more to questions of law than to those of history. Madison stated the key point in 1796, when he argued that questions about the meaning of the Constitution could be answered in the light of the debates over ratification, but *not* by consulting the intentions of the framers at Philadelphia. "Whatever veneration might be entertained for the body of men who formed our Constitution," he told the House of Representatives,

> the sense of that body could never be regarded as the oracular guide in expounding the Constitution. As the instrument came from them it was nothing more than the draft of a plan, nothing but a dead letter, until life and validity were breathed into it by the voice of the people, speaking through the several State Conventions. If we were to look, therefore, for the meaning of the instrument beyond the

face of the instrument, we must look for it, not in the General Convention, which proposed, but in the State Conventions, which accepted and ratified the Constitution.[22]

Although Madison had serious problems explaining how the views of the
latter were to be ascertained, his position has at least this in its favor: It
is fully consistent with the theory of popular sovereignty that was itself
one of the great rallying points of Federalist argument in 1787 and 1788.
The Constitution became supreme law not because it was proposed by the
Federal Convention of 1787 but because it was ratified by the state conventions of 1787–88. By this criterion, the intentions of the framers were
legally irrelevant to its interpretation, but the understandings of the ratifiers could provide a legitimate basis for attempting to fix the original
meaning of the Constitution.

Even the most intensive examination of the surviving records for the
debates of 1787 and 1788 will leave substantial gaps in our knowledge,
however. Similarly, the spare language of the Constitution does not make
explicit the broader assumptions about government on which it is clearly
based. The preamble to the Constitution cannot sustain the close theoretical analysis that has been lavished on the opening paragraphs of the Declaration of Independence.

To fill these gaps in the record and the silences of the Constitution,
many scholars have sought to reconstruct the larger intellectual context
that shaped the contours of American thought in the late eighteenth
century. That thought and the Constitution it produced were expressions
of the Enlightenment. There can be no question that the framers and
many of their contemporaries were familiar not only with the great
works of such luminaries as Locke, Hobbes, Montesquieu, Hume, and
Blackstone, but also with the richly polemical literature of seventeenth-
and eighteenth-century English politics, the moral philosophy and social
science of the Scottish Enlightenment, and the disquisitions on public law of such respected European authorities as Grotius, Pufendorf, and
Delolme. Moreover, it is clear that general historical reading informed
the way in which eighteenth-century Americans thought about politics.
When they spoke of learning from experience, they did not mean their
own so much as that of previous generations, running all the way back to
classical antiquity.[23]

All of these writings were somehow part of the intellectual universe
the framers inhabited. Yet again, their application to the interpretation of
the Constitution poses difficult problems.

Perhaps the most vexatious involves tracing the lines of influence between these authorities and their American audience. At certain points, it is clear, quite specific connections can be made. The way in which Hamilton and Madison both invoke "the celebrated Montesquieu" to introduce their respective discussions of the extended republic and the separation of powers in *The Federalist* (essays 9 and 47) demonstrates the authoritative status that the French baron's treatise *De l'esprit des lois* commanded.[24] Much has been made, too, of the inspiration that Madison found in David Hume's essay "Idea of a Perfect Commonwealth" as he sought to counter the familiar view that the republican form of government was suitable only for small and homogeneous societies, like the city-states of antiquity.[25] Or again, the Federal Convention's first discussion of executive power on June 1, 1787, presupposes a knowledge of William Blackstone's treatment of royal prerogative in his *Commentaries on the Laws of England*.[26]

Yet it is no easy matter to link specific provisions of the Constitution with the writings of prior authorities. The problem lies in a distinction that Americans at every level of politics understood: that between fundamental *principles* of government, on the one hand, and the actual *forms* that any individual government could take. On the principles of government, a broad consensus reigned. Government existed for the good of the many, and to protect the liberty, property, and equal rights of the citizen. The idea that representation would help the government to determine the common good was commonplace, and so was the belief that separation of powers was essential to the protection of rights. These and other principles were reiterated in all the political writings in which Americans were steeped. Their authority was axiomatic.[27]

Axioms alone, however, do not solve problems; specific calculations are always needed to derive the desired results. In practice, the entire enterprise of constitution making in revolutionary America centered on determining which forms of republican government were best suited to securing the general principles all accepted.[28] Decisions about forms touched such prosaic questions as the respective powers and privileges of the different branches of government or the two houses of a legislature, the basis of representation, terms of office, modes of election, and so on. Though statements by Hume or Montesquieu or Blackstone or Harrington occasionally seemed pertinent to a particular problem, more often a wide number of solutions could be made compatible with the first principles of republicanism. From their reading the framers of the Constitution could extract no simple formulas to determine the exact form the new government should take.

The intellectual world of the Enlightenment, then, provides only a general context within which the Constitution can be located. Though clearly important in its own right, it cannot readily be brought to bear to solve particular puzzles of constitutional meaning.

There is, however, a far broader context within which these writings can be located, and which in turn provides the true framework for recovering what was both original and derivative in the intentions and understandings of 1787–88. For the adoption of the federal Constitution culminated a century and a half of constitutional controversy, contestation, and innovation that gave the American revolutionaries a richly complicated legacy of ideas and practices from which to construct their new republican polity. With a modest risk of oversimplification, this prior history can be divided into four substantial phases.

It is evident, first, that the vocabulary of American constitutional thinking was profoundly shaped by the great disputes between the Stuart monarchs and their opponents (in Parliament and out) which reached a momentous climax in the Glorious Revolution of 1688–89. On a host of issues—ranging from the great paradigms of mixed government and separation of powers to the "inestimable" right to trial by jury—the contending positions of the Stuart era were still vividly recalled a full century later.

These positions remained vital, in the second place, because the structure of colonial politics gave seventeenth-century arguments a continuing vitality in eighteenth-century America. Colonists naturally regarded their own legislative assemblies as miniatures of the mother Parliament, and the provincial elites who ruled there sought to acquire for these bodies the same rights and privileges that the House of Commons had struggled so long to acquire (or regain, if one clung to the belief that the Norman conquest of 1066 had deprived England of its "ancient constitution" of Gothic liberty). The recurrence in the colonies of these classic quarrels between executive prerogative and legislative privilege made Americans receptive not only to the general principles that Locke had enshrined in his *Second Treatise* but also to the works of more obscure but equally impassioned writers who preserved the radical edge of seventeenth-century polemics amid the complacency of Georgian Britain.

Third, the imperial controversy that began with the Stamp Act of 1765 and ended with the Declaration of Independence sharpened the colonists' understanding of the striking differences between their own political practices and attitudes and those prevailing "at home" in Britain. These differences seemed most conspicuous in the practice of representation, but they were evident as well in the colonists' rejection of monarchy, aristocracy, and much (if not quite all) of the theory of mixed government.

Fourth, and arguably most important, independence necessitated the reconstitution of legal government within all the states (save the corporate colonies of Rhode Island and Connecticut), and it thus gave rise to the "experiment in republicanism" that the past generation of scholars has explored in such detail. The adoption of written constitutions of government in the mid-1770s was in one sense a wonderful accident made possible by the literal-minded way in which the colonists believed the collapse of royal government and the eruption of civil war had reduced them to something like a state of nature. But it also gave them the opportunity to establish new and superior forms of government, more in tune with the conditions of American society and republican principles. And once established, the operations of these state governments in turn provided the most visible examples of what republicanism meant in practice. Their failings not only drove the movement for constitutional reform that brought the framers to Philadelphia in May 1787, they also provided the experimental evidence upon which the Convention drew as it sought to fashion an improved model of republican government.[29] For the convention delegates of 1787–88 came to their task fresh not from research in their studies but from the business of managing a revolution and conducting public affairs at every level of government. Conscious as they were of the fate of other republics and confederacies, ancient and modern, the lessons of the past that they weighed most heavily were drawn from their own experience.

Yet if this decade of constitutional experimentation was the greatest influence on the debates of 1787–88, principles and lessons inculcated over the previous century and a half were not simply sloughed off as the detritus of an irrelevant, pre-Revolutionary ancien régime. Americans were as eclectic in their use of history as they were in their often selective reading of texts and authorities. Reconstructing how they reasoned about the great questions of the late 1780s may therefore require a review—in highly synthesized form—of aspects of Anglo-American politics and political theory that long predate the immediate debates over the Constitution. No simple formula or code can map how these strands of thought came together in 1787–88. Like any other historical effort to explain how texts emerge from contexts, the recovery of original meanings, intentions, and understandings is itself an act of interpretation—but one that can at least be bounded, though not perfected, by canons of scholarship.

Some may object that too great an emphasis on establishing the multiple contexts within which the framers and ratifiers acted risks historicizing the great moment of the Founding, reducing its profound expressions of principle to the prosaic level of mere interest and ideology, and subordinating its transcendent meaning in favor of a time-bound portrait of an eighteenth-century society that remains irretrievably lost and alien.[30] Against these charges, historians can respond in at least two ways. They can plead necessity: The evidence allows no other choice; our knowledge of the complexity of political controversy and debate during this period can sustain no other conclusion. Or they can plead innocence. Far from treating the political thought of the Revolutionary era as the mere product of a fevered ideology, the most important recent historical writing goes to great lengths to describe its originality and creativity. But it does so not by abstracting these creative acts and ideas from the circumstances of their origination but by exploring and explaining the relation between them.

ULTIMATELY, OF COURSE, HISTORIANS, political theorists, and legal scholars diverge in their approaches because they pose different questions and seek different answers. Working historians should have no illusions about their capacity to correct, much less prevent, the errors to which their colleagues seem prone. Nor should historians be surprised when their findings are put to uses they never intended or even contemplated. Surely J. G. A. Pocock, Bernard Bailyn, and Gordon Wood never imagined that their reconstruction of the early modern ideology of republicanism would provide the conceptual foundation upon which an entire school of legal scholars soon launched a "republican revival" of their own, in the process fashioning an originalism of the communitarian left to challenge the originalism of the new (and Republican) right.21[31] The forms of historical argumentation employed on both the right and left margins of contemporary scholarship (and politics) are not driven, of course, by the historian's old-fashioned and perhaps naïve desire to get the story right for its own sake. They represent, instead, only another chapter in the saga of the American search for a usable past. Historians certainly help this search to go forward, but they may also suggest why its goal is (and should remain) elusive. By taking the problem of "originalism" seriously, by considering the uses and potential misuses of different forms of evidence, it may be possible to advance a debate that is very much about a specific moment in history but is not about history alone.

CHAPTER II

THE ROAD TO
PHILADELPHIA

I SUSPECT THAT OUR POSTERITY will read the History of the last four Years with much Regret," wrote Secretary of Foreign Affairs John Jay in November 1786. Two months earlier, the abortive Annapolis Convention had called for a general convention to meet at Philadelphia the following May. The ever-cautious Jay doubted whether the proposed convention would succeed. When in late February he wrote again to John Adams, the American minister to Britain, Jay observed that he did not expect "much further immediate Good from the Measure than that it will tend to approximate the public Mind to the Changes which ought to take place."[1] In this he erred, and because he did, his other prediction of November proved equally wrong. Far from viewing the years immediately following the close of the Revolutionary War with "regret," posterity has preferred to treat this interval as a necessary prelude to the success of the Federal Convention.

Jay was only one of many correspondents who kept Adams abreast of events at home while he represented American interests abroad. Their views did not always accord. Alarmist reports of the state of politics, the economy, and public morality alternated with balanced appraisals of how well the country was recovering from a prolonged war that had placed unprecedented demands on government and citizens alike. "No people ever had a fairer opportunity to be what they have anxiously wished to be— none ever neglected their interest more," Tristram Dalton wrote Adams in July 1786. "From the seeds of division among us, much is to be dreaded." Far less gloomy was the report Adams received some months later from

Ezra Stiles. "We may be capricious, we may do 1000 foolish Things," Stiles wrote in March 1787, "without ruining the Federation or the growing Glory of the United States."[2] The letters Adams read during his service at the Court of St. James are filled with remarks like these. Some writers were even more discouraged than Dalton, others were as philosophical as Stiles, but all were concerned with how well Americans were vindicating the promise of their revolution and their new republican governments.

Adams expressed his own ideas about the dilemmas of American republicanism in his *Defence of the Constitutions of Government of the United States*, the first of whose three volumes appeared shortly before the Federal Convention assembled. With his usual modesty, Adams liked to think that this work had influenced the debates at Philadelphia. The delegates certainly knew the book, but most found its leading arguments—notably its praise for the limited monarchy of the British constitution—more objectionable than persuasive. "Men of learning find nothing new in it," James Madison complained to Thomas Jefferson, Adams's counterpart at the court of Versailles; "Men of taste many things to criticize."[3]

Adams exerted his greatest influence over the movement for constitutional reform not through the power of his writings but through his frustrations as a diplomat. From the first months of peace, Americans were continually reminded that their national interests remained closely tied to the character of relations with Great Britain. In London, Adams sought to negotiate a treaty of commerce with Britain, and to resolve the problems that arose when individual states violated provisions of the peace treaty of 1783. His failures owed nothing to his own faults as a diplomat and everything to the fundamental weaknesses of the Articles of Confederation. And this in turn illustrates a crucial truth about the political movement that ultimately led to the Federal Convention. In its inception it had important but limited goals. Far from contemplating the radical changes that suddenly seemed possible in 1787, those who sought to amend the Articles of Confederation were concerned, first and foremost, with enabling the Continental Congress to meet its accepted responsibilities, or at most, to extend its authority in modest ways. Only after these efforts proved uniformly abortive did it become possible to expand the agenda of reform far beyond what had seemed plausible or even desirable in the immediate postwar period.[4]

∞

EFFORTS TO AMEND the Articles of Confederation began even before the first federal charter of the United States took effect on March 1, 1781. Only weeks earlier, Congress had asked the state legislatures to approve an amendment authorizing it to collect a 5 percent impost on imported goods. This proposal was the outgrowth of the mounting financial problems that had plagued Congress since 1779, when the depreciation of paper currency forced it to close down its printing presses.

Like the Articles, amendments required the unanimous approval of the states. By the fall of 1782, it was evident that Rhode Island would never ratify the impost. A second, more ambitious effort to restore the credit of the national treasury began immediately, when Congress took up a set of measures proposed by Robert Morris, its superintendent of finance. Morris envisioned no radical shift in the essential purposes of the Union; his program was simply designed to enable Congress to discharge its existing duties under the Articles or the new responsibilities it would acquire with the anticipated creation of a national domain above the Ohio River.[5]

After months of furious politicking marked by the threats and cajolings of Morris and rumors of unrest and mutiny in the Continental army, Congress approved a comprehensive revenue plan on April 18, 1783. It had three major elements: an impost lasting twenty-five years, collected by officials appointed by the states; the appropriation by the states of supplemental taxes dedicated to federal use; and a revision of the formula in Article VIII of the Confederation for apportioning national expenses among the states, replacing an unwieldy and impracticable scheme based on the value of assessed land with a rule of population that would count enslaved African-Americans at a ratio of three-fifths of the free population. Though these resolutions fell short of the measures Morris originally proposed, their adoption reflected a genuine compromise that conceded the impossibility of persuading all thirteen states to approve a program that did not equitably balance their divergent interests. Congress accordingly presented its financial program as a package that the states would have to approve in its entirety.[6]

The idea that Congress could coax the states into approving such a compromise was not unrealistic. An encouraging precedent for balancing state and national interests could be found in the arduous process that had led individual states to yield their claims to western lands in the interest of creating a national domain. Moreover, the often-voiced expectation that the sale of these vast tracts would erase the national debt indicated that many of those who spoke most loudly against giving Congress any power of taxation did not oppose the financial autonomy of the

Union per se. "The western world opens an amazing prospect as a national fund," gushed David Howell, a leading opponent of congressional taxation, in February 1784; "it is equal to our debt."[7]

Yet while the history of the state cessions offered a hopeful precedent for the amendment of the Articles, Congress could not ignore the effect that a rejection of its revenue program would have on its plans for developing the West. Congress was too poor to maintain the troops needed both to restrain the frontiersmen who were already spilling across the Ohio and to intimidate the native tribes who resented the dictated treaties whereby Congress demanded the surrender of ancestral lands without fair purchase. Lacking adequate revenues, the Union risked losing control over the orderly sale of the national domain and even the allegiance of the settlers.[8]

Beyond the standing issues of finance and western lands, the postwar agenda of national politics was increasingly dominated by matters of foreign relations. Indeed, the most serious doubts about the adequacy of the Articles of Confederation arose over the inability of Congress to frame and implement satisfactory foreign policies. The emerging dilemmas of the mid-1780s were disturbing in two crucial respects. They revealed, first, that Congress lacked the formal authority it needed to protect American commercial interests—a crucial defect, because it was widely assumed that American relations with Europe would be commercial rather than political in nature. Second, the events of 1783–86 demonstrated that Congress no longer commanded the same internal consensus or popular support it had possessed in the early years of the Revolution. By the mid-1780s it was an open question whether there was, in fact, any longer a *national* interest that could be generally perceived or effectively pursued even by the relatively enlightened members of Congress, much less by their constituents in the state legislatures or the people "out-of-doors."[9]

Within a year of the peace of 1783, Congress confronted three external challenges to the national welfare. American merchants eager to restore prewar patterns of commerce found early cause for disappointment in the measures that Britain quickly took to close both home-island and West Indian ports to American shipping. At the same time, a stream of British ships sailed into American harbors, bringing goods sorely missed during the wartime years of deprivation while often cutting American importers out of their marketing. In theory, the United States should have pursued a retaliatory strategy of limiting British access to American ports until British harbors were opened to American shipping. But such a policy stood to fail on two counts. Lacking authority to regulate interstate or foreign commerce, Congress could neither devise nor impose a uniform set of restrictions on British ships. And this *constitutional* debility in turn diminished the prospects for advancing American trading interests through the negotiation of a satisfactory commercial treaty with Britain: What privileges could John Adams offer that British merchants did not already enjoy?[10]

The second great issue of foreign relations concerned the peace treaty itself. Article IV of the treaty provided that "creditors on either side shall meet with no lawful impediment" to the recovery of debts previously contracted in good faith. Under Article V, Congress was required to *recommend* that the states similarly permit British subjects and American loyalists to sue for the recovery of confiscated property. Both articles placed Congress in the awkward position of guaranteeing what it lacked the constitutional authority to deliver: the compliance of state legislatures and courts with a national commitment made to a foreign power. When individual states violated these clauses, Britain used their noncompliance as a pretext for retaining the northwestern forts (Oswego, Niagara, and Detroit) whose surrender had also been part of the treaty of peace. This in turn further jeopardized congressional plans for the national domain, since a continued British presence in the Northwest encouraged the hostile western tribes to resist encroachments on their lands.

The future of westward expansion was also implicated in the third major postwar problem of foreign policy. In April 1784, Spain closed New Orleans and the lower Mississippi River to American navigation, thus preventing frontier settlers living west of the mountain barrier from shipping their produce to the Gulf of Mexico and thence to other markets. This action, coupled with abortive separatist movements in Kentucky and what would become Tennessee, threatened to deprive the United States of the generous territorial settlement accorded by the Treaty of Paris. Should the weakness of the Union force western settlers to accommodate themselves to Spain, control of the regions lying between the Appalachian Mountains and the Mississippi would be lost to the United States. Furthermore, because the region below the Ohio was commonly viewed as an outpost of *southern* expansion, acquiescence in the Spanish action threatened to exacerbate sectional tensions within Congress. Southern leaders grew particularly outraged in 1786, when Secretary Jay went so far as to propose that the United States abjure its navigational rights in exchange for a commercial treaty with Spain. Jay's proposal evoked a sharp and bitter sectional division within Congress, giving sudden validity to vague speculations that the United States might eventually devolve into two or three regional confederacies.[11]

While the revenue plan of April 1783 made sluggish progress through the state assemblies and Congress pursued its efforts to organize the national domain, these concerns of foreign policy dominated efforts to strengthen the Confederation. Proposals for reform developed along two lines. One involved *clarifying* the authority that might be presumed already to lie in Congress by virtue of its general power to make treaties with foreign nations. Here the great challenge was to establish the principle that national obligations should prevail over the legislative acts of sovereign states. Thus in his seminal decision in *Rutgers* v. *Waddington*, James Duane set an important precedent for both the supremacy of federal treaties over state law and the judicial review of legislative acts.[12] The other avenue of reform centered on enhancing federal power in an area where experience indicated that the national interest required that Congress be given what it currently lacked: greater authority to regulate both foreign and interstate commerce. In 1784 Congress did submit new amendments asking the states for limited authority over foreign commerce; in 1785 and 1786 it considered committee reports proposing additional powers in the same area; and in September 1786 the Annapolis Convention met to ponder the same issue.[13]

All of these proposals foundered on the requirement of unanimous state ratification. In practice, the height of that constitutional hurdle discouraged those who supported a stronger Confederation from conceiving of the problems of federalism in terms that transcended the limited additional powers that Congress needed to respond to specific issues. Instead of contemplating the calling of a general convention, they pursued a prudent strategy of proposing discrete amendments whose piecemeal adoption and implementation, they hoped, would gradually make Americans less wary of a more efficient and potent national government. The desultory history of *all* the amendments that Congress had fruitlessly considered since 1781 indicated that more radical proposals stood little chance of adoption.

JUST AS THE MOVEMENT for independence a decade earlier had tapped beliefs and attitudes far more profound than mere opposition to parliamentary taxation, so the political events of 1787 and 1788 drew on deeper sources of concern than commerce, revenue, and western lands. Important as they were, the principal *national* issues of the mid-1780s could never alone have generated the sense of crisis that gave the struggle over the Constitution its urgent tenor. For most Americans, indeed, national politics mattered little. They knew more about the debates in Parliament, which were reported in American newspapers, than about the deliberations of their peripatetic Congress, which still met behind closed doors (though in different towns, until it finally settled in New York).[14] When Americans thought about politics at all, they directed their concerns toward local and state issues. These were the levels of governance whose decisions affected their daily lives, and which had to cope with the aftermath of a prolonged revolutionary struggle that had placed so enormous a strain on American society.

How the states were responding to this task became, by 1787, as important an element in the movement for constitutional reform as the more conspicuous failings of Congress. When enlightened leaders like James Madison or Alexander Hamilton fretted about the general condition of the Republic, they increasingly worried less about the "imbecility" of Congress than about the shortcomings of the individual governments of the states. Yet while the manifest defects of the Confederation were few and conspicuous, the problems of state government were more complex and difficult to diagnose. Nor was it evident how reforms at one level of government could benefit the other. Insofar as most proposals to amend the Articles sought to free Congress from its debilitating dependence on the states, the agenda of national reform seemed designed to reduce rather than strengthen the connections between state and national politics.

Directly and indirectly, perceptions of the problems of state politics and government influenced the movement for constitutional reform in three ways. The first and most obvious involved those areas where Congress and the states remained necessarily bound together. The failure of the states to approve proposed amendments to the Articles, to meet the financial requisitions of Congress, and to abide by the provisions of the Treaty of Paris all called into question the fundamental premise of the Confederation: that the states would exercise their sovereign powers in good faith to fulfill rather than frustrate essential national interests.

The relation between national politics and a second set of problems of state governance was more elusive yet potentially more powerful. Complaints about both the quality of domestic legislation—that is, laws regulating the internal concerns of the states—and the contentious character of state politics suggested that the promise of the Revolution was somehow being betrayed. Having won independence at great cost, Americans seemed unprepared or unable to manage their affairs wisely or peacefully. Much of this unease was a legacy of the final years of the Revolution, when inflation and its attendant evils strained both the resources of state governments and the public-spiritedness of their citizens. In the years after 1783, many of the states moved quickly to retire their accrued public debt. Though their efforts were effective, by mid-decade sorely pressed citizens were mounting increasing resistance to the collection of the requisite taxes.[15]

More worrisome than the impolicy of particular pieces of legislation, however, was the contentiousness of state politics in general. Discontent was directed against legislators and citizens alike—against both the mistakes of the lawmakers and the demands of their constituents. Officeholders complained about the unreasonable expectations of the people at large, while voters faulted those whom they elected for failing to remedy their immediate grievances. This disillusion, too, could in part be traced to the closing years of the war, when revolutionaries at every level of politics repeatedly contrasted the prevailing quarrelsomeness and disaffection with the patriotic enthusiasm of 1774–76. The memory of how unified Americans had been at the moment of independence was a nagging reminder of how far they had fallen during the short span of years since.

For all the complaints that state politics generated during the 1780s, it was far from apparent how the movement to amend the Confederation, even if successful, could simultaneously work to "prevent the local mischiefs which every where excite disgusts ag[ain]st the state governments." Perhaps the most important consequence of this generalized discontent lay in the ambiguous realm of mood, attitude, and perception rather than in any specific set of proposals. As Madison observed soon after the Convention, "the evils issuing" from the states "contributed more to that uneasiness which produced the Convention, and prepared the public mind for a general reform, than those which accrued to our national character and interest from the inadequacy of the Confederation to its immediate objects."[16]

By far the greatest influence that the experience of the states exerted on the deliberations of 1787 lay, however, in the area of constitutional theory itself. For when the framers set about designing the new national government, the crucial lessons they applied were drawn from their observation of the state constitutions written since independence. It was in the drafting of these charters, rather than the Articles of Confederation, that the revolutionaries had expressed their original notions of republican government most clearly. Some of these constitutions, notably Pennsylvania's, provoked controversy from the moment of their adoption; others were drafted hastily by conventions and legislatures distracted by other duties; others still, like the Massachusetts constitution of 1780, were approved only after prolonged debate and popular discussion. By the mid-1780s, however, all had come in for careful scrutiny and mounting criticism as the experience of war and the dissatisfactions of peacetime generated complaints about the shortcomings of state government. Rather than treat these failings as merely a function of poor decisions or intractable difficulties, the critics of state government sought constitutional explanations for political problems. How the framers at the Federal Convention thought about such major theoretical issues as representation and the separation of powers was largely a response to their assessment of the relevant provisions and practices of the state constitutions. The states had served, in effect, as the great political laboratory upon whose experiments the framers of 1787 drew to revise the theory of republican government.[17]

ALL OF THESE CONCERNS ultimately influenced the debates at Philadelphia, liberating the Convention intellectually and carrying its agenda well past the point where many delegates privately expected their explorations would end. Yet well into 1787, it seemed unlikely that the Convention would range much beyond proposing remedies to the most familiar problems of the Confederation—or that if it did, its recommendations would do little more, as John Jay noted, than "to approximate the public Mind to the Changes which ought to take place."[18]

Such skepticism reflected the discouraging political obstacles against which those who favored reforming both the Confederation and the state constitutions struggled. The record was hardly encouraging. The states had taken more than three years to ratify the Articles; during the six years that had elapsed since, not one of the amendments that Congress proposed to the states was approved. The requirement of unanimous ratification seemed insurmountable. Nor was that the only problem. Article XIII required that amendments to the Confederation first be approved by Congress. But by 1785 its reputation had fallen so low that any proposal Congress submitted to the states seemed tainted at its source.

Recognizing the force of these obstacles, the advocates of a stronger Confederation favored a strategy of piecemeal reform, hoping that the adoption of one or more of the modest measures Congress had proposed would reduce the objections against further amendments. By the early spring of 1786, however, this posture of patient optimism had become difficult to maintain. Not only did the commercial amendments of 1784 remain unratified, but the revenue plan of April 1783 also seemed doomed to rejection. In March 1786 the New Jersey assembly resolved that it would no longer comply with the financial requisitions of Congress; in April the New York legislature nominally approved the revenue plan, but only with conditions Congress deemed unacceptable because they conflicted with the corresponding acts already adopted by other states.[19]

With Congress clearly losing whatever influence it retained, the initiative for reform necessarily shifted to the states. The most important development took place in Virginia. In January 1786, at the very close of its session, the Virginia assembly adopted a resolution calling for an interstate conference to consider the utility of vesting Congress with adequate power to regulate commerce. Far from being a bold expedient to force the pace of reform, this measure was a weak substitute for other proposals, more immediately favorable to Congress, that the assembly balked at accepting. Thus Madison supported the resolution because it was "better than nothing," but for weeks after the legislature had adjourned, he thought that it was "liable to objections and will probably miscarry."[20]

Yet Madison soon realized that no other measure appeared more promising. While James Monroe, writing from Congress, at first objected that the agenda of the conference was too confined to do much good, Madison reasoned that "if anything can be done, it seems as likely to result from the proposed Convention, and more likely to result f[rom] the present crisis, than from any other mode or time."[21] Two considerations seemed crucial. First, amendments proposed by Congress stood little chance of approval. Nor was the Virginia assembly (or any other) as yet prepared to empower its commissioners to go beyond the single issue of commerce. More comprehensive reform was desirable in theory, but political caution still demanded a step-by-step approach.

Although eight states eventually accepted the Virginia invitation to meet at Annapolis, only twelve delegates from five states appeared at the appointed time in mid-September. No proposal issued by this small group could be expected to carry any weight with the states or Congress. Yet to adjourn without doing anything would amount to conceding that the movement to strengthen the Union had reached a dead end. Instead the commissioners chose a greater risk. Drawing on a clause in the instructions of the New Jersey members, they endorsed a report calling on the states to elect new delegates to attend a second convention, set for Philadelphia the following May, "to devise such further provisions as shall appear to them necessary to render the constitution of the federal government adequate to the exigencies of the Union."[22]

Given the potentially radical thrust of this proposal, the Annapolis Convention has always had a conspiratorial aura about it. Writing to Jefferson a month before it met, Madison reported that "Many Gentlemen both within & without Cong[res]s wish to make this Meeting subservient to a Plenipotentiary Convention for amending the Confederation."[23] The fact that those present at Annapolis included Madison, Hamilton, and John Dickinson—all prominent supporters of more effective national government—suggests that the commissioners welcomed the opportunity to ignore their assigned agenda. Yet even if they did, none underestimated the task ahead. In fact, the Annapolis report was as much a desperate maneuver of politicians who had exhausted all other alternatives as a bold stratagem of statesmen who knew exactly what they wanted, and how to get it. The sole advantage they could hope to exploit was that the failure of all previous measures to amend the Articles would finally rally the like-minded around the idea of a general convention—a measure that had long seemed too bold to have much chance of success. Yet this prospect alone could not miraculously overturn the obstacles that had blocked previous forays at amending the Articles—notably the requirement for unanimous ratification by the state legislatures, which might well oppose changes that would reduce their own powers.

Beyond the realization that the strategy of gradual reform had collapsed, one further consideration probably spurred the Annapolis commissioners to gamble on a second convention. By the fall of 1786, it could no longer be safely assumed that time lay on the side of reform. Sectional rifts within Congress over commercial policy and the navigation of the Mississippi had exposed the fault lines along which the Union might divide should the national government fail to satisfy the rival interests of different states and regions. While the idea that the Union might devolve into regional confederacies still seemed incredible, events since 1783 had called into question the very idea of national interest. Even during the war, the transcendent issue of independence had not always stifled the expression of sectional antagonisms; in peace, it became entirely permissible to ask whether divergent regional interests could sustain the "perpetual union" the Articles proclaimed.

In abandoning the strategy of piecemeal reform, the Annapolis Convention did not suggest that the mandate of the Philadelphia Convention should extend beyond the conspicuous failings of the Confederation to consider, as well, the internal problems of the states. By the early winter of 1787, however, events in Massachusetts had made it possible to cast the problems of the Republic in more comprehensive terms. Shays's Rebellion began as a protest movement among Massachusetts farmers laboring under the dual burdens of relatively heavy taxation and private debt; it escalated from a concerted effort to close county courts into a military confrontation pitting armed farmers from the interior against militia drawn largely from the seaboard counties. Although the government forces easily prevailed, that did not prevent concerned observers throughout the United States from taking alarm. Whatever else they thought about Massachusetts, its constitution was regarded as perhaps the best balanced of the Revolutionary charters—and that was exactly why Shays's Rebellion signaled a deeper crisis. If stable and seemingly well-governed Massachusetts could erupt in popular upheaval, what other state could claim to be more secure?

From his distant vantage point in Paris, Jefferson dismissed Shays's Rebellion with a characteristic aphorism: "[A] little rebellion now and then is a good thing," he wrote Madison on January 30, 1787, "and as necessary in the political world as storms in the physical."[24] Madison was hardly inclined to agree. Though reluctant to contradict his friend directly, he clearly felt that Jefferson, after three years in France, simply did not appreciate how grave the political situation at home had become. Madison allowed himself no such illusions. As he examined what he called "the vices of the political system of the United States" in the early months of 1787, he became convinced that the agenda of the coming convention could not be confined to the important but familiar problems of the Confederation alone. The time had come, Madison concluded, not only to free the Union from its dependence on the states but to free the states from themselves by taking steps that would undo the damage done by the excesses of republicanism.

Of all the developments that went into setting the agenda of the Federal Convention, James Madison's own preparations were perhaps the most important, and so deserve close attention in their own right.

THE MADISONIAN
MOMENT

EW BOOKS HAVE CONTRIBUTED more to our understanding of the larger world of ideas within which American constitutionalism took shape than J. G. A. Pocock's *The Machiavellian Moment*. In this influential study of the transmission of republican ideas from sixteenth-century Florence to seventeenth-century England and thence to eighteenth-century America, Pocock gave his title phrase two meanings. "The Machiavellian moment" was, first, the point in historical time when "Machiavellian thought made its appearance"—and why it did so thus deserves explanation. But the term has a second meaning. It is a specific problem not only *in* historical time but also *about* historical time itself, and the way in which Machiavelli and his contemporaries thought about the life cycle of republican polities. It was "the moment in conceptualized time in which the republic was seen as confronting its own temporal finitude, as attempting to remain morally and politically stable in a stream of irrational events conceived as eventually destructive of all systems of secular stability." In this second sense, the problem of the Machiavellian moment was eventually transmitted to the remarkable generation who "founded" the American republic.[1] And they bequeathed it in turn to those who would come after. For the argument that later interpretations of the Constitution should seek either to conform to or restore its original meaning is a much diluted yet still recognizable version of the Machiavellian notion of *ridurre ai principii*.

It was as a Machiavellian (in this sense) that James Madison spoke to his colleagues in Philadelphia on June 26, 1787. "In framing a system which we wish to last for ages, we shd. not lose sight of the changes which ages will produce," he observed. And whereas Machiavelli was concerned only with the fate of individual republics, Madison was prepared to give his republican project a universalist significance. "[I]t was more than probable we were now digesting a plan which in its operation will decide forever the fate of Republican Govt.," Madison reminded his colleagues—a sentiment which drew a quick second from Alexander Hamilton (even as he "acknowledged himself not to think favorably of Republican Government").[2]

The Madisonian moment of 1787 owed much, as Pocock suggests, to the heritage of Machiavelli and James Harrington, the crucial figure in transmuting Florentine concepts into the language of Anglo-American politics. But 1787 was Madison's moment in a more immediate sense. He had not consciously devoted his life to the goal of constitutional reform with the same ascetic fervor that later revolutionaries brought to their quests for justice (or power). Nor were his ambitions as relentless as those which drove later generations of democratic politicians to seek higher (or lower) office. But Madison went to Philadelphia in the grip of a deep passion, convinced that he had found a complete remedy for the vices of the American political system. Much of the history of the Convention can be written as the story of his efforts to persuade his colleagues that his diagnosis was accurate. By his own rigorous standards and high expectations, that effort fell short. But from the start, it elevated both the substance and the character of the debates well beyond the prevailing expectations.

FOR MADISON, AS FOR SO many of his contemporaries, the experience of revolution involved more than a transfer of political loyalties from Great Britain to the newly independent republic. It was also liberating in a profoundly personal way. On the eve of independence, Madison was a directionless young man with little apparent ambition. After completing his studies at the College of New Jersey in Princeton in 1772, he returned to Montpelier, the family plantation, where he spent his time reading and fretting about his health and his isolation in the Virginia piedmont, while avoiding any choice of vocation. The Revolution changed all that. At first through the influence of his father—the largest landholder in Orange County—and then in his own right, Madison acquired offices that thrust him directly into the Revolutionary struggle. Service in the Provincial Convention that drafted the state constitution in 1776 was followed by a two-year stint as a member of the Virginia Council of State; then, in the early spring of 1780, he joined the Virginia delegation to Congress. Here Madison spent three and a half years, returning home only when the clause in the Articles of Confederation limiting service to three years out of any six finally brought him back to Montpelier in the fall of 1783. His retirement from politics, however, was brief. In the spring of 1784 he entered the Virginia assembly as a delegate from Orange County, serving three terms until, with his eligibility restored, he returned to Congress in the winter of 1787.[3]

In politics Madison found a fulfillment that the management of a plantation or a law practice could never have provided. Few of his contemporaries shared his single-minded commitment to public life, and this offered a great advantage in an age when politics remained avocational, when officeholders typically saw themselves as discharging unpleasant duties rather than pursuing deeply held ambitions.[4] Short, slender, soft-spoken, and unprepossessing in person, Madison nevertheless exercised enormous influence in both Congress and the Virginia assembly. That influence rested in part on a willingness to take the initiative in lawmaking and an aptitude for the committee work in which so many of the details of legislation were worked out. But it also reflected the quality of mind that enabled Madison to dissect issues and alternatives with a rigor that even his opponents respected. When he was done briefing an issue, it was hard for anyone to avoid perceiving the problem in the terms he had used. Bookish Madison certainly was; he was indeed the very epitome of "the thinking revolutionary."[5] But his political intelligence was eminently pragmatic.

The crucial conclusions he drew about the debilities of the Republic reflected his experiences at both the state and national levels of government. Madison had entered Congress just as it was attempting to shift greater responsibility for sustaining the war effort to the states. His experience in Virginia led him to doubt whether the states were equal to the task, and with British troops operating almost at will in the South in 1780 and 1781, the experiment seemed all the riskier. Rather than rely on the good faith of the states, Madison concluded that Congress needed "coercive powers" to compel them to do their duty. Thus as soon as the Articles of Confederation took effect in March 1781, he drafted an amendment empowering Congress to use its armed forces "to compel" delinquent states "to fulfill their federal engagements." Though neither Congress nor the states were likely to approve so drastic a proposal, Madison remained persuaded that it offered an effective solution to the crucial problem of securing state compliance with national policy.[6]

The American victory at Yorktown in the fall of 1781 shifted congressional attention from problems of supplies to the issue of revenue. Here, again, Madison played an active role in supporting measures to provide Congress with independent sources of revenue. Though less closely associated with the ambitious plans of Robert Morris, the superintendent of finance, than were such colleagues as Alexander Hamilton and James Wilson, Madison generally favored the Morris program until it became clear that neither Congress nor the states could be expected to approve the comprehensive scheme of land, poll, and excise taxes Morris had requested. At this point, Madison broke with the superintendent and introduced the compromise that formed the heart of the revenue system Congress eventually approved in April 1783.[7]

His lengthy service in Congress left Madison a "nationalist" in this sense at least: He was convinced that Congress lacked the authority and resources to carry out even its existing duties under the Articles of Confederation. Whether he privately held more expansive notions of the potential scope of national power is less certain. Because the initial criticism of the Articles arose amid the urgency of the war, the delegates had little time and less incentive to imagine what role Congress would play after independence was secured. Robert Morris, his assistant Gouverneur Morris, and Hamilton may well have looked forward to a national government that could actively influence the development of the economy, but few of their colleagues were prepared to think so far ahead.

Members of Congress *were* the national government, and given the difficulties under which they labored, nearly every delegate ended his term convinced that Congress was too dependent on the states. But as the paid agents of their states, delegates were also repeatedly obliged to balance the demands of national policy against the interests of their constituents. Given the military threats to Virginia in 1780 and 1781, Madison found his dual obligations easy to reconcile. But on another crucial issue—the cession of Virginia's western lands to the Union—he acted as a delegate in the strict sense, faithfully defending the conditions that the state assembly insisted must be met in order for its cession to be completed. On occasion the efforts by other states to challenge the Virginia claims so alarmed Madison that he dared "to presume that the present Union will but little survive the present war."[8] But that bleak forecast marked the low point of his pessimism. Madison never thought that the Union should be dissolved; his deeper concern was to reverse the centrifugal political forces that rendered Congress increasingly impotent.

The recurring need to balance national and state loyalties shaped the development of Madison's political thinking in important ways. When it came to gauging the prospects for reform, he was a political realist who understood the obstacles that any attempt to amend the Articles would face. Only proposals commanding consensus within Congress could secure unanimous ratification by the states. That consensus could not be built by the scare tactics that Robert Morris had used in 1782 and 1783, when he tried to pressure Congress by fomenting unrest among the public creditors and within the Continental army, and by threatening to resign if his program was not approved. It would require instead a reasoned approach that would involve both accommodations among the interests represented in Congress and a prudent regard for the difficulty of mobilizing support for reform within the states. At the same time, Madison thought "it better to trust to further experience and even distress, for an adequate remedy," than to adopt "temporary" expedients which might prove inadequate to the permanent needs of the Union.[9]

This was the moderate and highly pragmatic strategy that Madison pursued when he framed the revenue plan of April 1783, when he entered the Virginia assembly the next year, and even as late as 1786, when he hoped the Annapolis Convention would provide a new mechanism for forming the Confederation. It was also the strategy that he finally abandoned as he prepared for the Federal Convention in the winter and early spring of 1787. Why he did so can be explained only in terms of his increasingly harsh assessment of the character and course of state politics, an assessment that largely reflected his experience in the Virginia assembly.

AS AN ASSEMBLY DELEGATE from Orange County during the mid-1780s, Madison had two great goals. The first was to inculcate an enlightened sense of national interest in legislators whose political instincts were innately parochial. In practice this meant urging approval of the revenue plan of 1783 and the commercial amendments Congress proposed in 1784, compliance with objectionable provisions of the Treaty of Paris, and levying the taxes necessary to maintain Virginia's contributions to the federal treasury. After 1784 he also grew increasingly concerned about the effect that Spain's closure of the Mississippi to American subjects would have on Virginia's underlying loyalty to the Union.

But the domestic concerns of Virginia seemed no less important. Madison was intent on securing the adoption of the comprehensive revision of the state legal code that a committee composed of Thomas Jefferson, Edmund Pendleton, and George Wythe had prepared in 1779. When the once dominant Anglican church sought public support for its recovery from the ravages of the war through the adoption of a general assessment that would provide funds for all Christian denominations, Madison led the fight that culminated in its defeat and the subsequent enactment of the Virginia Statute for Religious Freedom. To reduce British control of the state's commerce, Madison also proposed a bill restricting the access of foreign shippers to a small number of Virginia ports.

Madison took special pride in the defeat of the assessment bill and the victory for disestablishment that the Statute for Religious Freedom represented. In 1785 he also made substantial progress on the revised code before legislative fatigue and opposition to particular bills halted further deliberations. Other favored proposals fared less well. The port bill was so thoroughly amended to satisfy local interests that Madison regarded the final act as useless. His plan of court reform, though enacted by the assembly, was never implemented. The record on federal issues was similarly mixed. The assembly did its best to maintain its contributions to the federal treasury, but it balked at complying with the clause of the peace treaty requiring the states to open their courts to suits for the payment of prewar debts owed British merchants. Even the resolution calling the Annapolis Convention was hastily adopted as a weak alternative to the measure Madison originally proposed: a positive grant to Congress of a general power to regulate foreign commerce.

Madison was too seasoned a politician to expect victory on every issue, and he was not surprised that assembly deliberations were often mercurial and inefficient. Yet his frustration with legislative politics ultimately went well beyond the balance sheet of victories and losses or the erratic tenor of debate. More disillusioning than the rejection or dilution of particular measures was his cumulative assessment of the character of his fellow legislators, from his leading opponent, the great demagogue Patrick Henry, to the many backbenchers and one-term members whose votes finally mattered. By 1786 Madison had come to doubt whether most state legislators could ever be relied upon to act responsibly on either state or federal issues.[10]

Madison recorded his unease about the assembly in his letters to Jefferson, George Washington, and James Monroe. But he sent his most revealing early analysis of the problems of republican government to Caleb Wallace, an old college friend now residing in Kentucky, who had asked Madison to recommend "such a Form of Government as you would wish to live under" should he ever join the stream of migrants moving westward into Kentucky (which, though still part of Virginia, was expected to become a separate state in the near future). Madison replied immediately, seizing the occasion to collect his own thoughts about the defects of the Revolutionary constitutions.[11]

The most compelling need, he suggested, was for mechanisms to "give *wisdom* and steadiness to legislation," traits whose absence was "the grievance complained of in all our republics." Madison explained this defect of the constitutions historically, as a natural consequence of the colonists' long-festering resentment of the abuse of executive power under the British crown.[12] Experience since 1776 had exposed the fallacy of this preoccupation. Madison thought the establishment of a well-constructed Senate would provide the most effective check against the danger of faulty legislation. "As a further security against fluctuating & indegested laws," he recommended either a joint executive-judicial council of revision, armed with a limited veto, or at least the appointment of a "standing com[mi]ttee composed of a few select & skilful individuals" to undertake the actual drafting of legislation. The Virginia assembly, he noted, "give almost as many proofs as they pass laws of their need of some such Assistance."

But Madison did not confine his analysis to the failings of lawmakers alone. In suggesting that "some of the ablest Statesmen & soundest Republicans in the U States" favored replacing the sacred principle of the annual election of legislators with three-year terms, he implied that lawmakers would act more wisely if they were insulated from popular pressure. Even more significant, however, was his discussion of suffrage. Here he expressed his mounting fear that rights of property—or rather, the rights of the classes holding the most property—might be imperiled by economic legislation enacted at the behest of the mass of the population. To guard against this danger, Madison proposed setting different suffrage qualifications for the two houses of the legislature, leaving it reasonably broad for the lower house but narrowing it on the basis of property for the upper. "In a general vein," he observed, "I see no reason why the rights of property which chiefly bears the burden of Government & is so much an object of Legislation should not be respected as well as personal rights in the choice of Rulers." In distinguishing the social bases of representation in this way, Madison thus reflected a remarkable transformation in American thinking about property. From being a right attributed to all citizens, property was now increasingly regarded as an interest deserving protection against the envious and unjust designs of the less fortunate.[13]

The duality of Madison's concern with lawmakers and their constituents was also expressed in another noteworthy document of the summer of 1785, his *Memorial and Remonstrance Against Religious Assessments*. Because the *Memorial* was written to muster popular opposition to a bill already pending in the assembly, its most explicitly political passages cast the question of religious liberty as a struggle between legislators threatening to "exceed the commission from which they derive their authority" and a people who needed to recall that "prudent jealousy [was] the first duty of Citizens, and one of the noblest characteristics of the late Revolution." Such language echoed the rhetoric of the earlier Revolutionary conflict, and thus evoked the conventional image of an ongoing struggle between the power of rulers and the liberties of the ruled. But in his wide-ranging effort to identify all grounds of opposition to the assessment, Madison did not overlook the possibility that the bill might actually command the support of a popular majority. "True it is, that no other rule exists, by which any question which may divide a Society, can be ultimately determined, but the will of the majority," Madison conceded; "but it is also true that the majority may trespass on the rights of the minority."[14]

In the summer of 1785, however, it was still the danger of legislative misrule that most alarmed him. In a sense, it seemed easier to think of constitutional remedies and pragmatic reforms that might moderate the exercise of legislative power than to contemplate challenging the fundamental republican principle of majority rule. Yet in the months that followed his victories in the realm of religious legislation, this pregnant concern with the character of popular majorities emerged as the key element driving Madison's thought toward its great creative breakthrough— but only after he began to consider the defects of the Confederation in a more systematic way.

EVEN THE MOST ORIGINAL THINKER can harbor commonplace opinions. Many political leaders shared Madison's criticisms of the Articles of Confederation and the state constitutions. What allowed him to perform the crucial role he assigned himself in the movement for reform was not only the originality of his ideas but also their comprehensiveness. In the year preceding the Federal Convention, his political intelligence proved profoundly integrative, both in his perception of the deeper range of issues the delegates would confront and in his assessment of the political obstacles and opportunities they would encounter.

Madison took the first step in reordering the agenda of reform in the winter and spring of 1786. At home at Montpelier, he undertook a course of reading in the history of "ancient & modern confederacies," drawing upon two trunkloads of books that Jefferson had sent him from Paris. In a general way, he probably hoped this reading would better prepare him for the fall meeting at Annapolis. But given that the agenda set for An-napolis would be limited to commercial matters alone, it seems more likely that Madison wanted to consider the problems of federalism in a more thoughtful fashion. He closed each section of his notes on this read-ing with a short but pointed list of the "vices of the constitution" of the particular confederation he had just studied, the peculiar structural and political defects that compromised its strength and vigor.[15]

By the summer of 1786, his concern about the defects of the Amer-ican confederation was no longer confined to the familiar topics of reve-nue and commerce. The catalyst propelling Madison's thought was the question of American navigation rights on the Mississippi. From James Monroe, his trusted correspondent in Congress, Madison learned that Secretary of Foreign Affairs John Jay had asked for permission to abjure American claims in the hope of securing a favorable commercial treaty with Spain.[16] What Monroe personally told him of the divisions within Congress over this issue alarmed Madison even further when he visited New York before proceeding to Annapolis. Madison objected to Jay's re-quest for two closely connected reasons. First, as a matter of policy, he opposed any compromise of the American claim as a grave threat to the vital interests of the southern states and the western settlers, and as a po-tential source of division not only between northern and southern states but also between the existing Union and American settlers flooding into the interior. For the same reason, he also feared that Jay's request would have a disastrous impact not only on efforts to amend the Articles but also on the Union itself. Although the northern states had indeed revised Jay's instructions, they lacked the nine votes required to ratify whatever treaty he managed to conclude. Even an effort to negotiate on this dubi-ous basis would "be fatal," Madison feared, "to an augmentation of the federal authority, if not to the little now existing." Indeed, Jay's initiative made Madison's "personal situation . . . particularly mortifying. Ever since I have been out of Congress," he informed Jefferson, "I have been incul-cating on our assembly a confidence in the equal attention of Congress to the rights and interests of every part of the republic and on the western members in particular, the necessity of making the Union respectable by [granting] new powers to Congress if they wished Congress to negotiate with effect for the Mississipi."[17] If that confidence was found to be mis-placed, he would be unable to rally his own state to the cause of reform.

As he traveled through the middle states in the summer of 1786, Madison held frequent conversations about politics. It was clear, he wrote Jefferson in mid-August, that "[m]any Gentlemen both within & without Congs. wish to make" the Annapolis meeting subservient to a Plenipotentiary Convention for amending the Confederation. Tho' my wishes are in favor of such an event, yet I despair so much of its accomplishment at the present crisis that I do not extend my views beyond a Commercial Reform. To speak the truth I almost despair even of this.

But the failure of the Annapolis convention to draw enough members to pursue its prescribed agenda, coupled with the disruptive potential of the Mississippi affair, indicated that time no longer favored a strategy of gradual reform. Thus when Madison returned to Virginia in late October, a sense of urgency at last overcame the caution in his temperament. While continuing to work to neutralize the sectional rift the Mississippi dispute had opened,[18] Madison did not discount the political dangers it represented.

His travels also confirmed his pessimistic observations about the character of state lawmaking throughout the country. He was most troubled by "the general rage for paper money." In his lengthy mid-August letter to Jefferson, he provided a state-by-state survey of this "epidemic malady," which he feared would spare Virginia only if "the failure of the experiments elsewhere" and the presence of that stern republican, George Mason, could dissuade the assembly from its adoption. In fact it was Madison who took the lead in turning back a motion for an emission of paper money at the fall session of the assembly. Heartening as this victory was, he still worried that other states would make their depreciating paper money legal tender for the payment of debts. On this issue, he saw no virtue in moderation. The emission of an unsecured currency amounted to an "unjust" and "unconstitutional" assault on the rights of property; the more popular such measures appeared, the more he fretted that Americans were supporting a policy that would "disgrace Republican Govts. in the eyes of mankind."[19] Given the force of this concern, Madison was prone to suspect that the "great commotions" in Massachusetts were ultimately aimed toward "an abolition of debts public & private, and a new division of property."[20]

From his dual concerns with the politics of the Mississippi issue in Congress and the specter of unjust economic legislation, Madison now formulated the crucial problem that would shape his thinking. "There is no maxim in my opinion which is more likely to be misapplied, and which therefore more needs elucidation," he wrote Monroe on October 5, "than the current one that the interest of the majority is the political standard of right and wrong." That would be true if one took "the word 'interest' as synonomous with 'Ultimate happiness,'" he conceded.

But taking it in the popular sense, as referring to immediate augmentation of property and wealth, nothing can be more false. In the latter sense it would be the interest of the majority in every community to despoil & enslave the minority of individuals; and in a federal community to make a sacrifice of the minority of the component states.

In Madison's thinking, the right of western settlers to enjoy the navigation of the Mississippi was as essential as the right of property holders to be secured from the injustice of paper money. In both cases, decisions respectively favoring northern merchants or debtors stood to elevate "temporary and partial interests over those just & extended maxims of policy which have been so much boasted of among us."[21]

From his alarm over these two distinct problems of national and state policy, Madison began to fashion a powerful criticism of the majoritarian premise of republican government—a criticism he could apply to both Congress and the states. Privately, he continued to revolve the problem of majority misrule during the fall of 1786 and the winter of 1787. But for the time being, he resisted drawing the programmatic conclusions to which his analysis might lead the Philadelphia convention. Before Madison could begin to consider exactly what the Convention should do, the immediate challenge was to ensure that it would be well attended, and that it would assemble under favorable conditions. Satisfying the first of these conditions depended on the separate actions of the state legislatures; the second required preventing the congressional dispute over the Mississippi from inflicting any more damage on the Union itself.

The task of laying the groundwork for the Convention began well when the Virginia assembly unanimously approved the Annapolis recommendation for a second convention, issued a circular letter of invitation to the other states, and appointed an impressive delegation including George Washington, George Mason, Governor Edmund Randolph, the jurist George Wythe, and Madison. "It has been thought advisable to give this subject a very solemn dress," Madison informed Washington, "and all the weight which could be derived from a single state."[22] Madison also secured his own election to Congress, where his presence would strengthen the southern states in their opposition to Jay's foreign policy. Ten days after the assembly adjourned, he set off for New York, armed with a resolution (which he probably drafted) instructing the Virginia delegation in Congress to oppose the surrender of navigation rights on the Mississippi as "a flagrant violation of Justice, a direct contravention of the end for which the federal Government was instituted, and an alarming innovation of the System of the Union."[23] En route he stopped at Mount Vernon to continue the delicate courtship needed to persuade the general to attend the Convention.

Six other states had appointed delegates to the Convention by the time Madison returned to Congress on February 12, 1787. Nine days later, Congress gave its own approval to the Convention. The delegates were "much divided and embarrassed on the question whether their taking an interest in the measure would impede or promote it," as well as the possible impropriety of endorsing a device for amending the Confederation not mentioned in the Articles themselves.[24] Within days, New York and Massachusetts joined the states electing deputies, and Madison was confident that every state—including Rhode Island, generally regarded as the most retrograde member of the Union—would be represented. The Mississippi issue remained threatening, but a conversation with Gardoqui, the Spanish minister, convinced Madison that "the negociation is arrested," and he was heartened that the Pennsylvania and New Jersey delegations seemed inclined to support the southern position. It now seemed unlikely that "the Spanish project" would interfere directly with the Convention, though Madison worried that it would still tend "to foment distrusts among the Atlantic states at a crisis when harmony and confidence ought to have been studiously cherished."[25]

WITH CONGRESS MUSTERING too few members to do much business, Madison had time to prepare for the Convention. In early spring, he at last drew together the separate strands of his own political experience and education into a working memorandum analyzing the "[v]ices of the political system of the U. States." Madison opened this remarkable document by summarizing the defects of the Confederation, but he then proceeded to explain how "a compleat remedy" of "the evils which viciate" the Republic required confronting the internal failings of state government. In concurrent letters to Jefferson, Washington, and Randolph, he converted his general conclusions into the program he intended to pursue at Philadelphia.[26] For Madison's preparations were the acts not of "an ingenious theorist" speculating "in his closet or in his imagination," but of a veteran legislator intent on seizing the initiative from the opening moment of debate.[27]

At the most general level, Madison set out to demonstrate that the national government could be organized along republican lines. In doing so, he challenged the venerable association of republican government with small and homogeneous societies. Quite possibly he found some inspiration for his new position in the writings of David Hume, notably his brief essay "Idea of a Perfect Commonwealth."[28] But if there was a Humean dimension to Madison's thought, it lay less in the formulation of a specific hypothesis about the optimal size of republics than in the way in which Madison sought to derive general rules of politics from the experience of history. That experience certainly included knowledge gained from thoughtful reading in ancient and modern history and in respected treatises on public law and the science of politics. But this history that had to be pondered most carefully was that of the republican experiment of Madison's own era.

One central conviction lay at the heart of his analysis. Experience conclusively proved that neither state legislators nor their constituents could be relied upon to support the general interest of the Union, the true public good of their own communities, or the rights of minorities and individuals. From his perception of the essential parochialism of state politics and politicians, Madison forged a new connection between the distinct problems of federalism and of republican government within the states. The proper task of the Convention was not merely to free the Union from its debilitating dependence on the states but also to seize the occasion of reforming the national government to treat the internal defects of the states. At the same time, his ideas of how the national government should be reconstructed were profoundly influenced by his criticisms of the institutional defects of the state constitutions.

Madison opened his memorandum by surveying the ways in which the states had thwarted and obstructed the Confederation: by failing to comply with the requisitions of Congress, encroaching on its authority, violating treaty obligations, and refusing to grant the Union adequate powers to pursue objects of "common interest." Clearly the Articles lacked "the great vital principles of a Political Cons[ti]tution": the power to compel obedience to its decisions. "From what cause could so fatal an omission have happened?" Madison asked. Again he answered this question historically. The "mistaken confidence" that the framers of the Articles had placed in "the justice, the good faith, the honor, the sound policy" of the assemblies reflected both their own "enthusiastic virtue" and their "inexperience of the crisis" the war brought. It was, that is, the natural product of the heady patriotism that had flourished during the moment of independence.[29]

Madison's survey of the defects of the Articles was thorough but conventional. More important were his efforts to explain why a system resting on the "uniform and punctual obedience of 13 independent bodies

. . . ought not to be calculated on." One could hardly expect the state legislatures to take enlightened views of national affairs, for "the sphere of
life from which most of their members are taken, and the circumstances
under which their legislative business is carried on," would always militate
against it. Nor would thirteen dissimilar states ever be disposed to view
national measures in the same way. "Every general act of the Union must
necessarily bear unequally hard on some particular member or members
of it," Madison noted. The natural "partiality of the members to their
own interests and rights," reinforced by the demagoguery of "the Cour-
tiers of popularity," he observed, "will never fail to render federal measures abortive."

Had his analysis of the "vices of the political system" ended here,
Madison would already have fashioned a substantial agenda on which the
Convention could act. But when he reached the ninth point of his memorandum, his profound disillusion with the character of republican government in the states spurred him to extend his essential argument in a
radically innovative way.

> In developing the evils which viciate the political system of the
> U. S. it is proper to include those which are found within the States
> individually, as well as those which affect the States collectively, since
> the former class have an indirect influence on the general malady
> and must not be overlooked in forming a compleat remedy.

This quiet transition understated the power of the conclusions that followed. For Madison promptly went on to indict the state legislatures for
the "multiplicity," "mutability," and "injustice" of the laws they had enacted in the decade since independence. Of these three marks of a "vicious legislation," he deemed the last the most critical. "If the multiplicity
and mutability of laws prove a want of wisdom," he wrote (echoing his
1785 letter to Caleb Wallace),

> their injustice betrays a defect still more alarming: more alarming
> not merely because it is a greater evil in itself, but because it brings
> more into question the fundamental principle of republican Govern-
> ments, that the majority who rule in such Governments, are the saf-
> est guardians both of public Good and of private rights. To what
> cause is this evil to be ascribed?

Here at last Madison stood ready to derive a general theory of politics
from the historical lessons his own experience had taught. The issue was

no longer merely the "imbecility" of the Confederation or the parochial-ism of the state legislatures, but rather the majoritarian premises of pop-ular government itself.

With his characteristic fondness for drawing distinctions, Madison traced the sources of unjust legislation to both "the Representative bodies" and "the people themselves." Legislative office was sought for three rea-sons: "ambition," "personal interest," and a regard for "public good." But experience proved that the first two predominated, with woeful results. Artful legislators "with interested views" could always find ways to sacri-fice "the interest, and views, of their Constituents" for their own pur-poses, and then to have their "base and selfish measures, masked by pretexts of public good and apparent expediency." Even "honest" repre-sentatives would often fall prey to "a favorite leader, veiling his selfish views under the professions of public good, and varnishing his sophistical arguments with the glowing colours of popular eloquence."

In a few brief and (for him) unusually pungent sentences, Madison thus drew the bitter lessons he had gained from his own experience in the Virginia assembly and his monitoring of other states. But he now under-stood better that legislative misrule was itself often only a symptom of problems rooted in the larger society. "A still more fatal if not more fre-quent cause" of injustice, he wrote, "lies among the people themselves." While orthodox republican theory recognized that the people were often prone to unhealthy enthusiasms, it expected them to resist arbitrary acts of government corrosive of their own liberty. Ultimately it was the civic virtue of the people that would have to prevent republican government from degenerating into a mobocracy. Fearful of trusting human nature too far, previous writers had argued that stable republics could survive only in small and socially homogeneous communities, where the underlying sim-ilarity of interests would reduce the temptation one part of the commu-nity might feel to exploit another, and thus encourage citizens to exercise the essential virtue of subordinating private interest to public good.

It was this fanciful notion of social homogeneity that Madison now rejected as irrelevant to the American case. "All civilized societies," he wrote, "are divided into different interests and factions, as they happen to be creditors or debtors—Rich or poor—husbandmen, merchants or manufacturers—members of different religious sects—followers of differ-ent political leaders—inhabitants of different districts—owners of dif-ferent kinds of property &c &c." Just as Madison dismissed the restraints on legislative misrule as ineffective, so he now argued that neither "a pru-dent regard to their own good as involved in the general and permanent good of the community," nor "respect for character," nor even religion could be relied on to deter popular majorities united by "an apparent interest or passion" from "unjust violations of the rights and interests of the minority, or of individuals." These disparaging judgments rested on an arithmetic logic. Within a small republic—whether the city-states of ancient history or, by implication, the member states of the existing American Union—the wrong kinds of majorities could readily coalesce to pursue their evil purposes, while at the same time growing sufficiently numerous to relax the moral bonds ("respect for character" and religion) that might otherwise "restrain them from injustice."

Taken by itself, this perception of the play of interest and passion on politics was a commonplace of the eighteenth century. Madison's originality instead lay in his efforts to reconcile this image of society with the cause of republican government, to prove that the excesses of popular majorities were as dangerous as the ambitions of elected representatives, and yet to suggest that, "contrary to the prevailing theory," an extended national republic would better secure private rights than the more confined polities of the states. This diagnosis of the multiple causes of political disorder within the states provided the foundation upon which Madison built his entire program of constitutional reform. His ideas of federalism, representation, and the separation of powers—the crucial theoretical issues that the Convention would face—all reflected his disillusion with the failings of state legislators and citizens alike.

His least controversial conclusion concerned the manifest "imbecility" of Congress under the Confederation. The proper solution to its fatal reliance on the states was not to empower Congress to apply force against recalcitrant states—as he had proposed seven years earlier—but rather to create "a system which would operate without the intervention of the states" directly on the people by enacting, executing, and adjudicating its own laws. This single conclusion immediately led to another that was equally momentous: A union acting directly on the population through the processes of law would have to be reconstituted as a government in the normal sense of the term. In place of the anomalous institution of a unicameral Congress as the sole repository of national power, the federal government would have to comprise the three separate branches—including a bicameral legislature—that orthodox constitutional theory demanded.[30]

Madison realized that the deeper problems of federalism would not disappear even after the Union acquired an independent power of legislation. The respective jurisdictions of national and state government could never be neatly distinguished; to some extent the boundary between them must always remain problematic. Even with the best intentions of all concerned, two governments acting on the same population were bound to come into conflict at one time or another—if, for example, they sought to draw revenue from the same objects of taxation. But good intentions, he firmly believed, would not always prevail. The creation of an extended national republic would not by itself solve the residual problem of misgovernment within the states. There factious majorities would continue to form, and they could be counted upon not only to resist national laws and policies whenever interest dictated but also to enact those unjust laws that so disgusted and alarmed Madison.

It would accordingly not do for the Convention simply to identify the additional powers the Union needed. "Over and above this positive power" of legislation, he wrote Washington,

> a negative *in all cases whatsoever* on the legislative acts of the states, as heretofore exercised by the Kingly prerogative, appears to me to be absolutely necessary, and to be the least possible encroachment on the State Jurisdictions. Without this defensive power, every positive power that can be given on paper will be evaded & defeated.

Nothing better illustrated the reactionary quality of Madison's thought than this candid evocation of both the language of the parliamentary Declaratory Act of 1766 and the royal veto which Jefferson had vehemently denounced in the Declaration of Independence. But the most radical aspect of Madison's position was to extend the scope of this veto beyond avowedly national concerns so that it could also serve as a "controul on the internal vicisitudes of State policy; and the aggressions of interested majorities on the rights of minorities and of individuals." In this way, the national government would act as a "disinterested & dispassionate umpire in disputes between different passions & interests in the State"—that is, within the states individually—deciding even "local questions of policy" when they implicated fundamental questions of rights.[31]

So drastic a power could be vested safely in the Union, Madison believed, because the national government would act with a neutrality or disinterestedness that the states could rarely if ever attain. The principal basis of this belief rested on the general theory of faction for which he is best known—especially from his writings in *The Federalist*. At some point, Madison reasoned, the "enlargement of the sphere" of the republic would offset the regression in civic virtue that he associated with the sway of dominant interests or passions among the multitude,

not because the impulse of a common interest or passion is less predominant in this case with the majority; but because a common interest or passion is less apt to be felt and the requisite combinations
less easy to be formed by a great than a small number. The Society
becomes broken into a greater variety of interests, of pursuits, of passions, which check each other, whilst those who may feel a common
sentiment have less opportunity of communication and concert.

This diversity of interests would permit majorities to form only around a
broad consensus about the true public good. But as an "auxiliary desideratum," Madison predicted that representation in the national government
would involve "such a process of elections as will most certainly extract
from the mass of the Society the purest and noblest characters which it
contains, such as will at once feel most strongly the motives of their appointment, and be most capable to devise the proper means of attaining
it." In contrast to the petty demagogues and untutored novices who gave
state assemblies their sorry tone, a national congress could recruit a superior class of lawmakers whose decisions and deliberations would rise far
above the corresponding proceedings in the states.[32]

If Madison's attachment to a national veto was tied to his jaundiced
view of state lawmakers, his constitutional theory rested on a more profound insight into the nature of legislative power itself. The most striking
qualities of legislative power, he now understood, were its plasticity and
suppleness, its resistance to neat classification or limitation, and thus its
capacity to expand its reach. This insight allowed Madison to approach
the distinct issues of federalism and separation of powers as complementary aspects of one fundamental problem.

From the start, Madison conceded that the "consolidation" of the
states "into one simple republic would be as inexpedient as it is unattainable." Instead, he "sought for some middle ground, which may at once
support a due supremacy of the national authority, and not exclude the
local authorities wherever they can be subordinately useful." Therein lay
the problem. State officials "will be continually sensible of the abridgment
of their power, and be stimulated by ambition to resume the surrendered
portion of it." In this effort they would be aided not only by the political
support they might muster from their constituents but also by the "impossibility of dividing powers of legislation, in such a manner, as to be
free from different constructions by different interests, or even from
ambiguity in the judgment of the impartial." The more he examined different types of legislative power or different realms of law, the more Madison was persuaded of the imprecise and hence arbitrary basis of the

nominal distinctions between them. A state intent on thwarting a particular national act could always find a plausible pretext for asserting its own legislative authority in contravention of the Union. That was why the proposed national veto had to reach "all cases whatsoever."[33]

This same insight informed his approach toward the problem of separating powers within the sphere of national government alone. Madison believed that there were core functions of government that could be respectively labeled legislative, executive, and judicial in nature. Yet here, too, the purity of abstract definitions could not describe the nuances one met in practice. "Even the boundaries between the Executive, Legislative & Judiciary Powers," he wrote Jefferson, "though in general so strongly marked in themselves, consist in many instances of mere shades of difference."[34] He put the point even more directly in *Federalist 37*: "Experience has instructed us that no skill in the science of government has yet been able to discriminate and define, with sufficient certainty, its three great provinces, the legislative, executive, and judiciary," he observed. "Questions daily occur in the course of practice, which proves the obscurity which reigns in these subjects, and which puzzles the greatest adepts in political science." In monarchical regimes the chief danger arose from the excesses of the crown, but in a republic that distinction necessarily fell to the legislature. Not only did it enjoy the political advantages that flowed from direct popular election, it could also exploit its formal rule-making authority to circumscribe the discretion of the other branches, override particular decisions to which it objected, or use its power of the purse to make the other departments bend to its will. Nor was this concern merely speculative. Experience demonstrated that "[t]he legislative department is everywhere extending the sphere of its activity, and drawing all power into its impetuous vortex."[35]

Notwithstanding his hopes that Congress would be a more select body than its counterparts in the states, Madison thus recognized that legislative excess remained the crucial problem of republican constitutionalism. His proposed *institutional* remedies followed his 1785 letter to Wallace: the creation of a true senate, safely insulated from popular pressure, to check the lower house; and the establishment of a joint executive-judicial council of revision, armed with both a limited veto over national legislation and an advisory role in the negative on state laws. Alone, neither the executive nor the judiciary could resist a legislature speaking for the political will of the community; united in the council of revision, they might gain sufficient stature to correct its errors. The benefits this council would provide justified the threat it posed to the axiomatic view that the three powers of government had to be rigidly separated. Involving the judiciary in lawmaking would improve the quality of national legislation at its source, giving it "the perspicuity, the conciseness, and the systematic character" absent from the law codes of the states.[36] At the same time, Madison hoped that the senate and the council of revision would guard against laws violating particular claims of rights. In this sense, his approach to the separation of powers was tied directly to his theory of faction.

That theory was also directly relevant to the one issue that Madison believed the Convention would have to resolve at the outset. As he formulated his strategy in early spring, Madison decided that "the first step to be taken is I think a change in the principle of representation." In place of the equal state vote required by the Confederation, he insisted that some system for apportioning representation by population should be applied to both houses of Congress, and that this issue must be resolved *before* the Convention determined exactly what powers the new government would exercise. Madison had never doubted the justice of such a change; what was new was his belief that it had now become both "practicable" and necessary. The smallest states would oppose any change, but Madison assumed that in regional terms, apportionment would appeal to both the northern states, because of "the actual superiority of their populousness," and the southern, because of the "expected superiority" they would gain as population movements carried migrants southwest toward the Gulf of Mexico. "And if the majority of the large States concur," he concluded, "the fewer and smaller States must finally bend to them."[37]

In the confrontation that would ensue, Madison believed that the small-state delegates would "yield to the predominant will" once they realized that the large states would accept the changes all desired only if a rule of proportional representation was applied to both houses of Congress. Madison fashioned his general theory of faction in part to provide the rationale with which the large states' delegates could prevail in debate. By proving that an extended republic would protect *all* interests against factious majorities, Madison hoped to demonstrate that the small states could forego the security of an equal vote to protect them against outright domination by the large states.

Beyond explaining why the small states did not need equal representation, Madison's theory of faction further sought to demonstrate why they did not deserve it. To make their case conclusive, the large states would have to refute the claim that states deserved equal representation as the sovereign units of which the Union was originally and immutably composed. That was exactly what the modern image of society that formed the heart of Madison's theory of faction promised to do. Implicit in its logic lay the recognition that states *as such* were not real interests deserving representation. States possessed interests, but these were rooted in the attributes of individuals: in property, occupation, religion, opinion, and the uneven distribution of human faculties. Moreover, since congeries of interests could be found within any state, however small—witness Rhode Island—the principle of unitary corporate representation was further undercut. The larger a state was, the more complex and diverse its interests would be. Nor, finally, was size itself an interest capable of manifesting itself in any situation other than a constitutional convention, where the rules of voting would first have to be determined. Once government was under way, such disparate aggregates of interests as Virginia, Pennsylvania, and Massachusetts—the three most populous states—would never find common ground again, except, of course, when majorities of able legislators came together in pursuit of the true public good.

Thus little more than a month before the Convention was due to assemble in Philadelphia, James Madison fashioned a powerful and comprehensive analysis of the problems of federalism and republicanism. Much of his intellectual labor synthesized complaints that had been stated and restated throughout the 1780s. But his reassessment of these issues was neither merely intellectual nor merely synthetic. Its originality lay in part in its self-conscious willingness to challenge received wisdom, even if that wisdom often took the form of clichés about small republics and the separation of powers. Its deeper significance, however, was as much political as conceptual. In his grasp of the range and connectedness of the issues the Convention would face, Madison ranged well beyond the commonplace expectations of the postwar years. Rather than amend the Articles by identifying the additional duties the Union might discharge and modestly enhancing its authority over the states, he perceived the necessity and advantages of allowing the national government to act directly upon the population through the power of law. Rather than allow this authority to be vested in an anomalous unicameral Congress, he understood that the Union had to be reconstituted as a government in the normal sense of the term, and further, that the recent history of the individual states provided the critical experimental evidence from which a superior model of a republic could be constructed. And rather than confine the agenda of the Convention to issues of national governance alone, Madison was convinced that federalism also offered a solution to the problem of individual and minority rights. His agenda for the Federal Convention was not addressed to the woes of the Union alone, but to the underlying vices of the Republic.

IN HIS READING, Madison had often encountered the figure of "the lawgiver" or "the legislator" who loomed so large in both the records of history and the political science of his own era. "As a cultural hero, the legislator provided the Enlightenment's answer to the Christian saint or the Renaissance prince," the historian Harry C. Payne has observed. "Half-mythical, half-historical, the figure of the legislator who shapes and unifies his society dominates the political and historical writings of the philosophes." Nor were these examples confined to the dim mists of ancient history—to Solon, Lycurgus, and Numa Pompilius. In the royal and aristocratic courts of Europe, opportunities sometimes arose for such luminaries as Locke, Voltaire, Diderot, Holbach, and Rousseau to play the part they so admired in antiquity, advising kings and princes on codes of laws to bring their peoples a new measure of "social balance and harmony." Even provincial America could claim one such figure in William Penn, praised as "a true Lycurgus" by no less an authority than Montesquieu.[38] And perhaps there was something of the lawgiver in the project Thomas Jefferson had launched, and Madison had pursued, of revising the statutory code of Virginia to purge it of its unrepublican elements.

Did Madison also envision himself as a lawgiver-legislator as he prepared for the Convention? The thought must have crossed his mind more than once. Yet one crucial condition distinguished the opportunity he hoped to seize in Philadelphia from those that beckoned to the would-be "pragmatic philosophe-kings." In Europe laws could be given to the people through the act of a sovereign monarch relying on nothing more than the advice of his resident sage and the drafting skills of his chancellor. The lawgiver of the Enlightenment was a solitary figure; his legislation was not the product of collective deliberations but an imposition of individual wisdom. But in America whatever new law the Convention proposed would have to be accepted by the people, not given to them. And it would have to be framed, in the first instance, "by the intervention of a deliberative body of citizens."[35] For Madison to succeed as a lawgiver within the field of action the Convention would afford, he would have to use reason to overcome the play of interests he expected to encounter among its members. As much as his strategy for the Convention supposed that reason and justice would prevail, he could not escape regarding the grand meeting in Philadelphia in essentially political terms.

CHAPTER IV

THE POLITICS OF CONSTITUTION-MAKING

IN THE LEXICON OF AMERICAN politics, few words evoke as ambivalent a response as *compromise*. On the one hand, compromise (or better yet, its spirit) symbolizes the necessary pragmatism expected of politics in a pluralist society. It suggests a preference for consensus over confrontation, a willingness to meet opponents halfway rather than strive for ideological purity. Yet compromise just as often connotes moral failure, a weakness of nerve or, worse, of conscience. Here the willingness to compromise betrays a lack of inner conviction, a disposition to sacrifice vital principle to attain more tangible rewards.

Compromise, in all its ambivalence, is a staple theme of most narrative accounts of the Federal Convention of 1787, and with good reason. In the end, the framers granted concessions to every interest that had a voice in Philadelphia, and as the weeks wore on, they described these decisions as conciliatory gestures modeled on the crucial decision of July 16—the "great compromise" that gave each state an equal vote in the Senate. The Convention sounded the same note in its report to the Continental Congress: ". . . the Constitution which we now present, is the result of a spirit of amity, and of that mutual deference and concession which the peculiarity of our political situation rendered indispensable." Had each state consulted its own interest only, "the consequences might have been particularly disagreeable or injurious to others."[1] Federalists invoked this same spirit of compromise during the ratification campaign. "All the deputations composing the Convention were satisfactorily accommodated by the final act," James Madison told the readers of *Federalist* 37, "or were induced to accede to it by a deep conviction of the necessity of sacrificing private opinions and partial interests to the public good, and by a despair of seeing this necessity diminished by delays or by new experiments."[2]

Two compromises, both tied to questions of representation, proved essential to the political course of the Convention. The first, resolving the prolonged dispute over the Senate, is usually regarded as the great turning point of the Convention, and it thus symbolizes compromise in its positive and laudatory aspects. Had delegates from the large states not grudgingly accepted this verdict, the Convention might have broken apart—and once disbanded, the last best hope for preserving the Union might have evaporated as well. The second compromise, which enabled southern states to count three-fifths of their slaves for purposes of representation in the House, is more difficult to endorse, much less celebrate. Scholars still debate whether the success of the Convention required so abject an acknowledgment of the brutal reality of chattel slavery; nor can we avoid wondering whether the framers' failure to act against slavery doomed their deepest aspirations for a more perfect Union to the horror of civil war. The decisions over slavery thus embody compromise in its second, more troubling meaning. The Constitution, as the abolitionist William Lloyd Garrison later put it, was "a covenant with death and an agreement with hell."[3]

The contrast between these two momentous decisions cannot be drawn so starkly. In crucial respects the compromises over representation in each house of the new Congress were dependent and complementary; both sought to lock protection for specific minorities into the text of the Constitution. Nor was the evident moral disparity between them quite as pronounced as it appears at first glance. For while "the great compromise" over the Senate assured that the "vicious" principle of the equality of states would ever after remain part of the Constitution—immune even from the amending power of Article V—the impetus to protect slavery through the three-fifths clause had the ironic consequence of making the principle of one person, one vote the ultimate rule of popular representation in the House. But more important still, these two compromises cannot be treated solely in expedient or pragmatic terms, as the price on which the hard bargain of union was finally sealed. For just as the Convention approached both issues within the analytical framework that Madison had prepared before the meeting, so its eventual decisions illuminated both the power and the flaws in his theory of faction.

PUBLIC ASSEMBLIES IN eighteenth-century America often failed to meet on time. For all the great expectations the Convention commanded, only Pennsylvania and Virginia—the two states that were in effect its hosts—were adequately represented on the appointed day of Monday, May 14. Eleven days passed before a quorum of seven states finally assembled, enabling the Convention to elect George Washington as its chair and to appoint a committee to propose rules of debate.[4]

Having been coaxed to attend the Convention against his wishes, the former commander in chief did not treat this dilatory behavior lightly. "These delays greatly impede public measures," Washington grumbled on May 20, "and serve to sour the temper of the punctual members, who do not like to idle away their time." Madison, too, fretted over the delay, but he knew an opportunity when he saw one, especially when it involved setting the agenda on which others would act. He arrived in Philadelphia on May 5, the first member present from any state other than Pennsylvania. Once the appearance of George Mason brought their delegation to full strength on May 17, the Virginians took the initiative of drafting a plan of government to present to the Convention when it was ready to proceed. Meeting "two or three hours a day, in order to form a proper correspondence of sentiments," they approved eleven articles incorporating the essential elements of Madison's pre-Convention analysis.[5] Introduced by Governor Edmund Randolph on May 29, the Virginia Plan formed the basis of the Convention's first fortnight of debate.

Its preparation was nevertheless something of an accident. Had the other delegations appeared on time, they would not have turned to the Virginians for guidance. Then the delegates might first have had to feel their way gingerly into the business—perhaps by discussing the general state of the Union or by asking just what the national government should be expected to do—while postponing any discussion of its structure. This was the "more simple mode" of action that John Dickinson of Delaware proposed when the Virginia Plan was first discussed on May 30. Rather than seek agreement on broad principles, he argued, the Convention need only agree "that the Confederation is defective; and then proceed to the definition of such powers as may be thought adequate to the objects for which it was instituted."[6]

Dickinson was as well prepared for the Convention as Madison (who was nearly twenty years his junior). He had been a major figure in the resistance to Britain, first as author of the *Letters from a Farmer in Pennsylvania*, which rallied opposition to the Townshend duties of 1767, then as the leading congressional advocate of reconciliation in the months before the final break. Much of his hesitation reflected his long-standing fear that a union of thirteen sovereign states would prove inherently unstable. In part because this concern was so well known, and in part because other members of Congress hoped to coopt his continued participation in the cause, they gave Dickinson the leading role in preparing the first draft of the Articles of Confederation in June 1776 (though he left Congress before it debated the plan his committee submitted). That plan had been faulted for having "the vice of refining too much," but in 1787 Dickinson could direct the same charge against Madison, whose ideas of reform struck him as a formula for confrontation. Foreseeing that the equal state vote would come under assault, Dickinson and his colleague George Read had bolstered their position in the Convention by having the Delaware assembly instruct them to oppose any change in the existing rule of voting. Thus inclined by temperament to pursue conciliation and by principle to preserve the equal-state vote, Dickinson sensed that the Convention should first seek consensus on issues more tractable than representation.[7]

Nevertheless, it was Madison's insistence on solving the problem of representation first that set the course of debate. The large-state delegates privately discussed how to attain their goal even before the committee on rules reported on May 28. When the Pennsylvania delegates suggested "that the large states should unite in firmly refusing to the small States an equal vote" in the Convention itself, the Virginians convinced them that "it would be easier to prevail" on the small states "in the course of the deliberations" than to ask them "to throw themselves on the mercy of the large States" at the outset. But they delivered their ultimatum as soon as serious debate began. Madison flatly rejected the claim for an equal-state vote on May 30. "[W]hatever reason might have existed for the equality of suffrage when the Union was a federal one among sovereign States," he observed, "it must cease when a national Governt. should be put into place."[8] Madison and his principal allies—James Wilson of Pennsylvania, Alexander Hamilton of New York, and Rufus King of Massachusetts—presumed that their superior arguments would ultimately prove persuasive.

The Virginia Plan sought to further this preemptive strategy. While giving the new government substantial powers, it sought to defer discussion of their nature and scope until basic agreement was reached on its structure. Article 6 offered a general statement of the powers to be vested in its legislature. These were formidable, extending to "the Legislative Rights vested in Congress by the Confederation," to "all cases to which the separate States are incompetent, or in which the harmony of the United States may be interrupted by the exercise of individual legislation," to a national veto over state laws "contravening . . . the articles of union," and to the right "to call forth the force of the Union against any member . . . failing to fulfill its duty." On the key issue of representation, the plan called for "suffrage . . . to be proportioned to the Quotas of contribution, or to the number of free inhabitants, as the one or the other rule may seem best in different cases." But the states could only nominate their representatives in the upper house; the ultimate election of senators would be made by the popularly elected lower house. The Virginia Plan also provided for the establishment of an independent executive and judiciary, to be joined in a council of revision with a limited veto.[9]

All these provisions were discussed in early June, but it soon became evident that no serious progress could be made on any of them until the question of apportionment was resolved. This perception partly explains the deceptive ease with which the committee of the whole raced through the Virginia Plan between May 30 and June 13. But leading spokesmen for the small states immediately recognized where the logic of the Virginia Plan led. Dickinson revealed as much on June 2, when he observed that the conflict over representation "must probably end in mutual concession," in which "each State would retain an equal voice at least in one branch of the National Legislature." Roger Sherman of Connecticut—another major author of the Confederation—similarly grasped the key issue on June 11, when he declared that "the smaller States would never agree to the plan on any other principle" than an equal vote in the Senate. Dickinson made sure that the message was clear when he took Madison aside immediately after William Paterson introduced the New Jersey Plan on June 15. "You see the consequences of pushing things too far," Dickinson warned. "Some of the members from the small States . . . are friends to a good National government; but we would sooner submit to a foreign power, than submit to be deprived of an equality of suffrage, in both branches of the legislature."[10]

Madison was undeterred. Not only did he intently pursue his strategy for denying the principle of the equal-state vote, he also seized every opportunity to lay his new theory of republican government before the Convention. Between June 4 and 8, he raised the fundamental problem of the dangers of "interested majorities" no less than five times—in debates over the council of revision, the election of the legislature, and the negative on state laws. William Pierce of Georgia described the first of these speeches as "a very able and ingenious" summary of "the whole Scheme of the Government." Two days later, when Madison explained how an extended sphere of government would improve the character of representation, a more skeptical Hamilton noted that there was "truth" in his "principles but they do not conclude so strongly as he supposes."[11] Madison nonetheless enjoyed substantial support from other members. When the South Carolina delegates objected to "the vagueness" of the clause authorizing national legislation "in all cases to which the State Legislatures were individually incompetent," a chorus of large-state delegates responded that "it would be impossible to enumerate the powers which the federal Legislature ought to have." When Elbridge Gerry and Sherman argued that popular election of the lower house was unwise and unnecessary, Wilson and Mason replied: "There is no danger of improper elections if made by *large* districts."[12]

Madison's effort to use the opening fortnight to seize the higher ground fell short of its objectives in only two respects. First, he failed to convince his own delegation to extend the negative on state laws "to all cases whatsoever," and when Madison, Wilson, and Charles Pinckney of South Carolina offered an amendment to that effect on June 8, the committee of the whole rejected it, limiting the proposed negative to conflicts between state law and national interest.[13] A more serious reverse came on June 7, when Dickinson and Sherman moved to allow each state legislature to elect its senators. Wilson and Madison opposed this amendment vigorously, denying that legislative election would produce the benefits its supporters foretold. How could it work to bring "characters, distinguished for their rank in life and weight of property" into the Senate, as Dickinson suggested, or to "provide some check in favor of the commercial interest agst. the landed," as Gerry intimated? These objections elicited weak responses. But one additional argument was made in favor of the motion, and even some large-state delegates conceded its force. As Mason put it, "the State Legislatures also ought to have some means of defending themselves agst. encroachments of the Natl. Govt." It was probably this consideration that led all ten states present to approve the amendment.[14]

This decision threatened Madison's goals in several ways. A Senate elected by the parochial state legislatures could hardly possess the "wisdom and stability" and the broad view of the national interest that he sought. Nor was it likely to exercise the national veto on state laws as freely as he believed it should. Legislative election also jeopardized the principle of proportional representation by implying that the Senate would represent the states qua states—that is, as equal corporate units. At the same time, Madison may also have realized that he had not thought through the implications of applying any scheme of apportionment to the upper house. For if each state received at least one vote (as the Virginia Plan implied), proportional representation would make the Senate too large a body to retain the contemplative qualities that Madison desired. The upper house was meant to act "with more coolness, with more system, & with more wisdom than the popular branch," Madison observed. "Enlarge their number and you communicate to them the vices which they are meant to correct." For the time being, however, the consensus in favor of legislative election did not extend to the issue of voting in the Senate. On June 11, the committee of the whole voted, six states to five, to base suffrage in the Senate on the same proportional rule established for the lower house.[15]

Thus far no one had ventured to explain how the small states would be either injured or protected should proportional representation be instituted in both houses. The second phase of debate that began when Paterson read the New Jersey Plan on June 15 brought this issue to the fore. In appearance the New Jersey Plan resembled the amendments to the Confederation that had been discussed during the 1780s, and it thus offered a genuinely confederal alternative to the Virginia Plan. While it followed the Virginia Plan in proposing to establish three independent branches of government, it also preserved a unicameral Congress with each state having one vote. Since such an unchecked assembly could not safely exercise broad legislative authority, the New Jersey Plan could not pretend to grant the Union anything like the sweeping authority envisioned in its counterpart.[16]

This was such an obvious weakness that some members wondered whether Paterson meant his plan to be taken seriously. "The whole comes to this," Pinckney scoffed: "Give N. Jersey an equal vote, and she will dismiss her scruples, and concur in the Nati[ona]l system." Pinckney was a touch too sarcastic, but his analysis was near the mark. The supporters of the New Jersey Plan did not bother to defend Paterson's proposals as an adequate solution to the problems of union. Instead they argued that the Virginia Plan was at once illegitimate and impolitic. The Convention had no right even to consider any change in the basic principle of representation under the Confederation, Paterson and John Lansing of New York declared, and even if it did, there was no chance that so radical a revision could ever be adopted.[17]

If nothing else, the reading of the New Jersey Plan allowed the delegates to catch their breath after their almost headlong consideration of the Virginia Plan. Dickinson now saw an opening to play the mediator. Over the weekend of June 16–17, he drafted a new plan which included some elements of Paterson's but which also proposed a bicameral legislature and a triple executive chosen from each of the nation's major regions (a favorite idea of George Mason's). On Monday, June 18, Dickinson set out to introduce his plan by offering a prefatory resolution to postpone Paterson's. But as soon as this motion was approved, Hamilton gained the floor for the rest of the day while delivering a lengthy speech culminating in an even bolder plan—which he presented not as a formal "proposition to the Committee" but as potential future amendments to the Virginia Plan.[18] In this famous speech, Hamilton praised the British constitution in highly unrepublican terms, celebrating the House of Lords as "a most noble institution" and the monarchy as the very "model" of "a good executive," all to the end of suggesting that the Senate and executive of a well-constructed republic would both serve on the tenure of "good behaviour."[19] But the heart of this speech was an analysis of the "great & essential principles necessary for the support of Government," which Hamilton classified in his notes as:

I	Interest to Support it
II	Opinion of Utility & necessity
III	Habitual sense of obligation
IV	Force
V	Influence

In each case the states would retain a commanding *political* advantage over Congress, Hamilton argued, unless the Convention proposed such a scheme of government as would give a decided preeminence to the national government. Whether or not Hamilton described the Virginia Plan as *"pork still, with a little change of the sauce,"* his animus against the New Jersey Plan was clear.[20]

If there was one evening on which a historian would have liked to eavesdrop on the delegates' conversation, it was that of June 18, for Hamilton's speech surely provoked reactions ranging from outrage to bemusement. But his speech had at least one of its likely intended effects. When debate resumed the next day, Dickinson's motion to postpone the New Jersey Plan was repealed, and Madison then took the floor to review the inadequacies of the plan, making its manifest shortcomings a convenient foil for his own vision of national power. The New Jersey Plan, he argued, would not "provide a Governmt. that will remedy the evils felt by the States both in their united and individual capacities." After recounting his leading criticisms of the vices of the Confederation, Madison concluded that "[t]he great difficulty lies in the affair of representation, and if this could be adjusted, all others would be surmountable." And again, he rested his case on an appeal to justice, now reinforced by a reminder that the admission of new but initially underpopulated frontier states endowed with "an equal vote" would enable "a more objectionable minority than ever to give law to the whole."[21]

On its merits, then, Paterson's plan had little to commend it, and after Madison spoke, the committee of the whole rejected it seven states to three, with one divided. A revealing interlude followed. The opportunity that now beckoned the large-state leaders was to convert this majority into a durable coalition in favor of proportional representation in both houses. The campaign began at once as Wilson, Hamilton, and King took the floor one after another. In part their remarks were conciliatory. Wilson dissociated himself from Hamilton, who had implied that the state governments should be "swallow[ed] up"—whereupon Hamilton complained that he had been misunderstood, and that "he admitted the necessity of leaving in them, subordinate jurisdictions." But the three speakers also deepened the intellectual foundation upon which proportional representation in both houses could be vindicated. King explained why the states did not "possess the peculiar features of sovereignty" that true nations possessed, while Hamilton more pointedly reminded the small states that "all the peculiarities which distinguish the interests of one State from those of another" would operate to prevent combinations among Pennsylvania, Virginia, and Massachusetts.[22]

Only a brief rejoinder from Luther Martin of Maryland interrupted this appeal. But the silence of the New Jersey Plan's advocates is misleading, for they had already achieved their end. Their basic purpose was not to narrow the agenda of reform but to indicate that they would accept the broad changes of the Virginia Plan only if the small states retained an equal vote in one house of Congress. Should the large states persist in *their* ultimatum, the small states would accept nothing that went beyond the modest amendments of the mid-1780s. The real debate over the thrust of the New Jersey Plan thus began only *after* its rejection. Indeed, the most significant discussions of the next ten days nominally addressed issues that, as Mason complained, one "did not expect . . . would have been reagitated."[23]

It was during this period that the great issues between the two sides were clearly drawn in ways that made the strengths and weaknesses of the large states' position evident. Three motions introduced by opponents of bicameral proportional representation sparked the critical exchanges. The first, offered on June 20 by Lansing, would vest additional powers in the existing Congress.[24] The second, proposed by Lansing on June 28, was to base representation in the *first* house "according to the rule established by the Confederation."[25] When this was rejected the next day, Oliver Ellsworth of Connecticut immediately moved to give each state an equal vote in the Senate. After a day and a half of debate, the Convention reassembled on Monday, July 2, to reject this motion on a tie vote. This vote revealed that the effort to translate the majority against the New Jersey plan into a coalition in favor of proportional representation in both houses had failed, and it immediately led to the election of a committee to propose a compromise to break the impasse.[26]

The specter of deadlock encouraged the protagonists to bluff, cajole, and threaten on behalf of their constituents. Both sides had a natural incentive to emphasize the legislative authority of the new government. Because it needed to be so powerful, large-state delegates argued, justice demanded equitable principles of apportionment; if it would be so powerful, small-state delegates replied, their security required retention of the equal vote. But the opposing positions were less symmetrical than this juxtaposition suggests. The character and substance of the arguments the two sides presented were not equivalent, nor did their advocates use ideas in quite the same way. While the large-state spokesmen vindicated their position on its theoretical merits—or literally its justice—the central challenge confronting the small states was simply to retain a privilege they already enjoyed. In this endeavor consistency was useful but not always necessary.

In practice, the defense of the equal-state vote shifted along three parallel lines, any two of which could be abandoned as circumstances dictated. The first held that the interests of the small states would be ignored or overwhelmed if proportional representation prevailed in both houses. A second position held that the authority of the state governments could not be assured "without allowing them to participate effectually in the Genl. Govt.," and that this required "giving them each a distinct and equal vote for the purpose of defending themselves in the general Councils." Third, the same logic implied that the existence of the states "as political societies"—or as self-governing communities—depended on the principle of equal representation in the upper house. All three variations on this theme drew added force from the fear that a negative on state laws would enable the national government to grind down the effective jurisdictions of the states.[27]

The flaws in these positions were easy to detect, and the speakers from the large states hammered away at them relentlessly. It is difficult to resist concluding that the small-state delegates knew they had the weaker arguments. Time and again they were battered in debate. As during the debate over the New Jersey Plan, Madison, Wilson, and King were content to take the opposing claims at face value and refute them on their merits. And they did so, moreover, in terms that were essentially consistent with Madison's general theory of faction.

On what basis "was a combination of the large [states] dreaded?" Madison asked on June 28, after Luther Martin's two-day defense of the immutable sovereignty of the states rambled to a halt. What "common interest" would enable Pennsylvania, Virginia, and Massachusetts to coalesce against the other states? His answer restated his theory of faction. "In point of situation they could not have been more effectually separated from each other by the most jealous citizen of the most jealous state," Madison declared. "In point of manners, Religion and the other circumstances, which sometimes beget affection between different communities, they were not more assimilated than the other States." Nor did they share common economic interests. Hamilton echoed this point the next day, and Wilson returned to it on June 30, noting that "No answer has been given to the observations of [Madison] on this subject."[28] This at last goaded Ellsworth to object that "the danger of combinations among" the large states was "not imaginary." Yet even this response lacked conviction: Ellsworth immediately added that "altho' no particular abuses could be foreseen by him, the possibility of them would be sufficient to alarm him." In other words, the very prospect of dominance would lead the large states to discover suitable objects for mutual aggrandizement.[29]

But Madison's theory of faction also undercut the claim that the states or their legislatures deserved equal representation, whether as sovereign entities, coordinate governments, or distinct communities. If the state assemblies appointed senators, King warned, they "would constantly choose men subservient to their own views as contrasted with the general interest." And in a way that many members intuitively understood but never fully articulated, the combination of legislative election and an equal vote reinforced this fear of a parochial and indecisive upper house precisely because it evoked the prevailing image of the existing Congress. "A reform would be nugatory and nominal only," King complained, "if we should make another Congress of the proposed Senate."[30] Nor did states, as such, have interests greater than, or distinct from, those of their citizens. "The Interest of a State is made up of the interests of its individual members," Benjamin Franklin flatly stated on June 11. "If they are not injured, the State is not injured." The point could be extended to ask whether the interests of state governments were identical with those of their constituents. "A private citizen of a State is indifferent whether power be exercised by the Genl. or State Legislatures, provided it be exercised most for his happiness," Wilson argued on June 20 and again the next day. "His representative has an interest in its being exercised by the body to which he belongs."[31] Clearly the less populous states would lose influence. But this did not mean that their citizens would be either less free or less capable of reaping the benefits of union than the residents of larger states. And it was on this basis—rather than on its impact on the state governments—that the new government would ultimately be judged.[32]

The spokesmen for the small states declined to meet this argument on its own terms. They did not seek to identify the interests that gave their states a special coherence. Only at the close of the debate of June 30 did Ellsworth assert that true "domestic happiness" depended on the preservation of the rights of the states. For the most part, the small-state delegates were forthright about their concerns. "Can it be expected that the small States will act from pure disinterestedness," asked Gunning Bedford of Delaware, "when the large states [are] evidently seeking to aggrandize themselves at the[ir] expense?"[33]

Their strategy was directed, in any case, toward more calculated ends than reasoned persuasion. The three motions that Lansing and Ellsworth offered after June 20 were tests of strength which revealed that the large states could not translate the alignment of June 19 into a new coalition. More important, they provided leverage for the "compromise" that Ellsworth, Sherman, and Dickinson had solicited all along. Each defeat they suffered bolstered the claim for accommodation. This was why seemingly settled questions were "reagitated" after June 20. Ellsworth disclosed the logic of this gambit immediately after the defeat of Lansing's second motion on June 29. "He was not sorry on the whole" with the result, Ellsworth declared, for "he hoped it would become a ground of compromise with regard to the 2d. branch." He thereupon moved to give the states an equal vote in the upper house.[34]

Ellsworth justified this proposal with the image of a Union that would be "partly national; partly federal"; but the argument he pressed was the familiar one of "self-defence." The small states deserved the same protection in the Senate that the large states enjoyed in the lower house. "If security be all that the great States wish for," he argued the next day, "the 1st branch secures them." But security was not what the large states desired, Wilson and Madison replied. The true issue was not protection but legislation—that is, the ability of the national government to act, consistent with the will and interests of whatever majority would coalesce in Congress. Even if a popular majority were adequately protected in the first house, Madison replied, a majority of states could still injure their "wishes and interests" by blocking the measures they desired, by extracting "repugnant" concessions in exchange for their passage, or by using the "great powers" likely to be vested in the Senate alone to "impose measures adverse" to their concerns.[35]

It was at this point that Madison injected a new argument, broaching a subject so far left unexplored. His speech of June 30 is well known for its frank invocation of the danger of sectionalism. It was true "that every peculiar interest whether in any class of citizens, or any description of States, ought to be secured as far as possible," Madison agreed.

But he contended that the states were divided into different interests not by their difference of size but by other circumstances; the most material of which resulted partly from climate, but principally from <the effects of> their having or not having slaves. These two causes concurred in forming the great division of interest in the U. States. It did not lie between the Northern and Southern, and if any defensive power were necessary, it ought to be mutually given to these two interests. He was so strongly impressed with this important truth that he had been casting about in his mind for some expedient that would answer the purpose.

One solution to this problem was to apportion representation in one house to free inhabitants only, and in the other to total population. But "he was restrained from proposing this expedient by two considerations," Madison concluded; "one was his unwillingness to urge any diversity of interests on an occasion when it was but too apt to arise of itself—the other was the inequality of powers that must be vested" in the two houses.[36]

Madison had not discovered the danger of sectionalism only in the course of the Convention. He had dealt with it in Congress in the early 1780s and in Virginia thereafter.[37] If he was willing to interject a new source of division within the Convention, it was probably because he sensed that the tide of debate was turning against him. For the issue of sectional differences could be invoked to two distinct ends. It certainly could be used to suggest that the conflict between small and large states was not the true lasting danger the Union faced. But by calling attention to fundamental differences between the states and even regions, it gave new legitimacy to the argument for "security" by encouraging every delegation to ask how its constituents might be protected if the balance of power within Congress swung against their particular interests.

If these were the assumptions on which Madison now acted, his concerns were well founded. The vote of July 2 indicated that deadlock itself offered a sufficient rationale for compromise, regardless of the weight of argument. Immediately after rejecting Ellsworth's motion, the Convention—over the objections of Madison and Wilson—elected a committee to frame a compromise, and its composition revealed how strong the sentiment for accommodation had become. While the large states were represented by those delegates whose previous remarks augured best for conciliation—Gerry, Franklin, and Mason—the members elected from the small states included its leading partisans: Paterson, Ellsworth, Martin, and Gunning Bedford.[38]

The committee met on July 3, joined the other delegates in celebrating independence on the fourth, and reported on the fifth. Its members quickly discovered that no miraculous solution could be found in a small circle that could not be proposed in the Convention as a whole. They nevertheless struggled to fulfill their charge, which extended to the formula to be used for apportioning seats in *both* houses. At Franklin's urging, the committee proposed this compromise: Each state would have an equal vote in the Senate; but as a concession to the large states, all bills of appropriation would "originate" in the lower house and not be subject to amendment in the Senate. The committee also followed an earlier decision of the committee of the whole to allocate representation in the lower house "in proportion to the whole number of white and other free citizens and inhabitants of every age, sex, and condition . . . and three fifths of all other persons"—that is, slaves.[39]

The compromise was less than nominal. Restricting the power of the Senate to amending appropriations was inconsequential, Madison argued, when it could simply reject any measure it disliked. But this objection could not deflect the appeal enjoyed by a report explicitly presented as a compromise. Madison must have sensed that the opportunity for rational persuasion was evaporating. Of the nine days of debate that preceded the vote of July 16, the framers devoted only two to the upper house. With the Convention verging toward a deadlock, the supporters of the equal-state vote grew impervious to appeals for justice, however eloquent. Either states were corporate units deserving an equal voice in national government or they were not. On this issue there was little left to say.

∞

THAT WAS NOT THE CASE with the apportionment of seats in the lower house. Because this was the first item in the committee's report, this was where substantive discussion began on July 5. Almost immediately, however, Gouverneur Morris of Pennsylvania challenged the premise of the committee's recommendation. After attending the opening days of the Convention, Morris had missed all of June; he returned in July eager to make up for lost time. Morris faulted the proposed rule of apportionment on two grounds. He argued, first, that "property ought to be taken into the estimate as well as the number of inhabitants," because it "was the main object of Society"; and second, that "the rule of representation ought to be so fixed as to secure to the Atlantic States a prevalence in the National Councils," which could be "easily done by irrevocably fixing the number of representatives which the Atlantic States should respectively have, and which each new State will have." On July 6, Morris proposed recommitting this part of the report.[40] After some debate, the Convention appointed a new committee comprising four large-state delegates (Morris, Randolph, and two members from Massachusetts, King and Nathaniel Gorham) and John Rutledge of South Carolina, who agreed "precisely" with Morris that property should be the basis of representation. In its report of July 9, this committee proposed an initial allocation of 56 seats in the lower house, but it abandoned the formula of reapportionment the Convention had previously approved to recommend instead that the national "Legislature be authorized from time to time to augment the number of representatives," using its discretion to make both wealth and population the basis for apportionment.[41]

This report elicited two responses: one directed toward the initial composition of the lower house, the other concerned with its reapportionment. Pressed to explain "on what principles or calculations" seats were allocated, Gorham could only say that "The numbers of blacks & whites with some regard to supposed wealth was the general guide," while Morris conceded that "The Report is little more than a guess." General dissatisfaction with these answers led to the election of a second committee of one member from each state to produce a more informed estimate. Its report of July 10 expanded the initial membership of the house to 65. Though several southern delegates grumbled that their region "must be extremely endangered by the present arrangements," this allocation withstood not only several challenges to augment the representation of the Carolinas and Georgia but also Madison's motion to double the size of the house in the interest of promoting both "the confidence of the people" and the degree of "local information" that representatives would possess.[42]

The original committee of five was less diffident about justifying its rule of reapportionment. "The Atlantic States having the government in their own hands, may take care of their own interest," Gorham explained on July 9, "by dealing out the right of Representation in safe proportions to the Western States." Morris spoke no less bluntly the next day. "He dwelt much on the danger of throwing such a preponderancy into the Western Scale," Madison noted, "suggesting that in time the Western people wd. outnumber the Atlantic States." Only by avoiding any measure to "fetter" or "shackle" the legislature could the Atlantic states "keep a majority of votes in their own hands."[43]

This reasoning might have prevailed had this issue solely pitted the seaboard states against the prospective states of the interior. But reapportionment remained divisive even when the West was left out of the equation. If Madison was right to argue that the true division would lie "between the Northern & Southern" states, then southern delegates, speaking for the region which would have an initial minority in *both* houses, had cause to worry whether future adjustments of representation would give due weight to the peculiar form of human property to which their societies were committed. Nor was this an idle fear, for as early as July 9, Paterson opposed including slaves in any calculation of representation on the grounds that "he could regard negro slaves in no light but as property." If they were "not represented in the States to which they belong," he asked, "why should they be represented in the Genl. Govt."? Morris, too, warned that "the people of Pena. would revolt at the idea of being put on a footing with slaves." But his objection went less to the principle of treating slaves as wealth than to the impolicy of mentioning slavery in the Constitution. Better to trust to a future legislative discretion that would surely take the value of slaves into account, Morris implied, than to incorporate so offensive a rule into the Constitution and thereby risk its rejection.[44]

Remarks like these could only prompt southern delegates—particularly the South Carolinians—to favor a rule explicitly linking representation and slavery. But the Virginians found Morris's animus against the West nearly as alarming. In their calculations, the conditions for creating political parity between the great regional divisions of North and South depended on the equitable treatment of the West, because they believed that the dominant southwestern vectors of migration would operate to the political advantage of their own region. (That, again, was why the closure of the Mississippi to American navigation was a far more volatile issue from Virginia south than it was in the northern states.) In 1787 prospects for settlement north of the Ohio River were still difficult to assess. Most of New York remained the domain of the Iroquois peoples (though that would change dramatically the following year); farther west, a surge of unregulated settlement was already evoking violent resistance from the Indian villages and "republics" of the Ohio Valley which culminated in the frontier war of 1789–95. South of the Ohio, by contrast, settlement had proceeded far enough to sustain separatist movements in the Kentucky district of Virginia and the "Franklin" district of North Carolina.[45] Preserving the allegiance of these settlers, the Virginians believed, required not only a national government strong enough to break the Spanish chokepoint at New Orleans but also one in which western migrants would enjoy an equality of rights. "They will have the same pride & other passions which we have," Mason reminded the Convention on July 11, "and will either not unite with or will speedily revolt from the

Union, if they are not in all respects placed on an equal footing with their brethren."[46]

These dual concerns inclined southern delegates to question Morris's smooth assurances about the goodwill of future legislatures. The leading opponent of his position was Edmund Randolph. On July 10, Randolph moved to require the legislature to take a periodic census of the population and to "arrange the Representation accordingly"; the next day he accepted a substitute proposal from Hugh Williamson of North Carolina linking the census to the original rule of apportionment by population, with slaves again counted at three-fifths.[47] The three days of debate (July 11–13) the Convention devoted to this proposal and numerous suggested amendments elicited a broad spectrum of opinions about the wisdom of fixing constitutionally both the intervals between censuses and the rule of reapportionment.

The most difficult question was whether and how slaves were to be counted. The South Carolina delegation held one pole in this debate, demanding full representation for slaves not only as a matter of simple "justice" because they were "the labourers, the peasants of the Southern States: they are as productive of pecuniary resources, as those of the Northern States," but also because "The security the Southn. States want is that their negroes may not be taken from them which some gentlemen within or without doors have a very good mind to do."[48] But this fear ran well beyond the statements that northern delegates actually made. True, southern insistence on a population rule counting slaves provoked King and Morris to suggest that a union thus formed "could not be of long duration." If these regional distinctions were as "real" as the South Carolinians believed, Morris declared on July 13, "let us at once take a friendly leave of each other." But again, Morris and King did not oppose using calculations of wealth (including slaves) for apportioning representation, only a population-based rule that could be applied in turn, they feared, to subordinate the "commercial" or "maritime" states from Pennsylvania northeast to what Morris described as "the interior & landed interest" of the South and West.[49] The dominant view expressed by other northern delegates, however, accepted the accommodation with slavery as the price of union. There was no *principled* basis on which the three-fifths rule could be fully justified, Wilson observed on July 11. Are the "blacks" to be "admitted as Citizens? Then why are they not admitted on an equality with White Citizens?" he asked. "Are they admitted as property? Then why is not other property admitted into the computation?" But the answer seemed obvious. "These were difficulties however which he thought must be overruled by the necessity of compromise."[50]

After numerous motions and amendments, the Randolph-Williamson scheme was passed with a proviso suggesting that the three-fifths rule was primarily a rule for apportioning direct taxation among the states, and that the rule of representation simply followed the same formula. As Wilson noted, "less umbrage would perhaps be taken agst. an admission of slaves into the Rule of representation" if it posed as an extension of a rule of taxation.[51] The fact that few delegates expected such taxes to be levied posed no obstacle to a formula which was designed to legitimate a decision taken for political reasons. But the three-fifths clause had a deeper irony. By limiting the protected categories of property to a single, specified, and exceptional case, it narrowed the basis on which property in general could be protected more radically than the legislative discretion sought by Morris might have done. Because its advocates repeatedly held that "numbers of inhabitants; though not always a precise standard of wealth was sufficiently so for every purpose," a proviso nominally advanced to protect property had the effect of legitimating the principle that representation actually followed population. Nor was this an inadvertent result of either a reflexive adherence to slavery on the part of southern delegates or the expedient accommodation to its brutal reality by other delegates. Their position reflected an equally strong commitment to the fundamental principle of equality that Mason, Wilson, Randolph, and Madison all roundly stated to oppose discrimination against future states in the West. "If the Western States are to be admitted into the Union as they arise, they must," Mason insisted, "be treated as equals, and subjected to no degrading discriminations."[52]

The three-fifths clause, then, was neither a coefficient of racial hierarchy nor a portent of the racialist thinking of the next century. It was rather the closest approximation in the Constitution to the principle of one person, one vote—even if in its origins it was only a formula for apportioning representation *among*, as opposed to *within*, states, and even if it violated the principle of equality by overvaluing the suffrage of the free male population of the slave states. As much credence as this clause ultimately lent to abolitionist criticism of the Constitution, the concerns that drove southern delegates to insist upon constitutional rules for both a census and reapportionment had avowedly liberal aspects and consequences, if only because trusting to legislative discretion would have established no binding rule at all.[53]

Within the context of the Convention's other debate about representation, the sociology of sectionalism had a further advantage that Madison hoped to exploit. It described objective interests and differences that everyone understood were fated to endure long after the Convention ad-

journed, and that reflected in the most profound terms the underlying attributes of individuals, states, and entire regions. The same could not be
said about the mere size of a state, which in Madison's view could be a
source of division only within the Convention, when the rule of voting itself was under debate. If congressmen from Connecticut and New Jersey
later found themselves opposing their colleagues from Virginia, were their
differences more likely to arise from disparities in the size of their states
or in their economic and social systems? In this sense, the candor with
which the framers debated whether to count slaves buttressed the case
against equal-state representation by providing a superior model of the
rival interests that any national government would need to reconcile. In
a telling exchange on July 9, Madison even caught Paterson in an embarrassing contradiction when the New Jersey delegate opposed counting
slaves because "the true principle of representation" was to provide "an expedient by which an assembly of certain individls. chosen by the people
is substituted in place of the inconvenient meeting of the people themselves." Madison must have fairly leaped to his feet to remind Paterson
that such a "doctrine of Representation which was in its principle the
genuine one, must for ever silence the pretensions of the small States to
an equality of votes with the large ones."[54]

Yet the marginal gain this move promised did not outweigh its
costs. The more the delegates examined the apportionment of the lower
house, the more weight they gave to considerations of regional security.
Rather than treat sectional differences as an alternative and superior description of the real interests at play in American politics, the delegates
saw them instead as an additional conflict that had to be accommodated
in order for the Union to endure. In this sense, the apportionment issue
confirmed the claims that the small states had made all along. It called attention not to the way in which an extended republic could protect all interests but to the need to safeguard the conspicuous interest of North and
South. This defensive orientation in turn enabled even some large-state
delegates to find merit in an equal-state vote. If the security of a limited
number of interests was a primary object of the new government, a Senate in which states voted equally afforded a promising basis of reassur-
ance. No one could safely predict how shifting tides of migration and
population growth would affect the composition of the lower house. Calculations of influence based only on number of states were less daunting.
If the admission of new states was regulated by a Congress in which each
major region enjoyed particular influence in one house, it was possible to
foresee how a balance between (or among) the sections might be maintained over time.

Morris put the point with typical candor on Friday, July 13. The week before, in rejecting the claim that the equal-state vote was needed "to keep the majority of the people from injuring particular States," he had delivered the sharpest riposte imaginable. "But particular States ought to be injured for the sake of a majority of the people," he insisted, "in case their conduct should deserve it." Since then, however, he had opposed constitutional rules for apportionment with avowals of regional interest so transparent as to evoke Madison's complaint that Morris "determined the human character by the points of the compass." Yet inconsistency and insight are not always mutually exclusive. Even while lamenting that "there can be no end of demands for security if every particular interest is to be entitled to it," Morris revealed where this concern could lead. "The consequence of such a transfer of power from the maritime to the interior & landed interest," Morris declared, "will be such an oppression of commerce, that he shall be obliged to vote for the vicious principle of equality in the 2d. branch in order to provide some defence for the N. States agst. it."[55]

For lawyerly sophism, Morris had few peers. In their own final defenses of proportional representation, Madison, Wilson, and King opted for consistency. Almost everything that was said during the few days that were given to the main points of the proposed compromise recapitulated not only arguments made earlier but the basic asymmetry of the two positions. With compromise itself now the issue, the small states no longer defended their position on theoretical terms, while the large-state spokesmen could only cling to their previous arguments. Thus when a conciliating Gerry suggested that it might be better "to proceed to enumerate and define the powers to be vested in the Genl. Govt." before deciding the rule of voting, Madison repeated that such determinations had to await resolution of the rule of representation. Again, the arguments against the equal-state vote do not appear to have been effectively rebutted. When delegates from the large states dismissed as inconsequential the ostensible concession restraining the Senate from initiating or amending appropriations bills, they elicited only weak responses from the proponents of compromise. Paterson even declined to say whether it was "a valuable consideration or not."[56] Only on July 14 did the large-state delegates offer a tepid compromise, telescoping the allocation of seats in the Senate so that no state would have more than five votes. But they adhered to their major principles. King asserted that no credible threat to either the small states or the state governments had ever been identified; Wilson argued that the legislative election of senators would afford adequate security for the states; and Madison rejected Ellsworth's image of a Union "partly federal" by denying that there would be "a single instance in which the Genl. Govt. was not to operate on the people individually."[57]

In his final comments, Madison echoed his conclusions of June 30. An equal vote would not merely give the small states the security they craved; in practice it would also enable them to thwart the majority will. But he then cited one last "serious consideration" militating against the claim for an equal-state vote—and he did so in a way that implicitly challenged much of what he had argued hitherto. "It seemed now to be pretty well understood that the real difference of interests lay, not between the large and small but between the N. and Southn. States," Madison reminded his colleagues. "The institution of slavery and its consequences formed the line of discrimination," with the five states from Maryland south arrayed against the eight from Delaware north. The disparity would remain even should a scheme of proportional representation be adopted for both houses, "but not in the same degree [as] at this time; and every day would tend towards an equilibrium" of sectional power.[58]

Did "equilibrium" as Madison used it here mean anything different from the "security" that Ellsworth had sought for the small states? The debate over apportionment had exposed the central tension—or even contradiction—in the general theory that Madison labored so hard to develop. For the recognition that there was one overriding issue that threatened to establish a great "division of interests" between slave and free states could not be easily rendered compatible with the pluralist imagery of the diverse sources of faction. In both instances, it is true, Madison expressed concern for the protection of minority rights, by which he meant, principally but not exclusively, rights of property. Yet radically different inferences could be drawn from these two attempts to trace the origins of faction.

The theory of faction that Madison had formulated on the eve of the Convention promised to assure an array of minorities that their rights and interests would be treated justly in a national legislature that none of them could ever hope to control. But this conception of the multiple and mutable sources of faction purported to describe "all civilized societies" and was thus, in a sense, abstract and general. The same could not be said of the portrait of the United States that Madison etched when he raised the specter of sectional division. But what did one see when the new Republic was described in these gross regional terms: a society embracing a "multiplicity of interests" or a nation divisible into two great and potentially antagonistic factions, either of which could readily imagine how shifts in population and influence might threaten its prosperity, institutions, and values alike? And what notion of legislation was more compatible with this image: one that allowed majorities to govern while promising protection to all interests, defined principally in terms of the attributes of *individuals*; or one that implied that the first task in constructing a national legislature was to provide specific constitutional guarantees for certain broad groupings of *states*, whether large or small, northern or southern? And which political goal had become more important: overcoming the objections of the populous states against granting additional powers to a government founded (as King put it) on the "vicious constitution of Congs. with regard to representation and suffrage,"[59] or convincing the slave states that their interests would rest secure in a government in which they were the initial minority?

In the end, the framers could not avoid treating the states as constituent elements of the polity; nor could they deny that simple residence in a state would establish the most natural bond of civic loyalty. In all their efforts to prove that no objective interest could ever unite Massachusetts, Pennsylvania, and Virginia in the exercise of a federal condominium, the spokesmen for the large states never cited the diversity of interests within their own states to disprove the conspiracy theories of their antagonists. None of them ever suggested that representatives elected by small farmers in Pennsylvania and Maryland might have more in common with one another than they would with merchant congressmen from Philadelphia or Baltimore. Just as these ports eyed each other as competitive rivals, so the rural hinterlands they served might rise or fall with their entrepreneurial success. "If Va. should have 16 votes and Del[awa]re. with several other States together 16," Gorham reasoned, "those from Virga. would be more likely to unite than the others, and would therefore have an undue influence."[60] Nor did delegates from the small states argue that their constituents were no more likely to coalesce for obstructive purposes than were the large states in pursuit of domination.

There was one other reason why the case for proportional representation in both houses fell short of being persuasive. In his speech of July 14, King suggested that "the idea of securing the State Govts." logically required the creation of a tricameral legislature. If the first house represented the people directly, the second "was admitted to be necessary, and was actually meant, to check the 1st. branch, to give more wisdom, system, and stability to the Govt."; and once that was assured, a third house could then protect the "rights and dignities of the states."[61] Frivolous as this proposal might be, its rationale illustrated a crucial point. In King's conception as in Madison's, the Senate's representative character was incidental to its substantive functions and deliberative qualities. No sound republican could accept Hamilton's notion of a Senate composed of members serving for life, but the independence he sought did not differ at bottom from what Madison envisioned when he proposed a nine-year term that "should not commence until such a period of life as would render a perpetual disqualification inconvenient."[62] It was the Senate that would act as the great guardian of national interests, charged, as the framers originally expected it would be, with responsibility for war and foreign affairs. Within this framework, the proportional vote was no more designed to enable the Senate to reflect the actual distribution of interests within society than the aversion to legislative election was intended to make it more dependent on the popular will. The former was required merely to convince the large states to approve the desired augmentation of national power, the latter to prevent the Senate from becoming "another edition of Congs." through an improper solicitude for provincial concerns.[63]

The great flaw in this conception was that it risked ceasing to be a scheme of representation. The relation between senators and their constituents required only that the former possess some knowledge of local circumstances, without which they were unlikely to be chosen. Yet Madison never developed a clear or persuasive conception of how senators should be elected; nor did he explain how any form of proportional representation would preserve the elitist intimacy required for sober deliberation. His failure is the more striking because the place that the Senate initially occupied in his constitutional theory suggests that it, far more than the lower house, was meant to be the destination of those who he hoped would emerge from a refined system of elections. He knew better what he wanted to avoid than what he hoped to institute. "If an election by the people, or thro' any other channel than the State Legislatures promised as uncorrupt and impartial a preference of merit, there could surely be no necessity for an appointment by those Legislatures," he observed on June 7. But the vote of that date revealed that legislative election of senators, for all its faults, was preferred by a decisive majority of delegates.[64] From that point on, Madison hoped either to limit the damage without jeopardizing the cause of proportional representation or to use an eventual victory on apportionment to reverse the decision on election. But once the specter of sectional conflict legitimated the small states' appeal to security, that opportunity was lost.

WHEN THE TEST CAME on Monday, July 16, Gerry and Caleb Strong cast the key vote, dividing the Massachusetts delegation and thereby allowing the small-state coalition of Connecticut, New Jersey, Delaware, and Maryland to claim a narrow victory with the support of North Carolina.[65] There followed an interlude that revealed how the tensions of the past weeks still festered. For a few minutes parliamentary decorum prevailed, as the framers moved on to the next item on their agenda: the long-deferred article describing the legislative powers of the Union. When they reached the clause authorizing the national legislature to "legislate in all cases to which the states are incompetent," the South Carolina delegates moved for the appointment of a committee to provide a "specification of the powers comprised in the general terms." After this motion failed on a tie vote, Randolph observed that the decision on the Senate "had embarrassed the business extremely" because "all the powers given in the Report . . . were founded on the supposition that a Proportional representation was to prevail in both houses of the Legislature." Rather than proceed on this basis, Randolph added, the Convention should adjourn so "that the large States might consider the steps proper to be taken in the present solemn crisis of the business, and that the small States might also deliberate on the means of conciliation."[66]

Randolph thus revealed that the large-state leaders had approached the climactic vote still convinced that the small states would yield. Their immediate dismay left them unprepared to imagine how the deliberations could go forward. But Paterson, the next speaker, called them to their senses by giving Randolph's remarks a surprising cast. Paterson declared

> that it was high time for the Convention to adjourn that the rule of secrecy ought to be rescinded, and that our Constituents should be consulted. No conciliation could be admissible on the part of the smaller States on any other ground than that of an equality of votes in the 2d. branch. If Mr Randolph would reduce to form his motion for an adjournment sine die, he would second it with all his heart.

Randolph hastily protested that "his meaning had been so readily & strangely misinterpreted." While still urging the small states to ponder their victory, he insisted that he sought only an adjournment overnight. His motion was seconded by Paterson, who pointedly noted, however, that it was for "the larger states to deliberate further on conciliatory expedients." But when members from these states caucused the next morning, Madison noted, "The time was wasted in vague conversation on the subject, without any specific proposition or agreement." Some were willing to consider forming a rump convention without the small states; but the greater number, though dispirited, "seemed inclined to yield" even if that meant acquiescing in a constitution that might prove "imperfect &

exceptionable." Gouverneur Morris evidently dissented. When the Convention came to order a few minutes later, he made a last attempt to nullify the previous day's decision by suggesting that the Convention first consider "in the abstract the powers necessary to be vested in the general Government," deferring discussion of its form and structure until agreement could be reached on these points. But at this point the delegates were hardly disposed to accept an invitation to start afresh, and Morris's transparent motion went unseconded.[67]

Morris's gambit was only a distraction in a full and rich day of discussion that marked significant progress on several major questions, and which thus helped dissipate lingering ill feelings while pointing the delegates toward the work ahead.

The first of these issues turned on defining the general legislative powers of the Union. At least one member thought that the disarray of the large-state delegates might enable the Convention to pursue a more modest agenda. In May Roger Sherman had announced that he was not "disposed to Make too great inroads on the existing system," and he now offered a substitute motion to empower the national legislature to act "in all cases which may concern the common interests of the Union; but not to interfere with the Government of the individual States in any matters of internal police" not involving "the General welfare" of the nation. He explained his motion by reading "an enumeration of powers" which would limit congressional sources of taxation to duties on trade. This was probably a fatal defect, for his amendment lost, eight states to two. Instead, the Convention modestly amended the article as reported, preserving the Virginia Plan (as revised) as its working text, while leaving open the possibility that a specific enumeration of powers could be compiled later.[68]

One power which Madison deemed vital, however, did not survive the scrutiny of July 17. Thus far the Convention had endorsed the idea of arming the national legislature with a negative on state laws "contravening . . . the articles of union, or any treaties subsisting under the authority of the union." While balking at extending this power to "all Laws which it shd. judge to be improper," many framers presumably agreed that the national government required some power to protect itself against interfering laws of the states. But in the wake of the decision recognizing the equal sovereignty of the states, the negative seemed both impractical and improper. It was now attacked by the unlikely tandem of Sherman and Morris, though on slightly divergent grounds. Whereas Morris thought that the *national* judiciary and legislature would both retain the authority to supersede state law without the "terrible" weapon of the veto, Sherman argued that "the Courts of the States would not consider as valid any law contravening the authority of the Union, and which the legislature would wish to be negatived." Madison's effort to defend his proposal was un-availing. The negative was eliminated by a vote of seven states to three, and in its place the Convention adopted, without debate or dissent, a substitute resolution offered by Luther Martin. Reviving a key provision of the New Jersey Plan, Martin moved to make acts of the national leg-islature and national treaties the "supreme law of the respective states," binding on their judiciaries, "any thing in the respective laws of the indi-vidual States to the contrary notwithstanding." Here in seminal form was the supremacy clause of the Constitution—but ironically presented as a weak measure that failed to proclaim either the national constitution or its derivative acts superior to the authority of the state *constitutions*.[69]

The third major question the framers took up on July 17 returned to an issue they had ignored since early June: the executive. Once again Morris seized the initiative, denouncing the idea of allowing the national legislature to choose the executive as a formula for making its election "the work of intrigue, of cabal, and of faction." His remarks launched a flurry of motions, amendments, and counterproposals on the election and tenure of the executive that preoccupied the Convention for the next ten days, when it found itself exactly back where it had started: with a single executive to be elected by the legislature for the sole term of seven years. But its circularity notwithstanding, this debate marked a qualitative shift in the general tenor of the deliberations. For the various problems asso-ciated with the executive could only be considered on their merits—or rather, they could be answered only through a free discussion of the widely varying conceptions of the office that individual delegates favored. Unlike the politics of redesigning Congress, the presidency emerged not from the clash of naked wills to gain a long-contested point but from a series of ingenious efforts to design a new institution that would be suit-ably energetic but safely republican.

The session of July 17 also prefigured the more pragmatic course the Convention took until its adjournment exactly two months later. A nar-rative of this second great phase of debate cannot take the same form as the one that culminates on July 16. The brevity of Madison's notes after mid-July testifies not only to his mounting fatigue with his burdensome chore but also to the delegates' aversion for the long and polished speeches that were so frequent in June and July. Where the dynamics of the debate over representation spurred both sides to emphasize how po-tent a government they were creating, the framers could now ask exactly what purposes and functions they meant it (or its individual branches) to serve. In place of one overriding question, they now dealt with clusters of discrete issues, less momentous in their individual import yet cumulatively deciding the devilish details that gave the Constitution its original meaning. To the regret of later commentators, many of these clauses were adopted or amended with little debate. That was the case not only with the often-examined decision of August 17 substituting "declare" for "make" in the clause authorizing Congress to decide when the nation would be at war, but also with the modest but momentous revision that took place six days later, when the words "This Constitution" were added to Martin's formula affirming the supremacy of national laws and treaties.[70] But the quickened pace of debate reflected a changed mood among the delegates, as well as the recognition that the Convention would end in agreement rather than dissension.

FATIGUE, IMPATIENCE, AND HOMESICKNESS certainly contributed to this mood. "I believe the older men grow the more uneasy [the longer] they are from their wives," Oliver Ellsworth wrote to his wife, Abigail, on July 21. "Mr. Sherman and Doctor Johnson are both run home for a short family visit. As I am a third younger than they are I calculate to hold out a third longer, which will carry me to about the last of August." By then "the business of the convention" should "come to a close," he predicted, expedited by the appointment of "a smaller committee to throw into form and detail" the previous report of the committee of the whole, "after which it will undergo one revision more."[71] Ellsworth himself was a member of this committee of detail, joining Rutledge, Randolph, Gorham, and Wilson in the task of converting the resolutions adopted thus far into the working text of a constitution. While they labored from Friday July 27 through Sunday, August 5, their colleagues enjoyed a ten-day recess. (Washington literally went fishing with Robert Morris and Gouverneur Morris, taking time to visit "the old cantonment" of the Continental army at Valley Forge.[72]) When the framers reconvened on August 6, the committee of detail presented its report, which laid the basis for what became, in procedural terms, the third reading of the Virginia Plan.[73]

Committees often work best when their parent bodies weary of their labors. That may explain why they were appointed more frequently once hopes for a late-August adjournment began to slip away. On three separate occasions, the Convention gave the committee of detail additional tasks. On August 18, it referred two lists of supplemental legislative powers, submitted by Madison and Pinckney, to the committee. It took the same action two days later when Pinckney introduced a partial bill of rights and Morris proposed the establishment of an executive Council of State comprising the chief justice and five ministerial heads of department. On August 23, it referred the general subject of the treaty power to the committee after a full afternoon's debate revealed widespread discontent with the idea of placing that power solely in the Senate. By then the committee was itself breaking down, for August 23 was Ellsworth's last day in Philadelphia.[74] Like other unfinished matters—including the presidency—treaty-making thus fell to the "grand committee" (one member from each state) that was elected on August 31 to examine "such parts of the Constitution as have been postponed, and such parts of Reports as have not been acted on." This was in fact the fourth such committee elected in two weeks. Of the previous three grand committees, the most important was the one charged to balance conflicting regional concerns over the scope of a national power to regulate commerce.[75]

Taken together, this use of committees and the terse quality of debate convey the impression of a Convention moving restlessly toward conclusion, tying up loose ends, and trying to assuage the concerns of individual members without allowing their special pleas to impede the flow of proceedings. The final weeks were also spent resolving implications of the earlier preoccupation with the apportionment of representation. Those implications included not only issues largely ignored so far but also misgivings about the Senate the framers had struggled so long to construct, and whose defects contributed to the growth of presidential power during the final fortnight of debate. And as they moved to remedy defects in these earlier decisions, the framers simultaneously converted the bitter residue of the small states' victory of July 16 into the image of the compromise that proved so useful during the campaign for ratification.

The most notable change the committee of detail proposed in its report was to replace the open-ended formula previously used to describe the legislative authority of the Union with a list of specific powers. Perhaps this alteration was inevitable, and was delayed only by Madison's political strategy; but once it began, the delegates could fashion a more balanced if prosaic picture of the actual duties they expected the new government to assume. Even as augmented by the proposals that Madison and Pinckney had referred to the committee of detail, this list generated little sustained debate. The clause that proved most controversial during the ratification debate—authorizing Congress to "make all laws necessary and proper for carrying into execution" its enumerated powers—was unanimously approved on August 20 after only a brief discussion.[76]

The most vexatious recommendations of the committee of detail were found in the fourth and sixth sections of its seventh article. Section 4, which was likely inserted at the insistence of Rutledge, declared:

> No tax or duty shall be laid by the Legislature on articles exported from any State; nor on the importation or migration of such persons as the several States shall think proper to admit; nor shall such migration or importation be prohibited.

Section 6, which was probably the work of Randolph, required "the assent of two-thirds of the members present in each House" for the passage of any "navigation act." Though both clauses were the initiative of the committee, few delegates were surprised by the license it took. During the debate over the three-fifths clause, Paterson and Morris had both complained that its adoption would encourage southern states to continue importing slaves.[77] When the Convention discussed using a single formula to apportion both representation and taxation, Morris raised the possibility of taxing exports. This in turn prompted General Charles Pinckney to express his alarm over both the threatening tenor of Morris's remarks about the slave trade and the notion that exports might be taxed at all, because South Carolina would never receive representation "in proportion" to its annual exports of "£600,000 Sterling all which was the fruit of the labor of her blacks."[78] When Gerry moved the appointment of a committee of detail on July 23, Pinckney "reminded the Convention that if the Committee should fail to insert some security to the Southern States agst. an emancipation of slaves, and taxes on exports, he shd. be bound by duty to his State to vote agst. their Report."[79]

The South Carolinians were never bashful in their defense of slavery, and in Rutledge they had a powerful voice sitting on the committee of detail. Though Randolph, its other southern member, was more circumspect—"he lamented that such a species of property existed," a qualm never felt in South Carolina—he, too, agreed that the "security" southern delegates sought for slavery was legitimate. All three northern members of the committee had acknowledged the necessity of compromise over the apportionment of representation; only Wilson had voiced moral distaste for its evil. But how much accommodation was enough? What is striking about the report of the committee of detail was how much it claimed for the South. The limitations on the authority of Congress over exports or the slave trade were absolute, while the supermajorities required to pass navigation acts would make their adoption more difficult. Perhaps the committee calculated that the *later* modification of its recommendations could be portrayed as a compromise on the part of the South.[80] But whether or not that speculation is plausible, the tenor of their report clearly troubled northern delegates who were otherwise prepared, if grudgingly, to accommodate the South on representation.

For reasons that remain obscure, the report omitted a clear statement of the three-fifths rule for representation, and though this oversight was quickly corrected on August 8, sectional suspicions were already revived. "The admission of slaves was a most grating circumstance," King declared after the correction was made, and "it would be so to a great part of the people of America." It could be justified only if the South in turn evinced a willingness "to strengthen the Genl. Govt. and to mark a full confidence in it." But nothing would be gained in return if "the importations of slaves could not be prohibited—exports could not be taxed." Sherman immediately responded that "though the slave-trade was iniquitous," the issue of representation, "having been Settled after much difficulty," should not be reopened. Here, as on other occasions, the Connecticut delegates were the spokesmen for realpolitik, urging other northern delegates to treat slavery as a pragmatic interest to be balanced against their own special concerns. But Gouverneur Morris would have none of this. Slavery was "the curse of heaven on the States where it prevailed," he declared, its effects manifest in the contrast between the "rich & noble cultivation" of the "free regions of the Middle States" and "the misery & poverty which overspread the barren wastes" of the states from Maryland south; it would also make up "the most prominent feature in the aristocratic countenance of the proposed Constitution." Nor did Morris confine himself—as many Americans were wont to do—to the harm that slavery inflicted on the free population. He also denounced the slave trade as a crime against "the most sacred laws of humanity."[81]

Morris delivered these remarks in support of his amendment to apportion representation to "free inhabitants" alone. That motion was roundly rejected, with only New Jersey voting in its favor. But for all his rhetorical fire, Morris, like King, was more troubled by the political inequities of the committee's report than by its moral iniquity. Their objections against rewarding the "nefarious" slave trade with even greater representation were obvious enough, but these were not more pointed than their complaints about the costs the North would bear if exports were exempt from taxation. Morris was as keen a student of public finance as Hamilton. He knew that direct taxes were unlikely to be levied, and he could readily calculate that if national taxes were limited to duties and excises, the high living of a relatively small number of large planters could never compensate for the depressed consumption of a society in which so much of its population was sunk in slavery, incapable of obtaining more than its daily bread and the ragged garments that the mass of field workers wore. The South, in other words, could contribute its fair share of national revenues only if it allowed its agricultural commodities to be taxed.[82]

Taxation of exports was not solely a question of sectional interest; as Morris, Wilson, Dickinson, and Madison argued when debate reached this clause on August 21, other reasons of state justified giving Congress a power that was only discretionary, not mandatory. But though sectional concerns were not predominant in this debate, Butler and Mason did suggest that such a power would be especially "unjust and alarming to the staple States" of the South; and when the crucial test came over an amendment proposed by Madison and Wilson to permit taxation of exports by a two-thirds vote of both houses, the five states from Maryland south joined Connecticut to send it to a narrow defeat.[83]

The more heated debate began immediately, when Martin moved "to allow a prohibition or tax on the importation of slaves." Martin repeated two familiar arguments: first, that the three-fifths clause would encourage the slave trade; second, that "slaves weakened one part of the Union which the other parts were bound to protect." But he concluded on a more eloquent note: It was simply "inconsistent with the principles of the revolution and dishonorable to the American character to have such a feature in the Constitution."[84] Martin struck a nerve, for eight of the next nine speeches came from the Connecticut–South Carolina axis that manned the bulwarks in defense of slavery.[85] All were uncompromising and unapologetic. "Interest alone is the governing principle with Nations," Rutledge declared; it was as much in the interest of the North to encourage the economic growth that slavery made possible as it was in the interest of the planting states themselves. Ellsworth promptly agreed, adding, "The morality and wisdom of slavery are considerations belonging to the states themselves." A night's reflection may have left Ellsworth embarrassed over his indifference to the moral question that Morris— rarely regarded as an exemplar of virtue—had previously raised, for on August 22, he and Sherman voiced the pious hope that the abolition of slavery was already under way. But the South Carolinians were unrepentant. "If slavery be wrong, it is justified by the example of all the world," Pinckney declared. Left to themselves, he and Baldwin suggested, South Carolina and Georgia might voluntarily "stop importations"—but these states were not yet in the condition of Virginia, General Pinckney noted, which could only "gain by stopping the importations" because "she has more [slaves] than she wants."[86] The general aimed this reminder at Mason, the only delegate with the temerity thus far to interrupt the defense of the slave trade—and to do so on the same moral grounds as had Morris and Martin. Neither Virginia nor Maryland had a stake in the revival of the pre-Revolutionary slave trade, for in both states the demographic transition to a self-sustaining African-American population was sufficiently advanced to make them likely exporters of labor to the lower South and the colonizing regions of the interior.[87]

The northern demur to these claims began with Wilson, who ironically noted that if the southernmost states were likely to halt importations on their own, as alleged, they could not object to a national measure to the same end. Gerry, Dickinson, King, and John Langdon of New Hampshire echoed Wilson's concern. Though all their responses—save Dickinson's—stopped well short of a moral indictment of slavery, they elicited another bellicose retort from Rutledge, who warned that the lower South would never ratify the Constitution if slave importations were halted. But he joined General Pinckney in signaling a modest retreat by calling for the appointment of a committee on the clause in question, and in response Morris urged that the companion clauses concerning taxes on exports and the supermajority for navigation acts be committed as well. "These things may form a bargain among the Northern & Southern States," Morris noted, and most of the Convention quickly concurred in the appointment of a grand committee.[88]

The committee's report of August 24 made three major recommendations: No restriction of the slave trade could occur before 1800; duties could be collected on this trade (thereby ending its status as the only form of importation exempt from taxation); and navigation acts would no longer require two-thirds majorities.[89] Debate on the first two revisions was desultory. Only Madison criticized Pinckney's successful amendment to postpone the point at which Congress could halt slave importations until 1808. Morris then moved to restrict this twenty-year license for continued importations to the Carolinas and Georgia, but this was merely a final rhetorical sally which he quickly withdrew. After the amended clause was approved seven states to four, the recommendation permitting duties on imported slaves passed with even less difficulty.[90]

The issue of navigation acts proved more contentious when the delegates reached it on August 29, largely because Pinckney moved to postpone this part of the report in order to consider a proposal extending the original two-thirds provision from navigation acts to laws regulating both foreign and interstate commerce. On this point, however, Pinckney was abandoned by his own delegation, firmly if politely opposed by a number of northern and southern delegates, and vigorously supported by Mason and Randolph. After his motion was rejected, the committee's recommendation was approved without objection. The only alarming aspect of this debate was the evidence it provided that Mason and Randolph, who had both done so much to promote conciliation within the Convention, were moving toward a position of refusing to sign the completed Constitution.[91]

All of these decisions could be presented as concessions to the northern delegates. If the chief benefit their states sought from the Constitution was a government empowered to protect their great interests in commerce and shipping, the elimination of the two-thirds requirement for navigation acts was crucial. Morris had sounded the correct note when he spoke of a potential "bargain among the Northern & Southern states." The moral passion the earlier debate over slavery aroused had clearly abated. If a few delegates worried that these actions risked "bringing the curse of heaven" on Americans, most were relieved to resolve the sectional dispute without great rancor. In this atmosphere, the South Carolina delegates secured a further boon: the easy passage of a fugitive slave clause, providing that "any person bound to service or labor" in one state, escaping to another, "shall be delivered up to the person justly claiming their service or labor." When this proposal had been presented on August 28 in cruder form—"fugitive slaves and servants [were] to be delivered up like criminals"—Wilson and Sherman objected to "the public expense" states would incur; but when it was renewed in more refined language the next day, it went unopposed.[92]

These decisions did not quite complete the framework of compromises and bargains that the delegates now knew they were constructing. On August 24, the same day the grand committee on the sectional "bargain" presented its report, the Convention reached an impasse on another issue. Two test votes that day found the delegates almost evenly divided on the puzzling issue of how the president was to be elected, and because issues of election, length of term, and reeligibility were closely connected, the entire construction of the executive was left uncertain. This puzzlement coincided with growing doubts about the capacity of the Senate. The previous day's discussion of the treaty power, which the framers had so far assigned solely to the Senate, had crystallized an inchoate sense that the upper house would too closely resemble the Continental Congress to fulfill its grand responsibilities. The authority of these two institutions, and the relation between them, thus became part of the unfinished business that the last grand committee of August 31 was expected to resolve.[93]

Its report of September 4 fused the two major political compromises the delegates had struggled to craft on behalf of the interests they represented. The political logic of the electoral college almost exactly replicated the debate over representation. By allocating presidential electors among the states on the basis of their membership in both houses of Congress, it would honor both the three-fifths clause and the equal-state vote. This gave a slight weighting to the small states, but because collectively they could not command enough votes to make any single candidate formidable, they would prove unable to advance a nominee to the second round of voting that most framers thought would usually be needed in the decentralized polity the United States seemed destined to remain, where characters of truly national reputation would be hard to find. The large states would have an advantage in the first round, but the small states would have an equal vote in the second. It took some ingenuity on the part of Hugh Williamson and Sherman to devise the idea of having the state delegations in the House cast a unit vote rather than place the election in the Senate, as the committee proposed. But this in turn encouraged many delegates to accept the committee's proposal to place authority over treaties and appointments jointly in the president and Senate (so as to answer the objection that a president elected by the Senate would simply become its tool). Moreover, this reallocation of the treaty power partly compensated the South for allowing simple majorities to enact commercial legislation. For commerce with foreign nations could also be regulated by treaties which, once ratified, would be less easy to revise or revoke than unjust or invidious laws, which could always be repealed. Because flawed treaties could arguably do greater damage to regional interests than mere statutes, it was reasonable to require a two-thirds vote of the Senate for their ratification.[94]

It took nearly a week of debate (September 4–8) to resolve these points, but once that was done, the Convention elected a five-member committee (Johnson, Hamilton, Morris, Madison, and King) "to revise the stile of and arrange the articles which had been agreed to by the House."[95] After this committee presented its draft Constitution on Wednesday, September 12, the Convention considered a final flurry of widely varying amendments. A number of these emanated from the three dissenters who now indicated they were unlikely to sign the Constitution: Mason, Randolph, and Gerry. Some of their proposals were treated respectfully and even approved, in a final bid for their support; others, especially those coming from the maverick Gerry, were brusquely dismissed. Even at the proverbial eleventh hour, with everyone anxious to adjourn, potentially important issues were raised and noteworthy changes made. On September 12, for example, the majority required to override a presidential veto was reduced from three-fourths of both houses of Congress to two-thirds. Two days later, Franklin, Wilson, and Madison attempted to give Congress authority to build canals and to grant charters of incorporation when the national interest warranted, but this effort failed—helping to lay the groundwork for decades of controversy over the constitutionality of a national bank and internal improvements.[96]

In its last days the Convention also wrestled with issues relating to both the ratification and the subsequent amendment of the Constitution. The basic procedure for ratification had been formulated by late July, when the delegates agreed to submit the Constitution to popularly elected conventions in the states. On August 31, the framers fixed nine as the number of approving states required for ratification.[97] But the sole path for amendments as yet accepted required Congress to call a convention on the application of two-thirds of the state legislatures; nor had any rule been set for their ratification. When this article was reconsidered on September 10, the framers readily accepted Madison's revision making Congress the sole source of amendments, with ratification needing the approval of three-fourths of the state legislatures or conventions. This belated attention to the issue of future constitutional change also revived the insecurities of the two great minority interests that the bargains of mid-July and late August were meant to protect, for who could promise that what was done in Convention might not be undone by amendment? Rutledge immediately secured an amendment prohibiting any constitutional amendment adopted before 1808 from halting the importation of slaves or levying direct taxes by any rule other than the three-fifths clause.[98] By that time, Rutledge and other southern delegates assumed, another two decades of slave importations and the southwestern movement of population should place slavery beyond the reach of the amendment process.

On Saturday, September 15, the Convention reviewed the proposed Constitution a final time. It made one symbolic change that comported with northern members' pronounced aversion against allowing the word *slavery* to appear in the Constitution. The fugitive slave clause was modified to replace the defining phrase "No person legally held to service or labour in one state" with "No person held to service or labour in one state under the laws thereof." This was done, Madison noted, "in compliance with the wish of some who thought the term <legal> equivocal, and favoring the idea that slavery was legal in a moral view." Slavery, in other words, could be accepted as the positive law of the states, but the Constitution should not imply that slavery might be legal in a more fundamental sense.[99]

This change was made quickly, but more discussion was needed before the subject of constitutional amendments took its final form. One change came easily when the Convention, responding to a complaint from Mason, restored the provision requiring Congress to call a convention for purposes of amendments if solicited to do so by two-thirds of the states.[100] A second change was more ticklish. Taking a cue from Rutledge, Sherman moved to add to the proviso his South Carolina ally had secured on September 10 a further restriction "that no State shall without its consent be affected in its internal police, or deprived of its equal suffrage in the Senate." The first half of this formula offered further assurance to the South that slavery would exist in perpetuity—or at least until the ruling race acceded to its abolition. But this was also a formula that advocates of the autonomy of the states—notably Sherman—had used during the framing of the Confederation, and it marked one last venture by this taciturn but persistent political veteran to give the new system a strongly confederal twist. The import of Sherman's second proposal was self-evident.

"Begin with these special provisos," Madison objected, "and every State will insist on them, for their boundaries, exports &c." The weary delegates generally agreed, with only Connecticut, New Jersey, and Delaware from the original small-state coalition favoring the motion. But when Sherman's next motion to safeguard the equal-state vote by eliminating amendment procedures entirely was similarly rejected, "the circulating murmurs of the small States" impelled Morris to revive Sherman's second proposal in modified form: "[N]o State, without its consent shall be deprived of its equal suffrage in the Senate." This passed without dissent.[101] Sherman did not have quite the final word on this last day of debate,[102] but his success in guaranteeing that the "vicious" principle of the equal-state vote would remain the one clause of the Constitution safely insulated from the sovereign voice of the people was an apt tribute to his own persistence.

America has had more Shermans in its politics than Madisons, and arguably too few of either, but it was the rivalry between their competing goals and political styles that jointly gave the Great Convention much of its drama and fascination—and also permitted its achievement.

TWO DIVISIONS, TWO SETS OF COMPROMISES: These were what drove the politics of constitution-making at Philadelphia. There the ephemeral struggle between small and large states and the more durable and evil-fated rift between free and slave states defined the competing and conflicting interests that the framers had to resolve. Their accommodation was a necessary though not sufficient condition for the success of the Convention.

Which compromise was the greater act of statesmanship, which simply the fruit of expediency? It is easy to answer this question in favor of the vote of July 16, and not very difficult to condemn the bargains over slavery, in Garrisonian terms, as "a covenant with death." Embarrassed as many framers were to see human bondage acknowledged in the Constitution, euphemisms and indirection could never disguise its accommodation of slavery as a fundamental element in the structure of American politics and law. We may well ask whether that accommodation had to go as far as it did. Would South Carolina and Georgia really have bid defiance to the Union had the Constitution barred all further importations of slaves at a time when these states were facing renewed threats from Indian tribes along their frontier? Was the fugitive-slave clause a necessary part of the bargain? Did the electoral college have to give southern states additional votes on behalf of their slaves, when it could have been argued that if this form of property deserved any representation, the House alone should suffice?

Yet to say that the Convention conceded more to slavery than it needed to does not mean that the institution would have been any weaker had the northern delegates bargained better. It was not a superiority at bluffing that gave the South the edge at Philadelphia, even if its delegates carried to the statehouse skills gained at match races on court day or the card table in their plantation parlors. No bluff was needed to suggest that a Constitution that struck a serious blow at slavery would never survive the hurdles of ratification. Northern delegates who fretted about the umbrage their constituents would take at seeing slaves counted for representation could also foresee that southern citizens would act with exactly the same spirit should slavery not be given a place at the table of national politics.

So it was a compromise in the second, unhappy sense: a sacrifice of moral principle to attain a tangible political end. But a case can be made that this bargain turned out to have fewer costs than the other deal the framers had to strike to complete their task. It was not, after all, the three-fifths clause that gave the southern states the leverage they needed to keep the Union safe for slavery, but rather the Senate, where the later Compromises of 1819–20 and 1850 did more to preserve the political equilibrium Madison sought. And when, after 1865, that equilibrium dissolved and the South had to be reconstructed—precisely because freed but disenfranchised slaves would be fully counted for purposes of apportionment in the House—it was the Senate that continued to embody a vicious principle of representation, giving states with vastly disparate concentrations of population equal weight.

CHAPTER V

THE CONCEPT OF
RATIFICATION

O N SEPTEMBER 17, moments after the Convention adjourned for the last time, the Pennsylvania delegate Thomas FitzSimons took the literal first step toward ratification of the Constitution. From the legislative chamber on the main floor of the statehouse, he climbed forty-two stairs to the hall where the Pennsylvania assembly was also sitting to inform its members that their delegation stood ready to report at the first opportunity.[1] His was no impromptu errand. In late August Gouverneur Morris had urged the Convention "to hasten their deliberations to a conclusion" so that this session of the assembly could arrange the immediate election of a ratifying convention. Any delay was dangerous, Morris warned; the more "the people have time to hear the variety of objections" the Constitution would evoke, the more "doubtful" its fate would be. Now FitzSimons implied that the delegation could appear that afternoon, were it not that "after the accomplishment of so arduous a task," the framers wished "to enjoy a social meeting; which, on account of the departure of some of them this evening, had been appointed for today's dinner." The assembly accordingly agreed to hear their report in the morning.[2]

From the statehouse, the delegates "adjourned to the City Tavern, dined together and took a cordial leave of each other." True to the spare language of his diary, George Washington did not embellish this entry with anecdotes of the delegates' last repast. Did the thirty-nine signers extend the good humor of adjournment to George Mason, Edmund Randolph, and Elbridge Gerry, or did the dissenters sit in chastened silence while mutual congratulations went round the room? No doubt many complimented Benjamin Franklin for his concluding appeal for unanimity, so characteristic of the great sage in its wit and wisdom; but how many mustered the courage to salute the general personally for discharging the novel duties of presiding officer so well? Was the glass raised for the thirteen toasts that patriotic ritual prescribed for such celebrations—honoring Rhode Island in absentia, where many delegates were happy to leave it—or did a tankard of ale slake their thirst on a day when the mercury never rose above 50 degrees? Of these social details, Washington left no record; but he did note that from dining he returned directly "to my lodgings—did some business with, and received the papers [the journal] from the secretary of the Convention, and retired to meditate on the momentous w[or]k which had been executed" over the past four months.[3]

In these meditations the general was not alone; that evening all the delegates surely reflected on the summer's deliberations, the prospects for ratification, and the roles they expected to play in the struggle ahead. For most delegates this farewell dinner marked only a brief respite between the two stages of their constitutional labors. FitzSimons, George Clymer, and James Wilson immediately took the lead in the tumultuous politics of ratification in Pennsylvania, while ten framers quickly set off for New York, where as members of Congress they would be asked to transmit the Constitution to the states. In late September both the signers and the three dissenters acted to define the terms under which the Constitution would be debated through their efforts to influence the actions of Congress and the Pennsylvania assembly. But as assessments of the Constitution began to appear in the press, debate moved into the forum of res publica, where its fate depended on the complex politics of the thirteen American republics.

There is no simple way to characterize this debate, map its structure, or neatly separate its many lucid analyses of clauses and concepts from the wilder predictions of tyranny and anarchy that Anti-Federalists and Federalists volleyed back and forth. From their distant vantage point, historians can synthesize the many voices, motifs, and moods of this campaign by searching for underlying beliefs and imposing interpretive coherence on the contending arguments. But to many participants, the debate seemed as complex and multifaceted as the Constitution itself, given the absence of a truly national forum of decision and the publication of everything from the learned essays of *The Federalist* to sardonic squibs and polemical parodies.

From the start, however, it was apparent that this debate would take place at two levels or along dual helices: one held in the chambers of state legislatures and conventions, and therefore governed by parliamentary proprieties; the other waged freely in the newspapers, coffeehouses, taverns, and other meeting places, and therefore inherently unmanageable and even volatile. No one could anticipate how closely or at which point these two levels of debate would be joined, or how the uneven progress of the Constitution through states acting at different times would influence the ideas and tactics of the contending sides. Like the Constitution, ratification had both national and federal features. Its ultimate subject was the character of the nation Americans aspired to form; and the arguments of both sides were ultimately national as well. They swept across the country with no more respect for boundaries than thousands of Americans showed as they surged into the Appalachian backcountry and the Ohio Valley, in movements as vital to the history of the new Republic as the deliberations over the Constitution. Yet ratification was also a federal act. Each state remained a polity unto itself, and within its borders the fate of the Constitution rested on many factors: the openness of its press, the timing of its decision, the relative strength of the two parties, the intellectual and political acuity of its leaders, as well as calculations of parochial interests and partisan advantages.

All of these strictures need to be kept in mind before one can speak intelligently about what the Constitution meant to Americans at the moment of its adoption. But one further consideration deserves emphasis. However many understandings of the Constitution the ratifiers of 1787–88 entertained, in deciding its fate the intentions of its framers constrained them in one absolutely critical way. For among the many conceptual innovations the Constitution embodied, one of the most important was the idea of ratification itself. From the moment the Convention adjourned, Federalists struggled to prevent this powerful idea from overflowing the deep but narrow channel along which the framers intended to direct it. If the *debate* over ratification embraced as many topics and themes as Americans could conjure from their reading of history, their knowledge of the science of politics, their reflections on the Revolution, and their hopes and fears for the future, the *decisions* of 1787–88 ultimately devolved into the simplest of choices: to adopt or reject the Constitution in its entirety. Moreover, even as Anti-Federalists rallied around a strategy of insisting upon the adoption of amendments, Federalists waged their own successful campaign to prevent individual states from making ratification legally contingent upon the prior acceptance of the revisions each convention proposed.

A CONCEPT OF WHAT it might mean to ratify a constitution of government was not something that Americans had to fabricate entirely from whole cloth. As Samuel H. Beer has noted, *The Agreement of the People* drafted in England by the radical republicans of 1649 provided for popular approval of this proposed fundamental law, and James Harrington had also endorsed an idea of ratification for his commonwealth of Oceana.[4] But for all practical purposes, the framers' concept of constitution-making drew upon the experience of the states. All but two of the eleven constitutions written in 1776 and 1777 were drafted by the provincial conventions that acted as surrogate legislatures during the Revolutionary interregnum. Only Delaware and Pennsylvania framed constitutions by conventions specially elected for that sole purpose, though in several states the process was delayed to permit a fresh election of deputies by voters who understood that they would thereby authorize the creation of a new government. None of these constitutions were submitted to the people for approval; they were not *ratified* but simply promulgated by the bodies that drafted them. Pennsylvania was the only state in which the public was given an opportunity to comment on a draft constitution before its legal adoption. But after a mere three weeks of public discussion that did lead to some revisions in the text, the Pennsylvania convention simply pronounced the constitution adopted.[5]

At a time when revolutionaries were anxious to restore legal government and reluctant to divert attention from the war effort, any other procedure might have seemed risky and unwarranted. But these expedient concerns mattered less than the absence of any accepted criterion for endowing a written constitution with the status of fundamental law. Some early commentators recognized, as the Pennsylvania writer "Demophilus" observed, that

> every article of the constitution or *sett of fundamental rules* by which even the supreme power [the legislature] shall be governed, [should] be formed by a convention of the delegates of the people, appointed for that express purpose: which constitution shall neither be added to, diminished from, nor altered in any respect by any power besides the power which first framed it.

Yet John Adams probably voiced a common assumption when he implied (in his influential *Thoughts on Government*) that a constitution could be drafted and amended legislatively.[6]

Initial reservations about this process were directed more toward the character of the bodies that framed the constitutions than toward the absence of popular ratification. The fact that they were drafted by legislatures that were simultaneously discharging other ordinary (albeit revolutionary) functions of government carried ominous implications. If power was indeed as corrupting as good Whigs feared, it was hardly prudent to allow a group of sitting legislators to frame the very fundamental rules under which they were operating. Even if elections soon returned these framers to the body of the people, what was to stop them from knowingly designing a system which they or their closest connections could expect to dominate? But there was a more disturbing implication still. A constitution framed legislatively arguably possessed no greater authority than any statute; any subsequent legislature could in theory alter, amend, ignore, or even violate the constitution at will.

From an early point, then, critics of these charters understood that the authority of a constitution depended on the mode of its adoption. But only in Massachusetts did this concern, initially expressed at a handful of town meetings, attain sufficient force to persuade a reluctant General Court to accept the two cardinal principles that came to define the ideal standard: that a constitution should be proposed by a convention elected for that purpose alone, and subsequently ratified through some mechanism of popular consent. The contentious citizens of Massachusetts took nearly four years to agree on this point, but with their approval of the constitution of 1780, American thinking moved well beyond the half-formed ideas that prevailed at the moment of independence.[7]

Yet for all its theoretical significance, the Massachusetts precedent did not suddenly render the other state constitutions legally defective, nor did it produce a new consensus about the exact role of the people in establishing a constitution. A concept of popular ratification was certainly available to the framers by the eve of the Federal Convention, but it had yet to evolve into settled doctrine. Was the act of electing the framers of a constitution a sufficient measure of popular assent, or was their consent also required to ratify the actual document? Could the people feasibly do anything more than accept or reject a constitution in toto, or might they also judge its parts—and if they did, would it not take another meeting of the convention, or even a second convention, to determine which provisions were eliminated, revised, or retained? One problem with giving the people the final voice lay in devising the form that a popular referendum would take. Massachusetts had required the assent of two-thirds of the adult males in the state, but when the convention canvassed the town returns in June 1780, it discovered that it could not tidily aggregate their preferences because the town meetings had not posed the question in a uniform way. In the end, the convention exercised its own discretion to decide that the standard had been met, thereby allowing the first constitution framed by a special convention *and* formally ratified by an act of popular sovereignty to take effect.[8] But lesser forms of popular participation still seemed legitimate. In a trenchant critique of the South Carolina constitution of 1778—adopted by legislative fiat to replace the constitution of 1776—Thomas Tudor Tucker envisioned giving the people six months to review the proposals of an elected convention; but it would then reassemble with authority to accept or reject alterations and adopt the constitution in final form. Even Thomas Jefferson, the keenest critic of the procedures of 1776, would have confined the role of the people to the authorization and election of a convention.[9]

In an important passage of his *Notes on the State of Virginia*, Jefferson argued at some length that the charter of government drafted by his state in 1776 was not a true constitution. The voters had never understood that they were authorizing the convention to draft a permanent charter of government, Jefferson argued, nor did the constitution itself claim to have that status: "[I]t does not say that it shall be perpetual; that it shall be unalterable by other legislatures; that it shall be transcendant above the powers of those who they knew would have equal power with themselves." Nor did it matter that the convention had called its work a *constitution*, Jefferson continued, for in ordinary legal usage that word "invariably means a statute, law, or ordinance." Given these defects, Jefferson concluded, the constitution of 1776 could not repulse the legal challenge embodied in the familiar maxim *Quod leges posteriores priores contrarias abrogant:* In a conflict between two legislative acts of equal juridical status, the more recent enactment takes precedence. If a constitution was adopted under conditions that made it indistinguishable from a statute or ordinance, it could not bind or constrain subsequent legislatures.[10]

Jefferson shared this concern with Madison well before he raised the question in the *Notes on the State of Virginia*. After Jefferson took up his post as minister to France, Madison led an unsuccessful effort at the 1784 session of the Virginia assembly to call a convention to place a new constitution for Virginia on proper foundations. In his notes for a speech supporting this effort, Madison followed Jefferson's general reasoning about the errors of 1776 but added one point his friend had overlooked. Should "no change be made in the pres[en]t Const.," Madison noted, it would still be "advisable to have it ratified by [the people]," to make it "more stable and secured agst. the doubts & imputations under which it now labors." As it now stood, the "Constitution rests on acquiescence" only, a "dangerous basis" for sound government. It is not clear whether Madison believed that a constitution drafted by a properly deputed convention also required popular ratification. But he certainly thought that the constitution of 1776 would gain greater authority if it could be submitted (even at this belated date) to the people at large.[11]

Unlike the state constitutions, there was nothing uncertain about the juridical status of the Confederation. It had always been understood that articles of union could not be promulgated or imposed by Congress. The Confederation that Congress proposed in November 1777 was a compact among thirteen autonomous states, and its adoption required the unanimous consent of their legislatures. Eager to impress its new French ally with the durability of the Union, Congress staged a ceremonial signing of the Confederation by delegates from the eight states that had ratified it by July 1778; but nearly three years passed before Maryland's long-withheld assent allowed the Articles to take effect in March 1781. By then many national leaders agreed that further amendments were required. But to compound the frustration generated in the interval between the framing and ratification of the Confederation, all ensuing efforts at its amendment foundered over the rule of unanimity.[12]

Even so, before the spring of 1787 Madison was probably more concerned with the problem of how amendments to the Articles were to be proposed than with their ratification. Though initially fearful that the Annapolis convention of September 1786 would come to nought, he grew increasingly committed to its success as he came to believe that any amendment offered by Congress, as the Articles required, would be tainted at the source simply because its reputation and prestige had fallen so low. To comply with the Confederation, Madison still expected the Annapolis meeting to report to Congress, which would then presumably act as a neutral medium in transmitting its recommendation to the state legislatures. As his agenda for reform expanded in the winter of 1787, however, Madison realized that the ambitious proposals likely to emanate from Philadelphia would require a different disposition. "To give a new system its proper validity and energy, a ratification must be obtained from the people, and not merely from the ordinary authority of the Legislatures," he wrote Washington in mid-April. "This will be the more essential as inroads on the *existing constitutions* of the States will be unavoidable." Even "if such encroachments could be avoided," he wrote Edmund Pendleton a few days later, "a higher Sanction than the Legislative authority would be necessary to render the laws of the Confederacy paramount to the Acts of its members."[13]

The grounds for this opinion tracked Jefferson's concern about the state constitutions. Though several states had incorporated the Articles in their constitutions, "in others it has received no other sanction than that of the Legislative authority," Madison observed in his pre-Convention memorandum on the vices of the political system. "From this defect two evils result." If a state law and an act of Congress were "repugnant," he reasoned, "it will be at least questionable" which should "prevail." For if all legislative acts were equal, judges and juries resolving such a dispute would have to prefer the later act of a legislature to its prior ratification of the Confederation, according to the same legal maxim *(Quod leges posteriores priores contrarias abrogant).*[14] Madison extended this doctrine (more problematically) to suggest that a federal charter ratified by the legislatures created only "a league of sovereign powers"; and under a theory of compacts, "a breach of any of the articles of the confederation by any of the parties to it, absolves the other parties from their respective obligations, and gives them a right if they chuse to exert it, of dissolving the Union altogether."[15] These concerns would justify a resort to popular ratification even if the Federal Convention pursued a modest agenda. But should it go further, as Madison now hoped it would, a fundamental change in the rule of ratification would a fortiori be all the more necessary. A federal constitution ratified through an overt expression of popular sovereignty would rest on stronger foundations than all those state constitutions that had not been framed by special conventions or subsequently approved by the citizenry. On this basis, it could legitimately make "inroads" in the governing authorities of the states; and the ensuing conflicts between national and state law could be more readily resolved in favor of the federal government, even by judges holding commissions under the states.

Madison thus appropriated an argument developed to challenge the legitimacy of the state constitutions and transformed it into a principle of federalism. He clearly believed that the authority of a constitution depended on the form of its promulgation. Popular ratification provided more than a symbolic affirmation of popular sovereignty; it promised to render a constitution legally superior to ordinary acts of government that also expressed popular consent through mechanisms of representation.[16] But Madison and other framers went to Philadelphia aware that the Convention might have other reasons to circumvent the amending procedures of the Confederation. For they also knew that the reprobate state of Rhode Island had refused to send a deputation to Philadelphia, and though that did not preclude its later endorsement of the Constitution, it created a strong case for finally abandoning the rule of unanimity that had undermined all previous efforts at amending the Articles.

Such calculations had to be weighed against other scruples, however. In its resolution of February 21, 1787, endorsing the Philadelphia Convention, the Continental Congress had stated three conditions that, if read strictly, militated against a radical departure from the rules of the Confederation. First, the Convention was called "for the sole and express purpose of revising the Articles of Confederation," and it could be argued that a departure from its rules of amendment would violate this criterion. Second, the proposed revisions were to be "agreed to in Congress," and this implied that Congress retained a right to assess the merits of the plan of reform and even amend it. But third, the revisions were also to be reported to the state legislatures, and the confirmation of the states was, of course, also to be required. True, these conditions left room for interpretation. The resolution did not state what form the agreement of Congress must take, nor did it explicitly require the revisions to be confirmed by the state *legislatures*. But the onus of abandoning known rules (however cumbersome) for novel (and thus suspect) procedures ran its own risks.[17]

THE FRAMERS CAST ASIDE the first of these congressional conditions almost immediately. The objection that the Convention could not properly consider "a System founded on different principles from the federal Constitution" was raised as early as May 30, and it was restated more vigorously during the mid-June debate over the New Jersey Plan. What is striking about these objections, however, is how little force they carried. When William Paterson and John Lansing argued on June 16 that the Convention could not "discuss & propose" amendments that would violate the Articles in substance or form, Edmund Randolph replied that it could ignore its nominal mandate because "our business consists in recommending a system of government, not to make it," while James Wilson observed that he felt completely "at liberty to *propose any thing*" because he had power "to *conclude nothing*."[18] The principle of constitutional ratification thus carried the incidental benefit of licensing the delegates to consider whatever measure the public good demanded, regardless of the prevailing expectations and even their formal credentials. "When the salvation of the Republic was at stake," Randolph declared, "it would be treason to our trust, not to propose what we found necessary."[19] Whatever risks the framers took by proposing too radical a constitution would be mere errors of political judgment, not tyrannical acts of usurpation. The fact that the Convention could not simply promulgate a constitution on its own authority thus had an immensely liberating effect on its deliberations.[20]

This would have been true even had the convention abided by Article

XIII of the Confederation and submitted the completed Constitution to Congress and the state legislatures for their unanimous approval. But for obvious reasons, the issue of exactly how the work of the Convention would be ratified ranked low on its initial priorities. Consistent with Madison's pre-Convention planning, the concluding resolution of the Virginia Plan called for the "amendments" proposed by the Convention "after the approbation of Congress to be submitted to an assembly or assemblies of Representatives, recommended by the several Legislatures to be expressly chosen by the people, to consider & decide thereon."[21] But consideration of this issue presumed what no one took for granted: that the Convention would actually agree on a constitution. Accordingly, after an inconclusive debate of June 5, the question of ratification was deferred until July 23, and then not reexamined until the final two days of August. Even then uncertainty about the role of Congress in ratification led to a final debate on September 10.

In their early comments, the Virginia delegates rested the case for ratification by popular conventions on principled ground. Introducing the Virginia Plan on May 29, Randolph stressed the need to establish the supremacy of federal law. The Confederation was *"Inferior to State constitutions"* because it "had its ratification not by any *special appointment* from the people, but from the several assemblies," Randolph noted. "No judge will say that the *confederation* is paramount to a State constit[ut]ion." When this clause was debated on June 5, Madison reminded the delegates that the mere "legislative sanction" given the Articles would encourage "State Tribunals" of justice to decide conflicts between federal and state acts in favor of the states.[22] Mason reiterated the point on July 23, when he argued that legislative ratification was "wrong" because "succeeding Legislatures having equal authority could undo the acts of their predecessors"; while Madison linked popular ratification to the idea of judicial review. "A law violating a constitution established by the people themselves," he flatly declared, "would be considered by the Judges as null & void."[23]

By linking ratification to both the supremacy of national law and the doctrine of judicial review, the Virginians revealed how theoretically powerful a concept it was. But the discussion of ratification generally took a more pragmatic and political cast. Would it aid or impair the prospects for ratification to adopt some procedure other than that specified by the Articles? Had the framers been confident that legislators in every state would assess their work fairly and dispassionately, many of them would have preferred to abide by the existing rule of the Confederation. Perhaps because the other changes they were contemplating were so radical, they worried about the wisdom of violating Article XIII so flagrantly. On the other hand, it was absurd to expect all thirteen assemblies to approve a constitution circumscribing their legislative power and autonomy. If nothing else, the refusal of Rhode Island to send a delegation to Philadelphia provided a sound rationale for violating Article XIII at least in respect to the rule of unanimity; and once that first step was taken, why should the Convention worry about abiding by its other requirements?

The idea that the "perpetual union" of the Articles might be replaced with "a partial union" of a "plurality of States" was first advanced to threaten the small states during the debate over representation. Wilson's early hints on this score, Madison noted, were "probably meant in terrorem to the smaller states of N. Jersey and Delaware."[24] Once the small states gained their way in the Senate, however, the framers redirected their attention to the various obstacles that would threaten ratification. When discussion of this issue resumed on July 23, Oliver Ellsworth's motion to refer the Constitution to the legislatures was exposed to an array of critical responses that cut against both the rule of unanimity and the legal and political consequences of retaining ratification by the legislatures. "But will any one say that all the States are to suffer themselves to be ruined, if Rho. Island should persist in her opposition to general measures?" Nathaniel Gorham asked. New York was also a doubtful prospect, now that the departure of Lansing and Robert Yates left the state officially unrepresented in the Convention as well. Gorham argued further that the Convention should bypass the state legislatures "who are to lose the power which is to be given up to the Genl. Govt.," and whose decisions would likely be retarded both by their division "into several branches" and the distractions arising from the "variety of little business" they would simultaneously conduct. Randolph offered equally pragmatic reasons for bypassing the legislatures. "Whose opposition will be most likely to be excited agst. the System," he asked, if not "that of the local demagogues who will be degraded by it from the importance they now hold," and whose "full influence" was usually exercised in the legislatures?[25]

The framers roundly rejected Ellsworth's motion, leaving the proposal for popularly elected conventions intact. Though they did not yet attempt to determine how many states to require for ratification, they probably assumed that the rule of unanimity would be abandoned.[26] When this question was taken up on August 30–31, the Convention fixed nine as the number of states needed for ratification—a number "familiar to the people" because that was what the Articles required for major decisions in

Congress. But now the delegates found themselves divided on two other points: whether the states should determine their own mode of ratification; and, more puzzling, whether Congress should give the Constitution its "approbation" or simply submit it to the states.

When Gouverneur Morris proposed that the states should be allowed to decide whether to act legislatively or by conventions, he may have been responding to the special concern of the Maryland delegates. In Maryland the constitution could be altered only by the legislature; and if the new federal Constitution could be seen as revising the state constitution as well as the Confederation, "no other mode could be pursued in that state." In response, Madison, Rufus King, and Wilson gave the appeal to the sovereignty of the people a new force. The officers of every state were sworn to support their existing forms of government, Madison observed, all of which the new Constitution would effectively alter. But "the people were in fact, the fountain of all power, and by resorting to them, all difficulties were got over. They could alter constitutions as they pleased. It was a principle in the [state] Bills of rights, that first principles might be resorted to." King concurred: Though the Massachusetts constitution "was made unalterable until 1790," he noted, "[t]he State must have contemplated a recurrence to first principles before they sent deputies to this Convention."[27] Wilson justified ratification by fewer than thirteen states on the same grounds. "We must . . . go to the original powers of Society," he asserted on August 30. "The House on fire must be extinguished, without a scrupulous regard to ordinary rights."[28]

Nor were these heady statements hastily summoned to dispel the last-minute anxieties of the timid. Earlier debates had produced similar appeals as justifications for overriding the rules of the Confederation. As Wilson noted on June 16, "we expect the approbation of Cong[ress,] we hope for that of the Legis. of the several States [and] perhaps it will not be inconsistent w[i]th Revolution principles, to promise ourselves the Assent of the people provided a more regular establishment cannot be obtained" through existing procedures. Hamilton made the same point on June 18: "[I]f the Legislatures have no power to ratify because thereby they diminish their own Sovereignty the people may come in on revolution Principles." The great advantage of this appeal to popular sovereignty was that it promised to dissolve at one stroke all the legalistic qualms that still beset many delegates. While conceding that the approval of all the legislatures might be obtained, King indicated on July 23 that he "preferred a reference to the authority of the people expressly delegated to Conventions, as the most certain means of obviating all disputes &

doubts concerning the legitimacy of the new Constitution; as well as the most likely means of drawing forth the best men in the States to decide on it."[29]

It was easier to invoke "revolution principles" against the state legislatures, however, than against Congress. On August 31, the framers eliminated a clause to submit the Constitution to Congress "for their approbation"—in order to spare it the embarrassment of taking "an Act inconsistent with the Articles of Confederation." Ten days later, an unlikely alliance of Elbridge Gerry and Hamilton managed to reopen this question. Was it not just as "improper" and indecorous to treat Congress as a mere messenger, they implied? But this plaint only inspired another outburst from Wilson, who argued it would be "worse than folly" to rest the fate of the Constitution on the acquiescence of a Congress whose own assent could not be taken for granted if asked to evaluate the document on its merits.[30] Once the Articles had been breached in one respect, there was no reason to pay Congress a false obeisance as the symbol of the Confederation the framers hoped to supplant.

This reasoning proved decisive for all those delegates who were prepared to sign the Constitution. The closer they came to adjournment, the more attention they paid to the imperatives of ratification. Foreseeing that the Constitution would be exposed to wide-ranging criticisms, the framers acted to direct that debate toward a simple decision. In its final form, Article VII was "universally allowed," Randolph later observed, to require the state conventions to approve or reject the Constitution as a whole—not to ratify it in parts or make its adoption contingent upon subsequent revisions. The framers thereby sought to confine this exercise in popular sovereignty to the mere legal act of ratification.

But the three dissenters—Gerry, Mason, and Randolph—were prepared to give this radical concept a further meaning. Randolph justified his dissent by arguing "that the State Conventions should be at liberty to propose amendments to be submitted to another General Convention which may reject or incorporate them, as shall be judged proper." Popular sovereignty could thus evolve from a formal act of approval into a substantive expression of public opinion and an application of "revolution principles" far more energetic and assertive than anything the framers desired. For, as Mason observed in seconding Randolph's proposal on September 15: "This Constitution has been formed without the knowledge or idea of the people. A second Convention will know more of the sense of the people, and be able to provide a system more consonant with it."[31]

The framers hastily rejected this proposal as a prescription for chaos. "Nothing but confusion & contrariety could spring from the experiment,"

Pierce Butler responded; delegates "coming together under the discordant impressions of their Constituents" could never reach agreement. "Conventions are serious things," he went on—a point his fatigued colleagues could not deny—"and ought not to be repeated." No further rejoinder was needed to dismiss Randolph's motion by a vote of all the states.[32] Like other decisions about ratification, this one, too, was driven by pressing political considerations. A second federal convention would assemble encumbered by proposals for amendments of all kinds and bound by instructions that would make it impossible to replicate the process of persuasion, compromise, and bargaining from which the completed Constitution had so laboriously emerged.

Yet in seeking to restrain popular sovereignty to a merely legal act, the framers betrayed their awareness of its explosive potentialities. The alternative scenario sketched by Randolph and Mason was impractical and impolitic but not implausible, for the framers could readily imagine how public opinion would express itself once the Constitution was published. They also grasped the radical implications of the doctrine they were struggling to control. Once assembled, popularly elected conventions could claim to embody the sovereign will of the people more completely than any of the other bodies that would also participate in the adoption of the Constitution; and because they would meet for the special purpose of constitution-making, their authority would arguably be paramount to that of the legislatures whose enabling acts had summoned them into existence. In the abstract, there was no reason these bodies should have to obey the resolutions of the Convention and Congress and the relevant acts of their own legislatures. If the framers could plead "revolution principles" to justify abandoning the Articles of Confederation, why should the state conventions not enjoy equal liberty to propose amendments to the Constitution? If one or more conventions chose to vote on the Constitution by articles, or make ratification contingent upon the adoption of amendments, their actions could be faulted on *political* grounds, as ill-advised initiatives that would transform an orderly process of reform into a chaotic cacophony of incommensurable acts.[33] But Federalists would be hard-pressed to claim that the state conventions had exceeded their powers, when the precedent set at Philadelphia proved that deference to prescribed forms need not prevail during an appeal to "first principles."

The framers thus left Philadelphia fearful that their new concept of ratification, so useful a device to circumvent the Confederation, could be wielded against the Convention itself. Article VII had to be designed and construed to permit only wholesale assent or rejection rather than a clause-by-clause referendum on the Constitution, precisely because the framers knew that ratification would indeed involve something more than executing a legal fiction. The greater fiction was the one that they sought to perpetrate: that the only significant consequence of the debate over the Constitution could be confined to the ultimate question of its adoption.

THE FIRST SKIRMISHES over ratification occurred in New York and Philadelphia, as Congress and the Pennsylvania assembly discussed the Convention's recommendation for the election of conventions. In both places, debate echoed the competing conceptions of ratification that had appeared within the Convention. On the Federalist side, the framers who acted as the Convention's advocates urged a prompt, uncritical compliance with its recommendation. But the early critics of the Constitution had already taken counsel from the nonsigning delegates—especially Mason— and though outnumbered in both bodies, they entered the debate prepared to suggest that the state conventions might not be limited to the simple act of approval or rejection.

Eleven states were fully represented in Congress when the Constitution was read on Thursday, September 20; Maryland had a lone delegate present, while Rhode Island remained absent. To allow those members who had served in the Convention to return from Philadelphia, debate was postponed until the twenty-sixth. By then Richard Henry Lee had received letters from Mason and Randolph explaining their dissent and discussing the strategy he should pursue in Congress, and he also conversed at length with Gerry, an old ally, who carried to New York a copy of Mason's written objections to the Constitution.[34]

Skepticism about the Constitution came easily to Lee. A longtime leader of resistance to Britain who had served numerous terms in the Virginia assembly and Congress, Lee was an "old whig" whose ideological suspicion of constitutional change was reinforced by political rivalries that often placed him at odds with those who championed the project of a stronger national government after 1781. Having refused election to the Convention on the grounds that it was improper for members of Congress to "pass judgement at New York upon their opinion at Philadelphia," Lee believed that Congress should evaluate the Constitution on its merits, and in the deliberations of September 26–28, his maneuvers placed its supporters on the defensive.[35] Arguing that Congress "have no right to recom[men]d a plan subverting ye Govt.," Lee and Nathan Dane of Massachusetts moved to have Congress transmit the Constitution to the states without endorsing the conventions required by Article VII, while at the same time expressing its own grave doubts about the structure of the new government and the propriety of allowing the formation of a partial union of nine states. But Lee had another plan as well. Because the Constitution took the form of a "report," he argued, Congress was free "to amend if [they] thot. proper." Late on the twenty-seventh, Lee offered a lengthy set of amendments which included both "a declaration, or Bill of Rights," and such other changes as the creation of an executive "Council of State or Privy Council," the abolition of the vice presidency, and an alteration designed "to place the right of representation in the Senate on the same ground that it is placed in the House of Delegates."[36]

Perhaps this last proposition drew a brief smile from Madison, who certainly agreed with it in principle. But Madison had no intention of allowing Congress to tamper with the text of the Constitution. If any amendments were adopted, he warned, the Constitution would go forward as an act of Congress, thereby triggering the Confederation requirement for unanimous state ratification. Nor did Madison approve the neutral mode of submission proposed by Abraham Clark of New Jersey, under which Congress would endorse the calling of state conventions without commenting directly on the Constitution—even though that motion conformed to the position that the Convention itself had taken in declining to seek the "approbation" of Congress. "If either Lee's or Clark's motn. is adopted it implies disap[proval]," Madison argued; "ye ques. is wheth. on ye whole it is best to adopt it & *we* ought to say so."[37] Against the claim that Congress could not flagrantly defy the sources of its own authority, Madison, William Samuel Johnson, and Pierce Butler argued that "ye great principle of necessity or ye salus populi" outweighed any loyalty owed to the Confederation.

In going beyond the position taken by the Convention, Madison may have hoped that the endorsement of Congress would offset the damage done by the three nonsigners; or perhaps he was only preparing grounds for compromise by demanding a point he would readily yield. He knew that Congress would not approve Lee's amendments; as he later noted, "the contradictory objections" voiced against the Constitution indicated that "a discussion of its merits would consume much time, without producing agreement even among its adversaries." More alarming was the effect that evidence of division within Congress, or a simple delay in acting, would have on public opinion. If Lee demanded a roll call on his amendments, other delegates might support those changes that seemed least objectionable—such as the addition of a bill of rights. This was the concern to which Madison alluded when he informed Washington that

"These difficulties which at one time threatened a serious division in Congs. and popular alterations with the yeas & nays on the journals, were at length fortunately terminated" by the resolution Congress adopted, without dissent, on September 28. Under its terms, Congress took no position on the Constitution; but it explicitly asked the state legislatures to comply with the procedures recommended by the Convention. Though Madison still regretted not obtaining "a more direct approbation" of the Constitution, that approval was not worth securing at the cost of division, delay, or procedural confusion. Instead, he was heartened that "the circumstance of unanimity must be favorable every where."[38]

Lee found no such consolation. Although his proposals had "greatly alarmed the Majority & vexed them extremely," Lee wrote Mason, they also revealed that the advocates of the Constitution were determined "to push the business on with great dispatch, & with as little opposition as possible." Yet Lee did not explain why he accepted the "compromise" the majority offered. Aware that his amendments stood little chance of adoption, Lee used the threat of a protracted debate to deter Madison's demand that Congress approve the Constitution; he may also have calculated that the initiative for amendments might better come from the state conventions.[39] In the meantime, Lee warned Mason, Gerry, and his old ally, Samuel Adams, that Federalists hoped the unanimous vote for this resolution would be "mistaken for an Unanimous approbation" of the Constitution.[40]

The resolution of September 28 provided a measure of decorum to reassure those who were troubled by the procedural innovations of ratification. Events in Philadelphia soon revealed why decorum was so important—and so hard to preserve. After hearing its delegation report on September 18, the Pennsylvania assembly waited to receive the Constitution from Congress. But when ten days passed with no word from New York, the impatient Federalist majority decided to proceed with plans for organizing the state convention.[41] Ignoring all protests from the minority, the Federalists approved two resolutions setting general rules for the election of "deputies" to the convention; but when they returned for further action on the afternoon of the twenty-eighth, the absence of nineteen minority legislators deprived the assembly of its quorum. The sergeant at arms quickly located the absentees, only to be told that they would not attend the assembly. When they remained absent the next morning, a Federalist posse forcibly escorted two of the minority to the assembly, where they involuntarily provided the quorum necessary to enable the majority to complete legal preparations for a convention.[42]

By then the arrival of an express rider bearing news of the action of

Congress enabled George Clymer to insert language invoking its authority in the preamble of his resolution.[43] Yet only the day before, he and his allies had repeatedly mocked the authority of both Congress and the Confederation. When Robert Whitehill and William Findley protested that it was "unfederal" to act before Congress, FitzSimons replied that the Constitution "presupposes . . . that no Confederation exists; or if [it] does exist, it exists to no purpose." Congress and the assemblies were "but the mere vehicles to convey" the Constitution "to the people"; had they balked at this task, the people could still take their own measures for calling a convention. Hugh Henry Brackenridge spoke even more extravagantly. The assembly should realize that it was acting not on "federal ground," he exclaimed, "but on the wild and extended field of nature, unrestrained by any former compact" and entitled by "the principle of self-conservation" to ignore the Articles of Confederation, which in any case "have received sentence of death."[44]

In treating Congress so cavalierly and in demanding initially that the convention elections coincide with the assembly elections set for October, the Pennsylvania Federalists were clearly calculating the impact their actions would have on the ratification struggle elsewhere. Because their assembly was the first to receive the Constitution, any delay on its part would "undoubtedly have the appearance of our being unfriendly to the new Constitution," and even "occasion a delay in the other legislatures."[45] For the Pennsylvania Federalists, however, considerations of *state* politics were nearly as important. For a decade, this same political faction had sought to undermine the state constitution of 1776, with its unicameral assembly and weak plural executive; and they had challenged its legitimacy on the grounds that it had never received the popular approval now required for the federal Constitution. After carrying the state elections in 1787, the Federalists hoped to use the ratification debate to break the strength of the opposition Constitutionalists. A decisive victory would prepare the way for state constitutional reform, both by consolidating Federalist control of state politics and by setting up the federal Constitution as a superior model for Pennsylvania to emulate.

In their zeal, however, the Pennsylvania Federalists were actually jeopardizing ratification elsewhere. Even if they were justified in dragooning the attendance of the absentee members, their demand for immediate convention elections was easy to fault. Far from giving the Constitution the attention it deserved, R. H. Lee complained, the Pennsylvania Federalists were acting "[a]s if the subject of Government were a business of passion, instead of cool, sober, and intense consideration."[46] They hoped "to surprise you into a choice of members," the dissenting as-

semblymen warned their countrymen in a broadside of October 2, "to approve or disapprove of a Constitution, which is to entail happiness or
misery forever without giving time to the greatest part of the state even
to see, much less to examine the plan of government."[47] The manifestly
partisan character of these maneuvers thus cost Federalists some of the
political advantage they gained by ensuring that Pennsylvania acted
quickly. Because Philadelphia occupied a central location in the axis along
which information flowed in the new Republic, the assembly's precipitate
action evoked sharp criticism throughout the country well into 1788.

Most Federalists thought that a reasonable price to pay for having
Congress and Pennsylvania act so quickly. Though Anti-Federalists
faulted the Convention for exceeding its mandate, they did not seriously
oppose its appeal to the people as the arbiter of the final decision. In the
end, only the Rhode Island assembly balked at calling a convention, and
even its decision to hold a statewide referendum on the Constitution vindicated the theory of popular sovereignty the framers had invoked. The
Anti-Federalist leaders who participated in these first decisions conceded
the futility of insisting on preserving the requirements of Article XIII of
the Confederation. On this point, the three nonsigners of the Constitution, R. H. Lee in Congress, and even the Anti-Federalist leaders in
Pennsylvania agreed that state conventions were the proper forum for
decision.[48]

From the start, however, their understanding of what these conventions could decide went well beyond what the framers had intended. For
not one but two conceptions of ratification had emerged from the
Convention—and it was the nonsigners who forged the more radical if
problematic position. Their difficulty lay not in justifying the right of the
state conventions to claim greater authority than Federalists would have
allowed but in determining how this authority could be exercised. Where
the scheme proposed by the Convention had a great advantage of simplicity, the nonsigners' vague conception of the amending power of the
state conventions raised difficult, even intractable, problems. Who would
propose a suitable set of amendments? How could consensus be reached
among a sufficient number of states—presumably nine—acting separately? If five states ratified the Constitution unamended, would that preclude the adoption of amendments by the other eight? Would a second
federal convention be needed to attain consensus on the revisions? If so,
who would call and elect it? And would its decisions not have to be referred to the states in their turn? Once begun, how could this cycle of deliberation and revision ever end?[49]

Some of these problems occurred to the three nonsigners and Lee in the weeks following the Convention, but they failed to think them through systematically—and their lack of a common forum of decision only compounded the inherent problems of coordination that any strategy of amendments faced all along.[50] Nor did the Anti-Federalist cause benefit from having to rely on Mason, Randolph, and Gerry as its original voices of dissent. Mason personified the independent Whig whose influence rested on moral character and commitment to principle rather than on the political skills needed to build legislative coalitions or popular movements; Gerry's first concern after the Convention adjourned was to rejoin his young wife and daughter in New York; while Randolph balked at opposing the Constitution outright but posed instead as a potential supporter who understood better than its avowed friends just what changes its adoption required. Vacillating from the start, Randolph first suggested to Mason that the Virginia assembly should take the lead in proposing amendments to other states, then wrote Madison the next day to divulge his suggestion to the man who would command the campaign for ratification in Virginia.[51] The three nonsigners hardly formed the disciplined nucleus of leaders Anti-Federalists needed to overcome their initial tactical disadvantages.

Even so, if "indispensable amendments" were "proposed by a capital state or two, & a willingness expressed to agree with the plan so amended," R. H. Lee wrote Samuel Adams in early October, it might still prove possible "that a new general Convention may so weave them into the proferr'd system as that a Web may be produced fit for freemen to wear."[52] Among the "capital state[s]" that might be persuaded to pursue this course, Anti-Federalists could number New York, Massachusetts, and Virginia; and if even one of these states, much less all three, made the adoption of amendments a condition of ratification, such a strategy had a plausible chance of success.

ANTI-FEDERALIST WRITERS quickly grasped the uses to which the plan of ratification might be put if the conventions ignored the restrictions under which they were to operate. "An Old Whig" stated the crucial point in an essay that appeared just as the Pennsylvania convention was getting under way. "If the people in the different states have a right to be consulted, in the new form of continental government," this Philadelphia writer asked, "what authority could the late Convention have to preclude them from proposing amendments to the plan they should offer?" The answer seemed evident:

> The people have an undoubted right to judge of every part of the government which is offered to them. No power on earth has a right to preclude them; and they may exercise this choice either by themselves or their delegates legally chosen to represent them in the state convention. I venture to say that no man, reasoning upon *revolution* principles, can possibly controvert this right.

Nor need this lead to "irreconcilable discord," for the critics of the Constitution already shared "the very same sentiments" on its defects, though acting without "premeditated concert." If the state conventions united to demand a second general convention, the revised plan it would then propose would certainly secure adoption because "every good citizen of America pants for an efficient federal government."[53] So, too, the "Federal Farmer" closed his first series of letters by conceding that the state conventions might prove less "respectable" than the Federal Convention, but then again, the framers had "met without knowing the sentiments of one man in ten thousand in these states, respecting the new ground taken." Moreover,

> as the state conventions will probably consist of fifteen hundred or two thousand men of abilities, and versed in the science of government, collected from all parts of the community and from all orders of men, it must be acknowledged that the weight of respectability will be in them—In them will be collected the solid sense and the real political character of the country. Being revisers of the subject, they will possess peculiar advantages. To say that these conventions ought not to attempt, coolly and deliberately, the revision of the system, or that they cannot amend it, is very foolish or very assuming.

Like other Anti-Federalists, the "Federal Farmer" suspected that the unseemly haste with which the framers had returned to their states to "precipitate measures for the adoption of a system of their own making" proved the need for caution.[54]

Restraining the state conventions to their prescribed single decision thus required a political finesse that Federalists worked carefully to maintain, especially in the hotly contested conventions in Massachusetts, Virginia, and New York, the three states where the pressure to incorporate amendments in the act of ratification proved strongest. Though the legislatures could not resist asking their returning delegations to report on the debates at Philadelphia, Federalists prevailed in insisting that the only proper action the assemblies could take was to provide for the election of ratification conventions. When these bodies met, Federalists could similarly not prevent their opponents from raising whatever objections they wished, but they again insisted that the sole decision permitted was to approve or reject the Constitution in its entirety. So long as they held this ground, they even found it useful to give their opponents free rein, for the diversity and idiosyncrasy of Anti-Federalist objections confirmed the wisdom of that restricted choice. Efforts to examine the Constitution article by article often foundered as one objection tumbled pell-mell into another, exposing Anti-Federalist inconsistencies while enabling Federalists to complain about the delay in the proceedings—and to argue that the sum of potential flaws in the Constitution could never exceed its net advantages over the Confederation.

In pursuing this goal, Federalists adapted their strategies to the varying political circumstances of the states. They swept to early and easy victories in the first five conventions to debate the Constitution. The vote for the Constitution in Delaware, New Jersey, and Georgia was unanimous; in Pennsylvania, where Anti-Federalist leaders proved articulate and dogged in debate, it still carried by two to one; while in Connecticut, Federalists outpolled their opponents better than three to one in the vote of January 9, 1788, after a week of discussion. Debate in all of these states except Pennsylvania was brief and desultory. In New Jersey the Constitution was read and discussed "by sections," and according to one newspaper, "doubts and difficulties were raised" during three days of debate. But David Brearley, who had chaired the committee on postponed parts at the Convention, dispelled these doubts by providing "the necessary information" the ratifiers lacked to explain how the framers had labored "to fix general principles, which were, in a certain degree, accommodated to all the states."[55] In Georgia, Joseph Habersham reported, the Constitution was "read over paragraph by paragraph with a great deal of temper," but he also noted that it would probably have been approved immediately "if it had not been thought rather too precipitate."[56] In the Delaware convention the only significant discussion involved charges of electoral irregularities in Sussex County. In Connecticut a few Anti-Federalists managed to be heard over the "shuffling and stamping of feet, coughing, talking, spitting, and whispering" coming from a Federalist-packed gallery.[57] But if press reports are credible, their qualms were quickly overcome by the speeches of Oliver Ellsworth ("a complete master of the subject" whose "energetic reasoning bore down all before it"), William Samuel Johnson, and others; and after the Constitution was ratified 128 to 40, many of the minority reportedly left Hartford "above half convinced that the Constitution ought to be adopted."[58]

Federalists similarly dominated debate in two other states whose conventions met in the spring of 1788. In late April, after a week of debate in which the usually garrulous Luther Martin sat silent—reportedly sidelined by laryngitis—Maryland ratified by a vote of sixty-three to eleven. Debate in South Carolina lasted two weeks, but only because Federalists sought to mollify their opponents in the hope that they in turn would work to reconcile their constituents. That surmise is corroborated by the fact that the South Carolina convention was the only one of these six states to propose amendments, even though the two-to-one margin by which the Constitution was ratified on May 23 suggests that Federalists were under no pressure to attract moderate Anti-Federalists.[59]

In practical terms, then, serious Anti-Federalist efforts to convert the principle of popular ratification into a device for constitutional revision were confined to the six states where the Constitution was either warmly debated or closely contested between two evenly balanced parties. Pennsylvania and North Carolina met the first of these conditions but not the second; Massachusetts, New Hampshire, Virginia, and New York met both. The usual story that historians tell about the difficult passage of the Constitution through these states emphasizes the growing efforts of fair-minded Federalists—especially Madison, the fairest of them all—to placate their more reasonable opponents by agreeing that some amendments (in the form of a bill of rights) should be adopted. Participants would probably have told a different story. The true test was whether final ratification would be made conditional on the prior acceptance of amendments or the summoning of a second general convention. The real winner in this contest was not the Anti-Federalists, even if they secured the commitment that led to the Bill of Rights. It was the Federalists, who successfully struggled to keep the potent genie of popular sovereignty from escaping the narrow vessel in which it was bottled. To understand how close and arduous this struggle was, we have to survey the ways in which the mode of ratification was contested in these six states.

Pennsylvania. If the outcome of this first major convention was never in doubt, its impact on ratification elsewhere was on the minds of both parties as they jockeyed to set rules of procedure. Federalist strategy revolved around balancing firm control of the convention with the desire to prove that they meant "not to preclude, but to promote a free and ample discussion of the federal plan." That might take only a week, but the decision need not be "instantaneous," Thomas McKean noted. The crucial point was to confine the ultimate decision to a single question. "We do not come here to legislate," McKean told the deputies on November 24, the first full day of debate; "we have no right to inquire into the power of the late Convention or to alter and amend their work; the sole question before us is, whether we will ratify and confirm, or, upon due consideration reject, in the whole, the system of federal government that is submitted to us."[60]

Resisting this shackle, Anti-Federalists used the opening days of debate to press procedural motions designed either to slow the rush to judgment or to create a public record that would expose the Federalists as the enemies of candid deliberation. On November 24 and 26, John Smilie and Robert Whitehill urged the deputies to sit first as a committee of the whole, thereby ensuring two full rounds of debate. After this motion was rejected on the grounds that "no minutes could be taken of the proceedings [in committee], and that the people at large would thereby be kept in ignorance of them," Anti-Federalists tried to turn this argument to advantage by asserting a right to enter their objections to the Constitution on the official journal of the convention, and moreover to do so "upon every question that arises . . . whether in the intermediate or conclusive stages of the business." Surprised Federalists at first indicated that they would concede this privilege if it was confined to the one question of acceptance or rejection. But they withdrew this offer once they realized that Anti-Federalists meant to exercise it on "all questions where the yeas and nays were called." Conceivably, the minority could propose amendments to individual clauses, and use roll calls and the accompanying "objections" to turn the convention journal into a record of debate. McKean and Wilson now scoffed that the abuse of this privilege in the state assembly had only worked to "intrude" on its journals "language which would have disgraced a private club at a tavern" and which seemed better "adapted to the meridian of Billingsgate." The newspapers could offer adequate reports of the debates, Wilson declared, without "involv[ing] the public in expense" or bestowing "a stamp of authenticity" on opinions that would often betray "the acrimony of party."[61]

Futile as these motions were, Anti-Federalists clearly had a larger audience and a deeper purpose in mind. On November 27, Smilie linked the importance of maintaining a complete record of votes and their supporting reasons to the possibility that their publication might "produce a change in the minds of the people and incline them to new measures" which could be pursued *after* the convention ratified the Constitution. As authority for this claim Smilie cited the major speech that Wilson had delivered three days earlier. At that time Wilson had argued that "the people have a right at all times to alter and abolish government," Smilie recalled. If so, it followed that "if the people on better information or maturer deliberation should think it a bad and improper form of government, they will still have a right to assemble another body to consult upon other measures and either in the whole, or in part, to abrogate this federal work so ratified." And would they not then benefit from knowing the basis on which their first convention acted?[62]

Forced to weigh this version of popular sovereignty against the imperatives of ratification, Federalists did not hesitate to affirm the original rule of procedure. Anti-Federalists could criticize the Constitution as freely as they wished—Wilson's running count of their objections reached 240—but not propose votes or amendments on particular clauses. For a fortnight after November 28, most delegates sat passively while Whitehill, Smilie, and William Findley voiced their criticisms and Wilson, McKean, and a handful of Federalists responded. At times Federalist patience wore thin. On December 8, one member sparked "a very warm altercation" by complaining that the adversaries "had *abused* the *indulgence* which the other side of the house had granted to them in consenting to hear all their reasons" for opposing the Constitution.[63] Four days later, Whitehill and Findley moved to adjourn the convention to a later date, thereby enabling the people of Pennsylvania to consider the amendments they had prepared, as well as amendments emanating from other states. This motion and the two identical roll calls rejecting it and then ratifying the Constitution (forty-six to twenty-three) were entered on the journals of the convention; but to learn what amendments the Anti-Federalist delegates desired, citizens would have to turn to their newspapers and the dissent of the minority that was published in broadside form on December 18.[64]

Massachusetts. Anti-Federalists were a potential majority of the convention that met in Boston on January 9, 1788, and this obliged Federalists not only to hear their opponents out but to avoid even the appearance of procedural rigidity. The convention quickly accepted a motion from Caleb Strong proposing, first, that the Constitution "should be discussed and considered with moderation, candor, and deliberation" and "by paragraphs, until every member shall have an opportunity to express his sentiments"; and second, that they would "debate at large the question" of ratification "before any vote is taken expressive of the sense of the Convention, upon the whole or part thereof." To conciliate their opponents, Federalists not only promised "free conversation" and the "full liberty" of any member "to take up" any provision of the Constitution he believed "connected with the one immediately under consideration," but even acceded to a request to give Elbridge Gerry "a seat in the Convention, to answer any questions of fact . . . respecting the passing of the Constitution"—which arguably was unnecessary because the three other members of the state delegation in Philadelphia (Strong, King, and Gorham) were already present.[65] The first time Gerry spoke, however, Federalists objected that he was actually engaging in debate, and rather than endure further insult, Gerry declined to attend again.

Even had Gerry been a voting member, he was too eccentric to give Anti-Federalists the leadership they conspicuously lacked. A palpable sense of social inferiority and intellectual diffidence left them almost tongue-tied, while their educated antagonists defended the Constitution in polished speeches. In no other state did the division between the parties rest more on differences of social class than on specific objections to the Constitution, leaving Federalists puzzled as to how to allay the diffuse fears their opponents voiced. "Their objections are not directed against any part of the constitution," King informed Madison,

> but their opposition seems to arise from an Opinion, that is immoveable, that some injury is plotted against them, that the System is the production of the Rich, and ambitious; that *they* discern its operation, and that the consequence will be, the establishment of two Orders in the Society, one comprehending the Opulent & Great, the other the poor and illiterate. The extraordinary union in favor of the Constitution in this State, of the wealthy and sensible part of it, is a confirmation of their Opinion; and every Exertion hitherto made to eradicate it has been in vain.

Federalist speakers thus took on the added "Task, not only of answering, but also of stating and bringing forward, the Objections of their Opponents," in the hope that such candor would sway those moderate Anti-Federalists whose votes they needed.[66] In contrast to the studied oratory of Federalists like Theophilus Parsons and Fisher Ames, the most telling expressions of Anti-Federalist rhetoric occurred when General William Thompson of Topsham repeatedly offered the "pathetic apostrophe" of "O my country!" at the thought of the Constitution's adoption, or when Amos Singletary described its supporters as "these lawyers, and men of learning, and moneyed men, that talk so finely, and gloss over matters so smoothly, to make us poor little people swallow down the pill."[67]

After nearly three weeks of desultory debate, King and his allies reached an understanding with the two men who might have given the Anti-Federalists the leadership they lacked: Governor John Hancock, the commanding figure of state politics since 1780 and the elected president of the convention; and Samuel Adams, long eclipsed as the dominant force in Boston but still a parliamentary tactician of the first rank. Both men respected the strength of Federalist sentiment among the merchant and artisan classes of Boston; Hancock may further have been tempted by the prospect of his own election as president or vice president under the Constitution; while Adams, for all his deep suspicion of concentrated power, was also the one Revolutionary leader who had struggled the longest to forge an effective union of the American colonies in the years preceding independence. Pleading reasons of health, the gout-ridden Hancock did not attend until January 30, but the next day he gave its debates a decisive turn by proposing that the convention ratify but accompany its approval with a recommendation for the adoption of nine amendments. Whether this initiative came from Hancock or the Federalists is not clear.[68] But Federalists quickly made Hancock's proposals their own, rallying to the notion that the remaining state conventions and the future Congress would assuredly endorse amendments emanating from "the hoary head of Massachusetts."[69]

Far from welcoming Hancock's proposal as an invitation to debate the full range of amendments they desired, Anti-Federalist delegates took the surprising tack of denying that the convention "had authority to propose" amendments. William Widgery argued that "the Convention did not meet for the purpose of recommending amendments, but to adopt or reject the Constitution," while General Thompson flatly stated that "we have no right to make amendments. It was not . . . the business we were sent for." To answer these objections, Federalists made exactly the same radical appeal to popular sovereignty that their allies in Pennsylvania had struggled to silence. "If we have a right, sir, to receive or reject the Constitution," Charles Jarvis declared, "surely we have an equal authority to determine in what way this right shall be exercised." Their authority was "derived" neither from the Federal Convention nor Congress nor "even from the legislature itself," Jarvis added. "We are convened in right of the people, as their immediate representatives, to execute the most important trust which it is possible to receive; we are accountable, in its execution, to God only, and our own consciences." The contrary supposition rested on "ideas strangely derogatory to the influence and authority of our constituents." So, too, Fisher Ames equated Anti-Federalist scruples with the "quibbles" of a lawyer; the 355 delegates assembled in convention marked "the fullest representation of the people ever known, and if we may not declare their opinion, and upon a point for which we have been elected, how shall it ever be known?"[70]

In Massachusetts, then, Federalists adopted a position elsewhere associated with their opponents because it promised to attract the marginal votes required for ratification. Once the authority of the convention to propose amendments was affirmed, they preferred to see the ground of

further debate "totally shifted" so that the critical issue became the likelihood that Hancock's proposals would be "universally accepted." The
same conciliatory motives that inspired the convention to support amendments "of such a liberal, such a generous, and such a catholic nature and
complexion" would assure their adoption, Federalists insisted. But Federalists had to exaggerate the ultimate prospects for amendments because
they were intent on avoiding another danger. Amendments could be
safely proposed only so long as they were recommendatory to the new
government, not conditions to be met *before* Massachusetts gave its final
assent. Making ratification contingent on prior amendments, Jarvis
warned, "must operate as a total rejection" of the Constitution. The Anti-
Federalist failure to challenge this bluff was a tribute to the political en-
trepreneurship of the Federalists, who overcame their aversion to allowing
the state conventions to propose amendments in any form while avoiding
the uncertainties inherent in conditional ratification.[71]

New Hampshire. A week after Massachusetts ratified the Constitution on February 6, a bare quorum of delegates opened the convention at
Exeter. Here the exercise of popular sovereignty took yet another form.
Though observers thought that the prestige of Federalist leaders and the
result in Massachusetts favored ratification, the election of delegates in
New Hampshire had been closely contested; estimates of the relative
strength of the two parties varied, but committed Federalists were almost
certainly the minority. More important, a significant number of towns instructed their delegates to oppose ratification. Some delegates were prepared to challenge the legal force of these instructions, but not their
political implications. Rather than risk defeat, a coalition of Federalists
and eleven instructed delegates managed to adjourn the convention until
June. Federalists might have been tempted to follow the example of Massachusetts and rest content with recommendatory amendments, trusting
that this would enable the wavering instructed delegates to defend themselves before their spirited townsmen. But the weight of town instructions
and the fear of defeat apparently convinced John Langdon and other Federalists that discretion was the better part of valor.[72]

That calculation proved correct when the convention reassembled in
mid-June. Four months of renewed Federalist efforts to swing marginal
votes met success in a mere four days of desultory debate and carefully
plotted maneuver. After the Convention tabled a motion to make ratification contingent upon the prior adoption of amendments, Federalist
leaders moved for ratification with recommendatory amendments modeled largely on those of Massachusetts. As in South Carolina, Federalists
supported amendments primarily as a conciliatory gesture. On June 25,

1788, New Hampshire became the decisive ninth state required for ratification when its convention approved the Constitution by a ten-vote majority.[73]

Virginia. The convention at Richmond was already under way when the New Hampshire convention reassembled. After the fall 1787 session of the legislature set June 2, 1788, as the meeting date, Madison fretted that this delay would earn "no credit" for "a State which has generally taken the lead on great occasions."[74] But both sides thought they could exploit the intervening months to their advantage. Federalists hoped that the progress of ratification elsewhere would force Virginians to weigh the dangers of remaining outside a reconstituted Union all the more seriously. Should the Constitution lack the required nine states by June, Anti-Federalists calculated, their populous dominion might be well positioned to make the prior adoption of amendments the condition of its own accession to the Union.

For this strategy to work, however, Anti-Federalists had to improve the winter and spring of 1788 to forge connections with allies elsewhere. Patrick Henry clearly had that in mind when he asked the assembly to appropriate contingency funds to send deputies to "a second Federal Convention" or "to confer with the Convention or Conventions of any other State or States." This scheme presupposed that the convention could act in many respects as the voice of a sovereign people, at least to the extent of launching constitutional initiatives on its own authority (though not to usurp the legislative power of appropriation). But Federalists diluted this resolution to cover only the costs of communicating with other states, and in any case their opponents failed to develop adequate links with Anti-Federalists elsewhere.[75] Anti-Federalists also failed to foresee the wayward behavior of Governor Edmund Randolph, now moving in his erratic way back toward the Federalist camp. At least once, and perhaps twice, Randolph obstructed efforts to fashion an alliance in favor of amendments between Virginia and New York.[76] But opening formal communications among legislatures and conventions would be useful only if Anti-Federalists privately forged more specific agreement as to the amendments they would propose or the political gambits they would pursue. Even after an emissary from the Federal Republican Committee of New York arrived in Richmond on June 7, the Virginia Anti-Federalists could not fashion a coherent response. The letters from Henry, Mason, and William Grayson that Eleazer Oswald took back to New York offered statements of a common sympathy; they did not constitute a political strategy in any practical sense.[77]

Nor did the Virginia Anti-Federalists entirely agree on their own strategy for Richmond. While declining to attend himself, Richard Henry Lee had pressed Mason to insist that the convention thoroughly examine every part of the Constitution before allowing the "subtle managers" on the other side to force a decision.[78] But when Mason moved a resolution to that effect, he was surprised that Federalists supported it as well. Like their allies in Massachusetts, the Virginia Federalists knew that conciliation was the true rule of conduct in a closely divided convention. Mason's greater difficulty lay with Henry. As Madison was pleased to note, the two Anti-Federalist leaders "made a lame figure & appeared to take different and awkward ground."[79] Mason preferred a systematic examination of the Constitution as a means to determine which amendments commanded enough support to serve as a platform for a conditional act of ratification. But Henry pursued other ends. Far from confining himself to specific clauses or even whole articles, the legendary orator ranged widely, even wildly, across the whole text, repeatedly provoking Federalists to apologize for having to "transgress" the rules of the house to answer his charges. For all their power, Henry's speeches did little to advance the cause of amendments; nor could his listeners assume that amendments were his true goal, though occasionally he agreed with Mason on "the absurdity of adopting this system, and relying on the chance of getting it amended afterwards."[80] As Henry posed it, the true issue was whether Virginia could entrust its vital interests to a more powerful national government dominated by the northern states. In pursuit of this agenda, Henry even led the convention on an inquest into the politics of the divisive congressional debate over the navigation of the Mississippi.

Gradually the convention focused attention on the substance of the Constitution. Its four-day discussion of Article III, for example, probably offered the most closely reasoned examination of a particular aspect of the Constitution conducted in any of the conventions. Gradually, too, Mason was able to identify the most desirable amendments. What neither side could be certain of was whether Anti-Federalists could muster a majority in favor of a conditional ratification that would require either some prior adoption of amendments, a second convention, or even leave Virginia the option to abandon the Union should its requests not be met. The initial burden of disparaging these alternatives was assumed by Randolph, now returned to the Federalist fold. "The postponement of the convention, to so late a day" had converted the choice "between previous, and subsequent amendments" into a decision on the "dissolution of the Union," Randolph observed on June 4—and on this there could be no real choice.[81] But as discussion of the Constitution verged toward an end three weeks later, Federalists remained unsure whether they could withstand all appeals for amendments. While suspecting that Mason and Henry had doubts of their own, by June 22 Madison thought that "the nice balance of numbers, and the scruples entertained by some who are in general well affected," obliged Federalists to agree to "preface the ratification with a declaration of a few obvious truths which can not affect the validity of the act, and to follow it with a recommendation of a few amendments to be pursued in the constitutional mode."[82]

The climactic debate of June 24–25 was framed as a choice between a Federalist motion to ratify and recommend amendments, and Henry's rival proposal to submit amendments to the other states previous to ratification. Henry went so far as to warn the delegates that if the Constitution was adopted, Virginia would have no security against the emancipation of its slaves—a mark, perhaps, of political desperation. The principal responses to Henry came from Randolph and Madison, who stressed the procedural chaos Henry's scheme would produce. For conditional amendments to work, Madison explained, the people of each ratifying state would have to debate the Constitution again and elect new conventions. Presumably each convention would have to approve all forty of the amendments Henry had introduced—"a bill of rights which contains twenty amendments, and twenty other alterations, some of which are improper and inadmissible"—while resisting a temptation "to propose as many amendments" of its own. How could such a process produce a consensus, much less an unequivocal, coherent result?

In the decisive vote of June 25, the convention rejected Henry's motion eighty-eight to eighty and then approved the Federalist resolution eighty-nine to seventy-nine. It then appointed a committee to draft the recommendatory amendments the Federalists had promised to support. Madison hoped that his efforts to maintain "due decorum & solemnity" would promote a corresponding "acquiescence if not cordiality" among the Anti-Federalist rank and file, leading them to accept a temperate list of amendments. In this he was disappointed, for the convention endorsed several structural amendments that were "highly objectionable; but which could not be parried."[83] But the fact remained that they were recommendatory, not conditional. Had the balance of parties tipped a few delegates the other way, had Henry and Mason been more of one mind (and voice), or had Federalists acted a less conciliatory part, the Richmond convention might have done what Madison feared. Instead the high-handed behavior of the two leading Anti-Federalists, and perhaps the anti-unionist tenor of Henry's speeches, worked to the Federalists' advantage, keeping their slight majority intact while Henry and Mason despaired of wooing wavering Federalists.

After June 25, 1788, three states remained outside the new Union: New York, whose convention came to order in Poughkeepsie on June 17; North Carolina, whose delegates would meet in late July; and Rhode Island, to whose fate most Federalists were indifferent. Anti-Federalists outnumbered Federalist deputies forty-six to nineteen in the New York convention and in North Carolina by an equally lopsided margin of a hundred out of 268. Federalists in both states deployed powerful orators: Hamilton, John Jay, and Robert R. Livingston in New York, James Iredell in North Carolina; but in neither could they pretend to do anything more than encourage the majority to strike some suitable compromise that would preserve the Union without abandoning the project of amendments.

New York. The proceedings at Poughkeepsie divided into two segments. From June 17 until July 2, the delegates followed the usual procedure of debating the Constitution clause by clause, with the notable departure of allowing amendments to be introduced seriatim.[84] Though a report of New Hampshire's ratification arrived on June 25, Anti-Federalists held course for a week more until a courier arrived bearing the news from Virginia. At this point Federalists completely yielded the floor, allowing Anti-Federalists to finish their survey of the Constitution and introduce their entire list of amendments. During fully three ensuing weeks of maneuvering, different groups of Anti-Federalists attempted to agree upon their strategy while consulting with Federalist leaders who found themselves negotiating the terms on which their antagonists would pursue amendments.[85]

One option that Anti-Federalists quickly eliminated was that of rejecting the Constitution outright. Not only would that end any chance of New York City's remaining the national capital, it also made it difficult to imagine how conditional ratification would work in practice. Yet neither were Anti-Federalists willing to limit their dissent to a mere recommendation of amendments. They searched instead for a formula for conditional ratification that would keep the state in the Union while preserving a right to withdraw subsequently should its amendments not be adopted. More ingenious, however, were their efforts to divide the fifty-five amendments that John Lansing proposed on July 8 into three categories: "explanatory," "conditional," and "recommendatory."

The second category was *politically* the more controversial, largely because Federalists insisted that conditional amendments were tantamount to rejection. But in *theoretical* terms, the idea of "explanatory" amendments was the more radical. Here at last a state convention sought a formula to convert the legal act of ratification into an act of interpretation as well. In adopting the Constitution, the New York convention would also explain what it meant. Lansing's explanatory amendments stipulated that "the said Constitution shall in the cases above particularized receive the Constructions herein before expressed." Federalists indicated that they would accept the principle of "explanatory" amendments as early as July 11, when John Jay introduced a resolution declaring that "such parts of the Constitution as may be thought doubtful ought to be explained." Three considerations enabled the Federalists to concede this point so easily. First, most of the proposed "explanatory" amendments fell under the broad rubric of a bill of rights; few reached issues of the structure and authority of the federal government, and where they did, Hamilton and other Federalists persuaded the majority to transfer such proposals to the list of "recommendatory" amendments.[86] Though many Federalists still argued that a bill of rights was at best redundant and at worst dangerous, by now they could surmise that one would be added to the Constitution regardless of New York's action. The fact that the proposed explanatory amendments employed the advisory verb *ought* rather than the mandatory *shall* may also have made such a declaration acceptable.[87] Third, Federalists accepted explanatory amendments precisely because they were only that. Conditional amendments would have the result of removing New York from the Union; explanatory amendments would do nothing more than affirm principles that might later prove inconsequential to the actual conduct of government.

So opposed were Federalists to any form of conditional ratification that Hamilton even wondered whether they should agree that New York could reserve a right to "recede" from the Union should its desired amendments not be adopted—at least until Madison, back in New York City as a delegate to Congress, replied that the state "could not be received on that plan" either.[88] Federalists repeatedly denied that the new Congress would have the discretion to accept the convention's stipulations under the guise of negotiating the terms on which New York could join the new Union.[89] Though never in a position to dictate to the majority, Federalists exploited the uncertainties inherent in conditional ratification to foment disagreements among their opponents—most notably between Lansing and Melancton Smith, the two delegates who carried the burden of debate throughout the convention. By July 14, Smith and Lansing had seemingly agreed upon a formula whereby New York would ratify the Constitution *"upon condition nevertheless"* that the operation of four specific powers it granted to the national government would be suspended "until a convention shall be called and convened for proposing amendments."[90] But over the next ten days, the Federalist holding action persuaded Smith and a second delegate to accept a more ambiguous formula. In the climactic debate of July 24, they moved to replace the words "upon condition nevertheless" with "*in full confidence nevertheless,*" in effect substituting a political expectation for a legal qualification. On this motion, twelve Anti-Federalists joined the Federalists in a thirty-one to twenty-nine decision that held firm to reject Lansing's final effort to reserve a "right to withdraw." On the next day, Friday July 25, the convention approved the instrument of ratification, with its trinity of explanatory, anticipatory, and recommendatory amendments, by a vote of thirty to twenty-seven.[91]

To secure this result, Jay and Hamilton joined Lansing and Smith in drafting a circular letter urging the state legislatures to initiate the steps required to call a second constitutional convention. But the concession that Jay and Hamilton decided was necessary to bring New York into the Union was viewed with alarm by Madison, who thought it a myopic miscalculation that would revive Anti-Federalism just when it seemed close to dissolution. By late August, Madison was almost prepared to conclude "that the circumstances involved in the ratification of New York will prove more injurious than a rejection would have done." But as was often the case during these months, Madison was unduly pessimistic. A year later only New York and Virginia had passed resolutions for a second convention, and what little support this idea enjoyed evaporated after Madison persuaded the First Federal Congress to take up the subject of amendments.[92]

In New York, as in Virginia, the long delay in holding the convention worked to the Anti-Federalists' disadvantage. Perhaps their trifold scheme of amendments would have fared better had the state convention met earlier, or had they framed a common platform with their Virginia allies. There can be little doubt, however, that delay ultimately validated the underlying political strategy of the Federalists, even if their leaders in New York conceded more than Madison thought proper. In their efforts to classify types of amendments, the New York Anti-Federalists came closer than their counterparts elsewhere to wresting control of the concept of ratification from its original proprietors. Yet once Federalists succeeded in reducing the issue to a matter of union by balking at conditional amendments in any form, Anti-Federalist solidarity collapsed.

North Carolina was the one state where Anti-Federalists proved impervious to the equation of conditional ratification with rejection. Though the outcome was never in dispute, the debates at Hillsborough were spirited, with little rhetorical quarter asked or given by either side. Federalist speakers, led by Iredell and the framer William Davie, hoped that late word from New York might convince the majority merely to recommend amendments. But in a contentious, even raucous atmosphere, no concessions were forthcoming. Anti-Federalists insisted that North Carolina was not rejecting the Constitution outright, and they further intimated that the state would somehow remain in the Union—if not its new government—because the compact of the Confederation could be dissolved only with the consent of *all* its parties. Remarkably, Anti-Federalists even challenged the right of the Convention to abandon the Confederation, or to substitute "We the people" as the source of federal legitimacy for "we the states." Federalists responded predictably, emphasizing the improbability that North Carolina could dictate to the other states and the absurdity of denying itself a voice in the new Congress from which amendments would emanate.

For all their rhetorical power, these arguments proved unavailing. On August 2, the convention resolved to withhold ratification until its declaration of twenty specified rights and the twenty-six other amendments it sought "to the most ambiguous and exceptionable parts" of the Constitution were laid before Congress "and the convention of the states that shall or may be called for the purpose of amending the said Constitution." Interpreting its own action, the convention declared that it had "thought proper neither to ratify nor reject the Constitution"; and in an attempt to demonstrate how the state was remaining within the Union, it further urged the legislature to levy a new tax and "appropriate the money arising therefrom to the use of Congress." More than a year elapsed, however, before a second convention ratified the Constitution in November 1789.

Rhode Island, to no one's surprise, took even longer to act. Its convention finally met in March 1790 to recommend—in a gesture combining ideological purity and political futility—eighteen fresh amendments to those which the First Federal Congress had just proposed. Finally, in late May 1790, the convention met again to ratify the Constitution by a margin of two votes.[93] The original thirteen states again comprised a federal union.

THE ADOPTION OF THE CONSTITUTION has been described, with good reason, as the result of a series of acts that were illegal, even revolutionary, in character.[94] Refusing to be bound by either the requirements of Article XIII, or the sanctioning resolution of the Continental Congress, or the formal credentials of their states, the framers seized the main chance and then developed procedural and conceptual innovations to give their revolutionary act as much legitimacy as they could muster. True, it is difficult to imagine who would have pressed charges against the framers for subverting the Articles of Confederation and circumventing the authority of their own state legislatures, or in what court and under what law they might have been tried. Nor, of course, had the framers seized power for themselves in Philadelphia. Their stroke was not a coup d'état but a démarche—a sudden bold movement that shifted the country from a condition of political torpor and entropy into a feverish burst of activity. Yet in the end, as the legal scholar Bruce Ackerman has ably argued, the framers and many Federalists also knew they could never defend their decision to abandon the Articles of Confederation in strictly legal terms.[95] Madison conceded as much in *Federalist* 40, when he observed that "in all great changes of established governments, forms ought to give way to substance," for "a rigid adherence in such cases to the former, would render nominal and nugatory the transcendent and precious right of the people to 'abolish or alter their governments as to them shall seem most likely to effect their safety and happiness.'" If this mangled and ungrammatical citation from the Declaration of Independence suggests that this essay was hastily written, its appeal to Jefferson's revolutionary language confirms the more important point. In the critical situation in which the framers were placed, they would have deserved far more blame had they "taken the cold and sullen resolution . . . of sacrificing substance to form," Madison concluded. Even if all the charges of subversion that Anti-Federalists leveled against the framers were true, "does it follow that the Constitution ought, for that reason alone, to be rejected?"[96]

Yet if the framers were prepared to make the most of their opportunity, they were also attempting to establish new standards of constitutional legality as well as constitutional legitimacy. Building upon the precedent of Massachusetts, their scheme of ratification carried the logic of American constitutionalism to a conclusion that only a few of its original theorists of 1776 had even glimpsed. If most state constitutions and the Confederation itself rested on no authority greater than ordinary acts of legislation, two conclusions of enormous significance followed. First, the lawful decisions taken by the state legislatures to implement the recommendations of the Convention and Congress for ratification conventions could be said to supersede their earlier approval of the Confederation (again under the doctrine of *Quod leges posteriores priores contrarias abrogant*). As Forrest McDonald has suggested, a case can be made that these legislative acts constructively amended the Articles.[97] The road to ratification ran through Congress and the legislatures, not around them;

the trumpet of "revolution principles" was left unsounded. But in perceiving the advantages this new mode of ratification would have over the procedures of 1776, Madison and his allies were not merely plotting a course to evade Article XIII. For in the second place, the resort to popular sovereignty in 1787–88 marked the point where the distinction between a constitution and ordinary law became the fundamental doctrine of American political thinking. Far from being less legal than the other charters that had gone before it, the Constitution established a more profound criterion of legality itself.

It was this mobilization of popular sovereignty that created the theoretical foundation for the classic defense of judicial review that Alexander Hamilton presented in *Federalist* 78. The supremacy of original constitutional rules and norms over the lesser acts of government taken later, Hamilton argued, flowed from a simple principle: "[W]here the will of the legislature, declared in its statutes, stands in opposition to that of the people, declared in the Constitution, the judges ought to be governed by the latter rather than the former." The power of this principle depended on the elegance of the decision to which the framers and Federalists successfully struggled to restrict their countrymen, by force of argument, political skill, and a dose of guile. Whatever else might be said about the legality or illegality of this process, it produced a completely unambiguous result that ensured that the Constitution would attain immediate legitimacy.

But if this decision made the Constitution supreme law, its simplicity, rooted in the binary choice between approval or rejection, masked a second and far less tidy aspect of the struggle over ratification. For that decision was also the result of a more diffuse and complex debate over the meaning of individual articles, clauses, and even words. And it is to this debate over particulars, rather than the gross decision over the whole, that commentators must turn to ascertain what the Constitution originally meant.

CHAPTER VI

DEBATING THE CONSTITUTION

I T H A S B E E N frequently remarked," Alexander Hamilton observed in the opening paragraph of *The Federalist*, "that it seems to have been reserved to the people of this country, by their conduct and example, to decide the important question, whether societies of men are really capable or not of establishing good government from reflection and choice, or whether they are forever destined to depend for their political constitutions on accident and force." By 1787 this boast was so familiar that it was trumpeted by both sides in the debate over ratification: as much by Anti-Federalists, who accused their opponents of favoring an impulsive and precipitous decision, as by Federalists, who feared that squandering this opportunity would prove that this confidence in the "conduct and example" of the Americans was misplaced.[1] Both sides agreed, too, that this new opportunity stood in sharp contrast to the haste, distractions, and inexperience that had hampered constitution-writing in the states. For all the high hopes that John Adams so wonderfully captured when he exulted in being "sent into life at a time when the greatest law-givers of antiquity would have wished to live," the urgency of 1776 had limited the attention this project could command.[2] What was cause for exultation in 1776 now seemed a commonplace. Yet the sense of historical novelty and possibility that gave the Revolution its "enormous pathos" had not abated. "This is a new event in the history of mankind," Governor Samuel Huntington reminded the Connecticut ratifiers. "Heretofore, most governments have been formed by tyrants and imposed on mankind by force. Never before did a people, in time of peace and tranquility, meet together by their representatives and, with calm deliberation, frame for themselves a system of government."³

It was one thing to celebrate this renewed opportunity for "reflection and choice," however, another to believe that the "calm deliberation" exemplified in Philadelphia would carry over into the public debate. As Hamilton also observed in the first *Federalist*, the Constitution "affects too many particular interests, innovates upon too many local institutions, not to involve in its discussion a variety of objects foreign to its merits, and of views, passions and prejudices little favorable to the discovery of truth." Hamilton understood that Americans were prone to such "preconceived jealousies and fears," because they were steeped in a political culture in which innovation portended danger more often than it promised reform.⁴ The Anti-Federalist "Centinel" illustrated how powerfully this bias operated when he warned of the peril Americans would face if "this useful, this absolutely necessary jealousy of innovation in government" were ever lost.

> The science of government being the most abstruse and unobvious of all others, mankind are more liable to be imposed upon by the artful and designing in systems and regulations of government, than on any other subject; hence a jealousy of innovation confirmed by uniform experience prevails in most communities; this reluctance to change, has been found to be the greatest security of free governments, and the principal bulwark of liberty; for the aspiring and ever-restless spirit of ambition would otherwise, by her deceptive wiles and ensnaring glosses, triumph over the freest and most enlightened people.⁵

It was to counter this innate bias that the authors of *The Federalist* urged citizens of good faith to suspend their predispositions in order to consider dispassionately both the overall case for ratification and the merits of individual provisions of the Constitution. Much of the astonishing appeal that these essays exert over modern commentary surely reflects their lucidity and cool rationality, as well as the comprehensive and unmatched scope of their commentary on the text itself.⁶

But in fact *The Federalist* represented only one facet—and hardly the most influential—of the debate over ratification. That debate took the form not of a Socratic dialogue or an academic symposium but of a cacophonous argument in which appeals to principle and common sense and close analyses of specific clauses accompanied wild predictions of the good and evil effects that ratification would bring. The ease with which

Anti-Federalists uncovered seeds of tyranny nestled in obscure provisions guaranteed that much of what was written on both sides would be dedicated to assaying the merits and defects of particular clauses. But more general conceptions of human nature, society, economy, and government also came into play, and these in turn implicated larger clusters of ideas to which Americans—or different groups of Americans—were attracted.

How to comprehend this complex debate is no easy matter. As Bernard Bailyn has observed, "one easily loses track of any patterns or themes" amid this vast outpouring of writings, whose contents "rang[e] from rather silly lampooning squibs and jingle-jangle verses to scholarly treatises and brilliant polemical exchanges."[7] In another sense, the very extent and diversity of the records of ratification give intellectual license to a host of interpretative strategies, ranging from finely nuanced exegeses of key texts and broad thematic interpretations of the entire debate to a recent content analysis of 3,268 "summary sentences" in some 617 items that yield 178 "categories" of Federalist and Anti-Federalist ideas "based on subject matter, partisan origin, and argument or sentiment."[8] From such a body of writings, many an interpretation can be plausibly sustained, few conclusively verified or falsified. Were the Anti-Federalists "men of little faith" in the promise of the Constitution, votaries of the original political creed that carried the Americans into revolution, or bearers of a traditional agrarian *mentalité* that preferred the security of a decent "competence" and hard work to the risky allure of the market?[9] Were Federalists the political entrepreneurs of a commercial republic or a clique of patricians anxious to preserve gentry rule against rising populist forces, unable to perceive that their claims to espouse the public good only masked their own interested behavior?[10] Did the central axis of division pit Montesquieuian adherents of the virtues of small republics and a rigid separation of powers against the Madisonian exponents of an extended polity and pragmatic checks and balances? Did the two parties interpret and use history in different ways—Federalists opposing lessons drawn from their own revolutionary experience to the hoary maxims Anti-Federalists derived from the troubled histories of republics ancient and modern?[11] Did Federalists prevail because they "appropriated and exploited the language that more rightfully belonged to their opponents," leaving Anti-Federalists "holding remnants of thought that had lost their significance"? But was their triumph Pyrrhic at best, as their use of democratic rhetoric subverted the aristocratic conception of politics they hoped to advance?[12]

In contrast to the decisions on ratification taken by the state conventions, this public debate could never be brought to a single focus or confined to any single forum. Any effort to analyze this debate in the expectation of producing a definitive understanding of what the Constitution originally meant to Americans at the moment of its adoption must accordingly fall short of perfection. We possess neither the equations needed to convert expressions of individual opinion on particular provisions into collective understandings nor formulas to extract from the unstable compounds of hopes, fears, and expectations those elements that best predicted how the Constitution would operate in practice. Nor can one tidily graph how these perceptions shifted over time, as participants on both sides grappled with objections and counterarguments or thought through the implications of their own positions. The decisions of the state conventions thus represented both more and less than the sum of the arguments that the two sides used to assess the Constitution substantively: more because those decisions were finally about whether the Constitution offered a vision of union superior to the "imbecility" of the Confederation; less because the delegates could never conclusively analyze all the particular solutions to problems of republicanism and federalism that the Constitution offered.

ONE IRONY OF RATIFICATION was that both sides had to appeal to a public opinion in which they placed little confidence—not because they regarded the American people as an unwashed mass of the ignorant and selfish but because they feared that cunning leaders would manipulate even well-meaning citizens. A nagging skepticism about the basis on which citizens formed their opinions underlay the celebration of "reflection and choice." Federalists feared that the parochial demagogues of state politics would use their mischievous influence to poison the public mind; while Anti-Federalists worried that the prestige of the Convention would be invoked to ask that the Constitution be adopted on trust. Both parties accordingly placed great weight on their portrayal of the Convention.

This much was predictable. What better revealed prevailing assumptions about public opinion was the anxiety that the framers felt over their failure to achieve absolute consensus within the Convention. By any reasonable measure, the fact that only three members present the final day refused to sign the Constitution might have seemed inconsequential. Adding Luther Martin, John Lansing, and Robert Yates still left only six of its fifty-five members openly identified as foes of the Constitution.[13] Yet even this modest dissent alarmed the framers more than the numbers involved can explain. No doubt feelings of betrayal and annoyance colored their views of the dissenters. Martin's unswerving fealty to the primordial sovereignty of the states and Gerry's knack for moving idiosyncratic and futile amendments had worn thin over the course of the debates; so had Mason's self-serving penchant for casting himself as the vigilant patriot who was alone resisting the errors to which others were succumbing. As for Randolph, many framers suspected that he simply wanted to preserve his political options until he gauged the reception of the Constitution in Virginia.

But whatever resentment Federalists harbored mattered less than their deeper assumptions about popular politics. Gerry was a maverick; but in the spring 1787 elections his countrymen had repudiated Governor James Bowdoin and many legislators similarly identified with the suppression of Shays's Rebellion, indicating that the cause of sound government in Massachusetts rested on unfirm footing. Martin was a drunkard and a bore, but Maryland still carried an "anti-federal" reputation for delaying ratification of the Confederation and failing to send delegates to the conference held at its own capital of Annapolis. Yates and Lansing could be dismissed as faithful lieutenants of Governor George Clinton, whose wartime nationalism had long since faded—but that only confirmed that the Constitution faced a difficult prospect in New York. And should Mason and Randolph forge an alliance with Patrick Henry, the dominant figure in Virginia, the prospects for ratification in the largest state in the Union would seem bleak indeed.

These concerns rested on a conception of public opinion that still attached enormous importance to the authority of notable individuals. Not by chance did Hamilton list first among the factors favoring the Constitution "a very great weight of influence of the persons who framed it, particularly in the universal popularity of General Washington," and contrariwise, "the dissent of two or three important men in the Convention; who will think their characters pledged to defeat the plan."[14] Appeals to the collective stature of the Convention and the prestige of Washington and Franklin thus formed an important element of Federalist strategy. Heroic paeans to the Convention began to appear well before it adjourned, in part because its secrecy deprived newspapers of useful information but also because a predominantly Federalist press was already intent on preparing readers to accept its proposals. The framers were "a band of Patriots and Philosophers, who would have adorned the history of Greece and Rome, in their most brilliant aeras"; even the "punctuality" with which they assembled "and the long time they spend in the deliberations of each day (sometimes seven hours) are proofs, among other things, how much they are entitled to the universal confidence of the people of America."[15]

Other writers linked the collective virtues of the framers to the illustrious reputation of its two luminaries. "Bear witness," a correspondent of the *Pennsylvania Packet* beseeched the ghostly heroes of the Revolution, "with what solicitude the great council of America, headed by a *Franklin* and a *Washington*, the fathers of their country, have deliberated upon the dearest interests of men, and laboured to frame a system of laws and constitutions that shall perpetuate the blessings of that independence, which you obtained by your swords." Ratification of the Constitution "will enroll the names of the WASHINGTONS and FRANKLINS, of the present age, with those of the SOLONS and NUMAS, of antiquity," a Boston writer exclaimed. "Illustrious CHIEFTAIN! immortal SAGE!—ye will have the plaudit of the world for having twice saved your Country!"[16] All doubts should vanish simply because the two greatest Americans of their age had joined in framing the Constitution. How could either of these preeminent patriots possibly "set his hand to a constitution that would endanger your liberties?"[17] Equally revealing was the fawning letter that Gouverneur Morris wrote to the general in late October. "I am convinced that if you had not attended the Convention, and the same paper had been handed out to the world," Morris wrote, "it would have met with a colder Reception, with fewer and weaker Advocates, and with more and more strenuous Opponents." Nor could the general allow his service to end with the use of his name, Morris warned. "Should the Idea prevail that you would not accept of the Presidency" once the Constitution was adopted, "it would prove fatal [to ratification] in many Parts" of the country.[18] Advanced age spared Franklin from similar duty; his only sacrifice was to permit publication of his concluding speech to the Convention, in a transparent effort to portray the nonsigners as men too stubborn to learn Poor Richard's lesson: "that the older I grow the more apt I am to doubt my own Judgment and to pay more Respect to the Judgment of others."[19]

Washington and Franklin could be used in this way because they were, after all, barely mortal. Less exalted framers were reluctant to violate the rhetorical canons of their age by allowing their names to be attached to written defenses of the Constitution. With the noteworthy exception of James Wilson, whose October 6 speech in front of the Pennsylvania statehouse provided the one early exposition of the Constitution that could be directly linked to a member of the Convention, their initial contributions to public debate took the form of pseudonymous essays that left their identities unknown (if not beyond speculation): John Dickinson as "Fabius," Madison and Hamilton as "Publius," Ellsworth as "A Landholder," Roger Sherman as "A Countryman" and "A Citizen of New Haven." Only when the time came to defend the Constitution in legislatures and conventions did the framers publicly affirm their support for its adoption.

Conceivably, the *structure* of the public debate would have been more focused had other framers imitated the testimonial form of address with which Wilson was in effect experimenting. By honoring the conventions of anonymity, the framers sacrificed an opportunity to impose greater coherence on the overall public debate. Had they immediately provided firsthand accounts of their reasons for endorsing the compromises of the Constitution, they might have defused the suspicions of ulterior motives and dark plots that a people long disposed toward conspiratorial explanations of events were always ready to entertain.[20] But custom proved too strong to defy, and if other framers thought of emulating Wilson, the criticism his speech drew suggested that as much was to be lost as gained by investing public debate with personal authority. The framers who participated in the written debate accordingly restricted themselves to the kind of general arguments that Federalists naturally favored until mounting Anti-Federalist criticism required them to defend the Constitution more directly.

The nonsigning delegates shared the same inhibitions about the propriety of taking a *public* stand against the Constitution. Though in correspondence and conversations they helped to lay the initial basis of opposition, they did not rush to publish their reasons for dissent. It was the Federalist *Massachusetts Centinel* that first printed Gerry's letter to the General Court justifying his refusal to sign the Constitution, and then (on November 22) an incomplete version of Mason's objections, which had so far circulated only in manuscript.[21] Randolph's objections, drafted in mid-October, appeared in pamphlet form two months later.[22] But it was Luther Martin's serial history of the Convention—which began to appear in the *Maryland Gazette* of December 28, and was reprinted as *The Genuine Information Delivered to the Legislature of the State of Maryland*— that most alarmed his former colleagues.[23] Whereas other dissenters emphasized specific flaws in the Constitution, Martin lambasted the Convention itself. His highly charged account of its maneuvers and factions confirmed what many Anti-Federalists already suspected: that its secret history was a tale of subversion, and that the framers came to Philadelphia intent on defying the expectations and instructions that limited them to mere revision of the Confederation. At last Anti-Federalists possessed hard evidence that the delegates were something other than *"the most excellent body of men that ever appeared in the world"*; now the "monarchy men" who had gathered in "the *dark conclave*" appeared in true guise "as a set of the basest conspirators that ever disgraced a free country."[24]

The appearance of these objections and revelations provoked several framers to consider launching a frontal assault on the reputation of the nonsigners. Rufus King and Nathaniel Gorham drafted an elaborate refutation of Gerry's objections that presumably would have appeared under their signature had they not decided to withhold its publication.[25] Oliver Ellsworth proved less temperate. In his first three essays as "A Landholder," Ellsworth offered the kinds of general arguments that any Federalist could have presented: The Constitution promised new prosperity; its critics acted from selfish and even treasonous motives; their objections were palpably absurd. But the fourth essay abruptly veered to meet the just-published criticisms of Mason and Gerry. At first Ellsworth treated them politely. But in his sixth essay Ellsworth asserted that Mason's objections masked his disappointment over the Convention's refusal to require two-thirds majorities for navigation acts. Ellsworth called attention to Mason's complaint that the Constitution allowed the importation of slaves for another twenty years, suggesting that, as the owner of three hundred bondsmen, Mason favored its immediate suspension so that Virginians could profit from the internal slave trade with South Carolina and Georgia. Ellsworth closed his essay with a feeble disclaimer that he had heard these allegations made in the "presence of several" delegates to the Convention "who could not deny their truth"; but any reader could surmise that "A Landholder" had been a member of the Convention. His scruples overcome, Ellsworth devoted his eighth essay to a similar attack on Gerry, whose opposition to the Constitution flowed, he implied, from personal rage over the rejection of his "motion respecting the redemption of the old Continental money" of which "he was supposed to be possessed of large quantities."[26] Gerry published a short rebuttal in early January, and Martin rallied to his defense in a signed article for the *Maryland Journal*.[27] But by then Martin's own exposé of the Convention had made *him* a prime target for Federalist invective. His comeuppance came in February, when the *Maryland Journal* regaled readers with an account of the "many piercing mortifications" Martin had endured, notably his two-day speech of June 27–28, "which might have continued two months, but for those marks of fatigue and disgust you saw strongly expressed on whichever side of the house you turned your mortified eyes."[28]

If Madison felt the same annoyance with the dissenters, his prim sense of political propriety forbade him from stooping to personal attacks.

But he shared the same concern with the baneful public effect the testimonies of the dissenters could have. A week into the new year, Madison set down an assessment of public opinion in a remarkable letter to Randolph that illustrated his underlying doubts about democracy. Still hoping to woo his "dear friend" back to the Federalist side, Madison pointedly explained why Randolph's plan for a second general convention must end in failure. As much as he respected "the rights of private judgment" of ordinary citizens, Madison observed, there were clearly

> subjects to which the capacities of the bulk of mankind are unequal and on which they must and will be governed by those with whom they happen to have acquaintance and confidence. The proposed Constitution is of this description. The great body of those who are both for & against it, must follow the judgment of others not their own. Had the Constitution been framed & recommended by an obscure individual, instead of the body possessing public respect & confidence, there can not be a doubt, that altho' it would have stood in the identical words, it would have commanded little attention from those who now admire its wisdom.

Madison applied the same insight to the situation in Virginia. Had Randolph, Mason, Lee, and Henry endorsed the Constitution, Virginia "would have been as zealous & unanimous as she is now divided on the subject." If an effective national government were to "be ever adopted in America," he concluded, "it must result from a fortunate coincidence of leading opinions, and a general confidence of the people in those who may recommend it." But a second convention would never meet those conditions; it would destroy all confidence in the original Convention, while releasing a flood of "irreconcilable" opinions that would only confuse the public more than ever."

These reflections doubtless reflected the political anxieties of the moment, but they embodied as well Madison's most profound worries about the character of republican politics. A fear of the impulsive and dangerous influence that public opinion could exert over legislation lay at the core of his thinking in 1787 and 1788; indeed, it does not go too far to say that he regarded the neutralization of public opinion, or at least the creation of proper mechanisms for its safe expression, as the great desideratum of republican constitutionalism. The ironic dilemma that Madison and the Federalists faced was to have to appeal to the same public opinion whose excesses they feared to secure the adoption of a Constitution that they hoped would calm the populist surges that had roiled American politics since independence. Like other Federalists, Madison sought to resolve this dilemma by stressing the popular features of the Constitution. But he also went to some lengths in his public writings to explain why popular opinion posed the dangers it did, not only when it affected the ordinary business of government but also when it had to be mobilized for the extraordinary act of constitution-making.

Madison offered the clearest statement of this concern in three of his essays as "Publius." He opened *Federalist* 37—the essay which marked the transition in the entire series from the general advantages of union to the Constitution itself—with a lament echoing Hamilton's earlier account of the factors that would discourage impartial discussion of the Constitution. "It is a misfortune, inseparable from human affairs," Madison noted, "that public measures are rarely investigated with that spirit of moderation which is essential to a just estimate of their real tendency to advance or obstruct the public good; and that this spirit is more apt to be diminished than promoted, by those occasions which require an unusual exercise of it." Like Hamilton, Madison singled out "moderation" as the great virtue individuals needed to judge the competing claims of the "predetermined" advocates and opponents of the Constitution.[30] Moderation in this sense closely approximated the independent judgment expected of the republican citizen. Madison and Hamilton had good reason to appeal to this idealized class of citizens, for if they existed at all, their decisions might well determine the fate of the Constitution. But far from truckling to popular opinion, both men used their essays to lay their own political teachings before the public, and for Madison, this meant candidly discussing the fallibility of public opinion itself.

In *Federalist* 49 and 50, Madison extended this general critique of public opinion while examining a proposal made not by Anti-Federalists but by a more friendly source several years earlier. In his proposed constitution for Virginia, Jefferson had suggested that assaults by one branch of government on the constitutional rights of the others might be remedied by allowing the latter (acting in tandem) to call a convention for the purpose either of "altering the constitution, or *correcting breaches of it.*" While conceding that a "recurrence to the people" in such cases was justified because "the people are the only legitimate fountain of power," Madison faulted this proposal on three grounds. First, "frequent appeals" of this kind would "deprive government of that veneration which time bestows on every thing," sapping "the reverence for the laws" and the useful "prejudices of the community" that even "the most rational government" requires. Second, Americans would not always enjoy the favorable circumstances that during the Revolution had "repressed the passions most unfriendly to order and concord" and "stifled the ordinary diversity of opinions on great national questions." Constitutional "experiments are of too ticklish a nature to be unnecessarily multiplied," especially if they risked "disturbing the public tranquillity by interesting too strongly the public passions." Third, and most important, Madison feared that a public decision on a constitutional dispute

> could never be expected to turn on the true merits of the question. It would inevitably be connected with the spirit of preexisting parties, or of parties springing out of the question itself. It would be connected with persons of distinguished character and extensive influence in the community. It would be pronounced by the very men who had been agents in, or opponents of, the measures to which the decision would relate. The *passions*, therefore, not the *reason*, of the public would sit in judgment. But it is the reason, alone, of the public, that ought to control and regulate the government. The passions ought to be controlled and regulated by the government.

On constitutional questions, then, as on ordinary political issues, Madison believed that any coherent expression of public opinion would nearly always flow from the volatile forces of passion and interest that he was so eager to "control."[31]

All of these arguments were *prospective*; all anticipated the role that public opinion would play in future constitutional disputes. Arguably Madison might have believed that the special circumstances attending this original moment of constitution-making would allow a dispassionate and disinterested public reason to ground its decision on "the true merits of the question." But if this was his hope, the course of debate hardly diminished the pessimism about popular politics expressed in *The Federalist*. Even after the Constitution was ratified, his disgust with the New York Federalists for signing the circular letter calling for a second convention betrayed his persistent fear of public agitation of constitutional issues. "The delay of a few years will assuage the jealousies which have been artificially created by designing men and will at the same time point out the faults which really call for amendment," he wrote to Jefferson in August 1788. "At present the public mind is neither sufficiently cool nor sufficiently informed for so delicate an operation." When Randolph again argued that a second convention "will only incorporate the theory of the people with the theory of the convention; & each of these theories is intitled to equal respect," Madison echoed *Federalist* 49–50 by rejoining that "an *early* convention" would "be the offspring of party & passion, and will probably for that reason alone be the parent of error and public injury." The fact of ratification suggested that a majority or at least "a greater proportion" of the American people were content with the Constitution. "Should radical alterations take place, they will not result from the deliberate sense of the people," he concluded, "but will be obtained by management, or extorted by menaces." As late as September 21, he still fretted over "the feverish state of the public mind."[32]

For Madison and other framers, then, the appeal to public opinion in 1787–88 was both a reminder of the deepest promise and possibility of republican politics and a necessary evil. A full-fledged popular debate was required to meet the criteria of ratification they had adopted to circumvent the Articles of Confederation and establish the supremacy of the Constitution. But whether this debate would lead more to enlightenment or wholesale demagoguery remained unclear. "It is almost arrogance in so complicated a subject, depending so entirely on the incalculable fluctuations of the human passions, to attempt even a conjecture about the event," Hamilton observed in September 1787. Federalists entered the struggle highly uncertain of their ability to keep public debate as narrowly bounded as the decision of the state conventions would presumably be. The longer debate went on, the more worried they grew. "The same temper and equanimity which prevailed among the people" when the Convention was meeting "no longer exists," John Jay noted in April 1788. "We have unhappily become divided into parties; and this important subject has been handled with such indiscreet and offensive acrimony, that pernicious heats and animosities have been kindled, and spread their flames far and wide among us."[33] Far from confirming that recourse to "reflection and choice" came easily, the experience of ratification reminded many Federalists of how "ticklish" an exercise it was.

FEDERALISTS WOULD HAVE BEEN CONTENT to rest the case for ratification on the prestige and exemplary deliberations of the Convention, the promise of relief from the "imbecility" of the Continental Congress, and predictions that ratification would inaugurate a new era of prosperity. Beyond establishing these general points, however, they felt no compulsion to be any more specific than their opponents required them to be. Anti-Federalists thus enjoyed some discretion in choosing the ground where the substance and merits of the Constitution were to be debated.

Their first challenge was mounted in Pennsylvania. In late September the debate moved "out-of-doors" into the streets and press of Philadelphia, and then the countryside as preparations began for the convention elections in early November. Though outnumbered in the assembly and beleaguered in Philadelphia, the Pennsylvania Anti-Federalists were hardly disorganized. After conferring with George Mason, the "seceding assemblymen" who had attempted to break up the quorum published a broadside which justified their conduct, challenged particular features of the Constitution, and pointedly noted that three delegates "whose characters are very respectable" had refused to sign it. The seceders put their objections in the form of questions that asked their constituents whether they would be secure under a government that promised to be so expensive and burdensome and whose powers threatened the existence of the state governments. More striking, perhaps, were the dangers that the assemblymen found in the omission from the Constitution of a declaration of rights or other provisions explicitly securing "liberty of the press" or "trial by jury in civil causes."[34]

Though this broadside marked the first statement of many essential Anti-Federalist positions, its greater significance lay in the response it elicited from James Wilson in his widely reported statehouse speech of October 6. Wilson was an improbable figure to harangue a crowd. He had seen Philadelphians express other forms of enthusiasm than the "loud and unanimous testimonies of approbation" that "frequently interrupted" his remarks. In 1779 an angry mob had attacked his house in the so-called Fort Wilson incident that left several fatalities; four years later, as a member of Congress, he watched while unpaid Pennsylvania soldiers surrounded the statehouse in a clamorous protest that led Congress to flee Philadelphia for the torpor of Princeton. Wilson's close association with the merchant prince Robert Morris, his defense of unpopular economic measures, and his professional hauteur rendered him an easy target for caricature: "His lofty carriage indicates the lofty mind that animates him, a mind able to conceive and perform great things, but which unfortunately can see nothing great out of the pale of power and worldly grandeur."[35] Even the prevailing zeal for the Constitution in Philadelphia could not make Wilson a wholly popular figure—in November he lost an election for prothonotary of the Court of Pleas—but he remained the most effective spokesman Federalists could bring forward.

Wilson's speech marked the first notable effort by any framer to move beyond broad generalities and consider the Constitution on substantive grounds. Wilson did not offer a comprehensive review of the Constitution, but concentrated instead on rebutting the criticisms of the minority assemblymen: the omission from the Constitution of a bill of rights and an explicit guarantee of trial by jury in civil cases, its provision for a standing army, the "aristocratic" character of the Senate, its tendency to "annihilate" the states, and its grant to Congress of powers of direct taxation. This speech quickly became a focal point in the national debate, largely because Wilson explained the omission of a bill of rights by proposing a distinction that proved fundamental to all subsequent discussion. In the state constitutions, the people had "invested their representatives with every right and authority which they did not in explicit terms reserve," Wilson asserted, "and therefore upon every question, respecting the jurisdiction of the house of assembly, if the frame of government is silent, the jurisdiction is efficient and complete." By contrast, the Constitution required no bill of rights because the national government would exercise only those powers delegated to it by "positive grant expressed in the instrument of union." It would "have been superfluous and absurd to have stipulated with a federal body of our own creation, that we should enjoy those privileges, of which we are not divested either by the intention or the act, that has brought that body into existence." Not only would a bill of rights have been "nugatory," Wilson concluded, but "the very declaration might have been construed to imply that some degree of power was given" over crucial rights that the Constitution in fact did not place under the control of the new government. In the related matter of trial by jury, Wilson, condescending to "take advantage of my professional experience," explained that the diversity of practice among the states had deterred the Convention from fashioning "a general rule" that would neatly define all classes of civil cases for which jury trials should be required.

Even in the abbreviated form in which it was published, this "long and eloquent speech" was both sufficiently appealing and problematic to frame the terms of a debate that continued into 1788.[36] Federalists everywhere welcomed Wilson's statement as a simple, direct, authoritative response to the recurring argument over the necessity of a bill of rights. Yet they also had little choice about this, because the political costs of abandoning it outweighed whatever advantages they might gain by taking another tack—even when the reaction to his speech exposed its vulnerable gaps. If Wilson was correct, Anti-Federalists asked, why did the Constitution elsewhere establish "a partial bill of rights" by affirming the writ of habeas corpus or prohibiting bills of attainder or ex post facto laws?[37] By his own logic, these clauses, too, were "superfluous and absurd," for where had the Constitution empowered the government to violate the essential rights these provisions secured? Wilson's speech thus emboldened the opposition as much as it heartened his supporters. The candor and elegance that Federalists admired left an impression of glib casuistry that enabled Anti-Federalists to describe his speech as an exercise in "sophistry, so dangerous, as to require refutation." Some Anti-Federalists suggested that his "feeble attempt" to provide an "authoritative explanation" of the Constitution actually "disappointed and mortified" its supporters. "The Press has produced such Manly and well reasoned refutations of [Wilson] and his System," Richard Henry Lee informed Samuel Adams in late October, "that both have lost ground amazingly in the public estimation."[38] Wilson's "recourse to the most flimsey sophistry" seemed of a piece with the transparent desire of the Pennsylvania Federalists to hasten debate at an improperly brisk pace. "View them preventing investigation and discussion," "Centinel" warned, "and in the most despotic manner endeavouring to compel its adoption by the people, with such precipitancy as to preclude the possibility of a due consideration, and then say whether the motives of these men can be pure."[39]

Far from crushing early objections to the Constitution, then, Wilson gave Anti-Federalists something of the intellectual focus they initially lacked. In the nature of the case, they necessarily lagged behind their antagonists in framing a coherent body of arguments. True, Mason had counseled Anti-Federalist leaders in Philadelphia, and he soon circulated copies of his objections among likely allies in Virginia; Gerry did the same on his return first to New York and then to Boston. But for now their objections remained unpublished; nor were other Anti-Federalist writers prepared to undertake systematic criticism of the Constitution as soon as it appeared. By the time the Pennsylvania convention came to order on November 21, "Cato," a leading New York Anti-Federalist, had just sent his fifth essay to the printer; but "Brutus" and "Centinel," two other prominent opponents, had each published only three letters against the Constitution. The most coherent set of objections yet published were the five initial letters of the "Federal Farmer" that appeared In pamphlet form in early November; a week after it went on sale in Philadelphia, Anti-Federalist leaders purchased well over one hundred copies to distribute to their allies in the state convention and to supporters in the countryside.[40] While Anti-Federalists waited for their standard-bearers to emerge, Wilson provided an initial foil for their opposition.

Amid the general outpouring of polemical writings, however, the handful of isolated speeches and papers that clearly emanated from members of the Convention gave only a modicum of coherence to a debate that always threatened to swirl out of control. Important as Wilson's speeches were to framing discussion of a bill of rights, or Martin's revelations were to puncturing the heroic image of the Convention, other writers were free to enter the controversy wherever they chose. At the outset, Anti-Federalists rightly complained that many newspapers had begun to prepare their readers to accept the Constitution on trust; later they protested that a Federalist press was not acting as an impartial medium of debate. In some towns and even states—like Connecticut—Anti-Federalists found it difficult to gain access to the press; once they did, their essays were reprinted less frequently; and their speeches in the state conventions were less likely to be reported. When Thomas Lloyd published his notes of debates from the Pennsylvania convention, he relied almost exclusively on the speeches of Wilson and Thomas McKean; the Anti-Federalist position was reduced to a single question asked by John Smilie on December 11.[41] Perhaps the concentration of newspapers in urban areas also impaired Anti-Federalist efforts to mobilize support in the backcountry. But even taking these disadvantages into account, it seems doubtful that the course of public debate hinged on an imbalance in the dissemination of information and opinion. Surveying the northern press in late October, when Federalists held the political initiative, Madison informed Randolph that "one wd. suppose that the adversaries [of the Constitution] were the most numerous & the most in earnest.[42] Too many avenues of discussion remained open to keep objections against the Constitution from being early and widely known.

The greater difficulty that Anti-Federalists encountered stemmed from their inherent inability to give their arguments the same coherence that Federalists enjoyed. Their favored lines of attack evoked customary Whiggish fears of concentrated power and the specter of a potent central authority absorbing the residual powers of the state governments. Within this broad if predictable framework, however, Anti-Federalists were at equal liberty to call attention to a host of particular provisions that could be depicted as harbingers of tyranny. Some of the clauses they deemed most ominous were indeed essential components of the framers' plan for effective central government. Anti-Federalists would have been remiss to overlook the implications of the supremacy clause or the necessary-and-proper clause, and foolish to refrain from arguing that the small size of Congress violated prevailing norms of representation. But was it equally advisable to single out the power of Congress to "alter such Regulations" as the state legislatures might make for the election of congressmen, or to object to the prohibition on imposing religious tests for office? Once Anti-Federalists set about devising worst-case analyses of seemingly innocuous clauses, they could not easily separate their most telling criticisms from the wilder charges that Federalists were all too happy to ridicule.

Whereas Federalists could ring the changes on such simple themes as the vices of the Confederation and the chaos that would ensue if the states insisted on conditional amendments, Anti-Federalists had no comparable formula for reducing their multiple objections to a cohesive program of opposition. The political dilemmas they faced in the key conventions in Massachusetts, Virginia, and New York reflected their failure to fashion a platform that could rally a movement that was loosely coordinated from start to finish. Time could have worked to their advantage had they improved the staggered schedule of state conventions to frame a program that could be put forward as a reasonable corrective to the most troubling features of the Constitution. Instead, the longer their litany of dangers grew, the more evidence they gave that they could never themselves agree on an alternative plan of government. In an atypically barbed passage in *Federalist* 38, Madison recounted the babel of Anti-Federalist objections to imagine what would happen should the "most sagacious" and "zealous" critics form a second convention "for the express purpose of revising and remoulding the work of the first. Were the experiment to be seriously made," he observed, "I leave it to be decided by the sample of opinions just exhibited, whether, with all their enmity to their predecessors, they would, in any one point, depart so widely from their example, as in the discord and ferment that would make their own deliberations."[43] What Anti-Federalists needed was something more akin to a conference than a convention, a forum in which they could reduce their objections to manageable form without reprising the same disputes that the framers had to resolve in Philadelphia.

Had Anti-Federalists ever met in convention, however, they might well have been able to unite on a number of points that they generally shared.[44] For while their polemics often drifted off into implausible predictions of the tyranny lurking in obscure clauses, there were nonetheless a number of recurring themes to which most writers subscribed. Any short list of these central tenets would begin with the one conviction that is ritually invoked as a tribute to the enduring Anti-Federalist legacy: that no republican constitution could be complete or safe unless it contained a declaration of the reserved rights of the people, however partial or imperfect.[45] Yet for all the use Anti-Federalists made of this issue, the debate over a bill of rights was essentially static: Once the two sides formulated their basic positions, their arguments evolved little beyond the terms set by Wilson and his critics. A bill of rights was either utterly improper or absolutely necessary; between these stark positions, no middle ground appeared until Federalists in Massachusetts, Virginia, and New York found it expedient to accede to Anti-Federalist demands.

The demand for a bill of rights marked only the starting point of the Anti-Federalist inquest, however. Merely affirming that a declaration of rights was essential to *any* government—national as well as state, republican as well as monarchical—would not remedy all the other defects that Anti-Federalists attributed to *this* government; its adoption would correct a startling oversight but hardly reach other provisions demanding revision. Among these other objections, four broad categories define the common core of the Anti-Federalist attack on the substance of the Constitution. Anti-Federalists argued, first and foremost, that its central tendency would be to consolidate the federal Union into a unitary nation in which the governments of the original member states, if they survived at all, would operate as mere ciphers, all their real powers and resources being absorbed by the broad and potentially unlimited legislative and taxing authority of the new Congress. Second, the likelihood that Congress would abuse this authority at the expense of the jurisdictions of the states and the rights of their citizens was made more certain by the inadequacy of the proposed scheme of representation. No system that allotted so few representatives to the growing and dispersed population of so vast a country, or which would enable a select group of senators to cabal at the national capital for extended terms of office, could possibly conform to republican standards of accountability. Third, Anti-Federalists took equal alarm from the absence of barriers to secure the independence of the distinct branches and departments of the national government. Defying the principle of separated powers enshrined in the work of Montesquieu, the Constitution connected institutions that were best kept separate or vested functions where they did not belong, most notably by linking an aristocratic Senate and a protomonarchical president in the exercise of powers over foreign relations and appointments to office. Finally, the general concern that Anti-Federalists voiced about the security of liberty was compounded by the intense suspicion with which they regarded the national judiciary. Rather than welcome the establishment of a third independent branch of government as a check against the misuse of power by either Congress or the executive, Anti-Federalists drew upon an older tradition that treated the judiciary itself as an agent of arbitrary power.

Within each of these broad categories, Anti-Federalist writers ranged widely enough to generate the inconsistencies upon which their antagonists loved to pounce. So, too, lying beneath their specific constitutional worries lay clusters of other beliefs that informed the entire debate—beliefs about human depravity and the corruption of power, concerns with the impact that adoption of the Constitution would have on particular communities, regions, or classes—but which were even less susceptible of tidy resolution. Nevertheless, it was the Anti-Federalist obsession with the details of the Constitution that fueled the debate over ratification. For as they combed the text—from the "We the people" of its preamble to the concluding clause of Article VI barring religious tests for public office and the ratifying procedures of Article VII—they forced its supporters to move beyond broad generalities about union, prosperity, and patriotism to describe how the new government would actually work and explain why Anti-Federalist forebodings were ill-founded, illogical, and even fantastic. From sweeping denunciations of the potential for consolidation to minute quibbles about the jurisdiction of federal courts, Anti-Federalists raised questions that sometimes drew intemperate responses but often deserved precise answers. Federalists privately regarded many of these criticisms as the products of blatant demagoguery, to be dismissed with sarcasm and contempt. But because Anti-Federalist attitudes were deeply rooted in American political culture, Federalists finally had to treat them seriously. And sometimes they even welcomed the opportunity to justify the new ideas embodied in the Constitution and to challenge beliefs and attitudes they held accountable for the "vices" of republican politics. So began a sustained effort to fashion an original understanding of the Constitution.

IN MUSTERING THEIR ARGUMENTS, the polemicists of 1787–88 were not merely casting about for the appeals and warnings that each side felt would produce the decision it sought. More fundamentally, by ascribing meaning to the spare language of the Constitution, purposes noble and sinister to its framers, and implications benign and ominous to the imminent decisions of the state conventions, they initiated a process of interpretation that has continued ever since. Yet the original commentary of 1787–88 arguably possessed a unique authority that later interpretations can never equal even as they produce the legal doctrines and political practices that determine how the constitutional system has actually evolved and functioned. In this view, the ratifiers were not interpreting the Constitution merely to decide whether it would take effect; they were also investing their notions of its meaning in the document itself, thereby obliging later interpreters to treat those understandings as binding sources of authority. These understandings of 1787–88 thus become *original* in at least two senses: in point of time, as the *initial* forays in interpretation, providing the best historical evidence of what the Constitution meant to its adopters and thus explaining why it was adopted; but also as the *originating* source of its supreme authority, and therefore crucial to ascertaining legally binding meanings for later interpreters.

These original understandings were distinctive in one other respect. Where all later interpretative exercises could build upon intervening events, developments, and precedents, the debaters of 1787–88 could only predict what the Constitution would come to mean in practice. Acting in a moment suspended in historical time, they could freely indulge their imaginations to foretell the consequences of ratification. Federalists regarded many of the ensuing predictions less as serious forays in interpretation than as willful misreadings of the Constitution. Too many Anti-Federalist charges either distorted the plain text or rested on predictions so fantastic as to defy common sense and the limits of plausible speculation. True, Congress would be able to "make or alter such regulations" for congressional elections as the state legislatures "prescribed." But why would it compel all the voters of the "whole state" of New York to gather "at Poughkeepsie, at New-York, or, perhaps, at Fort Stanwix"— modern-day Rome—when the clause was obviously meant for occasions when a state deliberately thwarted the proper election of members of Congress.[46] It was arithmetically possible, too, for a handful of senators (two-thirds of a bare quorum) to collude with the president to approve a treaty betraying some vital interest to a foreign power. But was it credible that any clique of senators would actually perpetrate such a démarche, or that the country would supinely accede to their flagrant abuse of power? And if Congress used its purse and sword to create a standing army, would American soldiers therefore form a corps of "Turkish janizaries, better acquainted with plundering their country than fighting for its protection"? One could reach such conclusions, Madison complained, only by pyramiding improbable contingencies that appeared "more like the incoherent dreams of a delirious jealousy, or the misjudged exaggerations of a counterfeit zeal, than like the sober apprehensions of genuine patriotism."[47]

Had all Anti-Federalist objections been equally "delirious," the task of rebuttal would have been easy. But of course they were not uniformly or even preponderantly fantastic. There was nothing "incoherent" or trivial about the questions Anti-Federalists raised about the proposed scheme of representation, or the unlimited powers of taxation to be vested in Congress, or the jurisdiction of federal courts, or the omission of a bill of rights, or the arrogance of powerholders safely ensconced in their national capital. Here Anti-Federalists drew upon political orthodoxies to which Americans had long subscribed, and which were supported by authorities no less eminent than Washington and Franklin. Foremost among these was "the celebrated" or "excellent" Montesquieu, whose treatise *De l'esprit des lois* was repeatedly cited by Anti-Federalists on two crucial points: the optimal size of republics, and the true meaning of the doctrine of separation of powers. Beyond the oracular character of these familiar passages, the power of this great work lay in its canonical status in the political science of the Enlightenment. Whereas Federalists tended to regard Montesquieu as the author of allusive aphorisms whose own meanings required careful deciphering before their revelance to the American situation could be assayed, Anti-Federalists treated his writings as a source of incontrovertible rules that needed only to be quoted, not examined or assessed or interpreted. What was true of Montesquieu also held for the other sources and controlling ideas upon which the Anti-Federalist critique rested. In its extreme form, Anti-Federalism presented itself as a set of near-universal or absolute statements capable of predicting the destiny of all political systems.

Here Anti-Federalism also revealed its continuity with the dominant ideas and attitudes that had carried Americans from resistance to revolution a decade earlier. The same obsession with the corrupting and expansive properties of power was as essential to Anti-Federalist ideology in 1787 as it had been to American interpretations of British policy before 1776. Anti-Federalists expressed this animus most strongly when they examined those provisions of the Constitution that lay closest to the subjects on which generations of Anglo-American whigs had declaimed: the vital role of the jury in protecting local and customary rights against arbitrary acts of central power; the dangers of standing armies; the enormous threat that inhered in granting powers of taxation to a national government too loosely bound by ties of affinity and interest to a suffering citizenry which would bear the costs of the "vast number of expensive offices" it would doubtless create.[48] Yet if history rendered some threats more familiar and conspicuous than others, the genius of this political ideology lay in its ability to locate danger lurking anywhere—not merely in broad grants of power but also in seemingly minor choices of words.

Anti-Federalism resembled its Revolutionary antecedents even more profoundly in the grim *certainty* with which it forecast the consequences to which ratification must ineluctably lead. How could Anti-Federalists be so confident that particular clauses of the Constitution must end in the evil of consolidation, or that without a bill of rights Americans would lie utterly at the mercy of their rulers? As a mode of thinking about politics, Anti-Federalism combined a profound aversion to the perils of political innovation with a set of specific axioms of great explanatory and predictive power. The conviction that these axioms applied to all governments enabled Anti-Federalists to ransack the whole of history to sound suitable warnings against the peril of innovation. "It is a truth confirmed by the unerring experience of ages," wrote "Brutus," "that every man, and every body of men, invested with power, are ever disposed to increase it, and to acquire a superiority over every thing that stands in their way." For "Brutus" and other Anti-Federalists, "universal experience" taught lessons that it would be folly to deny.[49] Power once granted could never be reclaimed. "The history of the world furnishes many instances of a people's increasing the powers of their rulers by persuasion, but I believe it would be difficult to produce one in which the rulers have been persuaded to relinquish their powers to the people," wrote "A Plebeian." Such "observations are so well-founded, that they are become a kind of axioms in politics; and the inference to be drawn from them is equally evident": better to "err" on the side of granting rulers too few powers than too many.[50] Not only did "the uniform testimony of history, and experience of society" prove "that all governments that have ever been instituted among men, have degenerated and abused their power," a Pennsylvania Anti-Federalist wrote; Americans could look at the decision of the framers to cast aside their instructions as a fresh proof of this fact.[51] "You, gentlemen, the preachers up of the new Constitution, will not surely contest a fact proved by the records of all ages and of all nations," an Anti-Federalist broadside declared, *that the liberties and rights of the people have been always encroached on, and finally destroyed by those, whom they had entrusted with the power of government.*" Any group of men vested with power would "take a selfish and interested bias, tending invariably towards the encreasing of their prerogatives," the author went on; "this fact is as certain and incontrovertible a principle in politics, as universal attraction is in physics."[52]

As this comment suggests, Anti-Federalists were as Newtonian in their approach to politics as their adversaries. If the framers were Newtonians of one kind in seeking to set different political forces in equilibrial opposition to one another,[53] the Anti-Federalists were Newtonians of another stamp in thinking that the science of politics was grounded in universal laws. Their science comprised a fixed body of doctrine and cautionary lessons that were best applied to avert the risks of innovation. Events observed in the laboratory of history had long since produced results needing little further testing. By contrast, for Federalists the science of politics was becoming experimental and dynamic in a modern sense. It represented a way of knowing as much as what was already known, and therefore a field susceptible to fresh observations, improvement, and the testing of new principles. "The science of politics, like most other sciences, has received great improvement," Hamilton noted in *Federalist* 9. "The efficacy of various principles is now well understood, which were either not known at all, or imperfectly known to the ancients."[54] More to the point, Federalists believed that the discoveries Americans had made over the past decade superseded many stock lessons drawn from their reading. Where the lessons of history "are unequivocal, they ought to be conclusive and sacred," Madison wrote at the close of his survey of ancient and modern confederacies in *Federalist* 18–20. But "the important truth" he found there only corroborated what the experience of the Confederation had already proved: "that a sovereignty over sovereigns, a government over governments, a legislation for communities, as contradistinguished from individuals, as it is a solecism in theory, so in practice it is subversive of the order and ends of civil polity."[55]

What Federalists ultimately had to counter, then, was not only the specific axioms that their opponents invoked but also their tendency to think axiomatically. Federalists broke with this venerable disposition in thinking that the most useful lessons had to be drawn from cases that directly resembled the American situation, or better yet, from the immediate experience Americans had gained in their own experiments in government. Theirs was indeed a new "science of politics" whose predictions rested on a capacity for drawing distinctions, qualifying judgments, and accepting the possibility of innovation. Whereas Anti-Federalists always drew the same moral from the lessons of history, Federalists typically asked which cases from other periods and governments were pertinent, which irrelevant; which inferences they supported, or denied; and which authorities deserved to be respected, which criticized, or which ignored.

As students of these same authorities, Federalists were prepared to contest their proper interpretation and application and to expropriate their arguments for their own ends. In *Federalist* 9, for example, Hamilton argued that literal adherence to Montesquieu's strictures would require Americans either to break up many of their existing states—at least six of which far exceeded the "dimensions" that Montesquieu "had in view" when "he recommends a small extent for republics"—or "tak[e] refuge at once in the arms of monarchy."[56] Rather than cede the exclusive rights to Montesquieu to Anti-Federalists, Hamilton noted that *L'Esprit des lois* also recommended "a confederate republic" composed of a number of smaller societies as a "constitution that has all the internal advantages of a republican, together with the external force of a monarchical, government." Wilson cited the same passage a few days later in his widely reported speech to the Pennsylvania convention of November 24, 1787.[57]

Madison pursued much the same strategy when he took up the issue of separation of powers in *Federalist* 47. After first arguing that the British constitution that Montesquieu regarded as "the mirrour of political liberty" departed from a strict separation of powers in several crucial respects, Madison examined American practice to prove that "notwithstanding the emphatical and, in some instances, the unqualified terms in which this axiom has been laid down" in the state constitutions, "there is not a single instance in which the several departments of power have been kept absolutely separate and distinct."[58]

Well versed as they were in the political science of their age, these leading framers presented their findings as an extension of its known principles whenever they could. By linking the Constitution to the "great improvement" that had been made in the "science of politics" in modern times through the discovery of "various principles . . . which were either not known at all, or imperfectly known to the ancients," they implied that its reforms were less heterodox or radical than Anti-Federalists alleged.[59] Yet respect for received wisdom only partly disguised the sense of innovation that those who had participated in the Federal Convention palpably felt. If co-opting Montesquieu was rhetorically advantageous, refuting his dicta was more satisfying intellectually, especially for those leading framers who now believed that their grasp of republican theory excelled his oracular and aphoristic pronouncements. Notwithstanding their private misgivings about the Constitution, Madison, Wilson, and even Hamilton were too proud of what they had accomplished not to relish the opportunity to publicize those crucial ideas that they regarded as their own contributions to the science of politics.

The deeper challenge Federalists faced, however, was less to nullify or appropriate the strictures of Montesquieu than to undermine the mode of political reasoning exemplified in uncritical appeals to his authority. The assumptions on which their defense of the Constitution rested expressed more profound criticism and skepticism about the value of appealing to standard authorities, modern or ancient. One could indeed study the scattered examples of confederate republics encountered in the annals of history, as Madison had done in his preparations for the Convention. But in fact the sources of information about these bodies were so "defective," Wilson told the Pennsylvania convention, that few inferences relevant to the American case could be drawn from them. "Besides, the situation and dimension of those confederacies, and the state of society, manners, and habits in them, were so different from those of the United States," he added, "that the most correct descriptions could have supplied but a very small fund of applicable remark."[60] The same animus governed the way in which Wilson, Madison, and Hamilton framed the general question of representation, which they agreed was what made it possible to accommodate the principles of republican government with the establishment of an extended national polity. It was true that "Europe has the merit of discovering this great mechanical power in government," Madison conceded in *Federalist* 14; but only "Americans can claim the merit of making the discovery the basis of unmixed and extensive republics." Britain "may well boast, of the improvement she has made in politics by the admission of representation," Wilson told the Pennsylvania convention, but even there its operation was "confined" to "a narrow corner of the British constitution."⁶¹

In their zeal to refute the "trite" and "hackneyed" claims of their opponents, many Federalist writers shared the sensation of joining in the formulation of this new school of political science: Noah Webster, John Stevens, Alexander Contee Hanson, James Iredell, and others whose identities remain unknown. But probably it was felt most deeply by those framers who took as active a part in the public debates as they had at the Convention itself—notably Madison, Hamilton, Wilson, Ellsworth, Sherman, and King. Their writings and statements were interpretive in a dual sense, for the framers were involved in an effort not only to advance the arguments most likely to counter Anti-Federalist objections but to present as well their own understandings of the considerations that had prevailed at the Convention and their individual assessments of the Constitution. As much as the general structure of debate worked to produce a consensus among all Federalist writers, some of the framers still found ways to incorporate in their writings and speeches those ideas and concerns that engaged them individually. The powerful case for popular sovereignty that Wilson presented to the Pennsylvania convention flowed naturally from the arguments he had made to the Federal Convention. And whether or not *The Federalist* exhibited "a split personality"⁶²—the left brain of Madison contending with the right brain of Hamilton—there can be little doubt that even amid the hectic circumstances of its composition, the two authors repeatedly infused in their contributions their own distinctive ideas about the fundamental issues of republicanism and federalism. Not by chance did they divide their labors as "Publius" so that each addressed the topics that absorbed him most deeply—Hamilton in his treatment of taxation, executive power, and the judiciary; Madison in his essays on republicanism and representation.

The intellectual properties of complexity, breadth, and nuance that have turned the study of *The Federalist* into a growth industry of scholarship may well have detracted from its appeal to ordinary readers of

1787–88. Few of them knew or guessed the identity of its authors; nor could many readers have found the patience to wade through essay after essay with the ambition of mastering all its arguments or synthesizing its diverse themes. Nor did they know anything of the doubts that left both men privately convinced that the Constitution might prove seriously, even fatally, flawed because it lacked key provisions each respectively favored.

All of these qualifications need to be pondered before *The Federalist* is uncritically exalted as the definitive exposition of the original meaning of the Constitution. Yet precisely because Madison and Hamilton knew how extensive a network of compromises and partial solutions shaped the final text, they also knew that the Constitution could be accurately described only in its details, and that the very process that produced it belied the sinister motives Anti-Federalists attributed to its framers. It was their involvement in drafting the Constitution that enabled them to understand and thus explain why "the Convention must have been compelled to sacrifice theoretical propriety to the force of extraneous considerations" and "forced into some deviations from that artificial structure and regular symmetry which an abstract view of the subject might lead an ingenious theorist to bestow on a Constitution planned in his closet or in his imagination."[63]

Madison made this observation in *Federalist* 37. Amid a vast corpus of polemical writings, this essay marked a rare effort to rest the commonplace appeal for moderation in judgment not on the need to withstand the influence of demagogues or the prestige of names but on explaining why thinking about politics was itself so difficult. Madison took as his general subject "the difficulties inherent in the very nature of the undertaking referred to the convention," which he grouped in three broad categories: first, "combining the requisite stability and energy in government, with the inviolable attention due to liberty and the republican form"; second, "marking the proper line of partition between the authority of the general and that of the State governments"; and third, adjusting "the interfering pretensions" of different "combinations" of states. He opened this essay with a Franklinian appeal to readers not to "assume an infallibility in rejudging the fallible opinions of others," and he closed it in a similar key by suggesting that "the real wonder is that so many difficulties should have been surmounted" by the Convention "with a unanimity almost as unprecedented as it must have been unexpected." But in the central section of *Federalist* 37, devoted to the "proper line of partition" between levels of government, Madison offered fresh observations which justified the "candor" and "moderation" desired of citizens less on moral than on epistemological grounds—less because citizens should eschew "passion" and "interest" than because the issues submitted to their judgment resisted simplistic analysis.[64]

Madison introduced these reflections by asking his readers to consider two analogous efforts to "discriminate objects extensive and complicated in their nature." Just as "the most acute and metaphysical philosophers" have failed to "define" and "distinguish" the various "faculties of the mind," so "[t]he most sagacious and laborious naturalists have never yet succeeded in tracing with certainty the line which separates the district of vegetable life from the neighboring region of unorganized matter, or which marks the termination of the former and the commencement of the animal empire." In nature those "delineations" existed in "perfectly accurate" form; it was rather "the imperfection of the eye which surveys them" that accounted for the "obscurity" of human perceptions. When one turned "to the institutions of man," however, "obscurity arises as well from the object itself as from the organ by which it is contemplated," teaching us "the necessity of moderating still further our expectations and hopes from the efforts of human sagacity." To illustrate this point, Madison shifted from his ostensible topic of federalism to the distinct yet analogous subject of the separation of powers, where the experimental cases on which he could draw were more numerous than in the relatively novel field of federalism.

> Experience has instructed us that no skill in the science of government has yet been able to discriminate and define, with sufficient certainty, its three great provinces—the legislative, executive, and judiciary; or even the privileges and powers of the different legislative branches. Questions daily occur in the course of practice, which prove the obscurity which reigns in these subjects, and which puzzle the greatest adepts in political science.

Similar obscurity reigned in the realm of law. Here, too, "[t]he experience of ages, with the continued and combined labors of the most enlightened legislators and jurists, has been equally unsuccessful in delineating the several objects and limits of different codes of laws and different tribunals of justice." Even in Britain, "where accuracy in such subjects has been more industriously pursued" than elsewhere, the "precise extent" of various branches of law and "the jurisdiction of her several courts" remained "a source of frequent and intricate discussions."

Madison closed his account of the limits of political science with one final observation. "Besides the obscurity arising from the complexity of objects, and the imperfection of the human faculties," human language itself offered a further barrier to clarity and a source of "fresh embarrass-ment." The "perspicuity" that Madison desired in law must always prove elusive because "no language is so copious as to supply words and phrases for every complex idea, or so correct as not to include many equivocally denoting different ideas." Thus even if one "accurately" conceived how the powers of government should be separated, "the inaccuracy of the terms" in which these notions were expressed would introduce potential confu-sion, especially when the "complexity and novelty" of the subject com-pounded the difficulty. In a passage strongly echoing Locke—and nearly every other eighteenth-century writer on language—Madison observed: "When the Almighty himself condescends to address mankind in their own language, his meaning, luminous as it must be, is rendered dim and doubtful by the cloudy medium through which it is communi-cated." No one—least of all Madison—would pretend that the voices ad-dressing Americans in 1787 and 1788 were as luminous as the revelations of divinity.[65]

Set against the epistemological writings of Locke, Berkeley, Hume, or Kant, Madison's brief reflections are hardly noteworthy; their significance instead rests in the contrast they reveal between his understanding of the problem of constitutional interpretation and the more rigid mode of po-litical thinking he imputed to the Anti-Federalists. *Federalist* 37 chal-lenged their fundamental presumptions by identifying unavoidable sources of incertitude in politics. By construing constitution-making as an untidy effort to draw lines across terrain where different levels or branches of government were likely to assert competing claims, Madison disputed the controlling axioms of Anti-Federalist thought which held that *imperium in imperio*—a state within a state, or two sovereign authorities jointly rul-ing a common territory—was a "solecism" that must end in one level of government absorbing the other; and that any departure from a rigid sep-aration of powers would lead to tyranny. Just as federalism was an attempt to map a middle ground between the "individual independence of the states" and the "consolidation of the whole into one simple republic,"[66] so any serious survey of the boundaries separating the departments of gov-ernment revealed that their seemingly distinct fields of responsibility con-verged and overlapped in complex ways. No simple formula, however clear in its original conception, could capture this complexity; it could only be described in its details, and with the recognition that a measure of ambiguity was inevitable in any account.

If that were true, a second implication for the process of constitu-tional interpretation followed necessarily, and with rare economy, Madi-son managed to express this point in a single sentence. He concluded his discussion of the "indeterminate limits" of *legal* codes and jurisdictions by observing that "All new laws, though penned with the greatest technical skill, and passed on the fullest and most mature deliberation, are considered as more or less obscure and equivocal, until their meaning be liquidated and ascertained by a series of particular discussions and adjudications."[67] Because a constitution was more than a statute, "liquidating" its meaning might require other forms of review than those customarily applied to legislation. Yet no statute adopted in America had ever undergone "more mature" deliberation than the Constitution itself, and though Madison did not develop the point explicitly, the same maxim would surely govern its interpretation as well. "Is it an unreasonable conjecture," he asked in the next essay, "that the errors which may be contained in the plan of the convention are such as have resulted rather from the defect of antecedent experience on this complicated and difficult subject, than from a want of accuracy or care in the investigation of it; and consequently, such as will not be ascertained until an actual trial shall have pointed them out?" The best evidence for this conclusion could be found in "the particular case of the Articles of Confederation." For "among the numerous objections and amendments suggested by the States, when these articles were submitted for their ratification, not one is found which alludes to the great and radical error which on actual trial has discovered itself"— that is, the reliance the "compilers" of the Articles had placed on the voluntary compliance of the states with the recommendations of Congress.[68]

The special task of correcting *errors* by a process of constitutional amendment or revision should be distinguished, of course, from the ongoing enterprise of resolving "obscure and equivocal" *ambiguities* through "particular discussions and adjudications"—in a word, interpretation. But in both cases, again, only knowledge created by intervening developments could supply the "want of antecedent experience" felt by the framers. Anti-Federalists denied that such a "want" existed whenever they tapped the great reservoir of "universal experience" to identify the defects of the Constitution that required amendment before it was adopted. For Madison, however, the germane historical precedents again distinguished the fortuitous circumstances that justified the exalted image of the Convention sketched in *Federalist* 37 (and everywhere else in the literature of Federalism) and thus to support the claim that it was better to trust *future* experience to identify remediable defects in an adopted Constitution than to risk the uncertain event of a second convention. "It is not a little remarkable," he observed in *Federalist* 38, "that in every case reported by ancient history, in which government has been established with deliberation and consent"—or reflection and choice—"the task of framing it has not been committed to an assembly of men, but has been performed by some individual citizen of preeminent wisdom and approved integrity." If the labors of the Convention taught any lessons, they would "admonish us of the hazards and difficulties incident to such experiments, and of the great imprudence of unnecessarily multiplying them."[69] What made this experiment so "ticklish" was that the framers had indeed been required to resolve all the difficulties outlined in *Federalist* 37. Those who had conducted that experiment now knew what it meant to practice the science of politics as an applied discipline; those citizens who were now evaluating its results would have to be convinced that the Constitution was the product not of sinister design but of decisions shaped by complex and competing concerns. Only the experience of government under the Constitution could finally dispel Anti-Federalist visions of an imminent descent into tyranny. The original interpretations of 1787–y88 could yield nothing more than reasonable explanations and predictions of what the Constitution would mean. If events proved them false, or when ambiguities demanded resolution, intervening experience would provide the foundation for determining the course that the interpretation or revision of the Constitution should then take.

FEDERALISM

LTHOUGH *FEDERALIST* 39 ranks among James Madison's more illuminating contributions as "Publius," it falls a few degrees short of the high canonical status accorded several other essays. It lacks the full theoretical power and arresting phrases that we associate with the Tenth essay (which promises a "cure for the mischiefs of faction"), or the Fifty-first (which explains why "Ambition must be made to counteract ambition"), or Hamilton's Seventy-eighth (which describes the judiciary as "the least dangerous" department of government because "It may truly be said to have neither FORCE nor WILL, but merely judgment"). In contrast to the memorable formulations and bold hypotheses of these other essays, *Federalist* 39 presents a closely labored exercise in definitions and distinctions. After confirming that the Constitution possesses a "republican complexion" consistent "with the genius of the people of America," Madison asks which of its features can be described as "federal" or "national." Answering these questions requires nothing less than a five-pronged model of analysis that produces conclusions so untidy as to border on disingenuity. "The proposed Constitution" was neither national nor federal "but a composition of both," he argued.

> In its foundation it is federal, not national; in the sources from which the ordinary powers of government are drawn, it is partly federal and partly national; in the operations of these powers, it is national, not federal; in the extent of them, again, it is federal, not national; and, finally, in the authoritative mode of introducing amendments, it is neither wholly federal nor wholly national.

Such distinctions hardly assured Anti-Federalists who knew that the Constitution would form the states into a new Leviathan. "We may be amused if we please, by a treatise of political anatomy," Patrick Henry warned the Virginia ratifiers, rebutting a speech in which Madison re-stated this argument. "In the brain it is national: The stamina are federal—some limbs are federal—others national." But "[w]hat signifies it to me, that you have the most curious anatomical description of it in its creation?" Henry asked. "To all the common purposes of Legislation it is a great consolidation of Government."[1]

Madison was undeterred. In Richmond he again insisted that the only way to judge the Constitution was to "consider it minutely in its parts" while recognizing that "[i]t is in a manner unprecedented: We can-not find one express example in the experience of the world:—It stands by itself."[2] In its untidy complexity, *Federalist* 39 thus represented his un-derstanding of the federal system of the Constitution more "accurately" than did *Federalist* 10, which only explained how such a system was pos-sible. It also illustrated what the conceptual approach to the science of politics that he discussed in *Federalist* 37 meant in practice. If his efforts to define such terms as *federal, national,* and *republican* were too academic to escape Henry's sarcasm, they nevertheless attempted to correct the lin-guistic uncertainty that bedeviled all political discussion. His fivefold ac-counting of the federal and national features of the Constitution similarly sought to bring empirical precision to the task of classifying political phe-nomena. Whether this level of nuance could withstand the reductionist tendencies of public debate remained a vexatious question of national pol-itics long after 1788. Each passing decade taught Madison just how acute the analysis of *Federalist* 39 had been, and how hard it was to defend his original understanding of the subtleties of federalism against the simpler catechisms of national supremacy or state sovereignty.

The sources of this complexity ran deeper than the problems of ob-servation, description, and debate. The existence of the states was simply a given fact of American governance, and it confronted the framers at ev-ery stage of their deliberations. In the abstract, some of the framers could imagine redrawing the boundaries of the existing states, and a few hoped to convert the states into mere provinces with few if any pretensions to sovereignty. But in practice the reconstruction of the federal Union re-peatedly led the framers to accommodate their misgivings about the ca-pacities of state government to the stubborn realities of law, politics, and history that worked to preserve the residual authority of the states—and with it the ambiguities of federalism with which later generations would continue to wrestle.

∞

WHICH CAME FIRST, the Union or the states? Recourse to this hoary question of origins has offered an enticing avenue of escape whenever the task of disentangling the nuances of federalism becomes too tedious or threatening to pursue. Though not a central concern of the framers at the Convention, this question was disputed at least once, immediately after the rejection of the New Jersey Plan. To Luther Martin it seemed evident that the separation from Britain had "placed the 13 States in a state of nature towards each other," and that only then had these "separate sovereignties" formed a federal government for the dual purpose of "defend[ing] the whole agst. foreign nations" and "the lesser States agst. the ambition of the larger." For Martin and later theorists of states' rights, the idea that the states preceded and created the Union proved that they retained certain inherent powers that the Union could never supersede. James Wilson could not let this interpretation pass unchallenged. In his view, the colonies became states only by jointly declaring independence: "they were independent, not *Individually* but *Unitedly*." For Wilson and later nationalists, the idea that the states and nation emerged simultaneously, or that only a national act (either the Declaration of Independence *or* the Constitution) could give the states political identity, suggested that the rights they retained were not absolute. Just as the individual "purchase[s] civil liberty by the surrender of the personal sovereignty, which he enjoys in a state of nature," so the states should be willing "to purchase" what Wilson called "federal liberty" with "the necessary concession of their political sovereignty."[3]

Like other attempts to extract precise legal meanings from complex historical situations, the binary form of the which-came-first question reveals more about the difficulty of conceptualizing federalism than about the origins or character of the Union. In 1787 the binding authority of history mattered most to the opponents of innovation; for Wilson, by contrast, no claim of priority could outweigh the right of a sovereign people to replace a defective compact with "a more perfect union." Yet a good case can be made that Wilson was the better historian as well, for his understanding of the concurrent origins of the Union and the states rendered the developments of the mid-1770s far more accurately than Martin's effort to reduce these events to a neat, two-step process.

The states clearly preceded the Union in point of time, of course. While the Continental Congress had to be created de novo, the states were natural successors to the thirteen colonies whose legal origins could be traced to particular grants of rights of government by the Crown. Although the collapse of royal authority during the interregnum of 1774–76 suspended lawful government nearly everywhere, antecedent colonial laws remained in force, and the idea that Americans had to emerge from the state of nature into which a vengeful Crown had thrust them required only the restoration of legal government, not the formation of a new social compact. Just as revolution did not alter rights of property or the duties of family, so a map of America drawn in 1776 would show the same boundaries as one drawn in 1773. The same uncertainty over where Pennsylvania would intersect Lake Erie still existed; it was an open question, too, whether New York even had a western boundary, or whether its legal right to an eastern border at the Connecticut River would prove persuasive to the armed residents of Vermont. But along the seaboard, where most of the population resided, there was no doubt where the jurisdiction of one state ended and another began.

Territorial lines, however, offered only a minimal definition of statehood; in a revolutionary situation, the ultimate source of authority was the ability to command the loyalty of the people. Like all revolutions, the movement for independence required a mass mobilization at the local levels of politics, and it thus demanded an exercise of popular sovereignty in the most immediate sense. Yet the great emphasis that Americans placed on preserving the intercolonial consensus embodied in the Continental Congress, and the natural aversion that local leaders felt for undertaking actions that Congress had not approved, sharply reduced the autonomy that provincial conventions and county committees might have asserted. Just as Congress sought evidence that public opinion and the apparatus of resistance supported its policies, so local revolutionaries always preferred to commit treason with the explicit sanction of Congress. Power and legitimacy thus flowed reciprocally from one level of resistance to another, down from Congress as well as up from the people and their committees and conventions. The deference that provincial leaders showed toward Congress indicates that they were unprepared to assert that their authority rested solely on the popular support of their constituents. This deference extended to the crucial realm of constitution-making itself. Far from asserting their unilateral right to end the state of nature by restoring legal government, the colonies initiated the drafting of new constitutions only after receiving the permission of Congress—at first individually and then through its general resolutions of May 10 and 15, 1776.[4]

It was not, therefore, the factor of priority that eventually gave the state governments the advantage over Congress, but rather the political ties that kept them directly representative of the American people while an ineffective and isolated Congress receded below the horizon of public consciousness. Yet the debilities of the states were as formidable as those which afflicted Congress. After 1776 the states faced two fundamental challenges to their autonomy. The first flowed from the same legislative duties and representative qualities that made the states more effective than Congress. Because the states bore the brunt of the financial and economic problems that the Revolution created, they also offered the most conspicuous target for popular disenchantment with all government. While Congress was treated with derision, the state governments were held culpable for the failures of policy, and not only by the nationally oriented leaders who formed the nucleus of the Federalist movement but by resentful citizens as well. "In the contest between the states and the Congress the ideological momentum of the Revolution lay with the states," Gordon Wood has aptly noted; "but in the contest between the people and the state governments it decidedly lay with the people."[5]

States encountered a second challenge in the territorial and jurisdictional controversies that were fed by the relentless surge of population across state lines and into the backcountry. Separatist movements in Virginia, North Carolina, and Massachusetts (the future Kentucky, Tennessee, and Maine); the success of Vermont in wresting independence from New York while attracting dissident towns in western New Hampshire; and agitation to form a new state comprising Delaware and the eastern shore counties of Maryland and Virginia all indicated that states could not guarantee their territorial integrity. Moreover, the natural attachment that residents of long-settled communities felt toward their state governments came less readily to migrants from other states or overseas. Pennsylvania, for example, had to struggle to extend its control over not only defiant Connecticut Yankees settling the Wyoming Valley but also the restive Scots-Irish inhabiting the area around Pittsburgh, cut off from the eastern part of the state by the Appalachians. As Peter S. Onuf has argued, the challenge of securing these territorial claims did much to make the creation of an effective federal government the logical solution to the debilities of statehood. Far from sapping the vitality of the states, the formation of a more perfect Union capable of checking separatist movements, guaranteeing boundaries, and adjudicating territorial disputes could work to protect their authority against pressing threats. In this sense, vesting new powers in the Union need not constitute a net loss for the states.[6]

Territorial issues threatened the integrity of the states in another way. With the creation of a national domain in 1784, the Continental Congress at last began to plan for the orderly settlement of this vast territory—even while its peremptory treatment of Indian peoples and its inability to halt the movement of land-hungry settlers seeking a decent "competence" across the Ohio River threatened to transform these tracts into the anarchic borderland sober citizens feared they would become. The various plans of government Congress prepared—culminating in the Northwest Ordinance of July 1787—presumed that these territories would enter the Union on equal terms with its original members.[7] But this very capacity to organize states de novo demonstrated that the origins of the states were not lost in the foggy mists of time, and that statehood itself was artificial and thus malleable. Why should a future Congress empowered to create new states out of these "waste" lands not possess the authority to divide the existing states into more convenient units? Why should Americans honor the vague boundaries sketched by "ancient" royal charters when they could now organize their lands in more rational ways?

Beyond these real and latent challenges to the political authority of the states lay a deeper conceptual ambiguity about the nature of statehood itself. What, after all, was a state? The word itself was multivalent, and its various meanings shaded into one another in confusing and even ironic ways that nicely illustrated Madison's observation that "no language is so copious as to supply words and phrases for every complex idea, or so correct as not to include many equivocally denoting different ideas." The simplest usage of *state* was the one that Thomas Jefferson adopted in the Declaration of Independence and that Congress followed in formally styling itself "the United States in Congress assembled." A new condition demanded a new name; formerly dependent colonies now became "free and independent states," though as J. G. A. Pocock has noted, they could as easily have been called "commonwealths" or even "republics." But what attributes defined a state: its territorial limits (which were often contested); the people who inhabited it (though these might include enslaved African-Americans who had no political existence and Indians whom Article IX of the Confederation classified as "members" of states); or the form of government its citizens instituted to assert their political identity? Did it also matter that the colonies became states by leaving that version of the state of nature into which Americans literally believed King George III had thrust them, only to place themselves in that other state of nature where the nation-states of the world contended for power? But for purposes of war and peace, were the American states fully sovereign in the same sense as the kingdoms of George III and their ally Louis XVI? Or was their statehood not diminished by membership in the Union whose control of foreign relations they accepted both before July 1776 and after? And what relation did these states bear to one another?

As Pocock has wryly noted: "There are now thirteen 'states' in a 'state of nature' with respect to the 'state' (and people) of Great Britain; and the question must necessarily arise whether these thirteen are in a state of nature respecting one another—as they certainly are with respect to mankind—and what it is that keeps them from being so if they in fact are not." Locke had used the term "federative power" to describe that aspect of government concerned with relations among states, and in both an etymological and a substantive sense, the concept and practice of American federalism derived from the pressing need to fashion durable agreements to organize the relations of the thirteen states.[8] But again, insofar as the formation of an effective Union accompanied the transformation of colonies into states, American concepts of federalism and statehood were coeval in origin and mutually uncertain in meaning.

A decade of controversy over the structure of the British Empire might well have prepared the revolutionaries to scrutinize closely the relation between these independent states and the first federal government embodied in the Continental Congress.[9] But the process of drafting the Articles of Confederation took a different course. Little in the surviving records of debate and deliberation suggests that its congressional drafters were much troubled by questions about the location of sovereignty or the nature of the federal system. The divisions that delayed the drafting and ratification of the Articles were concerned instead with issues that pitted different clusters of states against one another on the basis of well-defined interests: the formula for voting in Congress, the apportionment of the expenses of war, and the control of western lands. When it came to allocating the powers of government, the Articles created two broad and largely exclusive spheres of authority for the Union and the states, and trusted to patriotism and the imperatives of war to persuade these two levels of government to cooperate for the public good. Congress would propose suitable measures through its resolutions, requisitions for funds, and recommendations, and the state legislatures would carry them out in good faith, with due attention to the specific circumstances of their constituents. The failure of the Articles to give Congress any power of "coercion" over the states arose naturally "from a mistaken confidence that the justice, the good faith, the honor, the sound policy, of the several legislative assemblies would render superfluous any appeal to the ordinary motives by which the laws secure the obedience of individuals," Madison aptly noted, "a confidence which does honor to the enthusiastic virtue of the compilers, as much as the inexperience of the crisis apologizes for their errors."[10]

This "fatal omission" was the crucial point of departure for everything the Convention undertook, for in giving the Union the power to act by law, it also had to ask how (and by whom) that law would be made, executed, and adjudicated. But the framers could not reconstitute the federal Union without attempting to reconceive the nature of statehood as well. If the *persistence* of the states was a given, their *status* was not. On the eve of the Convention, the factious and fractious pressures to which the thirteen states were exposed left their authority and autonomy vulnerable to attack. When Madison, Wilson, Hamilton, and King set out to trace the narrower orbits that they hoped the states would hereafter transit, those delegates who remained loyal to the principle of independent statehood had cause for alarm as well as surprise.

J UST AS NO WORKING MODEL of federalism could be deduced by definition alone, no single vector neatly charted the course the framers took in allocating power between the Union and the states. To evoke Madison's favored image, the new federal system would occupy a middle ground between a confederation of sovereign states and a consolidated nation. But the dimensions and contours of this terrain—or the placement of what Madison later called its landmarks—appeared only gradually, as the framers drew the boundaries between national and state governments, fixed the points where their sources of political influence would come into contact or overlap, and mapped the separate domains where each would exercise jurisdiction. Some of their decisions marked conscious efforts at compromise—that is, to find middle ground of another sort by halving the distances separating rival positions. Others grew from the recognition that seemingly simpler alternatives—either more national or more federal—offered no remedy for the defects of the Confederation.

Far from simplifying the concept of federalism, this course of debate led the framers to compound its nuances and uncertainties. Madison alluded to this progression in *Federalist* 37 when he asked whether it would "be wonderful if, under the pressure of all these difficulties, the Convention should have been forced into some deviations from that artificial structure and regular symmetry which an abstract view of the subject might lead an ingenious theorist to bestow on a Constitution planned in his closet or in his imagination?"[11] Writing as "Publius," Madison did not reveal the tacit irony of his comment. For these "deviations" carried the Convention away from the more "artificial structure and regular symmetry" that Madison had in mind when he proposed giving the national government an unlimited veto over all state laws. Compared to the lat-ticework of "federal" and "national" features sketched in *Federalist* 39, the program of *federal* reform that he incorporated in the Virginia Plan was far more national in respect both to the "extent" of the powers to be vested in the Union and to the "sources" from which those wielding these powers would be drawn.

That program rested on five essential propositions. First, the national government would act directly on the population rather than mediately through the states. Second, to assure that its measures would be framed with a broad regard for the public good, the national government had to be insulated from the political influence of the state governments. Third, while avowing "a strong bias in favor of an enumeration and definition of the powers necessary to be exercised by the national Legislature," Madi-son's "doubts concerning its practicability" inclined him to err on the side of giving the Union "all the necessary means" to secure "the safety, liberty, and happiness of the Community."[12] Fourth, to defend itself against pos-sible interference from the states, the Union should also possess a nega-tive on state laws, becoming, in effect, a supervisory branch of the state assemblies. And fifth, because the regulation of the daily affairs of Amer-icans would still fall largely to the states, Madison favored extending the negative to cover all state laws that the national legislature judged harmful not only to its own policies but also to the rights of minorities within the states. The net aim of this program was to render the Union politically independent of the states and the states legally dependent on national oversight.[13]

Only by abolishing the states altogether could Madison have moved to alter the structure of the Union more radically. This was indeed the dark motive that delegates from the small states imputed to him when they juxtaposed his hostility to the equal-state vote with the implications of the negative on state laws and the prospect that the national govern-ment would control the most productive sources of revenue. As early as June 2, John Dickinson complained that some members seemed to wish to "abolish altogether . . . the accidental lucky division of this country into distinct States," and other delegates concurred that the very "existence" of the states was in jeopardy.[14] Yet Madison and his allies were not dissem-bling when they insisted that the states had to be retained because "all large Governments must be subdivided into lesser jurisdictions."[15] Their purpose was rather to create a new definition that would relegate the state governments to some midpoint along the "gradation" of "political soci-eties" ranging from "the smallest corporation, with the most limited pow-ers to the largest empire with the most perfect sovereignty."[16] Yet neither did they sound reassuring when they hinted that "conveniency" provided the only valid objection against abolishing the state governments. "Were it practicable for the Genl. Govt. to extend its care to every requisite object without the cooperation of the State Govts.," Madison observed, "the people would not be less free as members of one great Republic than as members of thirteen small ones."[17] Expropriating a metaphor that Dickinson had introduced, Wilson and Madison held that the states should be confined to their "proper orbits" around a national "sun" that they could neither "warm [n]or enlighten," while the negative on their laws operated as "the great pervading principle that must control the[ir] centrifugal tendency" to "fly out of their proper orbits and destroy the order & harmony of the political system"[18] Nothing in these arguments suggested that they regarded the states as laboratories of liberty or nurseries of republican citizenship.

Statements so candid only inspired other delegates to articulate their notions of statehood with equal vigor, ultimately producing in recoil a reaffirmation of the vital place that the states would occupy in the federal system. Yet the framers did not reach this conclusion by choosing between the polar conceptions of statehood expressed by Martin, who portrayed the states as the immutable sovereign members of the Union, and Hamilton, who was prepared to treat the states as something akin to English shires. Rather, they amalgamated the less rigid opinions that most of them shared, and they did so only cumulatively, as they worked their way through clusters of discrete issues. In tracing this process, three sets of issues deserve particular attention: the further decisions that refined the character of the Senate; the replacement of Madison's negative on state laws with the judicial enforcement of the supremacy of national law; and the substitution of a list of enumerated powers for the broad and discretionary grant of legislative authority the Virginia Plan first proposed.

The Senate.   Nothing better symbolized the original ambiguities of American federalism than the mixed character of the Senate. After July 16, no one could deny that the Senate was intended to embody the equal sovereignty of the states and to protect their rights of government against national encroachment. These were the claims that the supporters of the equal-state vote advanced most consistently, and their victory clearly repudiated the efforts of Madison, Wilson, and King to ground the Senate on some principle—any principle—other than the representation of states. Yet the advocates of the equal-state vote did not extend the implications of this principle to other questions. If the Senate represented states in their corporate capacity, it was hardly consistent to allow senators to vote as individuals rather than as a delegation. Yet even before July 16,

Elbridge Gerry and Roger Sherman hinted that they favored per capita voting, and when Gouverneur Morris and King made a motion to that effect on July 23, only Maryland dissented, with Martin feebly objecting that this meant "departing from the idea of the *States* being represented in the 2d. branch."[19]

Equally revealing was the treatment of the payment of senatorial salaries. When the issue was first debated on June 26, a divided Convention could not agree whether senators should be paid by the states or out of the national treasury. Consistent with the vote of July 16, the committee of detail proposed that the states should pay both houses. But when this was taken up on August 14, it was Oliver Ellsworth who proposed restoring national payment because he was now "satisfied that too much dependence on the States would be produced" otherwise. A chorus of delegates from both sides of the earlier debate echoed his position, while again only Martin protested. Daniel Carroll immediately rebuked his colleague for forgetting that "The Senate was to represent & manage the affairs of the whole, and not to be the advocates of State interests." But he did not explain how he reconciled this image of the national responsibilities of the Senate with the representative obligations of senators. The Senate itself would embody the mixed character of the Constitution: It would be "federal" in origin but "national" in orientation, somehow protecting state sovereignty and the national interest simultaneously.[20]

Supremacy. The crucial issue of federalism, however, was not to determine how the political influence of the states would be projected in the national government. It was rather to decide how the anticipated rivalry of these two levels of government could be resolved short of overt resort to coercion. Those framers who argued most ardently for national supremacy often spoke as if the great challenge of federalism was to annul the political advantages the states would enjoy in commanding the loyalty of the people, and which would embolden the state governments to counteract or evade national measures as calculations of provincial interest dictated. This was the real thrust of Hamilton's famous speech of June 18—not its praise for the British constitution—and it was a concern that Madison fully shared.[21] James Wilson may have been the only member of the nationalist caucus who grasped the possibility that the political loyalties of the people might swing freely between rival levels of government as they competed to demonstrate their respective capacities for governance.[22] But the longer the framers revolved this question, the more they treated the disparity in *political* influence as a problem requiring a *legal* solution.

In determining how national acts could be enforced against potential opposition, the Convention could choose among three mechanisms: the use of coercive force against defiant states (which assumed that the Union would still rely on the states to implement its resolutions, requisitions, and recommendations); the negative on state laws; or the legal prosecution of individuals who violated or interfered with national law. These were not mutually exclusive alternatives. The Virginia Plan incorporated all three—although Madison quickly renounced coercion as "look[ing] more like a declaration of war, than an infliction of punishment"; the New Jersey Plan, both coercion and judicial enforcement.[23] The framers never doubted the need for judicial enforcement of national law. Their true disagreement lay on two other issues. First, should this responsibility be vested in a complete system of national courts, or divided between existing state courts and a national Supreme Court with appellate jurisdiction? Second, would judicial enforcement be adequate without the threat of either coercion or the negative to support it? Whereas Madison and Wilson viewed the negative as a benign alternative to coercion, William Paterson and his allies preferred the threat of coercion to the constant, intrusive oversight of state legislation implied by the negative.

Article 9 of the Virginia Plan proposed the creation of "one or more supreme tribunals, and of inferior tribunals," both to have jurisdiction over "questions which may involve the national peace and harmony." On June 5, John Rutledge denounced the idea of constitutionally mandated inferior courts as an "unnecessary encroachment on the jurisdiction of the state," a "right of appeal to the supreme national tribunal being sufficient to secure the national rights & uniformity of Judgmts." On his motion the committee of the whole first narrowly eliminated this provision but then accepted a motion from Wilson and Madison to give the national legislature a discretionary authority to create "inferior tribunals."[24] Article 4 of the New Jersey Plan built upon this aversion to an extensive federal judiciary by proposing to make "the Common law Judiciarys" of the state courts of "first instance" to try offenses against national acts, with the federal judiciary exercising appellate jurisdiction only. To provide some assurance that the state courts would discharge their national obligations in good faith, Article 6 of the New Jersey Plan declared that all acts of Congress and national treaties

> shall be the supreme law of the respective States so far forth as those
> Acts or Treaties shall relate to the said States or their Citizens, and
> that the Judiciary of the several States shall be bound thereby in
> their decisions, any thing in the respective laws of the individual
> States to the contrary notwithstanding . . .[25]

Here was a first attempt to state a principle of federal supremacy that would provide an interpretative rule for all those state judges whom many framers expected to exercise original jurisdiction over federal cases.

In opposing the New Jersey Plan, Madison and Wilson argued that a reliance on state courts was problematic on several counts. Merely proclaiming a principle of federal supremacy might not give state judges the independence and backbone they needed to withstand the control of their individual legislatures. An acquittal in state court of an individual accused of violating federal law could not be appealed, Madison observed, while state governors could simply pardon convicted offenders. Moreover, because the New Jersey Plan would require *legislative* ratification only, it could not render national acts "even legally *paramount* to the Acts of the States."[26] In their view, the negative on state laws and a broad jurisdiction for national courts remained a far more attractive alternative to the reliance on coercion and state courts.

After July 17, however, it was evident that the authority of the national government would depend on judicial enforcement. With the rejection of the negative that day, and the quick and unanimous restoration of the New Jersey Plan's version of a supremacy clause, the problem of balancing the respective authority of national and state courts came to the fore. Though Madison's persistent doubts about the efficacy of national judicial power and the loyalties of state judges could not save the negative, the framers still had to answer his reservations about the inherent weakness of judicial power. This process began in the committee of detail, whose five members included three future justices of the Supreme Court (Rutledge, Ellsworth, and Wilson), a leading author of the Judiciary Act of 1789 (Ellsworth), and the first attorney general (Edmund Randolph). Wilson, Randolph, and Nathaniel Gorham, the fifth member, already agreed "that the Courts of the States can not be trusted with the administration of the national laws"; they further opposed legislative ratification of the Constitution on the grounds that state courts would thereby remain free to subordinate national acts to state laws or even the common law.[27] By contrast, Rutledge and Ellsworth were more intent on preserving the jurisdictions of the state courts. But this concern required them to demonstrate that these courts could indeed be relied upon to act responsibly in the enforcement of national law (rather than serve as the first line of defense against national encroachment on state governments).

Article 9 of the committee's draft accordingly extended the supremacy clause to oblige the state courts to follow both the acts of the national legislature and national treaties, "any Thing in *the Constitution* or laws of the several States to the Contrary notwithstanding."[28] And when the

Convention reached this article on August 23, Rutledge proposed extending the assertion of national supremacy to the Constitution itself by adding the words "This Constitution" to the *beginning* of the clause. In this form, the supremacy clause was approved without debate or dissent—even from Martin, who later claimed that these changes rendered the original clause "worse than useless" because national acts "were intended to be superior [only] to the laws of our state government, where they should be opposed to each other," but not "to our *constitution* and bill of rights."[29] Quietly and uncontroversially, a clause which was originally offered as a weak alternative to the negative on state laws had been transformed into a potentially powerful basis for national supremacy.

This did not mean, however, that the framers were convinced that judicial power would provide a sufficient defense against the interference of the states. For when Charles Pinckney moved to restore the negative—a few minutes after this final action on the supremacy clause—a narrowly divided Convention turned back Madison's motion to refer the measure to a committee for "modification" by a single vote. "The firmness of Judges is not itself sufficient" to defend the national government, Wilson noted. "Something further is requisite—It will be better to prevent the passage of an improper law, than to declare it void when passed." Wilson and Madison had made this same argument during two previous debates on the negative, and its revival now illustrates their persistent skepticism about relying on the judiciary. But other delegates found the defects of the negative more alarming. "If nothing else, this alone would damn and ought to damn the Constitution," Rutledge declared. "Will any State ever agree to be bound hand & foot in this manner[?]" How would the negative possibly work in practice, Ellsworth asked in turn? Were all state laws to be submitted to Congress "previously to their taking effect?" Or would the national government not have to appoint a pro-consular authority to "have a controul over the State laws"?[30]

These unanswerable objections—so powerful because they were also so pragmatic—exposed the underlying defects in the negative that Madison never resolved. Madison and Wilson may have thought that its mere existence would operate as a deterrent against pernicious legislation.[31] Other delegates assayed its effects more literally. How could Madison's own constituents—much less the South Carolinians—tolerate a power that gave the national government a potent weapon to use against slavery? Like the discredited notion of coercion, the negative also presupposed conflict between the Union and the states. The supremacy clause held out the more hopeful prospect that conflicts between national and state law could be channeled into a forum where the rules and forms of adjudication would mute the overt clash of political wills.

The greater significance of the supremacy clause lies, of course, in its fundamental importance to the doctrine of judicial review of legislation. No account of this doctrine that slights its connection to federalism can do justice to the great question that is often treated as *the* crucial issue of American constitutional history: whether judicial review was originally intended or understood to be part of the Constitution. As the debate over the council of revision made clear, the framers did intend judicial review to apply to the realm of national legislation, where it would help maintain boundaries among the branches of national government. Yet the more likely sources of constitutional controversy requiring judicial review did not lie along the axis of the separation of powers—that is, within the realm of national government alone. They would arise instead along the uncharted borders where the powers of state and national governments would overlap. Their decisions on the structure of the national government gave the framers little reason to worry that Congress would enact or the president approve constitutionally improper statutes that the federal judiciary would feel compelled to overturn. But the institutional and political checks that would operate at the national level of government had no parallel in the states. There bicameralism was unlikely to dilute the perceptions of a coherent state interest that might encourage a legislature to challenge national policy; nor could the weaker executives and judiciaries established under the Revolutionary state constitutions be expected to impede the "impetuous vortex" of legislative power.

In this sense the supremacy clause marked an attempt to incorporate a principle of judicial review into all the state governments by the unilateral fiat of the Constitution. The delegates knew that the occasional efforts of state judges to exercise a power of judicial review had been bitterly contested by legislatures in New York and Rhode Island; but they also understood that a federal Constitution ratified by an act of popular sovereignty could effectively amend each state constitution by securing the approval of its citizens for "a more perfect Union." Yet even with the authority of the supremacy clause behind them, state courts might still construe national laws, treaties, or the Constitution itself improperly. The supremacy clause could only encourage state judges to aspire to the enhanced notion of judicial independence on which it was premised; it provided more of an incentive than a mandate, even if the framers hoped that incentive would evolve into a norm of judicial behavior. It seems evident, too, that the framers believed the ultimate judicial power to resolve conflicts between national and state laws would reside in the Supreme Court. Rutledge, the framer who struggled hardest to reconcile the authority of the state judiciaries with a robust principle of national supremacy, stated the key point on August 27, while opposing a motion authorizing the executive to remove federal judges "on the application" of Congress. "If the supreme Court is to judge between the U.S. and particular States," he observed, "this alone is an insuperable objection to the motion"—because it would prevent the Court from exercising the independent judgment its duties required.[32] Madison thus accurately captured the original intention of the framers in the single allusive sentence of *Federalist* 39 which noted that "in controversies relating to the boundary between the two jurisdictions" of national and state governments, "the tribunal which is ultimately to decide, is to be established under the general government." But that was no cause for alarm, for "The decision is to be impartially made, according to the rules of the Constitution; and all the usual and most effectual precautions are taken to secure this impartiality."[33]

This statement sounded the same confident note that Sherman struck when he flatly predicted that "the Courts of the States would not consider as valid any law contravening the Authority of the Union."[34] In fact Madison's bland assurance masked a tangle of doubts that troubled him until the end of his life, even as he repeatedly affirmed that the basic principle of *Federalist* 39 was the correct interpretation of the Constitution. Madison restated his reservations about judicial power in the extended defense of the congressional negative that he prepared for Jefferson five weeks after the Convention adjourned. "It may be said," he observed,

> that the Judicial authority under our new system will keep the States within their proper limits, and supply the place of a negative on their laws. The answer is, that it is more convenient to prevent the passage of a law, than to declare it void after it is passed; that this will be particularly the case, where the law aggrieves individuals, who may be unable to support an appeal agst. a State to the supreme Judiciary; that a State which would violate the Legislative Rights of the Union, would not be very ready to obey a Judicial decree in support of them, and that a recurrence to force, which in the event of disobedience would be necessary, is an evil which the new Constitution meant to exclude as far as possible.

Madison doubted whether adjudication alone could produce legally demonstrable and politically persuasive solutions, given "the impossibility of dividing powers of legislation, in such a manner, as to be free from different constructions by different interests, or even from ambiguity in the judgment of the impartial."[35] By giving the *separate* state judiciaries some responsibility for the enforcement of national acts, the Constitution promised to compound this inherent ambiguity, not reduce it. The mixed federal and national character of the judicial power must produce uncertainties as puzzling as those generated by the diverse legal codes and jurisdictions of Britain, which remained (as he observed in *Federalist* 37) "a source of frequent and intricate discussions, sufficiently denoting the indeterminate limits by which they are respectively circumscribed."[36] Indeed, the lines demarcating the rival jurisdictions of federal and state courts might prove even less "determinate" than the comparable divisions in British law, because the American states retained a residual sovereignty that subordinate institutions in Britain had never claimed.

The power to legislate. To the state and federal judiciaries, then, would fall the task of maintaining the boundaries between their respective governments. But the extent of the territories to be thus set off depended on how the framers defined the scope and limits of the legislative power of these two levels of government. In many ways the final irony of their approach to federalism was that the new Union was only marginally less of a confederation than the one it had replaced. Here, too, debate moved the Convention away from the implications of the Virginia Plan, with its indefinite notion of the powers of the national government, and toward a more modest set of duties that Madison plausibly described in *Federalist* 45 as "consist[ing] much less in the addition of NEW POWERS to the Union, than in the invigoration of its ORIGINAL POWERS."[37]

The chief difficulty in tracing this aspect of federalism through the Convention involves interpreting the motives underlying Article 6 of the Virginia Plan, which proposed

> that the National Legislature ought to be impowered to enjoy the Legislative Rights vested in Congress by the Confederation & moreover to legislate in all cases to which the separate States are incompetent, or in which the harmony of the United States may be interrupted by the exercise of individual Legislation . . .

This open-ended language may be interpreted in two ways. On the one hand, it may be viewed as an authentic formula for a national government whose legislative power would extend as far as its own discretion saw fit. On the other, it can also be read as a textual placeholder to be used so long as the great issue of representation remained unresolved, but then to be modified or even replaced by a list of particular powers. In the first view, Madison, Wilson, Morris, and King might indeed have attempted to secure a government with plenary legislative power had the vote of July 16 gone the other way; while the small states were certainly well advised to hold out for an equal vote in the Senate as a security against an omnicompetent national government. In the second view, the framers tacitly understood that an enumeration of legislative powers would eventually occur, but were prevented from moving in that direction by Madison's demand that issues of representation be resolved first.[38] Whether or not it was miscalculated, this strategy prevented consideration of any aspect of legislative power until the vote of July 16 signaled its failure.

Once past that hurdle, however, the record of debate indicates that the Convention was not hard-pressed to reach a general consensus about the powers of Congress. Although on July 17 it rejected Sherman's motion to substitute a list of enumerated powers for Article 6—and even broadened its language by accepting Gunning Bedford's motion to add the phrase "to legislate in all cases for the general interests of the union"—the previous day's tie vote over a motion to instruct a committee to report "a specification of the powers comprised in the general grant" already pointed to the course debate would take.[39] In practice, this was the charge under which the committee of detail operated in preparing Article VII of its report, which replaced the broad language of the Virginia Plan with a finite list of particular powers. Though it has been argued that this action marked a crucial, even subversive shift in the deliberations,[40] the fact that it went unchallenged suggests that the committee was only complying with the general expectations of the Convention. Where the committee lacked instructions, some of its actions clearly reflected special concerns of its members.[41] But the process that unfolded during its ten days of labor is better explained as an effort to identify particular areas of governance where there were "general Interests of the Union," where the states were "separately incompetent," or where state legislation could disrupt the national "Harmony."

What the committee's report instead revealed was the difficulty of enlarging the responsibilities of national government much beyond those that the Continental Congress already possessed or that it was generally agreed it should acquire. To "the Legislative Rights vested in Congress by the Confederation," the committee proposed to add the power to lay and collect taxes, regulate interstate and foreign commerce, establish a uniform rule of naturalization, subdue rebellion within individual states, raise an army without relying on the states for the recruitment of soldiers, and "to call forth" the militia to enforce national laws and treaties and to "suppress insurrections, and repel invasions." In practical terms, the committee thus defined the "common interests" to embrace little more than matters of foreign relations and general commerce. Its notion of the areas where independent action of the states could be deemed incompetent or unharmonious similarly expanded only slightly the restrictions already imposed by the Confederation.[42]

Far from being surprised by the report, most framers agreed that the scope of national lawmaking would remain modest. As ardent a nationalist as Gouverneur Morris even wondered if Congress would need to meet annually, as the committee proposed. This was "improper," he asserted on August 7. "The public business might not require it." Rufus King agreed. Earlier he had confessed that while he "doubted much the practicability of annihilating the states," he "thought that much of their power ought to be taken from them." Now King observed:

> The most numerous objects of legislation belong to the states. Those of the Natl. Legislature were but few. The chief of them were commerce & revenue. When these should be once settled, alterations would be rarely necessary & easily made.

Mason and Sherman thought this assessment too sanguine. "The extent of the Country will supply business," Mason argued, and even if it did not, annual meetings were "an essential safeguard of liberty" still required because Congress would also possess "inquisitorial powers, which can not safely be kept in suspension." This was the Whig orthodoxy to which Mason and Sherman remained faithful, but its continued sway did not disguise the expectation, as Wilson later noted, that "War, Commerce, & Revenue were the great objects of the Genl. Government."[43] Nor did the further legislative powers (beyond those listed by the committee of detail) that the Convention approved in August radically enlarge this conception.

Both the committee and the Convention were thus concerned less with broadening the objects of the national government than with guaranteeing that it would possess the powers necessary to secure its ends. This purpose was best expressed in the two clauses that authorized the national legislature to lay and collect taxes and to enact "all laws that shall be necessary and proper" to execute its powers and those vested in the other branches of the government. The Convention left one aspect of taxation deliberately ambiguous. "No one answd.," Madison noted on August 20, when "King asked what was the precise meaning of *direct* taxation"—that is, that class of taxes that were to be apportioned among the states according to the same three-fifths rule whose real purpose was to legitimate the sectional compromise over representation.[44] No such uncertainty arose when the framers considered whether the national legislature should be fully empowered to lay and collect taxes. Though a few delegates hinted that the new government might still resort to the "*federal principle,* of requiring quotas" in the form of requisitions upon the states,[45] experience had proved that the only workable revenue system was one that left the Union completely independent of the states. Consistent with their expectations about the modest responsibilities of the new government, the framers believed that its revenue needs would be met through a program of indirect taxation centering on import duties—the most productive and least burdensome forms of revenue available to the prudent statesman. But they balked at limiting its revenues to that source alone. The only restriction placed on the discretion of the legislature was to prohibit it from laying duties on exports.

Nor did the framers question the decision of the committee of detail to include the "necessary-and-proper" clause in its list of legislative powers. As with the quiet evolution of the supremacy clause, the lack of controversy over this clause suggests that they did not regard it as augmenting the powers already vested in the national government. The necessary-and-proper clause passed unanimously on August 20. Only at the close of the Convention did Randolph, Mason, and Gerry make its passage one of their objections to the Constitution.[46] There is no reason to think that the framers believed the necessary-and-proper clause would covertly restore the broad discretionary conception of legislative power in the Virginia Plan.

From the framers' perspective, the "more perfect union" embodied in the Constitution created a model of federalism far more complex than either the Confederation or the program that Madison had introduced, and which had dramatically enlarged his colleagues' understanding of their agenda even as they resisted the conclusions to which its author was most attached. The framers most closely followed Madison's thinking in enabling a fully formed national government to legislate directly on the population and in giving it the means to command the resources required to discharge its duties. But their decisions on issues of representation also compromised his image of a government liberated from the political influence of the state governments, while the replacement of the negative on state laws by a supremacy clause resting on the dual authority of national and state judiciaries offered at best a problematic solution to the radical vice of the Confederation.

∞

How to present an "accurate" account and defense of these arrangements was the great intellectual challenge that confronted the Federalists after September 17. It required a sustained effort to explain the
complex model of federalism the Constitution proposed, and to do so in
a highly charged atmosphere in which familiar axioms and an ingrained
distrust of innovation fanned conspiratorial explanations of what had
transpired in Philadelphia. For Anti-Federalists, the decisive fact about
the Constitution was how much more "national" it was than the Confederation; for the framers, by contrast, the greater irony was that it was
much more "federal" than the alternatives they had rejected. But this was
a difficult point to establish in debate, when fidelity to the rule of secrecy
limited what they could disclose of the reasoning behind their conclusions. While they could allude to the obvious compromises that had
shaped the Senate, they were not free to justify the supremacy clause by
comparing it with the negative, or to explain that the necessary-and-
proper clause gave less support to a doctrine of implied powers than did
the Virginia Plan's initial grant of discretionary legislative authority. Even
divulging that the Convention had rejected such measures could be taken
as proof that the framers had simply found more subtle means to pursue
their schemes of consolidation.

As Anti-Federalists used this loaded term, *consolidation* had two
distinct meanings: one descriptive, the other predictive. They did not entirely agree whether consolidation inhered in the "absolute and uncon-
troulable power" the Union would immediately possess over those
"objects" placed under its control; or whether it was better conceived as a
tendency that would unfold gradually but ineluctably as the new government deployed its powers and monopolized the most productive sources
of revenue to render the states impotent for all effective purposes of government. Used in the first sense, the Constitution amounted to consolidation merely because it ceased to be a pure confederation in which "the
state governments stand between the union and individuals" and "the laws
of the union operate only on states, as such, and federally."[47] Used in the
second sense, *consolidation* marked the ultimate destination toward which
the Constitution must verge. While conceding that "a partial consolidation" was possible in theory, or even that the Constitution "appears to be
partly federal," leading Anti-Federalists insisted that the Constitution was
"calculated ultimately to make the states one consolidated government,"
and dismissed Federalist rebuttals on this head as disingenuous.[48] Again

seizing on Wilson's speech of October 6, they argued that the various electoral functions of the states hardly dispelled the fear that the Constitution was "designedly framed, to reduce the state governments to mere corporations, and eventually to annihilate them." Far from giving the states a vital role in the federal system, these tasks would survive only as vestigial symbols of a hollow sovereignty. "Who is so dull as not to comprehend," wailed "Centinel"—in direct reply to Wilson, and with implicit homage to Machiavelli—"that the *semblance* and *forms* of an ancient establishment, may remain, after the *reality* is gone[?]"[49] The clause guaranteeing the states "a republican *form* of government" spoke all too "honestly," Thomas Tredwell told the New York convention; "the mere form" alone would remain while "the substance . . . is swallowed up by the general government."[50] What confidence or even interest would the people bestow on the state legislatures, his colleague Melancton Smith asked, should they be reduced to "meet once in a year to make laws for regulating the height of your fences and the repairing of your roads?"[51]

Common to both definitions of consolidation was a deeper assumption that set the larger dispute between the parties in its true light. For Federalists, the conceptual problem of federalism was to locate and map a middle ground between confederation and consolidation or—to use a different image—to explain how two levels of government could attain equilibrium. But the idea that such a middle ground could ever be discovered or any equilibrium long maintained was exactly what Anti-Federalists denied. No claim was more crucial to their entire case than that ratification of the Constitution could lead only to the "annihilation" of the states.

Anti-Federalists rested their argument for the inevitability of consolidation on three propositions. The first invoked the familiar axiom which held that "*imperium in imperio* was a solecism in politics." Two sovereign authorities could not coexist within one polity; one or the other had to be supreme; and because power itself was dynamic, the loser in the competition must expect its authority to continue to atrophy. The notion of *imperium in imperio* was so commonplace that it needed no further attribution, but the second axiom that Anti-Federalists cited appeared under a familiar banner. As even casual students of politics knew, Montesquieu had observed that a stable republic could safely operate only over "a contracted territory" whose citizens shared the same customs and interests, but manifestly not over as large a territory as the United States. Consolidation was inevitable because so arbitrary, aristocratic, or despotic a form of national government could never brook the rivalry of the states. The final presumption sustaining the case for consolidation bore the imprint of the ideology that had carried the colonists from resistance to revolution in the decade before independence: the belief that the innate human craving for power would exploit any opportunity to exercise dominion. Create a constitution that merely permitted the abuse of power, this theory predicted, and those who wielded it would soon find and exploit its weakest points for their own insidious and ambitious ends.

This third conviction was the force that drove Anti-Federalist writers to ask which features of the Constitution were most likely to prove vulnerable to manipulation. Most of the other, ostensibly distinct criticisms of the Constitution that figured in their writings—the adequacy of its schemes of representation and separation of powers, the potential aristocracy of the Senate, the necessity of a bill of rights—were at bottom designed to specify the paths and mechanisms that would produce the dread result. More than any other issue, the overarching problem of federalism elicited from Anti-Federalists the complete variety of arguments of which they were capable, from their mechanical application of tested axioms to their capacity to extract ominous portents of tyranny from seemingly minor and harmless clauses.

If the New York writer "Brutus" was not quite the first to sound the alarm about consolidation, his writings offered perhaps the most thorough and acute analysis of its likely sources that any Anti-Federalist provided. As "Brutus" observed in his opening essay of October 18, 1787, the "first question" to ask was whether the states "should be reduced to one great republic, governed by one legislature, and under the direction of one executive and judicial; or whether they should continue thirteen confederated republics, under the direction and controul of a supreme federal head for certain defined purposes only?" True, the Constitution did not "go to a perfect and entire consolidation, yet it approaches so near to it, that it must, if executed, certainly and infallibly terminate in it." The sources of consolidation lay not only in such obvious places as the necessary-and-proper clause and the supremacy clause, but also in the "unlimited" power of the national government over taxation and the "extensive" jurisdiction vested in the national courts. Taken together, these provisions revealed that "all ideas of confederation are given up and lost" because the powers of the national government were "absolute and perfect . . . with respect to every object to which it extends," and because those objects would "extend to every case that is of the least importance—there is nothing valuable to human nature, nothing dear to freemen, but what is within its power." Expansive as this claim might seem, it rested on one secure foundation. Taxation, "Brutus" noted, was "the most important of any power that can be granted; it connects with almost all other powers, or at least will in process of time draw all others after it"; it was "the great engine of tyranny and oppression." Here was where the ominous language of the necessary-and-proper and the supremacy clauses laid a constitutional basis for legislation by which "the government of a particular state might be overturned at a single stroke, and thereby be deprived of every means of its support." Even if the Constitution itself did not "warrant a law of this kind," "Brutus" concluded, the very fact that such a result was possible in theory predicted the inevitable outcome. For the "unerring experience of ages" proved that "every body of men, invested with power, are ever disposed to increase it, and to acquire a superiority over every thing that stands in their way."[52]

Having established that the Constitution invited consolidation simply because it permitted it, "Brutus" returned to his original question: "whether it be best the United States should be reduced to one great republic, or not?" Answering this query in the negative, he predictably invoked the authority of Montesquieu: "If respect is to be paid to the opinion of the greatest and wisest men who have ever thought or wrote on the science of government, we shall be constrained to conclude, that a free republic cannot succeed over a country of such immense extent, containing such a number of inhabitants, and these encreasing in such rapid progression as that of the whole United States." Did not the evidence of history prove that as small republics "extended their conquests over large territories," their forms of government were transformed "into the most tyrannical that ever existed in the world"?[53] For other writers, such appeals often served as little more than ritualized incantation, but in "Brutus" they inspired a sustained attempt to explain why "an extensive republic" was incompatible with the principles of "free government."

Beginning with assumptions essentially identical with those voiced by Madison, "Brutus" reached conclusions sharply opposed to the positions the framer was soon to publish in *The Federalist*. Like Madison, "Brutus" agreed that a free republic was best defined as a government in which "the people do not declare their consent by themselves in person, but by representatives"; he also recognized that a legislature elected from such "an extensive republic" would represent an extraordinary array of interests, manners, customs, and even climates, and that these differences would produce "a constant clashing of opinions" that would in turn complicate the adoption of legislation. For Madison, of course, it was precisely the existence of these differences in the larger society, coupled with his belief that a national assembly would recruit a superior class of lawmakers, that would hinder the adoption of ill-conceived measures—including those hinting at consolidation. "Brutus" drew a different lesson. If representatives found themselves unable to reconcile the "heterogeneous and discordant principles" for which they spoke, some other rule of action must fill the resulting vacuum.[54] "Brutus" found this rule in the play of ambition and influence within a small body in which a clique of "great and designing men" could use "their art and address, their soothing manners and civilities, and their cringing flattery, joined with their affected patriotism" to control their "honest and unsuspecting" colleagues. Again, this portrait of legislative politics closely resembled the harsh image of the state assemblies that Madison had sketched on the eve of the Convention; it differed only in denying that a national forum would render ordinary lawmakers more immune to the wiles of artful leaders.[55]

From their ambitious manipulations of the legislative process would presumably come those acts of taxation and usurpation that would erode the authority of the states. But "Brutus" went even further in explaining why the government would be led to enforce its law through the coercion of a standing army rather than the voluntary aid of the citizenry. "The confidence which the people have in their rulers, in a free republic, arises from their knowing them, from their being responsible to them for their conduct, and from the power they have of displacing them when they misbehave," he wrote. But the proposed Congress could never satisfy these conditions. So elite a body could not "resemble those who appoint them" or "represent the feelings, opinions, and characters of a great multitude"; its members would be little known to their own constituents, much less to residents of other districts who would have to vest trust in Congress collectively; while the very diversity of interests it represented would make it impossible for it to respond to the particular needs and concerns of individual states. Under such conditions, "Brutus" concluded, it was evident that the people "will have no confidence in their legislature, suspect them of ambitious views, be jealous of every measure they adopt, and will not support the laws they pass." For the designing rulers of this short-lived national republic, there could be only one recourse: to summon the armed forces, including the militia of the states, to execute national law upon a sullen populace. And a government that was prepared to enforce its dictates at the point of a bayonet could hardly permit the state governments to retain any authority that mattered.[56]

The claim that adoption of the Constitution would lead to armed tyranny struck Federalists as the most fantastic of their opponents' demagogic pronouncements. Though "Brutus" wrote less feverishly on this point than did other Anti-Federalists, he, too, held that the dangers of military despotism were not chimerical. Not only might rulers "employ [a standing army] for the purpose of promoting their own ambitious views," but an "equal, and perhaps greater danger is to be apprehended from their overturning the constitutional powers of the government, and assuming the power to dictate any form they please." Americans were not "so much better than the people of other ages and of other countries" in their capacity to withstand a Caesar or Cromwell. Had they not come perilously close to such treachery in 1783, when only Washington's intervention aborted a near-mutiny at the Newburgh encampment?[57]

From his treatment of the overt danger of standing armies, "Brutus" turned to a more subtle but arguably graver source of tyranny: the judicial power of the United States. While professing to lack the "degree of law knowledge" required to give this subject "that full and minute explanation" it deserved, the five concluding essays "Brutus" devoted to the "nature and extent of the judicial powers" rank among the most acute Anti-Federalist analyses of any aspect of the Constitution, and describe the theory of judicial review as acutely as the equivalent statement of Hamilton in *Federalist* 78.[58] As "Brutus" read Article III, the federal judiciary would clearly exercise a final power of interpreting the meaning of the Constitution and the laws, and because its jurisdiction extended to cases "in equity," it would also enjoy a considerable "latitude of construction." The judges "will give the sense of every article of the constitution, that may from time to time come before them," he wrote.

> And in their decisions they will not confine themselves to any fixed or established rules, but will determine, according to what appears to them, the reason and spirit of the constitution. The opinions of the supreme court, whatever they may be, will have the force of law; because there is no power provided in the constitution, that can correct their errors, or controul their adjudications. From this court there is no appeal. And I conceive the legislature themselves, cannot set aside a judgment of this court, because they are authorised by the constitution to decide in the last resort. The legislature must be controuled by the constitution, and not the constitution by them.

Thus far, "Brutus" treated judicial review as an aspect of separation of powers, but he soon indicated that its real force would lie along the axis of federalism, where it would "operate to effect, in the most certain, but yet silent and imperceptible manner, what is evidently the tendency of the constitution:—I mean, an entire subversion of the legislative, executive and judicial powers of the individual states." The "equivocal" and "ambiguous" language of key clauses and the broad purposes stated in its preamble would enable the Court to adopt "an equitable construction" of the

Constitution consistent with its "spirit, intent and design . . . as well as the words in their common acceptation." Moreover, just as federal judges would have a stake in "using this latitude of interpretation" to broaden the powers of Congress because that in turn would redound to "enlarge the sphere of their own authority," so judicial determinations would point out to Congress the "bounds" to which it could aspire.[59] In a telling and entirely unironic example, "Brutus" seized upon the preamble to demonstrate how far an equitable interpretation of the Constitution might carry. What did it mean to "form a more perfect union" of the American people? "Brutus" asked. "Now to make a union of this kind perfect," he answered, "it is necessary to abolish all inferior governments, and to give the general one compleat legislative, executive and judicial powers to every purpose." Such a result would not be accomplished by a single fiat, only with "as much celerity, as those who have the administration of [the general government] will think prudent," as courts struck down state laws interfering with the "exclusive jurisdiction" of Congress or areas of "concurrent jurisdiction."[60]

Whether or not this language was as malleable or enticing as "Brutus" supposed, he grasped the central thrust of Article III as clearly as any Federalist commentator, and his dark musings were no less plausible than Madison's bland assertion of the "impartiality" of federal judges. If "Brutus" did not always resist the Anti-Federalist tendency to locate grave threats in seemingly innocuous clauses or to sound the tocsin of military despotism, there was nothing disingenuous or demagogic about the importance he attached to the unlimited power of taxation, the relation between scales of representation and popular obedience to law, or the potential scope of judicial power; nor was it palpably wrongheaded to imply that the supremacy and necessary-and-proper clauses could be interpreted to enable the national government to undertake any project it favored. These were central features of the Constitution, and the criticisms "Brutus" directed against them merited serious rebuttal.

Other Anti-Federalists echoed these criticisms—though rarely with the cogency of "Brutus"—while locating additional threats of consolidation in other clauses. After mounting a sustained attempt to explain why the Constitution was far closer to a "consolidated government" than a properly organized "federal republic," the "Federal Farmer" devoted much of his final essay to the danger of empowering Congress to enact uniform bankruptcy laws and to exercise exclusive rights of government over both the national capital and such "places" as it might acquire from the states "for the erection of forts, magazines, arsenals, dock-yards, and other needful buildings."[61] But the ingenuity with which Anti-Federalists conjured up this parade of horribles mattered less than the common assumptions that gave underlying coherence to their separate visions of consolidation. On key points they shared a broad consensus. Republican government and an extended territory were incompatible; *imperium in imperio* was a solecism in politics; an unlimited power of taxation enforced by a federal judiciary armed with a supremacy clause was a formula to reduce state governments to indigence and impotence. If the exact path to consolidation remained hidden, these were the devices that ambitious rulers would utilize as their lust for dominion drove them to eliminate the states.

TO REFUTE THESE ALLEGATIONS of consolidation, Federalists ultimately had to answer two fundamental questions: How was federalism possible in theory? and How would it work in practice? The first question was arguably the more urgent because it forced Federalists to counter those prevailing axioms about the optimal size of republics and the "monstrosity" of *imperium in imperio*; but in many ways it was also easier to answer because Federalists could rally around the advantages of union and the necessity of replacing the Articles with an effective government. Answering the second question was a more prosaic but daunting (because tedious) task. Even such astute commentators as Noah Webster and Alexander C. Hanson balked at mounting the systematic inquiry needed to describe how federalism would operate in practice, with the tepid excuse that it would "require more time than I could bestow on it" or that it "would be a painful and needless undertaking."[62] Many Federalists preferred to rest their defense of federalism on simpler grounds. Often they discredited the case for consolidation by equating its more fantastic predictions with the obsessive tendencies of Anti-Federalist thinking. The power of Congress to alter state regulations for congressional elections gained surprising prominence, for example, not only because Anti-Federalists harped on it so often, but also because Federalists could readily defend it as a prudent measure to deal with contingencies unlikely to occur yet still worth anticipating.

Federalists also made a great virtue of necessity. Much of their case relied on general arguments for union that required little specific reference to the Constitution and which any intelligent writer could muster simply by recalling the events and concerns that had brought about the Convention. Merely reciting the litany of weaknesses ascribed to the Confederation could support the conclusion that this new model of federalism had to be tried because the older version had been weighed in the balance and found wanting. What alternatives to the Constitution did Americans have? Dickinson asked in his "Fabius" letters. Those who held to the "proposition" that "a very extensive territory cannot be ruled by a government of republican form" seemed to intend "to abolish all ideas of connection, and to precipitate us into the miseries of division, either as single states, or partial confederacies."[63] The belief that adoption of the Constitution was politically necessary made it all the easier to argue that federalism was theoretically possible.

Yet as Madison and Hamilton perhaps best understood, the truths of federalism lay as much in its details as in its grand premises. That was why they accepted the enormous burden in *The Federalist* of providing the comprehensive overview of federalism that other sympathetic commentators shrewdly avoided. Many of the individual points they developed were made by other writers, often with greater elegance and effect. But if the great conceptual problem was to see the federal system both as a whole *and* in its parts, then only a sustained examination could justly describe its inherent complexities and therefore ambiguities. No one else mapped the contours of federalism half as systematically—or with as much awareness of the difficulty of erecting and maintaining its essential landmarks. For as historians know better than ratifiers could have guessed, these two architects of the new federalism privately numbered among its great doubters. And that in turn gives their exposition a further ironic authority. For in dispelling the specter of consolidation, Madison and Hamilton could be entirely sincere because they still doubted that the Convention had in fact solved the dilemma of divided sovereignty in a way that would give the Union the decided advantage over the states.

Before a detailed exposition of federalism could proceed, crucial definitions and propositions had to be established. This was the task that Madison and Hamilton undertook in devoting early essays of *The Federalist* to restating Madison's theory of the extended republic, and which James Wilson also took on when he presented his doctrine of popular sovereignty to the Pennsylvania convention. As contributions to a general theory of federalism, these statements sought to clear away misconceptions that could only cloud popular thinking about the Constitution. But they were equally noteworthy as efforts to publicize ideas that their authors regarded as fresh contributions to the science of politics that they avowed the Constitution would "improve."

Wilson's attack on *imperium in imperio* is a case in point. When he first answered the charge of consolidation in his speech of October 6, Wilson merely argued that the role accorded the states in electing national officials proved that their continued vitality was essential to the federal scheme. He repeated this argument in Harrisburg, but now he embedded it within the more powerful doctrine of popular sovereignty. While accepting the conventional definition of sovereignty as a unitary entity, Wilson argued that it was fundamentally wrong to regard sovereignty as the property or attribute of *any* government, and that Americans had already rejected this notion by resorting to written constitutions. "To control the power and conduct of the legislature by an overruling constitution was an improvement in the science and practice of government reserved to the American states," Wilson observed. But it did not follow that sovereignty itself "was vested in the constitutions." Rather, it "*remains in the people*," who were free to alter "constitutions whenever and however they please," and thereby to delegate to particular governments the specific powers they wished them to exercise. "Unless the people are considered in these two views"—as "forming" two political communities whose respective powers were always subject to revision by a sovereign people—"we shall never be able to understand the principle on which this system was constructed." For Wilson, this conclusion was no rhetorical sleight of hand but a logical outgrowth of the underlying democratic theory that he had applied to the entire corpus of issues the Convention faced.[64]

Just as Wilson used popular sovereignty to subvert the maxim of *imperium in imperio*, so Madison directed *Federalist* 10 to undermine the axiom which held that republican government was incompatible with the administration of an extended domain. Read strictly, *Federalist* 10 does not directly address the principal problem of federalism: the allocation of power between levels of government. Rather, it compares two sizes of republics—national and provincial—to the end of predicting that one extended republic of United States might be superior on two counts. First, it would prove more resistant to the liberty-endangering effects of faction; second, it would recruit a superior class of legislators qualified to act as "proper guardians of the public weal." This was less a descriptive account of how federalism would work than a preliminary explanation of why it was possible, hinging on the crucial definition that republics of any size depended on the existence of "the scheme of representation." *Federalist* 10 followed Hamilton's immediately preceding essay in suggesting that a national republic will lend greater stability to the provincial republics from which it will be formed, but even then Madison went no further than to imply that outbreaks of factious behavior would be safely quarantined within the boundaries of individual states.[65]

Federalism, in the strict sense, emerged as a subject only in *Federal-*

ist 15. Although attributed to Hamilton, this essay bears strong marks of having been written either in collaboration with Madison or with his memorandum on the vices of the Confederation lying at Hamilton's side.[66] After a peroration decrying that "We may indeed with propriety be said to have reached almost the last stage of national humiliation," Hamilton took as his point of departure the observation that "the great and radical vice" of the Confederation lies "in the principle of LEGISLATION FOR STATES OR GOVERNMENTS in their CORPORATE or COLLECTIVE CAPACITIES, and as contradistinguished from the INDIVIDUALS of which they consist." This, indeed, accurately captured the crucial premise on which the Convention had acted; once that premise was accepted, it followed that any effective solution to the problems of national governance required the creation of a fully empowered national government. But the coauthors of *The Federalist* evidently felt that this premise had to be defended at length—and with the kind of historical reasoning their opponents respected—for in three succeeding essays (*Federalist* 18–20) Madison summarized his researches in the history of ancient and modern confederacies to support the same conclusion before Hamilton reviewed the defects of the Confederation in two further essays.

For all their power, these arguments offered only a preface to a more comprehensive exposition of federalism. Demonstrating that federalism was possible in theory was not the same as proving that consolidation would prove improbable in practice. For Anti-Federalist fears were directed less against the immediate legal authority the new government would exercise than against its aggrandizing tendencies over time. It still remained to be considered whether the dangers alleged to lurk in particular clauses were plausible or fanciful: whether uniting the purse and the sword in a government insufficiently attached to the rights of its constituents and armed with the necessary-and-proper and supremacy clauses might yet reduce the state governments to vestiges of their former power.

One problem that Federalists encountered in disputing these allegations was that it was not easy to juggle theoretical premises and practical details. Something of this fate befell the three letters that Tench Coxe (writing as "A Freeman") published in the winter of 1788 to rebut the dissenters of the Pennsylvania convention. Coxe opened his letters by rather fumblingly attempting to establish principled grounds for denying that it was the "*intention of the late convention*" to seek "*the final annihilation of separate state government or sovereignty, by the nature and operations of the proposed constitution.*" Coxe hit his stride only when he undertook to draw up a balance sheet comparing the limited powers to be given to Congress with the residual "state powers . . . that are so requisite to our system, *that they cannot be dispensed with.*" In rendering this account, Coxe's commercial training served him well. While noting the various roles that the states would play in selecting national officials, Coxe emphasized that most objects of legislation would remain the exclusive or preponderant preserve of the states: the regulation of religion; the law of descents and entail (where he endorsed in passing "a perfect equality, at least among the males, and possibly among the females"); altering and amending constitutions; chartering "corporations for literary, religious, commercial, or other purposes"; enforcing criminal law; and "all the innumerable disputes about property lying within their respective territories between their own citizens, such as titles and boundaries of lands, debts by assumption, note, bond, or account, mercantile contracts." Nor was even this catalogue exhaustive.

> 14thly. The several states can create corporations civil and religious; prohibit or impose duties on the importation of slaves into their own ports; establish seminaries of learning; erect boroughs, cities and counties; promote and establish manufactures; open roads; clear rivers; cut canals; regulate descents and marriages; license taverns; alter the criminal law; constitute new courts and offices; establish ferries; erect public buildings; sell, lease, and appropriate the proceeds and rents of *their lands*, and of every other species of *state property*; establish poor houses, hospitals, and houses of employment; regulate the police; and many other things of the utmost importance to the happiness of their respective citizens.

In his third letter, Coxe went on to note that the "lordship of the soil" which "remains *in full perfection* with every state" constituted "one of the most valuable and powerful appendages of sovereignty," and he further enumerated the various sources of revenue that the states would retain as "indisputable proofs of *sovereignty*." Coxe overreached himself perhaps only in his idiosyncratic and constitutionally dubious claim that states could apply their powers over treason and impeachments to punish any representative or senator "who may mediate the annihilation of the government of his state."[67]

Nowhere did Coxe display the theoretical acuity of Wilson or Madison. Yet his commonsense account of what government would actually do correctly anticipated that for decades to come the real burden of domestic governance would lie upon the states, while the federal government was content to deliver mail, collect customs duties, and manage its western territory.[68] But Coxe's defense of the Constitution could not completely answer the deeper fears on which the case for consolidation drew. How would the states be protected in those areas where their authority and that of the Union overlapped, or where these two levels of government competed directly for the loyalties of the people?

The most comprehensive answer to these charges was found in the several consecutive series of essays in *The Federalist* in which Hamilton examined issues of national defense (23–29) and revenue (30–36) and Madison considered the distribution of legislative powers (41–46). These essays followed the broad discussion of the advantages of union and the defects of confederation that began in *Federalist* 9–10, and they were punctuated by Madison's general reflections on constitution-making in *Federalist* 37–40. Read carefully, they illuminated three essential elements of the argument for federalism: the necessity for unrestricted national authority in certain crucial areas; the possibility of concurrent national and state action in others; and a comparison of the responsibilities and advantages that each would possess after the Constitution was adopted. As this progression suggests, the tenor of these essays moved from certainty and assertion toward indeterminacy and hesitancy—from arguments which presented the case for national power with near-inductive logic to a balanced weighing of the fluidity of political loyalty within a federal system.

No one was better prepared to state the nationalist case for federalism than Hamilton, especially when the powers to be justified fell under the rubric of defense and taxation. He had brooded on these problems for a decade, pondering the wartime experiences that made so many Continental officers supporters of the nationalist creed the Constitution inspired. But Hamilton was an exceptional convert. None of his contemporaries equaled his command of modern theories of public finance or his cold, sharp appraisal of the motives that animate nations in their endless struggles for power and advantage.[69] His treatment of national defense and revenue in *The Federalist* is striking for its lack of equivocation and its refusal to placate the venerable fears that gave the Anti-Federalist alarm over uniting purse and sword its resonance.

The central problem of federalism, Hamilton explained, was to "discriminate the OBJECTS . . . which shall appertain to the different provinces or departments of power" that would operate within the "compound" governments of the confederation, "allowing to each the most ample authority for fulfilling the objects committed to its charge." One could indeed debate whether any federal government was necessary, "but the moment it is decided in the affirmative, it will follow, that the government ought to be clothed with all the powers requisite to complete execution of its duty." Where any power of defense had to be vested at all, *Federalist* 23 asserted, it "ought to exist without limitation, *because it is impossible to foresee or define the extent and variety of national exigencies, or the corresponding extent and variety of the means which may be necessary to satisfy them.*"[70] Hamilton applied the same principle and adopted the same tone when he turned to taxation. In a noteworthy departure from the reliance "Publius" usually placed on experience as the primary source of political knowledge, *Federalist* 31 described "the necessity of a general power of taxation in the government of the Union" as the equivalent in "the sciences of morals and politics" of one of those "primary truths, or first principles upon which all subsequent reasonings must depend" in sciences such as geometry. Once it was agreed that "A government ought to contain in itself every power requisite to the full accomplishment of the objects committed to its care," it again followed that the power to raise revenue must be "unqualified."[71]

Between the cases of defense and revenue, however, lay one notable difference. It was much easier to ridicule the claim that Congress would rule by the sword than to explain how two governments could simultaneously derive adequate revenues from a people not known for their cheerful compliance with taxation. How could the purse and sword be improperly united when the authority to raise and command troops was distributed among three branches of government, one elected by the people at the same biennial interval when appropriations for defense would expire, the second by the same state legislatures whose authority would have to be crushed for consolidation to occur, and the third (the presidency) constitutionally independent of the other two in the conduct of military operations? Our fears of standing armies, Hamilton observed in *Federalist* 26, rested on "habits of thinking which we derive" from English history and which were being uncritically applied to American conditions. He was equally scornful of the "inflammatory ravings" of those "distempered enthusiasts" who imagined that the power to call the militia into national service would be used to march the citizen soldiers of one state hundreds of miles "for the purpose of riveting the chains of slavery upon a part of their countrymen."[72]

The question of taxation had to be treated more delicately. Because many Federalist writers took popular aversion to taxation so seriously, they were anxious to assure readers that the national government would rarely invoke its powers of direct taxation but rely instead on customs duties, which were commonly regarded as the most productive and least painful sources of revenue. By prohibiting states from levying their own duties on imports without the consent of Congress, the Constitution implied that they would have to rely on less popular forms of taxation, and to do so while net public costs would presumably grow as the national government expanded its activities. Therein lay the danger that moderate Anti-Federalists believed taxation posed. The problem was not that the leeches of the national government would drain the country of its wealth, or that its tax collectors would harry citizens in every nook and cranny of their farms, offices, and homes, as "Brutus" predicted in an especially lurid passage.[73] It was rather that the states must come out losers in an uneven competition. The Union could raise revenue easily and prosper; the states would prove vulnerable to constituent pressures, and wither.

Hamilton responded to this objection with a complex effort to make allowance for the needs of the states while affirming the priority of the Union. In *Federalist* 32—a text little studied today but closely read in the nineteenth century—he argued flatly that the states retained extensive powers of taxation over all categories of revenue except those explicitly reserved to the Union or denied to the states. "On all articles other than exports and imports," the two governments possessed "concurrent and coequal authority." While conceding that both governments might tax the same object, Hamilton identified several ways to mitigate potential conflicts. Though it was true that a federal tax "would be supreme in its nature and could not be legally opposed or abrogated" by the states, a national law "abrogating or preventing the collection" of a duly laid state tax would be "a usurpation of power not granted by the Constitution" and thus void. The mere prospect of dual taxation of one source of revenue would not of itself establish a "constitutional repugnancy" or "extinguish a pre-existing right of sovereignty" in the states. Hamilton did not fully explain, however, how this right would be affirmed or usurpation halted. *Federalist* 33 expressly stated that the supremacy clause did not cover "acts of the larger society which are *not pursuant* to its constitutional powers, but which are invasions of the residuary authorities of the smaller societies." Yet rather than seize this occasion to introduce the concept of judicial review that he would later develop at length in the concluding essays of *The Federalist*, Hamilton suggested that the judgment as to which taxes were permissible was essentially political. "If the federal government should overpass the just bounds of its authority and make a tyrannical use of its powers, the people, whose creature it is, must appeal to the standard they have formed, and take such measures to redress the injury done to the Constitution as the exigency may suggest and prudence justify."[74]

But politics might work to deter conflict in less drastic ways. Rather than assume that concurrent taxation must lead to confrontation, Hamilton intimated that "inconvenience," a sense of "reciprocal forbearance," and "sensible interest" would lead the national and state governments "mutually to abstain from those objects which either side may have first had recourse to."[75] Even more revealing was his effort to suggest that "in practice there is little reason to apprehend any inconvenience." Over time, "the wants of the States will naturally reduce themselves within *a very narrow compass*," he predicted in *Federalist* 34, while those of the Union would ultimately prove "altogether unlimited." Anti-Federalists need feel no alarm over the national advantage in taxation, Hamilton implied, because the revenue needs of the states would verge on insignificance! This prediction rested on a harsh but typically Hamiltonian view of world politics in which the great sources of public expense arose from the imperatives of national security—"wars and rebellions" were "the chief sources of expense in every government"—and the burden of debt they engendered.

> The expenses arising from those institutions which are relative to the mere domestic police of a state, to the support of its legislative, executive, and judicial departments, with their different appendages, and to the encouragement of agriculture and manufactures (which will comprehend almost all the objects of state expenditure), are insignificant in comparison with those that relate to the national defence.

Having the states retain exclusive rights to certain revenues—"internal" taxes on land and houses, for example—would thus be tantamount, in his "rough computation," to giving them "command of two thirds of the resources of the community to defray from a tenth to twentieth part of its expenses."[76]

Such an argument seemed calculated to prove that fears of consolidation were well founded. At the Convention Hamilton's fellow delegates had upbraided him when he spoke about the states with similar disdain, which makes it all the more puzzling that he could now couple a firm avowal of their constitutional rights with so slighting an account of their functions. What these essays make clear, in their emphasis on the necessity for *unlimited* national powers, is that Hamilton still believed that the great conceptual problem of federalism was not to explain how the states would retain sufficient sovereignty but to make Americans realize that a vigorous national government was essential to their security and welfare. He was prepared, however grudgingly, to offer the formal assurances that the politics of the ratification debate required, and in language so conclusive that Luther Martin gleefully cited it decades later when he championed the right of his state to tax the Second Bank of the United States in the landmark case of *McCulloch* v. *Maryland.* But Hamilton had left Philadelphia believing that the fate of the Constitution depended on more than its ratification, and he privately speculated on the additional conditions of its success in a loose set of "Conjectures about the new Constitution." At the minimum, a "good administration" under the likely presidency of Washington would be required to

> conciliate the confidence and affection of the people and perhaps en-
> able the government to acquire more consistency than the proposed
> constitution seems to promise for so extended a country. It may then
> triumph altogether over the state governments and reduce them to
> an entire subordination, dividing the large states into smaller districts.

But should this not occur, Hamilton ventured, "it is probable that the contests about the boundaries of power between the particular govern-ments and the general government and the *momentum* of the larger states in such contests will produce a dissolution of the Union."[77] Hamilton was already looking beyond ratification to consider what other measures and policies would be required to convert the ambiguous promise of the Con-stitution into the nation-state whose most ambitious architect he was in-tent on becoming.

Madison, too, had left Philadelphia worried that the Constitution "should it be adopted will neither effectually answer its national object nor prevent the local mischiefs which every where excite disgusts agst the state governments. The grounds of this opinion," he wrote to Jefferson on September 6, "will be the subject of a future letter." When he fulfilled his promise seven weeks later, he devoted the core of a seventeen-page summary of the Convention to an undiluted defense of the negative on state laws—a proposal he knew Jefferson must abhor but whose rejection he still lamented. Relying as it would on judicial power to maintain the boundaries between the Union and the "subordinate authorities" of the states, Madison concluded that the Constitution still "involves the evil of imperia in imperio." Nor did he think that the handful of restrictions im-posed on the state legislatures, even if obeyed, would be adequate "to se-cure individuals agst. encroachments on their rights."[78] The most to be hoped for, the penultimate paragraph of *Federalist* 10 suggested, was to quarantine outbreaks of legislative injustice within individual states and prevent them from infecting their neighbors or the Union at large.

The two principal authors of *The Federalist* differed little in their judgment of the defects of the Constitution, their opinions of state politics, or their assessment of the advantages the states enjoyed in commanding the loyalties of their constituents. Where they did diverge was in their understanding of exactly how "subordinate" or "inferior" a jurisdiction the states should retain. Unlike Hamilton, but more like Coxe, Madison recognized that most objects of governance would remain under their domain (which was why the negative on state laws was so essential). This difference was reflected in the systematic exposition of the Constitution that Madison launched with *Federalist* 37. When he reviewed powers of defense and taxation in *Federalist* 41, he echoed the positions Hamilton had taken. But as he moved on to the other powers of Congress and the relative strengths of national and state governments, Madison placed less emphasis on the necessity for unlimited national power than on understanding the limited ends to which that power would be directed and the residual authority and resources of the states.

Whereas Hamilton derived the case for unlimited powers of defense and revenue almost entirely from first principles, Madison used his transitional essays (*Federalist* 37–39) to explain why the effort to draw sharp and tidy lines between two distinct levels of government must be problematic. Some of the uncertainty of federalism inhered in the epistemology of political science. But it also reflected the framers' efforts to "combine" two principles that were not easily rendered compatible: the need for "the requisite stability and energy in government" with the "inviolable attention due to liberty and to the republican form." The effort to design a simple model of federalism must have been further complicated, he added, by the politics of the Convention—by the variety of interests that it represented. When Madison began to discuss federalism explicitly in *Federalist* 39, he had thus laid a basis for arguing more generally that "the real character of the government" was found in no single formula or definition, but could be discovered only by examining the entire system in its complexity.[79]

Once past these introductory formulations, Madison organized his discussion of federalism around two questions: "1. Whether any part of the powers transferred to the general government be unnecessary or improper? 2. Whether the entire mass of them be dangerous to the portion of jurisdiction left in the several States?"[80] The second question produced answers far more revealing than the first. Proving that the various powers vested in the national government were necessary and proper required little more than explaining why each was reasonable in itself. For the most part, Madison's survey of the legislative powers of Congress and the corresponding restrictions on the states was both brisk and sensible. In this survey, only two clauses of the Constitution received close analysis:

that guaranteeing each state a republican form of government, and the necessary-and-proper clause. An extended discussion of the first appealed to Madison because it allowed him to reprise his theory of faction—albeit in the extreme form of explaining why, contrary to "republican theory," a state might prove vulnerable to popular rebellion or subversion.[81] His discussion of the necessary-and-proper clause in *Federalist* 44 is arguably more significant, however, not only because the "sweeping clause" was vital to the case for consolidation but also because later dispute over its meaning helped launch the controversies that set Madison and Hamilton on opposite political courses after 1790.

Madison's analysis of this clause exhibited his penchant for resolving complex questions through carefully drawn distinctions. Madison considered but rejected four alternatives to the proposed clause. The Convention could have followed Article II of the Confederation by stipulating that the Union could exercise only powers "*expressly* delegated"; it could have compiled either a positive enumeration of powers necessary and proper to carry out the delegated powers or a negative enumeration of unnecessary and improper powers; or it could have rested entirely "silent on this head." The first remedy would risk crippling the government or inviting it to ignore the formal restraints; the second and third would require an impossibly long catalogue of acceptable or proscribed powers; while the last would produce exactly the result that Anti-Federalists dreaded because "[n]o axiom is more clearly established in law, than that wherever the end is required, the means are authorized." Something like the proposed clause was indeed necessary and proper, Madison concluded, but should Congress abuse it, two remedies remained. First, the "success of the usurpation will depend on the executive and judiciary departments, which are to expound and give effect to the legislative acts." And should they not act effectively, the people remained free, through the electoral process, to substitute representatives who would "annul the acts of the usurpers."[82]

Hamilton had reached the same conclusion in *Federalist* 33, but Madison pursued the argument further. The net losers in an act of congressional usurpation, he argued in *Federalist* 44, must be the state legislatures, and "these will be ever ready to mark the innovation, to sound the alarm, and to exert their local influence in effecting a change of federal representatives."[83] When he drafted the Virginia Resolutions opposing the Alien and Sedition Acts in 1798, Madison attempted to convert this prediction into a strategy of political opposition to meet a situation he had deemed improbable a decade earlier. The sources of his earlier skepticism could be found in the assessment of federal politics that Madison offered in *Federalist* 45 and 46 as he took up his second general question:

"whether the whole mass [of powers transferred to the federal government] will be dangerous to the portion of authority left in the several States." Echoing Wilson and Hamilton, Madison reminded readers that "The federal and State governments are in fact but different agents and trustees of the people, constituted with different powers, and designed for different purposes." He conceded, too, that "manifest and irresistible proofs of a better administration" might ultimately transfer popular loyalties and affection from the states to the Union.[84] But on balance it seemed likely that "The State governments will have the advantage of the Federal government" in every political respect, regardless of the legal force of the supremacy clause. Not only would the people at large feel more deeply interested in the activities of the state governments that would remain more intimately involved in the regulation of their ordinary affairs, but the rewards and benefits that they could bestow would exceed those emanating from a distant Union. Nor was it even likely that congressmen would possess great "prepossessions" in favor of enhancing national authority at the expense of the state. And in the unlikely event that national schemes to encroach upon the individual or collective rights of the states were launched, their governments would immediately provide an effective agency of resistance.[85]

Hamilton had said as much and more in his Convention speech of June 18. The acerbic tone in which both men had then derided the concept of statehood still resonated when Madison opened *Federalist* 45 by asking whether the Revolution had been fought to obtain whatever form of government seemed "essential to the happiness of the people," or simply to assure "that particular municipal establishments, might enjoy a certain extent of power, and be arrayed with certain dignities and attributes of sovereignty."[86] But if his assessment of the advantages of the states diverged little from the views he and Hamilton had voiced in June, the logic of the ratification debate led him to turn that perception to a different purpose. From his perspective—which Hamilton and Wilson still shared—the charge of consolidation was palpably false because the Constitution promised to fall far short of remedying all the vices they ascribed to the states. But whereas Hamilton was rash enough to predict that the functions of the states must decline in importance relative to those of the Union, Madison better grasped just how provincial American governance would long remain. Whereas Hamilton foresaw that war and security could prove as urgent to Americans as they did to Europeans, Madison tempered his estimate of the public concerns the Republic would face toward more pacific ends. "The operations of the Federal Government will be most extensive and important in times of war and danger," he wrote in *Federalist* 45; "those of the State Governments in times of peace and security. As the former periods will probably bear a small proportion to the latter, the State Governments will here enjoy another advantage over the Federal Government."[87]

WITHIN THE LANGUAGE of the Constitution, as it turned out, there was indeterminacy enough to confirm that both Federalists and Anti-Federalists were right in predicting how tempered or potent a government the Convention had proposed. Over the shorter run of a quarter century, Hamilton proved the superior prophet. The French Revolution, the wars it inspired, and the domestic disputes these contingent events provoked, encouraged both Hamiltonian Federalists and the Democratic-Republicans of Madison and Jefferson to apply national legislative power in ways that few supporters of the Constitution in 1788 might have envisioned. Over the longer run of the next century, Madison proved to have gauged the agenda of republican politics more accurately—though only after his party partly dismantled the Hamiltonian program for nationalism that had driven them into opposition within a few years of ratification. Whether the politics of the American republic would prove more "federal" or "national"—more oriented toward the statehouses of an expanding society or toward the drafty Capitol soon to be built in the federal district—was a function neither of the language of the Constitution nor of any grand principles that the framers implanted in their regime but of the various ways in which Americans weighed the advantages and disadvantages of pursuing their interests within the compound federal structure the Constitution both created and acknowledged. As James Wilson perhaps understood best, adoption of the Constitution would enable Americans to transfer their political loyalties and attachments from one level of government to another, but it could not by itself determine whether state or national institutions would prove most adaptable and responsive to these interests.

Here the intentions that ultimately mattered most were those not of the framers and ratifiers of 1787–88 but of the people themselves, both dispersed and united in congeries of interests, all seeking to mobilize one institution of government or another in their pursuit of happiness. The Constitution created a new framework within which their choices could be made, and the Supreme Court under Chief Justice Marshall enlarged it further by giving the necessary-and-proper clause and the supremacy clause expansive interpretations. But only politics (in the broadest sense) could determine how energy would flow within the complex array of institutions the American constitutionalists had inherited and only partly reformed. It took the better part of a century, civil war, and the transformation of the national economy to begin to convert the Union from a confederation into a polity more resembling a modern nation-state.

CHAPTER VIII

THE MIRROR OF
REPRESENTATION

IF ONE MAXIM reflected Americans' ideas of representation as much as the "solecism" of *imperium in imperio* governed their notions of sovereignty, it was the belief that a representative assembly "should be in miniature an exact portrait of the people at large. It should think, feel, reason and act like them."[1] So wrote John Adams in his *Thoughts on Government* of 1776. In Britain the idea that the people as a whole were somehow present in the House of Commons was a staple of Whig thinking, but when Adams invoked the metaphor of a "miniature" or "exact portrait," he gave the concept of representation a new precision that advocates of parliamentary reform had yet to attain.[2] Two years later Theophilus Parsons reworked Adams's language into the Essex County resolutions (commonly styled *The Essex Result*):

> The rights of representation should be so equally and impartially distributed, that the representatives should have the same views, and interests with the people at large. They should think, feel, and act like them, and in fine, should be an exact miniature of their constituents. They should be . . . the whole body politic, with all it's property, rights, and priviledges, reduced to a smaller scale, with every part being diminished in just proportion.[3]

The same sentiments were voiced when the Federal Convention first debated the popular election of the lower house. "The Legislature ought to be the most exact transcript of the whole Society," James Wilson declared on June 6. George Mason concurred a few minutes later. "The requisites in actual representation are that the Reps. should sympathize with their constituents; shd. think as they think, & feel as they feel," he observed; "so much so, that even the diseases of the people shd. be represented—if not, how are they to be cured?" Knowingly or not, Mason here echoed Edmund Burke, the Anglo-Irish parliamentarian and sometime agent for the colony of New York. Better a House of Commons "infected with every epidemical phrensy of the people," Burke had written in 1770, than one "wholly untouched by the opinions and feelings of the people out of doors."[4]

For the elite classes for whom both Mason and Burke spoke, this notion of sympathy connoted a measure of difference between a representative and his constituents. It was still a sentiment that had to be cultivated, like the condescension that enabled superiors to enter the mental world of their inferiors.[5] Pushed far enough, however, the idea that a representative body should be a miniature of society rested on the divergent assumption that only a concurrence or identity of interests could guarantee that legislators would act with the degree of accountability required to protect their constituents. Sympathy was most likely to exist, in other words, when electors and the elected *shared* underlying traits; sentiment alone would not do when the allure of power worked its charms. In this tension lay a fruitful source of disagreement.

As a specifically constitutional problem, the ambition of making a representative assembly into a sympathizing "mirror," "miniature," or "transcript" of society raised a number of other questions. One concerned the matter of *apportionment*, the problem that so perplexed the Convention. What were the appropriate constituencies to be represented: corporate entities (towns, counties, states) or aggregates of population (or population and wealth), and how equal (or proportional) a scale of apportionment should be followed? A second set of issues concerned *suffrage*. Who was eligible to vote in a republican polity: only the landed male property holders who possessed the full attributes of personal independence, or a wider community of adult males who could otherwise demonstrate their permanent attachment to the Republic—perhaps by risking their lives as its soldiers? And how, literally, were citizens to give their votes: by voicing their preference to the sheriff, who would then record their vote in a poll book, or by secret ballot; at a raucous public fete, with people gathered from miles around for the closest approximation to carnival a Protestant society could produce, or in widely separated polling places, with a decorum more suited to republican manners?

Important as these questions were, their solution was only instrumental to more profound ends. Was representation simply a device to replace the impracticable meeting of the people at large, in which case representatives should resemble their constituents as closely as possible? Or should representatives possess an independence of mind and a breadth of experience or knowledge that would provide a capacity for deliberation that ordinary citizens lacked? Did the "sympathy" desired of lawmakers require reinforcing the ties that bound them to the voters; or could it be attained, in adequate measure, through some act of imagination? The answers to these questions in turn reflected divergent definitions of the essential duties of representative institutions. Did they exist primarily to protect the people at large against arbitrary power by preventing government from acting without the expression of popular consent? Or did they not provide as well a mechanism whereby the people could authorize government to make law in the positive sense, actively adopting policies that would contribute to the prosperity of society and the happiness of its citizens?

John Adams hinted at the permutations and combinations of answers these questions could receive when he observed that "[o]f republics there is an inexhaustible variety, because the possible combinations of the powers of society are capable of innumerable variations."[6] In one form or another, all these questions came before the framers in Philadelphia and were reagitated during the debate over ratification. But two pairs of antinomies best capture the concerns that framed the debate over representation as it unfolded during these two phases of the adoption of the Constitution. At the Convention, the framers struggled to move beyond their preoccupation with the mechanics of representation—especially the dilemma of apportionment in *both* houses—to secure the qualitative improvement in the character of deliberation and legislation they desired. Once the Constitution was published, however, Federalists were hardpressed to defend this conception of representation against the more traditional norms to which Anti-Federalists clung when they worried that a small and elite Congress would lack the sympathy and local knowledge needed to protect the people at large against the abuse of power.

WHEN MADISON SET OUT to examine other federal systems in his pre-Convention researches, he had to cast a wide net to assemble a useful collection of samples. But Americans did not have to look far afield for the ideas, examples, and experiences on which to assess a scheme of national representation. Three sources lay close to hand: the Continental Congress that the Convention set out to reform or replace; the Parliament whose history framed the dominant narrative of Anglo-American constitutionalism; and the colonial and state assemblies in which Americans had fashioned their own understanding of the nature of representation and legislation.

Of these three sources, the existing Congress seemed to offer the most salient point of reference, but in fact it was useful largely as an example of everything a national legislature should not be. Indeed, by 1787 Congress had become such an object of scorn that it is a minor puzzle to explain why the framers retained its name for the new legislature. In ordinary usage, *congress* denoted a diplomatic assembly. This was the sense in which Burke once distinguished "a *congress* of ambassadors from different and hostile interests" from the true "*deliberative* assembly of *one* nation" that was Parliament; and conversely, when John Adams observed (in his *Defence of the Constitutions of Government of the United States*) that the Continental Congress was "not a legislative assembly, not a representative assembly, but only a diplomatic assembly," he implied that the name suited a body lacking the defining features of a legislature. Americans had used the term to describe an extraordinary meeting of deputies from individual provinces called to address issues of common concern, such as the Albany Congress of 1754 or the Stamp Act Congress of 1765. They naturally applied the same term to the delegates who gathered in Philadelphia in September 1774, even while they exalted the First Continental Congress not as a convocation of "hostile interests" but as the "collected wisdom" of the Continent. Once in place the name stuck, to be formalized in the Articles of Confederation as "The United States in Congress Assembled."

What kind of institution was Congress? Because its crucial duties involved matters of war and peace, powers traditionally identified in British practice as royal prerogatives, there were good grounds for regarding it as an essentially executive body—the successor less of Parliament than the Crown, which had exercised similar superintending powers over matters of common interest.[7] Its powers, one commentator noted in 1778, were those best described as "the external executive," while Congress itself was sometimes called a "supreme executive council" or "a deliberating executive assembly." Madison was clearly thinking in these terms when he observed in 1785 that "all the great powers which are properly executive [had been] transferd to the Federal Government."[8]

In its appearance and deliberations, however, Congress also resembled a legislature. It generally followed parliamentary rules, conducting routine business by electing committees that reported to the main body of delegates, who were often bogged down in procedural wrangles and prolonged debates of the sort that only a legislature could sustain. Congress was also a representative body: Its members served for (and were paid by) distinct constituencies, and its rule of voting embodied a principle of corporate representation. But if Congress looked like a legislature, it could neither enact statutes nor levy taxes—the two critical legislative powers. Instead, it ordinarily acted by resolutions and requisitions that it transmitted to the states for implementation through proper statutes; in a small number of cases requiring no intervening action by the states, it affixed the word *ordinance* to its decisions, indicating a note of uncertainty about their juridical character.[9]

As an institution, Congress was thus easier to describe than to categorize. When Thomas Jefferson read the first volume of Adams's *Defence*, its description of Congress was the sole point he singled out for comment. In Jefferson's view, Congress appeared "both legislative and executive," but "I doubt whether they are at all a diplomatic assembly." Adams conceded that the objection was a fair one.[10] A decade earlier, both men had participated in drafting the Confederation; what seems remarkable about this exchange is that two such expert commentators could disagree on so fundamental a point. From so anomalous an institution it was easier to draw lessons to avoid than solid precedents upon which to construct a true legislature.

Anomalies were inevitable in a body whose origins were more a response to an urgent revolutionary struggle than a considered effort to frame a durable national government. But a more profound objection precluded converting Congress into a true representative assembly. For were it to be elected by the people, as no less an authority than *Common Sense* proposed, what was to stop it from claiming equal powers with the legislatures of the states? When a debate over this question broke out in the spring of 1776 in Litchfield County, Connecticut, a worried member of the colony's delegation in Philadelphia explained why it would be dangerous to claim that the election of Congress was as much "the inherent birthright of every member of society" as the election of provincial lawmakers. Could such delegates "ever be called to acco[unt] by the assembly," Oliver Wolcott asked a friend back home, "or be displaced or receive any Instructions or advice from them more than from so many individuals"? But he then raised a more worrisome objection:

[A]nd would not the Colony be absolutely Bound (or rather I may say the people living within the present lines of the Colony, for upon this Idea they could hardly be called a Colony as they would have no separate Jurisdiction) by every Act their Delegates should do, as they would have all the Authority absolutely and independently which

the People could give them, as fully and compleatly as any of the
present Members of Parliament have, and if they should (being thus
Appointed) concurr in Adopting any Maxims intrenching never so
much on the Colony Constitution, would not the People be absolutely bound by their own Act? In a Word, would not the consequences (if attended to) reduce in a few years the Colony Jurisdiction
as low as the present Powers of our Selectmen—unless Imperium in
Imperio can exist?[11]

Wolcott transposed to Congress the same principle that cautioned against
colonial representation in Parliament. Representation was the mechanism
by which a people consented to be ruled, and if the colonies accepted
seats in the Commons, they would thereby bind themselves to obey its
acts. Eventually both Connecticut and Rhode Island permitted congressional delegates to be nominated by popular vote, but the state assemblies
retained the right of election.[12]

Keeping delegates accountable to the state legislatures was consistent
with the idea that Congress embodied a confederation of quasi-sovereign
states. Delegates were elected annually, and subject both to recall at any
time (though none ever were) and to instruction by their particular states.
On some issues, delegates clearly did act as ambassadors. The complicated maneuvers that surrounded the cession of western land claims and
the creation of a national domain constituted one such issue, and so did
numerous requests related to the financial and logistical burdens of the
war. But this ambassadorial model of the nature of representation in Congress often broke down in practice. Delegates frequently complained that
they lacked news of conditions in their home states, while communications with their official constituents in the legislatures were always erratic.
Overburdened and inefficient themselves, the assemblies often failed to
answer their delegates' requests for direction, much less generate instructions of their own. But when the delegates conducted their correspondence with the state executives, they had to deal with officials who often
had little if any influence over the legislatures. And under wartime conditions, any lag in correspondence made political coordination all the
more difficult. The accountability that the theory of confederation expected of delegates was thus frequently honored more in the breach than
the observance.[13]

While Congress remained something of a puzzle, a rich corpus of
historical and political writings made Parliament a vastly superior source
shaping American ideas of representation. The colonists had revolted
against Parliament before they renounced George III for upholding its

claims over America, and they had long since concluded that their own practice of representation was superior to the degraded institution whose decline they lamented from afar. Yet even after independence, Americans still regarded Parliament as a paradigmatic model of a representative assembly. Nor could they casually reject the great principles and lessons they associated with its history, when so much of their politics had revolved around securing for their own assemblies the same powers and privileges Parliament had confirmed for itself with the Glorious Revolution. This history influenced American thinking in three general respects: by stressing the traditional role of representation in protecting the rights of the people; by exposing the underlying contrast between the practice of representation in Britain and America; and by illustrating the emergence of a more modern conception of the nature of legislative activity itself.

In the traditional Whiggish theory to which the American revolutionaries subscribed, the great purpose of representation was to prevent the Crown and its subordinates from acting arbitrarily, without securing the consent of the people's representatives. In their efforts to govern without Parliament, and especially to raise something that looked very much like taxes without its consent, the Stuart kings had placed this question at the center of the great constitutional controversies of the seventeenth century. When the Glorious Revolution of 1688–89 resolved this great dispute by establishing the supremacy of Parliament, it did not convert the Crown into a mere executive agent of parliamentary will; it only confirmed that hereafter the Crown must conduct the affairs of state with the ongoing consent of Parliament. Supremacy did not liberate Parliament to make new law at its whim, much less inspire a politically awakened people to urge their representatives to pursue the policies they sought. Supremacy was rather a defensive concept whose overriding purpose was to prevent a recurrence of the arbitrary rule associated with the Stuart kings who had sought to raise revenues without the consent of Parliament, threatened customary rights and corporate liberties, and endangered the religious freedom of a Protestant people. As late as 1770, Edmund Burke gave voice to this conception of representation when he observed that the House of Commons was originally "designed as a control *for* the people," and that its "true characteristics" remained to provide "a vigilant and jealous eye over executory and judicial magistracy; an anxious care of public money; an openness, approaching towards facility, to public complaint."[14]

In the eighteenth century, however, this traditional notion of the constitutional role of Parliament was subject to at least two powerful stresses. The first was tied to the perceived use of influence and "corruption" to render Parliament the pliant tool of the Crown. How could Parliament possibly act as an independent check on the executive, much less maintain its supremacy, when successive ministries, beginning with the long reign of Robert Walpole (1721–42), could use patronage and influence to command stable and docile majorities in both houses? How could the House of Commons represent what Burke called "the express image of the feelings of the nation" when so many members were elected by a handful of easily managed voters in "pocket" and "rotten" boroughs, while populous towns went grossly underrepresented or not represented at all? How could the fiction that the whole people were virtually represented in the Commons be maintained when a limited franchise denied suffrage to entire classes of landholders as well as urban workers? If these conditions gave Georgian politics an underlying stability and complacency, they were not easily reconciled with the principle of parliamentary supremacy that gave Britain its "boasted," "vaunted" constitution. To a realist like David Hume, influence in all its forms might appear to be "necessary to the preservation of our mixed government," for the formal powers of Parliament would otherwise swamp the executive; but to its more ideological critics, and their American readers, the portents were more ominous.[15]

In place of the constitutional struggles of the Stuart era, the activities of Georgian parliaments increasingly involved the enactment of a host of statutes designed to support both the fiscal and military needs of a great imperial power and the development of the most dynamic economy in Europe. Here lay a second strain on the traditional image of Parliament, for it gave representatives other duties beyond monitoring the executive. Parliament was well on the way to becoming a legislature in the modern sense of the term. The idea that it might legislate in pursuit either of broad public good or on behalf of special interests purporting to serve the national good was not itself an eighteenth-century innovation. Numerous statutes in the past were ventures in social policy, including the Navigation Acts that helped propel Britain's economic transformation while defining the place of the colonies in a commercial empire. Many of the interests that this economy generated grew adept in the enterprise of securing legislative subsidies and exemptions to promote competitive advantage. A different source of this upsurge in lawmaking was the rash of penal statutes whose ready resort to capital punishment inspired one observer to wonder whether "the chief object of legislation in England" was "the extirpation of mankind."[16]

The point should not be overstated: Neither ministries nor parliamentary majorities nor electoral coalitions were formed to advance coherent legislative programs. "The great mass of legislation," one modern authority observes, "was personal and local in scope, largely consisting of enclosure bills, turnpike and canal bills, and naturalization bills . . . subjects that would now be regarded as questions for executive rather than Parliamentary decision."[17] But this surge in parliamentary lawmaking nonetheless had significant consequences. Complaints about the sheer growth of the statute book and Parliament's impulsiveness inspired reform proposals ranging from improving procedures for drafting bills and consolidating statutes to the sustained defense of the superiority of the remedies of common law and equity over the improvisations of statute. As David Lieberman has argued, such luminaries of eighteenth-century British legal theory as William Blackstone, Lord Chief Justice Mansfield, and Lord Kames shared a common project of defending (while reforming) traditional modes of adjuducation against the perceived vices of legislation. Whereas legislation was a blunt weapon, difficult to aim and prone to misfire, adjudication offered a more supple means of applying general rules to particular cases. But their concerns could not abate the pressure for legislation that arose from an enormous cluster of discrete interests, speaking not for the formal constituencies of boroughs and shires but for merchants, manufacturers, and all kinds of improvers seeking authority for the enclosure of commons and the construction of turnpikes, bridges, and canals. To advance these interests, "lobbyists"—literally those who solicited members in the lobby of the House of Commons—grew assiduous and skillful in their trade; while a small group of legal practitioners, led by one Robert Harper, developed a profitable business drafting the bills they sought.[18]

In this expansion of parliamentary lawmaking, we can see reflections of a more profound shift in British constitutional and legal theory. Once lawmaking became the essential activity of Parliament, it became easier to abandon the traditional understanding which regarded law as a restraint on the capacity of the Crown to act arbitrarily, and to accept in its place the modern notion which treated law simply as the command of the parliamentary sovereign. Good Whigs still paid lip service to the need to preserve the supremacy of Parliament over the Crown, but the reality was that Parliament was becoming an omnicompetent source of positive law. Perhaps the Commons could still respond to "the feelings of the nation," but in its unreformed state, it was more likely to pursue the interests of the propertied elite.

One assertion of this emerging theory of parliamentary sovereignty was the Declaratory Act of 1766, which affirmed that the American colonies were subject to Parliament "in all cases whatsoever." That assertion of sovereignty—of the power of parlimentary command—was the unresolvable issue on which the first British empire foundered. But in rejecting that claim, the colonists combined a healthy respect for the defensive purposes of representation with a marked awareness of the distinctiveness of American practice. Traditional ideas about representation retained a vitality in America they had lost "at home" because the structure of colonial politics preserved major elements of the Stuart struggles between royal prerogative and legislative privilege. Colonial governors exercised powers rendered obsolete in Britain—proroguing and dissolving assemblies, vetoing laws or suspending their operation, and appointing judges to serve at pleasure rather than during good behavior—and Americans could thus continue to believe that representative assemblies existed, in the first instance, to secure popular rights and liberties against arbitrary rule. The fears that political dissenters in England voiced over the erosion of parliamentary independence resonated in America because the colonial assemblies were still aspiring to secure the same powers they believed the Glorious Revolution had confirmed to Parliament.[19]

The colonists also knew, however, that representation was the one area of governance in which their practice already diverged most dramatically from that of Britain. They readily believed that the legitimacy of representation depended on maintaining close bonds between legislators and constituents; and they knew that the conditions of representation throughout America were superior to its degenerate state in Britain. By modern standards, obvious inequities still existed, of course. The franchise excluded not only the dependent classes of the unpropertied but a whole species of population whose bondage gave vivid meaning to the familiar definition of slavery as a condition in which laws were imposed on the governed without their consent. Yet by the standards of the era, access to the franchise and standards of apportionment were remarkably liberal and generous. Farmers' sons, tenants, and apprentices may have failed to meet property requirements for suffrage when they were enforced. But it was the absence of political competition, more than restrictions on the franchise, that kept the turnout in colonial elections low. New communities had generally received representation as they were organized—though the flood of new settlers into the interior in the final decades of the colonial era strained this principle, creating inequities that clearly favored the more densely settled seaboard.[20] "Pocket" and "rotten" boroughs simply did not exist, nor did Crown officials control the patronage needed to manage the legislative opposition they routinely encountered. The colonial assemblies thus possessed a measure of both independence *and* accountability that sharply departed from English practice.[21]

American practice likely diverged from the British model in one other respect. The circumstances of settlement had repeatedly led the assemblies to legislate in the active sense of the term, giving American lawmakers frequent occasion to innovate as they dealt with the range of problems the ordering of an entire social fabric entailed.[22] Often these conditions reflected the special characteristics of individual colonies. In Massachusetts and Connecticut, the impulse to legislate produced statutes requiring towns to implement the measures appropriate for a Puritan commonwealth. In the commodity-exporting colonies of the South, the most innovative legislation was found in the comprehensive slave codes that regulated the behavior of European and African-American populations alike. With a bench and bar far less developed than in Britain, Americans may also have regarded legislative initiative as a superior alternative to the gradual accretion of judicial doctrine.

Some caution is again required: The differences between colonial and parliamentary lawmaking may have been more of degree than kind. For all that has been written about "the rise of the assembly" in America, its legislative output has not been rigorously analyzed. It is instructive that in the presumably typical year of 1761 the Massachusetts General Court adopted only "three acts that were arguably legislative in the sense that they changed law or made new law." When statutes affecting an entire colony were enacted, they were likely to be acts of appropriation or taxation, or corrections of some common-law procedure. The ordinary business of any session was largely concerned with petitions requesting authority to undertake some enterprise promising particular benefits within the small compass of local communities. Other requests commonly involved appeals by individuals of decisions taken by local courts. Much of what passed for lawmaking in colonial America was still concerned with the petty affairs of a primarily agricultural society. In the memorable words of the eighteenth-century New York historian William Smith, the "views" of colonial legislators "seldom extended farther than to the regulation of highways, the destruction of wolves, wildcats, and foxes, and the advancement of the other little interests of the particular counties which they were chosen to represent."[23]

On the eve of the Revolution, then, representation in America was a hybrid of traditional ideas and modern practices. Decades of intermittent but recurring controversies with imperial authorities, and the lodestar of the Glorious Revolution, disposed Americans to continue to believe that representation existed, first and foremost, to protect the rights of their communities against the abuse of executive power. That conviction was only reinforced by the crisis of 1765–75. For even though this prolonged constitutional dispute pitted the rights of one set of legislatures against the mother Parliament, Americans believed they would lose the protective benefits of representation should they accept Parliament's jurisdiction. They did so because their standards of representation placed a far greater emphasis on accountability than the minuscule electorate of Georgian Britain and the oligarchic Parliament it supported could claim.

THE CRUCIAL DEPARTURES OCCURRED only with independence, which transformed American ideas of representation and legislation in several respects. By stripping the executive of its political independence and prerogatives, the new state constitutions gave the assemblies the same supremacy Parliament had enjoyed since 1689. Nor was this power merely theoretical, for the imperatives of mobilizing resources for war required the assemblies to use their supremacy to legislate vigorously in the positive sense of the term. Revolution also gave the political facets of representation a new urgency. The need to mobilize an entire people for the struggle encouraged new constituencies and segments of the population to gain a political voice, whether by correcting existing inequities in apportionment or by inspiring calls for an enlarged suffrage. Taken together, these conditions of active lawmaking and a highly responsive political system guaranteed that republican norms of representation would be tested under conditions far different from the humdrum routines of colonial governance.

When John Adams imagined an assembly as a "miniature" of society, he knew that the ferment of revolution was raising fundamental questions about exactly how representative a portrait it was necessary to sketch. Just as James Burgh's *Political Disquisitions* of 1774 offered Americans a trenchant criticism of the evils of a limited suffrage in Britain, so their own case against Parliament gave the dependent classes of colonial society a potent basis for challenging their exclusion from the franchise. Adams's *Thoughts on Government* appeared just as he was flippantly answering his wife Abigail's request that he and his male colleagues "[r]emember the Ladies" in "the new Code of Laws" they would soon form. While it is not clear that Abigail regarded suffrage as essential in itself, she clearly drew the connection between representation and the right to government by consent; and so did James Sullivan when he sent Adams a letter proposing to extend the franchise beyond its usual requirements of property. Adams's answer combined a sound rendition of Whig theory with a tacit recognition that rules of exclusion were arbitrary but necessary. Extend suffrage to the free male population, he argued, and one might as well extend it to women and children, whose lives and liberty were equally the objects of law, and who often had "as good Judgments, and as Independent Minds as those Men who are wholly destitute of Property," since the latter "were as much dependent upon others" for their wants as wives and children. Rather than "open So fruitfull a Source of Controversy and Altercation," it was better to abide by the general rule which made personal independence the best criterion of citizenship, in the expectation that an American society in which "the Multitude may be possessed of landed Estates" would enable most adult male voters to qualify for the suffrage, and thereby to preserve "the Liberty, Virtue, and Interest of the Multitude in all Acts of Government."[24] This was the logic that the constitution writers of the mid-1770s generally followed. While modifying property qualifications for suffrage, they still "expected all male adults to become voters because they would become property owners."[25]

The questions raised over apportioning representatives among communities were harder to resolve. On the one hand, a desire to mobilize the entire countryside and correct inequities in the late colonial distribution of legislative seats argued for giving each community of township or county its voice. The wartime legislatures were larger than their colonial forerunners, and frontier communities were more likely to send delegates. On the other hand, towns and counties were unequally settled, and with the war requiring continuous decisions on taxation and other economic issues, more densely peopled and wealthier communities could plausibly claim that representation should be proportioned to population or wealth or both. What then was the equality that Americans sought in representation: an equality of corporate communities, in which all towns were the same? or one in which the allocation of seats was tied to the actual distribution of population and (perhaps) the wealth upon which the states relied to prosecute the war? As democratic a writer as the anonymous author of *The People the Best Governors* illustrated the dilemma to which "this delicate point" could lead when he coupled his appeal for a government highly responsive to popular control with a defense of the Burkean claim that "each particular member in the legislature does not represent any distinct part, but the whole of the said body [politic]." His solution— which resembled Adams's for suffrage—was to assume that population would eventually distribute itself evenly across the landscape. That prospect made sense to farmers, who naturally imagined the progressive subdivision of land, but residents of more urbanized communities along the seaboard were already thinking in different terms.[26] The notion that legislatures might choose to give some incremental representation to urban areas did not satisfy those who thought, with the no less radical author of *Four Letters on Interesting Subjects*—possibly Thomas Paine—that equitable adjustments in the "natural right" of representation "ought not to depend upon the will and pleasure of future legislatures" but should be fixed constitutionally with due respect for the "encrease or decrease" of population.[27]

These questions were theoretically difficult in their own right, and they would continue to bedevil American politics for generations to come. But what gave them peculiar urgency during the Revolution was the new and radically enlarged impact that legislation had on the entire fabric of American society.

The burdens that the war imposed were without precedent in the colonial past. Once the sobering recognition that victory would not come easily replaced the sunshine patriotism of 1774–76, the assemblies were repeatedly impelled to use their legislative powers to mobilize the resources and manpower for a protracted struggle. The real stuff of wartime lawmaking did not involve drafting enlightened statutes to compact the debris of the colonial era into suitably concise and republican form, as in Jefferson's famous project to revise the legal code of Virginia. Nor did the amateur lawmakers who came and went every session spend much time thinking about ways of improving the republican manners of their constituents. Calling for fast days was easy enough; raising adequate numbers of soldiers or supplies of salt pork and blankets was more daunting. Matters at once prosaic yet urgent preoccupied the legislatures: laws setting the terms of military service, meeting congressional requisitions for men and supplies, regulating prices and markets in an unhappy effort to balance the rival needs of military commissaries, farmers, and urban artisans; currency emissions and the measures required to halt their depreciation; and all the other expedients the war required. Within each of the states, this legislation was intrusive and burdensome to an extent previously unimaginable.

The most sensitive and important categories of legislation concerned taxation, public debts, paper currency, and the control of markets—the broad arena of public finance and economic regulation. Here the legislatures repeatedly struggled against the open-ended demands of the war and the inflationary pressures generated by national and state reliance on currency finance.[28] To secure independence, Americans ironically had to accept economic restraints and financial measures far more onerous than any that Parliament would ever have dreamed of or dared to impose. At one time or another, every segment of society felt aggrieved either by the policies the states pursued or their inability to control the palpable economic dislocations of the war: a depreciating paper currency, shortages of goods, rising prices, profiteering. Sensitive to their complaints, the assemblies were reluctant to levy taxes commensurate with the costs of war, but this caution did not mitigate the impact the war had on ordinary families. After all, the inflation that inevitably resulted from these conditions was itself, as Benjamin Franklin observed, "a kind of imperceptible Tax."[29] Nor did the coming of peace in 1783 relieve the state legislatures of their burdens, since they still faced the problem of retiring the substantial and sometimes crushing public debt incurred during eight years of war. Their good-faith efforts to meet their obligations—to Congress as well as their own creditors—revealed their political vulnerability and administrative weakness.[30]

The legislatures thus had to govern actively, and to make decisions that were bound to aggravate one or another part of the community. It was in this sense that the war and ensuing efforts at recovery translated legislative supremacy from an abstract principle into a factual description of a functioning government. But this experience also subverted the republican belief that a representative assembly could both mirror society *and* pursue the general good to which all communities and classes could adhere. No assembly could distribute the burdens of war equally, or avoid persuading some that their interests were being treated unjustly. Nor could the assemblies escape the inevitable criticisms, resentments, and simply ornery complaints that arose because so much legislation affected property. As Americans increasingly questioned whether legislators truly represented (or sympathized with) their interests—a process that Gordon Wood has labeled the "disintegration of the concept of representation"— they were driven less by the logic of popular sovereignty than by complaints about the inability of the legislatures to manage all the economic evils the war had produced.[31]

Yet if these developments fed populist fears of legislative misrule, they also reinforced that traditional notion which held that the first duty of representation was to protect the people against unjust exercises of authority. In Britain that task was ascribed to the House of Commons collectively; in the United States it was an expectation that citizens and communities increasingly directed toward their individual representatives, and which often took the form of efforts to use instructions to bind their behavior. The metaphors which imagined a legislature as a mirror or miniature of society were inspired less by a majoritarian purpose of aggregating popular preferences than by a parochial (or, one might say, minoritarian) fear that local interests would be ignored or injured if they were obscured in the glass or omitted from the portrait. This concern expressed itself most strongly when schemes of taxation were to be decided, for no public act could do greater harm if framed in disregard of the circumstances that would enable particular communities to discharge their public obligations most easily.

It was, of course, the conviction that the existing forms of representation in America were unavoidably parochial, and thus incapable of perceiving and pursuing anything resembling a broad and coherent public good, that lay at the core of the Madisonian critique of legislative and popular politics in the states. While citizen gathered in town meetings or at county-court days to grumble that their interests were being ignored or impaired by one legislative act or another, Madison's bleak view of state politics suggested that their *cumulative* complaints were pulsing all too vigorously through the political system. The problem of representation was not to make legislators more accountable than they were already, but to find ways to dissipate the populist pressures of the people and improve the quality of lawmaking by reforming the character of the lawmakers.

Madison's thoughts about legislation also paralleled the criticism of parliamentary lawmaking offered by Blackstone, Mansfield, and Kames (authorities he likely read).[32] He, too, was troubled by the ease with which legislatures acted, by their lack of seriousness in deliberation, and the technical defects of their statutes. He was willing to consider reforms— from standing committees of skilled draftsmen to the more radical scheme of the Council of Revision—that would restore "perspicuity" to the legislative product. But while recognizing that "the principal task of modern legislation" was "the regulation of these various and conflicting interests" that the complex economies of "civilized nations" produced, Madison also denounced the "luxuriancy" of state legislation in nearly libertarian terms. "As far as the laws exceed [the] limit" required "to mark with precision the duties of those who are to obey them, and to take from those who are to administer them a discretion, which might be abused," he noted, they constitute "a nusance [sic] of the most pestilent kind." And when he later estimated the extent of lawmaking that future congresses would undertake should the Constitution be adopted, he intimated that after "the primeval formation of a federal code," the task would grow easier by the year—though it would still prove more demanding than the equivalent duties of the states.[33]

If the obligations of representatives were not limited to protecting popular rights, the talents and skills they needed would involve more than faithful attention to constituents' concerns, personal independence, and upright character (useful as these virtues remained). Being a *legislator*, in other words, might require other traits than those necessary for a *representative*—especially the experience and expertise that only public life itself could provide. These ideas began to percolate in proto-Federalist circles even before Madison brought his agenda for reform to fruition in April 1787. Jonathan Jackson, a Newburyport merchant who served briefly in Congress at war's end—and whose 1788 tract *Thoughts upon the Political Situation of the United States* made Madison's disgust with state politics seem pale in comparison—expressed this emerging sentiment well in a letter to John Adams in 1785. Returning from a disappointing voyage to England, Jackson was in no mood to be optimistic about either his own affairs or those of the public. "As I went away so have I returned," he noted, "tired of Politics and willing to leave them to any who know how to manage them." But where were such men to be found? Certainly not in a Congress which

> as at present appointed never appeared to me competent to the Business—they have not sufficient Stability collectively or individually— there is not permanency enough in their Appointment to induce them generally to qualify themselves for their Employment—to take it up and follow it as a Business.

Congress was not unique in this respect, for instability in office was a "capital *Defect* thro[ugh]out our appointments." To be effective, Jackson noted, government had to be made "the Business of a few—and made their Business both from Motives of Interest and Ambition." Benjamin Rush echoed this point a year later in his essay decrying the common tendency "to confound the terms of *the American Revolution* with those of *the late American war.*" "Government is a science, and can never be perfect in America, until we encourage men to devote not only three years, but their whole lives to it." No wonder "so many men of abilities object to serving in Congress," Rush concluded; who would wish "to spend three years in acquiring a profession which their country immediately afterwards forbids them to follow[?]"[34]

The ostensible target of this complaint was the clause in the Confederation restricting delegates to serving three years out of any six—a clause that numbered Madison among its first victims. That rule was itself the by-product of a cluster of beliefs that were expressed not only in the principle that rotation in office and annual elections were *rights* belonging to the people or in occasional populist surges among the electorate, but also in the attitudes of officeholders themselves. Throughout the Revolution and afterward, both Congress and the state legislatures suffered from high rates of turnover in membership. Inexperience and inefficiency went hand in hand, and much of the criticism directed against both levels of government could be traced, as Jackson argued, to the lack of a stable corps of capable legislators.³⁵ But this turnover was not primarily the result of the dissatisfaction of voters with the elected. It reflected instead the complaints of incumbents who found the burden of public life more than they wished to bear and who retired from office as soon as they gracefully could. However much homage Americans paid to the ideal of the citizen who virtuously subordinated private interest to public good, few of them learned to prefer the duties of public office to the contentments of private life. The civic life exalted in the classical republican tradition never became the dominant value of political behavior even during the war years, when patriotic appeals ran strongest. In time of peace, its appeal slackened further. The ennui that Madison felt when he was rusticated to Montpelier in 1783 was far less typical than the eagerness with which Cornelius Harnett, another delegate, had looked forward a few years earlier to retiring "under my own vine & my own fig tree (for I have them both) at Poplar Grove," his North Carolina plantation.³⁶

The notion that politics could become a profession or a business marked a significant departure from the conventional view that it was an avocation best pursued by men whose imminent return to a private station would remind them that they would be governed by the same laws they framed. Experience gained through tenure might support the monitory purposes of representation by enabling "honest but unenlightened" lawmakers to penetrate the "sophistical arguments" of demagogic leaders.³⁷ But the vision of representation that Madison, Jackson, and Rush shared also valued experience for a different reason: as a source of *expertise* of another kind than the awareness of local circumstances that would recommend a candidate to the voters of his neighborhood. National legislators would need an informed understanding not only of the conditions, laws, and customs of the diverse states of the American empire for which they would have to frame uniform acts, but also of the wider world in which the commercial and strategic interests of the United States would be immersed. This knowledge was of an order of magnitude greater than the concerns of state lawmaking; indeed, in Madison's harshest formulations, it seemed unlikely that any state legislator could appreciate the connection between his actions and the greater national interest.

Madison did not trust experience alone to give lawmakers the virtues they required. He also hoped to establish "such a process of elections as will most certainly extract from the mass of the Society the purest and noblest characters which it contains; such as will at once feel most strongly the proper motives to pursue the end of their appointment, and be most capable to devise the proper means of attaining it."³⁸ By treating this ideal of electoral reform as "an auxiliary desideratum for the melioration of the Republican form of government"—auxiliary to the benefits to be gained simply by extending a republic beyond its accepted territorial sphere—Madison illustrated the ambiguities in his attitude toward legislation. By making it more difficult for the complex interests a national republic would embrace to fashion the "requisite combinations" to convert their impulses into legislation, this theory promised relief from the "luxuriancy" of lawmaking that so alarmed him in the states. Yet if its electoral system worked as he hoped it would, such pieces of legislation as were enacted should possess the qualities he sought because they would be produced by a superior class of lawmakers.[39]

THE FRAMERS DELIVERED their headiest statements about representation when they initially considered whether or not to create a bicameral legislature. The first point that advocates of the Virginia Plan had to establish was that a popularly elected lower house was both proper in theory and feasible in practice. When this issue arose on May 31, Roger Sherman and Elbridge Gerry objected that the people "should have as little to do as may be about the Government. They want information and are constantly liable to be misled."[40] In reply, George Mason, James Wilson, and Madison quickly invoked the first principles of representation, and they did so on sweeping grounds.

The lower house was "to be our House of Commons—It ought to know & sympathise with every part of the community," Mason observed, and he went on to give this "democratic principle" a dual specificity. First, representatives should "be taken not only from different parts of the whole republic, but also from different districts of the larger members of it," which often had "different interests and views arising from difference of produce, of habits, &c &c." Mason then went on to endorse a broad suffrage as well. "We ought to attend to the rights of every class of the people," he added, noting that he "often wondered at the indifference of the superior classes of society to this dictate of humanity & policy." Did they not realize that "however elevated their situations" now, time might soon "distribute their posterity throughout the lowest classes of society"? (Of course, as the father of ten, Mason was not speaking completely disinterestedly.)[41]

Wilson thought popular election essential because "[n]o government could long subsist without the confidence of the people." Madison agreed that "the necessary sympathy between [the people] and their rulers and officers" would be "too little felt" unless one house was popularly elected, but he added a fresh point when he noted that "if the Election is made by the Peop. in large Districts there will be no Danger of Demagogues." In a first test vote, the committee of the whole approved the popular election of the lower house. A week later, however, it revisited the question when the South Carolina delegates moved to have members of the lower house elected by the assemblies. Again, Wilson, Mason, and Madison spoke nearly as one, defending popular election both because "[t]he Govt. ought to possess not only 1st. the *force* but 2dly. the *mind* or *sense* of the people at large," but also because "under proper regulation" it would have "the additional advantage of securing better representatives."[42]

The proponents of popular election quickly established two relations fundamental to their theory of representation. The first juxtaposed the sympathy of representatives and the confidence of the people. Without popular election, legislators would lack the requisite sympathy with (or for) the people, while the people would lack confidence in their representatives. The second relation tied the mode of election to the character and abilities of representatives. Here Wilson and Mason endorsed Madison's key hypothesis: that elections held in districts larger than the county and township units used to choose state legislators would encourage a superior class of lawmakers to gain national office, thereby enabling national law to be framed with a deliberation rarely found in the states. But on this point, another supporter of proportional representation had his doubts. Alexander Hamilton summarized Madison's proposition in these terms: "large districts less liable to be influenced by factious demagogues than small." But he then jotted down his own reservations.

> This is in some degree true but not so generally as may be supposed—Frequently small portions of [word mutilated in manuscript] large districts carry elections—An influential demagogue will give an impulse to the whole—Demagogues are not always *inconsiderable* persons—Patricians were frequently demagogues—Characters are less known & a less active interest taken in them.[43]

Hamilton may have been unduly skeptical, but his notes illustrate a crucial point. Madison's hypothesis, for all its theoretical power, was simply a prediction which experience might or might not confirm. Who could say whether elections would actually produce the desired results, obviating what Madison later called "the vicious arts, by which elections are too often carried"?[44] What was to stop some local demagogue from capturing an election if more qualified candidates split the virtuous vote?

Questions like these were worth pursuing, but the course of debate carried the framers in another direction. Once they agreed that the lower house should be elected by the people, they had no further reason to ponder the merits of extended districts or to consider "proper regulations" for elections, or even to ask how detailed a portrait of the people the lower house should provide. Through the first fortnight of July, they remained preoccupied with the dual questions of apportionment in House and Senate. And those questions were initially posed in terms of how to apportion representation *among* the states, not *within* them. They were concerned only with the weight each state would have, not with the methods each might choose to organize its population for electoral purposes.

Once the rules of apportionment were set, nothing prevented the Convention from considering precisely how a miniature of the political nation would be composed. Having already endorsed district elections, Madison, Mason, and Wilson could easily have pressed the case for incorporating a suitable rule in the Constitution, and even requiring the *states* to apportion seats on an equitable basis. Not only would such a rule support the principle of sympathy, and thereby forestall later objections to the Constitution; it could also be advanced as a logical extension of the constitutional mandate for reapportionment. Just as the balance of population among states would change over time, so it would doubtless alter within them—and the information gained by the census would enable the states to comply with the norm of equality at no expense.

Rather that proceed so boldly, the Convention took a less direct path. The report of the committee of detail included a clause authorizing each state legislature to determine "the times and places and manner of holding the elections" for both houses, but making these regulations subject "at any time" to alteration by Congress. When the Convention discussed this clause on August 9, the South Carolina delegates moved to strike out the latter provision.[45] Although their state's constitution of 1778 required periodic reapportionment on the basis of population and wealth, the legislature, dominated by the tidewater ruling elite, ignored this rule; and its spokesmen in Philadelphia evidently wished to preserve the assembly's power over national representative districts as well.[46]

The chief opponent of this motion was Madison, and his speech is notable for its concessions and assertions alike. On the one hand, Madison admitted that all essential decisions about the conduct of elections belonged to the state legislatures. "Whether the electors should vote by ballot or vivâ voce, should assemble at this place or that place; should be divided into districts or all meet at once place, shd all vote for all the representatives; or all in a district vote for a number allotted to the district; these & many other points would depend on the Legislatures," he observed. There lay the problem. The assemblies might "mould their regulations" for their own mischievous ends, in ways that would set the state governments at odds with the Union. Madison thus conceded that the election of senators was not the only device state legislatures might use to assert their influence in national politics. But he had another point to make: The "inequality of the Representation in the Legislatures of particular States, would produce a like inequality in their representation" in Congress—an inequality it should presumably be empowered to correct. Because Madison had long since concluded that equitable reapportionment of representation was an essential requirement of republican government, his defense of a national power to revise electoral procedures rested on the same rationale as the congressional negative on state laws. Both measures would enable Congress to intervene against acts of injustice within the states (though in this case the object of regulation would be a factious minority improperly holding on to power).[47]

The framers retained the clause, but they went no further in determining how elections would be conducted. Had they done so, they might well have reached an impasse in any case. For as electoral laws adopted in 1788 and afterward revealed, the smaller states did not regard the House as a mirror for local communities clustered in separate districts but preferred to have their delegations chosen statewide, with each citizen voting for as many candidates as the state had representatives.[48] By Madison's own standards, whatever was thereby lost on the index of sympathy might be offset by the net improvement in the character of those elected. For by the logic of his hypothesis, statewide elections should work at least as well and arguably better than district elections in encouraging qualified candidates to triumph over local demagogues.

There were two other ways to shape the relation between the people and their representatives, however. Qualifications could be set either for membership in Congress or for suffrage. On July 26, the day before the committee of detail set to work, the framers debated the wisdom of imposing property qualifications on members of Congress and other officials. While resisting efforts to disqualify various classes of public debtors, they did instruct the committee to propose "certain qualifications of property and citizenship" for all three departments.[49] The committee also discussed ways of setting qualifications for suffrage, for its papers include draft provisions proposing age, property, and residence requirements for voters, and also authorizing Congress to alter the qualifications set by the states. But its report disappointed those members who favored either requirement. The committee merely proposed empowering Congress "to establish such uniform Qualifications of the Members of each House, with

Regard to Property," as it deemed "expedient," while the electorate for the lower house of Congress would be the same as that for the lower houses in the states, and without any federal review.[50]

The Convention took up the suffrage question first. Gouverneur Morris, John Dickinson, and Madison all argued for limiting the national suffrage to freeholders, and they did so on the traditional ground that these independent landholders were "the best guardians of liberty." In the future "this Country will abound with mechanics & manufacturers who will receive their bread from their employers," Morris warned, and who would happily sell their votes to the rich. Madison was even gloomier, though a shade less agitated. "In future times a great majority of the people will not only be without landed, but any other sort of property," he predicted. They would either combine out of desperation to endanger "the rights of property & the public liberty," or "become the tools of opulence & ambition"—and hence of the same aristocracy whom Morris also professed to fear. Now was the time to restrict the vote to freeholders, Morris urged, when "9/10 of the Inhabs. are Freeholders."[51]

John Adams had reached much the same conclusion in 1776. It is a mark of how democratized American thinking had grown over the course of the intervening decade that the other framers—conservative, propertied leaders—were able to dismiss these arguments almost out of hand. There were, to be sure, expedient reasons to abide by the committee's recommendation to link state and national electorates. To create an invidious distinction between them was obviously impolitic. And as Wilson was quick to note, "It was difficult to form any uniform rule of qualifications for all the States." But it seems evident that many delegates opposed the pleas for a republic of freeholders on the principled grounds that landed property could no longer be treated as the preeminent source of political rights. "Every man having evidence of attachment & permanent common interest with the Society ought to share in all its rights & privileges," Mason asserted, and Franklin made this point even more poignantly when he recalled how American seamen captured during the war had refused to gain their freedom by agreeing to serve on British ships. This was a powerful plea, for seamen were often classed among the most despised ranks of "the lower orders," and if they could figure as objects in the mirror of representation, its perspective was broad indeed.[52]

In the end, the committee's recommendation to accept the existing state electorates was carried without dissent on August 9. That still left open the possibility of imposing qualifications for membership in Congress. When this issue was reached the next day, Charles Pinckney pointedly noted that the committee had departed from its instructions. He therefore moved a new clause requiring all national officeholders "to swear that they were respectively possessed of a clear unincumbered [i.e., debt-free] Estate."[53] The ensuing debate revealed that attempts to establish a property qualification were objectionable on practical and theoretical grounds. Two committee members explained why they had ignored their instruction. If a requirement was set too high, John Rutledge noted, it would anger the people; fix it too low, and it would prove "nugatory." Moreover, Ellsworth added, no constitutional standard could work equally well for different parts of the Union or at different periods in the history of the nation. These objections were so decisive that Pinckney's motion was rejected by a voice vote. That still left the proposal to allow property qualifications to be set by Congress, but this proved no more workable. Not only was it liable to the same problem of uniformity, it also violated the principle that "the qualifications of electors and elected were fundamental articles in a Republican Govt. and ought to be fixed by the Constitution." To give a legislature such discretion was to invite it to convert the government "into an aristocracy or oligarchy," Madison warned, or perhaps worse, Hugh Williamson added, to allow the lawyers who might dominate Congress to "secure future elections . . . to their own body."[54]

Decisions on other provisions that might have regulated eligibility for election also carried the Convention away from the idea of erecting significant barriers limiting access to office or tenure. Although the Virginia Plan proposed limiting representatives to a single term of office and making them subject to recall, this provision was deleted without debate or dissent.[55] Instead of requiring candidates to be "resident" in a state for a fixed period of years, the framers agreed that it was enough to be an "inhabitant" at the time of election.[56] When it came to deciding how legislators were to be paid, the delegates did not presume that members of Congress would be independently wealthy. Although this issue had divided the Convention in June, on August 14 it approved a new motion to pay congressional salaries from the national treasury.[57] The one area in which the framers narrowed access to the legislature was in raising the period of citizenship required for foreign-born candidates from the four years proposed by the committee of detail to seven years.[58]

In dealing with another set of restrictions, however, the Convention moved in the opposite direction by relaxing prohibitions against the appointment of legislators to other national offices. Of all the provisions relating to conditions of membership, this was the most hotly disputed, and it was not resolved—and even then only narrowly—until September 3. The committee of detail proposed barring legislators from accepting *any* federal office during the term of their election and further prohibited senators from "holding any such office for one year afterwards." Without such a restriction, Mason noted with typical irony, Congress would attract "those generous and benevolent characters who will do justice to each other's merit, by carving out offices and rewards" for their mutual profit. But equally candid arguments in favor of promoting ambition apparently swayed the bare majority who ultimately limited the prohibition only to civil offices "which shall have been created, or the emoluments whereof shall have been encreased" during a legislator's term. Wilson spoke as bluntly as Mason when he declared that "he was far from thinking the ambition which aspired to Offices of dignity and trust, an ignoble or culpable one." While consensus on this point proved unattainable, the majority clearly hoped that the experience and reputation acquired in Congress would make its best members eligible for other offices to which they could aspire for entirely proper reasons.[59]

It remained to be seen whether the Constitution was more likely to emulate "the policy of the Romans, in making the temple of virtue the road to the temple of fame," as Pinckney believed, or turn Congress into a haunt for the corruptible "office-hunters" whom Mason despised. Defying Mason's pessimism, most of the framers doubtless hoped that the Constitution would encourage a better class of leaders to acquire political power. But if it did so, it would not be because it had erected formidable criteria of membership. The Constitution required nothing more of legislators than relatively low requirements of age and citizenship—not even a religious test of the most innocuous kind. In the end, the framers rested their hopes on two plausible but problematic conditions: that a small Congress would give better-qualified candidates a political advantage over the ward heelers of their day; and that an open process of political recruitment, coupled with the promise of exercising serious responsibilities of national government, would somehow encourage the right men to seek office in the first place. For the new government to succeed in this respect, however, it would have to rely on the actual circumstances of political life rather than on the formal requirements that the framers failed to impose. Federalist expectations could be realized only if the enlarged sphere of the extended republic worked to filter talent upward while the prestige and power of national office drew qualified candidates away from their law offices, plantations, and countinghouses. In the meantime, they had first to defend the Constitution against the charge that even the lower house of Congress would become a nursery not of statesmen but of aristocrats.

∽

FROM THE MOMENT WHEN HE thanked the delegates for electing him their president, George Washington refrained from speaking on the issues before the Convention. It must have been wondrous, then, when he intervened to support the motion that Nathaniel Gorham offered on September 17, just after Wilson read Franklin's plea for unanimity. A week earlier, a proposal to increase the size of the House had failed by a single vote; then even Hamilton had argued that the House was drawn "on so narrow a scale as to be really dangerous, and to warrant a jealousy in the people of their liberties."[60] Now Gorham revived this concern. "If it was not too late," he asked, could the clause stating that "the number of representatives shall not exceed one for every forty thousand" be reduced to one for every thirty thousand, thereby "lessening objections against the Constitution" and giving future congresses "greater latitude" in reapportionment? When Washington rose to put the question, he first observed—in a tone probably more commanding than apologetic—that he, too, thought "the smallness of the proportion of Representatives" was "an insufficient security for the rights & interests of the people." The motion passed unanimously, even though it meant smudging the handsomely engrossed copy of the Constitution the framers were about to sign.[61]

Washington may have aimed his appeal at his old friend Mason, who already ranked the defects of the House second on his list of objections to the Constitution. "There is not the Substance, but the Shadow only of Representation," Mason wrote, "which can never produce proper Information in the Legislature, or inspire Confidence in the People: the Laws will therefore be generally made by Men little concern'd in, and unacquainted with their Effects & Consequences." Passage of Gorham's motion only partly assuaged Mason. To his objections he now appended a note admitting that this complaint "has been in some Degree lessened."[62] But well before his objections were published, other Anti-Federalists made the size of the House the leading point in their indictment of the national scheme of representation.

The first Anti-Federalists to press this issue seriously were also the most acute. The inadequacy of representation was a crucial theme in the early essays of "Brutus" and the initial *Letters from the Federal Farmer* that appeared in pamphlet form in November 1787 and the additional letters published in the winter of 1788. Although the identity of the "Federal Farmer" remains a subject of speculation, the striking similarities between his arguments about representation and the speeches of Melancton Smith, the moderate Anti-Federalist who played a key role in the New York rat-ification convention, corroborate the hypothesis that Smith *was* the "Fed-eral Farmer."⁶³ Whereas militant Anti-Federalists dismissed the feasibility of national representation out of hand, the "Federal Farmer" and Smith, though doubtful that any national government could conform to "the true doctrine of representation," still thought that a radical expansion of the House might render the Constitution acceptable.⁶⁴ In defending this po-sition, they avoided the shrill alarmism of other Anti-Federalists, while offering a description of political life as sensible as, and in some ways more vividly realized than, anything that Madison and like-minded Fed-eralists provided.

Their point of departure was conventional: "A full and equal repre-sentation," the "Federal Farmer" observed, was one "which possesses the same interests, feelings, opinions, and views the people themselves would were they all assembled." But this portrait now acquired a new precision. "Brutus" offered a remarkable example of the literalism of Anti-Federalist ideas of representation when he argued that "a stranger to the country" should immediately be able to learn "the character" of a people "by know-ing that of their representatives. They are the sign—the people are the thing signified." The "Federal Farmer" agreed: Representation "should be so regulated, that every order of men in the community, according to the common course of elections, can have a share in it—in order to allow pro-fessional men, merchants, traders, farmers, mechanics, etc. to bring a just proportion of their best informed men respectively into the legislature, the representation must be considerably numerous."⁶⁵ It was not enough for representatives to be generally conversant with the interests of all classes, Smith insisted, for only the knowledge acquired through "the kind of acquaintance with the common concerns and occupations of the people, which men of the middling class are in general much more com-petent to" possess, could assure that a legislature would "be disposed to seek their true interests."⁶⁶ But with each state selecting a bare handful of members, the "Federal Farmer" predicted, "nine times in ten, men of the elevated classes in the community only can be chosen." The "middle and lower classes" who form "the democracy" of the American people would not be present; instead, "the few men of wealth and abilities" who com-posed "the natural aristocracy of the country" would dominate.⁶⁷

In this formulation, the purposes of representation and legislation re-mained essentially conservative. The constitution and laws of a people who already enjoyed prosperity and equality and who were "unoppressed with riches or wants" should seek "to arrest them from national depravity, and to preserve them in their happy condition," the "Federal Farmer" argued. "A virtuous people makes just laws, and good laws tend to pre-serve unchanged a virtuous people." Representation should thus work to preserve the existing "national character and circumstances" and the "bal-ances" among "the several orders of men in a community." This equilib-rium would be endangered if a system of representation gave one of these orders "an undue ascendency."[68] But the form of aristocracy that alarmed the "Federal Farmer" and Smith was not the mere self-aggrandizing cliques of "unprincipled men" that radical Whig writers had denounced since the age of Robert Walpole. It was rather the "natural aristocracy" comprising holders of major public offices, "the most eminent profes-sional men, &c. and men of large property," and who could be distin-guished from "the other persons and orders" who "form the natural democracy . . . the yeomanry, the subordinate officers, civil and military, the fishermen, mechanics and traders, many of the merchants and profes-sional men." The distinction between these classes was not rigid; many Americans would prove "wavering and uncertain" as to where to place themselves in the social order. But the divisions did exist, and the task of representation was to balance these "orders" in ways that would prevent the natural aristocracy from oppressing the democracy.[69]

How could a natural aristocracy numbering perhaps five thousand prevail over a propulous democracy? The casual faith that Federalists placed in the people's ability to "elect good men" struck the "Federal Farmer" and Smith as naive. They accordingly set out to explain how under this constricted scheme of representation "men unfriendly to repub-lican equality will go systematically to work, gradually to exclude the body of the people from any share in the government."[70] The differences in at-titude and temperament that reflected the social conditions of the two classes would give the aristocracy disproportionate advantages.

> Men of the first class [the "Federal Farmer" wrote] associate more extensively, have a high sense of honor, possess abilities, ambition, and general knowledge; men of the second class are not so much used to combining great objects; they possess less ambition, and a larger share of honesty: their dependence is principally on middling and small estates, industrious pursuits, and hard labour, while that of the former is principally on the emoluments of large estates, and of the chief offices of government.[71]

Smith expounded the same point in a brilliant speech of June 21, 1788. If America lacked a legally privileged aristocracy, the "greater capacities" of "birth, education, talents and wealth" that "the author of nature has bestowed" would still "create distinctions as visible and of as much influence as titles, stars and garters." Not only would these conspicuous advantages "command a superior degree of respect" from the people at large, they would also leave "men in the middling class . . . not so anxious to be chosen." The aristocrats' natural superiority "will render the place of a representative not a desirable one to sensible, substantial men, who have been used to walk in the plain and frugal paths of life." The social advantages of aristocracy thus carried practical political dividends. Even more than Madison, who only *hoped* that talent and reputation would bestow electoral benefits, Smith *expected* that

> the influence of the great will generally enable them to succeed in elections—it will be difficult to combine a district of country containing 30 or 40,000 inhabitants, frame your election laws as you please, in any one character: unless it be in one of conspicuous, military, popular, civil or legal talents. The great easily form associations; the poor and middling class form them only with difficulty.

Their natural ease of manner would somehow enable these gentry to cooperate in ways that the restraint and shyness of the middling class would never permit.[72]

The "Federal Farmer" and Smith reinforced this insight into the social fabric of politics with a close assessment of the failure of the Constitution to specify how representatives were to be chosen. Whereas other Anti-Federalists treated the clause allowing Congress to revise state electoral laws as an invitation to the gross manipulation of state politics, the "Federal Farmer" argued that its likely use would be to prevent the states from adopting laws that fostered a close connection between representatives and their constituents. Nothing in the Constitution required states to be divided into electoral districts; or representatives to be residents of such districts, if created; or elections to be decided by a majority of voters. Not only would this absence of requirements benefit patrician candidates, the "Federal Farmer" argued, but once elected, they could use this clause to overturn state electoral laws that sought to give the House a more democratic cast. Rather than allow Congress this dangerous discretion, *or* leave electoral provisions solely to state regulation without a fixed rule, the "Federal Farmer" and Smith proposed to amend the Constitution to enlarge the House and to require its members to be elected in districts that would be small enough to make a choice by popular majorities effectual. In one sense, this was an unusual position for an Anti-Federalist because it would reduce the legislative power of the states. But it was consistent with the broader democratic principles that the "Federal Farmer" and Smith espoused.[73]

This proposal rested on an astute and by no means mistaken attempt to envision how a system of national representation would operate *politically*. In effect the "Federal Farmer" recalibrated the arithmetical component in the Federalist advocacy of large electoral districts. The difficulty of producing majorities in large districts would necessarily lead to plurality decisions in which the natural aristocracy could deploy its sources of "influence and corruption" to greatest advantage. Large districts would promote improper choices by making it all too easy to scatter votes among obscure or spurious candidates, and all too difficult to gather voters in the limited number of polling places that customary practice required, and where the very act of assembling would promote a knowledgeable choice. One New England Anti-Federalist refined this argument by asking what would happen if "the landed and mercantile interests" were combined in one district. Would not the seaport residents have a decided advantage over their rural brethren, he noted? Unlike farmers "scattered far and wide," the coastal residents were "more numerous; they live compact; their interests are one; there is a constant connection and intercourse between them; they can, on any occasion, centre their votes where they please."[74] Doubling or more the number of representatives would thus favor majoritarian choice by creating more convenient districts, but the "Federal Farmer" pushed his idea of reform further. While other Anti-Federalists denounced the Constitution for violating the sacred rule of annual elections, the "Federal Farmer" suggested that the two-year interval could be used to devise a two-stage process of nomination and election that would again foster an informed and majoritarian choice by making a "nomination" of a limited number of true candidates well in advance of the decision.[75]

Such positions can hardly be described as a small-minded refusal to recognize that republican norms of representation were compatible with national government. The "Federal Farmer" and Smith were willing to consider the claim for national representation on its merits, willing to boast (with Hamilton and Wilson) of the "very great improvements in representation" Americans had made and might yet make, and willing to agree (with Madison) that the stability of a republic required multiplying the interests present in the legislature.[76] Yet in the end, their ideas of representation still rested on traditional assumptions about its purpose. As much as their call for broad representation anticipated the avowedly democratic politics of the next century, its aim was far less to mobilize the American people to make law than to assure that the interests of the middling classes would not be trampled upon by an aristocratic clique. The majority deserved not so much to rule as to be protected from misrule; not so much to legislate in pursuit of its interests as to be secured against statutes that would reflect the high ambitions of the privileged class. A full representation was necessary for two purposes: to prevent the adoption of measures, especially taxes, that would distribute the *burdens* of government unequally across society; and to instill in the people the confidence in government that would obviate the need to resort to coercion (that is, armed force) to enforce the laws. Only members of the middling class, "from their frugal habits, and feeling themselves the public burdens," would have the sense to restrain government from excessive taxation, Smith warned the New York convention. By contrast, an aristocratic house, lacking "sympathy with their constituents" and by nature "being in the habit of profuse living," would prove correspondingly "profuse in the public expenses." The knowledge desired of legislators thus "requires something more than an acquaintance with the abstruse parts of the system of finance," Smith argued, or "just ideas of the commerce of the world," but also a detailed

> knowledge of the productions of your own country and their value, what your soil is capable of producing[,] the nature of your manufactures, and the capacity of the country to increase both. . . . It calls for a knowledge of the circumstances and ability of the people in general, a discernment how the burdens imposed will bear upon the different classes.[77]

Expertise of a different sort should indeed be expected of judges and executive officials whose "offices and duties require the information and studies of many years," and which few could be expected to attain. Not so representatives. "Some men of science are undoubtedly necessary in every legislature; but the knowledge, generally, necessary for men who make laws, is a knowledge of the common concerns, and particular circumstances of the people."[78] In this science of representation sympathy *was* the highest form of knowledge, but that sympathy could be attained only when the interests of elector and elected were one.

It was this preoccupation with the specter of capricious and onerous taxation that gave the Anti-Federalist doctrine of representation both underlying coherence and its rhetorical lien on the older ideology of resistance. With the exception of "Brutus," few other Anti-Federalists exhibited the same insight that enabled the "Federal Farmer" and Smith to explain how the social advantages of aristocracy could exploit the political ambiguities in the Constitution. They directed their ingenuity instead toward identifying the *powers* most likely to be misused—direct taxation, and the authority to raise armed forces and oversee the state militia—rather than toward explaining precisely why national legislators were so likely to abuse their trust. But then again, little nuance seemed necessary when simple arithmetic proved that Congress would be a mere fraction of the membership of the state legislatures or even the House of Commons, which some Anti-Federalists actually exalted as a superior model of equal representation. "We are to have one representative for every thirty thousand," moaned "Cincinnatus"; in Britain "they have nearly one for ten thousand souls."[79] Next to this lament, the criticisms that generations of Anglo-American Whigs had directed against a House of Commons never described as a miniature of the people it virtually represented seemingly counted for nothing. One Massachusetts Anti-Federalist even made the astonishing claim that members of Parliament, "on momentary occasions," were prone to "go home and consult their constituents, before they come to decision," something that congressmen at "a distant court" seemed unlikely to do.[80]

Anti-Federalists never glimpsed, much less grasped the advantage that the House of Representatives might derive as the sole institution of national government directly elected by the people, and therefore most likely to reflect the fluctuations of public opinion. Nor did they anticipate the dominant influence state legislatures would long exercise over the election of the House of Representatives, by virtue of controlling in the first instance every aspect of electoral law. Their obsession with the congressional power to alter these laws presumed that members of both houses (and the president) would collude to rig procedures to fragment the electorate, setting up polling places in obscure venues known only to the willing tools of incumbents. With so much invested in these bizarre scenarios, Anti-Federalists could do little more than complain that Congress was simply too small to be an effective representation. This point, once stated, needed little elaboration—but it was also an objection that leading Federalists thought they knew how to handle.

∝

LATE SEPTEMBER 1787 FOUND Hamilton, Madison, and Melancton Smith in New York City—Hamilton preparing to attend the October session of the state supreme court at Albany, Madison and Smith as members of the Continental Congress. Had these three men found the occasion to dine together, and had their conversation turned to the question of national representation, they could have found common ground on a number of points. At the outset, they could have quickly endorsed two rules defining the limits of size within which a representative assembly should fall. Such a body should not be so small as to permit a corruption founded on conspiratorial intimacy, or what Madison called in *Federalist* 10 "the cabals of a few." On the other hand, too large a body would prove "disjointed, unwieldy and incompetent," as the "Federal Farmer" condeded, and too prone, Madison thought, to "the confusion of a multitude."[81] In designing this assembly, they could further agree that the costs of an enlarged membership were trivial in comparison to the benefits to be gained. Madison had argued as much at the Convention, and the "Federal Farmer" offered a calculation placing the net increase in annual costs for a House doubled in size at $21,600 per year, which could be partly offset by reducing the size of the state assemblies. And because a House doubled in size was the minimal alteration that Madison and Hamilton had supported at the Convention, and which the "Federal Farmer" proposed in his *Letters*, that crucial point, too, could have been negotiable.[82]

At a more abstract level, they could have agreed that representative assemblies should balance the interests of the larger society in ways that discouraged the passage of "factious" legislation. But here the bases for disagreement would quickly have become evident. For Smith, the desired balance should prevent an aristocratic clique from trampling on the rights of the people at large; for his antagonists, it meant converting a system that seemed all too responsive to majoritarian pressures into one in which popular concerns should not be the basis for legislative decision. In the famous formulation of *Federalist* 10, the process of aggregating diverse interests into a republican majority should work to neutralize the parochial impulses of American politics, permitting laws to be framed on a more reflective and less reflexive basis. In Madison's calculations, doubling the size of the House would usefully complicate the formation of factious majorities by multiplying the interests to be represented without enlarging the chamber beyond the median point where the requisite deliberation could take place. Indeed, the very multiplication of interests would make deliberation more necessary.[83]

By this point, this putative conversation among these three acute commentators would have ended in an amiable agreement to disagree. Whatever their private opinions, Madison and Hamilton had to defend the initial allocation of seats in the House as reasonable if not ideal. Their more difficult task was to prove that the scale proposed for its future reapportionment would balance equally well the requirements of a democratized sympathy and the aristocratic virtues of deliberation. For while they understood that an expanded scale of representation would indeed foster popular confidence in the Constitution, they denied that the processes of deliberation and decision required making the membership of Congress as finely detailed a collective portrait of the people as Smith prescribed. Representation was not merely a convenient substitute for the popular meetings that any extended polity rendered impossible. It was also a mechanism whereby "the public voice pronounced by the representatives of the people, will be more consonant to the public good, than if pronounced by the people themselves convened for the purpose."[84] Lawmakers should *not* act as their constituents would if they met en masse, for the simple truth was that no substantial gathering of citizens could ever deliberate calmly or prudently. "In all very numerous assemblies, of whatever characters composed, passion never fails to wrest the sceptre from reason," Madison observed in *Federalist* 55. "Had every Athenian citizen been a Socrates, every Athenian assembly would still have been a mob."[85] And that rule applied as much to the deliberations of elective assemblies as to mass meetings of the citizenry.

To defend this model of deliberation, Federalists had to place the claims for sympathy in a new light—or rather, they had to defend the idea that sympathy was a sentiment that representatives could attain even if they did not possess all the social traits of their constituents. Though their allocation of duties left Madison the chief commentator on Congress, it was Hamilton who first considered this question in his essays on taxation. Without identifying either the "Federal Farmer" or "Brutus" (who made the same argument) as his targets, Hamilton devoted *Federalist* 35 to a rebuttal of the claim that "all classes of citizens should have some of their own number in the representative body, in order that their feelings and interests may be the better understood and attended to." That "altogether visionary" result could occur only if the Constitution "expressly provided . . . that each different occupation should send one or more members." The same qualities of modesty and frugality that the "Federal Farmer" hoped to bring into the legislature would always work, Hamilton warned, to discourage "mechanics and manufacturers" from seeking office, precisely because "They are sensible that their habits in life have not been such as to give them those acquired endowments, without which, in a deliberative assembly, the greatest natural abilities are for the most part useless." Members of these classes "will always be inclined . . . to give their votes to merchants" rather than their fellow workers, because artisans understood that the "superior acquirements" of the merchants would make them the most effective advocates for their common interests in promoting domestic manufactures and commerce.[86] Similar considerations would operate among the "landed interest" who comprised the mass of the population. When land was to be taxed, landholders of every description would share a common interest.[87]

Thus even if the House was substantially enlarged, electoral politics would rarely produce the result the "Federal Farmer" sought. Nor need one worry that representatives would lack the requisite sympathy. Any qualified candidate seeking "the favor of the people" would naturally "take care to inform himself of their dispositions and inclinations," Hamilton observed. But more important, it was erroneous to believe that merely local knowledge was the essential qualification of a legislator, especially in matters of taxation. Drawing upon his own deep studies of public finance, Hamilton reminded his readers (in a revealing slip of phrase) that

> There is no part of the administration of government that requires extensive information and a thorough knowledge of the principles of political economy, so much as the business of taxation. The man who understands these principles best will be least likely to resort to oppressive expedients, or to sacrifice any particular class of citizens to the procurement of revenue. It might be demonstrated that the most productive system of finance will always be the least burdensome.[88]

A sound program of public finance should be fashioned, in the first instance, by individuals or select boards who would "make a judicious selection of the objects proper for revenue." And the knowledge these representatives needed was not an encyclopedic accounting of the circumstances of every community but "a general acquaintance with its situation and resources."[89]

Hamilton expected the national government to rely on "commercial imposts"—which he called "the most convenient branch of revenue"— possibly supplemented by an excise on a limited number of items of internal production and the sale of western lands. He hoped to avoid the recourse to those forms of taxation, such as land and poll taxes, which would be assessed and imposed *directly* on the population, in favor of those to be quietly collected as individuals voluntarily purchased favored objects of consumption. In Hamilton's view, the lessons about taxation that Anti-Federalists drew from history were largely irrelevant to the real problems that the American state, in both its national and provincial incarnations, already faced and would continue to encounter. Because the Revolution had reinforced the aversion to taxation that was so deeply rooted in American political culture, Hamilton plausibly presumed that any scheme of representation adopted in the United States would leave legislators highly responsive to their constituents. The greater danger was not that Congress would levy onerous taxes on a docile people but that it would still lack the political will to solve the crisis of public finance. As the first secretary of the treasury, Hamilton set out to demonstrate that an enterprising minister could indeed frame a comprehensive system of public finance and make Congress his willing agent—actions that occasioned his break with Madison and the early emergence of national political parties.

In *The Federalist*, however, it was Madison's task to explain how national representation would work in practice. Rather than pursue Hamilton's speculations about the likely recipients of the people's suffrage, Madison framed his discussion to stress the similarities between the House of Representatives and the state legislatures—and in ways that qualified the claim of *Federalist* 10 that the creation of a national republic would encourage the recruitment of a superior class of legislators. In this account, Madison transposed to the House many of the traits he elsewhere ascribed to state legislators. "A local spirit will infallibly prevail much more in the members of Congress, than a national spirit will prevail in the legislatures of the particular states," he warned in *Federalist* 46. "Measures will too often be decided according to their probable effect, not on the national prosperity and happiness, but on the prejudices, interests, and pursuits of the governments and people of the individual States."[90] These prejudices would be enhanced by the high rates of turnover that Madison correctly surmised would long characterize tenure in the House. In any given session, most members would likely be newcomers who would need a two-year term simply to become "thoroughly masters of the public business" and thus to withstand "the snares that may be laid for them" by even a few incumbents whose "superior talents" and parliamentary experience might give them improper influence.[91] Madison returned to this theme in *Federalist* 62 when he invoked "the mutability in the public councils arising from a rapid succession of new members" to justify the existence of the Senate. "Every new election in the States is found to change one half of the representatives," he observed. A "due acquaintance with the objects and principles of legislation" could not be expected from "an assembly of men called for the most part from pursuits of a private nature, continued in appointment for a short time, and led by no permanent motive to devote the intervals of public occupation to a study of the laws, the affairs, and the comprehensive interests of their country."[92]

Of course, with Anti-Federalists denouncing the House as a haven for ambitious aristocrats, Madison had to stress the similarities between national and state representation. But in fact the assurances he offered as "Publius" accorded with his private opinions,[93] and Madison was far from certain that his hypotheses about the advantages of national representation would hold in practice. Some differences there surely would be, but would these amount to matters of degree or kind? Proud as he was of his contributions to the theory of representation, innate skepticism prevented Madison from confusing predictions with evidence. His own experience securing election to the First Federal Congress provided a salutary reminder of the nature of republican politics. Overcoming his original "inclination" and "judgment" to stand for election from his seat in the Continental Congress, Madison yielded to the "pressing exhortations" of his friends and returned to Virginia to wage an active campaign against his personal friend but current rival, James Monroe. "Whether I ought to be satisfied or displeased with my success, I shall hereafter be more able to judge," he wrote Edmund Randolph in early March 1789. "My present anticipations are not flattering." Scanning the list of new colleagues in the House, he found only "a very scanty proportion who will share in the drudgery of business." On March 29, with Congress weeks late mustering a quorum, he was still awaiting "experimental instruction" as to the true "genius" of the government. "Were I to advance a conjecture," he wrote to Jefferson, "it would be, that the predictions of an anti-democratic operation will be confronted with at least a sufficient number of the features which have marked the State Governments."[94]

In his earlier essays as "Publius" and in his speeches at the Virginia convention, however, Madison sought to balance the democratic aspects of representation with a candid statement of the Federalist ideal of deliberation. He could not deny that members of Congress would represent far more people than state legislators, nor could he dispute the fact that population growth would eventually require abandoning the ideal of one member for every thirty thousand people. But no simple ratio dictated "the number most convenient for a representative legislature," nor had the states adopted a single arithmetic scale of apportionment. A well-proportioned assembly was simply one that reconciled the need for information with the demands of deliberation—one that was too large for corruption but not so large as to take on "the confusion and intemperance of a multitude."[95] If one rule was certain, it was that "in all legislative assemblies, the greater the number composing them may be, the fewer will be the men who will in fact direct their proceedings," not only because of the resulting "ascendancy of passion over reason," but also because "the greater will be the proportion of members of limited information and of

weak capacities" who would fall prey to "the eloquence and address of
the few." Expanding representation in the name of democracy, Madison
warned, would only make "the soul that animates" government "more
oligarchic."[96]

As processes of national assimilation and integration made Americans
more like one another, Madison observed, the need to represent minute
interests should diminish further. While time would narrow the differences *among* states, he predicted, it would have a "contrary" effect on their
"internal affairs" by making their economies more complex.[97] But in justifying a reduced scale of representation, Federalists relied even more on
their definition of the objects to which Congress would direct its attention and the forms of knowledge most appropriate for its deliberations.
Here was where the standards of national and state representation most
sharply diverged. While state legislators could safely be presumed to be
"more or less conversant" with "the general affairs of the State" from the
moment of election, "the extensive information" that national "representatives ought to acquire" could be gained only in office. In challenging the
axiom " 'that where annual elections end, tyranny begins,' " Madison thus
defended the two-year term of the House on the grounds that the knowledge required to legislate for "the great theatre of the United States"
could be acquired only over the course of a session as members informed
each other of the "extremely diversified" laws, customs, and circumstances
of their individual states.[98] Nor need this information take the form of
minute accounts of the affairs of every district. Most of the knowledge
that Congress would need to regulate its primary concerns of commerce,
taxation, and the militia could be gained by studying the existing laws of
the states; and all of it could in fact be provided "by a very few intelligent
men, diffusively elected" from districts throughout any given state.[99] Here
again the *knowledge* desired of representatives transcended the "immediate
dependence on, & an intimate sympathy with, the people" that now appeared as minimal or threshold qualifications to be taken almost for
granted.[100]

This conception of representation was also a theory of federalism;
that is, it depended on a sharp distinction between the objects of general
and state government and the recognition that the responsibilities of
Congress were at once exalted but limited. If one considered "the vast variety and importance" of their duties, John Dickinson observed in his
"Fabius" letters, both houses "will actually be not only legislative but
diplomatic bodies, perpetually engaged in the arduous talk of reconcil-
ing, in their determinations, the interests of several sovereign states,"
and thus requiring "a competent knowledge of foreign affairs, relative to

the states."[101] State legislatures had to be more numerous than Congress, John Jay reminded the New York convention, because "[i]nnumerable things of small moment occupy their attention; matters of a private nature, which require much minute and local information." State legislatures remained bodies whose agendas were filled with petitions from communities and individuals, and whose oversight routinely extended to the activities of local governments in towns and counties. "The objects of the national government are not of this nature," Jay continued.

> They comprehend the interests of the states in relation to each other, and in relation to foreign powers. Surely there are men in this state fully informed of the general interests of its trade, its agriculture, its manufactures. Is any thing more than this necessary?[102]

The differences between state and national concerns were manifest, Oliver Ellsworth observed in his "Landholder" essays. "As the state legislatures have to regulate the internal policy, of every town and neighborhood," Ellsworth wrote,

> it is convenient enough to have one or two men, particularly acquainted with every small district of country, its interests, parties, and passions. But the federal legislature can take cognizance only of national questions and interests, which in their very nature are general, and for this purpose five or ten honest and wise men chosen from each state; men who have had previous experience in state legislation, will be more competent than an hundred.[103]

Edmund Randolph and John Marshall made the same point in the Virginia convention. "Can you believe that ten men selected from all parts of the State, chosen because they know the situation of the people, will be unable to determine so as to make the tax equal on, and convenient for, the people at large?" Marshall asked. It was safer to rely "on the virtue and knowledge of some few men," Randolph argued, than "the listlessness and inattention to the interests of the community" he had witnessed in larger assemblies.[104]

In moments of exasperation, Federalists lampooned the Anti-Federalist emphasis on sympathy. What did it mean to represent "the feelings of the people"? Robert Livingston asked the New York convention. If these feelings arose from anything more than "their interests," Livingston declared, "they ought not to be represented," for a legislator who responded to the "variable and inconstant" sentiments of the people would be a "political weathercock."[105] Hamilton was equally brusque when he told the same body that "one discerning and intelligent man will be as capable of understanding and representing the general interests of a state as twenty; because one man can be as fully acquainted with the general state of the commerce, manufactures, population, production, and common resources of a state, which are the proper objects of legislation."[106] Even in the states, financial measures were never produced through the equal participation of every member, Madison reminded the Virginia convention. "Our Assembly consists of considerably more than a hundred, yet from the nature of the business, it devolves on a much smaller number."[107]

From a modern vantage point, "the nature of the business" that Congress would transact appears modest. Next to the gross disparities that separate the objects of eighteenth-century governance from the regulatory concerns of the modern state, the disputes over public policy that pitted Hamiltonian Federalists against the Democratic-Republicans of Madison and Jefferson seem similarly slight—however real and principled they doubtless were to the participants. Yet in one sense at least, the advocates of the Constitution were on modern ground. For their defense of its scheme of national representation presupposed that legislation was the principal business of Congress, and that the qualities desired of its members accordingly transcended the independence and watchfulness that had been required (in theory) to maintain the supremacy of Parliament over the Crown. Unlike Parliament, Congress had not been called into existence to embody the consent of the people to the acts of another governing authority. The power to initiate legislation was not something it had to wrest from other sources; it was vested in Congress from the outset.

It was crucial to the formulation of the Federalist position that the objects of national legislation were at once vital but limited—that is, that they embraced the most important res publica while leaving the mundane affairs that preoccupied most Americans to the states. Had the Convention accepted the radical critiques of the state assemblies that Madison and Hamilton presented, with their corresponding proposals for much greater national oversight of state legislation than the Constitution ultimately afforded, the authors of The Federalist and other Federalists would have had to labor much harder to reconcile its scale of representation with the demands of sympathy. Then the Anti-Federalists' vivid specter of a central government whose laws and functionaries would intrude "into every corner of the city and country"—from "the ladies at their toilett" and "the professional man in his office or study" to the farmer in "the most obscure cottage"[108]—would have seemed far more plausible, and the demands for a great leap in the degree of sympathy required of representatives all the more persuasive.

RECENT COMMENTARY on the Federalist theory of representation has stressed the idea that the Constitution was designed to promote a "filtration of talent" in the election of Congress.[109] In a general sense this is correct. The framers had every reason to expect that large electoral districts serving a small Congress should produce more capable and distinguished legislators than the assemblies of the states. Anti-Federalists agreed that certain social advantages would conspire to make gentrified and cosmopolitan candidates the beneficiaries of this system. Yet the gap between these expectations and what the Constitution actually provided remains striking. The Constitution made no effort to reduce or regulate the size of the national electorate; or to impose significant qualifications on eligibility for office; or even to determine how national elections were to be conducted. By basing the House of Representatives on the existing electorates of the states, the framers shrewdly defused a potentially powerful objection against the Constitution. But by allowing the state legislatures so much discretion in setting electoral rules, they left the national government susceptible to both the aspirations and the abuses of democratic politics. That politics sometimes widened the claims for inclusion well beyond the propertied freeholders whom Madison idealized; but it also perpetuated unjust distortions in the form of the suffrage restrictions and gross malapportionment that proved so effective from the late nineteenth century until the 1960s. Equally important, the tension between the rival claims for sympathy and knowledge exposed a persistent fault line in American ideas of representation that the Federalist victory in 1788 hardly repaired. Not one but two sets of norms emerged from this debate, and in many ways the Anti-Federalist notion of responsiveness continued to command more adherents than the Madisonian ideal of deliberation. If Anti-Federalists erred in thinking that aristocrats, natural or otherwise, would make election to Congress the culmination of their ambition, their fears better reflected and predicted attitudes that continued to flourish in American political culture more generally. Given this ambiguous legacy, it is not surprising that disputes over how the mirror of representation is best polished remain as difficult to resolve today as they were contentious in 1787.

CHAPTER IX

CREATING THE PRESIDENCY

$\mathcal{E}$IGHT MONTHS after the Convention adjourned, the South Carolina delegate Pierce Butler recorded an observation that has misled some casual interpreters of the origins of the presidency. Acknowledging that its powers were "greater than I was disposed to make them," Butler doubted that "they would have been so great had not many of the members cast their eyes toward General Washington as President; and shaped their Ideas of the Powers to be given to a President, by their Opinions of his Virtue." Many framers and other Federalists certainly thought Washington's *election* would prove crucial to the fate of the Constitution. But Butler's observation hardly squares with the tangled record of proposals, tentative decisions, reconsiderations, and reversals from which the presidency finally, and belatedly, emerged.[1]

To derive a coherent theory of executive power from what Madison called these "tedious and reiterated" debates is not easy.[2] The uncertainties surrounding the executive reflect what Harvey C. Mansfield, Jr. has recently described as "the ambivalence of executive power." This ambivalence inheres in the disparity between the weakness of the executive as a subordinate, instrumental authority and the real advantages it enjoys in wielding power, advantages that its formal weakness often disguises and thus promotes.[3] But the difficulties the framers encountered owed as much in turn to *ambiguities* in the definition of executive power as to *ambivalence* in its exercise. The first sentence of Article II of the Constitution did little to dissolve this ambiguity when it baldly stated that "The executive power shall be vested in a president of the United States of America" without explaining what executive power is.

Deriving a single definition of executive power could never be a simple exercise. Multiple layers of historical experience shaped American thinking on this subject: the great disputes of Stuart England, which resonated still in eighteenth-century America; alarms over the rise of ministerial "corruption" under the Hanoverian kings; and lessons learned from the efforts of the early state constitutions to cabin executive power within strict republican limits. The conceptual confusion which arose as Americans sought to define executive power in nonmonarchical terms generated further uncertainty. They embraced the theory of separated powers without wholly abandoning the language of mixed government; they struggled to distinguish the administrative parts of governance from other powers that the British crown had exercised as its prerogative; and they were further puzzled to decide whether foreign relations was more nearly executive or legislative or a hybrid of both. Nor could they readily imagine the political dimensions of executive power. Was a republican executive best conceived as the equivalent of a "patriot king above party," a potential prime minister, or merely a general administrator?

These ambiguities in the definition of the executive made the other problems the framers faced in designing the presidency even less tractable, contributing to the cyclical debates Madison lamented. Yet the creation of the presidency was also their most creative act, and their achievement was all the more notable because leading framers thought about the executive in notably divergent ways. It was precisely because their views diverged so sharply that disagreements over the power of the presidency emerged as a potent source of constitutional controversy in the 1790s.

AMERICAN IDEAS OF THE EXECUTIVE developed within the two broad paradigms that eighteenth century commentators employed to explain why Britain's "boasted" constitution had attained its liberty-preserving stability. The first and more important was the ancient theory of mixed government that Charles I invoked in *His Majesties Answer to the XIX Propositions of Both Houses of Parliament* (1642); the second was the newer idea of the separation of powers that received its classic statement in Montesquieu's *De l'esprit des lois* (1748). As several studies have painstakingly explained, the relation between these two theories was fraught with ambiguity.[4] The English theory of mixed government held that the presence *in the legislature* of the three estates of monarchy, aristocracy, and people would prevent the constitution from degenerating into the corrupt forms of tyranny, oligarchy, or anarchy. By contrast, separation of powers emphasized the qualitatively distinct *functions* performed by the legislative, executive, and judicial departments of government.[5] In securing the *balance* that both principles were expected to promote, the two theories could be regarded as complementary, alternative, or even rival explanations of the "matchless constitution" that Britons and Americans revered. The two theories could be amalgamated, for example, if diverse tasks of governance were allocated to the institutions of monarchy, Lords, and Commons on the basis of the perceived characteristics of their members. But because mixed government presumed that royalty and nobility were part of the natural order, it proved vulnerable to the republican tendency of the Enlightenment to treat both estates as vestiges of feudalism. Separation of powers could then appear as a more attractive model of government because it did not depend on an archaic image of society.[6]

Both theories emerged from the great disputes of the mid-seventeenth century—the era of revolution and regicide, Long Parliament and Commonwealth, the Protectorate of Oliver Cromwell and the Restoration of Charles II. Responding to the royalist reliance on mixed government in the escalating conflict of the 1640s, several supporters of Parliament first sketched a theory of separated powers. In their view, the most objectionable prerogatives were those that enabled the king to govern without Parliament, veto legislation, and suspend or dispense with duly enacted statutes. If these powers were abrogated, the Crown would be restricted to truly executive functions. The regicide of 1649 and the ensuing abolition of the monarchy and House of Lords weakened the model of mixed government even more, while the theory of separation of powers ironically gained support from the mounting reaction against the excesses of a factious Long Parliament that thereafter "governed the country by appointing a host of committees dealing with all the affairs of state, confiscating property, summoning people before them, and dealing with them in a summary fashion." Its critics now ranged across the political spectrum, and they argued that Parliament's proper function was to enact general laws, framed in regular but relatively brief sessions, while the executive conducted the daily activity of governing subject to legislative review. With the restoration of the monarchy and the House of Lords in 1660, mixed government regained its dominant place, and separation of powers was relegated to its secondary position. But many accounts of the constitution now emphasized the special functions that Crown, Commons, and Lords were individually presumed to perform.[7]

In *classifying* the forms of public authority concerned with lawful governance within the realm, seventeenth-century English thinkers recognized only two powers: legislative and executive. The judiciary remained enfolded within the executive, while royal judges who had often acted as instruments of an arbitrary Crown at whose pleasure they served still commanded more distrust than respect. Yet because the process of doing justice also comprised nearly the entire corpus of executive duties, the administration of government still largely meant the administration of royal justice, while the truly executive aspect of this power was literally to carry out the judgments of the courts.[8] This equation of executive and judicial power also reflected the absence of anything like a national bureaucracy exercising broad administrative functions. Here the English Crown lagged far behind other European monarchies in developing the apparatus of a modern state. Not until its long isolation from European wars gave way after 1688 to prolonged international conflicts would conditions exist to construct a state in which executive power meant ministerial government of a kind unseen (if not entirely unfeared) in the Stuart age.[9]

The mid-century ideas of separated powers were certainly known to John Locke as he drafted his *Two Treatises of Government* around 1680.[10] Locke's primary contribution to these ideas was to add a third category of "federative" power covering relations "with all Persons and Communities without the Commonwealth." This power was "really distinct" in itself, not only in being directed toward external affairs but also in being "much less capable to be directed by antecedent, standing, positive Laws, than the *Executive*; and so must be left to the Prudence and Wisdom of those whose hands it is in." Yet Locke found underlying similarities between federative and executive power. Just as the executive derived from "the power every Man naturally had before he entred into Society" to preserve himself, so federative power concerned relations among communities in an international "state of nature." Moreover, both powers "requiring the force of Society for their exercise," it was "impracticable" to deposit them in different "hands," because the ensuing rivalry could end in "disorder and ruine." Locke's argument for prudence in the exercise of federative power further paralleled his willingness to allow the executive latitude in applying, ignoring, or even defying standing laws. Both forms of governance required the continuous exercise of a discretion that a legislature, meeting occasionally to frame general rules, would lack.[11] While affirming that executive and federative powers were both *"Ministerial and subordinate to the Legislative,"* Locke would allow the executive to retain the prerogatives of negativing and dispensing with legislation, and his thinking in this respect resembled that of the royalists of the 1680s.[12]

Other writers evoked the idea of separated powers in succeeding decades. Of these the most notable was Viscount Bolingbroke, whose 1738 tract, *The Idea of a Patriot King*, shaped American ideals of executive leadership by prescribing a model of governance in which the king would rise above party turmoil to embody a disinterested notion of the public good.[13] But it was Montesquieu who brought this principle closer to parity with mixed government in his famous examination of the English constitution in Book XI of *The Spirit of the Laws*. Montesquieu began by restating Locke's definitions: "In every government there are three sorts of power: the legislative; the executive in respect to things dependent on the law of nations; and the executive in regard to matters that depend on the civil law." A few paragraphs later, however, he offered a different triad of powers: "that of enacting laws, that of executing the public resolutions, and of trying the causes of individuals." This classification is commonly taken as the first statement of the modern theory of separated powers, and the ensuing discussion treated the legislative, executive, and judicial aspects of governance without further reference to external affairs.[14]

As an empirical observer of Georgian politics, Montesquieu left much to be desired. He ignored the concerns of those who fretted, like his friend Bolingbroke, that "corruption" was subverting the independence of Parliament, or the rival claims of those who held, with David Hume, that a Crown lacking influence would sink before an overmighty Parliament. Montesquieu instead followed Locke in thinking that the prerogatives of vetoing legislation and controlling the meeting of the legislature were essential sources of executive power. In fact the use of influence to manage Parliament had rendered the negative redundant since the reign of Queen Anne, while temptations more alluring than lust for power kept its members from sitting year-round in their drafty debating chambers. Nor did Montesquieu take account of other changes that were transforming the British state. The commanding figures of this newly modeled executive were its great ministers—beginning with Robert Walpole—who presided as virtual prime ministers from the stronghold of the Treasury. These men were still royal servants whose tenure depended on both their parliamentary skills and their relations with the king. But the government they administered was no longer the underdeveloped English state of the previous century, with its handful of bureaus and offices clustered around the Privy Council and royal household. In its place there now stood a growing apparatus of departments, boards, and most important, a revenue system that made the limited monarchy of Britain more efficient than its absolutist European rivals.[15]

Neither Britons nor Americans needed a French nobleman, however eminent, to explain the workings of their constitution. They celebrated Montesquieu because he celebrated their regime, and neither the flaws in his description nor his literary vices detracted from his influence.[16] But

Americans had more specific reasons for taking his aphoristic defense of the separation of powers to heart (even as they rejected his defense of particular prerogatives). His warnings against concentrating two forms of power in one set of hands appealed to the colonists for the same reason that first attracted the opponents of Charles I to the same idea. Recurring disputes between colonial assemblies and governors reprised the rival claims of parliamentary rights and executive prerogative that had been central to seventeenth-century English politics. In America royal governors retained the right to prorogue and dissolve assemblies, powers they freely used to send truculent legislatures home in the hope that a respite or new elections would make their next meeting more pliable. In Britain the abuse of this power was barred by statutes requiring Parliament to meet once every three years and elections to occur no more than seven years apart. Moreover, Parliament *had* to meet to vote on the supplies that the nation's strategic commitments required. But in America these prerogatives rendered the institutional life of the assemblies precarious, while the reduced urgency of government made their services more dispensable. And colonial governors routinely vetoed bills or insisted that they include clauses suspending final enactment for review and approval by the Privy Council, and they did so not on personal whim but in obedience to instructions from London and without regard to the circumstances warranting particular legislative acts.[17]

From the memory of the wrongs inflicted by generations of royal governors and the belief that ambitious monarchs and their ministers regularly threatened liberty, the American constitution writers of 1776 drew two great lessons. The first was to "strip" the new state executives of what John Adams called "those badges of domination called prerogatives"; the second was to affirm the principle of separated powers with the fervor that enabled the Virginia constitution of 1776 to declare "that the legislative, executive, and judiciary departments shall be separate and distinct; so that neither exercise the powers properly belonging to the other; nor shall any person exercise the powers of more than one of them at the same time."[18] As J. M. C. Vile has observed, this "was the clearest, most precise statement of the doctrine which had at that time appeared anywhere, in the works of political theorists, or in the pronouncements of statesmen," for it presupposed that there were three distinct forms of power that could be deposited in separate institutions whose members would serve in only one branch of government at a time. But the theoretical symmetry of this formula was belied in practice. "When Americans in 1776 spoke of keeping the several parts of the government separate and distinct," Gordon Wood has noted, "they were primarily thinking of insulating the judiciary

and particularly the legislature from executive manipulation"—not of sub-
jecting legislators to any external checks other than the good sense of the
electorate.[19]

The evisceration of executive power was the most conspicuous aspect
of the early state constitutions, which deprived the executive of its political independence and nearly every power that smacked of royal prerogative. Governors lost the ability to control the meetings of the assemblies,
much less veto or suspend their acts; most were subject to legislative election for the brief term of a year; they exercised only limited powers of appointment; and executive authority became merely that, the obligation to
carry out the legislative will.[20] When Thomas Jefferson drafted a constitution for Virginia, he went so far as to enumerate the specific prerogatives that his proposed "[a]dministrator . . . shall not possess." The
constitution that Virginia adopted while Jefferson was absent at Congress
declared more simply that the executive "shall not, under any pretence,
exercise any power or prerogative by virtue of any Law, statute, or Custom, of England," save a limited power to grant reprieves and pardons.
While this lack of detail did not satisfy Jefferson, the essential principle
remained the same.[21]

In reconstituting the executive, then, Americans paid homage to
Montesquieu's principle of separation without allowing his (or Locke's)
defense of prerogative to outweigh the lessons of their own history. The
reactionary character of their animus against the executive became trou-
blesome only after problems of wartime governance exposed the defects of
legislative supremacy. With the memory of monarchical power "before
our eyes," William Livingston recalled in 1783, "we improvidently raised
a battery against an attack that could never be made upon us, & accordingly constituted the Executive branch too weak & inefficatious to operate with proper energy & vigour." Madison reached the same conclusion.
"The want of *fidelity* in the administration of power having been the
grievance felt under most Governments, and by the American States
themselves under the British Government," he recalled in 1785, "it was
natural for them to give too exclusive an attention to this primary
attribute."[22]

Much the same impulse propelled an equally fundamental reconstitution of the colonial councils, the anomalous bodies which in nearly every
colony acted as an upper legislative chamber, an advisory executive council, and a high court of appeal (with the governor).[23] The closest analogue
to these bodies in the British constitution was the House of Lords, which
the theory of mixed government made the fulcrum balancing the more
volatile forces of king and Commons—even though the Lords were as

subject to the blandishments of "influence" as the Commons, and nearly always supported the governing ministry. In Britain this discrepancy between theory and fact mattered little, but in America the incapacity of the councils to play their prescribed mediating role seemed more troubling. Even before the Revolution, the councils were deemed defective not because they lacked the necessary formal powers but because the social conditions required to sustain mixed government seemed hopelessly absent. All the colonies had upper classes—some wealthy and cohesive, like the planter elites of South Carolina and Virginia, with its great cousinry; others a gentry only modestly superior to their neighbors, as in New Jersey and Connecticut—but none possessed an aristocracy in the proper sense. American councilors lacked the hereditary rights and great estates that presumably gave the British aristocracy its permanent stake in the weal of the realm; as creatures of Crown patronage, serving at pleasure, they were mere cogs in the machinery of influence that spanned the Atlantic, incapable of balancing either prerogative-wielding governors or the turbulent commons represented in the lower houses of assembly.[24]

When the revolutionaries began reconfiguring the structure of government, the councils were as much an object of reform as the governorships. Their claim to exercise all three forms of power violated the principle of separation as flagrantly as the "archaic" prerogatives of the governors. The state constitutions dispersed the multiple powers of the old councils among a new array of institutions: senates to act as upper legislative chambers, councils of state to serve as advisory boards for the executive, and high courts of appeal to cap the newly distinct judicial department of government.

Yet if this process of disaggregation simplified the task of making separation of powers the dominant constitutional paradigm, the older imagery of mixed government retained a residual hold on American thinking. By default, the new senates became the one institution expected to provide a measure of balance—a check—*within* government itself. In the absence of a legal aristocracy, it was not evident how an American senate could play the same mediating role as the House of Lords. Although seven states required either senators, their electors, or both to hold more property than members or electors of the lower house, the social distance between the chambers was trivial.[25] Yet so long as the notion survived that the senate represented a social elite, mixed government and the more functional theory of separated powers remained permeable. John Adams did not give the senate a distinct social character in his influential *Thoughts on Government*, yet the concept of mixed government still echoed faintly when he described it "as a mediator between the two extreme branches of the legislature, that which represents the people and that which is vested with the executive power." Mixed government resonated far more strongly in the tract that the Virginia planter Carter Braxton wrote in response to Adams, which called for an aristocratic "council of state" whose members would serve for life. At the other end of the spectrum of opinion, more populist writers imagined eliminating the senate entirely or giving it advisory powers only.[26]

Dispersing the multiple functions of the colonial councils affected the new shape of the executive in one other way: by requiring governors to act in consultation with councils of state whose members were elected either by the assembly or by the people at large. Just as legislative power was best divided between two houses, so executive power was to be vested in a plural body of which the governor was only the leading member. These councils were not conceived as a ministerial cabinet. Their members were not heads of administrative departments but advisers whose counsel the governor should take in the normal course of discharging executive duties. Should their advice be ignored, councilors were expected to make a formal record of their dissent. The state constitutions thus presumed that governors could not be trusted to act decisively on their own individual authority. Moreover, in most states governors lacked authority to appoint the subordinate officials for whose administration they were presumably accountable.[27]

To constitute a weaker executive would have been nearly impossible. Had Americans not learned the history of the Long Parliament and the dicta of Montesquieu so well, they might have moved to deconstitutionalize the executive entirely, leaving the legislature to delegate executive tasks as it saw fit. Or had they prudently foreseen the problems of governance that prolonged war would create, they might have anticipated that victory could depend more on the effective use of executive discretion than on fidelity to legislative supremacy. Respect for the idea of a balanced constitution ran deep enough for the executive to be recognized as a distinct department, but not to annul older lessons. Yet as powerfully as this anti-executive bias worked in 1776, it quickly began to wane. The New York constitution of 1777 marked a first step away by allowing the governor to be elected by popular vote for a term of three years. Thus freed from political dependence on the legislature, however, the executive could not be trusted completely. New York was the first state to create an external check on the legislature, but it vested this limited negative in a council of revision that included the chancellor and justices of the supreme court as well as the governor; powers of appointment were similarly placed in a second council made up of the governor and four senators. This movement to revitalize the executive continued in the Massachusetts constitution of 1780, but again ambiguously. Here, too, the people elected the governor, but for a term of only one year. Massachusetts was the first state to give the governor alone a limited veto over legislation. But in conducting "the executive part of government," including appointments to all civil offices, he was still obliged to act with the advice and consent of the council.[28]

The restoration of executive power in these states reflected the active part that John Jay, Gouverneur Morris, James Duane, and Robert R. Livingston took in drafting the New York constitution and which John Adams played in Massachusetts. All were actively involved in mobilizing the country for war, and their ideas of republican government were more prudent than enthusiastic. But the prevailing understanding of the executive was still tinged by anti-monarchical sentiments that had little room for reviving monarchical prerogatives or empowering governors to check the excesses of the legislature. Americans preferred a plural or conciliar executive to the idea that a single individual could hold the plenum of executive power, and they still regarded separation of powers more as a formula for restricting the executive than as a symmetrical balance among coequal departments. It is a mark of the misgivings that militated against the executive that as late as 1785 Madison could confess that he had formed "no final opinion whether the first Magistrate should be chosen by the people at large or whether the power should be vested in one man assisted by a council or in a council of which the President shall be only primus inter pares." The most promising remedy for the vices of republican misrule, he told Caleb Wallace, lay in creating true senates or a body like the New York council of revision.[29]

In this same letter, Madison identified a further ambiguity in American thinking when he suggested that the executive was no longer "entitled" to "the 2d place" in the structure of state government because "all the great powers which are properly executive [were] transferd to the Federal Government"—that is, the matters of war and diplomacy which were prerogatives of the British Crown. His comment suggests how the problem of federalism introduced a further complexity in defining the proper authority of a republican executive. The authority once claimed by the Crown had devolved on two levels of government, not only contributing to the weakness of the state executives but also complicating the task of understanding the nature of Congress itself, a body which had the appearance of a legislature but responsibilities customarily associated with the Crown.

Given its character as a "deliberating executive assembly," Congress was not so much an imbalanced government as an anomalous institution to which the concept of balance seemed irrelevant. True, it had a president, but his essential duties were to carry on correspondence and to act as a speaker of the house. The multiplicity of the functions Congress discharged frequently led more businesslike members to propose reforms that would transfer numerous tasks to an administrative bureaucracy. Daily reviewing what Robert Morris called the "damned trash" of routine expenditures and mundane matters, Congress seemed a monument to an inefficiency that was compounded by patterns of rotation and leave-taking which kept its membership in continual flux. Rank "mismanagement" was the necessary result, Morris charged, "because no man living can attend the daily deliberations of Congress and do executive parts of business at the same time."[30] A series of efforts to establish administrative boards finally led to the creation of four executive departments in 1781, with Morris returning from private life to become superintendent of the first organized and most important, the department of finance.

This effort to disaggregate the functions of Congress was part of "the efficiency side" of the separation of powers.[31] These pragmatic reforms were designed to unburden Congress of decisions that need not require its collective attention while delegating the administration of finance to an individual whose qualifications were widely respected. Morris's conduct in office, however, had the ironic effect of confirming both republican prejudices against the executive and the potential benefits of an "energetic" administration. His bold but ultimately rash efforts in 1783 to foment discontent among public creditors and the army in order to persuade Congress to adopt his financial program only reminded his detractors of the dangers of allowing ambitious minsters to manipulate legislative deliberations. On the other hand, to his admiring allies—congressional delegates James Wilson, Thomas FitzSimons, and Alexander Hamilton, and his assistant Gouverneur Morris—the vigor with which Morris acted contrasted sharply with the malaise they ascribed to the state and national officials who carried out essential functions of wartime governance. His political errors notwithstanding, Morris's administration illustrated the wisdom of placing executive powers in the hands of a single, energetic, responsible official.

Once Morris left office, Secretary of Foreign Affairs John Jay was the most prominent national official. A former president of Congress, minister to Spain, and peace commissioner, Jay had also had frequent occasion to ponder the problems Congress brought on itself by attempting to manage and discuss everything. When he accepted his new position in 1784, he insisted on the right to consult Congress in person and to conduct its foreign correspondence—signs that he regarded himself as a true minister rather than a glorified clerk. By the summer of 1786 Jay could write Jefferson that he was

> daily more convinced that the Construction of our Federal Government is fundamentally wrong. To vest legislative, judicial and executive Powers in one and the same Body of Men, and that too in a Body daily changing its Members, can never be wise. In my Opinion those three great Departments of Sovereignty should be for ever separated, as to serve as Checks on each other.[32]

Here Jay transposed to national government concerns more often generated within the states. Yet he was writing only a fortnight after he had urged Congress to support his plan to abjure immediate claims to the navigation of the Mississippi in order to secure a commercial treaty with Spain. The opposition Jay evoked from southern delegates did as much to confirm their reservations about the dangers of executive discretion as to illustrate the virtues of executive independence.

At the national level of government, then, Morris and Jay produced a mixed political legacy. No one with substantial experience of the inefficiency of Congress could fail to appreciate the benefits of delegating administrative responsibility to qualified executive officials. But at the point where administration and the formulation of policy overlapped, the lessons were less clear. For those who admired Morris and Jay, much could be said for transferring initiative from a quarrelsome Congress to competent ministers of state. Those who blamed the erratic quality of the American war effort on Congress, or recalled its difficulties in framing terms of peace, similarly wondered whether matters of war and peace were best decided by collective debates. But the prejudice against allowing executive ministers to manipulate legislative deliberations had deep roots—and neither Morris nor Jay had convinced their detractors that this prejudice was misplaced.

Among the delegates gathering at Philadelphia in May 1787, the greatest enthusiasts for an energetic executive were those framers most closely allied with Morris and Jay: Hamilton, Wilson, and Gouverneur Morris. By contrast, Madison's thinking on the executive had evolved little since 1785. Only weeks before the Convention met, he confessed to Washington that he had "scarcely ventured to form my own opinion either of the manner in which it ought to be constituted or of the authorities with which it ought to be cloathed."[33] He was certain of one thing only: that it was imperative to create an independent executive capable of withstanding overt manipulation by the legislature. Yet as important as it was to enable this weaker branch to defend itself against legislative encroachments, it remained difficult to imagine the executive as the crucial source of balance within the government as a whole. The Senate remained the most obvious candidate for that mediating role. Only after its limitations became apparent could a broader conception of the utility of the executive emerge to shape the development of the American presidency.

OTHER FRAMERS WERE LESS TENTATIVE and hesitant about the executive than Madison. But their early comments revealed a spectrum of opinions which ranged from the admiration that Hamilton and John Dickinson voiced for the limited monarchy of Britain to Roger Sherman's suggestion that no constitutional provision need be made for the executive because it was "nothing more than an institution for carrying the will of the Legislature into effect."[34] Moreover, the *structure* of this debate differed from the comparable discussion of representation in several respects. The choices the framers faced in constructing Congress were always fairly obvious, and their positions usually followed the manifest interests of their states. But the longer they discussed the executive, the more puzzled they grew; nor did their positions correlate neatly with the perceived interests of their states. The matrix of issues surrounding the election, term, reeligibility, and removal of the executive proved peculiarly complex. As the delegates repeatedly learned, a decision taken on one of these matters required revisions in one or more of the others. Under these conditions, no delegate or faction could control the course of a debate that proved frustratingly episodic and even circular. At crucial points, Wilson and Gouverneur Morris gave a decided twist to the debate, but at other times so did such lesser figures as John McClurg, William Houston, and Hugh Williamson.[35]

There were three distinct phases in the evolution of the presidency. The first (June 1–6) produced agreement on two major points: to vest the executive power in a single person, who would in turn wield a limited veto over legislation. During the second phase (July 17–26), the framers struggled to reconcile the general principle of an independent executive with different options for rules of election and tenure. Much of this discussion involved weighing the relative *dis*advantages of election by the legislature, the people, or an electoral college. These doubts persisted into the final stage of debate (September 4–8), but the decisions taken as adjournment neared also made the presidency the net beneficiary of growing reservations about the Senate.

The Virginia Plan offered only a minimalist approach to the problem of executive power. Article 7 proposed that the executive "be chosen by the National Legislature" for a single term of unspecified length, receive "a fixed compensation," and possess "general authority to execute the National laws" and "to enjoy the Executive rights vested in Congress by the Confederation." Whether those "executive rights" included matters of war and diplomacy was left unresolved; nor did the Virginia Plan make any provision for powers of appointment. Article 8 further proposed to join the executive "and a convenient number of the National Judiciary" in a council of revision armed with a limited veto over national legislation.[36]

The initial discussion of Article 7 was marked by a mixture of assertion and diffidence. Charles Pinckney opened debate on June 1 by declaring that "he was for a vigorous Executive but was afraid the executive powers" it would inherit from Congress "might extend to peace & war &c which would render the Executive a Monarchy, of the worst kind, to wit, an elective one." After Wilson moved "that the Executive consist of a single person," the delegates sat mutely until Nathaniel Gorham, chairing the committee of the whole, asked "if he should put the question." Serious debate began only after Benjamin Franklin and John Rutledge "animadverted on the shyness of gentlemen on this and other subjects." Thus inspired, two members faulted Wilson's motion on republican grounds: Sherman suggested leaving the entire subject to the discretion of Congress, while Randolph described "unity in the Executive magistracy" as "the foetus of monarchy" and criticized Wilson for taking the British constitution "as our prototype." Wilson replied that the royal prerogative did not provide "a proper guide in defining the Executive powers." Some of those prerogatives were actually legislative, including matters of "war & peace &c. The only powers he conceived strictly executive were those of executing the laws, and appointing officers" not otherwise "appointed by the Legislature." Far from encouraging a dangerous discretion, Wilson added, unity would reconcile the monarchical advantages of "energy" and "dispatch" with the "responsibility" demanded by republican orthodoxy.[37]

There debate on Wilson's amendment halted—the delegates "seeming unprepared for any decision on it." Madison then hinted that the Convention should first decide what powers to vest in the executive before determining whether it should be unitary or plural. Rather than pursue this hint—which ran opposite to his strategy on representation—the delegates turned to the issue of election and tenure. After another brief debate, the committee of the whole endorsed the clauses of the Virginia Plan calling for the executive to be elected by the national legislature for a single term now fixed at seven years. Two days later (June 4), the committee approved the idea of a unitary executive.[38]

The most revealing passage in this exploratory discussion occurred when the delegates took up the council of revision. Elbridge Gerry immediately moved to give a limited veto to the executive alone, and he prefaced his motion with the striking claim that the judiciary need not be involved in the veto because "they will have a sufficient check agst. encroachments on their own department by their exposition of the laws, which involved a power of deciding on their constitutionality. In some states," he pointedly noted, "the Judges had actually set aside laws as being agst. the Constitution." For Gerry and Rufus King, the joint council was doubly flawed because it would give the judges an improper role in legislating while making it difficult for them to "expound the law as it should come before them, free from the bias of having participated in its formation." Wilson and Hamilton then offered a rival amendment to give the executive an *absolute* veto. This was so offensive that only its movers and King voted in its favor. Gerry's proposal for a limited veto then passed nearly as decisively, eight states to two. But when Madison and Wilson renewed the case for the council of revision as a more prudent and effective check on the legislature, their motion failed eight states to three.[39]

This decision effectively completed the first round of debate on the executive. Notwithstanding the alarm that Mason and Randolph sounded against incipient monarchy, the delegates had already revived the executive in notable ways by creating a unitary office with constitutionally prescribed duties, a check on legislation, and a tenure that would render it independent of the legislature immediately after election. This was substantial progress, but it was made only by skirting issues that later proved vexatious.[40]

The second round of discussion brought the most perplexing passage of the entire Convention. It began deceptively when the delegates affirmed the principle of a unitary executive on July 17[41] and ended nine days later where it began, with an executive elected by the legislature for a single seven-year term. Between these two points, the framers cycled through a series of motions and counterproposals as they weighed the disadvantages of legislative election, rejected popular election while endorsing a plan for an electoral college, grappled with the issues of length of term and reeligibility as functions of these modes of election, reconsidered the council of revision, asked whether powers of appointment should be vested solely in the executive or jointly with the Senate, and then worked back to their starting position as qualms about both an electoral college and popular election prevailed over the desire to make reeligibility an incentive for sound administration.

Within this matrix, the nearest thing to a first principle or independent variable was the desire to enable the executive to resist legislative "encroachments." If that is kept in mind, the logic of the positions the framers took on nearly every other aspect of the executive becomes much more explicable. But another factor repeatedly worked to make consensus elusive. In their debates over Congress, the framers were content to allow the states to decide how representatives would be elected. But the rules for electing the executive had to be fixed constitutionally, and here they labored under doubts and uncertainties that reflected the very novelty of the office they were designing. The interplay of these two crucial factors becomes evident if we examine the major questions the framers considered between July 17 and July 26.

Election.   The framers considered three basic modes of election, and each proved vulnerable to serious criticism. The most obvious alternative was to give the choice to the national legislature, which had the advantage of placing the decision in the nation's most knowledgeable leaders. The countervailing concern, Morris warned, was that the result would inevitably be the "work of intrigue, of cabal, and of faction," producing a pliable official who would become the willing tool of his supporters.[42] The first alternative to this mode was election by the people, which Morris, Wilson, and Madison boldly endorsed on principle.[43] Its great defect was *not* that the framers feared the people would be easily duped by ambitious demagogues; two other objections loomed larger. First, "The extent of the Country renders it impossible that the people can have the requisite capacity to judge of the respective pretensions of the Candidates," Mason observed; they would naturally prefer citizens from their own states, and thus never produce a majority for any candidate. Second, if national majorities did form, Madison predicted, they would take a strongly sectional cast favoring the North, because in a vote taken at large the free white citizens of the South would be a permanent minority.[44]

The third option was to establish an electoral college, an idea first raised by Wilson on June 2, revived by Rufus King, and then revised further when Gerry and Ellsworth proposed to have the state legislatures appoint twenty-five electors.[45] The appeal of this scheme, which briefly took on the aura of a panacea, had little to do with the mode of election per se but rested instead on the support it gave to those who thought that eligibility for reelection would give the executive an important incentive to maintain his independence. Because the college would meet once and then forever dissolve, the executive could not be bound to toady to its demands. But the advantages of this proposal evaporated when some delegates questioned the inconvenience and expense of gathering electors from distant states, and more important, when they began to doubt whether electors would "be men of the 1st. nor even the 2d. grade in the States."[46] When the delegates gathered on July 26, Mason canvassed the defects in the various modes of election before concluding "that an election by the Natl Legislature as originally proposed"—for a single term of seven years—"was the best. If it was liable to objections, it was liable to fewer than any others." With the committee of detail about to begin its work, the Convention endorsed Mason's motion seven states to three (with Massachusetts unaccountably absent).[47]

Reeligibility. Mason could take this position because he strongly believed that it was "the very palladium of Civil liberty, that the great officers of State, and particularly the executive, should at fixed periods return to that mass from which they were at first taken, in order that they may feel & respect those rights & interests, which are again to be personally valuable to them." He had included that principle in the Virginia Declaration of Rights in 1776, and nothing since had altered his belief.[48] But other delegates regarded eligibility for reelection as valuable in itself. As Sherman and King both argued, "he who has proved himself to be most fit for an Office, ought not to be excluded by the constitution from holding it." Two votes on this issue indicated that a majority of delegates agreed, but only so long as they were satisfied that the power of election was safely placed outside Congress. When that prospect evaporated, the Convention had to restrict the executive to a single term.[49]

Length of term. But how long should that term be? If the underlying goal remained an executive capable of protecting his office from intrusive direction by Congress, it followed that the president should serve a reasonably lengthy term. Competence in the administrative aspects of government could not be gained in a day, nor should its benefits be yielded almost as soon as they were felt. Morris made this case forthrightly. When Dr. McClurg of Virginia offered a substitute motion for tenure "during good behavior" after the Convention initially voted for reeligibility, Morris exclaimed, "This was the way to get a good Government."[50] But statements like those could only spark a nervous reaction in those who worried that a president who grew too comfortable in office would acquire monarchical ambitions. No magic number defined the optimal term an executive should serve; this calculation also depended on the mode of election and the matter of reeligibility.

Impeachment. The longer the term the executive received, the more important it was to find a mechanism "for defending the Community agst the incapacity, negligence or perfidy of the chief Magistrate." But here, too, perplexing questions awaited. Was impeachment really necessary for an executive serving a fixed term? Why not limit its reach to the "coadjutors" of the president? What independence could the executive retain if this power was given to the legislature? But what body other than the legislature could exercise this formidable power?[51]

Council of revision. The discussion of all these questions of tenure was shaped by the framers' overriding concern with the need to curb legislative "encroachments." The debate over the joint executive-judicial council of revision, however, encouraged the framers to consider executive power and influence in broader terms—to ask what further purposes the executive might serve beyond the admittedly vital one of disproving the "maxim in political Science" which held "that Republican Government is not adapted to a large extent of Country because the energy of the Executive Magistracy can not reach the extreme parts of it."[52]

In early June, the committee of the whole had vested a limited negative in the executive. Simply reaching this point was a substantial step away from the republican orthodoxy of 1776, for it meant that the Convention already agreed that the legislature should be subject to an external "check." But Wilson and Madison remained strongly committed to the council of revision, and on July 21 they nearly deadlocked the Convention on its merits.

Their case for the council rested on three propositions. First, "the defence of the executive was not the sole object of the Revisionary power," Mason observed. It should also be used to discourage or annul the passage of "unjust and pernicious laws," and to make the executive, Morris added, "the guardian of the people, even of the lower classes, agst. Legislative tyranny, against the Great & the wealthy who in the course of things will necessarily compose the Legislative body."[53] Second, whatever injury a judicial role in lawmaking did to the strict separation of powers would be offset, Madison argued, by the "valuable assistance it would give in preserving a consistency, conciseness, perspicuity & technical propriety in the laws, qualities peculiarly necessary, & yet shamefully wanting in our republican codes."[54] But third, and most important, the case for a joint council assumed that the executive, acting alone, would lack the political resources to withstand the legislature. The key word here was "firmness," for Ellsworth, Madison, and Morris all asserted that without judicial support the executive would not possess the necessary "wisdom & firmness," the "confidence and firmness," the "auxiliary firmness & weight" to oppose a dominant Congress.[55] This pragmatic argument reflected the deeper difficulty the framers faced in imagining how a single official, however independent, could set his opinion against the collective weight and influence of a representative assembly.

The opponents of the council of revision were more inclined to emphasize the principle of separation of powers, and to limit their concern to enabling the two weaker branches to protect themselves separately against legislative encroachments. Judges would exercise their own negative, Luther Martin noted, by determining "the Constitutionality of laws."[56] But the case against the council had its own pragmatic side. Prior participation in lawmaking would in fact make it more difficult for judges to exercise their proper power and special knowledge when cases came before them. "The Judges in exercising the function of expositors might be influenced by the part they had taken, in framing the laws," Caleb Strong objected. They should never be asked "to give their opinion on a law till it comes before them," John Rutledge added; an executive needing bracing could turn to the other "officers of State, as of war, finance, &c.," without involving the judiciary in an improper activity.[57]

The pragmatic symmetry in these arguments reflected a nearly equal balance of opinion within the Convention, which now rejected the council by a vote of four states to three with two divided, and then unanimously reaffirmed the limited executive veto. That remained a crucial point of consensus. But nearly every other topic examined during this cycle of debate in late July revealed that the framers were still deeply uncertain about the fundamental political constitution of executive power; and with different members emphasizing particular problems—the need for rotation, the benefits of reeligibility, the danger of long terms—it was not evident how the Convention would pursue its general goal of securing executive independence. Nor was it yet certain that the executive would possess any powers other than administrative ones. At this point in their deliberations, the framers still expected the power to negotiate treaties and to make appointments to other major offices to reside in the Senate.

That expectation shaped the report of the committee of detail, which gave the Senate the "power to make treaties, and to appoint Ambassadors, and Judges of the supreme Court," and the quasi-judicial function of overseeing interstate disputes "respecting territory and jurisdiction."[58] The Senate would thus possess not only legislative but aspects of executive, federative, and judicial power alike. The president could convey information and recommendations to Congress; but his essential duties were to "take care that the laws . . . be duly and faithfully executed"; to "appoint officers in all cases not otherwise provided for"; and to act as commander in chief of the armed forces. Executive power in foreign relations involved only the ceremonial function of receiving ambassadors.[59]

Over the next five weeks, however, a growing reaction against the Senate worked in favor of the presidency, encouraging those framers who opposed legislative election and favored reeligibility to renew their efforts. Three days of debate marked turning points in this process. The first occurred when the Convention reconsidered the negative on August 15. After it rejected a new proposal by Madison requiring bills to be submitted separately "to the Executive and Supreme Judiciary Departments"—which inspired further criticism of the impropriety of judicial involvement in lawmaking—Morris and Wilson suggested that it would be better to give the executive an absolute negative, again implying that the Senate would not check the House when measures were afoot to promote legislative control of the executive. Their arguments were strong enough to carry an amendment raising the majority required to overturn a veto from two-thirds to three-fourths of each house.[60]

The other two debates that enhanced presidential authority fell within the realm of federative power. Late in the session of August 17, after a cryptic but momentous debate, the Convention modified the clause authorizing Congress "to make war" to read "to declare war." Madison's notes do not fully explain how the framers distinguished these verbs. If King expressed the sense of the meeting when he observed "that *'make'* war might be understood to 'conduct' it which was an Executive function," the substitution would preserve the capacity of the president to wage war with the essential attributes of energy and dispatch. Though Congress could still exert great influence through its power of the purse, allowing it to *make* war (in the sense of directing operations) was another form of encroachment that would compromise the benefits of holding the president as responsible for the conduct of war as for the administration of government.[61]

Could the same rationale apply to the conduct of foreign relations more generally? This much-examined debate of August 17 was not simply about the proper spheres of Congress and the president; it was no less concerned with the respective roles of the House and the Senate in matters of war and especially peace. While it seemed evident that a decision to go to war should be made bicamerally—not only because it required only a "simple and overt declaration" but also because war could only be waged if both houses voted the necessary supplies—"peace [was] attended with intricate & secret negotiations."[62] That point should have weighed in favor of the Senate. But as this debate and the discussion of the treaty power six days later revealed, a number of framers now thought that the Senate alone should not control American diplomacy. Their objections did not immediately work to enlarge the federative powers of the presidency. In fact, Morris and Wilson, who might be expected to have favored a broader presidential role, preferred to require treaties to be "ratified by a law"—in effect bringing both the president and the House into this process. But while the size of the House and the presumed inexperience of its members rendered it a doubtful partner in this delicate realm, the executive now emerged as the likely beneficiary of the misgivings that the framers were increasingly voicing about the Senate.[63]

The Convention took up the election of the executive on August 24. It first agreed, with difficulty, that Congress should ballot in joint session. Morris then roundly denounced legislative election as a formula for a supine executive who would be willing to "sacrific[e] his Executive rights." Two test votes now found the delegates evenly divided on the "abstract question" of restoring an electoral college. With this impasse, further consideration of the issue fell to the eleven-member committee that was appointed on August 31 to propose solutions to "such parts of the Constitution as have been postponed." Among its members were Morris and Madison, which assured that the arguments against congressional election would be thoroughly aired.[64]

The committee's deliberations were spirited, inventive, and completely satisfactory to no one. In its second report (September 4), the committee offered several proposals that bore directly on the election of the executive and its relation to the Senate. Most important was its revival of the electoral college, now modified to give each state the same number of electors as its membership in Congress. These electors would not meet as one faculty but gather separately in the states—thereby reducing the danger of cabal—to vote for two candidates each, at least one of whom must be an inhabitant of another state. Should the college not produce a majority, the decision would fall to the Senate, choosing from the five highest recipients, with the runner-up in either case being elected to the newly conceived office of vice president. The committee proposed three further changes. First, the president would serve for four years and be eligible for reelection. Second, the power "to make treaties" and to nominate and appoint "Ambassadors and other public Ministers, Judges of the supreme Court, and all other officers of the U.S. whose appointments are not otherwise herein provided for" was now given to the president, acting "by and with the advice and consent of the Senate." Third, the committee devised a removal procedure under which the House would impeach the president and the Senate try the charges brought against him.[65]

As three ensuing days of debate revealed, the link between the president and the Senate was liable to one critical objection. The committee had responded to the reservations raised about the Senate by giving the president a major role in treaty making and appointments, but it undercut this revision by empowering the Senate to elect the president whenever the electoral college failed to produce a majority. The objection to this clause would have been less severe had the framers thought the electoral college would make an "effectual" choice. In fact, few of them expected the electors to do anything more than nominate candidates. As Randolph, Mason, Wilson, Rutledge, Pinckney, and Williamson argued, the plan would give the Senate "such an influence . . . over the election of the President in addition to its other powers, [as] to convert that body into a real & dangerous Aristocracy," not least because it would then control all other executive and judicial appointments, down to the level of "tidewaiter."[66] Add its power to try impeachments and make treaties, Wilson complained, and one would see that "the Legislative, Executive, & Judiciary powers are all blended in one branch of the Government." When Morris responded that the report made the Senate less dangerous by allowing the executive to share powers previously given to the Senate alone, Williamson retorted that "The aristocratic complexion proceeds from the change in the mode of appointing the President which makes him dependent on the Senate."[67]

These objections did not outweigh the explicitly political calculations underlying the committee's proposal, which built on the "compromise" of July 16 by giving the large states the advantage in promoting candidates while the smaller states would enjoy greater influence when the final choice devolved on the Senate.[68] If either Congress or the House made this election, the large states would have the advantage at both stages. Unable to escape this dilemma, the Convention on September 6 approved both the electoral college and eventual election by the Senate. But almost immediately two committee members found an ingenious solution to the problem. Williamson first moved that the "eventual choice" be made by Congress "voting *by states* and not *per capita*," and Sherman then modified this idea to substitute the House of Representatives for the whole Congress. This had the twofold advantage of preserving the political compromise among the states while "lessening the aristocratic influence of the Senate." Sherman's amendment passed with hardly a word of debate and only Delaware dissenting.[69]

As this concern with the role of the House and Senate suggests, few of the framers anticipated, much less intended, that the election of the president would soon emerge as the most important stimulus for political innovation and the creation of alliances running across state lines. Madison came closest to foreseeing this result when he urged the delegates to recall that their aim was "to render an eventual resort to any part of the Legislature improbable" by encouraging the large states "to make the appointment in the first instance conclusive." Abraham Baldwin and Wilson also voiced a prescient hope that effective government and "the increasing intercourse among the people" would "multiply" the number of "Continental Characters" from whom electors could make a decisive choice.[70] But the prevailing expectation was that the electoral college would only limit, not eliminate, a legislative role in selecting the president.

Something of this ambiguity also marked the debates of September 7–8. By severing the electoral ties between the Senate and the president and placing the power to impeach in the House, the Convention enlarged the power of the executive at the expense of the Senate in the areas (treaties and appointments) where their authority overlapped. On the matter of diplomatic and judicial appointments, the framers reached near-consensus on the virtues of combining the "responsibility" of executive nomination with the "security" of senatorial advice and consent.[71] But the lengthier debate over the treaty clause revealed a greater disparity of opinion. Had the president been brought into this process as the logical agent to conduct whatever negotiations the Senate desired; or as a "check" on a Senate in which a handful of men (two-thirds of a bare quorum in the most fanciful scenario) might conclude treaties alienating the territory of entire states from the Union; or as "the general Guardian of the National interests"?[72] Only this last remark, offered by Morris, suggests an expansive conception of the executive as the one department best designed to embody a coherent national interest. No one else went as far. Wilson again tried to require the additional consent of the House for treaties, while Madison argued that peace treaties might be made "without the concurrence of the President," who would "derive so much power and importance from a state of war that he might be tempted, if authorized, to impede a treaty of peace." Both motions failed.[73] But the framers better revealed the limits of their conception of executive power by entertaining a flurry of amendments to modify the clause requiring treaties to be approved by two-thirds of the Senate. Although none passed, all presupposed that the Senate would remain the locus of decision for the exercise of this crucial power.[74]

Nothing in this debate suggests that the framers viewed the president as the principal and independent author of foreign policy, or that they would have reduced the advice and consent required of the Senate to the formal approval of treaties negotiated solely at the initiative and discretion of the executive. The prosaic aspects of foreign relations—routine correspondence, consular affairs, minor incidents of diplomacy—would clearly fall to the executive. Thinking of treaties as the cornerstones in the future structure of American foreign relations, and hardly foreseeing the dilemmas that a quarter century of European war soon posed for American diplomacy, few of the framers thought that the executive virtues of "energy" and "despatch" would come into play with quite the frequency or subtlety required of European rulers operating amid an ever-fluctuating balance of power. Yet by repeatedly expressing mistrust for the Senate, the framers indicated that they regarded the president as something more than a convenient conduit for negotiations. Much of the jockeying over the two-thirds clause reflected fears that particular regional interests might be "sacrificed" in a Senate that still closely resembled the Continental Congress. In 1779 and 1786, Congress had plunged into bitterly divisive debates, first over securing access to the Newfoundland fisheries, then over the free navigation of the Mississippi. Both disputes erupted while Congress was drafting instructions for treaty negotiations, and thus illustrated the problem of framing foreign policy in a quasi-legislative manner; both spilled beyond its chambers to foment public mistrust of Congress. Familiar as the framers were with these episodes, they could readily appreciate the diplomatic and political advantages of allowing the president a significant initiative in the conduct of foreign relations.[75] Interpreted in this way, this debate suggests that the placement of the treaty power in Article II was more than a quirk of draftsmanship but less than a complete endorsement of the idea that the general conduct of foreign relations was an inherently executive function derived from British precedent and the Lockean reasoning which explained why "federative power," though "really distinct" in itself, was most conveniently lodged in executive "hands."

This debate also illustrates the difficulty of converting the strong views that individual framers expressed about the executive into a coherent set of intentions for the Convention collectively. The growth of the presidency owed more to doubts about the Senate than to the enthusiasm with which Hamilton, Morris, and Wilson endorsed the virtues of an energetic administration. The electoral college similarly owed more to the perceived defects in alternative modes of election than to any great confidence that this ingenious mechanism would work in practice. Whether it would give the president the "firmness" to wield the veto not only to resist congressional encroachments but also to serve as a check against unjust legislation was far from certain. Moreover, precisely because the electoral college extended "the great compromise" over representation, with its dubious expectation that the division between small and large states would persist beyond 1787, its formal logic proved irrelevant to the actual politics of presidential election.

The problems that confounded the framers' efforts to imagine how any system of presidential selection would work anticipated the prolonged experimentation that accompanied the ebb and flow of party competition in the early Republic. No feature of the Constitution stimulated the organization of political parties more than the recognition that control of the national government depended on control of the presidency. That was hardly the result the framers intended, nor was it even an outcome that they could plausibly imagine. Had Britain progressed further toward the norms of cabinet government and strong party connections between executive and legislature that emerged in the next century, the framers might have reasoned differently about the political dimensions of executive appointment and leadership. But nothing like national political parties yet existed in Britain. Ministers still served at the pleasure of a Crown whose capacities for governance remained subject to the personality quirks and genetic vagaries of monarchy. In 1782 and 1783 the political turmoil accompanying the loss of America briefly disrupted the king's ability to control the selection of ministers, but by the election of 1784 George III had successfully restored the normal pattern in which the king personally chose ministers who would then use the resources of influence to manage a docile Parliament.[76] Attractive examples of the virtues of efficient administration and dynamic leadership could be found in the careers of such ministers as William Pitt, the great commoner and hero of the Seven Years' War, and Jacques Necker, the reforming director general of French finances in the 1780s. But the ideal of executive leadership that the framers favored remained, in a sense, apolitical. They saw the president not as a leader who would mobilize governing coalitions but as an executive who would rise like a patriot king above party, free from the habits of intrigue and corruption that the lessons of history ascribed to both Stuart kings and Georgian ministers.[77]

GEORGE MASON WAS THE ONLY one of the three nonsigners who placed the structure of the presidency high among his objections to the Constitution. At Philadelphia, Mason consistently favored a plural executive, first in the form of a troika with one member from each of the nation's three regions, then of a six-member council of state, also regional in composition, and empowered to "make all appointments and be an advisory body" to the president. Without such a "Constitutional Council," the president would

> be unsupported by proper information and advice, and will generally be directed by minions and favorites; or he will become a tool to the Senate—or a Council of State will grow out of the principal officers of the great departments; the worst and most dangerous of all ingredients for such a Council in a free country. . . .[78]

Mason's council was manifestly *not* a formula for a ministerial cabinet but a variant of the conciliar executive of the states. In this form it drew striking support when Mason moved (September 7) to instruct the committee on postponed parts to draft a suitable provision. Franklin thought it a useful way to avoid "caprice" in appointments; Wilson hoped that it could replace the Senate as "a party to appointmts"; and Dickinson argued that "it wd. be a singular thing if the measures of the Executive were not to undergo some previous discussion before the President." To placate his grumpy colleague, Madison also supported the proposed instruction, but its rejection only confirmed Mason in his dissent.[79]

Of the three likely sources of improper influence over the president—cronies, the Senate, or a cabinet—the one that most alarmed Mason was the Senate. Though he was as much its architect as any framer, Mason was also the one delegate most troubled by the Senate's "aristocratic" character. "His idea of an aristocracy was that it was the governt of the few over the many," Mason noted on August 8, while resisting a proposal to empower the Senate to "originate" money bills. "An aristocratic body, like the screw in mechanics, worki[n]g its way by slow degrees, and holding fast whatever it gains, should ever be suspected of an encroaching tendency."[80] The Senate would embody "the few" not in any representative sense—not as the institutional repository of "characters, distinguished for their rank in life and their weight of property" or of "family," as Dickinson urged; nor as a chamber in which "the rich" could be quarantined, as Morris argued[81]—but literally because it was small, hence potentially conspiratorial, and *if* its formal powers allowed it to control the springs of government. That was why Mason favored restricting its authority over money bills, and why he thought the reallocation of power between the Senate and the president would compound the danger of aristocracy. The factors that "will destroy any balance in the government,"

Mason noted, were the "great powers" the Senate would exercise "of altering all money bills," joining the executive in appointments and treaties, and trying impeachments, all of which "their duration of office and their being a constantly existing Body" would make more dangerous still. These "long continued sessions" could have been avoided had a formal executive council been created; instead the "alarming dependence and connection" between the Senate and the president would abet their "usurpations." By making treaties the "supreme laws of the land," the Constitution would also give the president and the Senate "an exclusive power of legislation." Though Mason professed to be uncertain whether a government that would "commence a moderate aristocracy" would evolve into "a monarchy, or a corrupt, tyrannical oppressive aristocracy," the source of its future imbalance was evident.[82]

Mason did not cite Montesquieu to support these claims, and he explicitly invoked the language of separated powers only when he objected to allowing "that unnecessary & dangerous Officer the Vice President" to preside over the Senate, "for want of other Employment." Other Anti-Federalists were less reticent about appealing to Montesquieu, but they did so largely to echo Mason's indictment of the Senate. When they faulted the Constitution for violating the separation of powers, their overarching concern was neither with the revival of an executive veto nor the specter of judicial review but with what the minority in the Pennsylvania convention called "the undue and dangerous mixture of the powers of government" in the Senate, the one "body possessing legislative, executive, and judicial powers." Its executive power inhered in its responsibility for appointments and treaties; its judicial power in the trial of impeachments, which it might use "to screen great delinquents from punishment," in effect acting as both "judge and party" because the "principal officers" of the government would "derive their offices in part from the senate." Whatever "weight and importance" the president enjoyed would depend on "his coincidence with the views of the ruling junto in that body." In practice, the president "may always act with the senate, but never can effectually counteract its views," the "Federal Farmer" warned, and in contests between the two houses of Congress, the executive might similarly "aid the senatorial interest when weakest, but never can effectually support the democratic [House] however it may be oppressed." Not only would this connection "destroy all independence and purity in the executive," the Pennsylvania minority declared, but the presidential power of pardoning, unregulated by any council, could in turn be used to "screen from punishment . . . his coadjutors in the senate."[83]

This was the formula that other Anti-Federalists repeated with little variation. The easy consensus they discovered created other conceptual difficulties, however. Committed as they were to defending state sovereignty, Anti-Federalists could not readily attack the Senate on representative grounds. They argued instead that senators serving six-year terms, without fear of recall, would have time enough to elevate personal ambition above loyalty to constituents. Anti-Federalists also had to differentiate the aristocracy they detected in the Senate from the aristocracy they attributed to the House. When the "Federal Farmer" took up this issue, he conceded that "the aristocratical and democratical interests" in American society were "too unequal . . . to produce a balance" between the houses. Instead of a Lords-like Senate formed "on pure principles" of "its numbers and wisdom, its extensive property, its extensive and permanent connections," Americans would have "a senate composed of a few men, possessing small property, small and unstable connections," whose influence would depend on their ability "to dispose of the public offices, and the annexed emoluments." In fact, the members of both houses would come from "the same grade in society," the "Federal Farmer" predicted, and "probably, if there be any difference, the senators will be the most democratic." Nor would there be much to distinguish the two chambers beyond "the partitions . . . of the building in which they sit," for they were likely to share "the same motives and views, and therefore pursue the same system of politics." Far from worrying that the proposed Senate would be too aristocratic, the "Federal Farmer" was thus driven to wish that the Senate could somehow be drawn "from a pure source" of prestige, wealth, and influence—that it could be made more aristocratic, because only thus could the government be properly balanced.[84]

In explaining why the Constitution threatened the separation of powers, Anti-Federalists thus took the peculiar position of exalting the British constitution in the language of mixed government. The great vice of the scheme of checks and balances proposed by the framers was that it lacked the *social* sources of stability that mixed government ascribed to the British constitution. This was the concern that inspired Patrick Henry to praise the British constitution in terms even Hamilton could not have surpassed. What made that government "superior . . . to any Government that ever was in any country," he told the Virginia convention in his restlessly impassioned speech of June 9, was that the House of Lords stood ever ready to "keep the balance" between the Commons and a Crown whose rivalry would necessarily endanger the "hereditary nobility" as well. The motive that inspired the Lords to do their constitutional duty was "self-love," by which Henry meant their personal interest in their permanent rights and estates; but such attachments hardly resembled the crude ambitions that Henry thought the Constitution would release. "The President and Senators have nothing to lose," he warned. "They have not that interest in the preservation of the Government, that the King and Lords have in England." The "real balances and checks" of the British constitution seemed far superior to the mere "checks on paper" the Constitution proposed. It would have been less "dangerous" to omit the usual republican prohibition against titles of nobility, Henry suggested, than to make "the perilous cessions of power contained in that paper."[85]

Henry's point was not that it would be better to establish a nobility but that in the absence of a true aristocracy, senators would seek to convert themselves into an aristocracy of ambition. Anti-Federalists disagreed whether senators were more likely to come from the upper strata of American society or from the ranks of the crassly ambitious, but once the cast was chosen, there seemed little doubt about the drama they would plot. By colluding with the president and exploiting its lengthier tenure and sessions, the Senate would use its legislative powers to overawe the House, its appointive powers to create a network of dependents (embracing pliable members of the lower House or their families), and the treaty power to legislate in its own right. In the most extreme scenario, a mere handful of senators (the proverbial two-thirds of a bare quorum required to conclude a treaty) could secretly assemble to strike some heinous deal with a foreign power—dismembering the Union, for example, or sacrificing the vital interests of individual states or entire regions—and thereby irrevocably confirm their own coup as the supreme law of the land. Like the Convention that had created it, the Senate loomed as a conspiratorial den.

This emphasis on the "baneful aristocracy" of the Senate, however, made it more difficult to criticize the presidency alone. Anti-Federalists depicted the president less as an independent wielder of power in his own right than as a senatorial co-conspirator, "a mere *primus inter pares*" but little more.[86] To be sure, they often suggested that the formal powers of the president equaled or exceeded the prerogatives of a British king. "[W]herein does this president, invested with his powers and prerogatives, essentially differ from the king of Great-Britain, (save as to name, the creation of nobility and some immaterial incidents)?" asked "Cato."[87] The president might not be "dignified with the magic name of King," warned "Tamony," but as "commander of the fleets and armies of America . . . he will possess more supreme power, than Great Britain allows her hereditary monarchs," notably because the president "may be granted supplies for two years, and his command of a standing army is unrestrained by law or limitation."⁸⁸ But their more compelling fear was not that the executive department would evolve into an *institutional* monarchy, exploiting the same sources of influence that enabled the Crown (king and ministry) to manage Parliament. They worried instead that ambition or desperation would drive *individual* presidents to attempt to set themselves up literally as kings. Rather than relinquish his rulership and endure the relegation that the republican rule of rotation required, would a retiring president not risk everything to retain power, ordering his ruthless janissaries in the standing army to repress whatever resistance appeared? "To be tumbled headlong from the pinnacle of greatness and be reduced to a shadow of departed royalty is a shock almost too great for human nature to endure," warned "An Old Whig." Were such a president "a favorite with his army" and devoid of "the virtue, the moderation and love of liberty which possessed the mind of our late general"—and when would another Washington appear?—he would "die a thousand deaths rather than sink from the heights of splendor and power into obscurity and wretchedness."⁸⁹ And what would happen, Henry asked, should a president be formally charged with "crimes" against his office? "Will not the immense difference between being master of every thing, and being ignominiously tried and punished, powerfully excite him to make this bold push [for the American throne]?"⁹⁰

Here again the Anti-Federalist case ironically owed as much to the language of mixed government as to the maxims of separated powers. The president and the Senate could not be made perpetually reeligible for office precisely because they must lack the hereditary rights and propertied estates—the social attributes—that gave British kings and nobility their *permanent* stake in the welfare of the realm. No Anti-Federalist writer developed this point more effectively than the "Federal Farmer." "Men who hold property, and even men who hold powers for themselves and posterity, have too much to lose, wantonly to hazard a shock of the political system," he argued, "to risque what they have, for the uncertain prospect of gaining more." But the case would be altogether different in the United States, where the temptations of power would overwhelm all restraint. "When a man shall get the chair, who may be re-elected from time to time, for life," the "Federal Farmer" predicted,

> his greatest object will be to keep it; to gain friends and votes, at any rate; to associate some favourite son with himself, to take the office after him: whenever he shall have any prospect of continuing the office in himself and family, he will spare no artifice, no address, and

no exertions, to increase the powers and importance of it; the servile supporters of his wishes will be placed in all offices, and tools constantly employed to aid his views and sound his praise.

This description would fit "nine-tenths of the presidents," he added. They "will have no permanent interest in the government to lose, by contests and convulsions in the state, but always much to gain, and frequently the seducing and flattering hope of succeeding." But with a rule of rotation, the situation would be reversed; presidents deprived of the temptations of succession might then be trusted with substantial power. Otherwise it would be better "to create a limited monarchy at once," with a presumed permanent interest in preserving the state, than to incite ambitious presidents "in attempts of usurpation."[91]

Predictions like these were faithful to the tales of liberty lost that were a staple of radical Whig literature. But precisely because they imagined how the entire constitutional system might collapse in extremis, they offered little insight into how Anti-Federalists thought executive power would be used in the course of normal governance. Their analyses left little room to assess the political advantages that might enable the presidency to emerge as the focal point of national governance without evolving into a surrogate of monarchy. Yet here the rhetorical Anti-Federalist tendency to leap to shrill conclusions reflected the genuine problem of anticipating how the presidency would work. Indeed, Anti-Federalists often shied away from examining the executive in any sustained way. It was symptomatic of this problem that "Brutus" could provide the most acute discussion of judicial power in the Anti-Federalist corpus yet never examine the executive in the sixteen essays he published between October 1787 and April 1788, or that in four weeks of deliberation, the Massachusetts convention spent only three days on the executive and judicial articles, and in terms that Benjamin Russell, reporting its debates, deemed unworthy of publication.[92] When the "Federal Farmer" finally reached the subject in his thirteenth and fourteenth essays, he was far more concerned with the modest limitations placed on the appointment of congressmen to offices than with the presidential veto, a topic he professed to take up "rather as a matter of amusement" and then dismissed in a single paragraph which concluded that the framers would have done better to imitate the New York council of revision (as Madison originally proposed).[93] Patrick Henry's fulminations at the Richmond convention largely spared the presidency. There the task of criticizing the executive fell to Mason, who mixed a moderate caution against presidential reeligibility with the xenophobic warning that "the great powers of

Europe" would be so "interested in having a friend in the President" that they would either "interpose" in his appointment by bribing the electors, or else offer him a "pension" to do their bidding.[94]

For the Virginia Anti-Federalists, however, such fears were less an abstract assessment of the foreign-policy powers of the executive than a reflection of two political concerns: anxiety about the security of southern interests in the navigation of the Mississippi, and a brazen appeal to the Kentucky members, who were regarded as the swing bloc within the convention. Whenever the electoral college failed to decide—as Mason insisted it must always fail to do—it would not matter that the choice would fall to the House, for a majority of northern states would select a president who would collude with their counterparts in the Senate to surrender southern rights and interests under the unassailable authority of the treaty power and supremacy clause. A president might negotiate "a partial treaty," then summon the Senate into session without notifying "those States whose interest he knew to be injured" by it, thus making it arithmetically possible for as few as ten northern senators from five states to "relinquish and alienate territorial rights, and our most valuable commercial advantages."[95] Even were southern senators present, William Grayson warned, they would have to be "nailed to the floor"; should they "be gone but one hour, a treaty may be made by the rest yielding that inestimable right" to navigate the Mississippi.[96]

Where did the greater danger lie: in the presidency or the Senate? Like other Anti-Federalists, Grayson assumed that the true danger lay in their collusion. And this in turn illustrates the great conceptual difficulty they faced in linking the presidency to the larger case for consolidation. Of the three departments of the federal government, the executive was the one which Anti-Federalists emphasized least. In their criticisms of Article II they found no middle ground between the specter of monarchy and the danger of cabal with the Senate; they could not imagine the president acting as an independent source of political influence within the government, much less being the focus of political agitation without. If the president proved to be a tool neither of foreign powers nor of his co-conspirators in the Senate, what role would he play?

FEDERALISTS NONETHELESS EXPECTED charges of monarchism to be leveled against the presidency. That was why Tench Coxe devoted the first substantive essay published anywhere in favor of the Constitution largely to contrasting the "nature and powers of the head" of Great Britain with those of "the ostensible head of ours." Those contrasts were pungently drawn. In Britain "the king is hereditary and may be an idiot, a knave, or a tyrant by nature, or ignorant from neglect of his education," Coxe noted, "yet cannot be removed, for *'he can do no wrong.'* " The president would be a creature of the people, and "cannot be an idiot, [and] probably not a knave or tyrant, for those whom nature makes so, discover it before the age of thirty-five." Nor would presidents possess the income and estates that elevated European monarchs above their subjects. It seemed more likely "that many citizens will *exceed* him in shew and expense, those dazzling trappings of kingly rank and power."[97] Nor was it difficult to explain why the presidency would not evolve into a "hereditary sovereign" or "elective monarchy." As "A Native of Virginia" put the case:

> No citizen of America has a fortune sufficiently large, to enable him to raise and support a single regiment. The President's salary will be greatly inadequate either to the purpose of gaining adherents, or of supporting a military force: He will possess no princely revenues, and his personal influence will be confined to his native State. Besides, the Constitution has provided, that no person shall be eligible to the office, who is not thirty-five years old; and in the course of nature very few fathers leave a son who has arrived to that age.

Where would a president find the "ensigns" of kingship? "He has no guards, no regalia, none of those royal trappings which would set him apart from the rest of his fellow citizens."[98] For Anti-Federalists it was the radical *absence* of these "royal trappings" from American society that would drive the desperately ambitious to pursue their desire for kingly preeminence. But from this same circumstance Federalists drew the opposite conclusion. Executive power in the United States could never turn monarchical because presidents must derive all their authority and influence from the Constitution itself.

When Anti-Federalists indicted the aristocratic tendencies of the Constitution in the language of mixed government, they inspired their adversaries to reply in more pragmatic, functional terms. In denying that any class of national officials could ever possess such independent sources of authority, Federalists thus proved more faithful exponents of the idea of separated powers than their opponents. The theory of separated powers could at last escape the shadow of mixed goverment because Federalists dismissed monarchy and aristocracy as obsolete categories of analysis, irrelevant to the new republican world the Revolution had created. However the tasks of government were now to be classified—as legislative, executive, judicial, or federative—and distributed, they would be defended in essentially *functional* terms. Though many Federalists hoped that the national government would indeed recruit its members from the elite ranks of society—and sometimes confessed as much in public[99]—they rarely described either the presidency or the Senate as the institutional embodiments of any distinct strata of the larger society.

Far from it: They defended these institutions in terms that almost transparently justified the overt provisions of the Constitution. Common sense and simple arithmetic suggested that the fixed terms of presidents and senators offered no formula for lifelong or hereditary office, while the arrival of a fresh class of senators every two years would preclude incumbents from pursuing their conspiracies. "Machiavel and Caesar Borgia together could not form a conspiracy in such a senate," John Dickinson noted in his second "Fabius" essay, "destructive to any but themselves and their accomplices."[100] If the president and the Senate used the power of appointment to corrupt members of the House, would not the prohibition against holding office under two departments still preserve its institutional integrity? Simple arithmetic also cautioned against equating the president's veto with the absolute negative of the British crown. As Coxe noted, this "modified and restrained power must give way to the sense of two-thirds of the legislature. In fact it amounts to no more than a serious duty imposed upon him to request both houses to reconsider any matter on which he entertains doubts or feels apprehensions; and here the people have a strong hold upon him *from his sole and personal responsibility.*" The negative was an incentive to deliberation—"a friendly office," one Virginia writer put it, likely to be used only on "capital occasions," or, another commentator observed, when "prejudices, passions, and partial views" hastened Congress into unwise measures.[101]

Points so easily made required little sustained theorizing. Nor were Federalists hard-pressed to defend the connection between the president and the Senate. They could not deny that the Senate would exercise some executive powers. This was manifestly true in the case of appointments, and arguably true as well in treaty-making. Wilson conceded the dual character of the Senate in his statehouse speech but denied that this would concentrate power unduly. Just as the Senate could not legislate by itself, so "in its executive character, it can accomplish no object, without the concurrence of the president."[102] Against the specter of collusion, Federalists emphasized the defects of Mason's favored scheme for a "privy" or "constitutional" council to the president, to be "made personally responsible for every appointment to office, or other act, by having their opinions recorded."[103] Was it likely that such a council would check the president more effectively than the Senate? "From the superiority of his talents, or the superior dignity of his place," observed "A Native of Virginia," the president "would probably acquire an undue influence over" a majority of his councilors, "at the same time that he would have the means of sheltering himself from impeachment, under that majority." In Britain royal councilors and ministers had to be held accountable for their conduct because the king himself could do no wrong, but to adopt that model for America would only dilute the "responsibility" that the Constitution rightly vested in "the first Magistrate [who] is the efficient Minister of the people, and as such, ought to be alone responsible for his conduct."[104] Moreover, the problem of constituting a council would replicate the dilemmas that had vexed the framers in designing the presidency. If it was appointed by Congress, Alexander C. Hanson asked, would that not violate the canon of separated powers by rendering the executive "dependent" on the legislature? But if councilors served on good behavior, that would require establishing a "tribunal" to judge their conduct, which in this case was less behavior or action than wisdom and opinion, for which "there can be no sure criterion."[105]

An independent Senate would thus provide a more prudent source of advice to the president than a body modeled either on a royal council or the executive boards in the states. Yet in making these comparisons, both sides largely ignored the form of council most likely to emerge in practice: a protocabinet in which the president would draw his advice from the heads of departments who constituted the actual government. James Iredell, the beleaguered Federalist spokesman in North Carolina, provided a rare exception to this neglect in his *Answers to Mr. Mason's Objections.* After faulting Mason for his loose allusions to British practice and for failing to explain how a constitutional council could be established, Iredell suggested that the clause authorizing the president to require "the opinion, in writing" of his principal subordinates was a better security.

> He is not to be assisted by a Council, summoned to a jovial dinner perhaps, and giving their opinions according to the nod of the President—but the opinion is to be given in the utmost solemnity, *in writing*. No after equivocation can explain it away. . . . From these written reasons, weighed with care, surely the President can form as good a judgment as if they had been given by a dozen formal characters, carelessly met together on a slight appointment.

Iredell's encomium on opinions presented solemnly *"in writing"* mirrored the Anti-Federalist fascination with councilors boldly recording their dissents in a book. Neither inspired a serious inquiry into the nature of collective decision-making within the executive. How cabinet officials would stand in relation to either the president or Congress was a matter that also went unexplored. For Iredell and other Federalists, it was enough to establish that a constitutional council promised no advantages over the advice of either the Senate or subordinate executive officials. If responsibility and prudence were the attributes that sound advice should foster, it was "infinitely more *safe*, as well as more *just*" to judge the *"conduct"* of a unitary executive than to hold councilors individually or collectively accountable for their mere advice.[106]

This emphasis on the virtue of concentrating responsibility in a single president complemented the response that Federalists wearily made to the charge that the Constitution would license rabid ambition to run amok. "This evil . . . of the possible depravity of *all public officers*, is one that can admit of no cure," Iredell complained. At times depravity indeed seemed the crucial issue. "The depraved nature of man is well known," Henry reminded the Richmond convention, while agitating the Mississippi question. "He has a natural biass towards his own interest, which will prevail over every consideration, unless it be checked."[107] But if depravity, ambition, and lust for power were the ruling passions of mankind, Federalists answered, no set of checks and balances could long preserve any government. Make universal depravity the premise of government and political debate might as well stop. Treat it not as a uniform rule of conduct but as a danger to be prudently guarded against, however, and the idea of making the president ultimately responsible for the administration of government, and jointly responsible with a distinct Senate for other executive functions, could be defended as a reasonable solution to a manageable problem.

⟡

ANTI-FEDERALISTS PROBABLY SURPRISED their opponents by deflecting much of the criticism they might have been expected to make of the presidency toward the Senate. "The objection against the powers of the President is not that they are too many or too great," Wilson remarked at the Pennsylvania convention, but rather that "they are so trifling that the President is no more than the tool of the Senate."[108] Wilson limited his comments on the presidency accordingly. This same economy impoverished the general Federalist treatment of the executive; few Federalists felt compelled to provide a comprehensive survey of Article II. The one exception to this was *The Federalist*. But modern interpretations of the original understanding of the executive do not rely on *The Federalist* merely because it is the most systematic or even in deference to its authors. For Madison's revisionist view of the separation of powers in *Federalist* 47–51 and Hamilton's examination of the presidency in *Federalist* 67–77 assume still greater importance in light of the process of constitutional contestation that unfolded as soon as the new government took effect in 1789—and which gave the meaning of Article II and "executive power" a critical place in the partisan conflicts of the 1790s. From this vantage point, Hamilton's essays loom larger, not least because they illuminate the conception of leadership on which the first secretary of the treasury acted. Yet in his essays on the presidency, Hamilton was careful to invoke the theoretical paradigm that Madison sketched in *Federalist* 47–51, which accordingly provides the appropriate context within which the general discussion of the executive may be situated.

Madison's essays say remarkably little about the specific constitutional arrangements he was ostensibly defending. A reader could hardly tell that the major charges leveled against the Constitution under the rubric of separated powers were the link between the president and the Senate and the improper concentration of all three forms of power in the Senate. Only a single paragraph tucked in the middle of *Federalist* 51 obliquely endorsed "the qualified connection" the Constitution would create "between this weaker department [the executive] and the weaker branch [the Senate] of the stronger department [Congress]." Though *Federalist* 48 clearly located the chief source of imbalance in the "impetuous vortex" of the legislature, Madison alluded to the remedies of bicameralism and an executive veto almost in passing, while ignoring the role of the judiciary.[109] In *Federalist* 49–50, he dwelled instead on an idea that was irrelevant to the actual debate of 1787–88: Jefferson's scheme to enable any two branches of government to call a popularly elected convention to propose revisions to a constitution whose walls of separation had been breached by the third department. And when Madison finally reached the structure of national government in *Federalist* 51, he concluded the entire discussion not with a round statement of the theory of checks and balances but by reiterating the ways in which an extended federal republic would break the play of faction—in other words, by reprising *Federalist* 10.

In what sense, then, did these essays provide a coherent restatement of the theory of separated powers that in turn prepared the ground on which Hamilton examined executive (and judicial) power?

Madison's initial step was to interpret the dicta of separation in light of his own reflections on the epistemology of the science of politics. While honoring Montesquieu for having brought this concept "most effectually to the attention of mankind," Madison insisted that its meaning must be ascertained empirically. In *Federalist* 47 he accordingly surveyed the working definitions and distributions of power evident in Britain and America to illustrate the crucial observation of *Federalist* 37 that "questions daily occur in the course of practice, which prove the obscurity which reigns in these subjects, and which puzzle the greatest adepts in political science." From this survey, Madison concluded that the principle of separation did not prevent *partial* distributions of the three forms of power across or among the departments; it only meant that "where the *whole* power of one department is exercised by the same hands which possess the *whole* power of another department, the fundamental principles of a free constitution are subverted."[110] On this basis, a number of partial distributions of power became acceptable in theory and discoverable in practice both in Britain and among all of the American state constitutions.

After this foray in definition, Madison took a second, more substantive step by restating the problem of separation in light of his underlying critique of the vices of republican politics. The apparent symmetry with which Montesquieu and the state constitutions stated the principle of separation was false. In a republic "the legislative authority, necessarily, predominates" through two decisive advantages: the political influence it derives from its close connection with the people, and the superior authority it wields through that very rule-making power that allows it to "mask, under complicated and indirect measures, the encroachments which it makes on the coordinate departments." Naturally preoccupied as the constitution writers of 1776 were with the "danger to liberty from the overgrown and all-grasping prerogative of an hereditary magistrate, supported and fortified by an hereditary branch of the legislative authority," they had errantly guarded against the wrong threat, making possible the legislative misrule that Jefferson had described in his *Notes on the State of Virginia* when he complained that "173 despots would surely be as oppressive as one."[111]

But *Federalist* 49 and 50 dealt with Jefferson in a more critical vein, taking as a foil his scheme to allow a popularly elected convention to repair breaches of the separation of powers. Such an idea might seem theoretically correct, Madison conceded, because "the people are the only legitimate fountain of power," but it would not remedy the most likely source of encroachment. In nearly every contest among the branches, all political advantage would fall to the legislature, whose numerous members would be better poised to influence public opinion. Indeed, Madison privately thought that the people were themselves the likely source of legislative encroachments on other departments, and though as "Publius" he let this point go unmentioned, he reached the ultimate conclusion it supported: No constitutional dispute within government could ever be safely remedied through an appeal to the people out-of-doors. These quarrels would prove too highly charged to be resolved on their merits, while recurring appeals to the people would erode the legitimacy of the Constitution itself.[112]

This conclusion explains why Madison found Jefferson's otherwise irrelevant proposal useful. In asking the people to act as constitutional arbiters, Jefferson merely modified the prevailing assumption that treated the separation of powers as a vehicle for protecting the legislature from the executive while the people themselves served as the principal check on the legislature. By denying that the people could meet that task, Madison eliminated the most important alternative to a reliance on a scheme of checks and balances. The first set of conclusions that *Federalist* 51 proposed followed readily. If the great danger to separation lay in the legislature, balance could be secured only by dividing its authority bicamerally, restoring a limited veto, and giving the Senate an incentive to support the executive in the exercise of its "constitutional rights."

Madison used this same phrase in the best-known passage of *Federalist* 51: "Ambition must be made to counteract ambition. The interest of the man must be connected with the constitutional rights of the place." Only by awakening new ambitions in the members of the *politically* weaker branches could the Constitution check the populist pressures and demagoguery that would spur the legislature on its encroaching path. The republican reliance on the check of popular election was not the solution to the problem of ambition; rightly channeled, ambition was the solution to the problem of republicanism. Yet *Federalist* 51 does not so much explain how these ambitions will work as assume that differences in election and tenure among the branches will foster the desired attachment between "personal motives" and "constitutional rights." Moreover, its final two paragraphs bring the entire discussion of the problem of separation of powers to a surprising conclusion by reminding those faithful readers who recalled *Federalist* 10 that the "multiplicity of interests" within the extended Republic will provide the chief solution to the deeper challenge of protecting "one part of the society against the injustice of the other part." The more effective this remedy proved, the less need would arise for "introducing into the government" the "precarious security" attained "by creating a will in the community independent of the majority—that is, of the society itself." In other regimes, that "will" was found in the "hereditary or self-appointed authority" of monarchy and aristocracy—the estates that Anti-Federalists implied they would trust more than the pale replica of Crown and Lords they saw in the president and the Senate. Madison thus answered this charge by suggesting that in an extended republic, the dominant popular house of Congress would be less likely to encroach on the weaker branches.[113]

Madison's treatment of the separation of powers is rich in nuance and theoretical implications; at crucial points it is also allusive and elliptical. In later years, Madison came to doubt whether *Federalist* 48 had been right to argue that "executive power being restrained within a narrower compass [than the legislature's], and being more simple in its nature, and the judiciary being described by landmarks still less uncertain, projects of usurpation by either of these departments would immediately betray and defeat themselves."[114] It was Hamilton's exploitation of the ambiguity of Article II that led Madison to reappraise this conclusion, and to review what his coauthor had written about the executive as "Publius." What he found there was ambivalent in its own way.

After Madison left New York in March 1788 to secure election to the Richmond convention, it was entirely appropriate that it fell to Hamilton to explain how the ambitions of the members of the weaker branches would operate in practice. In resuming the quill of "Publius," Hamilton did not have complete editorial liberty. He had to cast his general defense of the executive within the theoretical framework Madison had laid down, and to maintain positions other Federalists had taken. Discussing impeachment in *Federalist* 66, for example, he followed Madison in affirming that the doctrine of separation barred only a complete concentration of authority in one department. *Federalist* 71 again echoed Madison by evoking the "almost irresistable tendency" of the legislature "to absorb every other" authority, while *Federalist* 73 argued that the political advantages that representative assemblies possessed would prevent the executive from wielding the veto wantonly.[115] Hamilton also felt obliged to dispel certain misrepresentations about the presidency still swirling about the public debate, and to do so in ways that would appeal to his primary audience in New York.[116]

Yet Hamilton also embedded in these essays passages that presage the ambitious use of executive power he would make after 1789 when, as secretary of the treasury, he acted much like a prime minister. From his later *conduct* it is possible to discover in *The Federalist* those *conceptions* of the executive which seem most avowedly Hamiltonian—as opposed to the more conventional points he made in his opening essays. With the first sentence of *Federalist* 70, however, he took a deep, reflective breath and challenged his readers to reconsider the hoary assumption "that a vigorous

Executive is inconsistent with the genius of republican government." Nothing was further from the truth. "A feeble execution is but another phrase for a bad execution; and a government ill executed, whatever it may be in theory, must be, in practice, a bad government." And "energy," Hamilton proceeded to explain, was both a crucial "character in the definition of good government" and the defining attribute of the executive itself. It was also the one attribute that he emphasized in the succeeding seven essays as he described the "ingredients which constitute energy in the Executive[:] unity; duration; an adequate provision for its support; competent powers."[117]

In making energy the product of each of these "ingredients" of the executive, Hamilton drew a sharp contrast between the traits that republican values desired in a legislature and those most useful in the executive. Legislative deliberations and executive decisions could not be judged by the same criteria, he argued in *Federalist* 70. In a legislature "differences of opinion, and the jarrings of parties . . . often promote deliberation and circumspection"; but in the executive, "the disadvantages of dissension" would constantly "embarrass or weaken the execution of the plan or measures to which they relate." Nor was the "maxim of republican jealousy which considers power as safer in the hands of a number of men than of a single man" any more "applicable to the executive power."[118] He extended the argument in *Federalist* 71 when he denounced the impetuosity of representatives in terms Madison would readily have endorsed. It was true, Hamilton conceded, that

> The republican principle demands that the deliberate sense of the community should govern the conduct of those to whom they intrust the management of their affairs; but it does not require an unqualified complaisance to every sudden breeze of passion, or to every transient impulse which the people may receive from the arts of men, who flatter their prejudices to betray their interests.

Whatever "unbounded complaisance" the executive owed to the true "inclinations of the people" did not extend to "the humours of the legislature," and it was therefore entirely proper to provide the executive with a term in office long enough to encourage him to withstand the "imperious" acts of the legislature.[119]

All of this was consistent with the image of a president who had to be able to resist congressional encroachments for the laws to be faithfully executed. But when he turned to presidential reeligibility in *Federalist* 72, Hamilton introduced a more positive theme. "In its most precise signifi-

cation," the term "administration of government . . . is limited to executive details, and falls within the province of the executive department,"
and real advantages were to be gained, he added, by continuity in administration. A new president coming to office by defeating the incumbent
would naturally suppose that "the less he resembles [his predecessor], the
more he will recommend himself to the favor of his constituents." This
would "induce every new President to promote a change of men to fill the
subordinate Stations; and these causes together could not fail to occasion
a disgraceful and ruinous mutability in the administration of the government." Hamilton then proceeded to a remark that his biographers regard
as a crucial insight into his political psychology, but which also illuminates how he translated the abstract Madisonian praise of ambition into
a rule of conduct. The "hope of *obtaining*, by *meriting*, a continuance" in
office afforded the strongest "inducements to good behavior," Hamilton
argued, for "the desire of reward is one of the strongest incentives of human conduct," and "the best security for the fidelity of mankind is to
make their interest coincide with their duty." There followed perhaps the
least republican of the many observations of "Publius":

> Even the love of fame, the ruling passion of the noblest minds,
> which would prompt a man to plan and undertake the most exten-
> sive and arduous enterprises for the public benefit, requiring consid-
> erable time to mature and perfect them, if he could flatter himself
> with the prospect of being allowed to finish what he had begun,
> would, on the contrary, deter him from the undertaking, when he
> foresaw that he must quit the scene before he could accomplish the
> work, and must commit that, together with his own reputation, to
> hands which might be unequal or unfriendly to the task.

This was a formula for a government in which public good would be defined and pursued not only through the collective deliberations of the legislature but also through the carefully laid policies of executive ministers
of state, the real projectors or political entrepreneurs of government.[120]

Yet from this revealing statement, which so prefigures his later career,
Hamilton retreated to more conventional views. His additional reasons
for reeligibility, for example, stressed the benefits of experience and the
danger that "an avaricious man" limited to a single term might be
tempted "to make the harvest as abundant as it was transitory."[121] In *Federalist* 73, Hamilton portrayed the veto as a feeble weapon that would
rarely be used, and then largely to promote additional deliberation in
Congress. His analysis of the treaty power in *Federalist* 75 similarly pre-

sented no brief for broad executive discretion in the making of foreign policy. In a passage that resembled (but did not fully follow) Locke's concept of federative power, Hamilton suggested that treaty making was "a distinct department" that "belong[s], properly, neither to the legislative nor the executive." Like John Jay, who had treated this clause in *Federalist* 64, Hamilton emphasized the prudence of dividing this power between the Senate and the president, who would act "as the most fit agent" to conduct negotiations.[122] hamilton also steered a middle course when he discussed the appointment power in *Federalist* 76 and 77. Vesting this power solely in a legislature would produce "a full display of all the private and party likings and dislikes" that swirled among its members, while placing it in the president alone might give his "private inclinations and interests" free rein. A further restraint on the capricious exercise of this power existed, Hamilton added, because the consent of the Senate "would be necessary to displace as well as to appoint" a sitting officer, so that an incoming president could not "occasion so violent or so general a revolution" as would disrupt the "steady administration" of government.[123]

Although Hamilton repudiated this last position a year later, its appearance in *Federalist* 77 remains puzzling. It is difficult to imagine how a new president saddled with holdovers from the prior administration could provide the robust leadership Hamilton already favored. This was the situation that bedeviled John Adams in 1797, when he felt obliged to retain the cabinet he had inherited from Washington—and whose leading members looked more to Hamilton for guidance than to the president. Perhaps in the hurried and harried circumstances of 1788, Hamilton simply did not think through the implications of this statement—or perhaps this position better fit the rhetorical demands of the moment. The immediate challenge was not to expound his own expansive views of executive leadership but to answer the main Anti-Federalist objections within the general theoretical framework that Madison had laid down.

Hamilton's treatment of this single minor issue illustrates a further ambiguity in his thinking. Among all the participants in the debates of 1787–88, he was best qualified by experience, temperament, and intellect to grasp the "ambivalence of executive power"—its capacity to convert nominal constitutional weakness into overt political advantage. That perception may have been replicated in Hamilton's assessment of the relation between the debates of 1787–88 and the opportunities for governance that would arise once the Constitution was adopted. The theoretical questions that Madison felt driven to resolve did not bore Hamilton, but neither did they inspire or command his deepest intellectual powers. He was content to follow Madison's theoretical lead in part because he concurred with its essential tenets, but also because he was already more concerned with the uses to which the power of the new government could be put than with the exact basis upon which its authority would be established. Together, these two men were the great political entrepreneurs who most shaped American politics in the late 1780s and early 1790s, but they approached the task of legitimating the Constitution in strikingly different ways. For Madison the challenge of securing popular attachment to the Constitution depended in crucial ways on the character of the ratification process itself, which he increasingly regarded as an essential component of the larger project of nation-building. Concluded in the right way, it could provide political capital on which the new government could draw as it tackled real issues of public policy.

For Hamilton, by contrast, ratification was at most a hurdle to be surmounted. If the Constitution was rejected, he observed shortly after the Convention adjourned, the ensuing "struggles animosities and heats in the community," coupled with "the *real necessity* of an essential change in our situation will produce civil war." But if it were ratified, Washington's likely election as first president "will insure a wise choice of men to administer the government and a good administration," and this in turn "will conciliate the confidence and affection of the people and perhaps enable the government to acquire more consistency than the proposed constitution seems to promise"[124] Only then would deeper loyalties to the government be forged, and Hamilton made it his project to frame the policies that would best serve to attach the people to the government. In the meantime, the terms on which particular provisions were defended mattered primarily as they promoted ratification. Once the government was launched, Hamilton did not allow the rhetoric of 1788 to constrain his sense of the possible uses of the formal power and informal political initiative of the executive. To his chief detractors, Madison and Jefferson, these efforts displayed the ambivalence of the executive in a new light, spurring them to ask whether Hamilton was using the energy of the executive to attract support to the government, or the government to attract support to the executive.

CHAPTER X

RIGHTS

F IVE DAYS before the Convention adjourned, Elbridge Gerry and George Mason asked that a committee be appointed to draft a bill of rights to serve as a preface to the Constitution. This "would give great quiet to the people," Mason rightly predicted, "and with the aid of the State declarations, a bill might be prepared in a few hours." After a brief exchange between Mason and Roger Sherman, the motion was rejected without receiving the vote of a single state.[1] This was the one serious miscalculation the framers made as they looked ahead to the struggle over ratification. James Wilson only compounded its impact in his statehouse speech of October by glibly arguing that a bill of rights was superfluous because the Constitution gave the national government only limited powers.

Two centuries later the framers' oversight appears even more striking because disputes over the interpretation of the Bill of Rights pervade constitutional law and theory. These disputes are part of a broader debate about Americans' marked propensity to assert their claims in a language not merely of legitimate interest or net public good but of absolute entitlements. "Rights-talk," as it is called, has its adversaries and advocates. To such critics as Mary Ann Glendon, rights-talk impoverishes "our political discourse" through "its starkness and simplicity, its prodigality in bestowing the rights label, its legalistic character, its exaggerated absoluteness, its hyperindividualism, its insularity, and its silence with respect to personal, civic, and collective responsibilities."[2] To its advocates, like Ronald Dworkin, the belief that rights are "trumps" provides a principled basis for assessing the claims that individuals and groups make in both the public and private realms of life.³ And to less partisan observers, such as Thomas Haskell, "the curious persistence of rights talk in the 'age of interpretation' " raises a further puzzle: If the very concept of rights presupposes "the existence of an objective moral order accessible to reason," how can "rights-talk" flourish in an intellectual culture that treats all claims of this nature skeptically?⁴

These debates give the circumstances surrounding the passage of the Bill of Rights new importance, but also make its expedient politics a source of some unease. Understanding why James Madison overcame his doubts about the utility of these "parchment barriers" to force his "nauseous project" of amendments on a reluctant First Federal Congress makes for good political drama;⁵ but narrative alone cannot satisfy the deeper questions that the discourse of rights might put to the historical record. Surely, we sense, there must have been more to the story than this!

One response to the inadequacy of merely political accounts of the Bill of Rights takes the form of inquiries into the origins of its particular clauses. Recognizing that each of these rights possessed its own history, this monographic approach—pioneered by Leonard Levy—asks how the formulations of 1789 reflected the development of legal thinking in specific areas.⁶ Such studies serve us well by providing a baseline for measuring the doctrinal evolution of these clauses since 1789 (or 1868, in the case of the Fourteenth Amendment, whose interpretation has sustained the application of the Bill of Rights against the states). Even the origins of that constitutional joker, the Ninth Amendment, have been profitably examined—a matter of some import because its assertion that "The enumeration in this Constitution of certain rights shall not be construed to deny or disparage others retained by the people" suggests that fundamental rights not mentioned in the Constitution can secure constitutional recognition.⁷

Yet for all its merits, a clause bound approach to the Bill of Rights skews our understanding by implying that the original challenge the revolutionaries faced was to identify, enumerate, and define with textual precision the rights that Americans most valued. That issue *was* part of the debate of 1787–89, but it was only one element of a larger problem. Americans entered the Revolutionary crisis confident that they knew what their rights were; after independence, they modified these ideas only modestly. What did evolve, far more dramatically and creatively, were their ideas of *where* the dangers to rights lay and of *how* rights were to be protected. At the outset Americans believed that arbitrary acts of the Crown and its colonial officials, including judges of the higher courts, posed the greatest threat, and they accordingly treated the rights of representation and trial by jury as their chief securities against arbitrary rule. It took a decade of experience under the state constitutions to expose the triple danger that so alarmed Madison in 1787: first, that the abuse of legislative power was more ominous than arbitrary acts of the executive; second, that the true problem of rights was less to protect the ruled from their rulers than to defend minorities and individuals against factious popular majorities acting through government; and third, that agencies of central government were less dangerous than state and local despotisms. This reconception marked a significant departure in Anglo-American thinking about rights, and it helps to explain why Federalist qualms about the utility of bills of rights involved more than political oversight. It also has crucial and often overlooked implications for American ideas of judicial independence and judicial review, the distinctive doctrine that, over time, has given federal judges the special responsibility for protecting rights that Whig theory previously consigned to local juries.

THE LANGUAGE OF RIGHTS came naturally to the colonists; it was, they thought, their native tongue.[8] As eighteenth-century writers repeatedly argued, the original English settlers had carried all their rights with them, and passed these rights on to their descendants as a birthright and a patrimony. The belief that Britons and Americans enjoyed unparalleled liberty in the exercise of their rights permeated their political science and even popular culture. But the frequency and enthusiasm with which they celebrated their *rights* and *liberties* also gave those terms a flabby imprecision. No word was more multivalent than *liberty*. Along with life and property, it was one of the great triad of inalienable natural rights. But liberty was also a state of mind, the sense of personal security that enabled citizens to exercise other rights free from the fear of tyrannical rule. As Montesquieu put it, "The political liberty of the subject is a tranquillity of mind arising from the opinion each person has of his safety." Liberty was also a behavior that was often defined in relation to its deviant opposite, licentiousness. Much as the concept of rights often implied a set of duties and obligations, so true liberty had to be exercised with restraint.[9]

Any effort to think systematically about rights involved distinguishing the inalienable natural rights that individuals could never renounce from those alienable rights whose exercise was subject to the regulatory power of the state. Life, liberty, and property comprised the fundamental trinity of inalienable rights, though Americans tinkered with the formula by which these rights were expressed. The "life, liberty, and the pursuit of happiness" in the Declaration of Independence took a somewhat modified form in the state bills of rights, which preferred a triad of "enjoying and defending life and liberty, acquiring, possessing, and protecting property, and pursuing and obtaining happiness and safety."[10] To these familiar rights Americans were also inclined to add a fourth "natural and inalienable" right: "to worship Almighty God according to the dictates of their own consciences and understandings," or to enjoy "the free exercise of religion, according to the dictates of conscience," as the Virginia Declaration of Rights put it more simply. Presumably the class of alienable rights comprised all other rights that existed in the state of nature but which had subsequently been placed under the control of society. But in many ways this distinction was more theoretical than practical. Nearly all the activities that constituted the realms of life, liberty, property, and religion were subject to regulation by the state; no obvious landmarks marked the boundaries beyond which its authority could not intrude, *if* its actions met requirements of law.[11]

A different set of distinctions identified the multiple holders of rights. Rights did not pertain to individuals alone, nor did they come neatly bundled. The people as a whole had a right to be ruled by law. Communities, corporate bodies, and governing institutions all had rights, which they exercised on behalf both of the collective groups so constituted and their individual members. A farmer in Medway, Massachusetts, who voted for his town's deputy to the General Court simultaneously exercised an individual right of suffrage and a communal right of representation. In theory, he also had a stake in his deputy's right to speak freely at the General Court in Boston, and the assembly's sole right to levy whatever taxes would burden its constituents; while the assembly in turn had a right to chastise malcontents who criticized its decisions too severely.[12]

The realm of rights was not confined to these overt forms of political expression. A comprehensive overview of the rights of eighteenth-century Englishmen, as Forrest McDonald has noted, would run from the great natural rights to such prosaic aspects of daily existence as "grazing, wood gathering, hunting, passage, and the use of water" (and a host of others). The exercise of rights of property was subject to the supervisory authority of the state, which regulated markets, enacted sumptuary laws, granted monopoly privileges, and imposed various forms of takings through forfeiture, eminent domain, and taxation. Other civil rights defined the relation between the state and its subjects through such safeguards against arbitrary power as habeas corpus, rules for search and seizure, and trial by jury, "the genuinely crucial right." In England and America, freedom of conscience had gained broad and principled recognition, even if the exemptions that dissenters enjoyed varied with the strength of local establishments. Within the public realm, freedom of speech was still regarded more as a privilege of legislators than of citizens, while freedom of the press only prohibited prior restraint from publication, not prosecution for seditious libel.[13]

Rights thus came in many forms—and anyone who set out to catalogue them faced an exhausting task. To synthesize a philosophy of rights was no less challenging; while "many people certainly talked" of the rights of man in the eighteenth century, Knud Haakonssen has written, "few people understood exactly what they were talking about." The colonists in particular were often faulted in this respect, especially by their British governors. Their "reverence for rights was not grounded . . . in widespread intellectual mastery of the subject," James H. Hutson has noted; "there were frequent assertions and admissions that Americans did not fully understand the object of their devotion."[14] Yet this never deterred them from thinking that they knew what their rights were. As the legal historian John Phillip Reid has argued, the crucial problem the colonists faced after 1765 was not identifying rights but locating their sources. "The rights were British rights and well known," Reid observes. "Why Americans were entitled to them was more controversial and more complicated."[15]

Reid has examined the original understandings of rights that Americans brought to the imperial controversy more closely than any other scholar, providing a point of departure from which their evolving ideas can be measured. In a series of monographs that are archaeological in depth and taxonomical in approach, Reid has traced the colonists' multiple claims of rights to their primarily English sources and vindicated their positions as faithful expressions of older doctrines that had become problematic not because the Americans were grasping for pretexts to justify resistance but because British constitutional theory was itself changing in radical ways. The imperial debate brought two rival conceptions of the British constitution into irreconcilable conflict, Reid argues. Adhering to traditional notions, Americans saw themselves defending a body of customary rights that common law, precedent, and history had all secured. But this position collided with the emerging doctrine of parliamentary supremacy and "the constitution of arbitrary power that the British constitution was about to become."[16] Where law itself had been regarded as a set of procedural restraints on the exercise of arbitrary (royal) power, operating to protect customary (local) practices against its (centralizing) dominion, it was now being transformed into the mere command of the (parliamentary) sovereign. Once that doctrine was arrayed in full splendor, the notions that Americans espoused came perilously close to anachronism.[17]

Though Americans invoked broader claims of natural rights as the impasse with Britain verged toward civil war, their dispute was always about their *English* rights. Reid thus stands decidedly on one side of a venerable if trite debate over the relative importance of these two basic categories of rights—a debate that often seems reducible to the perceived tension in the Declaration of Independence between the preambular invocation of natural rights and the legalist appeal to specific English rights in the body of the text. Whether many revolutionaries felt this tension is doubtful. When it came to mustering citations, they were eclectic, pragmatic, and flexible in choosing among the potential sources of authority for rights. Nor did they regard English rights as a weak alternative to the great natural rights of mankind; English rights were the legal application of natural rights.[18] The greater challenge was to explain exactly why they were entitled to the English rights that would bar Parliament from legislating "in all cases whatsoever" or Crown officials from exercising "arbitrary" powers. Far from lacking a sound foundation for their claims, Reid argues, Americans drew upon no fewer than *ten* sets of plausible authorities or justifications:

(1) their rights as Englishmen; (2) natural law; (3) the emigration contract; (4) the original contract; (5) the original American contract; (6) the emigration purchase; (7) colonial charters; (8) equality with other British subjects, especially with Protestants in Great Britain and Ireland; (9) principles of the British constitution; and (10) principles of the customary American constitution.[19]

If this embarrassment of riches[20] explains how the colonists could assert their claims so insistently, it also illuminates the dilemma that the shift from the British to the American form of constitutionalism raised *after* 1776. Was it better to have one manifest locus of essential rights in the innovation of a written constitution or to rely on the multiple traditions and sources to which the colonists formerly appealed, none conclusive in itself but all testifying to the preexisting character of the rights they prized?

Americans escaped some of these perplexities by giving two rights preeminent importance. If the rights to representation and to trial by jury were left to operate in full force, they would shelter nearly all the other rights and liberties of the people. Neither right, strictly speaking, was natural in origin. Representation had not been necessary in the state of nature where the first social compacts had been formed. It was one of those "improvements" that distinguished the modern science of politics from its ancient antecedents, a right fashioned within the space of a known history that some seventeenth-century lawyers had examined well enough to learn that the rights of Parliament were less ancient than its advocates claimed.[21] The origins of the jury remained more obscure: Though confirmed by chapter 39 of Magna Carta, it was widely if wrongly believed to have descended from Saxon practice.[22] But as a uniquely English right, unknown to the Continental civil law, its avowedly historical character made Englishmen the envy of less fortunate peoples.

The commanding stature these two rights enjoyed was (again) a product of the seventeenth-century controversies which had inscribed the lesson that representative assemblies and juries existed first and foremost to protect the people against the abuse of power by an arbitrary Crown. Of the rights that representative legislatures protected, the most important was that of a people to be taxed only with their freely given consent. The notion was an "ancient" one, but the most immediate points of reference lay in the controversies that James I and Charles I provoked by seeking to raise revenue without the approval of Parliament.[23] The later efforts of Charles II and James II to use the royal courts to coerce and punish their opponents similarly worked to exalt the principle of jury trial. Just as the House of Commons served to protect the people as a whole, so juries shielded individuals from the injustice that would otherwise issue from feckless judges all too eager to serve their royal masters—at whose pleasure they still served. Proving that such fears were not idle required looking no further than the "bloody assizes" of the 1680s, or the concurrent efforts of the Crown to pack juries or prosecute jurors who refused to render the verdicts it desired. A cluster of other rights regulating bail, search and seizure, habeas corpus, and punishment also provided security against the coercive might of the state, but trial by jury remained the great *institutional* barrier behind which they sheltered.

Although representatives and jurors deliberated differently, they thus shared parallel constitutional duties. William Penn illustrated how representation and jury trial could form the basis for a simplified theory of constitutional rights in his 1675 tract, *England's Present Interest Considered*. "Those rights and privileges which I call *English*, and which are the proper birth-right of Englishmen . . . may be reduced to these three," Penn wrote:

I. An ownership, and undisturbed possession: that which they have is rightly theirs, and nobody's else.

II.   A voting of every law that is made, whereby that ownership or propriety may be maintained.

III.   An influence upon, and a real share in, that judicatory power that must apply every such law; which is the ancient, necessary and laudable use of juries: if not found among the *Britons*, to be sure practiced by the *Saxons*, and continued through the *Normans* to this very day.

As this rubric suggests, representation and jury trial were dual securities for the first great class of personal rights. Penn restated the point a decade later. What "is truly and properly called *an Englishman's liberty*," was to be ruled by law rather than "the mere will of the Prince," and thus "to be freed in person and estate from arbitrary violence and oppression," he wrote on the eve of the Glorious Revolution. "And this Birth-right of Englishmen shines most conspicuously in two things: 1. PARLIA-MENTS. 2. JURIES." The first gave Englishmen "a share in the Legislative (or lawmaking) Power"; the second "in the executive part of the law."[24]

Penn had good reason to value jury trial so highly. He was a defendant in the proceedings that led to the landmark decision in *Bushell's Case* of 1670, in which jurors who had defied both the evidence and the law to acquit Penn and a codefendant were jailed and starved for their conduct but then sued successfully for their freedom, in the process establishing the principle that jurors could not be punished for exercising their discretion.[25] But Penn feared that the settlers in his new colony in America would forget their true "birth-right" of English liberty from a lack both of "leisure from their Plantations" and of appropriate "Law-books." He need not have worried. Whatever other amenities of English life they missed, there was no shortage of rights consciousness among colonists whose dual motives for emigration included both tender matters of religious conscience and the pursuit of property. Even had colonists inexplicably neglected to carry their rights in their baggage, the structure of their governments and politics assured that knowledge of their precious birth-right would not be lost. What the colonists instead seemed to forget, Penn and other governing officials soon lamented, was that the exercise of English rights entailed the sense of "duty and allegiance" that kept liberty from degenerating into license.

One mark of this consciousness was the presence in early colonial charters and legal codes of declarations affirming the English rights and liberties that their inhabitants would enjoy. From a later vantage point, these documents afforded legal proof that the original settlers had never alienated the rights that the resisting colonists now claimed. Neither in

1675 nor 1765 would the colonists have believed that such statements *created* the rights they described. Yet Americans had reason to treat their charters as something more than declarations of preexisting entitlements. These were not mythic notions like the social contract or the true original contract of government but documents issued at known moments, with the evident intent of stating the conditions under which settlements would be organized and the risks of migration borne by the colonists.[26] These charters provided a potent authority to which Americans could appeal whenever the status of their rights within the empire was controverted.

These colonial declarations accordingly had greater political utility than the document that eighteenth-century Anglo-Americans venerated as the paradigmatic statements of the rights they treasured: the Declaration that the Convention Parliament presented to William and Mary in 1689, subsequently adopted in statutory form as the Bill of Rights. In Britain there was little need after 1689 to treat this document as anything more than a symbol of the turmoil England had avoided. Though a good case can be made that the Bill of Rights had radical implications, its prevailing interpretation after 1689 was essentially cautious: It had "simply reaffirmed the ancient liberties of the nation," creating neither new law nor new rights. This view, which was initially the product of uncertainty about the legal authority of the Convention Parliament, was later reinforced by the conservative tenor of Georgian politics and the reaction against the French Revolution.[27] A *declaration* might affirm certain preexisting rights, but it need not be regarded as an essential source of their authority—especially if these rights were regarded as an ancient inheritance that individual kings had often usurped but never rightfully alienated from their original holders.

The Declaration of 1689 informed American thinking in another sense. The Declaration asserted both parliamentary and popular rights; but its crucial feature was that *all* the rights it proclaimed were to be protected against abuse by the Crown, the great and even sole danger to English rights and liberties. Every article of the Declaration "touched on the prerogative of the king" under one of three broad headings: "(1) royal power with respect to law—the right to suspend and dispense with laws, the right to create an ecclesiastical commission, and several legal procedures; (2) royal military authority with respect to a standing army in time of peace, and the right of the subject, under certain restrictions, to bear arms; and (3) royal power of taxation."[28] Although the Declaration of 1689 added little of substance to the ideas of rights the colonists already possessed, its anti-monarchical animus fit the circumstances of American politics well into the next century. Believing that they were equal heirs with their English countrymen to the Glorious Revolution, the colonists had every incentive to appropriate its settlement in their own struggles with royal officials. The model of extensive parliamentary privilege set the standards to which all colonial assemblies aspired. If the rights of Englishmen depended on the rights of Parliament, American rights similarly required that colonial assemblies enjoy equal privileges vis-à-vis Crown and proprietary governors.[29]

THE COLONISTS' COMMITMENT to the right of representation is, of course, the controlling theme in the narrative of the American Revolution—and as such, it needs little explication. But their ideas of the nature of judicial power are much less familiar. To understand how a new conception of the judicial protection of constitutional rights emerged after the Revolution, it is first necessary to grasp the hold that older notions of the proper roles of judges and juries retained in American thinking down to independence and even beyond.

The credit for recognizing judicial power as a third aspect of internal government, distinct from the executive, customarily falls to Montesquieu. His treatment of this subject in Book XI of *De l'espirit des lois* was the most important innovation in his account of the separation of powers. What made this power (in his striking phrase) "so terrible to mankind" was that it marked the point where the authority of the state intersected the lives of its subjects—where fear of the misuse of power threatened the equanimity, vital to liberty, that existed only when the subject was free of the "apprehensions" that "tyrannical laws" might be enacted and enforced "in a tyrannical manner." This equation of liberty and security was unoriginal; it was a commonplace of English thought grounded in the turmoil—the prevailing insecurity—of the previous century.[30] Yet Montesquieu's account of "the judicial function" was so abstract, J. M. C. Vile notes, as to "bear little relation to the actual practice in England." It allowed no place for a professional judiciary but instead vested *le puissance de juger* in "persons taken from the body of the people at certain times of the year" to form "a tribunal that should last only so long as necessity requires"—that is, a jury drawn from "the same rank as the accused." Whether they would exercise discretion in interpreting law seems doubtful, because Montesquieu also described "the national judges"—by which he still meant jurors—as "no more than the mouth that pronounces the words of the law, mere passive beings, incapable of moderating either its force or rigor."³¹ His modern appreciation of the distinctiveness of judicial power did capture an older English bias against arbitrary judges whose discretion only exposed their role as lackeys of an unrestrained monarchy, but his ideal type of an English constitution offered little guidance for anyone wrestling with the thorny question of determining the respective authority of judge and jury. That explains why Sir William Blackstone, usually his faithful pupil, did not follow Montesquieu too closely when he described the integrity of the judiciary as an institutional *department* of government. While repeating the dictum against joining the judges with the executive or legislature, Blackstone was careful to note that one "main preservative for the public liberty" lay in the existence of the judges as "a peculiar body of men, nominated indeed, but not removeable at pleasure, by the crown."³² This was exactly what Montesquieu had denied.

Blackstone here referred to the Act of Settlement of 1701, which established the key principle that judges would serve on good behavior *(quam diu se bene gesserint)*. The independence that English judges now enjoyed was not absolute. They were free only of overt Crown control and manipulation, not of statutory correction by Parliament or of review by the House of Lords, acting as the high court of appeal. As members of a cohesive ruling elite, judges were unlikely to challenge either Crown or Parliament. But this shift in tenure nonetheless made it possible to consider the benefits of a professional, independent judiciary in more serious, sustained, and fundamentally *institutional* terms than paeans to the exemplary behavior of a few distinguished judges—notably Sir Edward Coke—could support. If judges could be trusted as independent, specially qualified sources of legal knowledge, the rationale for regarding juries as competent triers of law as well as fact would be weakened. Juries could still act to protect individuals in the exercise of their rights, but with independent judicial tenure established in law and parliamentary supremacy confirmed as the dominant theory of the constitution, the need to preserve the role of the jury as an absolute security against arbitrary power was diminished. By mid-century a movement to restrict the law-finding power of juries and enlarge that of judges was well under way in England, a policy initiated by Chief Justice Holt and pursued after 1756 by his successor, Lord Mansfield.³³

These eminent judges had few admirers in America. There a different set of understandings dominated legal practice and the political disputes that sometimes erupted over the place of the judiciary in the colonial constitutions. Americans were naturally partial to Montesquieu's equation of *le puissance de juger* with the determinations of juries because colonial judges, down to the local justices of the peace who were the bedrock of the system, were both appointed and removable by the Crown. The efforts of the assemblies to place their tenure on the standard of good behavior were negatived either by governors or the Privy Council. This disparity was compounded by the fact that governors and their appointive councils—also removable at pleasure—constituted the highest courts of appeal within the colonies. Seventeenth-century prejudices were also confirmed whenever British authorities sought to try offenses committed against the empire in courts where the protection of the jury did not operate. The principle of judicial independence thus initially meant little more to Americans than insulating judges from the overt control of the Crown. It did not yet require them to articulate a substantive conception of the judiciary as a third branch of government.[34]

In practice an overbearing Crown did not impose slavish justices of the peace on a resentful population; judges were drawn from the same communities whose customary law they followed and defended. But that sense of local accountability, coupled with the underdeveloped condition of the colonial bar, meant that few justices brought anything resembling legal expertise to their duties. This was little cause for alarm. That judges should be independent and honest was evident; whether they need also be repositories of a refined knowledge beyond the ken of ordinary citizens was less certain. The dense texts that the young John Dickinson pored over so earnestly when he studied law at the Inns of Court in the 1750s were of modest use when he returned home to practice.[35]

Besides, legal expertise was irrelevant to many of the routine duties of courts. In colonial America, most politics, in the sense of competition for influence and power, was provincial; but most governance was local, and its vehicle was the courts, which everywhere exercised "extensive administrative powers," Richard Ellis has observed.

> They assessed local taxes and administered their spending on the building and repairing of roads, bridges, jails, workhouses, and courthouses. Their approval was necessary to establish a ferry, or to build a road or bridge, and it was the neighborhood justice who determined over whose land a road would pass. Courts set and paid bounties on wild game, settled quarrels between servants and masters, and issued licenses to innkeepers and merchants who wished to sell excised goods.[36]

Though judges could thus be said to exercise judicial, executive, and even legislative functions, few colonists worried that this seemingly improper concentration of all three powers in one set of hands violated the doctrine of Montesquieu; to question them would mean revising the entire framework of local government.

When courts exercised their properly judicial (as opposed to administrative) functions, the decision-makers were the juries. The most striking feature of colonial justice was the bare modicum of authority that judges actually exercised. "Americans of the prerevolutionary period expected their judges to be automatons who mechanically applied immutable rules of law to the facts of each case," William Nelson observes in his survey of the eighteenth-century Massachusetts legal system.[37] The competence of the jury extended to matters of law and fact alike, and juries used this authority freely. In cases tried before panels of judges, a jury might hear multiple explanations of the relevant law from judges speaking seriatim, as well as from the rival attorneys. It was then free to decide the case on any basis it chose, and though appeals could be taken from its decision, the devices that English judges could use to set unreasonable jury verdicts aside were left largely untapped in America. Only rarely were colonial juries limited to reaching *special verdicts* in which they decided narrow questions of fact, leaving the legal consequences of their findings to the bench; far more often they rendered *general verdicts* resolving questions of law and fact at once. And they did so less by applying general principles drawn from external sources of authority than by invoking local custom. Not only did "the vast power of juries" reduce judges to handling "only a few rather simple law tasks," largely by applying well-known precedent almost "mechanically," Nelson concludes; more important, it also meant "that the representatives of local communities assembled as jurors generally had effective power to control the content of the province's substantive law."[38]

Generalizing from Massachusetts to other colonies (and states) is always risky, but in this area its experience probably did not diverge substantially from that of other colonies. Pressures there may well have been by the late colonial era to align American legal practice with British norms, but in these decentralized polities, reform and innovation could overcome the inertia of habit and custom only slowly. Equally important, this preference for jury over judges still retained important normative sanction. For the conviction that juries were essential to the protection of rights remained an article of Whig faith on both sides of the Atlantic. The "strong and twofold barrier" of requiring indictment by one jury and trial by another, Blackstone told his readers, was "the sacred bulwark" erected between "the liberties of the people, and the prerogative of the crown."[39] As a slew of British officials discovered as they sought to enforce the Navigation Acts, colonial juries were happy to play their rights-protecting role, determining facts and interpreting law to guard their neighbors against the despotism of imperial bureaucrats, and entertaining the countersuits that defendants routinely filed to challenge the misuse of power. In the most famous of these actions, the New York jury trying Peter Zenger in 1735 upon the charge of printing a seditious libel against Governor William Cosby balked at delivering a special verdict determining merely whether Zenger had published the words in question; instead it issued a general verdict of acquittal based on its interpretation of the criminal law per se.[40] But if the Zenger jury deserves special mention because its decision foreshadowed substantive changes in the law of libel, the law-finding authority it assumed was by no means anomalous. It was precisely because colonial common-law courts had frustrated imperial officials all too often that the Revenue and Stamp Acts of 1764–65 provided for enforcement in vice-admiralty courts where juries did not hold sway.

Thus when John Adams entered a rough draft of an essay on juries in his diary of February 12, 1771, he wrote in terms that William Penn could readily have endorsed. Adams was alarmed that he was beginning to hear "[d]octrines, advanced for law, which if true, would render Juries a mere Ostentation and Pageantry and the Court absolute Judges of Law and Fact." When arcane matters of law did stump juries, Adams thought, they were likely to defer to the learning of the court. But, he added,

> 1000 Cases occur in which the Jury would have no doubt of the Law, to one, in which they would be at a Loss. The general Rules of Law and common Regulations of Society, under which ordinary Transactions arrange themselves, are well enough known to ordinary Jurors. The great principles of the Constitution, are intimately known, they are sensibly felt by every Briton—it is scarcely extravagant to say, they are drawn in and imbibed with the Nurses Milk and first Air.[41]

Here again the language of rights makes birthright its metaphor. But coming from an ambitious attorney who had struggled long and hard—as only an Adams could—to master the law, this tribute to the capacity of juries attests to the depth of the conviction Adams endorsed.

This deference also offers a vital insight into the role juries played in defining the nature of citizenship. Accustomed as we are to thinking of suffrage as the test of membership in the polity and jury duty as a burden, we overlook the difference between the occasional act of voting—which meant little when elections went uncontested and were more often occasions for raucous conviviality than sober debate—and the serious deliberations that jury service required. "A substantial segment of the male freeholding population was called on to furnish services on juries and jurylike bodies," David T. Konig concludes from a close study of York County, Virginia, and many "served on dozens—even hundreds—of juries," giving their decisions "a quasi-professional consistency" and fostering "a widespread sense of citizen engagement in the legal system."[42] Transposed to Massachusetts, this experience explains why Adams could speak so confidently about the knowledge jurors carried. But it also illustrates two other aspects of colonial political culture. First, a population used to participating in the multifaceted business of the courts could preserve its attachment to English rights and liberties without having to peruse the "law books" whose scarcity had worried Penn. Second, the dominant role that courts played in everyday affairs illuminates the localist bias that Americans brought to government. Although the provincial assemblies had the authority to give law to these local bodies, they generally deferred to their customary practices. If Americans expected their provincial assemblies to protect their collective rights against the excesses of imperial authority, they were little less eager to protect the rights of communal self-government against the external authority of their own legislatures—or any other body that threatened the sanctity of customary practice.

THUS ON THE EVE OF INDEPENDENCE, seventeenth-century norms for the protection of rights still flourished in America. John Adams reiterated the familiar equation in his diary entry of 1771. "As the Constitution requires, that the popular branch of the Legislature, should have an absolute Check . . . upon every Act of the Government," he observed, "it requires that the common People should have as compleat a Controul, as decisive a Negative, in every Judgment of a Court of Judicature." He had put the same point even more pungently in 1766. "In these two powers, consist wholly the liberty and security of the people," Adams declaimed.

> They have no other fortification against wanton, cruel power: no other indemnification, against being ridden like horses, fleeced like sheep, worked like cattle, and fed and cloathed like swine and hounds: No other defence against fines, imprisonments, whipping posts, gibbets, bastenadoes and racks.[43]

The imperial debate reinforced this creed in self-evident ways. When Parliament claimed it could tax the colonists or legislate for them "in all cases whatsoever," it confirmed that basic rights of property and liberty would be insecure unless each colonial assembly retained its full privileges. When it created vice-admiralty courts to enforce its new measures, it similarly placed the benefits of trial by jury under grave assault. "In these Courts, one Judge presides alone!" Adams had the Braintree resolutions against the Stamp Act exclaim. "No Juries have any Concern there!"[44] Nor did patriots rest easy when the ministry of Lord North provided the judges of the Superior Court of Massachusetts with salaries from the Crown civil list. Far from encouraging judges to support colonial rights, this form of judicial independence promised to turn them into even more pliant tools of the Crown.[45]

The great anomaly of the imperial debate of 1765–76 was that it made Parliament the ostensible threat to American rights. The logic of the imperial quarrel led the colonists to appeal to George III to intervene on their behalf by vetoing parliamentary acts violating their rights, redressing their grievances, and generally acting, in Jefferson's phrase, as "the balance of a great, if well-poised empire."[46] But if this wildly improbable and constitutionally inconceivable solution skewed the usual identification of the principal threat to rights, it confirmed the Americans' belief that their rights could be secure only if their own assemblies retained full authority.

In 1776, then, most Americans thought their existing forms of representation and justice were adequate to protect their fundamental rights. Simple reforms could remove whatever impurities had crept in under the ancien régime of the empire. The new constitutions of 1776 promised to narrow even further the distance between constituents and legislators while placing the judiciary on a proper tenure. By emphasizing the capacity of legislators to provide a "miniature" of a relatively homogeneous society, republicanism supposed that the people and their elected representatives shared common concerns—including a common stake in their mutual rights. Yet the very devices that would keep the miniature true to scale—annual elections, rotation, a broad franchise, equitable apportionment—also betrayed doubts about the trustworthiness of any lawmaking authority. Republican confidence in the promise of representation thus merged with a residual measure of republican mistrust of the vices of representatives.[47] Even in 1776 some Americans were prepared to fear that their own assemblies could go astray. "If once the legislative power breaks in upon [the constitution]," the author of *Four Letters on Interesting Subjects* warned, "the effect will be the same as if a kingly power did it."[48]

In theory the early constitutions might have guarded rights by enumerating specific powers that legislatures might or might not exercise. But that would have run counter to the general idea of legislation that the colonists inherited from Britain, for no plausible object of regulation could lie beyond its reach.[49] It was easier to define principles for enacting and enforcing law than to fix a point where legislative authority did not extend. Rather than prohibit the exercise of specific powers, the early constitutions expected political mechanisms to keep lawmakers accountable. If a legislature violated its trust, the proper remedies lay with the citizenry, who could petition or instruct their representatives, or eject errant lawmakers through the device of annual elections, which orthodox republicans regarded as a sufficient protection for all popular rights. "While all kinds of governmental power reverts [sic] annually to the people, there can be little danger of their liberty," observed "Demophilus," one of the more radical writers of 1776. "Because no maxim was ever more true than that, WHERE ANNUAL ELECTION ENDS, SLAVERY BEGINS."[50]

It was easier to turn that principle into a constitutional rule, however, than to determine how to preserve the clarity of the legislative mirror over time. Those who recalled the rotten boroughs of England and Crown efforts to block the creation of new electoral districts in America, advanced the crucial argument that rights of suffrage—including the right to an "equal" representation—had to be protected against future legislative abuse. "A constitution should lay down some permanent ratio, by which the representation should afterwards encrease or decrease with the number of inhabitants," the author of the *Four Letters* observed, "for the right of representation, which is a natural one, ought not to be dependent upon the will and pleasure of future legislatures." That premise could be extended to other rights as well. "And for the same reason," the author added, "perfect liberty of conscience, security of person against unjust imprisonments, similar to what is called the Habeas Corpus Act; the mode of trial in all law and criminal cases; in short, all the great rights which man never mean, nor ever ought, to lose, should be *guaranteed*, not *granted*, by the Constitution, for at the forming a Constitution we ought to have in mind, that whatever is secured by law only, may be altered by another law." The same animus informed the Concord town resolutions which explained why the Massachusetts constitution must be drafted by a special convention appointed for that purpose alone:

first, because we conceive that a Constitution in its proper Idea intends a System of principles Established to Secure the Subject in the

Possession and enjoyment of their Rights and Privileges, against any Encroachment of the Governing Part—2d Because the same Body that forms a Constitution have of Consequence a power to alter it. 3d—Because a Constitution alterable by the Supreme Legislative is no Security at all to the Subject against any Encroachment of the Governing part on any, or on all of their Rights and privileges.

The Concord resolutions not only recognized that legislatures could endanger rights but also grasped the more sophisticated point that a mere legislative declaration could in fact weaken their authority by leaving them vulnerable to modification by a future legislature.[51]

For all its precocious insight into the distinction between a statute and a constitution, this was still a relatively advanced position. Americans could as yet only speculate about the future dangers that legislatures might pose to rights, but they already possessed an ample historical record of the harm the executive had inflicted. That bias continued to inform their ideas about the role of the judiciary as well. It was one thing to render judges independent of the executive, another matter entirely to regard them as coequal in authority with the legislature. True, in *Thoughts on Government* John Adams seemed to move some distance from his earlier defense of juries by portraying judges as "men of learning and experience in the laws, of exemplary morals, great patience, calmness, coolness and attention"—all of which traits would enable "the judicial power" to act as a "check upon both" the legislature and executive, "as both should be checks upon" the judiciary. With independent tenure, judges could be given greater authority. But others still found it difficult to distinguish judicial from executive power—and thus to escape the traditional bias against judges. "However we may refine and define," the *Four Letters* observed, "there is no more than two powers in any government, viz., the power to make laws, and the power to execute them; for the judicial power is only a branch of the executive, the CHIEF of every country being the first magistrate."[52] Nor did many Americans think that courts should be free from legislative correction or review. The author of the quasi-populist *The People the Best Governors* voiced a widely held view when he argued that judicial discretion in interpreting the law, which was made necessary because the "circumstances [of cases between man and man] are so infinite in number, that it is impossible for them all to be specified by the letter of the law," ineluctably led judges to "assume what is in fact the prerogative of the legislature, for those, that made the laws ought to give them a meaning, when they are doubtful."[53]

On balance, then, the starting position for American ideas about the protection of rights in 1776 was closely tied to the concerns that shaped the institutional structure of the new state governments. The concept of legislative supremacy assumed that the assemblies would protect the rights of the people, especially if annual elections reminded lawmakers that they would soon be governed as citizens by the very measures they framed. Converting the governorship into a literally executive office would severely reduce the real danger this historical enemy of rights posed. Judges would no longer be tools of executive power, but the greater security for rights within the judicial department still resided in the jury box, not on the bench.

To establish these new institutions, however, Americans had to leave the state of nature into which they were thrust when George III refused to uphold their claims against Parliament. It was the literal-minded way in which Americans conceived this transition that explains why bills of rights accompanied most of the early state constitutions. If these declarations are read as coherent statements of a theory of rights, they raise more questions than they resolve. But their simple promulgation testifies to the deep anxiety over the status of rights that Americans shared—not least at the local levels of governance, where suspicions of external authorities percolated so readily.

These early bills of rights were problematic in at least three respects. First, their relation to the actual constitutions was ambiguous. It was not clear whether bills of rights were part of this new organic law or merely rhetorical flourishes of principles that deserved to be honored but did not establish legally binding or enforceable rules. The Virginia Declaration of Rights, arguably the most influential of these statements, was separately adopted more than a fortnight before the actual constitution, which made no explicit reference to the prior document. Moreover, the marked preference in nearly all the state bills of rights for the monitory verb *ought* rather than the mandatory *shall* testifies to their legal ambiguity; taken literally, most of the rights were affirmed in language that was advisory rather than obligatory or prohibitive.

This ambiguity was compounded, in the second place, by the potpourri of rights the state declarations affirmed. As Gordon Wood has noted, these documents offered "a jarring but exciting combination of ringing declarations of principles with a motley collection of common law procedures." Wood goes too far in describing these procedural safeguards as "motley," for the idea that government must act through defined procedures was essential to the entire concept of rule by law, but he captures a key point nonetheless.[54] State bills of rights spoke at several levels of generality, from the avowal of first principles of government to the guarantee of specific civil liberties. The early declarations reminded Americans of their overarching right to be free of arbitrary government by stating, for example, that all officials "are the trustees of the public, and, as such, accountable for their conduct"; that "The doctrine of non-resistance, against arbitrary power and oppression, is absurd, slavish, and destructive of the good and happiness of mankind";[55] that "the people have a right, at such periods as they may think proper, to reduce their public officers to a private station."[56] Other statements took the form of moral homilies addressed to the conscience of the citizenry, as in Article 15 of the Virginia Declaration: "That no free Government, or the blessing of liberty, can be preserved to any people but by a firm adherence to justice, moderation, temperance, frugality, and virtue, and by frequent recurrence to fundamental principles."[57] Here the basic popular right of self-government was tied to the equally basic duty of the individual citizen to govern himself.

Yet the state declarations also contained a number of articles identifying specific civil rights, most frequently when they addressed powers historically associated with the Crown. For example, Article 7 of the Virginia Declaration—echoed in other states—harked back to the Stuarts when it warned "that all power of suspending laws . . . without consent of the Representatives of the people, is injurious to their rights, and ought not to be exercised." Succeeding articles guaranteed those common-law procedural rights that guarded individuals against the coercive powers of the courts. All of these provisions—trial by jury and the accompanying rights to know the charges of which one was accused, to confront witnesses, and to "call for evidence"; the prohibition of excessive bail and fines and of cruel and unusual punishment; the admonition against general warrants permitting unrestrained searches or arrests without specific accusation—addressed matters of law subject to legislative regulation, and the relevant articles in the Virginia and other declarations could thus be regarded as injunctions to the assemblies.[58] But Americans knew that the abuse of these rights had customarily emanated from the Crown and its courts, and it was their power that these provisions sought to curtail.

Insofar as these articles did address the legislature, they were meant to *guide* it in exercising its discretionary authority rather than to *restrain* legislative power by creating an armory of judicially enforceable rights. "The most common format" these documents used, Donald S. Lutz has concluded after surveying the relevant provisions, "permits rights to be withdrawn or modified by the legislature acting in the name of the majority of the people." Most rights *were* alienable, Lutz adds, in the sense that their exercise was subject to legislative control. "The first state constitutions often permitted the legislature to confiscate property, limit speech, require a religious test for office, negate trial by jury, and affect just about every other right we today consider inalienable."[59] These declarations thus affirmed the rights the people retained against the legislature not by circumscribing its powers but by reminding legislators and citizens alike of the principles whereby they "ought" or "ought not" to act. When Article 5 of the Virginia Declaration of Rights called for rotation in office, it did not affect the rules of tenure fixed by the state constitution; it only reminded citizens that officials would best "be restrained from oppression, by feeling and participating the burdens of the people" and "return[ing] into that body from which they were originally taken." Similarly, when Article 12 declared "[t]hat the freedom of the press is one of the greatest bulwarks of liberty, and can never be restrained but by despotick Governments," it did not create an exemption that courts could confidently enforce against legislative despotism; it only endorsed a principle that the legislature should respect, and to which its constituents might rally if it did not.[60]

Even had the state declarations explicitly restricted the legislative authority, they were vulnerable to the same criticism that Jefferson and Madison directed against the constitutions more generally. Derived as they were from the same quasi-legislative bodies that promulgated the constitutions, bill of rights were not legally superior to the will of subsequent legislatures. Here lay a third general problem that the early declarations raised but did not resolve, and which the ambiguity of *declaring* rights only compounded. For the authority of bills of rights not only depended on the evolution of the doctrine that made written constitutions supreme law; it was also complicated by the conviction that fundamental rights were not created by some positive act but instead existed as an amalgam of natural rights and customary tradition. In the wake of the Revolutionary dispute with Britain, which repeatedly forced the colonists to explain why they were entitled to the rights they claimed, it was only natural that the constitution writers of 1776 should attach statements of rights to the new charters of government. Some of them doubtless hoped that such formal declarations would reduce the ambiguities about the sources of rights they had just encountered. But that did not mean that rights left undeclared would lose their authority or be relegated to a lower status. "The much-vaunted" Virginia Declaration, Leonard Levy observes, "omitted the freedoms of speech, assembly, and petition; the right to the writ of *habeas corpus*; the right to grand jury proceedings; the right to counsel . . . and freedom from double jeopardy and *ex post facto* laws." Other states committed similar oversights.[61] But this was evidence less of a systematic attempt to distinguish fundamental and lesser rights than of the hectic circumstances under which the declarations were drafted and the uncertainties surrounding the entire subject. Did the failure of New York, South Carolina, and Georgia to issue such a declaration make rights in those states less secure?

Arguably it did not. Yet in one noteworthy case—the failed Massachusetts constitution of 1778—the lack of a bill of rights clearly contributed to the breakthrough in constitutional doctrine that the state achieved in 1780. It was the opinion of the townspeople of Westminster, for example, "that no Constitution Whatsoever ought to be Established, till previously theirto the bill of Rights be Set forth, and the Constitution formed theirfrom: That So the Lowest Capacity may be able to Determine his Natural Rights, and judge of the acquiteableness of the Constitution theirby." The town meeting of Lexington developed the point in greater detail. It was essential that the

> [r]ights intended to be retained (at least those that are fundamental to the well-being of Society and the Liberty and Safety of Individuals) should be, in the most explicit Terms, declared.—And that, not only that Government, and Persons in Authority, might know their stated Limits and Bounds; but also the Subjects, and all Members of Such Societies, might know when their Rights and Liberties are infringed or violated; and have some known and established Standard to which they might, with becoming Confidence, appeal, for the Redress of Grievances and Oppressions, whether real or supposed.[62]

Of the dual audiences this declaration would address, the people were more important than their rulers. For if one assumed, as good Whigs did, that rulers inevitably abused their powers, a bill of rights would prove most beneficial when it provided the people with the standards to judge the conduct of their governors. That explains why the early bills of rights contained so many statements of general principles that seemed to lack legal effect. Lurking behind this recitation of commonplace ideas was the fear—again ingrained in Whig thinking—that other peoples had fallen into slavery because they had literally forgotten what rights they owned. Even if the right to resist arbitrary government was unalienable, a people habituated to tyranny and wallowing in political ignorance might lose the confidence required to vindicate their rights or restore their constitution.

In a republican polity, the rulers whom the people would have to fear most were the legislators whose constitutional supremacy now meant something more than the capacity to check the abuse of an arbitrary executive. By default, the evisceration of the executive after 1776 made the legislature the active force in government, just at a moment when the demands of the war required lawmakers to mobilize the resources of society to an extent unknown in the colonial past. This shift in the balance of political power and governance made it possible for Americans to cast the problem of rights in a new mold, to reconsider the dominant paradigm they had inherited from the seventeenth century and preserved in their own struggles with imperial authority. The great pioneer in this shift was James Madison.

MADISON'S CONCERN WITH ISSUES of rights can be traced to an early age. In his autobiography he recalled that he had been "under very early and strong impressions in favor of liberty both civil and religious." If anything, his commitment to the cause of religious liberty predated his interest in politics. His first notable public action was to secure an amendment to the Virginia Declaration of Rights of 1776, altering the article that originally promised "the fullest toleration in the exercise of religion" to the broader affirmation that "all men are equally entitled to the free exercise of religion, according to the dictates of conscience." But Madison's crucial contribution to religious liberty came in the mid-1780s, when he successfully opposed a general assessment bill providing public funds for all teachers of Christianity, and then capitalized on this victory to secure passage of the Bill for Religious Freedom that Jefferson originally drafted in 1779.[63] If the two friends did not completely concur in their personal ideas of religiosity, their conceptions of the constitutional significance of the free exercise of conscience and disestablishment were in accord, and they provide a crucial point of departure for reconstructing a Madisonian theory of rights.

Madison expressed his ideas about religious liberty most completely in his *Memorial and Remonstrance against Religious Assessments* of 1785, which he published anonymously to rally public opposition against the pending assessment bill. As a reflection of a general theory of rights, the *Memorial* combined conventional and original motifs. Its most explicitly political passages echoed the language of the dispute with Parliament. Lawmakers who would enact such a law were "tyrants," while "The People who submit to it are governed by laws made neither by themselves nor by an authority derived from them, and are slaves." Virginians should "take alarm at the first experiment on our liberties," emulating the patriots of 1776 who "did not wait until usurped power had strengthened itself by exercise, and entangled the question in precedents." So, too, an assembly that succeeded in violating this one right could proceed to "sweep away all our fundamental rights" as well.[64]

Yet if this rhetoric sounded familiar, the campaign against the assessment bill led Madison toward more radical conclusions. To describe legislators as "rulers" was itself problematic; it was precisely because they were representatives that Madison could appeal to public opinion to reverse the assembly's initial judgment in favor of assessment. But the assessment bill raised a more troubling question: How were rights to be protected if the institution customarily regarded as the bulwark of popular liberty took the part of "tyrant"? The question could be answered in two ways. The conventional answer was to mobilize the people to defend their rights—the strategy that eventually sent the assessment bill to defeat. The *Memorial* was circulated as one of several petitions that collectively gained more than ten thousand signatures, and this graphic expression of popular opinion proved decisive when the assembly resumed discussion of the bill at its fall session of 1785.[65]

The more innovative solution, however, lay in the action that Madison then took by pressing the assembly to enact the Bill for Religious Freedom, which is rightly regarded as a landmark in the struggle for religious liberty that was so much the project of the Enlightenment. Its underlying presumptions about both the sources of religious knowledge and the role of the state in the regulation of religion can only be understood within the larger context of the massive transformations of epistemology and politics that the Reformation had unleashed.[66] It is obvious, too, that Madison and Jefferson owed a substantial philosophical debt to previous writers on these subjects, notably John Locke and Frances Hutcheson. But with his characteristic mixture of philosophical radicalism and political prudence, Locke never denied that the state had legitimate reasons to proscribe both atheists and those churches that rejected the imperatives of toleration.[67] Jefferson and Madison similarly did not deny that the state had an interest in regulating some aspects of behavior on behalf of religiosity: The Revisal of Laws of which the Bill for Religious Freedom was a part also contained a bill to punish Sabbath-breakers. Yet this measure was a bare vestige of the deep concern with public order that Locke had expressed—a remedy that was more likely to be applied against unruly Presbyterians given to loosing their hounds on Anglican ministers in the southern backcountry than to preventing the forms of persecution and sectarian violence Locke had known. Madison and Jefferson were not mere tolerationists; they countenanced a constitutional solution to the religion question, renouncing the authority of the state to regulate the one aspect of behavior that had most disrupted the peace of society since the Reformation. For at the heart of their support for disestablishment and free exercise lay the radical conviction that nearly the entire sphere of religious practice could be safely deregulated, placed beyond the cognizance of the state, and thus defused as both a source of political strife and a danger to individual rights.

By treating religion as a matter of opinion only, Jefferson and Madison identified the one area of governance in which the realm of private rights could be enlarged by a flat constitutional denial of legislative jurisdiction, thereby converting the general premise that all government rested on a delegation of authority from the people into a specific refusal to permit government to act over an entire area of behavior. In this sense religious liberty differed markedly from other civil rights that Americans valued. These other rights were essentially *procedural*; they assumed that government had the authority to act, but that it had to do so in conformity to the due processes of law that legislatures and courts both followed. In the realm of religion, however, what Madison and Jefferson contested was the capacity of the state to act at all. And they did so not on behalf of the collective right of a people to be free from arbitrary rule, but rather to protect autonomous individuals as the bearers of rights. The free exercise of religion was the most "liberal" of all the rights Americans could claim, the one right that placed the greatest trust in the capacity of private choice, and the one least dependent on positive law. In the state declarations, "[f]reedom of religion was universally said to be an unalienable right," Michael McConnell has noted; by contrast, "the status of other rights . . . was more disputed and often considered derivative of civil society."[68]

Yet this distinction did not resolve the legal perplexities that troubled Jefferson when he drafted the Bill for Religious Freedom or Madison when he secured its passage. Because the assembly held "no power to restrain the acts of succeeding assemblies," the final paragraph of the bill conceded, "to declare this act irrevocable would be of no effect in law; yet . . . if any act shall be hereafter passed to repeal the present, or to narrow its operation, such act will be an infringement of natural right."[69] Here again Jefferson confronted the problem of distinguishing an act meant to possess constitutional force from the lesser majesty of statutory law. But what did this distinction mean when applied to the realm of rights? If a right was natural and unalienable, in what sense did its existence and exercise depend on the statute? If a later assembly repealed or narrowed the statute, would the right not in fact be diminished or infringed? Or could it be rendered secure only if it rested on a truly constitutional—rather than a merely statutory—footing?

The difficulty of resolving these questions conclusively should not obscure the progress that the religion problem enabled Madison to make. Rather than rely on representative assemblies to protect rights, he now began to ask how rights were to be secured against legislative abuse. This question was clearly on his mind when he pondered the vices of state constitutionalism only a few weeks after the *Memorial and Remonstrance.* "If it were possible," he wrote,

> it would be well to define the extent of the Legislative power but the nature of it seems in many respects to be indefinite. It is very practicable however to enumerate the essential exceptions. The Constitution may expresly restrain them from medling with religion—from abolishing Juries from taking away the Habeas corpus—from forcing a citizen to give evidence against himself, from controuling the press, from enacting retrospective laws at least in criminal cases, from abridging the right of suffrage, from seizing private property for public use without paying its full Valu[e,] from licensing the importation of Slaves, from infringing the Confederation &c &c.

Save for the reference to slavery—which of course raises a host of questions about the prevailing conception of rights—this compendium is not exceptional; what distinguishes it instead is the explicit recognition that it is against the legislature that such prohibitions must now be made.[70]

The crucial departure in his thinking, however, occurred *after* 1785, and it involved asking *why,* in a republic, the purposeful decisions of the legislature posed a greater threat to rights than did capricious acts of the executive. Legislators might sometimes act as "rulers," pursuing private ambitions in public guise, but far more often they acted in response to the passions and interests of their constituents. And this meant that the problem of rights was no longer to protect the people as a collective whole *from* government but to defend minorities and individuals against popular majorities acting *through* government. This in turn led Madison away from the ostensible lesson of the fight over the assessment bill. Rather than infer from its defeat that appeals to public opinion could prove effective, he now concluded that the people themselves, acting through their representatives, were the chief danger. He similarly came to doubt whether formal limitations of legislative authority—either through the enumeration of particular powers or the constitutional exemption of specific rights—could restrain a legislature bent on mischief from enacting unjust laws. And as he revolved these dual problems of legislative *and* popular misrule, Madison further concluded that the greatest dangers would necessarily arise within the states, where the wrong kinds of majorities could more readily form to pursue their vicious ends. His new opinion of bills of rights was a product of this analysis. He disparaged their value not because it was difficult to enumerate rights worth protecting but because he doubted whether any bill of rights, however carefully drawn or exhaustive, could counter the real forces of republican politics.

The radical tenor of Madison's new thinking about rights was distilled in a single sentence of his pre-Convention memorandum:

> 11. If the multiplicity and mutability of laws prove a want of wisdom, their injustice betrays a defect still more alarming: more alarming not merely because it is a greater evil in itself, but because it brings more into question the fundamental principle of republican Government, that the majority who rule in such Governments are the safest Guardians both of public good and of private rights.[71]

From this succinctly stated discovery flowed both his explanation of the sources of faction and his solution to the crisis of republicanism. Republican majorities ruled through the mechanism of legislation, and when this led to injustice, it did so because the play of interest and passion among the people impelled their representatives to do wrong.

To reach this conclusion, Madison drew upon his experience in the Virginia assembly and his observation of the course of legislation in other states. His concern about the security of private rights was rooted in a palpable fear that economic legislation was jeopardizing fundamental rights of property. Paper-money laws, debtor-stay laws, and the specter of Shays's Rebellion in Massachusetts all alarmed him terribly. So did the grim prospect he sketched at the Federal Convention when he warned that even in the United States a factious majority might eventually form from "those who will labour under all the hardships of life, & secretly sigh for a more equal distribution of its blessings." The constitution writers of 1776 had erred in assuming that by protecting "the rights of persons" they would also protect "those of property." Now he understood "that in all populous countries the smaller part only can be interested in preserving the rights of property." Although other classes of rights still concerned Madison, his analysis of the dangers to property was paradigmatic for the program of reform he carried to Philadelphia in May 1787.[72]

When rights of property were at stake, Madison feared, neither the enumeration nor the denial of specific legislative powers would provide adequate safeguards. In this sense his solution to the problem of religion—denying government any authority to legislate—could never wholly apply to economic regulation and public finance.[73] His clearest statement on this point appears in *Federalist* 10. He closed his famous passage explaining how the forms of property divided society into different "interests" by noting that "The regulation of these various and interfering interests forms the principal task of modern Legislation, and involves the spirit of party and faction in the necessary and ordinary operations of Government." But he then denied that acts of economic regulation were solely legislative in character. "What are so many of the most important acts of legislation, but so many judicial determinations, not indeed concerning the rights of single persons, but concerning the rights of large bodies of citizens; and what are the different classes of legislators, but advocates and parties to the causes they determine?" The examples of regulation that Madison cited reveal that he regarded *all* decisions of economic policy as implicating questions of justice and thus of private rights: laws relating to creditors and debtors, to the protection of domestic manufactures and the restriction of foreign goods, to the apportionment of taxes.[74] Economic rights thus differed from rights of conscience in a fundamental sense. While government could safely abstain from religious matters, it could never avoid regulating the "various and interfering interests" of a modern society; and any legislative decision would necessarily affect the rights of one class of property holders or another. Nor was this a merely speculative danger. For by 1787 a decade of state legislation had enabled Madison to perceive how economic and financial issues could forge broad coalitions across society, which could then actively manipulate the legislature to secure their desired ends.

This strikingly modern perception of what legislatures could do reflected not only discontent with the sheer busyness of American lawmaking but a recognition of "the impossibility of dividing powers of legislation, in such a manner, as to be free from differing constructions, by different interests, or even from ambiguity in the judgment of the impartial." In the realm of economic legislation, the interests to be regulated were so complex, the ends and means of legislation so intertwined, that no simple formula could defeat the "infinitude of legislative expedients" that artful lawmakers could always deploy.[75] By its very nature, legislative power was too supple and plastic to be neatly confined. Moreover, the legislature possessed other advantages than the plasticity of its power. Its superiority was political as well as legal, a function of its greater intimacy with, and influence over, its constituents.

From this analysis, two programmatic conclusions followed, both derived from the arithmetic logic of Madison's theory of faction. First, majorities inimical to rights were unlikely to form or endure at the national level of government. Second, and more important, the true problem of protecting rights was to curb injustice *within* the individual states, where most laws affecting property and religion (and all other ordinary activities) would still originate. That was why an unlimited veto on state laws was indispensable to preserving private rights against "vicious" state legislation. Armed with this power, the national government could act as a "disinterested & dispassionate umpire in disputes between different passions & interests in the State"—that is, within the *individual* states—and thus curb "the aggressions of interested majorities on the rights of minorities and of individuals."[76] A proposal more offensive to the autonomy of the states could hardly be imagined, especially when Madison explicitly compared the veto to the same prerogative the Crown had wielded over colonial legislation. But the negative was the one remedy that would most effectively reach the populist and legislative sources of injustice.

From these two propsitions, a third proviso followed, if only implicitly. Whatever their rhetorical value, Madison saw little evidence that the state declarations of rights had any efficacy in securing their avowed objects. Not only had they failed to restrain the state assemblies, they had done nothing to brake the factious passions swirling among the people at large. Bills of rights were as much "parchment barriers" as the formal affirmations of the principle of separation of powers had been found to be—and not coincidentally, since these cautions against the concentration of powers commonly appeared in the declarations of rights rather than in the main texts of the state constitutions. At the national level of government, Madison believed, a bill of rights would prove redundant or pointless. Solving the problem of rights ranked high among his priorities at Philadelphia, but it never occurred to him that drafting an improved declaration of rights should be part of the enterprise.

NOR APPARENTLY DID ANY of the framers think otherwise until Mason and Gerry raised the matter in the waning days of debate. The committee of detail had in fact considered the issue a good seven weeks earlier, in a memorandum sketching the outline of a constitution, evidently drafted by Edmund Randolph and John Rutledge. "A preamble seems proper," it noted, but "[n]ot for the purpose of designating the ends of government and human polities." Such a "display of theory, howsoever proper in the first formation of state governments, *is* unfit here; since we are not working on the natural rights of men not yet gathered into society, but upon those rights, modified by society, and *interwoven with* what we call the rights of states." The committee thought it would suffice to draft a preamble stating the general purposes for which the Federal Convention had been called.[77]

This brief comment helps to explain why the framers could omit a bill of rights so readily. If these documents were regarded less as compilations of legally enforceable civil rights than as general reservations of natural rights, there was less reason to issue such a declaration in 1787 than there had been in 1776. Then Americans had removed themselves from a condition that seemed close enough to a state of nature to warrant a public declaration reserving fundamental rights. Now they were only modifying the existing structures of government, forming "a more perfect union" that would leave the powers of state government largely intact if somewhat circumscribed and the fundamental rights of their citizens unimpaired. The Union would not assume powers that the people had never vested in government; it was only acquiring from the states and the people the resources and authority to exercise its essential tasks.[78]

Disparaging the need for a bill of rights did not mean omitting all references to rights from the Constitution. The committee of detail inserted in its draft constitution several rights that had gone unmentioned in prior debates, including jury trial in criminal cases and the guarantee that "[t]he Citizens of each State shall be entitled to all privileges and immunities of citizens in the several States." Additional rights made their way into the Constitution in late August. Charles Pinckney offered a set of resolutions on the 20th which included the writ of habeas corpus (subject to legislative suspension) and a ban on religious tests for office, both of which the framers eventually endorsed; but four other rights-like statements (one affirming liberty of the press, the other three relating to the military) fell by the wayside.[79] A week later the Convention added a prohibition on the power of the states to "emit bills of credit" and then considered Rufus King's motion for a further "prohibition on the States to interfere in private contracts." Gouverneur Morris and Mason both thought "[t]his would be going too far," because "a thousand laws" could be construed to affect contracts, while Madison argued in response that the "inconveniences" would be "overbalanced by the utility." The Convention initially rejected King's proposal, preferring Rutledge's motion to ban bills of attainder and ex post facto laws. But in revised form the proposal reappeared in the report of the committee of style—King and Madison were members—and was easily approved on September 14.[80]

One other late decision contributed to the subsequent public debate over rights: the rejection on September 12 of a Mason-Gerry motion to make the same provision "for juries in Civil cases" it had made for criminal cases. Mason conceded that the cases in which civil juries should be provided "can not be specified" by a simple constitutional rule, but he still thought that "A general principle laid down on this and some other points would be sufficient." The two dissenters used this motion as the occasion (or pretext) to propose a general bill of rights, but the Convention remained unconvinced on both points.[81]

Some rights, then, *were* protected in the Constitution, but the list was clearly piecemeal in composition and partial in coverage. None of these provisions invoked the natural rights and first principles that Americans expected a declaration of rights to contain. The omission left the framers open to the charge that they had contrived to deprive the people of their fundamental rights. They thought the charge absurd, but its repetition carried greater conviction as Federalists struggled to justify their oversight.

FEDERALISTS LEARNED EARLY that the omission of a bill of rights would weigh heavily against them. Though Mason made it the first of his objections to the Constitution, Federalists took their earliest alarm from the amendments that Richard Henry Lee proposed when Congress debated how to convey the Constitution to the states, and from the published dissent of the minority assemblymen in Pennsylvania. Both had seen Mason's objections before they acted, but while the assemblymen simply restated his points as rhetorical questions, Lee better indicated the general concerns that Anti-Federalists soon shared.[82]

While describing the Constitution as a "Social Compact" and invoking "Universal experience" to mark the value of "express declarations and reservations" of rights against "the silent, powerful, and ever active conspiracy of those who govern," Lee avoided broad statements of natural rights and first principles. Instead he detailed the specific rights that needed explicit protection: freedom of religious conscience and the press; prohibitions on excessive bail, cruel and unusual punishment, and unreasonable searches and seizures; assurances of free elections, independent judges, and the right to petition; and restrictions on standing armies in peacetime. Lee's most carefully drafted proposals, however, related to the administration of justice. Lee proposed two sets of changes to the Constitution. First, the declaration of rights he sought should affirm that the right to trial by jury in criminal and civil cases and other common-law protections in criminal prosecutions "shall be held sacred." But Lee also proposed amending Article III to assure that these general principles would be applied in detail, by providing for criminal trials "by a Jury of the Vicinage," and by preventing "the vexatious and oppressive calling of Citizens" to have their cases tried "in far distant courts," because "in a multitude of Cases, the circumstances of distance and expence may compel men to submit to the most unjust and ill founded demands." Even at this early stage of ratification, these recommendations illustrated the great sensitivity that Anti-Federalists displayed toward the administration of justice as the crucial test of the security of rights.[83]

Had Federalists been able to limit debate to the questions of religious conscience and the more political matters of freedom of press, assembly, elections, and standing armies, their case for the redundancy of a bill of rights would probably have proved strong enough to withstand their adversaries' claims. What would a declaration of the virtues of frequent elections or the evils of standing armies add to the constitutional provisions that already regulated these features of governance? How could matters of religious conscience ever come under federal purview—and even if they did, how could a fractious Protestant society ever agree on the norms to be enforced? But Anti-Federalist claims about the insecurity of trial by jury and other common-law rights, though more prosaic, were politically more potent. Not only did they resonate deeply in American political culture, they also exposed what was most problematic in Federalist arguments while illustrating the dilemma Americans now faced in weighing the advantages and disadvantages of grounding the authority of rights in a written constitutional text.

While Lee was failing in his effort to convince Congress to propose amendments, the minority legislators in Pennsylvania were placing the issue of rights squarely before the public. Americans should "wonder whether the trial by jury in civil causes is become dangerous and ought to be abolished," they observed in their address of September 29. James Wilson answered this charge in his public speech a week later. Smugly apologizing for having to "take advantage of my professional experience," he explained that the diversity of procedures in the states and the fact that admiralty and equity matters were resolved without juries prevented the framers from drawing a constitutional "line of discrimination" to indicate where civil juries were necessary or not. Instead they "left the business as it stands," confident that Congress, as "a faithful representation of the people," would adopt suitable regulations, and that "the oppression of government is effectually barred" by the guarantee of criminal juries.[84]

Wilson's speech proved even more controversial in its assertion that the difference between state and national constitutions obviated any need for a federal bill of rights. Accepting the social-compact imagery that dominated American thinking about the formation of the state constitutions, Wilson argued that while in the states the people had "invested their representatives with every right and authority which they did not in explicit terms reserve," in the proposed federal Constitution, "everything which is not given, is reserved." There was no need to affirm the freedom of press, for example, because nothing in the Constitution could be plausibly read to give the federal government any "power to shackle or destroy that sacred palladium of national freedom." From this position Wilson drew a further conclusion. The very insertion of a provision to protect a particular right might be falsely "construed to imply that some degree of power" to regulate its exercise "was given, since we undertook to define its extent."[85]

In seeking to quash his opponents, Wilson miscalculated how easily they could exploit his simple if elegant distinctions between types of juries and constitutions alike. Within days Anti-Federalists were gleefully exposing the embarrassing contradiction that Wilson left open to attack. Did not the guarantee which the Constitution extended to trial by jury in criminal cases and its prohibitions against suspension of habeas corpus and the enactment of ex post facto laws comprise a partial bill of rights? If these were fundamental rights, why did they need to be mentioned in the text? And if they were explicitly recognized, were other rights not thereby rendered vulnerable to congressional regulation and even abrogation? Viewed from this perspective, the distinction between types of juries seemed to contradict the deeper distinction between state and federal constitutions on which Wilson relied.[86]

This anxiety over civil juries, however, was only one count in a more sweeping indictment of Article III. The fact that even criminal trials need occur only "in the State where the said crimes shall have been committed" implied that the right to trial by jury "in the vicinage" was also abolished, and that the burden of producing witnesses and evidence at a distance would sorely press defendants. Pity the poor Virginians to be tried by a jury "collected 500 miles from where the party resides," Patrick Henry implored the Richmond convention, "no neighbours who are acquainted with their characters, their good or bad conduct in life, to judge of the unfortunate man who may thus be exposed to the rigour of that Government."[87]

More ominous still was the fundamental grant of jurisdiction given to the Supreme Court and to the inferior courts Congress might create. What did Article III mean when it gave the Supreme Court "appellate jurisdiction, both as to law and fact"? In the most severe analyses, this amounted to an effort to replace the common-law birthright of Americans with the dread civil law of continental Europe. "The word *appeal*, if I understand it right, in its proper signification includes the *fact* as well as the law, and precludes every idea of a trial by jury," wrote "A Democratic Federalist" in mid-October. "It is a word of *foreign growth*, and is only known in England and America in those courts which are governed by the civil or ecclesiastical law of the *Romans*."[88] Even if civil juries were provided by law, Anti-Federalists warned, federal appellate judges could retry virtually every aspect of every civil case and reach fresh verdicts unconstrained by the decisions of juries below. An appellate court was by definition juryless, the "Federal Farmer" argued, for in both ancient and modern usage, "court, or curia" referred to judges only, just as "we uniformly speak of the court and jury, and consider them distinct." Even when a criminal jury acquitted, some Anti-Federalists reasoned, an appeal of legal issues might permit a higher court to revisit issues of fact.[89] If "the general government is not satisfied with the verdict of the jury," Luther Martin argued, "its officer may remove the prosecution to the supreme court, and *there* the *verdict of the jury is to be of no effect*."[90] And how many parties could afford to carry appeals to the national capital where the Supreme Court must sit, given the impracticality of its touring the American countryside?

Anti-Federalists attained as great a consensus on these repeatedly elaborated points as they found on any other issue. Here again, however, flights of rhetorical excess proved impossible to stifle. The least temperate writers took the abolition of civil juries as an accomplished fact. "It is a law maxim, that the expression of one part is an exclusion of the other," a New York writer asserted. "In legal construction therefore, the preservation of trial by jury in criminal, is an exclusion of it in civil cases."[91] And in the fevered atmosphere of Pennsylvania, Anti-Federalists delighted in blaming these provisions on Wilson ("James the Caledonian"). For his "extraordinary and unwearied exertions in the cause of despotism," who could make so "suitable and deserving" a chief justice of the Supreme Court? "Centinel" asked. "Here he would be both Judge and jury, sovereign arbiter in law and equity. In this capacity he may satiate his vengeance on patriotism for the opposition given to his projects of dominion," unhindered by any "intervening jury to shield the innocent, or procure redress to the injured."[92]

Yet as fantastic as many of these charges seemed, they triggered deep concerns because the daily business of governance and the regulation of property fell preponderantly under the purview of courts and juries that enforced local norms with little oversight by external institutions. It was this ingrained sensitivity to the workings of the legal system that enabled the Virginia convention to spend the better part of five days debating the details of Article III with a degree of care that it rarely sustained at other times, as Mason and Henry disputed no less impressive a trio of speakers than Edmund Pendleton, John Marshall, and Madison.[93] Nor were these fears merely expressions of a ritualized faith. For the more sophisticated Anti-Federalist analyses raised questions of the first importance to a general theory of rights. Only a handful of Anti-Federalists glimpsed—or at least voiced—the great insight that the "Federal Farmer" fleetingly offered when he noted that the two offices of juror and representative were "the means by which the people are let into the knowledge of public affairs," the "situation" in which they "acquire information and knowledge in the affairs of government and society."[94] Yet even when other Anti-Federalists overlooked the relation between jury service and citizenship, they understood how much the multifarious duties of courts defined the essence of government in a society completely devoid of anything resembling a bureaucracy or the apparatus of a modern state.

The most important aspect of the criticism of Article III, however, was that it located the danger to rights not in the courts per se but in *Congress.* True, Anti-Federalists often clothed federal judges in the sinister robes of civil-law magistrates, officials who would become habituated "to secret and arbitrary proceedings—to taking evidence secretly—exparte, &c. to perplexing the cause"—and far more subject to bribery, the "Federal Farmer" added, than jurors who normally "possess the honest characters of the common freemen of a country," and whose identity "is not, generally, known till the hour the cause comes on for trial."[95] They were anxious, as well, to defend the competence of juries to try matters of law and fact alike, thus preserving the traditional suspicion of judges as high priests of recondite legal knowledge. But in this account judges remained more the agents of despotism than its source. Slighting the importance of the life tenure they would now enjoy, Anti-Federalists emphasized the arbitrary rules that Congress could instruct those judges to enforce. When Federalists insisted that Congress had to be trusted to fashion arrangements for civil juries, they only encouraged their adversaries to regard it as the institution against which rights had most to be protected. For if the Constitution itself did not unilaterally abrogate the right to a civil jury, "An Old Whig" warned, Congress could still do so at a stroke, using the supremacy clause to prohibit civil juries "in any of the United States."[96]

A bill of rights was required less to guide judges in the administration

of justice than to prevent Congress from voiding the common-law procedures that Americans venerated. Henry illustrated this point vividly when
he warned that "the Necessity of a Bill of Rights" was "greater in this
Government, than ever it was in any Government before" because without it Congress would violate one right after another. "Congress from
their general powers may fully go into the business of human legislation,"
he claimed. "Are you not therefore now calling on those Gentlemen who
are to compose Congress, to prescribe trials and define punishments without [the] controul" that Virginians enjoyed because their Declaration of
Rights prohibited excessive bail and fines and cruel and unusual punishments? Without an explicit affirmation of the common law, Congress
may "introduce the practice of the civil law" and the modes of torture
common in France, Spain, and Germany. Its members might perhaps
be trusted if they were given written "knowledge of the extent of the
rights retained by the people," Henry said. "But if you leave them otherwise, they will not know how to proceed; and being in a state of uncertainty, they will assume rather than give up powers by implication."[97]

This was a curious conclusion to an impassioned argument, for Henry
did not explain how a bill of rights would work in practice. He could not
propose that it would empower the federal judges to act as vigilant guardians of rights, because the Anti-Federalist case against Article III rested
on mistrust of judicial authority (though a few Anti-Federalists, including
Samuel Adams, thought a bill of rights would enable judges to check
abuses of federal power).[98] Henry instead seemed to suppose that a bill of
rights would operate as a moral restraint on Congress—though if its
members were as rapacious as he supposed, it was not clear why they
should suddenly be reformed. Other Anti-Federalists offered a different
explanation of the efficacy of a bill of rights. As John Smilie told the
Pennsylvania convention, a bill of rights would provide "a plain, strong,
and accurate criterion by which the people might at once determine
when, and in what instance, their rights were violated" by their future
"governors" and "rulers." "So loosely, so inaccurately are the powers which
are enumerated in this Constitution defined, that it will be impossible,
without a test of that kind, to ascertain the limits of authority and to declare when government has degenerated into oppression."[99] The "Federal
Farmer" expressed the same idea in more abstract terms. "What is the
usefulness of a truth in theory," he asked, "unless it exists constantly in
the minds of the people, and has their assent?" A bill of rights did not
create the rights it declared; a people were entitled to their rights "not because their ancestors once got together and enumerated them on paper,
but because, by repeated negociations and declarations, all parties are

brought to realize them, and of course to believe them to be sacred." The differences among societies in their attachment to rights was almost reducible to "the effect of education, a series of notions impressed upon the minds of the people by examples, precepts and declarations."[100]

Here was a theory of rights that owed less to the *Second Treatise* than to Locke's writings on epistemology and education. Bills of rights were educational documents; they provided the standards of certainty that enabled citizens to assess doubtful acts of government; and they worked best by inculcating the values they espoused among the people *and* their rulers. But in political terms this argument still supposed that the problem of rights was to protect the people from their governors, the ruled from their rulers. That was the traditional paradigm that few Anti-Federalists escaped. Yet the rulers whom they feared were now demonstrably those who would exercise the unbounded and indefinite legislative powers the Constitution would bestow on Congress. And in this sense at least, Anti-Federalists were no less inclined than Madison to locate the threat to rights in the power of the legislature.

There was, of course, an obvious difference between the nature of the legislative threats that Anti-Federalists and Federalists perceived. Congress was threatening in a way that the state legislatures were not, because its members lacked the accountability that enabled their provincial counterparts to fulfill their rights-protecting duty. Whether doubling or trebling the size of the House of Representatives would have left Anti-Federalists less anxious over the absence of a bill of rights is doubtful. But the structure of this debate enabled some Anti-Federalists to make the same crucial theoretical transition that drove Madison to his more radical hypotheses.

Nor was that the only leap in the theory of rights that Anti-Federalists managed to make. As faithful as they remained to tried axioms, as zealously Anglophilic as they were in naming the rights they cherished, Anti-Federalists came close to adopting a modern, positive law position on the authority that rights, however ancient or natural their origins, would have once the Constitution was ratified. By implying that traditional rights and liberties would be rendered insecure if they went undeclared, Anti-Federalists in effect suggested that the existence of these rights *depended* upon their positive expression. An American bill of rights would thus be something more than a declaration of preexisting rights; for though its adoption could be interpreted as merely verifying the birthright Americans already possessed, its omission would fatally impair their authority. Anti-Federalists sensed that the supremacy clause of a written, popularly ratified constitution could indeed sweep aside all prior claims of rights and authority. The multiple sources for the authority of rights that the colonists had once invoked now seemed obsolete because the Constitution would create its own self-sufficient standard of legality. The argument that rights would cease to be rights if they were not explicitly constitutionalized thus rested on venerable concerns, but it also addressed the modernity of the Constitution in forthright terms.

THE FEDERALIST RESPONSE to these charges labored under two constraints, one political, the other rhetorical. The appeal for a bill of rights was not a distinct proposal in itself but part of a broader demand that the Constitution receive structural amendments prior to ratification. Federalists resisted all these appeals because they could only produce political and procedural uncertainties that would jeopardize the entire enterprise of reform. Wilson's speech created a second constraint. Even when its crucial distinctions proved vulnerable to attack, its stature as the definitive pronouncement of an authoritative commentator obliged Federalists to rally to its support. Few Federalists found this obligation troubling, however; most were probably grateful to Wilson for rebutting the Anti-Federalists in such simple but powerful terms, challenging them only to devise new metaphors to express his essential point. "To have made a formal declaration, that all the rights and powers not mentioned nor defined are reserved, would have been as great an afront to common sense," a western Massachusetts writer remarked, "as if after having made a grant of a certain tract of land . . . in a deed or bill of sale, I should add a particular enumeration of my every other piece of land and article of property, with a declaration in form, that none of these are meant to be granted." What did it matter that liberty of the press was not guaranteed? Oliver Ellsworth asked in his sixth "Landholder" essay, rebutting Mason. "Nor is liberty of conscience, or of matrimony, or of burial of the dead; it is enough that Congress have no power to prohibit either, and can have no temptation." Endless variations on this theme were possible. "As well might a Judge when he condemns a man to be hanged, give strong Injunctions to the Sheriff that he should not be beheaded."[101]

Some of this sarcasm reflected rank annoyance with their adversaries' exploitation of this issue. Yet there is little evidence that Federalists felt embarrassed about justifying the Convention's oversight. They remained adamant that bills of rights had no place in the new federal regime; and they often extended this criticism to deny that they had any value in the states either. Their reservations echoed the criticisms that led Madison to describe bills of rights as "parchment barriers"—useless when their eloquence was arrayed against the real political forces of a republican polity and redundant when republican politics operated in its proper channels. If legislators "determined among themselves to use their efforts to effect the establishment of an aristocratical or despotick government," James Sullivan asked, "would a bill of rights be any obstacle to their proceedings?"[102] But no less than their opponents, Federalists also confronted the fundamental question that the transition to a written constitution posed for an American theory of rights. Was the cause of liberty better served by explicitly incorporating rights in the text of a constitution, or might their enumeration and textual definition actually weaken the protection a declaration was meant to provide?

Federalist objections were premised on the different roles that bills of rights played in monarchies and republics. "The very words" of Magna Carta declared the rights and liberties it recognizes "to be the gift or grant of the king," Wilson reminded the Pennsylvania convention, "and under the influence of that doctrine, no wonder the people should then, and at subsequent periods, wish to obtain some concession of their formal liberties by the concessions of petitions and bills of rights." But in America "the fee simple of freedom and government is declared to be in the people." Nor did that mean that these ancient rights had been the Crown's to grant, only that the continuous challenge of recovering them from the heirs of William the Conqueror made their formal recognition all the more important. "How different then is our situation from the circumstances of the British nation?" Thomas Hartley asked the delegates at Harrisburg, for "from that instant" when independence was declared, "all our natural rights were restored to us." From this it followed "that whatever portion of those natural rights we did not transfer to the government was still reserved and retained by the people." Some rights "from their preeminence in the scale of political security, deserve to be particularly specified," Hartley concluded, but that did not negate the general point that all rights were reserved unless a positive grant of power to the government indicated otherwise.[103] In England bills of rights were inspired by the "usurpations of the Crown," James Iredell observed, and made necessary only because "no original constitution is to be found." But had such "a solemn instrument delegat[ing] particular powers to the Crown at the formation of their government" existed in England, no bill of rights would have been required even there. The Declaration of 1689 was a poor model for Americans to imitate; its articles "were never intended to limit the authority of Parliament." Bills of rights had been "eagerly adopted" by the states "without a due attention to the difference of the cases," at a moment when "the minds of men then being so warmed with their exertions in the cause of liberty, as to lean too much towards a jealousy of power to repose a proper confidence in their own government."[104]

Nothing would have been lost, then, had the states omitted to declare rights in 1776; liberty was as secure in those states which lacked bills of rights, Wilson told the Pennsylvania ratifiers, as in those that had adopted them.[105] The true security lay in the system of representation, the mutuality of interests between legislators and electors, and the virtue of a people whose liberties "never can be lost," a Virginia writer declared, "until they are lost to themselves, in a vicious disregard of their dearest interests, a sottish indolence, a wild licentiousness, a dissoluteness of morals, and a contempt of all virtue."[106] "No bill of rights ever yet bound the supreme power longer than the *honey moon* of a new married couple, unless the *rulers were interested* in preserving the rights," Roger Sherman wrote in his second "Countryman" letter. "The sole question . . . ought to be, how are Congress formed? how far are the members interested to preserve your rights? How far have you a controul over them?"[107] Hamilton nearly reduced this argument to a single sentence when he asserted that "the Constitution is itself, in every rational sense, and to every useful purpose, A BILL OF RIGHTS."[108] Like most Federalists, he found the clamor for a bill of rights hard to credit; his treatment of the topic in *Federalist* 84 was essentially an afterthought that restated conventional arguments.

Federalists displayed the same disparaging attitude toward the claim that the Constitution would erode the right to trial by jury. Yet here they had to tread more carefully. The essay preceding Hamilton's dismissal of a bill of rights was by far the longest in the entire work. Hamilton devoted much of *Federalist* 83 to a tedious examination of the cases in which juries were and were not required in the various states—an obvious attempt to prove the futility of imposing a uniform constitutional rule when actual practice was so diverse. In fact, Hamilton argued, if "the friends and adversaries" of the Constitution differed when it came to "the value they set upon the trial by jury," it was only that while Federalists regarded it "as a valuable safeguard to liberty," Anti-Federalists "represent it as the very palladium of free government." But that was true only in "relation to criminal proceedings," for "Arbitrary impeachments, arbitrary methods of prosecuting pretended offenses, and arbitrary punishments upon arbitrary convictions, have ever appeared to me to be the great engines of judicial despotism." By contrast, "I cannot readily discern the inseparable connection between the existence of liberty, and the trial by jury in civil cases."[109]

A few Federalists went much further. The North Carolina framer

William Pierce published a letter ridiculing the civil jury as a feudal relic that Americans could safely jettison; "the opinion of its utility is founded more in prejudice than in reason."[110] Hamilton was more discreet. Yet by placing the subject of the jury last in the six essays he devoted to Article III, he illustrated a shift in emphasis that did distinguish Federalist and Anti-Federalist perceptions of judicial power. For the dominant theme of *Federalist* 78–83 is the advantage the federal republic will gain from a judicial department whose key members are judges, not jurors. The jury remains important, but its function is also taken for granted; it is the role of the judges that requires explication. Much of their importance springs from the exigencies and even the logic of federalism. Among the multiple republics of a federal union, the uniformity and supremacy of national law can be maintained only by vesting just the sort of appellate jurisdiction in the Supreme Court that Anti-Federalists found so ominous. Not only will such a system of overlapping jurisdictions require judges who can resolve complex legal issues; it will also need to counteract the localist biases of state courts (including juries) and legislatures that would possess greater political resources than the national government.

Hamilton considered this issue as early as *Federalist* 22, and he returned to in his later essays. Yet as his defense of the theory of judicial review in *Federalist* 78 makes clear, the advantages that a corps of professionally qualified, independent judges will provide are not confined to the formidable task of policing "infractions of the Constitution" by the political branches of government, both federal and state. They extend as well to providing remedies for "the injury of the private rights of particular classes of citizens, by unjust and partial laws." The formal limits on legislative authority that Anti-Federalists sought "can be preserved in practice in no other way than through the medium of courts of justice," Hamilton wrote. "Without this, all the reservations of particular rights or privileges would amount to nothing."[111] No doubt judges would share that responsibility with juries and even defer to their decisions; yet in comparison to traditional conceptions of judges as presiding officials and juries as deciders of law and fact, Hamilton's account marked an important shift in the balance between the two.

Would a positive enumeration of rights better enable judges to meet their responsibilities? On this point Hamilton wrote with a measure of ambiguity. If federal judges were regarded not as unlettered local magistrates but as professionally qualified officials, appointed because they "unite the requisite integrity with the requisite knowledge" of the laws, they should need far less recourse to a bill of rights than the people at large, who Anti-Federalists worried would forget their rights if they were not publicly proclaimed. Yet Hamilton also defined the "limited Constitution" that judges should maintain as "one which contains certain specified exeptions to the legislative authority; such, for instance, as that it shall pass no bills of attainder, no *ex-post-facto* laws, and the like." These were the provisions that both Federalists and Anti-Federalists regarded as evidence that the Constitution contained at least a partial bill of rights, and presumably their inclusion in the text made them of some use. Hamilton nonetheless followed other Federalists in insisting that a more thorough rendering of rights would prove "not only unnecessary in the proposed Constitution, but would even be dangerous." The two realms where this danger was most likely to arise, Federalists generally insisted, were liberty of the press and freedom of conscience. How could one affirm that either right was to be protected, Hamilton asked, without conveying "a clear implication, that a power to prescribe proper regulations concerning it was intended to be vested in the national government"?[112]

The force of this objection reflected the deeper tendency in eighteenth-century thinking to regard rights not as absolute barriers against public regulation but rather as guarantees that when the state acted it must do so lawfully. But the Federalist concern was directed to a more profound issue. If one began with the premise that rights were properly secure only when explicitly protected, it followed that any enumeration undertaken to rectify the omissions of the Convention would have to be comprehensive or risk creating new dangers of its own. Had the framers assumed the laborious task of enumerating "every thing, which the citizens of the United States claim as a natural or civic right," Alexander Contee Hanson wrote, they would have exposed the Constitution to greater criticism, for "[a]n omission of a single article would have caused more discontent, than is either felt, or pretended, on the present occasion." Moreover, such an effort might suffer not only from partiality but also from an unavoidable lack of foresight. If a bill of rights was indeed necessary to erect the standard to which the people must resort to judge their rulers, it had to be drawn with the greatest care, Jasper Yeates told the Pennsylvania ratifiers, "for, it might be argued at a future day by the persons then in power—you undertook to enumerate the rights which you mean to reserve, the pretension which you make is not comprised in that enumeration, and, consequently, our jurisdiction is not circumscribed."[113] Nor was omission the only danger. "Our rights are not yet all known," Benjamin Rush told the Pennsylvania convention; how then could they be properly enumerated?[114]

To prove the absurdity of enumerating rights, Federalists lampooned one of the amendments proposed by the minority in the Pennsylvania convention, which would have affirmed that Americans would retain the "liberty to fowl and hunt in seasonable times, and on lands they hold . . . and in like manner to fish in all navigable waters, and others not private property, without being restrained" by Congress. Nearly transported by "laughter at this clause," Noah Webster proposed a further "restriction:— 'That Congress shall never restrain any inhabitant of America from eating and drinking, *at seasonable times*, or prevent his lying on his *left side*, in a long winter's night, or even on his back, when he is fatigued by lying on his *right*.' "[115] Such barbs came easily to Federalist jesters, but the issue both sides addressed remained serious enough. By specifying some rights, the framers had obviously not meant to disparage others, least of all venerable common-law procedures. But a lack of sinister intentions just as obviously did not obviate the theoretical problem of determining whether the Constitution had left the glass of rights half empty, half full—or full. As exaggerated as Anti-Federalist fears were, they confronted a theoretical problem of the first magnitude. Once a partial set of rights had received textual recognition as supreme law, did that not relegate all other rights to some lesser or more problematic status, even if they were originally derived from the variety of preexisting sources to which the colonists had appealed before 1776?

MADISON SHARED THESE RESERVATIONS, but his analysis of the inadequacy of bills of rights was far more profound. Yet so, too, were his reasons for concluding that the first Congress to meet after ratification should place the adoption of suitable amendments high on its agenda. And this conviction in turn was a crucial, even decisive factor in the politics of the amendment process. For were it not for Madison, a bill of rights might never have been added to the Constitution. Contrary to the usual story, the concessions that Federalist leaders offered to secure ratification in such closely divided states as Massachusetts, Virginia, and New York did not establish a binding contract to provide a bill of rights. By the time the First Congress mustered a quorum in April 1789, it was not evident that action on amendments was imperative. Most Federalists had grown indifferent to the question, nor were former Anti-Federalists now sitting in Congress any more insistent, largely because they knew that the substantive changes they desired in the Constitution lay beyond their reach. Nearly all Madison's colleagues in Congress thought the entire subject could be deferred until the new government was safely operating, by which point the desire for a bill of rights might well have evaporated. But Madison insisted that Congress had to act sooner, not later, and the amendments it eventually submitted to the states in September 1789 followed closely the proposals he introduced in June. Madison was not merely one participant among many or even primus inter pares; he was the key actor whose purposes deserve scrutiny for that reason alone.

His path to authorship of these amendments was not direct. Madison had left Philadelphia fearful that the Constitution would not provide a satisfactory solution to the pervasive problem of protecting rights. When he explained "the grounds of this opinion" in his letter to Jefferson of October 24, 1787, he went out of his way to defend the absolute veto on state laws as the optimal solution to the problem of rights. It was true, he observed, that the Constitution did afford some basis for the protection of economic rights. Yet even if its restraints on emissions of paper currency and laws impairing the obligation of contracts proved "effectual as far as they go, they are short of the mark," Madison observed. "Injustice may be effected by such an infinitude of legislative expedients, that where the disposition exists it can only be controuled by some provision which reaches all cases whatsoever." Because such a provision would not have to identify specific rights, Madison's reservation was the corollary of his concern that "legislative expedients" could always circumvent a formal ban proscribing the exercise of particular powers. In effect, Madison feared that an enumeration of rights would prove restrictive in a way that the enumeration of legislative powers could not. Nor could the federal judiciary be trusted to remedy wrongs. "[I]t is more convenient to prevent the passage of a law [through a national veto], than to declare it void after it is passed," he observed, especially "where the law aggrieves individuals, who may be unable to support an appeal agst. a State to the supreme Judiciary."[116]

Nothing that transpired during the next year altered this opinion—including the knowledge, conveyed both in personal correspondence (which met extraordinary delays) and published letters, that Jefferson had thrown his prestige behind the demand for a bill of rights, even wishing, with characteristic impulsiveness, "that the 9 first conventions may receive, & the last 4 reject" the Constitution, obliging the majority "to offer a declaration of rights in order to complete the union." This no more amused Madison than Jefferson's earlier letter that responded to Shays's Rebellion in Massachusetts with the calculation that "one rebellion in 13 states in the course of 11 years" was all to the good.[117]

When Madison finally answered Jefferson on October 17, 1788, he coupled a somewhat disingenuous assertion that he had "always been in favor of a bill of rights; provided it be so framed as not to imply powers not meant to be included in the enumeration," with a disarming explanation why "I have not viewed it in an important light." To some extent he accepted Wilson's argument that a bill of rights was less necessary for the federal government because it was vested with limited powers; and also because the independent existence of the states would "afford a security" against an abuse of federal power. Too, there was "great reason to fear that a positive declaration of some of the most essential rights could not be obtained in the requisite latitude"—especially if "rights of conscience" were considered. To reduce a broad principle to an inadequately formulated text might have the same limiting effect on the actual protection of rights as an incomplete enumeration.

Madison saved for last the argument that expressed his most profound doubts. "Experience proves the inefficacy of a bill of rights on those occasions when its controul is most needed," he observed. "Repeated violations of these parchment barriers have been committed in every State." The crucial point followed.

> Wherever the real power in a Government lies, there is the danger of oppression. In our Governments the real power lies in the majority of the Community, and the invasion of private rights is *cheifly* [*sic*] to be apprehended, not from acts of Government contrary to the sense of its constituents, but from acts in which the Government is the mere instrument of the major number of the constituents. This is a truth of great importance, but not yet sufficiently attended to: and is probably more strongly impressed on my mind by facts, and reflections suggested by them, than on yours which has contemplated abuses of power issuing from a very different quarter.

Madison thus set his own observations about American politics against the inferences Jefferson had drawn from four years of service as minister in France, inferences that allowed him to preserve the traditional paradigm of protecting the ruled from the rulers. In a monarchy, Madison continued, a bill of rights could serve "as a standard for trying the validity of public acts, and a signal for rousing the superior force of the community" against "abuses of power" by "the sovereign." But in a republic, "the political and physical power" were both lodged "in a majority of the people, and consequently the tyrannical will of the sovereign is not [to] be controuled by the dread of an appeal to any other force within the community."

If Madison's deepest concern was still for rights of property, he nevertheless applied this general analysis to other categories of rights. He remained convinced that some form of religious establishment could yet be adopted in Virginia, if the assembly "found a majority of the people in favor of the measure," and "if a majority of the people were now of one sect," notwithstanding the "explicit provision" protecting rights of conscience in the state constitution and "the additional obstacle" which the Statute for Religious Freedom "has since created." He doubted whether the provisions for rights that Jefferson desired should be cast in "absolute" terms. "The restrictions however strongly marked on paper will never be regarded when opposed to the decided sense of the public," he warned, "and after repeated violations in extraordinary cases, they will lose even their ordinary efficacy." "No written prohibitions on earth" would deter a people alarmed by civil turmoil from suspending habeas corpus, nor would an article prohibiting standing armies as a danger to liberty do much good if Britain or Spain massed forces "in our neighbourhood."

What value, then, Madison asked rhetorically, would a bill of rights have in a republic? He saw two uses for it "which though less essential than in other Governments, sufficiently recommend the precaution." The first was educative: "The political truths declared in that solemn manner acquire by degrees the character of fundamental maxims of free Government, and as they become incorporated with the national sentiment, counteract the impulses of interest and passion." By his own standards, this seems remarkably optimistic: Everywhere else in his concurrent writings he concluded that ordinary citizens would rarely find appeals to principle more persuasive than the impulses of interest and passion.[118] He was equally doubtful about the second rationale he conceded: that occasions could arise when "the danger of oppression" would lie more in "usurped acts of the Government" than in "the interested majorities of the people," or even that "a succession of artful and ambitious rulers, may by gradual & well-timed advances, finally erect an independent Government on the subversion of liberty." But Madison treated even this more as a speculative possibility than as a serious threat. In the American republics, the greater danger was that government would experience a progressive "relaxation" of its power to restrain the populace, "until the abuses of liberty beget a sudden transition to an undue degree of power."

With these monitory strictures in mind, Madison was prepared to endorse the call for a bill of rights, if suitably framed, and to assume personal responsibility for the adoption of appropriate amendments. Yet this grudging acceptance of political necessity reflected no sudden realization that a national bill of rights would have great practical value. The original failure of the Federal Convention to accept the programmatic reforms he valued most—the national veto and the council of revision—could not be remedied by the adoption of a federal bill of rights that would not reach the cases (or the arena) where rights remained at greatest risk. Legislation affecting property, conscience, and the legal procedures (civil and criminal) to which Americans would be subject remained the province of the state legislatures, and Madison simply could not see how the acceptance of cautionary limitations on the exercise of national power would do much good.

Given the continuing force of these reservations, Madison's colleagues in Congress had reason to interpret his public statement favoring amendments as a campaign conversion inspired by his difficult election contest against James Monroe. Senator Robert Morris of Pennsylvania scoffed that Madison had "got frightened in Virginia and 'wrote a Book' "—that is, published letters revising his known views about amendments.[119] Yet as important as political concerns were in convincing Madison to take the lead in promoting amendments, his libertarian convictions were never in doubt. When the time came to enumerate rights meriting constitutional recognition, he had no problem drafting an expansive list of civil rights in language that by contemporary standards can only be described as advanced. His subsisting objections to bills of rights were more pragmatic and functional than principled. Madison simply regarded the adoption of a federal bill of rights as an irrelevant antidote to the real dangers that republican politics would generate—unless it applied to the states. Nor could he imagine how rights of property could ever be codified with the same ease and precision with which procedural rights could be guaranteed.

Just as Madison's deepest reservations survived intact, so he found it impossible to dissemble when the time came (both in Virginia and Congress) to present his reasons for accepting and sponsoring the requisite amendments. For all the aggrevation his stewardship of the eventual amendments caused him, he did not shrink from offering a final and largely unmodified defense of his essential views. Rather than endorse the Anti-Federalist claim that a constitution lacking a bill of rights would prove dangerous, he carefully explained why standard Federalist arguments against amendments were at once plausible yet less than persuasive. He stressed that the most important reason for proposing amendments was to reconcile to the Constitution all those "respectable" citizens whose "jealousy . . . for their liberty . . . though mistaken in its object, is laudable in its motive." Similarly, Madison used his speech introducing amendments to reiterate central elements of his own teachings about republican government. He reminded his colleagues, and the public who read his speech in the newspapers, that a declaration of rights needed to be aimed against the legislature, not against the relatively weak executive.

But in fact, "the greatest danger" to liberty was "not found in either the executive or legislative departments of government, but in the body of the people, operating by the majority against the minority."[120]

Far from bowing to Anti-Federalist arguments or public opinion, Madison thus restated his essential convictions. So, too, he sought once again to restrict the abuse of state power by proposing an additional amendment declaring that "No state shall violate the equal rights of conscience, or the freedom of the press, or the trial by jury in criminal cases." Though far more limited than the national veto, this measure marked a last effort to salvage his earlier critique of the preeminent dangers to rights within the states. In subsequent debate, Madison boldly described this clause "as the most valuable amendment on the whole list." Would the people not be equally grateful, he asked, if "these essential rights" were secured against the state as well as the national governments? This logic prevailed in the House but not the Senate, which acted to protect the rights of its legislative constituents in the state assemblies against national encroachment.[121]

In his speech of June 8, Madison did make one notable point he had not endorsed previously. If a declaration of rights was "incorporated into the constitution," he observed,

> independent tribunals of justice will consider themselves in a peculiar manner the guardians of those rights; they will be an impenetrable bulwark against every assumption of power in the legislative or executive; they will be naturally led to resist every encroachment upon rights expressly stipulated for in the constitution by the declaration of rights.

The inspiration for this statement came from Jefferson.[122] But however attractive this prospect seemed in the abstract, Madison did not expect the adoption of amendments to free judges to act vigorously in defense of rights—at least over the short run. The true benefits of a bill of rights were to be found in the realm of public opinion, whose workings so intrigued Madison. Beyond the immediate boost in allegiance to the new government that the prompt approval of amendments would produce, Madison hoped a bill of rights would reinforce the stability of government over a longer period. "In proportion as Government is influenced by opinion, must it be so by whatever influences opinion," Madison privately noted in December 1791. "This decides the question concerning a bill of rights, which acquires efficacy as time sanctifies and incorporates it with the public sentiment."[123] As greater popular respect for individual and minority rights developed over time, perhaps the judiciary would eventually act as Madison very much hoped yet initially doubted it would. But the greater benefit would occur if acceptance of the principles encoded in rights acted to restrain political behavior, tempering improper popular desires *before* they took the form of unjust legislation. Perhaps that in turn explains why Madison insisted that Congress take up the subject of amendments at its first session. The logic of this demand was consistent with the concern with public opinion that drove his constitutional thinking. By closely linking the adoption of amendments with the ratification of the Constitution, and by treating both as extraordinary acts of reflection and choice, Madison hoped to attach to this conception of rights "that veneration which time bestows on every thing, and without which perhaps the wisest and freest governments would not possess the requisite stability."[124]

Few of his insights better illustrate what Bernard Bailyn has called "the hard, quizzical, grainy quality of mind that led Madison to probe the deepest questions of republicanism . . . as an operating, practical, everyday process of government capable of containing within it the explosive forces of society."[125] Madison was not entirely alone in thinking that the value of a bill of rights was primarily educative; Melancton Smith, the putative "Federal Farmer," developed a similar argument.[126] There was, nevertheless, a crucial difference between Madison's tersely sketched position and that taken by his contemporaries. Other writers—Anti-Federalists and Federalists alike—still regarded bills of rights as standards that would enable the people to judge the behavior of their governors, to know when their legitimate rights and interests were being violated. Madison foresaw a more sophisticated use: Bills of rights would best promote the cause of republican self-government if they enabled republican citizens to govern themselves—to resist the impulses of interest and passion that were the root of factious behavior.

JEFFERSON HAD ADDRESSED the same problem of the self-governing citizen in his *Notes on the State of Virginia* when he condemned slavery as "a perpetual exercise of the most boisterous passions, the most unremitting despotism." Only a "prodigy" could "retain his manners and morals undepraved by such circumstances," he concluded, which were hardly the circumstances to nurture the manners and morals of republican citizens. Jefferson went on to reflect on the greater evil of "permitting one half the citizens thus to trample on the rights of the other," urging his readers to ponder this question: "And can the liberties of a nation be thought secure when we have removed their only firm basis, a conviction in the minds of the people that these liberties are of the gift of God?" Once again the existence of the fundamental right to liberty ultimately depends on inner conviction, not the forms of constitutionalism; once again, the limitations of Jefferson's anti-slavery become evident in the weakness of his conclusion: "We must be contented to hope," Jefferson wrote, that "the various considerations of policy, of morals, of history natural and civil" that urged "a total emancipation" of the slaves "will force their way into every one's mind." And if they did not? Better it come "with the consent of the masters," Jefferson warned, "than by their extirpation" in the rebellion he feared.[127]

Of the many questions this passage raises, not the least curious is Jefferson's description of slaves as one half of the citizenry, with due claims to rights. That hardly constituted an accurate description of their status in the new Republic. Madison came nearer the mark in *Federalist* 43 when he defended the clause of the Constitution guaranteeing each state a republican form of government because it would enable the federal government to quell local insurrections. Here he alluded to slaves as "an unhappy species of population . . . who, during the course of regular government, are sunk below the level of men"—and who thus have no rights to claim—"but who, in the tempestuous scenes of civil violence, may emerge into the human character." Yet at the Convention Madison had described racial slavery as "the most oppressive dominion ever exercised by man over man," grounded on "the mere distinction of colour." And a few years later, he cited "the case of Black slaves in Modern times" as an example of "the danger of oppression to the minority from unjust combinations of the majority"—a restatement of the republican dilemma that echoed Jefferson's reference to slaves as citizens manqué.[128]

Nothing in the Bill of Rights alleviated this radical deprivation of liberty, of course. But Madison's carefully guarded thoughts on slavery expose a further puzzle in his thinking. Among the many objections that militated against an unlimited veto on state laws, the criticism it must have sparked in his native region would have doomed the Constitution once his fellow planters grasped that it would extend to the law of slavery. Could Madison possibly have overlooked this implication? Or might he have hoped that the pressing need to reconstitute the Union would somehow carry the veto in its wake, and thereby provide an entering wedge to weaken the hold of slavery and its evil effects? If he at least glimpsed this possibility, can we not speculate whether the Civil War amendments—especially the Fourteenth—are the most Madisonian elements of the

American Constitution? For on what other basis did the federal government acquire the authority that Madison sought for it in 1787: to act as
an umpire mediating the various forms of injustice that he expected to
flourish within the states?

So it is that an original intention is sometimes fulfilled long after its
author has outlived even himself.*

---

*I allude here to a letter Madison wrote in 1831, when he and Charles Carroll of Carrollton were the
last survivors of the political leadership of the Revolution. "Having outlived so many of my contemporaries," Madison wrote Jared Sparks on June 1, 1831, "I ought not to forget that I may be thought to have
outlived myself." *Letters and Other Writings of James Madison* (Philadelphia, 1865), IV, 182.

CHAPTER XI

MADISON AND THE
ORIGINS OF ORIGINALISM

P ERRY MILLER, the great historian of the American mind, opened his most famous essay by revolving the dual meanings of the "errand" that sent an earlier set of American founders—the Puritans—into their wilderness. By the seventeenth century, Miller noted, *errand* had come to mean both the journey, usually short, "on which an inferior is sent," and "the actual business on which the actor goes, the purpose itself, the conscious intention in his mind." New England's confusion of mission after 1660 reflected this ambiguity. Was its settlement only a step in the broader Reformation still under way in Europe, "or was it an end in itself?" Miller answered his question with this memorable sentence: "Having failed to rivet the eyes of the world upon their city on the hill, they were left alone with America."[1]

Where John Winthrop's generation failed, James Madison and his succeeded (or so they thought, and with reason). But Miller's poignant contrast between the purposes of founders and heirs is as relevant to the fate of the Constitution as it was to the Puritan covenant. Moreover, the same duality of meaning that Miller relished in *errand* applies to the two words that describe the subject of this book: *constitution* and *interpretation*. The framers believed that their concept of a constitution broke decisively with the prior understanding they inherited from Britain. Yet in one sense that break was less radical than it seemed. For since 1789 Americans have always possessed two constitutions, not one: the formal document adopted in 1787–88, with its amendments; and the working constitution comprising the body of precedents, habits, understandings, and attitudes that shape how the federal system operates at any historical moment. The problem of originalism is about the relation between these two constitutions. Originalism asks whether some aspect of law or governance should be brought nearer to its constitutional source. It is what remains in American politics of the Machiavellian concept of *ridurre ai principii*—the belief that the preservation of the republic requires a periodic return to its founding principles and condition.

Interpretation bears a dualism of meaning even closer to Miller's *errand*. It, too, is both a process and its result, both the act of interpreting a text and the legal action to which it leads. To its advocates, originalism offers a means of making both this process and its results less capricious. It rests on the belief—or legal fiction—that most clauses of the Constitution possessed a clear meaning at their inception. It strives to ask how its language "would have been understood at the time," as Robert Bork has observed, and to recover its "public understanding," as "manifested in the words used [in the text] and in secondary materials, such as debates at the conventions, public discussion, newspaper articles, dictionaries in use at the time, and the like." Nothing in Bork's own principal defense of originalism suggests that he has ever tested his thesis against this evidence; his citations to *The Records of the Federal Convention of 1787* indicate that he has encountered the debates only as they happen to be excerpted in a standard legal text.[2] But his definition fairly states one of two critical assumptions on which the strong form of originalism rests. The other is that the original meaning of the Constitution is binding because it represents the highest exercise of popular sovereignty possible within the constitutional system.

A historically grounded approach to originalism poses the problem differently. It begins by recognizing, as the framers themselves did, that the Constitution would inevitably be subject to two phases of interpretation. One began as soon as it was submitted for ratification; the second could unfold only when the business of governance commenced. Interpretation, in the strict sense, was not a process that followed ratification; it began with the publication of the Constitution on September 19, 1787, and has continued ever since. From the essays of "Publius" to the ranting of the most fearful Anti-Federalist, every commentator on the Constitution was interpreting its meaning. An obvious temporal line would separate these two phases, but in 1787 no one could anticipate how the initial bounded phase of interpretation would affect the actual decision-making required to convert the Constitution into a government. Originalism, then, is not only about the relation between the Constitution of 1787 and the constitutions of later periods; it is also about the relation between the interpretative predictions of 1787–88 and the interpretative processes that developed afterward. Would the debates of these months themselves become evidentiary sources on which later interpreters would rely, or would the "construction" of the Constitution depend on other rules and methods?

Though volumes have been written about constitutional interpretation after 1789, these questions have received little attention—with two notable exceptions. In an influential article published in 1985, H. Jefferson Powell argued that existing norms available to the earliest interpreters of the Constitution left little room to look beyond the explicit language of a legal text. Although some commentators implied that interpretation should strive to recover the subjective purposes of the parties to a document, in practice that intention was almost always reducible to and discoverable in its language. There was no notion or tradition of construing a statute by examining its legislative history—committee reports or records of debates, which in America rarely existed. In case of ambiguity, interpreters might consider the purposes declared in the preamble, but they relied far more on the rules and precedents of common-law adjudication. Knowledge of the intention of a statute, Powell concludes, was far less a *guide* to interpretation than its *product*, an understanding formed and refined over time through a course of reasoning and practice.[3] This was very close to Madison's observation that "All new laws, though penned with the greatest technical skill, and passed on the fullest and most mature deliberation, are considered as more or less obscure and equivocal, until their meaning be liquidated and ascertained by a series of particular discussions and adjudications."[4] The modern theory that equates intention with the subjective purposes of identifiable historical actors was simply not part of the arsenal from which interpreters could draw.

Charles Lofgren, a skillful practitioner of originalist analysis, has challenged these conclusions on two grounds. Reviewing Powell's use of sources, Lofgren discovers a cavalier approach to evidence that weakens his argument. More important, Lofgren argues that Powell errs in limiting his inquiry to the relevance of the intentions of the framers of the Constitution while ignoring the understandings of its ratifiers. Some disputants in the political debates of the 1790s clearly thought that the known expectations, understandings, and intentions of the ratifiers could serve as a restraint on doubtful constructions, Lofgren concludes. And he goes a step beyond Powell in intimating that this view was then, and remains now, doctrinally sound.[5]

Much can be said both for Powell's account of the prevailing interpretative norms of 1787 and Lofgren's distinction between framers and ratifiers. But the story is more complicated still. Neither Powell nor Lofgren asks how the political struggles of the early 1790s affected the evolution of theories of interpretation, or shaped the curiously intertwined role that Madison and Hamilton, the great collaborators turned protagonists, played in their development. Neither considers, in other words, how the permeable border between politics and the Constitution influenced the form of originalist interpretation which appears to have become legitimate by the winter of 1796, when the House of Representatives conducted a celebrated debate over its role in implementing the Jay Treaty. In the course of that debate, James Madison delivered a speech which can be cited as a definitive early statement of the theory that the original understanding of the ratifiers of the Constitution can indeed provide an essential guide to its interpretation. Retracing how Madison reached that position offers a fascinating (and not unironic) concluding commentary on what the Constitution originally meant.

AT PHILADELPHIA, THE FRAMERS clearly kept the two phases of interpretation in mind. That was why they repeatedly labored over the wording of individual clauses, down to the last day of debate. Some of their editorial tinkering was driven by the looming challenge of ratification. But most revisions were directed toward creating a text that could be easily implemented. The framers generally followed the advice that Edmund Randolph gave the committee of detail in July. "In the draught of a fundamental constitution, two things deserve attention," he observed:

> 1. To insert essential principles only; lest the operations of government should be clogged by rendering those provisions permanent and unalterable, which ought to be accommodated to times and events; and
> 2. To use simple and precise language, and general propositions, according to the example of the constitutions of the several states. (For the construction of a constitution necessarily differs from that of law.)[6]

This formula left little room for flights of rhetorical embellishment, even in the preamble. Unlike the Declaration of Independence, which Jefferson (we now know) wrote to be read aloud, literally performed, the prosaic text of the Constitution was best read silently, not for inspiration but for direction.[7] (If it had to be read aloud, in Congress or a courtroom, that was a sure sign that its meaning was not self-evident.) Its wording bore the mark of the numerous attorneys present at Philadelphia, a group that included King, Ellsworth, Hamilton, Wilson, Morris, Paterson, Dickinson, Randolph, and Rutledge. But other framers unschooled in the fine points of legal draftsmanship also worried how its clauses would be read. Madison was not a lawyer, and neither were Gerry, Sherman, Mason, Williamson, Butler, and Baldwin—all of whom demonstrated close concern with the language they were adopting. The framers worried about how the Constitution would be interpreted not as lawyers but as legislators.

The predictions that both sides offered in 1787–88 were directed toward the overriding question of ratification. For Federalists, this meant explaining how the Constitution's prudent distribution of power would preserve equilibrium within the national government and between it and the states. For their adversaries, it meant exposing the loosely worded provisions and frail safeguards that later power-wielders could exploit for the purposes of consolidation. Their rival claims sought not to create an evidentiary record (or potted history) to guide later interpreters but to advance the arguments most likely to influence the course of ratification.

The closest the polemicists of 1787–88 came to imagining how their exchanges might affect later interpretations was when Federalists warned that repetition of the wilder Anti-Federalist charges could produce the very results dreaded. One such instance is found in *Federalist* 33, where Hamilton answered the "virulent invective and petulant declamation" being directed against the necessary-and-proper clause. This "sweeping clause" would in fact obviate the need for "construction" without enlarging the powers the Constitution vested in Congress, Hamilton argued. But suppose Congress wrongly impinged on the authority of a state. The "forced constructions" needed to support such palpably unconstitutional acts would be so apparent that "the people" could then readily "appeal to the standard they have formed"—the Constitution—"and take such measures to redress the injury done to the Constitution as the exigency may suggest and prudence justify." "If there should ever be a doubt on this head," he concluded, "the credit of it will be entirely due to those reasoners who, in the imprudent zeal of their animosity to the plan of the convention, have labored to envelop it in a cloud calculated to obscure the plainest and simplest truths." In other words, if the people were later confused about the limits of the powers of Congress, it would only be because Anti-Federalist invective had turned the necessary-and-proper clause into the engine of tyranny it was never meant to be.[8]

James Iredell verged toward a similar argument when he asked the North Carolina ratifiers to imagine how future rulers bent on invading a fundamental right might reason historically about its omission from a bill of rights.

> Would they not naturally say, "We live at a great distance from the time when this Constitution was established. We can judge of it much better by the ideas of it entertained at the time, than by any ideas of our own. The bill of rights, passed at that time, showed that the people did not think every power retained which was not given, else this bill of rights was not only useless, but absurd."

Later interpreters would naturally assume that their "ancestors," scrupulous in "their attachment to liberty," had incorporated every right they deemed worthy of protection. Yet even in this effort to think of interpretation as a process of historical recovery, Iredell assumed that interpreters would have no useful sources to examine beyond the Constitution itself. Acting "long after all traces of our present disputes were at an end," they would not examine documentary evidence to reconstruct the debate to which he was contributing. They would read the Constitution as Federalists were reading it now, relying on its plain language and structure to ascertain its meaning. If some rights were enumerated and others not, they would need no other evidence to conclude that the omissions were deliberate.[9]

Oliver Ellsworth stated the assumptions on which this notion of interpretation relied in his fifth "Landholder" essay. Answering Gerry's published objection "that some of the powers of the Legislature are ambiguous, and others indefinite and dangerous," Ellsworth replied that this charge "may be brought against every human composition, and necessarily arises from the imperfection of language." Even "the most perspicuous and precise writers" were guilty of ambiguity; others "never attain to the happy art of perspicuous expression"; and still others (like Gerry) "thro' a mental defect of their own, will judge the most correct and certain language of others to be indefinite and ambiguous." But that charge could not be lodged against the Constitution, which was "expressed with brevity, and in the plain common language of mankind." The alternative was in fact far more dangerous.

> Had the Constitution swelled into the magnitude of a volume, there would have been more room to entrap the unwary, and the people who are to be its judges, would have had neither patience nor opportunity to understand it. Had it been expressed in the scientific language of law, or those terms of art which we often find in political

compositions, to the honourable gentleman it might have appeared more definite and less ambiguous; but to the great body of the people altogether obscure, and to accept it they must leap in the dark.

The people would be in "much more danger of a deception" if the powers vested in Congress came "loaded with provisos, and such qualifications, as a lawyer who is so cunning even to suspect himself, might have intermingled." Interpretation would then be open to sophistry and manipulation; but the Constitution as written was nearly transparent in its meaning.[10]

Like other framers, Ellsworth grasped the concept of judicial review. A month later, he told the Connecticut ratifiers that the courts would simply void any national or state law which attempted to "overleap [the] limits" of their respective authority.[11] The lines of demarcation that the plain words of the Constitution made visible to the people would be all the more evident to legal minds possessing the perspicuity that Ellsworth (like Madison and Wilson) admired. But in his "Landholder" essay Ellsworth posed more as a republican than as a lawyer. That is, he wrote as if the people would have a role as well as a stake in interpreting the Constitution. Their *political* capacity to police its boundaries of power depended on the clarity of its language. Hamilton drew the same inference in *Federalist* 33, and so did Anti-Federalists who argued that only a forthright declaration of rights would enable the people to know when government overstepped its proper authority.

Most Federalists thought that the people would rarely make such judgments. The real interpretation of the Constitution would occur as decisions taken within government gradually settled its operations in regular channels. Madison shared this hope. But as was often the case, his concerns had a more profound dimension. For he also understood that the purposes of constitutional and statutory interpretation might diverge in crucial ways. The purpose of statutory interpretation was to ascertain or "liquidate" meaning by applying a general rule to particular circumstances. The end of constitutional interpretation was to determine which branch or level of government possessed the right to act in a particular area of governance, and in doing so, to preserve the equilibrium among institutions that the Constitution intended to establish. This last concern in turn identified the interpretative purposes that Madison initially believed were most urgent to establish at the outset. For here, as everywhere else in his thinking, the great challenge was to curb the excesses of legislative misrule and the unruly surges of popular interest and opinion that made republican politics so tumultuous.

Madison's initial approach to constitutional interpretation was thus an extension of his general theory of republican government. Whereas other Federalists and even Anti-Federalists argued that a clear and lucid Constitution would enable the people to police the boundaries of power, Madison literally went out of his way in *Federalist* 49 and 50 to explain why the people should never act as arbiters of constitutional disputes through the "occasional" or "periodical appeals" to their authority that Jefferson had proposed in his *Notes on the State of Virginia*. Their judgment "could never be expected to turn on the true merits of the question. It would inevitably be connected with the spirit of preexisting parties, or of parties springing out of the question itself."[12] Such appeals, if repeated, would sap the very legitimacy of the Constitution. Equally important, the logic of Madison's entire theory of faction led to the conclusion that the most likely source of constitutional encroachments was the House of Representatives, where the people's impulses would be felt most quickly and powerfully.

Madison fittingly pursued this point in the final lines he wrote as "Publius." "The irresistible force possessed by that branch of a free government, which has the people on its side," he wrote in *Federalist* 63, made the prediction that the Senate might "transform itself, by gradual usurpations, into an independent and aristocratic body" utterly frivolous. Should the Senate seek to do so, "the House of Representatives, with the people on their side, will at all times be able to bring back the Constitution to its primitive forms and principles." Not so the obverse situation. "Against the force of the immediate representatives of the people, nothing will be able to maintain even the constitutional authority of the Senate, but such a display of enlightened policy, and attachment to the public good, as will divide with that branch of the legislature the affections and support of the entire body of the people."[13]

Nothing that transpired during the ratification debate or the first federal elections shook this opinion. While waiting for Congress to assemble, Madison predicted that the new government would share many of the democratic "features" of "the State Governments." When Congress conducted its first serious constitutional debate, he wrote Randolph that he favored a sole presidential power over the removal of executive officials because "I see, and *politically feel* that that will be the weak branch of the government." This concern recurs in a letter to his mentor, Edmund Pendleton. "In truth, the Legislative power is of such a nature that it scarcely can be restrained either by the Constitution or itself," Madison almost sighed. "And if the federal Government should lose its proper equilibrium within itself, I am persuaded that the effect will proceed from the Encroachments of the Legislative department." If the choice of evils lay between the Senate and the president, Madison added, there was more to fear from the upper house. But "I remain fully in the opinion," he concluded, "that the numerous and immediate representatives of the people, composing the other House, will decidedly predominate in the Government."[14]

Over the next seven years, however, events led Madison to rethink these fundamental premises of his thought. By 1796 he was prepared to support an evident encroachment of the House on the treaty powers of the president and the Senate; to join in converting this constitutional dispute into a vehicle for rallying public opinion to the banner of his opposition party; and to imply that the records of the ratification debates offered a legitimate means to determine the meaning of the Constitution. To understand how he reached these positions, we must review several episodes in the constitutional politics of these years: the debate of 1789 over the power of the president to remove subordinate officers; the dispute of 1791 over the constitutionality of a national bank; and the controversy of 1796 over the role of the House in implementing the Jay Treaty.

The removal debate. When the House took up a bill to organize the executive branch in mid-May 1789, Madison moved to create departments of foreign affairs, war, and treasury, each headed by a secretary "who shall be appointed by the president, by and with the advice and consent of the senate; and to be removeable by the president." The "advice and consent" clause was deleted after William L. Smith of South Carolina objected that it was "superfluous" to repeat what the Constitution already stated. But the next clause was perplexing because the Constitution made no comparable provision for the removal of officers—other than by impeachment. Though Smith went unsupported in concluding that impeachment was therefore the only acceptable procedure, no consensus greeted the other alternatives. Should not the consent of the Senate be required for removal as well as appointment? Or was this an inherent aspect of the executive power that the Constitution vested solely in the president, who otherwise could not be held responsible for the conduct of his subordinates? Yet could it not be argued that the discretion Congress must exercise in creating departments covered conditions of tenure, though that would place the House in the awkward position of asking the Senate to share a power it could claim as its own?[15]

Egbert Benson, a veteran New York legislator and Hamilton ally, proposed the eventual solution with an amendment providing that the chief clerk of the department would take charge of its records whenever the president removed the secretary.[16] The House could thereby indirectly endorse the idea that the removal power was inherent in "the executive power" without implying that it was asserting that position of its own authority. And what if this interpretation still seemed unsound? Even in 1789 some representatives assumed that the judiciary would have the final say on the question. Congress could then accept suspect legislation, confident that the courts would decide the matter conclusively. Smith stated this position in extreme form when he argued that the House should take no position at all, and simply leave the question to the judiciary, which could act whenever an aggrieved official sued to retain his post. For Congress "to give a legislative construction of the Constitution," he added, would amount to "an infringement of the powers of the judiciary."[17]

Smith directed this point to Madison, who had defended the proposed clause not as a positive grant of authority but as an "explanatory" statement "of the meaning of the Constitution."[18] In reply, Madison acknowledged that "in the ordinary course of government . . . the exposition of the laws and constitution devolves upon the judicial" branch. But when it came to "the limits of the powers of the several departments," none "of these independent departments has more right than another to declare their sentiments on that point." And lest his colleagues conclude that he regarded such a declaration as advisory only, Madison wondered whether "this question could come before the judges" at all.[19] Nor was this an impulsive response; he had reached a similar conclusion eight months earlier, at a time when the issue of judicial review was actively being discussed in Virginia.

> In the State Constitutions & indeed in the Fedl one also, no provision is made for the case of a disagreement in expounding them; and as the Courts are generally the last in making their decision, it results to them, by refusing or not to execute a law, to stamp it with its final character. This makes the Judiciary Dept paramount in fact to the Legislature, which was never intended, and can never be proper.

Here Madison recognized that courts will exercise a power that sounds very much like judicial review, while implying that this power is both unintended in design and improper in principle. It arises circumstantially, literally through the chronology of action—yet absent any conflicting provision, it expresses the latent intent of the document itself.[20]

Though this hesitant treatment of judicial review seems troubling,

Madison's puzzlement can be reduced when set within the immediate context of the removal debate. Was it really better to defer to the judiciary, Madison asked, or to await the first occasion when the president removed an official? That would postpone this issue to a moment when it would already be politicized, when a displaced officeholder might seek patrons in the Senate, while trusting the judiciary to find the courage to challenge two more powerful branches of government.[21] But if the House acted now, when "the imagination of no member here, or of the senate, or of the president himself, is heated or disturbed by faction," it would set a valuable precedent merely by declaring its opinion.[22] Not only would it strengthen the presidency by discouraging officials from seeking alliances with patrons in the Senate; by insulating senators from "those questions of a personal nature, which in all Governments are the most frequent & violent causes of animosity and party," it would also keep the Senate "in a fit temper to control the capricious & factious counsels" and "the passions" of the House.[23] And if the House now declined to use its own power to establish terms of office legislatively, it might set a valuable precedent for its future conduct.

On balance, Madison had cause to be satisfied with this debate, especially after the Senate narrowly followed the lead of the House, thereby executing a self-denying act of its own.* Like other congressmen, he agonized over the "mortifying tardiness" with which Congress was acting, but he also understood that "the novelty and complexity of the subjects of Legislation" explained the delay. "Among other difficulties, the exposition of the Constitution is frequently a copious source," he wrote on June 21, "and must continue so until its meaning on all great points should have been settled by precedents."[24]

In settling this first precedent, only one of the nineteen former framers present in Congress alluded to the deliberations at the Federal Convention, and Abraham Baldwin did so more to chastise Elbridge Gerry than to enlighten the House.[25] As an exercise in interpretation, the removal debate followed the prevailing rules of construction that called for a closely reasoned analysis of the text emphasizing manifest language, internal consistency, and fidelity to general principles. Congressmen dis-

---

*Had he been in the Senate, he might have been less sanguine. Sitting behind closed doors (as they would until 1795), senators had no need to strive for the high seriousness that marked the House debates. They could insult each other freely, and if the caustic account in the diary of Senator William Maclay is to be trusted, the intimacy of the upper house did as much to foster mutual irritation as the measured deliberations the framers had desired. At one point, Ellsworth compared depriving the president of the removal power to stripping a tree from a farmer's justly purchased land; at another, a speech by William Paterson and the "recantations" of several other senators reminded Maclay of the "war songs" Indians recited to raise their "spirits" to the point where they could do the noble deeds they avowed. (For citation see n. 15 below.)

agreed not about these rules per se but about matters of definition and the weight to be given to specific passages and principles.

One noteworthy effort to draw a leading inference from the records of ratification was made, however. After failing to prove that removal required impeachment, William L. Smith insisted that the consent of the Senate was constitutionally required to remove as well as appoint. This opinion was supported by "[a] publication of no inconsiderable eminence, in the class of political writings on the constitution," Smith told the House on June 16. He then read a passage from *Federalist 77* affirming that "The consent of [the Senate] would be necessary to displace as well as appoint." But a rude shock awaited Smith. As he wrote to Edward Rutledge, the brother of the framer, shortly thereafter:

> the next day Benson sent me a note across the House to this effect: that *Publius* had informed him since the preceding day's debate, that upon mature reflection he *had changed his opinion* & was now convinced that the President alone should have the power of removal at pleasure; He is a Candidate for the office of Secretary of Finance!

The candidate was, of course, Hamilton; and Smith probably knew that Madison was the other of the "two gentlemen of great information" who had written as "Publius." Neither man felt obliged to stand by their joint work. So ended the first effort to use extrinsic evidence taken from the period of the adoption of the Constitution to interpret its meaning.[26]

The bank bill.   While Madison was wearily pushing his constitutional amendments through the First Congress, he found time to ask Edmund Randolph for a text of the "introductory discourse" with which he had presented the Virginia Plan to the Convention. Randolph replied that he could not re-create his speech, for he did not trust his own memory to "[separate] much of what I have heard since . . . from what occurred then." Madison would have to make do with the rough notes that Randolph now forwarded. Madison's own account of his "particular reasons" for "preserving this as well as the other arguments in that body" never suggested that his records could be used to resolve the constitutional disputes that continued to arise.[27] When Jefferson hinted in January 1799 that publication of the notes might turn the tide against the reigning Federalists, Madison replied with the usual caution he brought to their collaboration. "The whole volume ought to be examined with an eye to the use to which every part is susceptible," he warned. "In the Despotism at present exercised over the rules of construction, and the Counter reports of the proceedings that would perhaps be made out & mustered for the occasion, it is a problem what turn might be given to the impression on the public mind."[28] Nor did the passage of the years change his opinion. The publication of his notes "should be delayed till the Constitution should be well settled in practice," he wrote in September 1821, "& till a knowledge of the controversial part of the proceedings of its framers could be turned to no improper account."[29]

Here, of course, lay one basis for his distinction between the intentions of the framers and the understanding of the ratifiers. But Madison's aversion to using the records of the Convention had a more personal source. For he was not entirely consistent in avoiding recourse to his own knowledge of the proceedings in Philadelphia. On one crucial occasion, that knowledge provided a pretext, and perhaps a rationale, for his decision to oppose Secretary of the Treasury Hamilton's proposal that Congress incorporate a national bank, and to argue further that evidence drawn from the records of 1787–88 could legitimately guide the interpretation of the Constitution.

Explaining his opposition to the bank bill in his House speech of February 2, 1791, Madison passed from "a general review of the advantages and disadvantages of banks" to ask how a Constitution of "limited" powers was to be interpreted. He introduced this topic by noting that his reservations were "the stronger, because he well recollected that a power to grant charters of incorporation had been proposed in the general convention and rejected."[30] That proposal was in fact his own, numbered among a list of "proper" powers referred to the committee of detail on August 18, 1787. When no such power was reported, Madison renewed his motion (on September 14) to authorize Congress "to grant charters of incorporation where the interest of the U. S. might require & the legislative provisions of individual States may be incompetent." Rufus King and James Wilson clearly thought this proposal embraced banks, for they disagreed whether its approval would damage the prospects for ratification by exciting the financial rivalries of Philadelphia and New York. The proposal was abandoned after the delegates rejected a test vote on a "modified" motion "limited to the case of canals." Nothing in Madison's notes indicates that the motion was thought superfluous because the necessary-and-proper clause already reached the power in question. On the other hand, just as Wilson thought that a power to create "mercantile monopolies" was "already included in the power to regulate trade," so other framers may have reasoned that a power to charter banks could derive from other clauses.[31]

Madison did not claim that this tidbit of history was conclusive in itself; he merely sought to demonstrate that his scruples were not contrived for the moment. Instead, as "preliminaries to a right interpretation," he proceeded to offer several "rules." The first two argued that when the "meaning" of a provision was "doubtful, it is fairly triable by its consequences," especially when "the very characteristic of the government" might be threatened. Madison's next two rules laid the groundwork for an originalist method of construction.

> In controverted cases, the meaning of the parties to the instrument, if to be collected by reasonable evidence, is a proper guide.
> Contemporary and concurrent expositions are a reasonable evidence of the meaning of the parties.[32]

As H. Jefferson Powell has noted, existing rules of statutory construction permitted looking beyond the text for "reasonable evidence" of its meaning, though again this ordinarily meant attempting to "read acts of Parliament against the background of the common law."[33] But here Madison implied that the Constitution was less like a statute than a contract among unspecified "parties" whose purposes were material to its meaning.

Most of Madison's speech took the conventional path of examining the express language and structure of the Constitution to ask whether a national bank was necessary and proper. Necessary, as Madison used the term, was akin to indispensable. He denied that a power of incorporation was merely an incidental means to other expressly stated ends. The legal powers such acts created were so substantial as to amount to a separate category of legislation in its own right, and thus to require an explicit delegation by the Constitution. Madison could advance this argument without pioneering a new mode of interpretation. But appealing to the "contemporary expositions" of 1787–88 was more innovative. Ignoring *The Federalist*, which offered little support for his position, Madison looked elsewhere. While conceding the mixed quality of the "publications which he quoted," he read passages from the debates in Pennsylvania, Virginia, and North Carolina to affirm that Federalists had repeatedly argued "that the powers not given" to the national government "were retained; and that those given were not to be extended by remote implications"; and further, "that the terms necessary and proper, gave no additional powers to those enumerated." Madison did not describe these opinions as anything more than expositions; they only confirmed arguments that could be advanced on more familiar grounds. But the germ of an interpretative theory of original understanding was nonetheless present.[34]

This argument exposed Madison to a charge of inconsistency. In the well-remembered removal debate of 1789, he had denied that that power had to be explicitly mentioned in the Constitution, but instead relied on "construction and implication" to prove that it was inherent in the grant of executive power. Why was a legislative act of incorporation designed to advance other express purposes of government any different? And "was it not rather late in the day to adopt" this doctrine? asked Fisher Ames. During the past two years "we have scarcely made a law, in which we have not exercised our discretion, with respect to the true intent of the constitution."[35]

In this debate, Madison's appeal to historical evidence was no more than a distraction. But it did elicit a thorough rebuke from Gerry, of all people, who traveled even further from his own position in the removal debate to take on Madison. Dismissing Madison's rules as "being made for the occasion," Gerry invoked the "sanctioned" authority of Blackstone to propose that the House follow more settled rules. "The fairest and most rational method to interpret the will of the legislator," Blackstone had written, "is, by exploring his intention at the time when the law was made, by *signs* the most natural and probable; and these signs are either the words, the context, the subject matter, the effect and consequences, or the spirit and reason of the law." Gerry did not identify the "legislator" whose "will" and "intention" he was analyzing, but he offered telling objections that grasped the problem of recovering a coherent collective intention by aggregating individual opinions. As for Madison's appeal to the Federal Convention, Gerry asked,

> are we to depend on the memory of the gentlemen for an history of their debates, and from thence to collect their sense? This would be improper, because the memories of different gentlemen would probably vary, as they have already done, with respect to those facts; and, if not, the opinions of the individual members, who debated, are not to be considered as the opinions of the convention.

Gerry then demonstrated the fallibility of his own memory by wrongly claiming that the proposition the Convention entertained was one "to erect *commercial* corporations." But the force of his objection was strengthened when he turned to Madison's use of the ratification conventions. It was well known that these records were "partial and mutilated,"

Gerry noted. Even if that bias was discounted, the speech "of one member" could not be taken "as expressing the sense of a convention." Finally, Gerry recalled how the urgency of the ratification proceedings led both "parties to depart from candor, and to call in the aid of art, flattery, professions of friendship" and other doubtful tactics. "Under such circumstances," he concluded, "the opinions of great men ought not to be considered as authorities, and, in many instances, could not be recognised by themselves."[36]

Madison did not answer these points in his second speech of February 8—except to marvel at how far Gerry had come since 1787: "The powers of the constitution were then dark, inexplicable and dangerous—but now, perhaps as the result of experience they are clear and luminous!"[37] After Congress approved the bill, the president asked Attorney General Randolph, Secretary of State Jefferson, and Hamilton to brief the issue. Only Jefferson followed Madison's lead in looking to the evidence of 1787–88, and he did so merely to note that the Convention had rejected the power in question. But Randolph, while also opposing the bill, thought that neither the "almost unknown history" of the Convention nor opinions given during ratification could be regarded. Hamilton rebutted the argument even more vigorously. "No inference whatever can be drawn" from the unauthenticated and "very different accounts" that might be given of the Convention's action. Hamilton concluded this discussion by restating the familiar rule of interpretation. Jefferson could "not deny, that, whatever may have been the intentions of the framers of a constitution, or of a law, that intention is to be sought for in the instrument itself, according to the usual and established rules of construction."[38] Washington signed the bill.

This first serious foray in originalism was manifestly a failure. Most scholars agree that Hamilton got the better of his antagonists on the dual issues of policy and constitutionality that the bank bill raised.[39] It would be easy to conclude that Madison appealed to the disputable evidence of 1787–88 only to buttress a weak position. If so, it matters little whether he was driven by distrust of Hamilton; or his conviction, which other southern congressmen shared, that a bank would not benefit their region; or ideological suspicions of the danger monied interests posed to republican virtue. His constitutional objections would remain merely instrumental and contrived.

Yet that judgment is questionable on several counts. First, Madison's reservations did not arise on the spur of the moment. When the Continental Congress issued a charter of incorporation to the Bank of North America ten years earlier, Madison was one of a handful of delegates who opposed the measure, evidently on constitutional grounds.[40] More important, his motion at the Convention to grant Congress a power of incorporation obviously presumed that such authority did not yet exist elsewhere in the Constitution (a position that Wilson, no strict constructionist, seemed to endorse). Other framers, including Hamilton, were free to think differently, especially on an issue hastily considered at the last minute; but they were also less likely to agonize over constitutional distinctions with Madison's intensity. It is noteworthy, too, that Madison had reasoned similarly about the Constitution a year before the bank controversy erupted, when Tench Coxe proposed a scheme to set aside national lands as a fund to lure European inventors to bring their machinery to America. Though Madison had proposed a similar provision at the Convention, it had been whittled down to the sole incentives of limited patents and copyrights. "This fetter on the National Legislature tho' an unfortunate one, was a deliberate one," Madison concluded. "The latitude of authority now wished for was strongly urged and expressly rejected."[41] Here, in a speculative exchange, Madison espoused essentially the same view he advanced on an analogous issue a year later.

Most important, Madison's objections to a broad construction of the necessary-and-proper clause fully comported with the critique of legislation on which his constitutional theory rested. The great problem of republicanism was to develop constitutional mechanisms and political understandings to limit the plasticity of legislative power and the irresistible forces of public opinion behind it. Licensing Congress to make its discretion the test of its authority was the last precedent this still-experimental phase of government should set. The true point of comparison between the positions Madison took in the removal and bank debates did not lie in the seeming contradiction between the implied power he was willing to grant the president in 1789 and the strict rule of construction he wished to impose on Congress in 1791. It rested instead on the way in which this asymmetry served the great purpose of making legislative encroachments more difficult. The rule of interpretation mattered less than the support each construction gave to preserving "the exact balance or equipoise contemplated by the Constitution."[42]

The Jay Treaty. After 1791, foreign affairs overtook domestic policy as the chief source of partisan conflict in the widening breach between Hamilton and his Virginia opponents. This development, an outgrowth of the eruption of European war, forced Madison to reconsider fundamental premises of his theory of government. The imperatives of diplomacy not only placed a premium on the energy and dispatch the framers had envisioned for the presidency, they also gave the administration a political initiative to which the opposition Republicans in Congress could only react. The constitutional implications of this dispute were first laid out in a famous exchange between Hamilton and Madison. Defending the administration's April 1793 decision to issue a proclamation of neutrality without consulting Congress, then in recess, Hamilton (writing as "Pacificus") argued that the conduct of foreign relations was inherently executive in nature, except in those cases (treaties, diplomatic appointments, declarations of war) where the Constitution explicitly dictated otherwise.

Madison (writing as "Helvidius") replied that this improper view of executive power seemed to derive from two sources. The first was the ideas of such European authorities as Locke and Montesquieu, who suffered from having written before the era of the American Revolution, and whose views were "evidently warped" by their admiration for the British constitution. Madison dismissed the use of such authorities as "a field of research which is more likely to perplex than to decide."[43] The second, more likely source for the doctrines of "Pacificus," Madison maintained, was the model of executive prerogative in foreign affairs that British theory and practice placed in the Crown. In preferences to these sources, he concluded, one need only read the works of a recent American writer: Hamilton himself—or rather "Publius," though the authors of *The Federalist* were by now publicly known. Drawing on *Federalist* 69 and 75, Madison quoted passages which contradicted the claims of "Pacificus," while noting that those claims were "made at a time when no application to *persons* or *measures* could bias: The opinion given was not transiently mentioned, but formally and critically elucidated: It related to a point in the constitution which must consequently have been viewed as of importance in the public mind." Had the Federalists of 1788 been privy to the analysis of "Pacificus," Madison concluded, they could only have thought it " 'an experiment on public credulity.' " This last uncredited quotation came from *Federalist* 24, as only Madison and (perhaps) its author, Hamilton, were likely to know.[44]

Madison's recourse to *The Federalist* was made largely for rhetorical effect; he did not suggest that "Pacificus" was wrong *because* he contradicted "Publius," only that these essays exposed the fallacy in Hamilton's reasoning. Originalism itself was not at stake in 1793. But it did become a serious question in 1795–96, after the Senate narrowly approved the controversial treaty, resolving the outstanding issues of Anglo-American relations, that Chief Justice John Jay brought back from Britain. Only then was the treaty published, eliciting a storm of protest that alarmed Washington but failed to deter his ratification of the treaty in August 1795. At this point the Republican opposition sought to fashion constitutional barriers to its implementation, hoping to capitalize on their majority in the House when the Fourth Congress convened in December.

Treaty opponents made three claims on behalf of the constitutional authority of the House in treaty making. Should not a treaty which affected foreign trade require the approval of the House (which shared the congressional power to regulate commerce)? If public funds had to be expended to implement the treaty, should the House not judge those appropriations on their merits? And how could it exercise this traditional power without considering the treaty proper, which might in turn justify examining other records relating to its negotiation? [45] Though Madison was reluctant to take this ground, he was also the principal author of a widely reprinted petition to the Virginia assembly whose fourth major complaint held that "The President and Senate by ratifying this Treaty, usurp the powers of regulating commerce, of making rules with respect to aliens, of establishing tribunals of justice, and of defining piracy"—all powers of Congress. The petition then noted that "A formal demonstration of every part of this complex proposition is not requisite"—nor perhaps was it, since the text and logic on which the objection rested were hardly obscure. [46]

The burden of defending the treaty fell largely to Hamilton, now retired to his legal practice but still the dominant figure of his party. In thirty-eight numbers of "The Defence," Hamilton and Rufus King justified the Jay Treaty largely on its merits, reaching the constitutional questions only in the final three essays published just after the new year. In the first of these essays, Hamilton argued that the plain text of the supremacy clause bound the House no less than the states to adhere to duly made and ratified treaties. The next essay argued that the claims made for the House would render the formal treaty power of the president and the Senate "altogether nominal," thereby violating the rule of construction which required "that every instrument is to be so interpreted, that all the parts may if possible consist with each other." If the claims made for the House were allowed, plausible pretexts could always be found to assert that a treaty trenched upon some aspect of legislation, thereby emptying the ostensible language of the treaty clause of *any* meaning. [47]

The last essay was implicitly addressed to Madison. Here Hamilton asked how the treaty power "was understood by the Convention, in framing it, and by the people in adopting it." No "formal proof of the opinions" of the framers existed, Hamilton conceded. "But from the *best opportunity of knowing the fact*"—thus intimating that "Camillus" was himself a framer—it was evident that the framers thought the treaty power was comprehensive in its reach. For the truth of this claim he appealed to the memories of the two former framers—Madison and Abraham Baldwin—expected to "obstruct execution" of the Jay Treaty in the House. Hamilton then cited George Mason's and Gerry's objections to the Constitution as proof that the treaty power vested "an *exclusive power of legislation*" in the president and Senate. Nor was this an Anti-Federalist opinion alone, for in a lengthy footnote, Hamilton quoted two of Madison's essays as "Publius" to confirm that Federalists had argued that the joint role of the president and the Senate left the treaty power "sufficiently guarded."[48] When "Publius" was concerned, turnabout was fair play.

In March 1796, Washington asked the House to appropriate funds to implement the treaty. Republicans then introduced a resolution asking the president to provide the House with the executive papers that would enable it to place the treaty in its proper light. Federalists answered this request by applying the conventional norms of legal construction. "Are we to explain the Treaty by private and confidential papers, or by anything extraneous to the instrument itself?" asked Daniel Buck of Vermont. A challenge to a treaty "should be determined from the face of the instrument," William L. Smith argued on March 7; "a knowledge of the preparatory steps which led to its adoption, could throw no light upon it." The President would not "examine the Journals of the House" to test the constitutionality of a law, Smith added, nor would the Supreme Court do so in its imminent decision determining whether the federal carriage tax should be classed as a direct tax to be apportioned according to the three-fifths rule (the first case in which the Court would clearly test the constitutionality of a congressional statute).[49]

When the Republicans persisted, however, the focus of debate shifted from the treaty to the Constitution. Though Madison had misgivings about this strategy, he joined the fray in a lengthy speech on March 10. His argument rested on text and inference alone, not on history. If Federalist arguments were given full force, he asserted, the House could be obliged to forfeit its "deliberation & discretion" and to support indefinitely a war triggered by a treaty of alliance framed by the president and the Senate alone, regardless of its power over war, armies, and appropriations. Acknowledging some role for the House was the only way to give "signification to every part of the Constitution," even if the formal holders of the treaty power had to cope with the difficulties created.[50]

The immediate response to Madison's delayed entrance into the debate came from Smith, well known as Hamilton's spokesman. Smith "appeal[ed] to the general sense of the whole Nation at the time the Constitution was formed," noting that through these "cotemporaneous expositions," formed "when the subject was viewed only in relation to the abstract power, and not to a particular Treaty, we should come at the truth." Madison had made the same claim for *The Federalist* in his "Helvidius" letters, but Smith went one step further. Had the Virginia convention in which Madison served thought that the legislative authority of the House could check the treaty power, it would not have proposed an amendment to require commercial treaties to be ratified by two-thirds of all senators (rather than a quorum).[51] Theodore Sedgwick also made Madison his target. Did not Madison's "known caution and prudence" oblige him to explain how the Federal Convention could have neglected to express the "true meaning" he had so belatedly discovered? Sedgwick wondered. Madison and other framers "certainly knew what they had so recently intended" at Philadelphia when they defended the treaty power in the state conventions. But they had never answered objections to the treaty clause with the theory Madison now maintained; they had instead argued that the power was well secured by the mutual check of the president and the Senate. And responding to a complaint that Smith "had not quoted any part of the proceedings on the subject, or of the reasons that led to the amendment," Sedgwick read at length from the Virginia records, citing speakers on both sides to re-create the structure of its debate.[52]

Sedgwick thus implied that the intentions of the framers *were* relevant, and one other major Federalist speech developed the point further. It was well known that the politics of the Convention revolved around the compromise between small and large states over the Senate, Benjamin Bourne of Rhode Island reminded the House. That, too, indicated that the House did not possess the authority claimed. But Bourne also relied on speeches in the ratification conventions to make his point; he agreed, with Sedgwick, that "the real inquiry was, what opinion was entertained on this subject by those who ratified the Constitution."[53] That was the question which engaged the other speakers who examined the evidence of 1787–88. In this inquiry, both Federalists and Republicans suggested that the ratifiers and, beyond them, the American people had in some sense consented to the particular interpretation each side was now advancing. "The people have declared that the President and Senate shall make Treaties, without a single exception," Isaac Smith declared, "and, lest there should be any mistake or cavilling about it, they have put it in written words, as they thought, too plain to be doubted, too positive to be contradicted."⁵⁴ On the other side, Republicans argued that the Constitution itself might never have been ratified had the people realized that the president and the Senate would possess this "uncontrollable power."⁵⁵ Several speakers asked whose original understandings were to be treated as more authoritative, the majority or the minority? William Findley, the leading Pennsylvania Anti-Federalist now turned Republican, even found himself ironically reflecting that he did not "expect the sentiments of a minority, acting under peculiar circumstances of irritation, and consisting of but one-fifth of the members [at the Harrisburg convention], to be quoted as a good authority for the true sense of the Constitution."⁵⁶

From these remarks, it seems apparent that the House was prepared to entertain interpretations reconstructing the positions of framers, ratifiers, and "the people." The ensuing disagreements prompted a few representatives, on both sides, to suggest that recourse to historical evidence was futile. Edward Livingston, the author of the original motion seeking the treaty papers, even declared that "we were now as capable at least of determining the true meaning of that instrument as the Conventions were; they were called in haste, they were heated by party, and many adopted it from expediency, without having fully debated the general articles."⁵⁷ But that did not stop him from undertaking his own originalist analysis, nor did it recall the House to traditional rules of construction. In these exchanges, Federalists gained the upper hand, leading Republicans to rely on the analogical reasoning to the British constitution that Madison had spurned in "Helvidius." If the British king submitted treaties to Parliament when they required further legal action, they reasoned, did it not follow that the American House retained at least equal authority? Federalists dismissed this reasoning in the same terms that Madison had condemned "Pacificus" in 1793. "The practice and prerogatives of that despotic Court" were irrelevant, Daniel Buck exclaimed. "What have they to do with a Constitution, which is the express will of the great body of the people of America, prescribing rules for her own self-government?"⁵⁸

Notwithstanding the problems they faced in rebutting such blunt remarks, the Republican majority approved the call for presidential papers. In his short but cogent reply of March 30, Washington made little use of the extended memorandum that he had solicited from Hamilton—with the exception of one point. Hamilton reminded Washington that the Convention had "overruled" a motion to involve the House in treaty making, and the president made this the concluding point of his reply. If one consulted the Convention journal, which Washington (its custodian) had since deposited in the Department of State, "it will appear" that a motion to require treaties to be "ratified by a Law" had been "explicitly rejected."[59] Had Hamilton been present in Philadelphia when Gouverneur Morris made this motion on August 23, 1787, he might also have reminded Washington that Madison had first "suggest[ed] the inconvenience of requiring a legal *ratification* of treaties of alliance for purposes of war," then wondered whether the Convention should distinguish types of treaties which might or might not require "the concurrence of the whole Legislature."[60] If that evidence implied that the exclusion of the House from treaty-making troubled Madison in 1787, it also confirmed the crucial point of how the Constitution, as written, was to be interpreted *now*—for, of course, no such distinction had been made.

When the House continued to pursue the issue after learning of the president's refusal, Madison felt compelled to reenter a debate he had worriedly observed since early March. His speech of April 6, 1796, offers perhaps the clearest (and most frequently cited) statement of his acceptance of a version of originalism. It was framed partly in response to Washington's appeal to the journal of the Convention, which Madison now judged improper even though he had reasoned much the same way in 1791. But Madison had also been stung by the criticism he had personally suffered when William Vans Murray, a young congressman from Maryland, appealed directly to him during a lengthy speech of March 23. In what must have been a dramatic moment, Murray first praised Madison as the man to whose "genius and patriotism, in a great degree, he had always understood, were we indebted for the Constitution." But he then urged Madison to rescue the House from its confusion.

> If the Convention spoke mysterious phrases, and the gentleman helped to utter them, will not the gentleman aid the expounding of the mystery? If the gentleman was the Pythia in the temple, ought he not to explain the ambiguous language of the oracle? To no man's expositions would he listen with more deference.

Yet Murray could not have disguised the mocking taunt that lurked beneath the praise, the implication that Madison had said little because the evidence did not sustain his position.

Nor did Murray halt there. In language that carried Madison back to his researches of 1787, Murray noted that "the historian and the commentator" who study other constitutions have "to resort to records unintelligible" or "to the uncertain lights of mere tradition." But Americans no longer had to settle for this obscurity. They had known "the Constitution from its cradle" and "its infancy," better than any other society had ever known its constitution. But if the perplexing "doubts" the House now faced could be raised "upon some of its plainest passages," what hope was there that posterity would maintain the boundaries of power?

> One hundred years hence, should a great question arise upon the construction, what would not be the value of that man's intelligence, who, allowed to possess integrity and a profound and unimpaired mind, should appear in the awful moments of doubt, and, being known to have been in the illustrious body that framed the instrument, should clear up difficulties by his contemporaneous knowledge? Such a man would have twice proved a blessing to his country.

Again, the younger man's homage could not conceal a hint of mockery.[61]

Madison answered both Murray and the president on April 6. His speech was less an affirmation of the possibilities of using the understandings of the ratifiers to fix the meaning of the Constitution than an attempt to nullify any appeal to the authority and intentions of the framers. Madison disclaimed having either the resources or the obligation to speak for "the intention of the whole body" of the Convention. That would be a matter of some "delicacy," because the framers had disagreed in their opinions (though some, he added, supported his current position). Moreover, he had a personal reason to avoid this mode of argument, for had he not been roundly criticized when he "incidentally" referred to the Convention during the bank debate of 1791? Nor had any other dispute yet been settled this way. And then Madison reached the critical transition.

> But, after all, whatever veneration might be entertained for the body of men who formed our constitution, the sense of that body could never be regarded as the oracular guide in the expounding the constitution. As the instrument came from them, it was nothing more than the draught of a plan, nothing but a dead letter, until life and validity were breathed into it, by the voice of the people, speaking through the several state conventions. If we were to look therefore, for the meaning of the instrument, beyond the face of the instrument, we must look for it not in the general convention, which proposed, but in the state conventions, which accepted and ratified the constitution.

This conclusion was entirely consistent with the great political and theoretical insight that had enabled Madison to persuade the Convention to follow his agenda. But as he then applied the evidence of ratification to the issue at hand, his qualified conclusions revealed more of the limitations attending this mode of interpretation than the blinding light it would shed on the true meaning of the Constitution.[62]

Again ignoring *The Federalist*, Madison limited his analysis to two categories of evidence. As to the first category—the published record of the conventions (Pennsylvania, Virginia, and North Carolina) where the treaty power was debated seriously—he had little to say. While noting that the speakers had regarded the treaty power as "limited" in nature, Madison ignored the Federalist objection that this limitation inhered in the division between president and Senate. Instead he pursued the analogy to the British constitution, which he weakly corroborated with an irrelevant allusion to the pardoning power. Madison concluded this part of the argument by conceding that even the Virginia debates, as published, "contained internal evidences in abundance of chasms, and misconceptions of what was said."[63]

The second category—the amendments proposed by the state conventions—was a "better authority," but not free of liabilities. No one could "expect a perfect precision and system" in these measures, given "the agitations of the public mind on that occasion, with the hurry and compromise which generally prevailed in settling the amendments to be proposed." Madison nonetheless plunged ahead to consider the amendments as they related to the allocation of the treaty power. Here, again, his argument did little more than speculate that the framers of those amendments would have favored the construction now advanced by the Republican majority. Madison then considered two other classes of amendments: those which had denied that laws could be suspended without the assent of the legislature and those to require supermajorities for legislation relating to war, commerce, and appropriations. He concluded this analysis with another speculative question. Could the authors of these amendments, all of which touched upon powers whose exercise could be constrained by the treaty power, have supposed that they had given the president and the Senate "an absolute and unlimited power" free of any control by the House?[64]

At no point did Madison explain how proposals designed to remedy perceived defects in the Constitution—proposals that he himself had ignored in compiling his amendments of 1789, and which went unadopted—could prevail over the explicit language of the treaty clause. He never explained how criticisms of the Constitution could be transformed into interpretations of its meaning when the opposite inference was more logical. Nor did he explain how partial and hasty expressions of opinion

in individual states could trump the contrary position that Federalists occupied in this debate when they treated the language of the Constitution
as an expression of the "intention" of a sovereign people. At only one
point did Madison briefly stumble upon an answer to these seemingly fatal objections, when he described an amendment to the treaty power proposed by North Carolina as "intended to ascertain, rather than to alter
the meaning of the constitution."[65] But developing this point would only
have exposed his position to another powerful objection. How could an
unadopted amendment proposed by a state rejoining the Union *after* the
Constitution had taken effect be regarded as authoritative?

When this prospect was raised in 1788, Madison vehemently denied
that states might ratify the Constitution conditionally in the expectation
that specific amendments would be adopted later. Where else could such
a process end except in a second general convention whose prospects for
success must be far worse than that of the meeting at Philadelphia? Madison could hardly have drafted his speech of April 6 without recalling this
concern; the manifest problems he now encountered in articulating his
ideas may have been a mark of the intellectual embarrassment he felt.
That embarrassment had a deeper source still. For by 1796 the politics of
opposition had placed Madison in a position he had never expected to occupy. At least through 1791, he remained firmly convinced that legislative
encroachments, most likely emanating from or through the lower house,
would pose the greatest danger to constitutional equilibrium. But after
1793, the growing prominence of questions of foreign policy led him to a
new conclusion: that it was the executive that wielded the greatest degree
of power and initiative, and that the powers of the House had accordingly
to be extended. Yet what was to distinguish the dubious claim for the
House that Madison was now defending, however reluctantly, from the
category of "complicated and indirect measures" that enabled the legislature to "mask . . . the encroachments which it makes on the co-ordinate
departments"?[66]

If this was originalism that Madison was defending in his speech of
April 6, he was not yet prepared to make the most of it. His best-known
statement of the theory was marred by unresolved problems. Whatever
clarity he gained by distinguishing framers from ratifiers was clouded by
the difficulty of using the ambiguous debates and failed amendments of
1787–88 to offset an express constitutional provision. After balking at using these sources in his first speech on the Jay Treaty, he was later driven
to invoke their authority less by his belief that they provided a viable
method of interpretation than by the arguments of other speakers, the
president's message, and Murray's pointed appeal. In this debate, the

more successful originalists were the Federalists, whom Madison else-where accused of using the loose canon of Hamiltonian construction to enlarge the meaning of the Constitution. When Smith, Sedgwick, Bourne, and Murray appealed to the evidence of 1787–88, they could plausibly argue that these opinions merited consideration because they were formed at a moment when partisan wrangling over a particular treaty was not a bias.[67] But if originalism could thus be defended as a neutral mode of interpretation, the temptation to resort to it was manifestly political. It was dictated not by the prior conviction that this was the most appropriate strategy to ascertain the meaning of the Constitution but by considerations of partisan advantage.

That did not prevent commentators from forming opinions with greater or lesser degrees of neutrality, nor did it banish the ideal of neutrality from the temples of constitutional judgment. It merely demonstrated that neutrality could rarely be attained when the Constitution was so highly politicized, or when politics was so highly constitutionalized. This was not what Madison had intended in 1787, nor what he desired a decade later; but he contributed as much to this result as any of his colleagues and contemporaries, and he lived long enough to foresee its most tragic implications.

CODA

Democracy has no forefathers, it looks to no posterity, it is swallowed up in the present and thinks of nothing but itself.

John Quincy Adams, 1833

THE LATE JUDITH SHKLAR took this passage from the memoirs of the sixth president as the epigraph for a lecture on "Democracy and the Past: Jefferson and His Heirs," which she presented at Stanford University in April 1988.[1] The quotation, and Professor Shklar's meditation on it, have engaged me ever since. They go to the heart of the puzzle that underlies this book. Democracy—and especially American democracy—is an endless present, a polity that occasionally looks forward but rarely looks back (except through mists of nostalgia and myths of origins that little resemble the complexities of the past). American culture has long since lost whatever patriarchal character it once had, though the reading rooms of historical societies and libraries are filled with old and young tracking their genealogies. Why, then, in a society not otherwise known to defer to past wisdom, do appeals to the original meanings of the Constitution and the original intentions of its framers still play a conspicuous role in our political and legal discourse?

The short answer might be that originalist appeals are used for instrumental purposes alone. They offer a form of argument to be employed whenever rhetorical convenience or the imperatives of law-office history and its political variants promise some tangible advantage. No doubt this explanation carries a great deal of truth. But if that is so, one purpose of this book—to treat original meaning/intention/understanding as a serious historical question—would merit little attention, beyond giving historians another occasion to muse on the abuse of history and the misuse of "the lessons of the past."

Yet there is another reason why an anti-patriarchal society may find this appeal attractive. For better or worse, the Revolutionary era provides Americans with the one set of consensual political symbols that come closest to universal acceptance. Those symbols are less gripping and compelling, but also less divisive, than those we associate with the Civil War; reaffirming them, even for superficial purposes, may accordingly have some value in preserving "that veneration which time bestows on every thing, and without which perhaps the wisest and freest governments would not possess the requisite stability." So Madison wrote in *Federalist* 49, and so he continued to believe, not only when he soon discussed with Jefferson whether or not it was a good idea to recognize the right of each generation to write its own constitution, but also when he looked with growing alarm on the conflicts over constitutional interpretation that became an independent disruptive force in American politics so soon after 1789. Two centuries later, when events in the world around us illustrate how difficult the transition to stable forms of constitutional governance must be, we have good reason to ponder Madison's teaching.

Yet Jefferson's concern about the stale veneration of the past retains its force as well. "Some men look at constitutions with sanctimonious reverence, and deem them like the ark of the covenant, too sacred to be touched," he wrote to a correspondent in the last year of Madison's presidency. "They ascribe to the men of the preceding age a wisdom more than human, and suppose what they did to be beyond amendment. I knew that age well; I belonged to it, and labored with it. It deserved well of its country. It was very like the present, but without the experience of the present; and forty years of experience in government is worth a century of book-reading; and this they would say themselves, were they to rise from the dead."[2] Hence our problem. As Professor Shklar noted, "Jefferson's heirs were torn irresolutely between his contempt for tradition and Madison's prudent fondness for it." In the end, it was Jefferson who better grasped the habits of democracy, Madison who better understood its perils. But perhaps Jefferson also saw more clearly than his friend what the experience of founding a republic finally meant, even to the conservative framers themselves. Having learned so much from the experience of a mere decade of self-government, and having celebrated their own ability to act from "reflection and choice," would they not find the idea that later generations could not improve upon their discoveries incredible? How could those who wrote the Constitution possibly understand its meaning better than those who had the experience of observing and participating in its operation? It is one thing to rail against the evils of politically unaccountable judges enlarging constitutional rights beyond the ideas and purposes of their original adopters; another to explain why morally sustainable claims of equality should be held captive to the extraordinary obstacles of Article V or subject to the partial and incomplete understandings of 1789 or 1868.

Yet language, or at least the language constitutive of a polity, cannot be infinitely malleable. If nothing in the text of the Constitution literally constrains or even instructs us to read it as its framers and ratifiers might have done, we may still have soundly Madisonian reasons for attempting to recover its original meanings. But then we also have to ask why we are doing so. Is it because we truly believe that language can only mean now what it meant then? Or is it because the meditations about popular government that we encounter there remain more profound than those that the ordinary politics of our endless democratic present usually sustains?

A NOTE ON SOURCES

A vast literature is devoted to the adoption and interpretation of the Constitution, and it swells annually at a prodigious rate. The following notes do not provide an elaborate, much less comprehensive, set of references to the entire corpus of scholarly writings concerned with the topics discussed. They identify instead those books and articles that have contributed most to my formulation of questions and answers, or that laid a foundation for particular points of interpretation.

Readers interested in pursuing the public and scholarly debate over a "jurisprudence of original intention" should consult the bibliography to my reader *Interpreting the Constitution: The Debate over Original Intent* (Boston, 1990), which identifies a number of leading articles by legal scholars and historians alike. Two critical review essays provide valuable overviews of the outpouring of writings that made the scholarly bicentennial of the Constitution more productive than might have been expected: Peter S. Onuf, "Reflections on the Founding: Constitutional Historiography in Bicentennial Perspective," *William and Mary Quarterly*, 3d. ser., 46 (1989), 341–75; and Richard B. Bernstein, "Charting the Bicentennial," *Columbia Law Review*, 87 (1987), 1565–1624. Also quite valuable is the bibliographic essay by Patrick T. Conley in the collection of essays which he coedited with John P. Kaminski, *The Constitution and the States: The Role of the Original Thirteen in the Framing and Adoption of the Federal Constitution* (Madison, Wis., 1988). Their colleague Gaspare Saladino performs a similar service in another volume the same two coeditors have produced: *The Bill of Rights and the States: The Colonial and Revolutionary Origins of American Liberties* (Madison, Wis., 1992).

This book was written, as history must be, primarily through an immersion in the primary sources. These sources are often multiply reprinted, and with some misgivings I have decided to emphasize convenience and ease of access over scholarly purity in providing citations. Although I have some reservations about the editorial methods of the *Documentary History of Ratification* project (cited fully below), when completed it should become the definitive scholarly source, and I have accordingly made it my preferred locus of citation even for *The Federalist*. There is a sense, I now understand, in which the problem of fixing an editorial strategy for the presentation of this rich and complex body of materials parallels the conceptual problem of making sense of the debate it records. In many ways, the thematic organization that distinguishes Bernard Bailyn, ed., *The Debate on the Constitution* (New York, 1993) presents these materials in the most accessible form, but there is merit, too, in the rather different model adopted by Philip Kurland and Ralph Lerner in *The Founders' Constitution* (also cited below).

NOTES

SHORT TITLES USED IN CITATIONS

American Political Writing Charles S. Hyneman and Donald S. Lutz, eds., *American Political Writing during the Founding Era, 1760–1805* (Indianapolis, 1983), 2 vols.

Complete Anti-Fed. Herbert Storing, ed., *The Complete Anti-Federalist* (Chicago, 1981), 7 vols.

Doc. Hist. Merrill Jensen, John Kaminski, and Gaspare Saladino, eds., *The Documentary History of the Ratification of the Constitution* (Madison, Wis., 1976–), 10 vols. to date

Elliot's Debates Jonathan Elliot, ed., *The Debates in the Several State Conventions, on the Adoption of the Federal Constitution . . .* , 2d ed. (Washington, 1836), 4 vols.

Founders' Constitution Philip Kurland and Ralph Lerner, eds., *The Founders' Constitution* (Chicago, 1987), 5 vols.

Hutson, ed., *Supplement* James H. Hutson, ed., *Supplement to Max Farrand's The Records of the Federal Convention of 1787* (New Haven, 1987)

Papers of Madison William T. Hutchinson, William M. E. Rachal, Robert Rutland, et al., eds., *The Papers of James Madison* (Chicago and Charlottesville, 1962–91) 17 vols. (covering 1751–1801)

Records Max Farrand, ed., *Records of the Federal Convention of 1787*, rev. ed. (New Haven, 1937 [reprinted 1966]), 4 vols.

WMQ *William and Mary Quarterly*, 3d series (1944–)

CHAPTER I THE PERILS OF ORIGINALISM

1. Madison to William Eustis, July 6, 1819, *Letters and Other Writings of James Madison* (Philadelphia, 1865), III, 140; Max Farrand, ed., *The Records of the Federal Convention of 1787*, rev. ed. (New Haven, 1937), III, 550 (hereafter *Records*).
2. Madison to Edward Everett, March 19, 1823, *Letters*, III, 308–9.
3. J. Allen Smith, *The Spirit of American Government* (New York, 1907); Charles Beard, *An Economic Interpretation of the Constitution* (New York, 1913).
4. James MacGregor Burns, *The Deadlock of Democracy: Four-Party Politics in America* (Englewood Cliffs, N.J., 1963); Robert A. Dahl, *A Preface to Democratic Theory* (Chicago, 1956).
5. For two major statements, see Hadley Arkes, *Beyond the Constitution* (Princeton, 1990), and Walter Berns, *Taking the Constitution Seriously* (New York, 1987).
6. *Records*, III, 551.
7. *Youngstown Sheet & Tube Co.* v. *Sawyer*, 343 U.S. 579, 634–35 (1952).
8. I refer to William Winslow Crosskey, *Politics and the Constitution in the History of the United States*, 2 vols. (Chicago, 1953); a third volume, completed by his student William Jeffrey, Jr., was published in 1980; for the exegesis of the meaning of commerce, see vol. I, part I, "The National Power over Commerce."
9. Gordon S. Wood, "Ideology and the Origins of Liberal America," *William and Mary Quarterly*, 44 (1987), 632–33 (hereafter *WMQ*). Wood here draws on an important article by William E. Nelson, "History and Neutrality in Constitutional Adjudication," *Virginia Law Review*, 72 (1986), 1237–96.
10. By way of example, see the essays by John M. Murrin, "Fundamental Values, the Founding Fathers, and the Constitution," and Isaac Kramnick, "The Discourse of Politics in 1787: The Constitution and Its Critics on Individualism, Community, and the State," in Herman Belz, Ronald Hoffman, and Peter J. Albert, eds., *To Form a More Perfect Union: The Critical Ideas of the Constitution* (Charlottesville, 1992), 1–37, 166–216.
11. Leonard Levy, *Original Intent and the Framers' Constitution* (New York, 1988), 284–398; William E. Nelson, *The Fourteenth Amendment: From Political Principle to Judicial Doctrine* (Cambridge, 1988), 5; and see the earlier but still valuable study, Charles A. Miller, *The Supreme Court and the Uses of History* (Cambridge, 1969). In her forthcoming *Faith of Our Fathers: The Spell of the Warren Court* (to be published by Yale University Press), Laura Kalman provides an intellectual history of modern legal scholarship that pays substantial attention to the different versions of originalism which have flourished in the legal precincts of the American academy over the past generation.
12. Amazingly enough, vestiges of that debate are still heard today. See Raoul Berger, *Federalism: The Founders' Design* (Norman, Okla., 1987), 21–76; and H. Jefferson Powell, "The Modern Misunderstanding of Original Intent," *University of Chicago Law Review*, 54 (1987), 1513–44.
13. Gordon S. Wood, *The Creation of the American Republic, 1776–1787* (Chapel Hill, 1969), 483–99; Wood further develops this theme in *The Radicalism of the American Revolution* (New York, 1992).
14. *Records*, III, 85 (Morris); II, 648, (Franklin). The best short narrative account of the Convention is still Max Farrand, *The Framing of the Constitution of the United States* (New Haven and London, 1913); for popular narratives, see Catherine Drinker Bowen, *Miracle at Philadelphia: The Story of the Constitutional Convention* (Boston, 1966); Clinton Rossiter, *1787: The Grand Convention* (New York, 1966); and Christopher Collier and James Collier, *The Constitutional Convention of 1787* (New York, 1986).
15. Hutson, ed., *Supplement*, 325–37.

16. *Records*, I, 423–24.

17. James H. Hutson, "The Creation of the Constitution: Scholarship at a Standstill," *Reviews in American History*, 12 (1984), 463–77; and "Riddles of the Federal Constitutional Convention," *WMQ*, 44 (1987), 411–23, both provide useful short summaries of the state of scholarship. On the duality of concerns operating at Philadelphia, see William E. Nelson, "Reason and Compromise in the Establishment of the Federal Constitution, 1787–1801," ibid., 458–84.

18. Calvin C. Jillson, *Constitution Making: Conflict and Consensus in the Federal Convention of 1787* (New York, 1988), is the most recent and comprehensive of several efforts by political scientists to use roll-call analysis in this way; and see Robert A. McGuire, "Constitution Making: A Rational Choice Model of the Federal Convention of 1787," *American Journal of Political Science*, 32 (1988), 483–522.

19. Thus Leonard Levy: "[M]uch of the Anti-Federalist literature was trash based on hysterical assumptions or on political calculations intended to deceive and incite fear of the Constitution." Levy, *Original Intent*, 4.

20. Kenneth Stampp, *The Imperiled Union: Essays on the Background of the Civil War* (New York, 1980), 3–36.

21. James H. Hutson, "The Creation of the Constitution: The Integrity of the Documentary Record," *Texas Law Review*, 65 (1986–87), 1–39, reprinted in Jack N. Rakove, ed., *Interpreting the Constitution: The Debate over Original Intent* (Boston, 1990), 158–62.

22. *Records*, III, 374. The context of these remarks is discussed in the concluding pages of Chapter 11, below.

23. On this point, the classic essay is Douglass Adair, " 'Experience Must Be Our Only Guide': History, Democratic Theory, and the United States Constitution," in Trevor Colbourn, ed., *Fame and the Founding Fathers: Essays by Douglass Adair* (Chapel Hill, 1974), 107–23; and more generally, Trevor Colbourn, *The Lamp of Experience: Whig History and the Intellectual Origins of the American Revolution* (Chapel Hill, 1965).

24. *Federalist* 9 and 47, in Merrill Jensen, John Kaminski, and Gaspare Saladino, eds., *The Documentary History of the Ratification of the Constitution* (Madison, Wis., 1976–), XIV, 160–62, XV, 499–501 (hereafter *Doc. Hist.*).

25. Adair, " 'That Politics May Be Reduced to a Science': David Hume, James Madison, and the Tenth Federalist," Colbourn, ed., *Fame and the Founding Fathers*, 93–106; the essential point is developed far more elaborately in Garry Wills, *Explaining America: The Federalist* (Garden City, 1981). For a broader examination of the influence of Hume, see Morton White, *Philosophy, The Federalist, and the Constitution* (New York, 1987).

26. *Records*, I, 64–74.

27. On this point, see especially Willi Paul Adams, *The First American Constitutions: Republican Ideology and the Making of the State Constitutions in the Revolutionary Era*, trans. Rita and Robert Kimber (Chapel Hill, 1980), 118–28.

28. John Adams put the key point in his *Thoughts on Government* of 1776. The "animating principle" of all republican government, Adams wrote, was its commitment to "an impartial and exact execution of the laws." But, he added, "Of republics there is an inexhaustible variety, because the possible combinations of the powers of society are capable of innumerable variations." Reprinted in *American Political Writing*, I, 403.

29. That is the great lesson to be learned, I believe, from Gordon Wood's epochal study of republican constitutionalism—rather than the hackneyed and increasingly sterile debate over the respective weight of the republican and liberal strains of American political ideology.

30. For two powerful statements of this theme, see Ralph Lerner, *The Thinking Revolutionary: Principle and Practice in the New Republic* (Ithaca, 1987), 1–38; and Thomas L.

Pangle, *The Spirit of Modern Republicanism: The Moral Vision of the American Founders and the Philosophy of Locke* (Chicago, 1988) 28–39.

31. A good place to begin is Cass Sunstein, "Beyond the Republican Revival," *Yale Law Journal*, 97 (1988–1989), 1539–90 (part of a special issue devoted to a Symposium on the Republican Civic Tradition); for a general summary (and post mortem?) on republicanism, see Daniel T. Rogers, "Republicanism: the Career of a Concept," *Journal of American History*, 79 (1992), 11–38; and see Kalman, *Faith of Our Fathers*, chap. V.

CHAPTER 11 THE ROAD TO PHILADELPHIA

1. John Jay to John Adams, New York, Nov. 1, 1786, and Feb. 21, 1787, Adams Family Papers, Massachusetts Historical Society (microfilm reel 368).

2. Dalton to Adams, Boston, July 11, 1786; Stiles to Adams, Yale College, Mar. 10, 1787; Adams Family Papers, Mass. His. Soc. (reel 368).

3. Madison to Jefferson, June 6, 1787, in William T. Hutchinson, William M. E. Rachal, Robert Rutland, et al., eds., *The Papers of James Madison* (Chicago and Charlottesville, 1962–91), X, 29.

4. This chapter summarizes the interpretation of problems of national government that is developed in much greater detail in Jack N. Rakove, *The Beginnings of National Politics: An Interpretive History of the Continental Congress* (New York, 1979), 275–399.

5. For divergent accounts of the Morris program and its fate, see ibid., 297–324; E. James Ferguson, *The Power of the Purse: A History of American Public Finance, 1776–1790* (Chapel Hill, 1961), 78–110; Clarence L. Ver Steeg, *Robert Morris: Revolutionary Financier* (Philadelphia, 1954), 125–45; E. Wayne Carp, *To Starve the Army at Pleasure: Continental Army Administration and American Political Culture, 1775–1783* (Chapel Hill, 1984), 189–217; for documentary evidence, see E. James Ferguson et al., eds., *The Papers of Robert Morris, 1781–1784* (Pittsburgh, 1973–).

6. Worthington C. Ford, ed., *Journals of the Continental Congress, 1774–1789* (Washington, 1904–37), XXIV, 207–9.

7. David Howell to Jonathan Arnold, Feb. 21, 1784, in William R. Staples, ed., *Rhode Island in the Continental Congress* (Providence, 1870), 479.

8. Two excellent overviews of these issues are found in Peter S. Onuf, "Settlers, Settlements, and New States," and James S. Merrell, "Declarations of Independence: Indian-White Relations in the New Nation," both in Jack P. Greene, ed., *The American Revolution: Its Character and Limits* (New York, 1987), 171–223; and see Jack N. Rakove, "Ambiguous Achievement: The Northwest Ordinance," in Frederick D. Williams, ed., *The Northwest Ordinance: Essays on Its Formulation, Provisions, and Legacy* (East Lansing, 1989), 1–19. The turbulence of relations between the Indian "republics" of the Ohio Valley and migrating American republicans is brilliantly examined in Richard White, *The Middle Ground: Indians, Empires, and Republics in the Great Lakes Region, 1650–1815* (Cambridge, Eng., 1991), 366–468.

9. Rakove, *Beginnings of National Politics*, 342–52; and for a broader survey of postwar foreign relations, see Frederick W. Marks, III, *Independence on Trial: Foreign Affairs and the Making of the Constitution* (Baton Rouge, La., 1973), 3–95.

10. Postwar economic conditions are surveyed in Richard B. Morris, *The Forging of the Union, 1781–1789* (New York, 1987), 130–61; and Cathy D. Matson and Peter S. Onuf, *A Union of Interests: Political and Economic Thought in Revolutionary America* (Lawrence, Kan., 1990), 67–100.

11. H. James Henderson, *Party Politics in the Continental Congress* (New York, 1974), 387–99; Drew McCoy, "James Madison and Visions of American Nationality in the Con-

federation Period: A Regional Perspective," in Richard Beeman, Stephen Botein, and Edward C. Carter II, eds., *Beyond Confederation: Origins of the Constitution and American National Identity* (Chapel Hill, 1987), 226–58, locates this critical episode within a broader context of ideas of expansion.

12. The record for this case is reprinted in Julius Goebel, Jr., ed., *The Law Practice of Alexander Hamilton: Documents and Commentary* (New York, 1964), vol. I.

13. Rakove, *Beginnings of National Politics*, 345–52, 361–76.

14. Lawrence D. Cress, "Whither Columbia? Congressional Residence and the Politics of the New Nation, 1776–1787," *WMQ*, 32 (1975), 581–600.

15. Roger H. Brown, *Redeeming the Republic: Federalists, Taxation, and the Origins of the Constitution* (Baltimore and London, 1993).

16. Madison to Jefferson, Sept. 6, and Oct. 24, 1787, *Papers of Madison*, X, 163–64, 212.

17. Wood, *Creation of the American Republic*, 306–467, provides the best analysis of these developments, nicely juxtaposing the limited role that concern about the Confederation played in the general unease of the 1780s with the more pervasive anxiety over state politics.

18. Jay to John Adams, Feb. 21, 1787, Adams Family Papers, Mass. His. Soc. (reel 368); Rakove, *Beginnings of National Politics*, 378–79 and n. 37.

19. Linda Grant De Pauw, *The Eleventh Pillar: New York State and the Federal Constitution* (Ithaca, 1966), 31–42.

20. Madison to James Monroe, and to Jefferson, Jan. 22, 1786, *Papers of Madison*, VIII, 483, 476–77.

21. Madison to Monroe, Mar. 14 and 19, 1786, ibid., 497–98, 505–06.

22. The proceedings are reprinted in Philip Kurland and Ralph Lerner, eds., *The Founders' Constitution* (Chicago, 1987), I, 185–87; Rakove, *Beginnings of National Politics*, 368–75.

23. Madison to Jefferson, Aug. 12, 1786, *Papers of Madison*, IX, 95–97.

24. Jefferson to Madison, Jan. 30, 1787, ibid., 247–48.

CHAPTER III   THE MADISONIAN MOMENT

1. J. G. A. Pocock, *The Machiavellian Moment: Florentine Political Thought and the Atlantic Republican Tradition* (Princeton, 1975), vii–viii.

2. *Records*, I, 422–24.

3. In this chapter I draw on my short biography of *James Madison and the Creation of the American Republic* (Glenview, Ill., 1990) as well as other essays that I have written about him, including "Mr. Meese, Meet Mr. Madison," *The Atlantic* (Dec. 1986), 77–86, and "The Madisonian Moment," *University of Chicago Law Review*, 55 (1988), 473–505. Like other Madison scholars, I tend to prefer Ralph Ketcham, *James Madison: A Biography* (New York, 1971) to Irving Brant, *James Madison*, 6 vols. (Indianapolis, 1941–61). There are, of course, numerous interpretations of his political thinking in the 1780s that rely almost exclusively on his contributions to *The Federalist* and his speeches in the Philadelphia and Virginia conventions. But for more historically minded approaches to the *development* of his ideas in the 1780s, one should consult the following: Charles Hobson, "The Negative on State Laws: James Madison, the Constitution, and the Crisis of Republican Government," *WMQ*, 36 (1979), 215–35; three essays by Lance Banning: "James Madison and the Nationalists, 1780–83," ibid., 40 (1983), 227–55; "The Hamiltonian Madison: A Reconsideration," *Virginia Magazine of History and Biography*, 92 (1984), 3–28; and "The Practicable Sphere of a Republic: James Madison, the Constitutional Convention, and the Emergence of Revolutionary Federalism," in Beeman et al., eds., *Be-*

yond Confederation, 162–87. John Zvesper, "The Madisonian Systems," *Western Political Quarterly*, 37 (1984), 236–56, is a valuable assessment of the apparent contradictions between the Madison of the 1780s and the 1790s. Drew R. McCoy, *The Last of the Fathers: James Madison and the Republican Legacy* (Cambridge, Eng., 1989) is a wonderful reflection on Madison's retirement, but this sensitive sketch informs our view of his entire life.

4. I discuss this facet of Revolutionary politics in *Beginnings of National Politics*, 216–39.

5. Here (not for the first time) I borrow a title from Ralph Lerner, whose book *The Thinking Revolutionary* has inspired a few thoughts of my own.

6. Madison to Jefferson, Apr. 16, 1781, and Proposed Amendment, [Mar. 12, 1781], in *Papers of Madison*, III, 71–72, 17–19. Madison drafted this amendment as a member of a three-man committee appointed to prepare a plan for giving Congress "full and explicit powers for effectually carrying into execution all acts or resolutions passed agreeably to the Articles of Confederation." For general background, see Rakove, *Beginnings of National Politics*, 285–92.

7. Ibid., 297–324; Banning draws similar conclusions in "The Hamiltonian Madison." For a different interpretation of this episode, see Ferguson, *Power of the Purse*, 109–76.

8. Madison to Jefferson, Nov. 18, 1781, *Papers of Madison*, III, 308. The best analysis of this issue is Peter S. Onuf, *The Origins of the Federal Republic: Jurisdictional Controversies in the United States, 1775–1787* (Philadelphia, 1983), 75–102.

9. Madison to Washington, Dec. 9, 1785, *Papers of Madison*, VIII, 438, discussing measures relating to vesting powers over commerce in Congress.

10. My conclusions echo the sparkling passage on Madison's disillusionment in Gordon S. Wood, "Interests and Disinterestedness in the Making of the Constitution," in Beeman et al., eds., *Beyond Confederation*, 73–77.

11. Wallace to Madison, July 12, 1785; and Madison to Wallace, Aug. 23, 1785; *Papers of Madison*, VIII, 321, 350–57.

12. For the expression of a similar sentiment, see William Livingston to the Baron van der Capellen, Nov. 18, 1783, in Carl E. Prince et al., eds., *The Papers of William Livingston* (New Brunswick, N.J., 1988), V, 56–57.

13. On this point see especially Wood, *Creation of the American Republic*, 214–22.

14. The *Memorial* is reprinted in *Papers of Madison*, VIII, 295–306. It has received extensive critical attention from historians and other scholars, in part because of the light it sheds on Madison's understanding of the concept of "an establishment of religion." So, too, the relation between Madison's commitment to religious liberty and the development of his general political ideas has also merited close examination. See, especially, Thomas E. Buckley, S.J., *Church and State in Revolutionary Virginia, 1776–1787* (Charlottesville, 1977); Thomas J. Curry, *The First Freedoms: Church and State in America to the Passage of the First Amendment* (New York, 1986); Leonard W. Levy, *The Establishment Clause: Religion and the First Amendment* (New York, 1986); Lance Banning, "James Madison, the Statute for Religious Freedom, and the Crisis of Republican Convictions," in Merrill D. Peterson and Robert C. Vaughan, eds., *The Virginia Statute for Religious Freedom: Its Evolution and Consequences in American History* (New York, 1988), 109–38; William Lee Miller, *The First Liberty: Religion and the American Republic* (New York, 1986), 77–150; and Robert S. Alley, ed., *James Madison on Religious Liberty* (Buffalo, 1985).

15. Notes on Ancient and Modern Confederacies, *Papers of Madison*, IX, 3–24; see 22, n. 1, for a discussion of the dating of these notes.

16. Monroe to Madison, May 31, 1786, ibid., 68–70.

17. Madison to Jefferson, Aug. 12, 1786; and to James Madison, Sr., Nov. 1, 1786; ibid., 96–97, 154.

18. Thus Madison sought to use his old friendship with John Witherspoon, president of

the College at New Jersey, and his association at Annapolis with Abraham Clark, a former New Jersey delegate to Congress, to bring that state to support the southern position on the Mississippi question. See Madison to Monroe, Aug. 12 [11], 1786; and Clark to Madison, Nov. 23, 1786, ibid., 90–91 and n. 3, 177.

19. Madison to Jefferson, Aug. 12, 1786; and see his outline and notes for a speech opposing paper money, ca. Nov. 1, 1786; ibid., 94–95, 156–59.

20. Madison to James Madison, Sr., Nov. 1, 1786, ibid., 154.

21. Madison to Monroe, Oct. 5, 1786, ibid., 141.

22. See Madison's draft of "A Bill for appointing deputies" and his letter to Washington, Nov. 8, 1786, ibid., 163–64, 166.

23. Ibid., 181–84.

24. Madison to Washington, Feb. 21, 1787, and Notes of Debates in Congress, same date, ibid., 285, 290–92.

25. Madison to Jefferson, March 19, 1787, ibid., 319–20. In an autobiographical sketch written much later, Madison recalled that "his main object in returning" to Congress was the "cancelling of the project of Mr Jay for shutting the Mississippi which threatened an alienation of Kentucky, then a part of Virginia, from any increase of federal power, with such an evidence in view of a disposition in those possessing it to make that sacrifice." Douglass Adair, ed., "James Madison's Autobiography," *WMQ*, 2 (1945), 202.

26. The memorandum is in *Papers of Madison*, IX, 345–57; the crucial letters are to Jefferson, Mar. 19, 1787; to Randolph, Apr. 8, 1787; and to Washington, Apr. 16, 1787; ibid., 318–19, 369–71, 383–85.

27. The quoted phrases are from *Federalist* 37, *Doc. Hist.*, XV, 348.

28. On this connection, see the seminal essays of Adair, "The Tenth Federalist Revisited," and " 'That Politics May Be Reduced to a Science,' " in Colbourn, ed., *Fame and the Founding Fathers*, 75–106; and Edmund Morgan, "Safety in Numbers: Madison, Hume, and the Tenth Federalist," *Huntington Library Quarterly*, 49 (1986), 95–112.

29. Quotations in this and the following six paragraphs are taken from the memorandum of April 1787, *Papers of Madison*, IX, 351–57.

30. Madison to Randolph, Apr. 8, 1787, ibid., 369–70.

31. Madison to Washington, Apr. 16, 1787, ibid., 383–84.

32. Vices of the Political System, ibid., 356–57.

33. Madison to Washington, Apr. 16, 1787, and to Jefferson, Oct. 24, 1787, ibid., IX, 383, X, 211.

34. Ibid.

35. *Federalist* 37 and 48, *Doc. Hist.*, XV, 346, XVI, 4.

36. Speech of June 6, 1787, *Papers of Madison*, X, 35.

37. Madison to Randolph, Apr. 8, 1787, and to Washington, Apr. 16, 1787, *Papers of Madison*, IX, 369–70, 383.

38. Harry C. Payne, *The Philosophes and the People* (New Haven and London, 1976), 61–62; for the reference to Penn, see Montesquieu, *The Spirit of the Laws*, bk. IV, chap. 6.

39. Madison reflected on the difference between classical law-giving and the deliberations of the Convention in *Federalist* 38, which is quoted here; *Doc. Hist.*, XV, 353–54.

CHAPTER IV THE POLITICS OF CONSTITUTION-MAKING

1. A draft of the letter, in the handwriting of Gouverneur Morris, was reported by the committee on style on September 12 and adopted without revision; the official letter was signed by Washington in his capacity as presiding officer. *Records*, II, 583–84 and n. 3a,

666–67. For two discussions of the motif of compromise, see Nelson, "Reason and Compromise," *WMQ*, 44 (1987), 458–84; Peter B. Knupfer, "The Rhetoric of Conciliation: American Civil Culture and the Federalist Defense of Compromise," *Journal of the Early Republic*, 11 (1991), 315–38. A classic (and widely reprinted) essay offering a variant of this theme is John P. Roche, "The Founding Fathers: A Reform Caucus in Action," *American Political Science Review*, 55 (1961), 799–816, which emphasizes calculated pragmatism more than compromise per se.

2. *Doc. Hist.*, XV, 348.

3. On this much agitated question, see Paul Finkelman, "Slavery at the Constitutional Convention: Making a Covenant with Death," in Beeman et al., eds., *Beyond Confederation*, 188–225; idem., *An Imperfect Union: Slavery, Federalism, and Comity* (Chapel Hill, 1981), 20–45; Don E. Fehrenbacher, *The Dred Scott Case: Its Significance in American Law and Politics* (New York, 1978), 20–27; William W. Freehling, "The Founding Fathers and Slavery," *American Historical Review*, 77 (1972), 81–93; William M. Wiecek, *The Sources of Antislavery Constitutionalism in America, 1760–1848* (Ithaca and London, 1977), 62–83; and James Oakes, "The Rhetoric of Reaction: Justifying a Proslavery Constitution," *Cardozo Law Review* (forthcoming).

4. *Records*, I, 1–4.

5. Washington to Arthur Lee, May 20, 1787; Mason to George Mason, Jr., May 20, 1787, *Records*, III, 22–23.

6. *Records*, I, 42 (notes of James McHenry; Madison makes no mention of this speech). In suggesting that the Virginians benefited from the delay of the other delegations, I do not overlook that Randolph and Madison had briefly discussed the idea that "some leading propositions at least would be expected from Virga."; I simply mean to note that there is no evidence that the Virginia Plan itself was drafted before the delegation as a whole could caucus. Randolph to Madison, Mar. 27, 1787, and Madison's reply, Apr. 8; *Papers of Madison*, IX, 335, 369.

7. It is noteworthy that in 1775 Dickinson had pursued a similar ploy with the Pennsylvania assembly, eliciting instructions that would enable him to resist the movement toward independence. For his role in resistance and in drafting the Articles of Confederation, see Rakove, *Beginnings of National Politics*, 72–74, 84, 151–62; Edward Rutledge to John Jay, June 29, 1776, in Paul H. Smith, ed., *Letters of Delegates to Congress, 1774–1789* (Washington, D.C., 1976–) IV, 338.

8. *Records*, I, 10–11 (Madison's note), 37.

9. *Records*, I, 20–23.

10. *Records*, I, 87, 201, 242 n.

11. *Records*, I, 108, (Madison's speech of June 4, as noted by King), 110 (Pierce's comment), 138–40 (Madison's speech of June 6), 146 (Hamilton's comments). For other speeches in which Madison drew directly upon his analysis of the vices of republican government, see ibid., 151–52, 164–65, 168.

12. *Records*, I, 53, 59–60, 132–34.

13. *Records*, I, 164–68.

14. *Records*, I, 150–56, 158–60.

15. *Records*, I, 151, 201–2.

16. After announcing on Friday, June 14, that alternative resolutions were in preparation, Paterson presented his plan the next day. *Records*, I, 240–45.

17. The Plan was debated on June 15; *Records*, I, 249–56.

18. Two versions of Dickinson's plan are printed in Hutson, ed., *Supplement*, 84–91; for the prefatory resolution, see *Records*, I, 282; Hamilton's speech follows.

19. *Records*, I, 288–89 and Articles III and IV of Hamilton's plan of government, 291–92.

20. *Records*, I, 284–85, 305 (for Hamilton's own outline). The "pork still" comment appears in Robert Yates's notes of Hamilton's speech; but these were printed only in 1821, with editorial liberties evidently being taken by their editor, the celebrated Citizen Edmond Genet—no admirer of Hamilton—and their accuracy, as Hutson has demonstrated, is questionable. See Hutson, "The Creation of the Constitution," in Rakove, ed., *Interpreting the Constitution*, 156–58.

21. *Records*, I, 313–22.

22. *Records*, I, 322–25, 329–32.

23. *Records*, I, 338.

24. *Records*, I, 336.

25. *Records*, I, 445.

26. *Records*, I, 468–70, 482–93 (the debate of June 30), 510–16 (vote of July 2 and discussion of committee).

27. *Records*, I, 355, 461–62 (quoting William Samuel Johnson of Connecticut in both cases); cf. the remarks of his colleague Sherman on July 14, stressing the equal-state vote as a means to defend the state governments rather than the interests of the small states.

28. *Records*, I, 447–48, 466, 483–84. Nor had this argument been answered eleven years earlier, when the Continental Congress debated the issue of voting under the proposed Articles of Confederation. Then John Adams, Benjamin Rush, and Wilson had reminded the delegates supporting the equal-state vote that "the larger colonies [sic] are so providentially divided in situation as to render every fear of their combining visionary." Jefferson, Notes of Proceedings in the Continental Congress, July 30–August 1, 1776, Julian P. Boyd et al., eds., *The Papers of Thomas Jefferson* (Princeton, 1950–), I, 326–27.

29. *Records*, I, 484–85.

30. *Records*, I, 356–57, 359, 489; cf. the similar remarks of William Davie, ibid., 488.

31. *Records*, I, 199 (Franklin), 343–44, 359 (Wilson).

32. Hamilton, June 29, *Records*, I, 466.

33. *Records*, I, 491–92 (Bedford speaking first).

34. *Records*, I, 468.

35. *Records*, I, 482–87, 496–97, 504.

36. *Records*, I, 486–87; the words in angled brackets indicate a later addition to Madison's manuscript.

37. He was also the author of the original version of the three-fifths clause, which had first appeared in the congressional revenue plan of April 18, 1783, as a formula for apportioning federal expenses among the states; see Madison's notes of debates in Congress, Mar. 28, 1783, *Papers of Madison*, VI, 407–8.

38. *Records*, I, 510–16. In electing committees, the entire Convention voted by individual ballot for individual members. This rule extended to the so-called grand committees of one member from each state, so that the member chosen to represent each delegation would be appointed by the Convention rather than by his own state.

39. *Records*, I, 522–23 (Yates's notes); 526–27.

40. *Records*, I, 533–34, 540.

41. *Records*, I, 540–42, 557–59.

42. *Records*, I, 559–70.

43. *Records*, I, 560, 571.

44. *Records*, I, 561 (Paterson), 593 (Morris).

45. McCoy, "Madison and Visions of American Nationality," in Beeman et al., eds., *Beyond Confederation*, 226–58; on the implications of western separatism, see Onuf, *Origins*

of Federal Republic, 33–41; Indian policy is surveyed in Reginald Horsman, *Expansion and American Indian Policy, 1783–1812* (East Lansing, Mich., 1967), 3–52. In 1788 New York undertook purchases of substantial lands of the Iroquois peoples, possibly anticipating that implementation of the Constitution would weaken its authority to negotiate directly with them.

46. *Records*, I, 578–59.

47. *Records*, I, 570–71, 579.

48. *Records*, I, 596 (Charles Pinckney), 605 (Pierce Butler).

49. *Records*, I, 595 (King, July 12), 604 (Morris, July 13).

50. *Records*, I, 587.

51. *Records*, I, 591ff. (quotation at 595).

52. Both quotations come from Mason's speech of July 11, *Records*, I, 578–79.

53. In making this claim, I do not mean to slight the far greater importance of the Four-teenth Amendment, only to remind readers that the framers had to debate seriously whether representation was about people or property or both, and that the formula of re-apportionment at legislative discretion was a far less liberal alternative.

54. *Records*, I, 561–62.

55. *Records*, I, 551–53, 584 (Madison), 604. This claim is again based on the initial north-ern dominance in the Senate.

56. *Records*, I, 551.

57. *Records*, II, 6–11. On June 25 Pinckney appears to have suggested that for purposes of allocating seats in the Senate, the "States ought to be divided into five Classes—to have *from one to five votes.*" Hutson, ed., *Supplement*, 112.

58. *Records*, II, 9–10.

59. *Records*, II, 7.

60. *Records*, I, 404–5.

61. *Records*, II, 6–7.

62. *Records*, I, 289–92 (Hamilton), II, 421–23 (Madison).

63. *Records*, I, 490 (Madison).

64. *Records*, I, 154.

65. *Records*, II, 15.

66. *Records*, II, 17–18.

67. *Records*, II, 18–20, 25.

68. *Records*, I, 34–35, II, 25–26. The proposals Sherman presented on July 17 are almost certainly those which Farrand reprinted in Appendix E of the *Records*, III, 615–16. It is puzzling that Farrand failed to identify this document with Sherman's motion, but linked it instead with the preparation of the New Jersey Plan.

69. *Records*, II, 27–29; I, 245 (New Jersey Plan). At first glance, Morris's notion that Congress could effectively repeal or supersede a state law that presumably violated a na-tional statute seems puzzling if not paradoxical. The debate immediately preceding the discussion of the negative, however, had produced a slight revision of the report of the committee of the whole that extended the power of the national legislature "to legislate in all cases for the general interests of the Union, and also in those to which the States are separately incompetent, or in which the harmony of the U. States may be interrupted by the exercise of individual Legislation."

70. The committee of detail had previously diluted Martin's motion of July 17 by making national acts superior to the state constitutions. *Records*, II, 183, 389.

71. Ellsworth to Abigail Ellsworth, July 21, 1787; and to Gov. Samuel Huntington, July 26, 1787; in Hutson, ed., *Supplement*, 177, 194.

72. Washington, diary entries July 30–Aug. 4, 1787, ibid., 199–204.

73. For the proceedings of the committee of detail, see *Records*, II, 95–96, 106, 129–89, and Hutson, ed., *Supplement*, 207–12.

74. For the additional matters referred to the committee of detail, see *Records*, II, 324–26, 340–42, 392–94. As late as August 29, the Convention came close to reconstituting this committee when it referred the forerunner of the comity clause to the other four members still in attendance plus William Samuel Johnson in place of the departed Ellsworth; ibid., 447–48.

75. In order of appointment, the four grand committees were charged with considering (1) both an assumption of state debts and the regulation of the militia (August 18); (2) the matrix of issues concerned with the size of majorities needed for the passage of navigation acts and the limitations on powers of regulating commerce (August 22); (3) the designation of official ports of entrance for the importation of foreign goods (August 25); and (4) the committee on postponed parts (August 31); *Records*, II, 327–28, 330–33; 373–75; 417–18; 481.

76. Such debate as took place was concerned with another Madison-Pinckney amendment to insert "and establish all offices" between "laws" and "necessary," an idea that a respectable chorus of Morris, Wilson, Rutledge, and Ellsworth all dismissed as superfluous; *Records*, II, 344–45.

77. *Records*, I, 561 (Paterson, July 9), 588 (Morris, July 11).

78. *Records*, I, 592 (emphasis in the original).

79. *Records*, II, 95.

80. Certainly it is difficult to imagine Wilson, the Convention's most consistent majoritarian, quietly accepting a two-thirds rule for navigation acts on any other basis.

81. *Records*, II, 178, 182–83 (for the relevant articles in the report of the committee of detail), 219–23 (for the debate of August 8). The confusion apparently arose because Article IV, section 4, of the report linked apportionment "to the provisions herein after made" without explicitly mentioning the rule of direct taxation.

82. *Records*, II, 222–23.

83. *Records*, II, 359–64; in the immediately succeeding vote to adopt the article as initially proposed, Massachusetts joined this coalition to produce a majority of seven states to four.

84. *Records*, II, 364.

85. This debate carried the Convention through adjournment on the twenty-first and well into the next day's session. The speakers were Rutledge, Charles Pinckney twice, General Pinckney, Ellsworth twice, Sherman, and Abraham Baldwin (a Connecticut native who had migrated to Georgia, a state which was still something of an outpost of its northern neighbor).

86. *Records*, II, 364–65, 369–72.

87. For the social background to these political questions, see the essays by Richard S. Dunn, "Black Society in the Chesapeake, 1776–1810"; Philip D. Morgan, "Black Society in the Lowcountry, 1776–1810"; and Allan Kulikoff, "Uprooted Peoples: Black Migrants in the Age of the American Revolution, 1790–1820"; in Ira Berlin and Ronald Hoffman, eds., *Slavery and Freedom in the Age of the American Revolution* (Charlottesville, 1983), 49–171.

88. *Records*, II, 372–75.

89. *Records*, II, 400. A fourth recommendation preserved Section 5 of the committee of detail's report, which stipulated that capitation taxes must be laid in conformity to the three-fifths clause.

90. *Records*, II, 414–17.

91. *Records*, II, 449–53. Randolph virtually announced his opposition in his speech of the twenty-ninth; Mason's position became evident by the thirty-first; ibid., 479.

92. *Records*, II, 443, 453–54.

93. *Records*, II, 400–4 (presidency); 392–94 (Senate); 481 (committee on postponed parts).

94. This paragraph summarizes much of a whole week of debate (Sept. 4–6), which is examined in Chapter 9. For the committee's report, see *Records*, II, 496–99.

95. *Records*, II, 553. This was not in fact the last committee to be elected. In a gesture evidently meant to humor Mason, the Convention on September 13 elected another five-member committee to consider his bizarre proposal to prepare "articles of Association for encouraging by the advice the influence and the example of the members of the Convention, œconomy frugality and american manufactures." The committee never reported. Ibid., 606–7.

96. *Records*, II, 585–87, 615–16.

97. *Records*, II, 88–93, 468–69, 475–78. This question is examined in Chapter 5.

98. *Records*, II, 557–59.

99. *Records*, II, 628.

100. Mason's concern was that the people would otherwise have no avenue open to them for securing amendments against "the Government should [it] become oppressive." Set in the context of recent debates about the need for amendments to require balanced federal budgets or to limit congressional incumbency, Mason's point has a certain populist appeal. But Madison's response, as usual, has a characteristic virtue of its own: It anticipates the reservations many scholars have expressed about the difficulty of restraining the actions of any subsequent constitutional convention, given the opportunistic precedent the framers themselves set in 1787. Madison did not object to "providing for a Convention for the purpose of amendments, except only that difficulties might arise as to the form, the quorum &c. which in Constitutional regulations ought to be as much as possible avoided." *Records*, II, 629–30. Shortly before his death, Mason alleged, in conversation with Jefferson, that Morris and King, as members of the committee of style, had connived at giving Congress a monopoly over amendments, but that allegation seems to be contradicted by the Journal as well as by Madison's notes, which record Madison as the author of this amendment; cf. Jefferson's account of this conversation with the records of debate of September 10, ibid., III, 367–68, 555–59.

101. *Records*, II, 629–31.

102. Mason then moved to require two-thirds majorities for navigation acts until 1808. When this failed, Randolph, Mason, and Gerry briefly stated the reasons that would prevent their signing the Constitution. The two Virginians argued that no constitution should be adopted until the state ratifying conventions had been given the opportunity to propose amendments to a second general convention.

CHAPTER V   THE CONCEPT OF RATIFICATION

1. I am grateful to Mr. Daniel Rakove for counting the number of stairs during a visit to the statehouse on May 30, 1993.

2. For FitzSimons's report, see *Doc. Hist.*, II, 58–59; I attribute the remarks about the urgency of action by the Pennsylvania assembly to Morris on the basis of Luther Martin's address "To the Citizens of Maryland," which almost certainly refers to Morris's speech of August 31, though Madison's notes of this speech do not contain this specific point. *Maryland Journal*, Mar. 21, 1788, *Doc. Hist.*, XVI, 458–59; *Records*, II, 478.

3. Washington, Diary, Sept. 17, 1787, Hutson, ed., *Supplement*, 276.

4. Samuel H. Beer, *To Make a Nation: The Rediscovery of American Federalism* (Cambridge, 1993), 310–12. Beer locates this point within a discussion of the American concept of ratification with which I fundamentally agree, but which has a rather different emphasis from the one developed below.

5. John N. Shaeffer, "Public Consideration of the 1776 Pennsylvania Constitution," *Pennsylvania Magazine of History and Biography*, 98 (1974), 415–37. Procedures for adopting the new constitutions are surveyed in Adams, *First American Constitutions*, 63–98. In the spring of 1776 a group of New York City mechanics also proposed popular ratification of a state constitution, but the British occupation of the city and the care with which conservative leaders managed the process of adopting a constitution effectively nullified this demand. See Edward Countryman, *A People in Revolution: The American Revolution and Political Society in New York, 1760–1790* (Baltimore and London, 1981), 162–23.

6. [Adams], *Thoughts on Government*, in *American Political Writing*, I, 406 (emphasis added); in fairness to Adams, his passage may refer only to arrangements for executive and judicial officers, rather than legislators, whose manipulation of their own terms of office would remind Americans of the Septennial Act of 1716 under which a House of Commons elected for three years extended its term of office to seven.

7. The entire documentary record of this process is presented in Oscar Handlin and Mary Handlin, eds., *The Popular Sources of Political Authority* (Cambridge, 1966). For two important early expressions of this animus, see the Concord resolutions of Oct. 21, 1776; and the Berkshire County protest of Nov. 17, 1778; ibid., 153, 374–79. For further discussion, see Adams, *First American Constitutions*, 86–93.

8. As the leading students of the 1780 constitution have observed, "Some [communities] voted on the document as a whole; others on each clause; and still others joined to their decision qualifications of greater or lesser significance. When the convention examined the results in June it declared the Constitution ratified; but, though it tried to do so, it was not able to cast up a coherent statistical account that would show just how many were in favor and how many opposed." Handlin and Handlin, eds., *Popular Sources of Political Authority*, 25.

9. See [Thomas Tudor Tucker], *Conciliatory Hints, Attempting, by a Fair State of Matters, to Remove Party Prejudice* (Charleston, 1784), reprinted in *American Political Writing*, II, 619–20; Jefferson's 1783 Draft of a Constitution for Virginia omits any provision for popular ratification; Boyd, ed. *Papers of Jefferson*, VI, 294–95. See the general discussion in Donald S. Lutz, *Popular Consent and Popular Control: Whig Political Theory in the Early State Constitutions* (Baton Rouge, 1980), 72–84; and Wood, *Creation of the American Republic*, 328–43.

10. Jefferson, *Notes on the State of Virginia*, ed. William Peden (Chapel Hill, 1955), 121–25; and see Gerald Stourzh, "*Constitution*: Changing Meanings of the Term from the Early Seventeenth to the Late Eighteenth Century," Terence Ball and J. G. A. Pocock, eds., *Conceptual Change and the Constitution* (Lawrence, Kansas, 1988), 35–54.

11. Notes for a Speech, [June 14 or 21, 1784], *Papers of Madison*, VIII, 77–78 (and see the valuable headnote, 75–77); I have eliminated the editorial marks in the quotation.

12. Rakove, *Beginnings of National Politics*, 135–91, 285–96.

13. Madison to Washington, Apr. 16, 1787, and to Pendleton, Apr. 22, 1787, *Papers of Madison*, IX, 385, 395; Rakove, *Beginnings of National Politics*, 368–80. In her essay, "The Founders' Unwritten Constitution," *University of Chicago Law Review*, 54 (1987), 1146ff., Suzanna Sherry suggests that ideas of using the ratification process to affirm the status of the Constitution as positive laws evolved only during the debates. But Sherry seemingly did not read Madison's pre-Convention writings, and thus misses the important point that he had considered this problem before May 1787.

14. Madison's language seems to transpose his intended meaning, as it is interpreted here: "Whenever a law of a State happens to be repugnant to an act of Congress, particularly when the latter is of posterior date to the former, it will be at least questionable whether the latter must not prevail." *Papers of Madison*, IX, 352 and 358 n. 8, for evidence that "someone other than" Madison later corrected the manuscript to invert its literal meaning. The interpretation given here is consistent with Madison's corresponding Convention speeches of June 5 and July 23. In the latter, after first comparing the Confederation to a treaty, Madison restated the point this way: "A law violating a treaty ratified by a preexisting law, might be respected by the Judges as a law, though an unwise and perfidious one." *Records*, I, 122; II, 93. The basic rule of statutory construction, of course, is that a more recent enactment takes precedence over a previous act of the same body.

15. *Papers of Madison*, IX, 352–53. The legal validity of this argument has recently been defended in Akhil Amar, "The Consent of the Governed: Constitutional Amendment Outside Article V," *Columbia Law Review*, 94 (1994), 457–508; and vigorously criticized by Bruce Ackerman and Neal Katyal, "Our Unconventional Founding," *University of Chicago Law Review*, 62 (1995), 475–573, which they kindly let me read in manuscript.

16. The idea that popular sovereignty is best imagined (or represented) as a fiction is the controlling motif in Edmund S. Morgan, *Inventing the People: The Rise of Popular Sovereignty in England and America* (New York, 1988). But though Morgan concludes his account of the development of this Anglo-American concept with the adoption of the Constitution, he curiously says little about the constitution-ordaining facet of popular sovereignty, emphasizing instead the fictive quality of the claims made on behalf of political representation.

17. *Doc. Hist.*, I, 185–87.

18. No fewer than five delegates preserved notes for this debate of June 16; the fullest is Madison's, *Records*, I, 249–56, but the quotations from Wilson and Randolph are taken respectively from the notes of Rufus King and Robert Yates, ibid., 266, 262. Also extant is the outline of Wilson's prepared speech comparing the New Jersey and Virginia plans, which, however, does not contain any reference to the issue of the Convention's authority, perhaps because Wilson did not anticipate the emphasis that the advocates of the New Jersey Plan placed on that point.

19. *Records*, I, 255.

20. In the strict sense, then, the charge that the Convention somehow acted "illegally" still seems somewhat puzzling, at least if one asks under what law the framers might have been prosecuted for ignoring the formal recommendations under which they were meeting. In the broader sense, of course, the argument for illegality is that the framers (and ratifiers, for that matter) deliberately ignored the legally adopted provisions of the Articles of Confederation to pursue the project of constitutional reform, and that at least until the new Constitution took effect, their actions in doing so were necessarily subversive. This argument might also be mitigated, however, by the maxim *quod leges posteriores priores contrarias abrogant*, for were the individual legislatures not entitled to supersede the acts of previous assemblies in endorsing the Confederation? The crucial point is not the issue of the "illegality" of the procedures proposed for ratification of the Constitution but the recognition that through the combination of legislative assent to the calling of conventions and the expression of popular sovereignty they would provide, the legal defects of the existing state constitutions would become apparent in the light of the new understanding of what was required to make *any* constitution supreme law. The case for "illegality" is made in Richard McKay, "The Illegality of the Constitution," *Constitutional Commentary*, 4 (1987), 57–80; and see Bruce Ackerman, *We the People*, vol. 1, *Foundations* (Cambridge, 1991), 41–42, 173–79.

21.   *Records*, I, 22. In theory the use of the phrase "assembly or assemblies of Representatives" left open the possibility that the Constitution could be adopted by a single ratification convention embodying a national citizenry, as opposed to conventions meeting in the separate states. But this option was never debated, and when Gouverneur Morris moved on July 23 "that the reference of the plan be made to one general Convention, chosen & authorized to consider, *amend*, & establish the same," he was not seconded; ibid., II, 93. Given that this motion was made only a week after the crucial vote of July 16, Madison's emphasis on *"amend"* implies that Morris may have contemplated using such a convention to attack the crucial decision regarding the Senate. But the theoretical implications of both the original proposal and Morris's unseconded amendment extend further still. For a single assembly of representatives elected by the people would arguably have greater authority than any other political body in the country: Congress, the state legislatures, or the Federal Convention.

22.   *Records*, I, 22, 26 (notes of Randolph's speech taken by McHenry), 122 (Madison).

23.   *Records*, II, 88–89, 92–93.

24.   *Records*, II, 123. On the issue of ratification, Wilson regularly took the most aggressive stand in favor of ignoring the Confederation.

25.   *Records*, II, 88–93. In noting that some legislatures were divided into "several branches," Gorham included not only the twelve states where bicameralism was the rule but also those states where the assent of the governor was required for the enactment of legislation, making the executive in that sense a third branch of the legislature.

26.   In its report of August 6, the committee of detail proposed that "The ratifications of the Conventions of   States shall be sufficient for organizing this Constitution." The blank could still have been filled with thirteen, of course, but the use of "sufficient" indicates the direction of the committee's thinking. *Records*, II, 189.

27.   *Records*, II, 476–77. By implicitly equating "the State" of Massachusetts with its legislature, which had, of course, appointed the delegates to the Convention, King begged the question whether a resort to first principles should not have been initiated by the sovereign people upon whose consent the state constitution of 1780 rested. It is equally important to note Madison's earlier objection to legislative ratification: "These changes [proposed by the new constitution] would make essential inroads on the State Constitutions, and it would be a novel & dangerous doctrine that a Legislature could change the constitution under which it held its existence." Ibid., 92–93.

28.   *Records*, II, 469. In the initial debate of June 5, Wilson had also spoken strongly in favor of placing "the provision for ratifying . . . on such a footing as to admit of a partial union," prompting Madison to note that "This hint was probably meant in terrorem to the smaller states of N. Jersey & Delaware" over the issue of representation." Ibid., I, 123.

29.   Wilson, June 16 (King's notes); Hamilton, June 18 (King's notes); King, July 23, *Records*, I, 266, 301; II, 92.

30.   *Records*, II, 478–79, 559–63.

31.   Randolph to the Speaker of the Virginia House of Delegates, Oct. 10, 1787; speeches in Convention, Aug. 31, Sept. 10 and 15; *Records*, III, 125–26; II, 479, 560–61, 631–32. It is worth noting that Randolph had considered the mode of ratifying whatever proposals the Convention would produce prior to its meeting. Writing to Madison on March 27, 1787, he suggested that the amendments to be "grafted on the old confederation"—as he supposed—should "be so detached from each other, as to permit a state to reject one part, without mutilating the whole." In his reply of April 8, Madison identified the obvious problems that such a procedure would generate. He doubted "that it will be practicable to present the several parts of the reform in so detached a manner to the States as that a partial adoption will be binding. Particular States may view the different articles as con-

ditions of each other, and would only ratify them as such. Others might ratify them as independent propositions. The consequence would be that the ratification of both would go for nothing." *Papers of Madison*, IX, 335, 369.

32. *Records*, II, 632–33.

33. Aristides [Alexander Contee Hanson], *Remarks on the Proposed Plan of a Federal Government* . . . [Annapolis, 1788], in *Doc Hist.*, XV, 540.

34. Randolph had written Lee on September 17, the day the Convention adjourned; Mason wrote the next day. These letters are now missing, but their contents can be inferred from Lee's responses to Mason of October 1 and to Randolph of October 15; *Doc. Hist.*, VIII, 28–30, 61–67. Mason predicted that Madison and the other framers would insist upon "this [the Constitution] or nothing," and he also proposed the strategy of having the conventions propose amendments to be adopted—whether by Congress or a second convention is unclear—prior to ratification.

35. R. H. Lee to John Adams, Sept. 3, 1787, *Doc. Hist.*, VIII, 9. There is no satisfactory scholarly biography of Lee, who certainly merits one; the best interpretive sketch of his political career is the essay in Pauline Maier, *The Old Revolutionaries: Political Lives in the Age of Samuel Adams* (New York, 1980), 164–200.

36. The relevant motions and debates for the proceedings of September 26–28 are reprinted in *Doc. Hist.*, XIII, 231–42, quotations in this paragraph are at 232, 238. Notes of debates for September 27 were kept by Melancton Smith, a moderate Anti-Federalist who later played a key role in the ratification of the Constitution in New York.

37. *Doc Hist.*, XIII, 235. According to Smith's notes, Madison opened this short speech by saying that he "cant. accede to it," which the editors take to refer to Lee's motion; but as the subsequent text suggests, Madison found both motions defective, though admittedly Lee's more than Clark's.

38. Madison to Washington, Sept. 30, 1787, in *Doc. Hist.*, XIII, 276.

39. Writing to Caleb Strong on October 10, Nathan Dane echoed Lee in noting that "the warmest friends" of the Constitution "appeared to be extremely impatient to get it thro Congress, even the first day that it was taken up"; but he also reported that "very few members wanted any alterations." *Doc. Hist.*, XIII, 357.

40. Lee to Mason, Oct. 1, 1787, and to Samuel Adams, Oct. 5, 1787, *Doc. Hist.*, XIII, 281–82, 323. Under the Articles of Confederation, "any delegate" could request a roll call once a motion was properly before Congress; and Lee's colleague, William Grayson, would have happily seconded his motion.

41. On September 26, the Philadelphia *Independent Gazetteer* published an extract of a letter purportedly written by a member of Congress, dated September 23, lamenting that the assembly might adjourn before the Constitution would "pass through the necessary formalities of Congress," and implying that the assembly should nevertheless proceed with the calling of a state convention, from which "Pennsylvania will derive great consequence and consideration"—possibly a reference to the anticipated competition over the location of a permanent national capital. *Doc. Hist.*, XIII, 246.

42. For these proceedings, which have a touch of "Duck Soup" about them, see *Doc. Hist.*, II, 99–110.

43. In its original form, the preamble cited only the proposed Constitution itself and a handful of petitions hastily presented to the assembly as evidence of "the sense of great numbers of the good people of this state" to justify the calling of a convention; *Doc. Hist.*, II, 65–66, 101.

44. For the debates on this point, see *Doc. Hist.*, II, 74–94; the speech of FitzSimons is at 89–90.

45. *Doc Hist.*, II, 85 (George Clymer), 92 (Brackenridge).

46. Lee to Samuel Adams, Oct. 5, 1787, *Doc. Hist.*, XIII, 324–25. In this same letter, Lee indicated a revealing uncertainty about the amending procedures proposed in the Constitution itself when he argued that it would be wrong to trust Congress to correct "the defects in this new Constitution." For even should Congress do so, "a subsequent Assembly may repeal the Acts of its predecessor for the parliamentary doctrine is 'quod legis posteriores priores contrarias abrogant' "; ibid., 323 [citing Sir Edward Coke].

47. *Doc. Hist.*, III, 113.

48. Enclosing a copy of his objections to the Constitution in a letter to Washington of October 7, Mason pointedly noted that he was "most decidedly of opinion, that it ought to be submitted to a Convention chosen by the People, for that special Purpose." *Doc. Hist.*, XIII, 348.

49. [Hanson], *Remarks on the Proposed Plan*, in *Doc. Hist*, XV, 539–41.

50. Upon returning to Virginia, Randolph wrote Mason to suggest that the Virginia *assembly* could propose amendments to the other states, so that "before the meeting of the convention an answer may be obtained." Mason offered a variant on this scheme in a letter to Gerry in late October. "It would be fortunate for America, if the Conventions cou'd meet upon this important Business about the same time, by a regular & cordial Communication of Sentiments, confining themselves to a few necessary amendments, & determining to join heartily in the System so amended, they might, without Danger of public Convulsion or Confusion, procure a general Adoption of the new Government." Randolph refined his ideas when he drafted a letter explaining his dissent to the Virginia assembly on October 10—but the letter went unsent and was not published until December. Randolph to Madison, Sept. 30, 1787 (describing his letter to Mason, not extant); Mason to Gerry, Oct. 20, 1787; Randolph's letter to the assembly; *Doc. Hist.*, VIII, 25, XIII, 421, XV, 117–35 (with a headnote tracing composition and printing of this document).

51. Randolph to Madison, Sept. 30, 1787, *Doc. Hist.*, VIII, 25; a month later, Randolph wrote again to ask why Madison had not yet commented on this idea, adding that "I am not convinced of the impropriety of the idea, but I wish to open to you without reserve the innermost thoughts of my soul, and was desirous of hearing something from you on this head." Madison finally responded on November 18, explaining that he had not conveyed his sentiments because he assumed that Randolph would have known what they were, but adding that he deemed Randolph's proposal impracticable because several states would already "have provided for a Convention, and even adjourned before amendatory propositions from Virginia could be transmitted." Ibid., 134, 166–67.

52. Lee to Adams, Oct. 5, 1787, *Doc. Hist.*, XIII, 324–25.

53. "An Old Whig," Philadelphia *Independent Gazetteer*, Nov. 10, 1787, *Doc. Hist.*, II, 300–3.

54. *Doc. Hist.*, XIV, 51.

55. "Unitas," *Pennsylvania Mercury*, Jan 5, 1788, *Doc. Hist.*, III, 194–95. The standard narrative history of the politics of the ratification struggle is Robert A. Rutland, *The Ordeal of the Constitution: The Antifederalists and the Ratification Struggle of 1787–1788* (Norman, Okla., 1986), which this chapter and the next hardly pretend to supplant; and see Jackson T. Main, *The Anti-Federalists: Critics of the Constitution, 1781–1788* (Chapel Hill, 1961), 187–248.

56. Joseph Habersham to John Habersham, Dec. 29, 1787, *Doc. Hist.*, III, 272.

57. Hugh Ledlie to John Lamb, Jan. 15, 1788, *Doc. Hist.*, III, 576.

58. Enoch Perkins to Simeon Baldwin, Jan. 15, 1788; *New Haven Gazette*, Jan. 24, 1788, *Doc. Hist.*, III, 583–84, 594.

59. For useful interpretations of ratification in these two states, see Peter S. Onuf, "Maryland: The Small Republic in the New Nation," and Robert M. Weir, "South Car-

olina: Slavery and the Structure of the Union," in Michael Gillespie and Michael Lienesch, *Ratifying the Constitution*, (Lawrence, Kansas, 1989), 171–234 (esp. 225–26 for the prolongation of debate in the latter state); and James W. Ely, Jr., " 'The Good Old Cause': The Ratification of the Constitution and Bill of Rights in South Carolina," in Robert J. Haws, *The South's Role in the Creation of the Bill of Rights* (Jackson, Miss., 1991), 101–24.

60. Thomas McKean, Nov. 24, 1787, *Doc. Hist.*, II, 333–34, 337.

61. For the procedural maneuvers of November 26–27, see *Doc. Hist.*, II, 364–82.

62. Smilie, Nov. 27, 1787, *Doc. Hist.*, II, 375–76. Beyond its use in the ongoing struggle over ratification, the publication of an extensive record of votes and the reasons behind them could serve one further purpose, which Whitehill best articulated while denying that press coverage of the debates would prove adequate. "A public paper is of a transient and perishable nature," he observed, "but the Journals of this house will be a permanent record for posterity, and if it ever becomes a question, upon what grounds we have acted, each man will have his vote justified by the same instrument that records it." In imagining subsequent uses for these records, Whitehill did not suppose that later generations would find in them conclusive or unambiguous evidence of what the Constitution had originally meant to its ratifiers. For by definition the occasion for recording votes and dissents arose when consensus could not be attained, and when a minority anxious to "justify" its conduct sought to dissociate itself from those who stood to prevail. The views that the Anti-Federalists most wished to preserve were those that had to be rejected in order for the Constitution to be adopted in Pennsylvania; and the end for which these views were to be recorded was not to lay a foundation for its legal or political interpretation but to provide historical evidence that would identify which party had better foreseen its true tendency. Ibid., 377.

63. *Pa. Herald*, Dec. 12, 1787, *Doc. Hist.*, II, 529–31.

64. *Doc. Hist.*, II, 589–91; "The Address and Reasons of the Dissent of the Minority," 618–40 (amendments at 623–25).

65. *Elliot's Debates*, II, 3, 6.

66. Rufus King to Madison, Jan. 27, 1788, *Papers of Madison*, XI, 436–37; and see the discussion in Wood, *Creation of the American Republic*, 486–90. This perception of the social and intellectual disadvantages of Anti-Federalist delegates to the Massachusetts convention was widely shared; see "Centinel," XV, Philadelphia *Independent Gazetteer*, Feb. 22, 1788; *Doc. Hist.*, XVI, 190–91.

67. *Elliot's Debates*, II, 16, 32, 68, 102.

68. The best discussion of this point is Michael Gillespie, "Massachusetts: Creating Consensus," in Gillespie and Lienesch, eds., *Ratifying the Constitution*, 151–61, making a strong case that the initiative for recommending amendments came from Hancock and Adams rather than the Federalists; cf. the discussion in *Doc. Hist.*, XVI, 60–64.

69. *Elliot's Debates*, II, 170 (Turner).

70. Ibid., 138 (Widgery), 140 (Thompson), 151–52 (Jarvis), 154–55 (Ames).

71. Ibid., 154 (Ames); 152 (Jervis); 170 (Turner).

72. I rely here on Jere Daniell, "Ideology and Hardball: Ratification of the Federal Constitution in New Hampshire," in Patrick T. Conley and John P. Kaminski, *The Constitution and the States: The Role of the Original Thirteen in the Framing and Adoption of the Federal Constitution* (Madison, Wis., 1988), 181–200; and Jean Yarbrough, "New Hampshire: Patriotism and the Moral Foundations of America," in Gillespie and Lienesch, eds., *Ratifying the Constitution*, 235–40 (arguing that Federalist failure to pursue the Massachusetts precedent may have been a miscalculation).

73. Daniell, "Ideology and Hardball," in Conley and Kaminski, eds., *Constitution and the*

States, 194–98; and Yarbrough, "New Hampshire," in Gillespie and Lienesch, eds., *Ratifying the Constitution*, 250–55.

74. Madison to Pendleton, and to Washington, both Oct. 28, 1787; Edward Carrington to Jefferson, Nov 10, 1787; John Dawson to Madison, c. Nov. 10, 1787, *Doc. Hist.*, VIII, 126–27, 149, 150. For the proceedings in the assembly, see ibid., 110–18.

75. For these proceedings, see *Doc. Hist.*, VIII, 183–93.

76. On December 27, the assembly instructed Randolph to convey the act of December 12, with its reference to the possibility of communications among the states or their conventions, to the executive and legislature of the other states. For reasons that remain obscure, but which Anti-Federalists attributed to Federalist manipulation of the mails, the letter to New York was not received until March 7, 1788; its assembly adjourned two weeks later without fashioning any response to the Virginia act. When Clinton wrote Randolph on May 8, he accordingly noted that his letter should be regarded "as expressive of my own sentiments" only, though likely reflective of the views of "a majority of the People of the State." The date that Randolph received the letter is not known, but in any case, it was presented not to the convention but to the assembly only on June 23, two days before the Constitution was ratified. See the headnote and documents in *Doc. Hist.*, IX, 788–93.

77. For further discussion of this point, see DePauw, *The Eleventh Pillar*, 204–12.

78. Lee to Mason, May 7, 1788; and compare Lee to Edmund Pendleton, May 26, 1788, *Doc. Hist.*, IX. 784–86, 878–82.

79. Madison to Washington, June 4, 1788, *Papers of Madison*, XI, 77.

80. *Doc. Hist.*, IX, 1070.

81. Randolph, speech of June 4, 1788, *Doc. Hist.*, IX, 933.

82. Madison to Hamilton, and to King, June 22, 1788; and to Washington, June [23], 1788, *Papers of Madison*, XI, 166–68.

83. For Madison's comments, see his letters to Hamilton, King, and Washington, June 25, 1788, to Hamilton, June 27, 1788, and to Washington, June 28, 1788; ibid., 177–78, 181–83.

84. Although the third and fourth rules of procedure originally adopted for the convention on June 18 contemplated that members could make motions at any point, and that roll calls would be taken at the request of two members, on June 19 Robert Livingston moved, and the committee of the whole agreed, that it would not vote upon any clause or article of the Constitution or any proposed amendment until the entire document had been considered. *Elliot's Debates*, II, 207–8, 216.

85. The definitive history of the New York convention is DePauw, *The Eleventh Pillar*, 183–254, upon which I have relied

86. See, for example, Hamilton's eighth and ninth speeches of July 19, Harold C. Syrett and Jacob E. Cooke, eds., *The Papers of Alexander Hamilton* (New York, 1960–78), V, 183–84 and accompanying notes.

87. The final text of the explanatory amendments is reprinted as Appendix B in DePauw, *Eleventh Pillar*, 293–96. The one proposed explanatory amendment that unambiguously possessed structural implications stated "[t]hat no Treaty is to be construed so to operate as to alter the Constitution of any State," which would seem to contradict the supremacy clause of the Constitution on a fundamental point. Two possible considerations may explain why the convention would have insisted upon this point. First, in 1784 New York had been the locus of the famous decision in *Rutgers* v. *Waddington*, in which James Duane (a member of the convention) had denied a claim for damages in trespass arising under a New York statute because it conflicted with provisions of the federal treaty of peace of 1783. Second, and in my view somewhat more intriguing, this reservation may

have been tied to the state's imminent plans to acquire by treaty purchase a substantial portion of the lands occupied by its aboriginal Iroquois inhabitants. Under the New York constitution, the state claimed the exclusive preemptive right to the purchase of Indian lands, but given a prior history of conflict with the Continental Congress over land claims and Indian relations, both Federalist and Anti-Federalist delegates may have worried that adoption of the Constitution could jeopardize the state's policy. I plan to pursue this subject in a future monograph; but see J. David Lehman, "The End of the Iroquois Mystique: The Oneida Land Cession Treaties of the 1780s," *WMQ*, 47 (1990), 523–47.

88.   Hamilton to Madison, [July 19, 1788]; Madison to Hamilton, [July 20, 1788], *Papers of Madison*, XI, 188–89. As Madison noted, the same idea, when proposed in Virginia, was regarded "as a conditional ratification which was itself considered as worse than a rejection."

89.   See especially the various notes and accounts of Hamilton's speech of July 12, *Papers of Hamilton*, V, 154–60.

90.   The text of Smith's resolution, which was presented as an amendment to Jay's resolution of July 11, is printed in *Elliot's Debates*, II, 411. The four powers specified related to terms of militia service, and congressional power over elections, excises, and direct taxes.

91.   Pending the publication of the relevant volume in the *Documentary History of Ratification* project, many of the pertinent motions essential to tracing the concluding three weeks of maneuvers in the New York convention are most easily consulted in the editorial notes accompanying Hamilton's speeches during the period July 2–24, 1788, in *Papers of Hamilton*, V, 141–96; and see especially notes for Hamilton's first speech of July 24, ibid., 193–95. The complete text of the act of ratification is reprinted in DePauw, *Eleventh Pillar*, 293–302. The roll call on the "full confidence" amendment and the final vote on ratification can be found in *Elliot's Debates*, II, 412–13.

92.   Madison to Washington, Aug. 24, 1788, *Papers of Madison*, XI, 240; DePauw, *Eleventh Pillar*, 265–79. Madison's misgivings were exacerbated by his belief that the New York Federalists had yielded in order to improve the prosects that New York would be designated as the meeting place of the new government, a point then in agitation in Congress (and on which he had competing ambitions of his own to pursue).

93.   Patrick T. Conley, "Rhode Island in Disunion, 1787–1790," *Rhode Island History*, 31 (1972), 99–115.

94.   See the sources cited in nn. 14, 19, *supra*.

95.   Ackerman, *We the People*, I, 41–42, 173–79; Ackerman and Kaytal, "Our Unconventional Founding."

96.   *Federalist* 40, *Doc Hist.*, XV, 407–9. The sentence from the Declaration properly reads: "That whenever any Form of Government becomes destructive of these ends, it is the Right of the People to alter or to abolish it, and to institute new Government, laying its foundation on such principles and organizing its powers in such form, as to them shall seem most likely to effect their Safety and Happiness."

97.   Forrest McDonald, *Novus Ordo Seclorum: The Intellectual Origins of the Constitution* (Lawrence, Kan., 1985), 279. This counts the action of the Rhode Island assembly to call a popular referendum on the Constitution as a de facto thirteenth vote mofidying Article XIII.

CHAPTER VI   DEBATING THE CONSTITUTION

1.   *Doc. Hist.*, XIII, 494. Compare Hamilton's much-quoted observation with this passage from an anonymous Anti-Federalist: "Almost all the governments that have arisen

among mankind, have sprung from force and violence. The records of history inform us of none that have been the result of cool and dispassionate reason and reflection: It is reserved for this favoured country to exhibit to mankind the first example." *Address from a Plebeian* (New York, 1788), in *Complete Anti-Fed.*, VI, 142. In 1784 the author of the strikingly original pamphlet, *The Political Establishments of the United States*, endorsed the possibility of federal reform in much the same language. Edmund S. Morgan, ed., "Political Establishments," *WMQ*, 23 (1966), 288, 300, 304.

2. [Adams], *Thoughts on Government*, in *American Political Writings*, I, 408. In this judgment I obviously diverge from the position of Wood, *Creation of the American Republic*, 127–32.

3. Hannah Arendt, *On Revolution* (New York, 1963), 27; Huntington, quoted in *Conn. Courant*, Jan. 14, 1788, *Doc Hist.*, III, 557.

4. *Doc. Hist.*, XIII, 494–5.

5. "Centinel," XV, *Doc. Hist.*, XVI, 189–90.

6. *Federalist* 1, "Centinel," letter XIV, *Doc. Hist.*, XIII, 494–96, XVI, 189–90. As Bernard Bailyn has observed, the enormous scholarly literature on *The Federalist* "inundates everything written on the history of the Constitution and on American political thought," attaining "an exquisite refinement of analysis that would have amazed the harried authors, who wrote polemically, to help in a political battle." Bailyn, "The Ideological Fulfillment of the American Revolution: A Commentary on the Constitution," in *Faces of Revolution: Personalities and Themes in the Struggle for American Independence* (New York, 1990), 270–71 n. 12 and accompanying text, 230–31. The differences between modern and previous approaches to the essays is discussed in Jack N. Rakove, "Early Uses of *The Federalist*," in Charles R. Kesler, *Saving the Revolution: The Federalist Papers and the American Founding* (New York, 1987), 234–49; other essays in this volume provide a representative sample of the approach to *The Federalist* taken especially by political theorists. Other recent important discussions include: David Epstein, *The Political Theory of the Federalist* (Chicago, 1984); Morton White, *Philosophy, The Federalist, and the Constitution* (New York, 1987); Daniel W. Howe, "The Language of Faculty Psychology in *The Federalist Papers*," in Ball and Pocock, eds., *Conceptual Change and the Constitution*, 107–36; and Albert Furtwangler, *The Authority of Publius: A Reading of the Federalist Papers* (Ithaca, N.Y., 1984). Though it is too late in the day to restore correct usage, it should be noted that the commonly employed title, *The Federalist Papers*, is a modern corruption that can probably be traced to the popular classroom edition prepared by the late Clinton Rossiter.

7. Bailyn, "Ideological Fulfillment of the Revolution," 229–30.

8. William H. Riker, "Why Negative Campaigning Is Rational: The Rhetoric of the Ratification Campaign of 1787–1788," *Studies in American Political Development*, 5 (1991), 224–83 (quotation at 234). A sound summary of objections to the Constitution can be found in Main, *The Anti-Federalists*, 119–86.

9. Cecilia Kenyon, "Men of Little Faith: The Anti-Federalists on the Nature of Representative Government," *WMQ*, 3d ser., 12 (1955), 3–43; Bailyn, "Ideological Fulfillment of the Revolution," 232–46; Isaac Kramnick, "The Discourse of Politics in 1787: The Constitution and Its Critics on Individualism, Community, and the State," in Belz et al., eds., *To Form a More Perfect Union*, 188–93; and for a more radical effort to emphasize the range of Anti-Federalist sentiments, see Saul Cornell, "Moving Beyond the Canon of Traditional Constitutional History: Anti-Federalists, the Bill of Rights, and the Promise of Post-Modern Historiography," *Law and History Review*, 12 (1994), 1–28.

10. Gordon S. Wood, "Interests and Disinterestedness in the Making of the Constitution," in Beeman et al., eds., *Beyond Confederation*, 69–109.

11. Michael Lienesch, *New Order of the Ages: Time, the Constitution, and the Making of*

Modern American Political Thought (Princeton, 1988), 119–37; Jack P. Greene, " 'An Instructive Monitor': Experience and the Fabrication of the United States Constitution," *Proceedings of the American Philosophical Society*, 131 (1987), 298–307.

12. Wood, *Creation of the American Republic*, 519–64 (quotations at 562, 524).

13. Lansing and Yates left on July 10, Martin on September 4; *Records*, III, 588–90.

14. Hamilton, Conjectures about the new Constitution, [Sept. 1787], *Doc. Hist.*, XIII, 277.

15. Boston *American Herald*, Aug. 6, 1787; *Pa. Gazette*, Aug. 22, 1787; both in *Doc. Hist.*, XIII, 185, 190; and see, generally, John K. Alexander, *The Selling of the Constitutional Convention: A History of News Coverage* (Madison, Wis., 1990). To a modern reader, of course, the idea that punctual attendance for a seven-hour day offered a proof of extraordinary industry and duty is a revealing illustration of differences between eighteenth-century and postindustrial attitudes toward time; cf. discussion of the work habits of the Continental Congress in Rakove, *Beginnings of National Politics*, 223–24.

16. *Pennsylvania Packet*, Sept. 22, 1787; Boston *American Herald*, Oct. 1, 1787; *Doc. Hist.*, XIII, 222, 286.

17. *Pennsylvania Gazette*, Oct. 10, 1787, *Doc. Hist.*, XIII, 364.

18. Hamilton, Conjectures about the new Constitution, [Sept. 1787]; Morris to Washington, Oct. 30, 1787; *Doc. Hist.*, XIII, 277–78, 513–14.

19. *Doc. Hist.*, XIII, 212–14.

20. Bernard Bailyn, *The Ideological Origins of the American Revolution* (Cambridge, 1967), 94–159; Gordon S. Wood, "Conspiracy and the Paranoid Style: Causality and Deceit in the Eighteenth Century," *WMQ*, 39 (1982), 401–41.

21. *Doc. Hist.*, XIII, 546–50 (Gerry), 346–51 (Mason).

22. *Doc. Hist.*, VIII, 260–75.

23. For convenience, this may be most easily read in *Complete Anti-Fed.*, II, 19–82; the dissents of the other five delegates, including Yates and Lansing, are found here as well.

24. "Philadelphiensis," X, Philadelphia *Freeman's Journal*, Feb. 20, 1788, *Doc. Hist.*, XVI, 159.

25. *Doc. Hist.*, XIII, 550–55.

26. "Landholder," VI and VIII, *Conn. Courant*, Dec. 10 and 24, 1787; *Doc. Hist.*, XIV, 398–404, XV, 75–79.

27. *Massachusetts Centinel*, Jan. 5, 1788, *Doc. Hist.*, XV, 273; though unsigned, the letter was clearly authoritative.

28. *Md. Journal*, Feb. 29, 1788, *Doc. Hist.*, XVI, 265–71, and see the discussion of authorship in the headnote. Though signed "Landholder," this essay was almost certainly the work not of Ellsworth but of another Maryland framer.

29. Madison to Randolph, Jan. 10, 1788, *Papers of Madison*, X, 354–56; cf. the strikingly similar opinions of the Anti-Federalist "Centinel," I, Philadelphia *Independent Gazetteer*, Oct. 5, 1787, *Doc. Hist.*, XIII, 329–30. Of course, few Federalists were prepared to utter such sentiments in public. For one noteworthy exception, see "Publicola," [Archibald Maclaine], *State Gazette of North Carolina*, March 20, 1788, arguing against popular instructions for the delegates to the state convention because "[t]he greatest part of you have not the means of information, and being unaccustomed to think of government, few of you are competent judges of it." *Doc. Hist.*, XVI, 438.

30. *Doc. Hist.*, XV, 343–44. This essay appeared only a few days after Madison discussed public opinion in his letter to Randolph.

31. *Doc. Hist.*, XVI, 16–19, 29–31 (quotations all come from *Federalist* 49).

32. Madison to Jefferson, Aug. 10, 1788; Randolph to Madison, Aug. 13, 1788; Madison to Randolph, Aug. 22, 1788; Madison to Jefferson, Sept. 21, 1788, *Papers of Madison*, XI,

226, 231, 237, 258. Writing to Jefferson on August 23, Madison again noted: "An early convention is in every view to be dreaded in the present temper of America. A very short period of delay would produce the double advantage of diminishing the heat and increasing the light of all parties." Ibid., 238.

33. Hamilton, Conjectures on the new Constitution, [Sept. 1787], *Doc. Hist.*, XIII, 276; [John Jay], *An Address to the People of the State of New-York, On the Subject of the Constitution* [New York, 1788], in Paul L. Ford, ed., *Pamphlets on the Constitution of the United States* (Brooklyn, 1888), 80.

34. *Doc. Hist.*, II, 112–17; Washington to Madison, Oct. 10, 1787, ibid., VIII, 49–50.

35. "An Office of the Late Continental Army," Philadelphia *Independent Gazetteer*, Nov. 6, 1787, in *Doc. Hist.*, II, 213. Responding to this caricature, "Plain Truth" explained Wilson's "lofty carriage" in this way: "[A] man who wears spectacles must keep his head erect to see through them and to prevent them from falling off his nose," *ibid.*, 217.

36. The speech was first published in the *Pennsylvania Herald*, Oct. 9, 1787, where it was introduced by a note indicating that the newspaper was providing the "outlines" of "a long and eloquent speech." The text is, however, a polished text, leaving the reader uncertain how or to what extent it was condensed for publication. By year's end, the speech had been republished in at least thirty-four newspapers, and in every state but Delaware and North Carolina. *Doc. Hist.*, XIII, 344 n. 1.

37. "Federal Farmer," IV, *Complete Anti-Fed.*, II, 248–49.

38. "Cincinnatus," *New York Journal*, Nov. 1, 1787; "A Republican," *New York Journal*, Oct. 25, 1787; Lee to Adams, Oct. 27, 1787; *Doc. Hist.*, XIII, 530, 477, 484.

39. "Centinel," II, Phila. *Freeman's Journal*, Oct. 24, 1787, *Doc. Hist.*, XIII, 459, 468.

40. *Doc. Hist.*, XIV, 15–18.

41. *Doc. Hist.*, II, 41.

42. Madison to Randolph, Oct. 21, 1787, *Papers of Madison*, X, 199.

43. *Doc. Hist.*, XV, 357–58.

44. See the observations on this point in Herbert Storing, *What the Anti-Federalists Were For* (Chicago, 1981 [*Complete Anti-Fed.*, I]), 5.

45. This judgment, it should be noted, is present-minded in the most radical way—that is, it depends far more upon the important and indeed central place the Bill of Rights came to occupy, somewhat abruptly, in American constitutionalism after 1950 than on any continuous influence that in fact it failed to exert during the first century and a half after its ratification.

46. "Cato," VII, *Complete Anti-Fed.*, II, 125.

47. "Philadelphiensis," III, Phila. *Freeman's Journal*, Dec. 5, 1787; *Federalist* 46; *Doc. Hist.*, XIV, 351; XV, 192–93.

48. "A Federal Republican," *A Review of the Constitution Proposed by the Late Convention Held at Philadelphia, 1787* (Philadelphia, 1787), in *Doc. Hist.*, XIV, 264. My general formulation here is clearly indebted to Bailyn, "Ideological Fulfillment," 232–48, which makes a persuasive case for the continuity between the pre-Revolutionary ideology of the colonists and the fundamental beliefs and attitudes of anti-federalism.

49. "Brutus," I and II, *New York Journal*, Oct. 18 and Nov. 1, 1787, *Doc. Hist.*, XIII, 416, 526–27.

50. *Address by a Plebeian*, in *Complete Anti-Fed.*, VI, 130.

51. "A Farmer," Phila. *Freeman's Journal*, Apr. 23, 1788, *Complete Anti-Fed.*, III, 191.

52. The author used a similar analogy to defend the proposition that the amount of power to be vested in an officer should be inversely related to his term of office: "This may be held as certain an axiom in politics as this is in mechanics; that we cannot increase

force but at the expence of velocity, nor increase velocity but at the expence of force." "A True Friend," broadside (Richmond, 1787), in *Doc. Hist.*, XIV, 373–77.

53. See, for example, the characterization of Madison in Richard Hofstadter's classic essay "The Founding Fathers: An Age of Realism," chap. I of *The American Political Tradition and the Men Who Made It* (New York, 1948), 8.

54. *Doc. Hist.*, XIV, 159. Wilson developed the same point in his widely reprinted speech of November 24, 1787, to the Pennsylvania convention; it is tempting to speculate whether he had already seen *Federalist* 9, which was published in New York three days earlier; *Doc. Hist.*, II, 353–54.

55. *Doc. Hist.*, XIV, 413.

56. Francis Corbin echoed the point at the Virginia convention when he argued that "the objection that an extensive territory is repugnant to a republican Government, applies against this and every State in the Union, except Delaware and Rhode-Island. Were the objection well founded, a republican Government could exist in none of the States except those two." *Doc. Hist.*, XIV, 160 (Hamilton); IX, 1011 (Corbin).

57. *Doc. Hist.*, XIV, 161, II, 352.

58. *Doc. Hist.*, XV, 499, 501.

59. *Federalist* 9, *Doc. Hist.*, XIV, 159.

60. Speech of Nov. 24, 1787, *Doc. Hist.*, II, 353.

61. *Doc. Hist.*, XIV, 314 (*Federalist* 14); II, 353–54 (Wilson).

62. Alpheus T. Mason, "The Federalist—A Split Personality," *American Historical Review*, 57 (1952), 625–43.

63. *Federalist* 37, *Doc. Hist.*, XV, 347–48. Can we juxtapose the use of "compelled," "force," and "forced" in these passages with the notion of force in *Federalist* 1?

64. *Doc. Hist.*, XV, 343–45.

65. *Doc. Hist.*, XV, 345–47 (for preceding two paragraphs).

66. Madison to Washington, Apr. 16, 1787, *Papers of Madison*, IX, 383.

67. *Doc. Hist.*, XV, 346.

68. *Federalist* 38, *Doc. Hist.*, XV, 354–55.

69. *Doc. Hist.*, XV, 353–54.

CHAPTER VII   FEDERALISM

1. *Federalist* 39; Henry, June 9, 1788; *Doc. Hist.*, XV, 380–86, IX, 1067–68.

2. June 6, 1788, *Doc. Hist.*, IX, quotations at 989, 995–96.

3. *Records*, I, 166.

4. This paragraph draws broadly on the discussion of the politics of resistance during this period in Rakove, *Beginnings of National Politics*, chaps. 2–5.

5. Wood, *Creation of the American Republic*, 362.

6. Onuf, *Origins of the Federal Republic*, passim; for a good short restatement (among several), examining to the relation between the general issue and the constitutional politics of 1787–88, see Onuf, "State Sovereignty and the Making of the Constitution," in Ball and Pocock, eds., *Conceptual Change and the Constitution*, 78–98; and for a formulation with broader implications still, see Peter Onuf and Nicholas Onuf, *Federal Union, Modern World: The Law of Nations in an Age of Revolution, 1776–1814* (Madison, Wis., 1993).

7. For the making of territorial policy, see Jack Eblen, *The First and Second United States Empires: Governors and Territorial Government, 1784–1912* (Pittsburgh, 1968), 17–51; Robert F. Berkhofer, Jr., "Jefferson, the Ordinance of 1784, and the Origins of the American Territorial System," *WMQ*, 29 (1972), 231–62; and Arthur Bestor, Jr., "Constitutionalism

and the Settlement of the West: The Attainment of Consensus, 1754–1784," in John Porter Bloom, ed., *The American Territorial System* (Athens, Ohio, 1973), 13–44.

8. I rely here on J. G. A. Pocock, "States, Republics, and Empires: The American Founding in Early Modern Perspective," in Ball and Pocock, eds., *Conceptual Change and the Constitution*, 57–61 (quotation at 59).

9. For a general discussion, see Jack P. Greene, *Peripheries and Center: Constitutional Development in the Extended Polities of the British Empire and the United States, 1607–1788* (Athens, Ga., 1986).

10. Vices of the political system of the U. States, [Apr. 1787], *Papers of Madison*, IX, 351. In this paragraph I summarize the broader argument in Rakove, *Beginnings of National Politics*, 135–91.

11. *Doc. Hist.*, XV, 348.

12. May 31, *Records*, I, 53.

13. For a more moderate assessment of Madison's federal agenda, see Banning, "Practicable Sphere of a Republic," in Beeman et al., eds., *Beyond Confederation*, 162–87, which I believe understates the reactionary quality of Madison's thinking about the states.

14. *Records*, I, 85, 87 (wording in second quotation has been transposed).

15. Wilson, June 19, *Records*, I, 322.

16. Madison, June 29, *Records*, I, 463–64.

17. *Records*, I, 359, 357.

18. *Records*, I, 153–54 (Dickinson, Wilson), 165 (Madison).

19. *Records*, II, 5, 94–95.

20. *Records*, I, 426–28, II, 180, 290–92. Madison illustrated the difficulty of resolving the tension between these attributes in *Federalist* 62 and 63. Whether out of lingering bitterness or a refusal to offer a principled rationale for decisions taken on other grounds, Madison treated the "federal" aspects of the Senate in a dismissive way. He allotted all of three sentences to its mode of election (a subject "unnecessary to dilate on"); justified the equal-state vote with a double negative ("it does not appear to be without some reason"); and then concluded that "it is superfluous to try, by the standard of theory, a part of the Constitution which is allowed on all hands to be the result, not of theory, but 'of a spirit of amity, and that mutual deference and concession which the peculiarity of our political situation rendered indispensable.'" But as he went on to explore the Senate's other attributes—its capacity as a select and stable deliberative body to form a coherent conception of the national interest—these perfunctory comments gave way to the more sophisticated insights that typified his writings as "Publius."

21. *Records*, I, 281–86.

22. For thoughtful studies of Wilson's political ideas, see the chapter describing him as "The Democratic Federalist Alternative" in Jennifer Nedelsky, *Private Property and the Limits of American Constitutionalism: The Madisonian Framework and Its Legacy* (Chicago, 1990), 96–140; Beer, *To Make a Nation*, 341–77; and Stephen A. Conrad, "Metaphor and Imagination in James Wilson's Theory of Federal Union," *Law and Social Inquiry*, 13 (1988), 1–70.

23. *Records*, I, 21–22, 54 (Madison), 243–45.

24. *Records*, I, 21–22, 124–25.

25. *Records*, I, 245.

26. *Records*, I, 252, 317. Cf. Madison's criticisms of the dependence of state judges during the House debates over the Judiciary Bill of 1789, in Charlene Bangs Bickford et al., eds., *Documentary History of the First Federal Congress of the United States of America* (Baltimore and London, 1992), XI, 1359–60.

27.　See the remarks of Gorham and Randolph on July 18, when the clause authorizing legislative creation of inferior federal tribunals was under review; *Records*, II, 46.

28.　*Records*, II, 169 (emphasis added).

29.　Martin argued that his intention would also be subverted by the likely creation of a system of inferior federal courts, because he had contemplated that state courts would act as original trial courts in cases involving national laws and treaties. Martin, "To the Citizens of Maryland," *Md. Journal*, Mar. 21, 1788, *Doc. Hist.*, XVI, 452–53.

30.　*Records*, II, 390–91. Pinckney was bold enough to concede that the state executives should be appointed by the national government, and presumably given some role in making an initial determination of the need to implement a particular law before it could be submitted for national review.

31.　Madison raised this point as early as June 8. *Records*, I, 164.

32.　*Records*, II, 428. Rutledge was speaking in opposition to a motion from Dickinson and Gerry authorizing the executive to remove federal judges on "application <by> the Senate and House of Representatives."

33.　*Doc. Hist.*, XV, 385.

34.　July 17, *Records*, II, 27.

35.　Madison to Jefferson, Oct. 24, 1787, *Papers of Madison*, X, 211.

36.　*Doc. Hist.*, XV, 346.

37.　*Doc. Hist.*, XV, 480.

38.　*Records*, I, 551.

39.　*Records*, II, 25–27.

40.　John C. Hueston, "Altering the Course of the Constitutional Convention: The Role of the Committee of Detail in Establishing the Balance of State and Federal Powers," *Yale Law Journal*, 100 (1990), 765–83.

41.　This was clearly the case in matters dealing with the regulation of commerce, the continuation of the slave trade, and the committee's recommendation to prohibit taxes on exports, subjects of special importance to its two southern members, Rutledge and Randolph; *Records*, II, 183.

42.　*Records*, II, 181–82, 187.

43.　*Records*, II, 197–99, 275; I, 324 (for King's earlier remarks).

44.　*Records*, II, 350. It was Gouverneur Morris who on July 12 had suggested adding the word "direct" to his initial motion proposing "that taxation shall be in proportion to Representation," but who subsequently suggested (July 24) that the Convention "strike out the whole of the clause proportioning direct taxation to representation" on the grounds that "He had only meant it as a bridge to assist us over a certain gulph;"—that is, the issue of whether slaves should be counted at all—"having passed the gulph the bridge may be removed." Ibid., I, 591–92, II, 106.

45.　Sherman, July 14 and 16, *Records*, II, 11, 26.

46.　*Records*, II, 344–45, 563, 633, 640.

47.　"Federal Farmer," XVII, *Complete Anti-Fed.*, II, 331–32.

48.　"Federal Farmer," I and II, *Complete Anti-Fed.*, II, 228–34.

49.　"Centinel," II, Phila. *Freeman's Journal*, Oct. 24, 1787, *Doc. Hist.*, XIII, 459. On the connection to Machiavelli, see Paul Rahe, *Republics Ancient and Modern: Classical Republicanism and the American Revolution* (Chapel Hill, 1992), 527 and epigraph 521.

50.　*Elliot's Debates*, II, 403.

51.　June 25, 1788, *Complete Anti-Fed.*, VI, 166.

52.　*Doc. Hist.*, XIII, 411–21.

53.　*Doc. Hist.*, XIII, 417.

54.　*Doc. Hist.*, XIII, 418–19.

55. "Brutus," IV, *New York Journal*, Nov. 29, 1787, *Doc. Hist.*, XIV, 298–99.

56. *Doc. Hist.*, XIII, 419–20, XIV, 299–301; see "The Address and Reasons of Dissent of the Minority of the Convention of the State of Pennsylvania," ibid., II, 637.

57. "Brutus," X, *New York Journal*, Jan. 24, 1788, *Doc. Hist.*, 462–63.

58. Here I agree with Storing that the discussion of judicial power by "Brutus" was "the best in Anti-Federalist literature." *Complete Anti-Fed.*, II, 358.

59. "Brutus," XI, *New York Journal*, Jan. 31, 1788, *Doc. Hist.*, XV, 512–16.

60. "Brutus," XII, *New York Journal*, Feb. 7, 1788, *Doc. Hist.*, XVI, 72–75.

61. "Federal Farmer," XVIII, *Complete Anti-Fed.*, II, 339–49.

62. [Noah Webster], *An Examination into the Leading Principles of the Federal Constitution . . .* (Philadelphia, 1787), in Ford, ed., *Pamphlets*, 47; [Hanson], *Remarks on the Proposed Plan*, in *Doc. Hist.*, XV, 523.

63. "Fabius," VIII, in Ford, ed., *Pamphlets*, 204.

64. Wilson, Nov. 24 and Dec. 4, 1787, *Doc. Hist.*, II, 361–62, 471–73.

65. *Doc. Hist.*, XIV, 175–81.

66. Compare Hamilton's discussion with the seventh item of Madison's memorandum. Where Hamilton writes, "Government implies the power of making laws. It is essential to the idea of a law, that it be attended with a sanction," Madison had noted "A sanction is essential to the idea of law, as coercion is to that of Government." Hamilton proceeds to reflect on the revolutionaries' patriotic expectation of uniform state compliance with the recommendations of Congress; so had Madison. Hamilton explains why "bodies of men" cannot be expected to "act with more rectitude or greater disinterestedness than individuals," noting that regard to personal reputation diminishes "when the infamy of a bad action is to be divided among a number"; Madison pursued the same thought in item 11 of his memorandum. Hamilton describes how each state considers itself entitled to judge of the "propriety" of congressional recommendations; Madison developed the same concern in item 7. *Federalist* 15, *Doc. Hist.*, XIV, 328–31; *Papers of Madison*, IX, 351–52, 355–56.

67. *Doc. Hist.*, XV, 454–58, 508–11, XVI, 50–51.

68. On this point, see especially John Murrin, "The Great Inversion, or Court versus Country: A Comparison of the Revolution Settlements in England (1688–1821) and America (1776–1816)," in J. G. A. Pocock, ed., *Three British Revolutions: 1641, 1688, 1776* (Princeton, 1980), 425; and Harry Scheiber, "Federalism and the American Economic Order, 1789–1910," *Law and Society Review*, 10 (1975–76). In making this claim, I do not overlook the ambitious uses of national power either promoted by Hamilton in his financial program of the early 1790s or forced upon both Federalist and Republican administrations after 1793 by the course of events in Europe. I mean only to suggest that once this transitional period came to a close with the end of the War of 1812, the essential allocation of power between state and national governments indicated that the United States was little less a confederation when Madison died in 1836 than it had been when he set off for the Annapolis conference half a century earlier.

69. In reaching this conclusion (which does not come easily for a biographer of Madison), I have been much influenced by the treatments of Hamilton in Gerald Stourzh, *Alexander Hamilton and the Idea of Republican Government* (Stanford, 1970); Stanley Elkins and Eric McKitrick, *The Age of Federalism* (New York, 1993); and Rahe, *Republics Ancient and Modern*, 651–86.

70. *Federalist* 23, *Doc. Hist.*, XV, 4–7.

71. *Doc. Hist.*, XV, 211–13. On the epistemological significance of this "move," see Morton White, *The Philosophy of the American Revolution* (New York, 1978), 81–94, reprised in White, *Philosophy, **The Federalist**, and the Constitution*, 34.

72. *Doc. Hist.*, XV, 65–69.

73. "Brutus," VI, *New York Journal*, Dec. 27, 1787, *Doc. Hist.*, XV, 113–14.

74. *Federalist* 32–33 was published as one essay in the *New York Independent Journal* of Jan. 2, 1788, but was reprinted in two parts in the McLean edition of 1788; *Doc. Hist.*, XV, 216–23. (Hence readers of the *Doc. Hist. of Ratification* will note that its editors assign two numbers to the succeeding essays; as do they, I follow the conventional numbering used in all book-length editions of *The Federalist*.)

75. *Federalist* 36, *Doc. Hist.*, XV, 305.

76. *Doc. Hist.*, XV, 259–63.

77. *Doc. Hist.*, XIII, 278.

78. Madison to Jefferson, Sept. 6 and Oct. 24, 1787, *Papers of Madison*, X, 163–64, 209–14.

79. *Doc. Hist.*, XV, 344–45, 347, 383.

80. *Federalist* 41, *Doc. Hist.*, XV, 418.

81. It was an error, Madison argued, to conclude "that force and right are necessarily on the same side in republican governments." A minority of citizens might seize power in various ways: through "superiority of pecuniary resources, of military talents and experience, or of secret succors from foreign powers," or with the support of "alien residents, of a casual concourse of adventurers," and the disfranchised—including even slaves. *Federalist* 43, *Doc. Hist.*, XV, 443–44.

82. *Federalist* 44, *Doc. Hist.*, XV, 471–73.

83. *Doc. Hist.*, XV, 473.

84. *Federalist* 46, *Doc. Hist.*, XV, 488–89.

85. *Federalist* 45 and 46, *Doc. Hist.*, XV, 478, 490–91.

86. *Doc. Hist.*, XV, 476; Hamilton, June 18, *Records*, I, 284–87.

87. *Doc. Hist.*, XV, 479–80.

CHAPTER VIII   THE MIRROR OF REPRESENTATION

1. [Adams], *Thoughts on Government*, in *American Political Writings*, I, 403.

2. I say probably because I have been unable to locate a prior English usage of this metaphor, and because two leading authorities, John Phillip Reid and J. R. Pole, concur that Adams seems to offers a new image. (Letter from Reid to author, May 28, 1993; and from Pole to author June 30, 1993.) Cf. J. R. Pole, *Political Representation in England and the Origins of the American Republic* (Berkeley and Los Angeles, 1966), 184. There is an excellent discussion of this general question in Hanna Fenichel Pitkin, *The Concept of Representation* (Berkeley and Los Angeles, 1967), chap. 4, "'Standing for': Descriptive Representation," but save for one passing reference to the Monarchomachs (p. 73)—a term of opprobrium applied to sixteenth-century Huguenot opponents of the French monarchy—Pitkin's account also seems to confirm the originality of the metaphor.

3. [Theophilus Parsons], *Result of the Convention Holden at Ipswich in the County of Essex . . .* (Newburyport, 1778), in Handlin and Handlin, eds., *Popular Sources of Political Authority*, 341; and cf. the instructions endorsed by the town of Beverly for their representative in the General Court, calling for an assembly that would "be a fair and exact Epitome of the whole People"; ibid., 293.

4. *Records*, I, 132–34, 142; Burke, *Thoughts on the Cause of the Present Discontents* (1770), in *Founders' Constitution*, I, 391 (excerpt).

5. Wood, *Radicalism of the American Revolution*, 224, 234–40.

6. [Adams], *Thoughts on Government*, in *American Political Writings*, I, 403.

7. This conception of the origins and character of Congress is developed at great length

in Jerrilyn Greene Marston, *King and Congress: The Transfer of Political Legitimacy,*
1774–1776 (Princeton, 1986).

8. [Parsons], *Result of the Convention,* in Handlin and Handlin, eds., *Popular Sources of*
Political Authority, 337; Madison to Caleb Wallace, Aug. 23, 1785, *Papers of Madison,*
VIII, 352. The "Federal Farmer" reached the same conclusion while contrasting the size
of the Continental Congress with the far more numerous representation he proposed for
the new Congress: "[T]he present Congress is principally an executive body, which ought
not to be numerous." *Complete Anti-Fed.,* II, 284.

9. Richard P. McCormick, "The 'Ordinance' of 1784?" *WMQ,* 50 (1993), 112–20. For a
detailed analysis of congressional procedures, written from the vantage point of the new
institutionalist approach in political science, see Calvin C. Jillson and Rick K. Wilson,
Congressional Dynamics: Structure, Coordination, and Choice in the First American Con-
gress, 1774–1789 (Stanford, 1994).

10. Jefferson to Adams, Paris, Feb. 23, 1787; and Adams to Jefferson, Mar. 1, 1787, Boyd,
ed., *Papers of Jefferson,* XI, 177, 189–90. Though Congress itself could not act judicially,
its power extended to the appointment of both admiralty courts and independent commissions to adjudicate disputes between states.

11. For evidence of this debate, see *Connecticut Courant,* Apr. 1, May 27, June 3, 17, 1776;
Sept. 15, 29, 1777. Wolcott to Samuel Lyman, Apr. 17, 1776, Smith, ed., *Letters of Delegates*
to Congress, IV, 552–54.

12. Richard Buel, Jr., *Dear Liberty: Connecticut's Mobilization for the Revolutionary War*
(Middletown, Conn., 1980), 213–15.

13. Rakove, *Beginnings of National Politics,* 127–32.

14. Burke, *Thoughts on Present Discontents,* in *Founders' Constitution,* I, 391 (excerpt). My
general interpretation owes a great deal to the work of John Phillip Reid, especially *The*
Concept of Representation in the Age of the American Revolution (Chicago, 1989), though he
cannot be held culpable for the uses to which I put his ideas.

15. Burke, *Thoughts on Present Discontents,* in *Founders' Constitution,* I, 391; Hume, "Of
the Independency of Parliament," in David Hume, *Essays, Moral, Political, and Literary,*
Eugene F. Miller, ed. (Indianapolis, 1985), 45.

16. William Eden, *Principles of Penal Law,* 2d ed. (1771), 306.

17. P. D. G. Thomas, *The House of Commons in the Eighteenth Century* (Oxford, 1971),
46–47.

18. David Lieberman, *The Province of Legislation Determined: Legal Theory in Eighteenth-*
Century Britain (Cambridge, Eng., 1989); John Brewer, *The Sinews of Power: War, Money,*
and the English State, 1688–1783 (New York, 1988), 221–49, offers a good discussion of the
relation between legislation and the need for information; for a more technical discussion,
see Sheila Lambert, *Bills and Acts: Legislative Procedure in Eighteenth-Century England*
(Cambridge, Eng., 1971).

19. Bernard Bailyn, *The Origins of American Politics* (New York, 1968), 66–70.

20. Rosemarie Zagarri, *The Politics of Size: Representation in the United States* (Ithaca,
1987), 42–46.

21. The contrast between American and British practice is a recurring theme in the
scholarly literature; see Reid, *The Concept of Representation;* Pole, *Political Representation,*
3–165; Bailyn, *Ideological Origins,* 161–75; and Beer, *To Make a Nation,* 163–77.

22. Bailyn, *Origins of American Politics,* 101–4; Reid, *Concept of Representation,* 29–30.

23. William E. Nelson, *Americanization of the Common Law: The Impact of Legal Change*
on Massachusetts Society, 1760–1830 (Cambridge, 1975), 14. The three acts Nelson adjudges
legislative were "an act making robbery a capital offense, an act prohibiting the arrest of
royal soldiers or sailors for debt, and an act for incorporating the Society for the Propa-

gation of Christian Knowledge." Nelson describes the overall work of the session in these terms: "The great bulk of the General Court's acts in that year were essentially administrative, involving questions of raising and appropriating money, organizing and granting jurisdiction to local units of government, and responding to specific local needs. The court also acted on a number of occasions in a quasi-judicial capacity when it granted new trials to litigants in pending actions." For other accounts, see Thomas L. Purvis, *Proprietors, Patronage, and Paper Money: Legislative Politics in New Jersey, 1703–1776* (New Brunswick, 1986), 176–99; Allan Tully, *William Penn's Legacy: Politics and Social Structure in Provincial Pennsylvania, 1726–1755* (Baltimore and London, 1977), 98–102; and Robert Zemsky, *Merchants, Farmers, and River Gods: An Essay on Eighteenth-Century Politics* (Boston, 1971), 10–27. The validity of the comparison between British and American attitudes toward legislation requires a systematic assessment of legislative output in the two societies. As Purvis aptly notes, "Little is presently known regarding either the disposition of petitions or the general range of statutes enacted by provincial governments in eighteenth-century America." For a partial response to this lament, see the monograph by Raymond C. Bailey, *Popular Influence upon Public Policy: Petitioning in Eighteenth-Century Virginia* (Westport, Conn., 1979). William Smith's portrait of colonial legislators is quoted in Bailyn, *Origins of American Politics*, 85.

24.   Abigail to John Adams, Mar. 31, 1776, and John to Abigail Adams, Apr. 14, 1776, in L. H. Butterfield and Marc Friedlaender, eds., *Adams Family Correspondence* (Cambridge, 1963–), I, 370, 382; John Adams to James Sullivan, May 26, 1776, in Robert Taylor et al., eds., *Papers of John Adams* (Cambridge, 1977–), IV, 208–12.

25.   Adams, *First American Constitutions*, 196–217 (quotation at 216), and see accompanying appendix surveying property qualifications in each of the states, 293–311.

26.   ([Hartford], 1776), reprinted in *American Political Writings*, I, 390–400 (quotations at 395, 396).

27.   Ibid., I, 387. For a more general discussion, see Zagarri, *Politics of Size*, 36–60. A strong if not entirely conclusive case for Paine's authorship of the *Four Letters on Interesting Subjects* is made in A. Owen Aldridge, *Thomas Paine's American Ideology* (Newark, Del., 1984), 219–39.

28.   For all that has been written on state politics during the Revolutionary War, more attention could well be paid to the problem of mobilization and regulation at the state level—that is, to the *use* of power—as opposed to the more familiar themes of struggles for "democracy" or the opening up of the political system to new groups. The best study for these purposes is Buel, *Dear Liberty*; and see Ronald Hoffman, *A Spirit of Dissension: Economic, Politics, and the Revolution in Maryland* (Baltimore and London, 1973); and Edward C. Papenfuse, "The Legislative Response to a Costly War: Fiscal Policy and Factional Politics in Maryland, 1777–1789," in Hoffman and Albert, eds., *Sovereign States in an Age of Uncertainty*, 134–56.

29.   Quoted in Ralph V. Harlow, "Aspects of Revolutionary Finance, 1775–1783," *American Historical Review*, 35 (1929), 62–63.

30.   This point is well developed in Roger H. Brown, *Redeeming the Republic*, 32–138.

31.   Wood, *Creation of the American Republic*, 363–76. Here as elsewhere, in my view, Wood's illuminating account of the directions in which American thought was moving after 1776 pays insufficient attention to the specific issues of public policy to which both public officials and their constituents were responding. See Jack N. Rakove, "Gordon S. Wood, the 'Republican Synthesis,' and the Path Not Taken," *WMQ*, 44 (1987), 617–22.

32.   In his letter to Caleb Wallace, for example, Madison indicated his familiarity with the contrary positions of Bacon and Kames on the merits of chancery jurisdiction; *Papers of Madison*, VIII, 353, 357 n. 6.

33. *Federalist* 10 and 53, *Doc Hist.*, XIII, 177, XVI, 100 ("primeval formation"); *Papers of Madison*, IX, 353 (for "pestilent" legislation).
34. Jonathan Jackson to John Adams, Aug. 10, 1785, Adams Family Papers, Mass. His. Soc. (reel 365). Rush's essay first appeared under the pseudonym "Nestor" in the Philadelphia *Independent Gazeteer*, June 3, 1786; it is reprinted in *Doc. Hist.*, XIII, 46–49.
35. See the discussion of congressional recruitment and tenure in Rakove, *Beginnings of National Politics*, 216–29.
36. Quoted ibid., 231–32.
37. Madison, Vices of the political system, [Apr. 1787], *Papers of Madison*, IX, 354.
38. Ibid.
39. The question of exactly how important this "auxiliary desideratum" was in the overall theory of the extended republic is a recurring point of dispute in Madisonian scholarship. In my view, Paul Rahe goes too far in suggesting that in comparison to the benefits to be derived from extending the sphere, "the procedures designed to encourage the election of men of character and intelligence were a relatively minor concern" for Madison. Rahe, *Republics Ancient and Modern*, 1056–57 n. 60. Rahe ignores the extent to which Madison was concerned with both the popular and the institutional sources of the factional politics he observed in the legislatures. Madison's difficulty (as I argue below) was that he lacked any more precise means of converting the ideal into constitutionally mandated rules for improving the quality of elections and the character of the legislators they were designed to produce.
40. *Records*, I, 48 (quoting Sherman), 50 (in which Gerry suggests a system of popular nomination and legislative election of representatives similar to the procedures used by Rhode Island and Connecticut to elect delegates to Congress).
41. *Records*, I, 48–49.
42. *Records*, I, 48–49, 56, 132–35.
43. *Records*, I, 146–47.
44. *Federalist* 10, *Doc. Hist.*, XIV, 180.
45. *Records*, II, 179, 239–40.
46. Zagarri, *Politics of Size*, 46–53.
47. *Records*, II, 240–41. Cf. the speech of Theophilus Parsons in the Massachusetts ratifying convention, defending this power on the grounds that state legislatures might regulate the election of representatives in ways that "would render the rights of the people insecure and of little value. They might make an unequal and partial division of the states into districts for the election of representatives, or they might even disqualify one third of the electors." *Elliot's Debates*, II, 27. For Madison's prior thoughts on this point, see his Aug 23, 1785 letter to Caleb Wallace, *Papers of Madison*, VIII, 353–54.
48. Zagarri, *Politics of Size*, 105–50, carries this story down to the congressional law of 1842 requiring representatives to be elected by districts.
49. Mason had originally proposed setting "qualifications of landed property" while "disqualifying all such persons as are indebted to, or have unsettled accounts with the United States." *Records*, II, 121–26.
50. *Records*, II, 151, 153, 163–64, 178–79. The idea of suffrage requirements was first mentioned on the 26th by Morris, who observed that "If qualifications are proper, he wd. prefer them in the electors rather than the elected."
51. *Records*, II, 201–10, 215–16, 225. Madison agonized over this question all his life, eventually coming to the conclusion that his position in 1787 had been too severe, though not improper in principle. See the discussion in Drew McCoy, *The Last of the Fathers*, 194–98.
52. *Records*, II, 201–5.

53. *Records*, II, 248–49.
54. *Records*, II, 248–50.
55. *Records*, I, 20, 217.
56. *Records*, II, 216–19.
57. *Records*, I, 371–74, 385, 426–49; II, 180, 290–92.
58. *Records*, II, 235–39, 268–73.
59. *Records*, II, 283–89 (quotations at 284, 288), 489–92.
60. *Records*, II, 553–54. It is not clear whether this motion was concerned with the original size of the House or the scale to be used for subsequent reapportionment, or both. Its author, Hugh Williamson, had indicated on September 5 that he would move to reconsider "the number of Representatives, which he thought too small," but he also noted that he thought the single member allowed Rhode Island in the initial allotment inadequate. Ibid., 511. The Convention could, of course, have expanded the initial membership of the House to assuage fears that it would immediately take on too "high-toned" a cast, while trusting to a formula limiting the later expansion of its membership.
61. *Records*, II, 643–44. On several occasions Madison recorded how Washington had voted within the delegation.
62. *Records*, II, 638.
63. On this point I find the argument for Smith's authorship presented in Robert H. Webking, "Melancton Smith and the *Letters from the Federal Farmer*," *WMQ*, 44 (1987), 510–28, persuasive. Gordon S. Wood first challenged the traditional identification of Richard H. Lee as the "Farmer" in "The Authorship of the *Letters from the Federal Farmer*," ibid., 31 (1974), 299–308; for further discussion, see Storing, *Complete Anti-Fed.*, II, 215–16. Of course, Smith could simply have appropriated the "Farmer's" arguments, but as Webking notes, the formulations used by both seem too close to suggest mere borrowing. In the following paragraphs I refer to both the "Federal Farmer" and Smith in order to clarify the separate sources of quotations.
64. Smith, June 20, 1788, *Complete Anti-Fed.*, VI, 154. Because the relevant volumes of the *Documentary History of Ratification* project that would cover both the publication of the *Additional Number of Letters from the Federal Farmer* (New York, 1788) and the debates in the Poughkeepsie Convention have not yet appeared, I will cite to *Complete Anti-Fed.* in the following paragraphs.
65. "Federal Farmer," II, *Complete Anti-Fed.*, II, 230; "Brutus," III, *New York Journal*, Nov. 15, 1787, *Doc. Hist.*, XIV, 122.
66. Smith, June 21, 1788, Complete Anti-Fed., VI, 157.
67. "Federal Farmer," III, ibid., II, 235.
68. "Federal Farmer," VII, ibid., 266.
69. "Federal Farmer," VII, ibid., 266–68; cf. Smith's speech of June 21, 1788, ibid., VI, 159–60.
70. "Federal Farmer," X, ibid., II, 285.
71. "Federal Farmer," VII, ibid., 267, 269.
72. Ibid., VI, 157–8; cf. letter IX, ibid., II, 276.
73. "Federal Farmer," XII, ibid., 294–301. In the New York convention, Smith proposed an amendment to the Constitution stipulating "that each state shall be divided into as many districts as the representatives it is entitled to, and that each representative shall be chosen by a majority of votes." *Elliot's Debates*, II, 327.
74. "Cornelius," *New Hampshire Chronicle*, Dec. 18, 1787, in *Complete Anti-Fed.*, IV, 143.
75. "Federal Farmer," XII, ibid., II, 299.
76. "Federal Farmer," VII, ibid., 265.
77. Smith, June 21, 1788, ibid., VI, 159, 157.

78. "Federal Farmer," XI, ibid., II, 291–2.

79. "Cincinnatus," IV, and "Brutus," III, *New York Journal*, Nov. 22 and 15, 1787, in *Doc. Hist.*, XIV, 189, 124.

80. General Heath, Jan. 15, 1788, *Elliot's Debates*, II, 13.

81. *Federalist* 10, and "Federal Farmer," III, both in *Doc. Hist.*, XIV, 180, 32.

82. "Federal Farmer," IX, Storing, *Complete Anti-Fed.*, II, 277–8; Madison, July 10, 1787, *Records*, I, 568–69.

83. As Samuel H. Beer has succinctly put it: "As increasing diversity breaks down parochialism, the opportunity is widened for rational deliberation to perceive common problems and to discover common solutions for them. In sum, as a decline in pluralism diminishes the influence of reason, an increase heightens it and raises the prospect of agreement on the public interest." Beer, *To Make a Nation*, 261.

84. *Federalist* 10, *Doc. Hist.*, XIV, 179. Fisher Ames made the same point in the Massachusetts convention. "Much has been said about the people divesting themselves of power, when they delegate it to representatives; and that all representation is to their disadvantage, because it is but an image, a copy, fainter and more imperfect than the original, the people, in whom the light of power is primary and unborrowed, which is only reflected by their delegates. I cannot agree to either of these opinions. The representation of the people is something more than the people." *Elliot's Debates*, II, 8.

85. *Doc. Hist.*, XVI, 112.

86. One obvious objection to this argument is that merchants importing manufactures from overseas might have rather different interests from those vending domestic products. But Hamilton's argument can be seen as peculiarly framed for the postwar economy in which the large-scale dumping of British imports and the use of direct auction sales provided a basis for American merchants and artisans to have common cause.

87. *Federalist* 35, *Doc. Hist.*, XV, 270–1. The thought is briefly pursued in the opening paragraphs of the next essay.

88. *Doc Hist.*, XV 272.

89. *Federalist* 36, *Doc. Hist.*, XV, 303.

90. *Federalist* 46, *Doc. Hist.*, XV, 490.

91. *Doc. Hist.*, XVI, 100–1.

92. *Doc. Hist.*, XVI, 235.

93. Compare, for example, the quotation from *Federalist* 46 in the preceding paragraph with Madison's letter to Jefferson of Oct. 24, 1787, *Papers of Madison*, IX, 211.

94. Madison to Randolph, Mar. 1, 1789, and to Jefferson, Mar. 29, 1789, *Papers of Madison*, XI, 453, XII, 38. I discuss this transition from theoretical prediction to practice in "The Structure of Politics at the Accession of George Washington," in Beeman et al., eds., *Beyond Confederation*, 261–94.

95. *Federalist* 55, *Doc. Hist.*, XVI, 111–12.

96. *Federalist* 58, *Doc. Hist.*, XVI, 157.

97. *Federalist* 56, *Doc. Hist.*, XVI, 131; and see the earlier discussion in *Federalist* 53, ibid., 100.

98. *Federalist* 53, *Doc. Hist.*, XVI, 99–100; William Maclaine, speech of July 24, 1788 (N.C.), *Elliot's Debates*, IV, 29.

99. *Federalist* 56, *Doc. Hist.*, XVI, 130–31.

100. *Federalist* 52, *Doc. Hist.*, XVI, 84.

101. Ford, ed., *Pamphlets*, 170.

102. Jay, June 23, 1788, *Elliot's Debates*, II, 283.

103. "Landholder," IV, in *Doc. Hist.*, XIV, 233.

104. *Doc. Hist.*, IX, 1122, 1025.

105. *Elliot's Debates*, II, 275–6.
106. *Elliot's Debates*, II, 265–6.
107. *Doc. Hist.*, IX, 1147–48.
108. "Brutus," VI, *Doc. Hist.*, XV, 113–14.
109. Wood, *Creation of the American Republic*, 506–18.

CHAPTER IX CREATING THE PRESIDENCY

1. Pierce Butler to Weedon Butler, May 5, 1788, *Records*, III, 302. Yet Butler was the only delegate to propose giving the executive "a power to suspend any legislative act" for a limited term, or to argue that the power to make war could be safely vested in the president alone; ibid., I, 103–4, II, 318.
2. Madison to Jefferson, Oct. 24, 1787, *Papers of Madison*, X, 208.
3. This is itself, and necessarily, only the crudest summary of the complex argument developed in Harvey C. Mansfield, Jr., *Taming the Prince: The Ambivalence of Modern Executive Power* (New York, 1989), xv-20 (for essential definitions); and see idem, "The Ambivalence of Executive Power," in Joseph M. Bessette and Jeffrey Tulis, eds., *The Presidency in the Constitutional Order* (Baton Rouge and London, 1981), 314–33.
4. In this discussion I rely primarily on M. J. C. Vile, *Constitutionalism and the Separation of Powers* (Oxford, 1967), which should be read in conjunction with the other leading study, W. B. Gwyn, *The Meaning of the Separation of Powers: An Analysis of the Doctrine from Its Origin to the Adoption of the United States Constitution* (New Orleans, 1965 [Tulane Studies in Political Science, IX]).
5. I ignore the distinction between mixed government and mixed monarchy emphasized in Corinne Weston, *English Constitutional Theory and the House of Lords, 1556–1832* (London, 1965), esp. 29–41, largely because it carries a degree of refinement unnecessary to explain the American point of departure.
6. Vile, *Constitutionalism*, 98–99.
7. Ibid., 37–58 (quotation at 43).
8. Ibid., 28–32, 54–6.
9. Brewer, *Sinews of Power*, 3–24.
10. Vile, *Constitutionalism*, 58; Gwyn, *Meaning of Separation of Powers*, 70. The question of whether Locke should be regarded as a theorist of separated powers remains controversial. Peter Laslett maintains that Locke "cannot be said to have contemplated" anything resembling the understanding of separated powers for which Montesquieu and the American constitution writers professed to find inspiration in his writings. John Locke, *Two Treatises of Government*, Peter Laslett, ed., 2d. ed. amended (Cambridge, Eng., 1970), 117–21. Vile and Gwyn both argue (in my view convincingly) that Locke's awareness of prior writings developing this idea support the conclusion that the relevant passages of the *Second Treatise* can indeed be read as part of the evolution of this doctrine.
11. Locke, *Two Treatises*, 364–66 (chap. XII, sect. 143–48, "Of the Legislative, Executive, and Federative Power of the Commonwealth"), 369, 374–80 (chap. XIV "Of Prerogative"). For discussion, see Vile, *Constitutionalism*, 58–68; Gwyn, *Meaning of Separation of Powers*, 66–81, and Mansfield, *Taming the Prince*, 181–211, who makes the strongest case for Locke's significance as a theorist of executive power.
12. Gwyn, *Meaning of Separation of Powers*, 78–80. Locke's position has to be understood within the context of the use of the prerogative of dispensation to extend toleration to both Catholics and nonconforming Protestant dissenters, against the provisions of the Test Act. Richard Ashcraft, *Revolutionary Politics and Locke's Two Treatises of Government* (Princeton, 1986), 479ff.

13. On this point see especially Ralph Ketcham, *Presidents Above Party: The First American Presidency, 1789–1829* (Chapel Hill, 1984), 51–68.

14. Montesquieu, *Spirit of the Laws*, bk. XI, chap. 6 (reprinted in *Founders' Constitution*, I, 624–25). In his first tripartite definition, Montesquieu equated the first form of the executive with Locke's federative power and the second with the administration of justice, seemingly excluding nonjudicial functions from the domain of internal executive power. His second set of definitions seem concerned with domestic governance alone. In effect, as Vile notes, Montesquieu identifies four (not three) forms of power, three of which are in one sense or another executive. Vile, *Constitutionalism*, 86–90.

15. On the status of the ministry in this period, see the general discussion in Betty Kemp, *King and Commons, 1660–1832* (London, 1959), 113–40; for administrative changes, Brewer, *Sinews of Power*, 64–87.

16. Vile, *Constitutionalism*, 96–7.

17. Bailyn, *Origins of American Politics*, 66–70.

18. [Adams], *Thoughts on Government* (1776); Virginia Constitution of 1776; both in *Founders' Constitution*, I, 109, 7. Justices of the peace were exempted from this prohibition.

19. Vile, *Constitutionalism* 119; and idem., "The Separation of Powers," in Jack Greene and J. R. Pole, eds., *Blackwell Encyclopedia of the American Revolution* (Cambridge, Mass., and Oxford, Eng., 1991), 678 (an excellent short statement); Wood, *Creation of the American Republic*, 157. The statement of this theory in the Virginia constitution marks the transition from the opening denunciation of the various acts of tyranny ascribed to George III to the substantive provisions of the constitution proper.

20. Wood, *Creation of the American Republic*, 132–50; for a somewhat different view, emphasizing that the constitution writers did not go even further, see Adams, *First American Constitutions*, 271–75.

21. Jefferson's ideas and their relation to the constitution of 1776 can be traced in Boyd, ed., *Papers of Jefferson*, I, 329–86; for the passages relating to the executive (or "Administrator"), see 341–42, 349–50, 359–60, and 380 (for the clause as adopted).

22. Livingston to Baron van der Capellen, Nov. 18, 1783, in Prince, ed., *Papers of Livingston*, V, 56–57; Madison to Caleb Wallace, Aug. 23, 1785, *Papers of Madison*, VIII, 351.

23. The question of whether councils still exercised appellate judicial functions deserves further examination, which the research of Mary Bilder will provide.

24. Bailyn, *Ideological Origins*, 275–79; Wood, *Creation of the American Republic*, 208–14.

25. New Hampshire, Massachusetts, New Jersey, and South Carolina had higher requirements for candidates; New York for electors; and Maryland and North Carolina for both. Adams, *First American Constitutions*, appendix, 293 307.

26. One can nicely survey this spectrum of opinion in the pamphlets reprinted in *American Political Writing*, I: [Adams], *Thoughts on Government*, 405; Braxton, *An Address to the Convention . . . of Virginia* (Williamsburg, 1776), 336–37; *Four Letters on Interesting Subjects* (Philadelphia, 1776), 385–86; and *The People the Best Governors: Or a Plan of Government Founded on the Just Principles of Natural Freedom* ([Hartford], 1776), 393–94.

27. Wood, *Creation of the American Republic*, 138–39.

28. Countryman, *A People in Revolution*, 167–69; Bernard Mason, *The Road to Independence: The Revolutionary Movement in New York, 1773–1777* (Lexington Ky., 1966), 213–49; and see the general survey in Charles C. Thach, Jr., *The Creation of the Presidency, 1775–1789* ([reprint] New York, 1969), 25–54. For the Massachusetts constitution of 1780, see *Founders' Constitution*, I, 17–19.

29. Madison to Caleb Wallace, August 23, 1785, *Papers of Madison*, VIII, 350–52.

30. Morris to Committee of Secret Correspondence, Dec. 16, 1776, and to John Jay, Feb. 4, 1777, in Smith, ed., *Letters of Delegates*, V, 609, VI, 216. See the discussion in

Rakove, *Beginnings of National Politics*, 198–205. For further comments on the presidency of Congress, see Jillson and Wilson, *Congressional Dynamics*, 76–88.

31.   Louis Fisher, "The Efficiency Side of Separated Powers," *Journal of American Studies*, 5 (1971), 113–31.

32.   Jay to Jefferson, Aug. 18, 1786, Boyd, ed., *Papers of Jefferson*, X, 272. For a short summary of Jay's career, see Richard B. Morris, *Witnesses at the Creation: Hamilton, Madison, Jay, and the Constitution* (New York, 1985), 142–60. There is no good scholarly biography.

33.   Madison to Washington, Apr. 16, 1787, *Papers of Madison*, IX, 385. On this issue, at least, his thinking seems to have evolved little if at all since 1785, when his letter to Caleb Wallace was nearly as tentative in its discussion of executive power.

34.   Sherman, June 1, *Records*, I, 65.

35.   Two excellent collections of scholarly essays on the origins of particular aspects of presidential power are Bessette and Tulis, eds., *Presidency in the Constitutional Order*, and Thomas E. Cronin, ed., *Inventing the American Presidency* (Lawrence, Kan., 1989), parts I ("Structure") and II ("Powers").

36.   *Records*, I, 21. The language of Article 8 suggests that in the national review of state legislation, the council of revision would act after the legislature had decided to veto a state law; a dissent by the council from the veto would "amount to a rejection" unless overridden by a supermajority in the legislature. In his April 1787 letters to Randolph and Washington, Madison had alluded to a council of revision "including the great ministerial officers" while omitting any mention of a judicial role. At that point Madison seems to have supposed that the "national supremacy" was to be imposed on the "Judiciary departments" of the states rather than vested in something resembling a Supreme Court, though he did believe that "some national tribunals" would be required. *Papers of Madison*, IX, 370, 384–85.

37.   *Records*, I, 64–66.

38.   *Records*, I, 66–69, 96–97.

39.   *Records*, 97–104, 138–40. Madison and Wilson renewed the issue of the council of revision immediately after the committee of the whole approved Gerry's amendment on June 4; but at the request of Hamilton, debate was postponed until Wednesday the sixth. There is some question whether the lengthy speech that Madison recorded himself giving on June 6 was presented on the fourth, the sixth, or conceivably divided between the two days.

40.   One further debate took place on June 9, when Gerry offered an amendment to have the national executive selected by the state executives; but this was vigorously criticized by Randolph and then roundly rejected. *Records*, I, 175–76.

41.   The consensus on this point is striking, not only because the New Jersey Plan and the draft that Dickinson prepared in mid-June both envisioned a plural executive but also because Hamilton's concurrent defense of the British constitution in his speech of June 18 could have triggered all the fears of the "foetus of monarchy" that Randolph had voiced at the outset. *Records*, I, 244; Hutson, ed., *Supplement*, 87, 90–91.

42.   July 17, *Records*, II, 29.

43.   Morris and Wilson (July 17), Madison (July 19 and 25), *Records*, II, 29–30, 56–57, 110–11.

44.   Mason (July 17), and Madison (July 19), *Records*, II, 31, 57. Pinckney did raise the specter of the people being "led by a few active & designing men" (July 17), ibid., II, 30.

45.   *Records*, I, 80; II, 55–59. The best account of the creation of the electoral college is Shlomo Slonim, "The Electoral College at Philadelphia: The Evolution of an Ad Hoc Congress for the Selection of a President," *Journal of American History*, 73 (1986), 35–58.

46.   *Records*, II, 95, 99–101 (July 24).

47.   *Records*, II, 118–21.

48.   July 26, *Records*, II, 119–20.

49. King, July 19, echoing Sherman, July 17, *Records*, II, 55–56, 33–34; and for the votes on these two dates, ibid., 33, 58.
50. *Records*, II, 33–36 (July 17).
51. *Records*, II, 64–69 (quoting Madison at 65). See the fine study by Peter C. Hoffer and N. E. H. Hull, *Impeachment in America, 1635–1805* (New Haven and London, 1984), 96–106.
52. *Records*, II, 52 (Morris, July 19).
53. *Records*, II, 78 (Mason), 52 (Morris, July 19), 30 (Wilson, July 17).
54. *Records*, II, 74, restating the point he had made in his speech of June 6, ibid., I, 138–39.
55. *Records*, II, 73 (Ellsworth), 74 (Madison), 76 (Morris), and see Madison's speeches of June 4 and 6, ibid., I, 99–100, 138.
56. *Records*, II, 76.
57. *Records*, II, 75 (Strong), 80 (Rutledge), and see the similar remarks of Gerry, Gorham, and Martin during this debate.
58. *Records*, II, 183; the last provision was borrowed from Article IX of the Confederation.
59. *Records*, II, 171–72.
60. *Records*, II, 296–301. The provision for an override by two-thirds of both houses was restored only on September 12, on a close vote of six states to four with one divided; ibid., 585–87.
61. The meaning of all the remarks uttered during this debate has been subject to intensive scrutiny in recent years as a function of ongoing controversy over the extent of the executive authority to undertake military action without the approval of Congress and the constitutional status and practicality of the War Powers Act of 1973. The best historical examination of this debate can be found in Charles A. Lofgren, "War-making Under the Constitution: The Original Understanding," *Yale Law Journal*, 81 (1972), 672–702, reprinted in Lofgren, *"Government by Reflection and Choice": Constitutional Essays on War, Foreign Relations and Federalism* (New York, 1986), 3–38.
62. *Records*, II, 318–19 (Ellsworth).
63. *Records*, II, 392–94; for a more detailed discussion, see Jack N. Rakove, "Solving a Constitutional Puzzle: The Treatymaking Clause as a Case Study," *Perspectives in American History*, n.s. 1 (1984), 240–42.
64. *Records*, II, 401–07, 473.
65. *Records*, II, 493–95.
66. *Records*, II, 501–2, 511–13 (quoting Randolph).
67. Sept. 6, *Records*, II, 522–24.
68. Sherman and King, Sept. 5, *Records*, II, 512–14.
69. *Records*, II, 527.
70. *Records*, II, 513 (Madison), 501 (Williamson, Wilson).
71. *Records*, II, 538–40.
72. Sept. 7, *Records*, II, 540–41.
73. Sept. 7, *Records*, II, 538, 540–41.
74. *Records*, II, 540–41, 547–50.
75. On "sacrifice," see Gerry's remarks on Sept. 7, *Records*, II, 541. For a more sustained exposition of this point, see Rakove, "Solving a Constitutional Puzzle," 267ff.
76. For a succinct summary by the leading historian of late-eighteenth-century British politics, see Ian Christie, "Great Britain in the Aftermath of the American Revolution," in Greene and Pole, eds., *Blackwell Encyclopedia of the American Revolution*, 490–94.
77. This is the general argument of Ketcham, *Presidents Above Party*.

78.   *Records*, II, 638–39; this passage also appears in the fourth letter of the Anti-Federalist writer "Cato," *New York Journal*, Nov. 8, 1787, which appeared two weeks before the *Mass. Centinel* first published Mason's objections; *Doc. Hist.*, XIV, 9, 150.

79.   *Records*, II, 541–42.

80.   *Records*, II, 224.

81.   *Records*, I, 150, 153 (Dickinson, June 7), 510–14 (Morris, July 2).

82.   *Records*, II, 637–40; this text, originally written on Mason's copy of the text of the Constitution printed for the Convention on Sept. 12, differs slightly from the manuscript copy he later circulated, as printed in *Doc. Hist.*, XIII, 346–51.

83.   Dissent of the Minority, Dec. 18, 1787, *Doc. Hist.*, II, 634–5; "Federal Farmer," III, *Complete Anti-Fed.*, II, 237–38.

84.   "Federal Farmer," XI, *Complete Anti-Fed.*, II, 287–88.

85.   Henry, June 9, 1788, *Doc. Hist.*, IX, 1062–63.

86.   "Federal Farmer," XIII, Storing, *Complete Anti-Fed.*, II, 304.

87.   The parenthetical passage at the close of this sentence ends with the ambiguous and possibly garbled phrase "the offspring of absurdity and locality." *Complete Anti-Fed.*, II, 115.

88.   *Va. Independent Chronicle*, Jan. 9, 1788, in *Doc. Hist.*, VIII, 287.

89.   "An Old Whig," V, Philadelphia *Independent Gazetteer*, Nov. 1, 1787, *Doc. Hist.*, XIII, 542.

90.   June 5, 1788, *Doc. Hist.*, IX, 964.

91.   "Federal Farmer," XIV, Storing, *Complete Anti-Fed.*, II, 312–13.

92.   *Elliot's Debates*, II, 109.

93.   *Complete Anti-Fed.*, II, 301–14; the discussion of the veto appears in the final paragraph. One of the best Anti-Federalist discussions of the veto can be found in "The Impartial Examiner," IV, but this essay was printed relatively late, in the *Virginia Independent Chronicle* of June 11, 1788.

94.   Mason, June 17, 1788, *Doc. Hist.*, X, 1365.

95.   Mason and Henry, June 18, 1788, *Doc. Hist.*, X, 1381.

96.   *Doc. Hist.*, X, 1383.

97.   "An American Citizen," Philadelphia *Independent Gazetteer*, Sept. 26, 1787, *Doc. Hist.*, XIII, 249–51.

98.   A Native of Virginia, *Observations upon the Proposed Plan of Federal Government* (Petersburg, Va., 1788), in *Doc. Hist.*, IX, 679.

99.   Thus Alexander C. Hanson suggested that "The senate will, in all human likelihood, consist of the most important characters, men of enlightened minds, mature in judgment, independent in their circumstances, and not deriving their principal subsistence from their pay"—but the point of this description was to justify the advantage of the Senate as an advisory and appointive council to the president, as opposed to the distinct executive council sought by Mason and other Anti-Federalists. *Remarks on the Proposed Plan*, in *Doc. Hist.*, XV, 529.

This is an appropriate place to note a recent work that I find quite flattering but perversely wrongheaded: Elaine K. Swift, "The Making of an American House of Lords: The U.S. Senate in the Constitutional Convention of 1787," *Studies in American Political Development*, 7 (1993), 177–224, which argues that the framers really did intend the Senate to be an Americanized version of the upper chamber of Parliament. Though her reasoning is unpersuasive, Swift earns my profound thanks for this sentence: "If, according to Madison, Tocqueville, Rakove, and others, the Senate was to be a representative of the states, why did the Framers act to effectively minimize any influence states might have over Senators?" (ibid., 180).

100. "Fabius," II, Ford, ed., *Pamphlets*, 173.

101. [Coxe] "An American Citizen," I, Philadelphia *Independent Gazetteer*, Sept. 26, 1787; "Cassius," I, *Va. Independent Chronicle*, April 2, 1788; A Native of Virginia, *Observations upon the Proposed Plan*, in *Doc. Hist.*, XIII, 250, IX, 644, 669. "Cassius" followed Coxe's phrasing: With the veto the president "may entreat both houses to calmly reconsider any point, on which he may entertain doubts, and feel apprehensions."

102. *Doc. Hist.*, II, 341.

103. "Centinel," II, Oct. 24, 1787, *Doc. Hist.*, XIII, 465; see Lee's proposed amendments to the Constitution, Sept. 27, 1787, ibid., 239.

104. A Native of Virginia, Apr. 2, 1788, *Doc. Hist.*, IX, 679–80.

105. [Hanson], *Remarks on the Proposed Plan*, in *Doc. Hist.*, XV, 529.

106. [James Iredell], "Marcus," Answer to Mr. Mason's Objections, II, *Norfolk and Portsmouth Journal*, Feb. 27, 1788, *Doc. Hist.*, XVI, 243–47.

107. Iredell (as "Marcus"), ibid.; Henry, June 12, 1788, ibid., X, 1220–21.

108. *Doc. Hist.*, II, 566, alluding to John Smilie's remark of December 6, ibid., 508.

109. Although it could be argued that the famous passage "Ambition must be made to counteract ambition[; t]he interest of the man must be connected with the constitutional rights of the place," applies best to the judiciary, the one branch whose members have a life interest in their office; *Federalist* 51, *Doc. Hist.*, XVI, 44–45. For "impetuous vortex," see *Federalist* 48, ibid., 4; and cf. Madison's speech of July 21, *Records*, II, 74.

110. *Doc. Hist.*, XV, 343, 499–500.

111. The first quotation appears in *Federalist* 51, the second in *Federalist* 48; *Doc. Hist.*, XVI, 44, 4–5; Peden, ed., *Notes on Virginia*, 120.

112. *Federalist* 49 and 50, *Doc. Hist.*, XVI, 16–19 (quotation at 16), 29–31.

113. *Federalist* 51, *Doc. Hist.*, XVI, 45–47.

114. *Federalist* 48, *Doc. Hist.*, XVI, 5.

115. *Doc. Hist.*, XVI, 355, 413 (I have compressed the phrasing), 448–50.

116. He devoted *Federalist* 67 largely to refuting the specious claim that the president could appoint senators when the Senate itself was in recess. When he compared the presidency with the British crown and the state governorships in *Federalist* 69, anxiety about the prospects for ratification in New York clearly led him to make its governorship the touchstone for his analysis, and he pursued the same comparison while discussing the power of appointment in *Federalist* 77.

117. *Federalist* 70, *Doc. Hist.*, XVI, 396. I follow the usage in the printed McLean edition, which excised the adverbs ("firstly" etc.) with which Hamilton listed each of these qualities.

118. *Federalist* 70, *Doc. Hist.*, XVI, 398–99, 401.

119. *Federalist* 71, *Doc. Hist.*, XVI, 412.

120. *Federalist* 72, *Doc. Hist.*, XVI, 422–23; and see Stourzh, *Hamilton and the Idea of Republican Government*, chap. III (especially pp. 99–106), and the title essay in Colbourn, ed., *Fame and the Founding Fathers*, 3–26.

121. *Doc. Hist.*, XVI, 423–24.

122. *Doc. Hist.*, XVI, 482–83. Locke's federative power is a broader construct than treaty making per se, because it embraces the entire corpus of international relations, including all those matters where the absence of a common sovereign places nations in a mutual condition resembling the state of nature. By contrast, Hamilton is concerned in this essay with building legal agreements among nations.

123. *The Federalist*, Benjamin Wright, ed. (Cambridge, 1961), 481–85 (cited here because the published volumes of Jensen, Kaminski, and Saladino, eds., *Doc. Hist.*, have not yet reached the final essays of *The Federalist*). For further discussion of the removal power,

which occasioned the first constitutional debate in the new Congress, see pp. 347–50, below.

124. Hamilton, Conjectures about the new Constitution, [Sept. 1787], *Doc. Hist.*, XIII, 277–78.

CHAPTER X RIGHTS

1. *Records*, II, 587–88. Gerry offered the motion only after Mason suggested he would second such a proposal if another delegate made it.

2. Mary Ann Glendon, *Rights Talk: The Impoverishment of Political Discourse* (New York, 1991), x.

3. The best-known exposition of this view arguably is Ronald Dworkin, *Taking Rights Seriously* (Cambridge, 1977).

4. Thomas Haskell, "The Curious Persistence of Rights Talk in the 'Age of Interpretation,'" *Journal of American History*, 74 (1987), 984–1012.

5. For these phrases, see Madison to Richard Peters, Aug. 19, 1789; and to Jefferson, Oct. 17, 1788; *Papers of Madison*, XII, 346, XI, 297. For a general narrative history, see Robert A. Rutland, *The Birth of the Bill of Rights, 1776–1791* (Chapel Hill, 1955).

6. Levy's writings in this vein include *Origins of the Fifth Amendment: The Right against Self-Incrimination* (New York, 1968), and *Emergence of a Free Press* (New York, 1985), a significantly revised version of his *Legacy of Suppression: Freedom of Speech and Press in Early American History* (Cambridge, 1960). Levy summarizes many of his findings about rights in *Original Intent and the Framers' Constitution* (New York, 1988). Two useful collections of essays are Jon Kukla, ed., *The Bill of Rights: A Lively Heritage* (Richmond, 1987); and Eugene W. Hickok, Jr., ed., *The Bill of Rights: Original Meaning and Current Understanding* (Charlottesville, 1991), which is ideologically weighted toward conservative interpretations and somewhat uneven in quality. The Second Amendment has become the most hotly contested battleground for this kind of approach; see Joyce Malcolm, *To Keep and Bear Arms: The Origins of an Anglo-American Right* (Cambridge, 1994).

7. See the essays collected in Randy E. Barnett, ed., *The Rights Retained by the People: The History and Meaning of the Ninth Amendment* (Fairfax, Va., 1989). Closely related to, but in some senses distinct from the question of the original meaning of the Ninth Amendment, is the problem pursued by Thomas Grey and Suzanna Sherry in complementary articles on the relation between ideas of fundamental law, written constitutionalism, and judicial review: Grey, "Do We Have an Unwritten Constitution?," *Stanford Law Review*, 27 (1975), 703–18; idem., "Origins of the Unwritten Constitution: Fundamental Law in American Revolutionary Thought," ibid., 30 (1978), 843–93; and Sherry, "The Founders' Unwritten Constitution," *University of Chicago Law Review*, 54 (1987), 1127–77. Although these essays have influenced my general approach in this chapter, the argument of this chapter draws more directly on other sources cited below and my particular interest in making sense of Madison's reservations about bills of rights.

8. Or as Professors Lerner and Kurland put it, "From the beginning, it seems, the language of America has been the language of rights." *Founders' Constitution*, I, 424.

9. "Liberty fascinated eighteenth-century English-speaking people as much as an abstraction as a practical constitutional principle. . . . The extent to which eighteenth-century legal, constitutional, and political commentators discussed liberty in the abstract is simply amazing." John Phillip Reid, *The Concept of Liberty in the Age of the American Revolution* (Chicago, 1988), 11, 32–38 (relation of liberty to licentiousness). For other discussions of this point, see Bailyn, *Ideological Origins*, 55–93; and Linda Colley, *Britons: Forging the Nation, 1707–1837* (New Haven and London, 1992), 30–54. Montesquieu's

definition appears at the beginning of the discussion of the English constitution in *Spirit of the Laws*, book XI, chap. 6, excerpted in *Founders' Constitution*, I, 624.

10.   Art. I of the Pennsylvania Declaration of Rights, 1776, *Founders' Constitution*, V, 6, which slightly revises the formula of the Virginia Declaration: "the enjoyment of life and liberty, with the means of acquiring and possessing property, and pursuing and obtaining happiness and safety," and which was in turn modestly revised in the Massachusetts Declaration of 1780: "the right of enjoying and defending their lives and liberties; that of acquiring, possessing, and protecting property; in fine, that of seeking and obtaining their safety and happiness." Ibid., I, 6, V, 7.

11.   On this point see especially James H. Hutson, "The Bill of Rights and the American Revolutionary Experience," in Michael J. Lacey and Knud Haakonssen, eds., *A Culture of Rights: The Bill of Rights in Philosophy, Politics, and Law—1791 and 1991* (Cambridge, Eng., 1991), 74–82.

12.   Some of these examples would seem to blur the distinction between right and power; but as Hutson has argued, those words were themselves often closely linked in both usage and conception; ibid., 92–95.

13.   I draw here on the brisk survey of "The Rights of Englishmen" in McDonald, *Novus Ordo Seclorum*, 9–55 (quotations at 29, 40), which provides a wonderful introduction to the subject.

14.   Knud Haakonssen, "From Natural Law to the Rights of Man: A European Perspective on American Debates," in Lacey and Haakonssen, eds., *Culture of Rights*, 61; Hutson, "Bill of Rights," ibid., 62–63. The question of the origins of rights thinking in the political theory and moral philosophy of early modern Europe lies far beyond the scope of this chapter, which is concerned with more explicitly constitutional issues; but in addition to Haakonssen's essay, one could begin with Richard Tuck, *Natural Rights Theories: Their Origin and Development* (Cambridge, Eng., 1979), and two more recent works: A. John Simmons, *The Lockean Theory of Rights* (Princeton, 1992), and Michael P. Zuckert, *Natural Rights and the New Republicanism* (Princeton, 1994). Leo Strauss, *Natural Right and History* (Chicago, 1953) remains, of course, a work of brooding power and controversial effect.

15.   John Phillip Reid, *Constitutional History of the American Revolution*, vol. I, *The Authority of Rights* (Madison, Wis., 1986), 65–66.

16.   Reid, *Authority of Rights*, 237.

17.   Reid, *Concept of Liberty* 60–63.

18.   Reid's emphasis on "The Englishness of [the] Rights" the colonists claimed seems designed to challenge the view, still dearly held in some circles, that natural rights provided the dominant conceptions of the rights that Americans cherished. See Reid's essay, "The Irrelevance of the Declaration," in Hendrik Hartog, ed., *Law in the American Revolution and the American Revolution in the Law* (New York, 1981), 46–89.

19.   Reid, *Authority of Rights*, 66.

20.   Modern lawyers use the term "belt and suspenders" to characterize this form of argumentative overkill. I owe this phrase to Jeffrey Bates.

21.   J. G. A. Pocock, *The Ancient Constitution and the Feudal Law: English Historical Thought in the Seventeenth Century* (Cambridge, Eng., 1957).

22.   McDonald, *Novus Ordo Seclorum*, 40; for a more thorough introduction to this immensely important topic, see Thomas Andrew Green, *Verdict According to Conscience: Perspectives on the English Criminal Trial Jury, 1200–1800* (Chicago, 1985).

23.   See the general discussion in Clive Holmes, "Parliament, Liberty, Taxation, and Property," in J. H. Hexter, ed., *Parliament and Liberty from the Reign of Elizabeth to the English Civil War* (Stanford, 1992), 122–54.

24.   Penn, *England's Present Interest Considered, with Honour to the Prince, and Safety to*

the People (1675); *The Excellent Priviledge of Liberty and Property Being the Birth-Right of the Free-Born Subjects of England* (1687); excerpts from both reprinted in *The Founders' Constitution*, I, 429, 432 (and for quotations in the next paragraph).

25. Green, *Verdict According to Conscience*, 200–64, discusses the origins and implications of this case at some length.

26. I here follow Reid, *Authority of Rights*, 132–38, on the distinction between the (Lockean) social contract and the idea of an original contract of government; I also draw more broadly on the entire discussion of rights derived from migration and colonial contract, ibid., 114–68.

27. Lois G. Schwoerer has recently challenged this interpretation by arguing that the acceptance of the Declaration by William and Mary as a condition of their accession did indeed constitute a substantive change in the nature of kingship, resolving many of the issues of rights that the Stuart crown and its opponents had contested. My concern here, however, is with the subsequent understanding of the document, not its "original meaning." Schwoerer, *The Declaration of Rights, 1689* (Baltimore and London, 1981), 3–7 (for historiography).

28. Ibid. 58ff.

29. The literature on the general topic of the rise of the colonial assemblies and their quarrels with the representatives of the Crown is massive. Two books by Jack P. Greene, the synthetic *Peripheries and Center*, and his great monograph, *The Quest for Power: The Lower Houses of Assembly in the Southern Royal Colonies, 1689–1776* (Chapel Hill, 1963), provide the best introduction. It could of course be argued that the "ancient" rights claimed by Parliament and confirmed to it by the Glorious Revolution were either less venerable or legally secure than their advocates asserted; see Schwoerer, *Declaration of Rights*, 58–101, which surveys the sources of particular claims. In theory this would have made it more difficult for the colonists to claim that equivalent or identical rights had been vested in their assemblies *ab initio*; in practice, both American and English Whigs had good reason not to press their historical scholarship too far, but simply state their claims as given. As Bernard Bailyn has argued, the constitutional sources of political strife in eighteenth-century America can be traced to the retention by Crown authorities in America of prerogative powers that the Glorious Revolution and its aftermath had rendered archaic in Britain; Bailyn, *Origins of American Politics*, chap. II. For a wonderful account of how "rights-talk" functioned in the politics of one particularly disputatious colony, see the chapter on "The Rights of the People," in Richard L. Bushman, *King and People in Provincial Massachusetts* (Chapel Hill, 1985), 88–134; cf. Gary Nash, *Quakers and Politics: Pennsylvania, 1681–1726* (Princeton, 1968), 273–305.

30. Reid, *Concept of Liberty*, 68–73. "Almost everyone in Restoration England felt insecure," one historian has recently argued. "The people were repeatedly gripped by panic fears of popery," while the Crown and its opponents fell equally prey to their respective fears of "rebellion and republicanism" or "absolutism or arbitrary government." J. R. Jones, *Country and Court: England, 1658–1714* (Cambridge, 1978), 3.

31. Montesquieu, *Spirit of the Laws*, Book XI, chap. 6; in *Founders' Constitution*, I, 625, 627. Montesquieu leaves it to the upper chamber of the legislature (the House of Lords) "to moderate the law in favor of the law itself, by mitigating the sentence," bypassing the idea that juries of the vicinage were best prepared to balance legal principle, local custom, and knowledge of the parties and the circumstances of the case.

32. Blackstone, *Commentaries*, I, 259.

33. I draw here on the argument of Shannon C. Stimson, *The American Revolution in the Law: Anglo-American Jurisprudence before John Marshall* (Princeton, 1990), 10–33, a valuable book for my purpose even though it does not directly address the debates of

1787–88. This is an enormously complicated subject, and I make no pretense of having mastered its nuances; my point, again, is to provide a context within which to understand why Americans thought the power of juries to consider law and fact so important. For further discussion, see Green, *Verdict According to Conscience*, 265–355.

34.   On the general problem of judicial tenure, see the editorial headnote to Joseph Galloway's tract, *A Letter to the People of Pennsylvania* (Philadelphia, 1760) in Bernard Bailyn, ed., *Pamphlets of the American Revolution*, (Cambridge, 1965), I, 249–55.

35.   For Dickinson's account of his studies, see H. Trevor Colbourn, ed., "A Pennsylvania Farmer at the Court of King George: John Dickinson's London Letters, 1754–1756," *Pa. Magazine of History and Biography*, 86 (1962).

36.   Richard E. Ellis, *The Jeffersonian Crisis: Courts and Politics in the Young Republic* (New York, 1971), 5–6. In Pennsylvania, justices of the peace "performed singly or in pairs important administrative functions such as assigning servants, authorizing overseers of the poor to levy township poor taxes, judging claims for bounties on predators, and performing marriage ceremonies." Tully, *William Penn's Legacy*, 104–5. In Massachusetts, William Nelson has similarly noted, the quarterly Court of General Sessions "possessed broad supervisory powers over town governments and over the local economy. Sessions courts approved the establishment and alteration of roads and bridges; appointed holders of ferry licenses, liquor licenses, and licenses to sell coffee, tea, and china; approved town bylaws, provided that they were not on subjects regulated by the provincial legislature; supervised town administration of the poor law; punished vagabonds; levied county taxes; approved county accounts and expenditures; regulated the county prisons; and performed a number of other miscellaneous functions. Sessions was, in effect, the county government; the only significant regulatory power it lacked was that of control over public health procedures." Nelson, *Americanization of the Common Law*, 15.

37.   Ibid., 19; Nelson here seems to echo a letter in which Jefferson called for the "strict and inflexible" apportioning of punishments by judges who would act as "mere machine[s]"); Jefferson to Edmund Pendleton, Aug. 26, 1776, Boyd, ed., *Papers of Jefferson*, I, 505.

38.   Nelson, *Americanization of the Common Law*, 18–35.

39.   *Founders' Constitution*, V, 255. Cf. the discussion of Blackstone's attitude toward juries in Lieberman, *Province of Legislation Determined*, 56–60.

40.   For a short account, see Leonard Levy, "Did the Zenger Case Really Matter? Freedom of the Press in Colonial New York," in Levy, *Constitutional Opinions: Aspects of the Bill of Rights* (New York, 1986), 72–79; for more detailed treatment and the documentary record, see Stanley N. Katz, ed., *A Brief Narrative of the Case and Trial of John Peter Zenger*, by James Alexander, 2d ed. (Cambridge, 1972). The English background of jury action in trials for seditious libel is examined in Green, *Verdict According to Conscience*, 318–55.

41.   L. H. Butterfield, ed., *Diary and Autobiography of John Adams* (Cambridge, 1961), II, 3–5.

42.   David T. Konig, "Country Justice: The Rural Roots of Constitutionalism in Colonial Virginia," in Kermit L. Hall and James W. Ely, Jr., *An Uncertain Tradition: Constitutionalism and the History of the South* (Athens, Ga., 1989), 72–73.

43.   "Clarendon," *Boston Gazette*, Jan. 27, 1766, in Taylor, ed., *Papers of Adams*, I, 169.

44.   Braintree Instructions, October 10, 1765, ibid., 141.

45.   The importance of this development in the onset of the Revolution cannot be slighted, for it launched the chain of events that led to the organization of the Boston Committee of Correspondence, the provocative debate between the General Court and Thomas Hutchinson in early 1773, and thus (not entirely indirectly) to the Boston Tea Party and the adoption of the Coercive Acts.

46. [Jefferson], *A Summary View of the Rights of British America* (Williamsburg, 1774), in Boyd, ed., *Papers of Jefferson*, I, 134–35; Rakove, *Beginnings of National Politics*, 35–36.

47. This formulation parallels, I believe, Gordon Wood's efforts to trace the American attachment to republicanism and its promise of "moral reformation" to the contradictory images that the colonists held of themselves, as a people uniquely virtuous, yet also actively in pursuit of the self-interest that republicanism abhorred. This tension was also manifested, Wood argues, in the conflict between a persistent attachment to the norms of virtual representation, and the pressures, apparent from the start, to make the legislatures susceptible to popular will. Wood, *Creation of the American Republic*, 91–124, 178–196.

48. *Four Letters on Interesting Subjects* (Philadelphia, 1776), reprinted in *American Political Writing*, I, 389.

49. The colonists' aversion to the concept of prerogative—that is, to the capacity of the executive "to act according to discretion, for the publick good, without the prescription of the Law, or sometimes even against it" (Locke, *Two Treatises*, ed. Laslett, 375)—may have made it more difficult for them to imagine how legislative authority could be less than plenary.

50. "Demophilus," *The Genuine Principles of the Ancient Saxon, or English Constitution* (Philadelphia, 1776), reprinted in *American Political Writing*, I, 353–54.

51. Ibid., 387; for the Concord resolutions of Oct. 21, 1776, see Handlin and Handlin, eds., *Popular Sources of Political Authority*, 153.

52. [Adams], *Thoughts on Government*, in *American Political Writing*, I, 407; *Four Letters*, ibid., 387.

53. *The People the Best Governors: Or a Plan of Government Founded on the Just Principles of Natural Freedom* ([Hartford], 1776), reprinted ibid., 399–400.

54. Wood, *Creation of the American Republic*, 271. This criticism of Wood was drummed home to me by Professor Reid.

55. Maryland Declaration of Rights, Article IV, Francis N. Thorpe, ed., *The Federal and State Constitutions, Colonial Charters, and Other Organic Laws of the States, Territories, and Colonies . . .* (Washington, D.C., 1909), III, 1687.

56. Pennsylvania, Art. VI, following Virginia, Article 5, *Founders' Constitution*, V, 7, I, 6.

57. Ibid., I, 7. The version of this statement in Article XIV of the Pennsylvania Declaration of Rights implies that these are the traits the people should look for in their officials.

58. *Founders' Constitution*, I, 6–7; compare the prefatory Massachusetts declaration in the constitution of 1780, ibid., 11–14.

59. Lutz, *Popular Consent and Popular Control*, 50.

60. *Founders' Constitution*, I, 6.

61. Levy, *Emergence of a Free Press*, 227; I have omitted Levy's inclusion of "separation of church and state" from this list because that implicates a realm of rights and liberty that remained more controversial.

62. Westminster resolutions, May 15, 1778; Lexington resolutions, June 15, 1778; Handlin and Handlin, eds., *Popular Sources of Political Authority*, 312, 317.

63. Adair, ed., "James Madison's Autobiography," *WMQ*, 2 (1945), 198. On Madison's early views, see his letters to his college friend William Bradford of Dec. 1, 1773; Jan. 23, 1774; and Apr. 1, 1774, *Papers of Madison*, I, 101, 106, 112, 172–75 (for the 1776 Declaration). The progress of disestablishment in Virginia has been studied extensively; see especially Buckley, *Church and State in Revolutionary Virginia, 1776–1787*, and the essays collected in Peterson and Vaughan, eds., *The Virginia Statute for Religious Freedom*.

64. *Papers of Madison*, VIII, 299–304.

65. As the editors of the *Papers of Madison* observe (VIII, 295–99), the signatures to

Madison's *Memorial* numbered less than a fifth of all those collected in the petitions against the assessment submitted to the assembly.

66.   The subject is enormous, and the relevant literature nearly overwhelming. Among recent works that emphasize the relation of American developments to this broader context, see (again) the essays collected in Peterson and Vaughan, eds., *Virginia Statute for Religious Freedom*; Miller, *The First Liberty*; and Leonard Levy, *Blasphemy: Verbal Offense Against the Sacred from Moses to Salman Rushdie* (New York, 1993). For a more general account, emphasizing Britain but with important implications for America, see J. C. D. Clark, *The Language of Liberty, 1660–1832: Political Discourse and Social Dynamics in the Anglo-American World* (Cambridge, Eng., 1994).

67.   On these influences, see White, *Philosophy of the American Revolution*, 195–213; James Tully, *An Approach to Political Philosophy: Locke in Contexts* (Cambridge, Eng., 1993), 57–58.

68.   Michael W. McConnell, "The Origins and Historical Understanding of Free Exercise of Religion," *Harvard Law Review*, 103 (1989–90), 1455–56 and ff.

69.   Boyd, ed., *Papers of Jefferson*, II, 546–47.

70.   Madison to Caleb Wallace, Aug. 23, 1785, ibid., 351–52. Madison here echoes the comments of William Livingston, the venerable New Jersey Whig, writing anonymously as "Scipio" in the *New Jersey Gazette* of June 14, 1784, in defense of fixed salaries for state judges: "[T]he purity of their courts of justice," Livingston wrote of England, "is now perhaps the only remaining band that (amidst the wreck of publick and private virtue) holds together the pillars of that tottering nation." Prince, ed., *Papers of Livingston*, V, 137.

71.   *Papers of Madison*, IX, 353–54.

72.   June 26, 1787, *Records*, I, 422–23; Observations on Jefferson's Draft of a Constitution for Virginia [Oct. 1788], *Papers of Madison*, XI, 287–88. The centrality of Madison's concern with property appears in numerous scholarly accounts of his thinking, but see especially Nedelsky, *Private Property and the Limits of American Constitutionalism*, 16–66.

73.   I do not mean to deny that Madison still *hoped* that a diversity of economic interests would have the same beneficial effects as "a multiplicity of sects," only to suggest that he was more confident that Protestant sectarianism would continue to work in wonderfully divisive ways than he was about the consequences of economic development. Nathan O. Hatch, *The Democratization of American Christianity* (New Haven, 1989) provides a provocative account of the fusion between Jeffersonian-Madisonian principles, on the one hand, and the sectarian creativity of the Second Great Awakening. On Madison's economic ideas, see Drew McCoy, *The Elusive Republic: Political Economy in Jeffersonian America* (Chapel Hill, 1979).

74.   *Federalist* 10, *Doc. Hist.*, 177–78.

75.   Madison to Jefferson, Oct. 24, 1787, *Papers of Madison*, X, 211–12. The point was developed as well in *Federalist* 37 and 48.

76.   Madison to Washington, April 16, 1787, *Papers of Madison*, IX, 383–84.

77.   Hutson, ed., *Supplement*, 183; I have omitted from the quotation alternative phrasing that appears in what was a working draft, including an incomplete parenthetical phrase reading that the "business [of designating the ends of government], if not fitter for the schools, is at least sufficiently executed" in the state constitutions. It is worth noting that this document is found among the papers of George Mason in the Library of Congress.

78.   Hutson, "The Bill of Rights," in Lacey and Haakonssen, eds., *Culture of Rights*, 90.

79.   *Records*, II, 187 (for committee of detail), 341–42 (for Pinckney's resolutions, which also opposed keeping up troops in peacetime except with the consent of Congress; affirmed the superiority of civil to military authority; and banned the peacetime quartering of troops in private houses without the consent of the owner).

80. *Records*, II, 439–40, 597, 619.

81. *Records*, II, 587–88. A final effort on the fifteenth by Gerry and Pinckney to guarantee trial by jury in civil cases also failed; ibid., 628.

82. *Doc. Hist.*, XIII, 348–50 (Mason).

83. For Lee's amendments, see *Doc. Hist.*, XIII, 238–40.

84. *Doc. Hist.*, II, 116, 168–69.

85. *Doc. Hist.*, II, 167–68.

86. For a nearly definitive statement of the Anti-Federalist position, see "Brutus," II, *New York Journal*, Nov. 1, 1787, *Doc. Hist.*, XIII, 524–29.

87. Patrick Henry, June 23, 1788; Mason, June 19, 1788; *Doc. Hist.*, X, 1465–66, 1407; and see Thomas Tredwell in the New York convention, July 2, 1788, *Elliot's Debates*, II, 400.

88. "A Democratic Federalist," *Pennsylvania Herald*, Oct. 17, 1787, in *Doc. Hist.*, XIII, 387–90.

89. *Complete Anti-Fed.*, II, 319; Mason invoked the same usage of court in his June 19, 1788 speech at Richmond; *Doc. Hist.*, X, 1407.

90. Martin, *Genuine Information*, in *Doc. Hist.*, XVI, 9.

91. "Cincinnatus," II, *New York Journal*, Nov. 8, 1787, *Doc. Hist.*, XIV, 13.

92. Phila. *Independent Gazetteer*, Jan. 30, 1788, in *Doc. Hist.*, XV, 506.

93. See the debates of June 19–23, 1788, in *Doc. Hist.*, X, 1398–1466. Two monographs help to place the deep concern of Virginians with these questions in a broader context: F. Thornton Miller, *Juries and Judges versus the Law: Virginia's Provincial Legal Perspective, 1783–1828* (Charlottesville, 1994); and A. G. Roeber, *Faithful Magistrates and Republican Lawyers: Creators of Virginia Legal Culture, 1680–1810* (Chapel Hill, 1981), which, however, has surprisingly little to say about juries.

94. *Complete Anti-Fed.*, II, 320, 249.

95. *Complete Anti-Fed.*, II, 321.

96. "An Old Whig," III, Phila. *Independent Gazetteer*, Oct. 20, 1787, in *Doc. Hist.*, XIII, 427–28.

97. Henry, June 16, 1788, *Doc. Hist.*, X, 1328–32; cf. "Agrippa," *Mass. Gazette*, Jan. 14, 1788, Paul L. Ford, ed., *Essays on the Constitution of the United States, 1787–1788* (Brooklyn, 1892), 95.

98. See Adams's statement endorsing the first of John Hancock's proposed amendments to the Constitution, reserving to the states all powers not explicitly delegated to Congress: This alone was "a summary of a bill of rights," Adams observed. It would give "assurance that, if any law made by the federal government shall extend beyond the power granted by the proposed Constitution, and inconsistent with the constitution of this state, it will be an error, and adjudged by the courts of law to be void." Speech of Feb. 1, 1788, in *Elliot's Debates*, II, 131. For similar views, see "An Old Whig," II, in the Phila. *Independent Gazetteer*, Oct. 17, 1787; and "The Address and Dissent of the Minority of the Convention of the State of Pennsylvania to their Constituents," Dec. 18, 1787; *Doc. Hist.*, XIII, 402; II, 636.

99. Smilie, Nov. 28, 1787, *Doc. Hist.*, II, 392; and see Samuel Spencer in the North Carolina convention, July 28, 1788, *Elliot's Debates*, IV, 137.

100. "Federal Farmer," XVI, *Complete Anti-Fed.*, II, 324–25.

101. "Objections," I, *Norfolk and Portsmouth Journal*, Feb. 20, 1788; "Anti-Cincinnatus," Northampton (Mass.) *Hampshire Gazette*, Dec. 19, 1787; "Landholder," VI, *Conn. Courant*, Dec. 10, 1787; [Iredell], "Marcus," "Answer to Mr. Mason's Objections," *Doc. Hist.*, XV, 37, XIV, 401, XVI, 164.

102. [James Sullivan], "Cassius," *Mass. Gazette*, Dec. 14, 1787, Ford, ed., *Essays*, 28.

103. Wilson, Nov. 28, 1787; Hartley, Nov. 30, 1787, *Doc. Hist.*, II, 383–84, 430.

104. [Iredell], "Answer to Mr. Mason's Objections," *Doc. Hist.*, XVI, 163, 381.

105. See Wilson's widely reported speeches of Nov. 28 and Dec. 4, 1787, *Doc. Hist.*, II, 388, 480.

106. "Civis Rusticus," *Va. Independent Chronicle*, Jan. 30, 1788, *Doc. Hist.*, VIII, 335.

107. "A Countryman," *New Haven Gazette*, Nov. 22, 1787, *Doc. Hist.*, XIV, 173–74.

108. Wright, ed., *The Federalist* (no. 84), 536.

109. Wright, ed., *The Federalist* (no. 83), 521–22.

110. Pierce to St. George Tucker, Sept. 28, 1787, published in the *Gazette of the State of Georgia*, Mar. 20, 1788; *Doc. Hist.*, XVI, 444–45.

111. Wright, ed., *The Federalist* (no. 78), 490–95.

112. Wright, ed., *The Federalist* (no. 78), 496, 491; (no. 84) 535.

113. [Hanson], *Remarks on the Proposed Plan*; Yeates, Nov. 30, 1787, *Doc. Hist.*, XV, 537, II, 437.

114. Rush, Nov. 30, 1787 (Wilson's notes, quoted here in their entirety), *Doc. Hist.*, II, 440; and see Iredell, July 28, 1788, *Founders' Constitution*, I, 476.

115. [Noah Webster], "America," *New York Daily Advertiser*, Dec. 31, 1787, *Doc. Hist.*, XV, 199.

116. Madison to Jefferson, Sept. 6 and Oct. 24, 1787, *Papers of Madison*, X, 163, 211–12. This section draws on my essay "Parchment Barriers and the Politics of Rights," in Lacey and Haakonssen, eds., *Culture of Rights*, 98–143; and see Paul Finkelman, "James Madison and the Bill of Rights: A Reluctant Paternity," *Supreme Court Review*, 1990 (Chicago, 1990), 301–47.

117. Jefferson to Madison, Feb. 6, 1788, Dec. 20, 1787, *Papers of Madison*, X, 474, 338.

118. The obvious texts to be consulted on this point include *Federalist* 10, 49, and 50.

119. Morris to James Wilson, Aug. 23, 1789, Willing, Morris, and Swanwick Papers, Pennsylvania Historical and Museum Commission, Harrisburg.

120. Speech in the House of Representatives, June 8, 1789, in *Papers of Madison*, XII, 196–209, quotations at 198, 204.

121. Ibid., 202, 208, 344.

122. Ibid., 206–7. "In the arguments in favor of a declaration of rights [included in Madison's letter of October 17, 1788]," Jefferson had written on March 15, 1789, "you omit one which has great weight with me, the legal check which it puts into the hands of the judiciary." Ibid., 13.

123. This observation appears in the notes Madison kept for his *National Gazette* essays of 1791–92. In the printed essay on "Public Opinion," the corresponding passage reads: "In proportion as government is influenced by opinion, it must be so, by whatever influences opinion. This decides the question concerning a *Constitutional Declaration of Rights*, which requires [sic; "acquires" was probably the intended word] an influence on government, by becoming a part of the public opinion." Ibid., XIV, 162–63, 170.

124. *Federalist* 49, *Doc. Hist.*, XVI, 17.

125. In a comment comparing Madison and Paine, in Bailyn, *Faces of Revolution*, 82.

126. See the discussion *supra*, at n. 100. Herbert Storing has also suggested that "The fundamental case for a bill of rights is that it can be a prime agency of that political and moral education of the people on which free republican government depends." *What the Anti-Federalists Were For*, 69–70.

127. Peden, ed., *Notes on Virginia*, Query XVIII, 162–63.

128. *Federalist* 43; speech of June 6, 1787; Notes for essays in the *National Gazette*; *Papers of Madison*, X, 415, 33, XIV, 157, 160. One can also speculate about the device Madison used in *Federalist* 54, where the defense of the three-fifths clause is placed, in effect, in the voice of "one of our southern brethren"; ibid., X, 500.

CHAPTER XI   MADISON AND THE ORIGINS OF ORIGINALISM

1.   Perry Miller, *Errand into the Wilderness* (Cambridge, 1956), 3, 15.

2.   Robert H. Bork, *The Tempting of America: The Political Seduction of the Law* (New York, 1990), 144, 318 nn. 18–20.

3.   H. Jefferson Powell, "The Original Understanding of Original Intent," *Harvard Law Review*, 98 (1984–85), 885–948; reprinted in Rakove, ed., *Interpreting the Constitution*, 53–115 (which I cite below).

4.   *Federalist* 37, *Doc. Hist.*, XV, 346.

5.   Charles A. Lofgren, "The Original Understanding of Original Intent?" *Constitutional Commentary*, 5 (1988), 77–113, reprinted in Rakove, ed., *Interpreting the Constitution*, 117–50. For some examples of this pioneer at work, see Lofgren, "*Government from Reflection and Choice*," 3–115.

6.   Hutson, ed., *Supplement*, 183.

7.   Jay W. Fliegelman, *Declaring Independence: Jefferson, Natural Language, & the Culture of Performance* (Stanford, 1993), 1–28, 166.

8.   *Federalist* 33, *Doc. Hist.*, XV, 220–22.

9.   Iredell, July 28, 1788, *Founders' Constitution*, I, 476.

10.   "Landholder," V, *Conn. Courant*, Dec. 3, 1787, *Doc. Hist.*, XIV, 335.

11.   Jan. 7, 1788, *Doc. Hist.*, III, 553.

12.   *Federalist* 49, *Doc. Hist.*, XVI, 19.

13.   *Federalist* 63, *Doc. Hist.*, XVI, 297–98.

14.   Madison to Jefferson, March 29, 1789; to Randolph, May 31, 1789; and to Pendleton, June 21, 1789, *Papers of Madison*, XII, 38, 190, 252–53.

15.   The debate can be followed in Charlene Bangs Bickford et al., eds., *Documentary History of the First Congress*, X, 718–40 (for the initial debate of May 19, 1789), XI, 842–1036 passim (for the debates of June 16–22, culminating in the adoption of the amendments moved by Benson). This did not resolve the question, of course, since the bill then went to the Senate, whose debates are described in vivid and at times hilarious terms by the irascible senator from Pennsylvania, William Maclay; ibid., IX (*The Diary of William Maclay and Other Notes on Senate Debates*), 109–16. There it took the tie-breaking vote of Vice President John Adams to accept the House language. For analysis of the issues in this debate, see Donald R. Morgan, *Congress and the Constitution: A Study of Responsibility* (Cambridge, 1966), 49–57.

16.   There is a good sketch of Egbert Benson in Edward Countryman, "Some Problems of Power in New York, 1777–1782," in Hoffman and Albert, eds., *Sovereign States in an Age of Uncertainty*, 157–84.

17.   Smith, June 16, 1789; Gerry, June 19, 1789, Bickford, ed., *Doc. Hist. of First Congress*, XI, 876, 1022.

18.   Madison, June 16, 1789, ibid., 866–69.

19.   Madison, June 17, 1789, ibid., 926–27.

20.   Observations on the Jefferson's draft of a Constitution for Virginia [Oct. 1788] *Papers of Madison*, XI, 293; and see Alexander White to Madison, Aug. 16, 1788; and Monroe to Madison, Nov. 22, 1788; *Papers of Madison*, XI, 233–34, 361, discussing the recent controversy in Virginia sparked by a judicial reform act which had in turn been challenged by the judges of the state's higher courts. I do not pretend to resolve the even more interesting question of whether or not constitutional decisions would be made in the first instance by juries (trying law and fact) or judges, though it is easy to see how Madison's concern with the establishment of appellate jurisdictions could be interpreted as a re-

sponse to the danger that local juries would act as soi-disant defenders of their own understanding of the Constitution.

21. On this point, see the comments of Theodore Sedgwick and Abraham Baldwin; Bickford, ed., *Doc. Hist. of First Congress*, XI, 962, 1007–8. "Let gentlemen consider themselves in the tribunal of justice, called upon to decide this question on a mandamus," Baldwin exclaimed. "What a situation!"

22. June 18, 1789, ibid., 987.

23. See Madison's letters to Pendleton and Randolph of July 15, 1789, *Papers of Madison*, XII, 290–91.

24. Madison to Jefferson, June 30, 1789; and to Samuel Johnston, June 21, 1789, ibid., 268, 250.

25. June 19, 1789, Bickford, ed., *Doc. Hist. of First Congress*, XI, 1003–4 and n. 32.

26. June 16, 1789, ibid., 861; Smith to Rutledge, June 21, 1789, *South Carolina Historical Magazine*, 69 (1968), 8.

27. Madison to Randolph, Aug. 21, 1789; Randolph to Madison, Sept. 26, 1789, *Papers of Madison*, XII, 349, 421.

28. Jefferson to Madison, Jan. 16, 1799; Madison to Jefferson, Feb. 8, 1799, ibid., XVII, 209–10, 229.

29. Madison to Thomas Ritchie, Sept. 15, 1821, *Records*, III, 447.

30. Because the standard source for this debate (the *Annals of Congress*) will soon be superseded by additional volumes of Bickford, ed., *Doc. Hist. of First Congress*, for convenience I will cite to M. St. Clair Clarke and D. A. Hall, eds., *Legislative and Documentary History of the Bank of the United States* (Washington, 1832 [reprint ed., New York, 1967]). For Madison's speech, see pp. 39–45. The debate as a whole is analyzed in Benjamin B. Klubes, "The First Federal Congress and the First National Bank: A Case Study in Constitutional Interpretation," *Journal of the Early Republic*, 10 (1990), 19–42; and see Elkins and McKitrick, *Age of Federalism*, 223–34.

31. *Records*, II, 325, 615–16. In 1798, Baldwin recounted to Jefferson a conversation he had had with Wilson when the bank bill was under discussion, in which Baldwin recalled and Wilson agreed that Robert Morris had moved in Convention to give Congress a specific power to incorporate banks, but Gouverneur Morris had opposed the idea with the political arguments that Madison's notes ascribe to King. Ibid., III, 375.

32. Clarke and Hall, eds., *Legislative History*, 40–41.

33. Powell, "Original Understanding," in Rakove, ed., *Interpreting the Constitution*, 60.

34. Clarke and Hall, eds., *Legislative History*, 44. This statement is noteworthy for suggesting that the states were the contracting "parties" to the constitutional compact—a position anticipating the Virginia Resolutions of 1798.

35. Feb. 3, 1791, ibid., 46.

36. Feb. 7, 1791, ibid., 75–81.

37. Feb. 8, 1791, ibid., 83.

38. Jefferson, Opinion, Feb. 15, 1791; Randolph, Opinion no. 2, Feb. 12, 1791; Hamilton, Opinion, Feb. 23, 1791; ibid., 92, 90, 101; the respective *Papers* of both Jefferson and Hamilton reprint their opinions with scholarly annotation.

39. Elkins and McKitrick, *Age of Federalism*, 233.

40. Worthington C. Ford, et al., eds., *Journals of the Continental Congress, 1774–1789* (Washington, D.C., 1904–37), XX, 545–47; *Papers of Madison*, III, 175 n. 20.

41. Coxe to Madison, March 21, 1790; Madison to Coxe, March 30, 1790; ibid., XIII, 112–13, 128.

42. Speech of Feb. 8, 1791, ibid., 383.

43. "Helvidius," no. 1, Phila. *Gazette of the U. S.*, Aug. 24, 1793, ibid., XV, 67–68.

44. "Helvidius," nos. 1 and 3, ibid., 72–73, 97 (emphases in quotations from *The Federalist* added by Madison); *Federalist* 24, *Doc. Hist.*, XV, 40.

45. For an introduction to the constitutional questions, see Abraham Sofaer, *War, Foreign Affairs and Constitutional Powers: The Origins* (Cambridge, 1976), 85–93, and the fascinating article by Ruth Wedgwood, "The Revolutionary Martyrdom of Jonathan Robbins," *Yale Law Journal*, 100 (1990–91), 260–66.

46. This point does not appear in the draft version of this petition which the editors of the *Papers of Madison* have recently identified, and it is possible its addition came at the urging of Jefferson, whom the Madisons visited only days before the petition was first printed. *Papers of Madison*, XVI, 62–69 headnote (esp. 66), 102.

47. "The Defence," XXXVI, XXXVII, [New York] *The Herald*, Jan. 2, 6, 1796, *Papers of Hamilton*, XX, 3–10, 13–22.

48. "The Defence," XXXVIII, [New York] *The Herald*, Jan. 9, 1796, *Papers of Hamilton*, XX, 22–24.

49. William W. Seaton and Joseph Gales, Jr., *Debates and Proceedings in the Congress of the United States* (Washington, 1834–56) (commonly known and cited here as *Annals of Congress*), V, 432, 438–41.

50. March 10, 1796, *Papers of Madison*, XVI, 255–63 (I prefer this source because no scholarly reprinting of the *Annals* for any Congress other than the First is likely).

51. *Annals of Congress*, V, 495–96.

52. *Annals of Congress*, V, 519–20, 522–27; the complaint that no recourse had been made to the actual debates came from William Branch Giles of Virginia; ibid., 502.

53. *Annals of Congress*, V, 567 ff., 526–27.

54. *Annals of Congress*, V, 627 (Smith), 516 (Sedgwick).

55. *Annals of Congress*, V, 543–46 (Holland), 635 (Edward Livingston).

56. *Annals of Congress*, V, 578–80 (Richard Brent), 591–92 (Findley).

57. *Annals of Congress*, V, 635, 647 (Milledge, a Republican, citing the necessary-and-proper clause to uphold the authority of the House!), 657–58 (Coit, a Federalist, then proceeding to reflect on the conduct of Baldwin and Madison).

58. *Annals of Congress*, V, 703–10 (quotations at 709–10). This analogy had been made frequently since the start of the debate, especially by the rising Republican star Albert Gallatin; ibid., 464ff.

59. Hamilton to Washington, Mar. 29, 1796; Washington to Hamilton, Mar. 31, 1796, *Papers of Hamilton*, XX, 85–105 (Hamilton's reference to the Convention is on p. 100).

60. *Records*, II, 392–94. Hamilton was away in New York at the time.

61. *Annals of Congress*, V, 700–2.

62. *Papers of Madison*, XVI, 294–96.

63. Ibid., XVI, 296.

64. Ibid., 296–99.

65. Ibid., 298.

66. *Federalist* 48, *Doc. Hist.*, XVI, 5.

67. Even this claim might be considered problematic, given the extent to which the concern over Mississippi navigation underlay the debate over the treaty power in 1788.

CODA

1. The Robert Wesson Lecture in Democracy, Apr. 1, 1988 (manuscript in possession of author); for the epigraph see *The Memoirs of John Q. Adams* (Philadelphia, 1874–87), VIII, 519.

2. Jefferson to Samuel Kercheval, July 12, 1816, in Andrew Lipscomb, ed., *The Writings of Thomas Jefferson* (Washington, 1903), XV, 40.

INDEX

A NOTE ABOUT THE AUTHOR

Jack N. Rakove was born in Chicago in 1947. He received his B.A. at Haverford College in 1968 and his Ph.D. from Harvard University in 1975. He taught at Colgate University from 1975 to 1980. Since 1980 he has been at Stanford University, where he is currently professor of history. He is the author of *The Beginnings of National Politics: An Interpretive History of the Continental Congress* (1979) and *James Madison and the Creation of the American Republic* (1990), and he is the editor of *Interpreting the Constitution: The Debate Over Original Intent* (1990).

A NOTE ON THE TYPE

This book was set in a modern adaptation of a type designed by the first William Caslon 1692–1766. The Caslon face, an artistic, easily read type, has enjoyed over two centuries of popularity in our own country. It is of interest to note that the first copies of the Declaration of Independence and the first paper currency distrubuted to the citizens of the newborn nation were printed in this typeface.

Composed by Creative Graphics, Allentown, Pennsylvania
Printed and bound by R.R. Donnelley & Sons, Harrisonburg, Virginia
Designed by Robert C. Olsson
Calligraphy by Carole Lowenstein